THE ORGANS
OF SOVIET ADMINISTRATION
OF JUSTICE :
THEIR HISTORY AND OPERATION

STUDIEN ZUR GESCHICHTE OSTEUROPAS
STUDIES IN EAST EUROPEAN HISTORY
ÉTUDES D'HISTOIRE DE L'EUROPE ORIENTALE

HERAUSGEGEBEN VON / EDITED BY / ÉDITÉ PAR

W. PHILIPP
Freie Universität Berlin

P. SCHEIBERT
Universität Marburg

UNTER MITARBEIT VON / IN COLLABORATION WITH / AVEC LE CONCOURS DE

A. M. AMMANN S.J.
Pontificio Istituto Orientale, Roma

F. T. EPSTEIN
Indiana University, Bloomington, Ind.

C. E. BLACK
Princeton University, Princeton, N.J.

R. PORTAL
Institut d'Études Slaves, Paris

XIII

SAMUEL KUCHEROV

THE ORGANS
OF SOVIET ADMINISTRATION
OF JUSTICE :
THEIR HISTORY AND OPERATION

LEIDEN

E. J. BRILL

1970

THE ORGANS
OF SOVIET ADMINISTRATION
OF JUSTICE :
THEIR HISTORY AND OPERATION

BY

SAMUEL KUCHEROV

WITH A FOREWORD BY

JOHN N. HAZARD

LEIDEN
E. J. BRILL
1970

To Michael

TABLE OF CONTENTS

PART ONE

INSTITUTIONS OF JUSTICE

PART TWO

MEN OF LAW

AUTHOR'S PREFACE

Fifty years have passed since the Bolsheviks seized power in Russia.

The October Revolution—the first socialist revolution in the world—had as its purpose not to improve the political and social structure of Russia, but to build a completely new society based on Marx's doctrine of socialism and communism. The guiding slogan at that time was : "in order to build a new home, it is necessary to tear down the old one".

Thus, the Tsarist system of administration of justice, with all its institutions, organs and codes, went down the drain together with the entire state apparatus.

The new system of administration of justice which was erected on the ruins of the old one and developed during the time of Soviet rule, does not differ to any extent—on paper—from other systems accepted in the West. However, the Soviet state assumed from its very beginning a totalitarian character which it has retained up to the present time. This meant the primacy of state interests over those of the individual in the process of meting out justice and the unrestricted rule of the Communist Party over all aspects of Soviet life—including the administration of justice.

As a result, a yawning abyss between the written law and its implementation was created, and flagrant violations of legality take place whenever the Party chooses to interfere with the administration of justice. Conditions of permanent violation of legality existed during the period of the "cult of personality" under Stalin. After Stalin's death, these violations acquired a sporadic character.

Collective farmer Chudrov, one of the characters in the novel "After the Marriage" by the Soviet writer D. Granin [1], complains to another collective farmer from a neighboring farm that his *kolkhoz* has been ruined by an "appointed chairman, a drunkard".

"What do you mean, 'appointed' ?" Chudrov's interlocutor exclaims. "Did you not elect him yourself ?"

"Don't you know that they are hand picked ?" Chudrov retorts. "A goat also goes where it chooses, except that it is on a leash."

The Soviet judge's independence is established on paper, but in

---

[1] *Oktyabr'*, 1958, No. 7, p. 87.

reality he, too, is "on a leash", and the other end of the leash is still firmly in the hands of the Party—as the trials of 1966-1968 make clear.

At the same time, however, there occurred in connection with these trials a phenomenon unknown in the Soviet Union since the end of the twenties, when Stalin crushed the last opposition : the phenomenon of protests against violations of legality in the administration of justice. These protests took the form of street demonstrations, of hundreds of letters to Soviet authorities signed by Soviet citizens with their full names and addresses. The bare fact that people dare to express their discontent and criticism openly is a sure sign of a certain clearing of the air, of some degree of liberalization undergone by the Soviet Union after 1953.

Certainly, the process of liberalization is developing more slowly in the Soviet Union than in some other Communist countries. Nonetheless, in the opinion of the present writer, this development is inescapable, in spite of the attempts of the present Soviet administration to hold it in check at home and even to inhibit it in other Communist countries. The process of liberalization has to continue in the Soviet Union, because it corresponds to the desires and expectations of the new generation which will come to power sooner or later.

The pendulum of history swung sharply from right to left in Russia in 1917. It was retained in its position by Lenin and Stalin, with the help of measures which it would be impossible to repeat today. After Stalin's death, the pendulum began to move in the opposite direction. How fast and how far it will go, nobody knows. But its movement will bring a gradual narrowing of the gap between written law and reality.

* * *

I am very grateful to the Library of Congress, for the assignement of a study desk greatly facilitating my work. Doctors Nizankowski, Rusis and Krivickas of the Foreign Law Division, Library of Congress, were very helpful in providing me with the necessary literature. Mr. Edmond Jahn, Chief of the Foreign Law Division, read the entire manuscript.

Heartfelt thanks go to Mrs. Jacquelyn Flynn who typed this manuscript with diligence and good humor.

My thanks are extended to the Editors of the Bulletin of the Institute for the Study of the USSR for the permission to reprint my article, The Nature and State of *Arbitrazh* (1966, No. 11); *Osteuropa-Recht* for the authorization to reproduce from my article, The Jury of Tsarist Russia and the People's Assessors of the Soviet Union (1966, No. 3); the American Journal of Comparative Law for the permission to quote extensively from my article, The Legal Profession In Pre- and Post-Revolutionary Russia (1956, No. 3), and to Mrs. Sophie Grynberg for authorization to reprint from the minutes of the Brodsky Trial (*Vozdushnyye puti*, N.Y., 1965, pp. 279-303).

FOREWORD

V.I. Lenin had no blueprint for the judicial arm of the Marxian socialist state when he created the courts of the Russian revolution. He seems to have been intent on establishing only a few fundamental principles : the foremost of which were simplicity and popularity. He was content to let matters develop as they might in evolution of these fundamentals.

As a lawyer Lenin must have expected tradition to influence the course of his new epoch, but as a social revolutionary he wanted to minimize it. His courts were proudly proclaimed as something new, differing from anything the world had known. In a sense they were to be the people themselves : acting militantly against enemies, but in fraternal fashion with their co-workers who proved to be slow in grasping the message of the new day. They were to be the people themselves playing the first act of a drama of undetermined length but with a final act which would inevitably terminate in the withering away of the state.

Outsiders can criticize Lenin as lacking in realism. History shows that such criticism is unwarranted, for he knew what needed doing to keep power, but on the issue of the withering away of the state he seems in 1917 to have been an ardent believer. He anticipated a future, perhaps very distant, but perhaps not too far away, when mankind in the society he hoped to create would no longer need to be goaded into conformity with the regulations of public order. Education and abundant production were expected to work their wonders in creating a new system of social control.

Lenin's dream of a society without state compulsion had vast appeal among adherents who participated in a revolution which seemed at the time to be directed against authority of all kinds. Sophisticated men with good legal training wrote proudly of the anticipated achievement of a society which could function effectively without judges, prosecutors or lawyers; a society which would bring to mind the organization of primitive people but would prevail in a community which would be no longer primitive. This was the Communist Party's declared goal, and Lenin's first decree on the courts was designed as a step in what outsiders believed to be a utopian direction.

Soviet society of today has moved far from the dreams of 1917. It has evolved with much experimentation during which there has been conscious and unconscious balancing of traditions of the Russian Empire and the revolutionary ideas inspired among Russians by the works of Karl Marx and his colleague Friedrich Engels. History shows that as pressing problems of public order have been faced by Lenin's successors, they have been prone to search their Marxist doctrine for suggestions as to a solution but to resort in the final balancing to policies mindful of the Russian past.

Philosophers say that old forms have been imbued with new content from which have emerged new forms. Dr. Samuel Kucherov seems to draw such a conclusion, for he finds that the forms of today do not differ greatly from those he knew as a lawyer under the Tsar. Still, he notes a radical change of content because of the administration by the Communist Party of the formal instruments of public order. His narrative gives strong support to the theory that the Soviet legal system has taken shape as a result of pressures springing from the necessity of governing, but in the selection of instruments appropriate to the necessity there has been inspiration from both theory and practice inherited from the past. Shades of both Marx and the Romanovs stalk his pages.

Dr. Kucherov is admirably fitted to examine both elements of influence upon those who have shaped the Soviet system. He has lived through the tumultuous years. He was a lawyer before the revolution, graduated from the gymnasium in Kiev at the very moment when the first blows of the revolution were being felt with the assassination in the Opera House of Prime Minister Stolypin. He is one of the last remaining lawyers of the Imperial time who concerned themselves with what Lenin introduced. He knows his native country, its traditions, its possibilities, its temptations, its sorrows and its joys. He has studied Marxist theory and traced its development by Lenin, Joseph Stalin and Nikita Khrushchev. He is, of course, a master of the language and during his years in the Library of Congress he has had access to its incomparable collection on the history of Soviet legal institutions.

Perhaps Dr. Kucherov's disappointements at the turn of events in 1917 when the liberals in whom he had faith were driven from power by the Bolshevik militants has influenced his thinking. He quite properly singles out for attention not only the excesses of the early years but the continuing excesses of current times. He finds little progression from the class conscious system devised by Lenin. What hope of liberalization emerged under Khrushchev seems to him to have faded with the trials of authors since Khrushchev's ouster. These trials are examined in detail with ample quotation from the records. But these are the records of what can be seen and heard in the courtroom, and in that fact lies the problem in any interpretation of trends.

Soviet society is developing increasingly courageous groups unwilling to accept dictation of thought. There is conflict within the Central Committee of the Communist Party. The majority evidently still reacts in what was the tradition of authoritarianism when facing problems of social control. This majority believes in the "hard line". But there are others, and notably Communists with legal training and knowledge of the experience of other countries, who doubt the wisdom of following such a line in contemporary conditions.

The realists of the Party still present a force which cannot be measured and which must remain muted to outsiders, but it is there. They are not without success, for there is today no dictator like Stalin. The purge dramas have been eliminated from the arsenal of those responsible for maintaining public authority. The arbitrary executions which characterized Stalin's time have been stopped. Dr. Kucherov notes these changes and believes that the reformers can progress further.

The great unsolved question for analysts of Soviet legal development is that posed by the young generation of Communists. Dr. Kucherov has not tried to evaluate this factor, and it is indeed elusive. He has limited himself to the past and present. If the past is really prologue, and there is strong reason to conclude that it is, the reader can gain from Dr. Kucherov's pages the elements needed to anticipate the probable future. No one has yet attempted in English as thorough an account of Soviet legal institutions and of the men who man them. Even Soviet authors can offer no such view, for they still sense an obligation to present their system with sympathy, and this has made in their histories for a selection of data that presents less than the full story as Westerners want it.

John N. HAZARD.

ABBREVIATIONS AND TRANSLITERATIONS

The following abbreviations are used in this book :

Sob. post.	for *Sobraniye postanovleniy i rasporyazheniy pravitel'stva soyuza sovetskikh sotsialisticheskikh respublik* (Collection of Decisions and Orders of the Government of the Union of Soviet Socialist Republics)
Sob. uz., RSFSR	for *Sobraniye uzakoneniy i rasporyazheniy raboche-krestyanskogo pravitel'stva RSFSR* (Collection of Laws and Orders of the Workers' and Peasants' Government of the RSFSR)
Sob. zak., SSSR	for *Sobraniye zakonov i rasporyazheniy raboche-krestyanskogo pravitel'stva SSSR* (Collection of Laws and Orders of the Worker's and Peasants' Government of the USSR)
Sots. zak.	for *Sotsialisticheskaya zakonnost'* (Socialist Legality)
S.G.P.	for *Sovetskoye gosudarstvo i pravo* (Soviet State and Law)
Sov. yust.	for *Sovetskaya yustitsiya* (Soviet Justice)
V.V.S., RSFSR	for *Vedomosti Verkhovnogo Soveta, RSFSR* (Journal of the RSFSR Supreme Soviet)
V.V.S., SSSR	for *Vedomosti Verkhovnogo Soveta SSSR* (Journal of the USSR Supreme Soviet)

Transliteration is made according to the system used by the Board of Geographic Names with the exception of family names : for instance, Vyshinsky is not transliterated "Vyshinskiy" as it should be and "Izvestiya" is spelled Izvestia in order to conform to the more usual transliteration method and avoid misunderstanding.

PART ONE

INSTITUTIONS OF JUSTICE

CHAPTER ONE

THE FIRST COURTS

A. COMMUNIST THEORY ON COURTS

a) *Lenin on Courts*

The creator of the Soviet State, V.I. Lenin, expressed his views on courts before and after the Bolshevist Revolution of October 1917. He strongly criticized the tsarist courts and was in a very high degree instrumental in the destruction of the old courts and the creation of new ones under the Soviets.

Lenin received a legal education, was a junior member of the Bar in Petersburg and practiced law there for a time. These circumstances should have aided him in the formation of an objective opinion on the functions of the administration of justice under the tsars of his time. However, Lenin's thinking was completely dominated by Marxism. What Marx and Engels thought and wrote was for him as relevant and indisputably true as the gospel teaching is to a pious Christian. Naturally, also his views on courts, their structure and functioning were under the influence of what Marx and Engels wrote on these subjects.

Thus, since Marx wrote in "The Civil War in France" that "There developed in the nineteenth century originating from the days of absolute monarchy, the centralized state power with its ubiquitous organs of standing army, police, bureaucracy, clergy and judicature", [1] Lenin accepts and adopts as his own the assertion that the courts are organs of the State and no more. And since, according to Marx, "the state is an organ of domination and oppression of one class by another", [2] state organs, including the court, became instruments of domination and oppression by the ruling class.

The culmination point of this activity of "domination" and "oppression" by the state is ascribed by Lenin, to the period of imperialism, the last stage of capitalism, which definitely ripened

---

[1] Quoted in V.I. Lenin, *State and Revolution* (International Publishers) N.Y., 1954 (revised translation), p. 36.

[2] *Op. cit.*, p. 9.

in the 20th century, producing the deterioration of legal elements and of the work of individual organs of the state, including the courts. The conclusion follows that "the court was chiefly the implement of oppression, the instrument of bourgeois exploitation" in capitalist countries. [1]

Although the bourgeois court personified the protection of order, in reality, it was "a blind, subtle instrument of merciless suppression of the exploited, defending the interests of the money-bag". [2]

These oppressive features of a capitalistic state and its organs are in no way attenuated by the measure of democracy or liberalism existing in a state, according to Lenin. On the contrary, "the more free" or "democratic" a bourgeois country is, "the more the capitalist gang rages and brutalizes the workers revolution".

The United States serves as an example for Lenin's allegation. "Do not forget" he wrote, "that in the case of America we have the most free, the best, perhaps the most democratic republic, but that does not prevent the fact that imperialism acts there in the same beastly way, that internationalists are not only lynched there, but that the mob dragged them into the street, stripped them naked, poured tar on them and ignited it, that they [the Americans] are not only not for peace, but not for pacifism in general". [3]

Consequently, Lenin asserts, the bourgeois court is not only a medium for the oppression and exploitation policy of the capitalist state with regard to the people, but performs this role under the mask of an independent and impartial administration of justice.

Lenin attempts "to tear the mask from the capitalist court", and to prove that its alleged democratic premises—independence from the government, publicity of procedure and participation of the people in court decisions—are completely fictitious.

The independence of bourgeois judges is excluded because nobody can argue making himself free from the influence of his class. Also a public worker, including the members of the judiciary, simply cannot make himself free from the influence of his class, even in judicial decisions. "By what wonder can ... the conclusion be made, that a public worker should not sympathize with this or that class, that he is not supposed to do it", [4] Lenin asks.

---

[1] Lenin, *Works*, XXII, p. 424.

[2] Lenin, XXII, p. 212.

[3] Lenin, XXIII, p. 216.

[4] Lenin, II, p. 335.

"It is ridiculous even to speak about duty in such a case because *not a single human being can avoid to put himself on the side of this or that class* ... to rejoice in the successes of a given class, deplore its short-comings, to be indignant with those who are hostile to this clas ... -" [1]

As an example of this unscrupulous allegiance of every man to his class, including the bourgeois judge, Lenin quotes the case of a beating-up of a strike-breaker by a worker. The case was related by Justice Ginsberg who took part in the trial, at the Congress of Criminology in Vienna, in 1912 at which Lenin was present. According to Lenin, the judge, "who strongly wanted the setting of a heavy punishment on the worker", related that he had best make the greatest effort in order that the accused should not be acquitted; one of the assessors, a socialdemocrat, told the judge that he (the judge) does not understand the worker's psychology. "But I understand the psychology of the beaten-up very well" was the answer of the judge. [2]

Even the election of judges by the people in a capitalistic state, as for instance, the United States, does not save them from the dependence upon their class of society which shapes all their actions, including decisions of the courts.

This viewpoint of Lenin exactly corresponds to Marx's opinion that elected jurors also cannot free themselves from their class mentality in a capitalistic state since a court with jurors is still "a class court of privileged classes, created with the purpose of filling the gaps of law with the width of bourgeois conscience". [3] "But what about the conscience of the jurors, you will reply to us. Conscience—is there a better guarantee necessary? *Ah, mon dieu*, conscience depends upon consciousness, upon the whole life of a person. The republican has a conscience different from that of a royalist, the wealthy person—one different from that of the indigent, a thinker—a conscience different from that of one who never thinks. A man who is required to be a juror only because of his property qualifications has accordingly a conscience qualified by property. The point is that the conscience of the privileged is a privileged conscience". [4]

---

[1] *Ibid.*

[2] It seems to the author that the example brought forward by Lenin speaks against and not for the theory he advances. Indeed the strike-breaker was evidently also a worker and the fact that Justice Ginsberg, who belonged to the bourgeoisie, understood his psychology proves that the judge was not under the influence of his appurtenance to the bourgeoisie.

[3] K. Marx and F. Engels, *Sochineniya*, M. 1928-1939, VIII, p. 558.

[4] *Op. cit.*, VII, p. 495-496.

Democracy in a bourgeois state does not prevent the worst abuse of judicial power when the class struggle becomes acute. "Then", as Lenin writes, "penal laws passed with direct scope to help the government in the political fight against the proletariat ... are mercilessly pushed back by direct political struggle, open street skirmishes. 'Justice' takes off the mask of impartiality and loftiness and takes to flight, leaving the field of action to police, gendarmerie and kosacks ..." [1]

Such a time existed for Lenin not only under the Tsars, during the intensive fight against the menacing revolution, but also when Kerensky tried to repulse the Bolshevik onslaught in 1917.

When Lenin and Zinov'yev were summoned to appear in court to respond to accusation leveled against them, Lenin refused and gave the following explanation for his refusal. "The court is a state organ. Liberals forget it sometimes, it is a sin for Marxists to forget it ... I did not commit anything illegal. The court is just. It will examine. The trial will be public. The people will understand. I will appear. These arguments are naive to the point of childishness. Not a trial but a persecution of internationalists, that is what the power wants. To grab and keep them ... that is necessary to Messrs. Kerensky and Co. It was so [in England and France] It will be so [in Russia.] Many internationalists work illegally, but do not make the mistake of appearing (in court)".

Lenin contends that "to give oneself up to state power now would mean to surrender to the hands of Milyukov, Aleksinsky and Pereverzev, to the hands of raging counter-revolutionaries, for whom all accusations against us are simple episodes of the civil war. There is no guarantee of justice in Russia at the present time". [2]

The murder of Karl Liebknecht and Rosa Luxemburg in Germany in 1919, during the Weimar Republic, inspired Lenin to write that "if the arrested, i'e., [those] taken by [the] state power under its protection could have been killed by officers and capitalists with impunity under a government of social-patriots, the democratic republic in which such a thing could occur, is a dictatorship of the bourgeoisie ... . 'Liberty' in one of the most free and advanced republics of the world, in the German Republic, is liberty to kill with impunity, arrested leaders of the proletariat. And it cannot be otherwise since the development of democracy does not deaden, but intensifies class struggle ..." [3]

---

[1]   Lenin, IV, p. 116.

[2]   Written July 21 (8) 1917, Lenin, XXI, p. 24/25, 32.

[3]   Lenin, XXIV, p. 11.

The Administration of justice does not lose its class character under any government in a capitalist state, i.e., a state where the struggle between classes rages. That is why "if you (a proletarian) steal a loaf of bread, you will be jailed, but if you (a bourgeois) steal a railroad, you will be appointed a senator". [1]

Basically denying that a capitalist court has the capacity of meting-out impartial justice to proletarians, Lenin still urged them to use capitalist courts for the propaganda of Bolshevist ideas. On the occasion of a trial of workers, he wrote to them : "Comrades, you have ... to use the open doors of the court for a direct statement of social-democratic views, hostile not only to tsarism in general, but also to social-chauvinism of all kind of shades". [2]

In the beginning of 1905, Lenin received a letter from comrades in the Moscow jail with the inquiry as to how they should behave during the forthcoming trial. His opinion was especially asked as to the following three kinds of behavior the accused should adopt in court : 1. To ignore the court and directly boycott it; 2. To ignore the court and not participate in the proceedings at the trial; 3. To use the court for political agitation and take part in the proceedings in court with the help of counsel in order to show the illegality of the trial and summon witnesses (proof of alibis, etc). Lenin answered this letter on 19, 1905 :

"Much depends in my opinion upon *the kind* of trial which will take place, i.e., as to whether there is a possibility to use it for agitation or is there no such possibility ? In the first alternative the tactic No. 1 is out of place; in the second alternative, it is appropriate, but also only after a definite energetic protest and declaration. But if there is a possibility to use the court for propaganda, then tactic No. 3 is advisable. A speech with a *profession de foi* is very desirable in general, very useful, in my opinion, and in a majority of cases, would have chance to play a propagandistic role". [3]

But Lenin thought it also advisable to seek the protection of capitalistic courts even in disputes between members of the social-democratic party. An example is the case of R.V. Malinovsky, Vice-Chairman of the Socialist-Democratic Fraction in the fourth State Duma, accused by Martov and Dan of being an *agent provocateur.* "Yet those who shield Dan and Martov or the nervous members of the intelligentia who

---

[1] Lenin, XV, p. 155.
[2] Lenin, XVIII, p. 130.
[3] Lenin, VII, p. 59-60.

believe in rumors (set afloat) by these gentlemen, sigh when they think about a bourgeois court. We cannot be intimidated by it. Against blackmailers we are always and unconditionally for the bourgeois legality of a bourgeois court. If a man says : give me 100 rubles or I shall disclose that you are unfaithful to your wife and have an affair with NN ... this is criminal blackmail. We are for a bourgeois court in this case. When a man says : make political concessions to me, recognize me as a fulfledged member of the Marxist entity with equal rights, or I shall vociferate rumors concerning Malinovsky's provocation— this is political blackmail. We are for a bourgeois court in this case", Lenin declared. And he made the following challenge : "Come forward with a direct accusation signed by you, in order that a bourgeois court could expose and punish you (there is no other means to fight blackmail) or remain with the stigma of men whom representatives of 10 workers' professional societies have publicly called slanderers. This is a choice for you, Messrs. Martov and Dan". [1]

This was written by Lenin in an article in the periodical "Prosvesh-cheniye" in June 1914.

However, what Lenin demanded from Martov and Dan—i.e., to revert to a tsarist court, he did not apply to himself when the District Attorney made public an accusation against him and some other Bolshevists of having organized the armed insurrection of July 3-4, 1917 and having acted as a German spy. Lenin preferred to go into hiding although there no longer was any tsarist court in Russia, but the court of a democratic government.

Lenin also wanted the capitalistic court to shield the proletariat from the misuse of administrative power. He complained that "the government answered to strikes with wild persecutions, arrested and banded masses of workers without a trial". [2]

In a proclamation of the "Association for the Fight for Worker's Class Liberation", he wrote : "They (the government) enumerated to the public how many socialistic leftists there were, but did not give the figures of arrests of workers and socialists, how many families were ruined, how many were banned and thrown in jail without trial". [3]

---

[1] Lenin, XVII, p. 498-499. Lenin continued to defend Malinovsky in spite of evidence of his role of an *agent provocateur*. But when, after the October Revolution the Bolshevists gained access to the secret documents of *Okhranka* (Tzarist political police), and that of what Martov and Dan accused Malinovsky in 1918 was made evident, Malinovsky was summarily executed in 1918.

[2] Lenin, II, p. 129.

[3] Lenin, I, p. 457-458.

In a draft of a social-democratic party program written by Lenin in jail in 1895-6, he demanded that "the right to prosecute in court every official without reverting to his superior [1], should be given to every citizen" and that "industrial courts should be established in every branch of industry with judges equally elected by capitalists and workers". This claim was extended to agricultural courts by Lenin for every agricultural branch in a later draft (1899). Judges of these courts had to be elected in the same way by employees and workers. [2]

Another provision demanded by Lenin in the draft of 1899 was that the agricultural court should be empowered to lower the extraordinarily high rents (paid by peasants to landowness for the lease of land) and to declare one-sided agreements without force. [3]

In Lenin's opinion industrial courts were very important and he wrote a special article on this subject at the end of 1899. [4] Lenin understood industrial courts to be courts composed of elected representatives of workers and appointed representatives of plant owners. jurisdiction of such courts was to extend to inequities on questions of hiring and working conditions, wages for regular and over-time work, etc. ... in all disputes arising from labor relations between workers and their industrial employers. Such courts existed in the majority of European countries but not in Russia. [5]

According to Lenin the first advantage of the industrial court in comparison with a regular one is its increased accessibility to the worker : to lodge a complaint with the regular court it is necessary to put it on paper and hire an attorney to this effect, to pay court fees, to wait a long time for the judgment, to attend the court's sessions, leaving work. [6]

Then an appeal to a higher court is possible, which takes another

---

[1] Tsarist political police.

[2] According to tsarist law a complaint against the official had first to be lodged with his superiors.

[3] Lenin, II, p. 426.

[4] Lenin, II, p. 16.

[5] Lenin, II, p. 557-568.

[6] When serfdom was abrogated in 1861, a commission for the recommendation of regulations concerning the work of handicrafts and industrial workers was established. It studied European legislation on the subject and in 1865, 5 vols. on the findings were published. Among other recommendations the commission suggested the introduction of industrial courts with judges equally elected by employers and workers. This measure was not adopted by the Russian government.

amount of time and costs. An industrial court, however, requires only a verbal complaint, the formulation of which before its own worker-comrades is not difficult at all. Sessions of industrial courts are usually held on Sundays or at a time when workers are not at work. Preceedings in such a court are much shorter than in a regular court.

The second advantage of industrial courts for workers is that the judges understand much better factory and plant affairs : they are not strange officials, but local men, versed in worker's life conditions and matters of production, half of them being workers who "always will be just with regard to a worker and will not look upon him as a drunkard or impudent fellow, ignoramus, as the majority of professional judges recruited from the bourgeois class, from the well-to-do classes do, and who almost always keep relations with the bourgeois society, with manufacturers, directors, engineers and are separated from workers as by a Chinese Wall..."

And then comes a diatribe against professional judges which is worthy to be quoted *in extenso*.

"Professional Judges (officials)", writes Lenin, "care most of all that the case should develop smoothly, according to documents : only that order should be in the documents; the official does not care for anything else, and he strives only to get his salary and curry favor with his supervisors. That is why so much red tape, bigotry and chicanery occurs in regular courts : you wrote something wrongly on a paper, were not able to put something on record at the proper time—the case is lost, although it was a just case ... The professional judge casts a look into the workbook, reads the rule and does not want to hear anything else : the rule is, namely, violated, so you are responsible and I do not want to know anything else.

But judges elected from employers and workers do look not only into papers, but also at what occurred in reality. Indeed, sometimes the rules remain on paper, but in reality something else takes place.

A regular simple worker who receives minimum wages cannot afford a good lawyer and that is why, as all workers know very well, judges-officials pass down most cruel and senseless decisions in labor cases. You can never expect complete justice from judges-officials : we mentioned already that these judges belong to the bourgeois class and are in advence prejudiced in favor of everything advanced by the employer and do not believe the worker. The judge looks into the Code—an employment contract... and it makes no difference to him, as to whether an engineer, physician, factory director or an unschooled laborer is hired by the factory owner; the judge thinks (thanks to his paper soul and bourgeois stupidity) that an unschooled laborer must know his rights and how to safeguard them in the contracts, like a director, physician or engineer ... If a worker wants to complain against unjust rejection of defective work or fines, he should not think even to address his complaint to an official-judge or to the official—the Factory Inspector. The official will repeat over and over again : 'the law gives the right to the employer to fine workers and to reject defective work, and it is namely, his business to establish when the work is defective and when the worker was at fault'. That is why the workers so seldom direct such complaints to courts ..."

Thirdly, industrial courts are advantageous for workers because the latter get acquainted with laws at these courts. The working masses do not know the laws and regulations governing their activities, although officials and judges-officials demand from them the knowledge of these laws and regulations. "If a worker replies, when an official points out a law, that the law is not known to him", writes Lenin, "the official (or the judge) will laugh at him or scold him : nobody has the right to excuse oneself by ignorance of the law ... that is the basic Russian law. That is why every official and every judge assumes that every worker knows the law. But this assumption is a lie, a lie invented by propertied against the non-propertied ; a similar presumption is that the worker concludes a 'free contract' with the employer". [1]

A fourth advantage of the industrial courts "is the training of workers for the independent participation in public, state affairs (because the court is a state institution, the activity of the court is a part of state activity ..." [2]

A fifth advantage Lenin sees in the fact that industrial courts would provide more publicity to industrial legislation and all aspects of factory life.

Lenin summarizes the advantages for workers of industrial courts to the effect that they consist of elected representatives of employers and workers, asserting that these courts are very important because they are more accessible to workers than regular courts, they have much less red tape and written procedure ; judges in these courts understand the conditions of factory life, and render more equitable judgements, they make one better acquainted with laws, they train

[1] Lenin, *op. cit.*, p. 561-562.
[2] *Op. cit.*, p. 563.

workers in the election of their representatives and the participation in state affairs, they increase the publicity of factory life and of the workers' movements, they accustom factory owners to a direct relationship with workers and to correct bargaining with workers, as with persons equal to them. [1]

However, in spite of the dithyrambs to the industrial courts by Lenin, still such courts were not established in Russia when the time came for Lenin to realize his views on the courts : the court competent in labor cases consisted as a regular court of an official judge and two assessors, not necessarily workers, and the procedure was not much less complicated as in regular court.

In his booklet "To the Village Poor" written in 1903, Lenin gives an explanation as to the purpose of agricultural courts, also included in the Program of the Social-Democratic Party. According to Lenin these courts, consisting of judges, one half freely elected by farm hands and the poorest peasant and the other half by landowners, should have the right to lower the rent for leased land set too high by the landowner, thus misusing the need of the peasant (on the land), and to regulate wages agreed upon between the landowner and the worker : if, for instance, the landowner hired the peasant in the winter for summer work for half-the-price, the court would decide on an equitable price. The jurisdiction of the court was to extend to any litigation between landowner and peasant. [2]

Also, the agricultural courts never came into existence either in tsarist or Soviet Russia.

But Lenin's suggestions with regard to courts were included in the draft of the program worked out by the editing boards of "Iskra" and "Zarya". [3]

In the official program of the Russian Social-Democratic Party adopted by the Congress of 1903, Lenin's suggestions were amended and appeared in the following wording :

The provision on the right of every citizen to prosecute officials in court without filing a complaint with his superiors, was formulated as follows : "The right of every man to prosecute an official in the usual way in a court with jury". Thus, the participation of jurors and not assessors was demanded.

---

[1] *Op. cit.*, p. 565-566.

[2] Lenin, V, p. 305.

[3] Two newspapers published in Russian abroad, of which Lenin was one of the editors.

Also this particular right was never emphasized in Soviet Codes. The provision on the competence of courts, the lowering of rent established by a one-sided contract was retained in Lenin's wording. A new provision was added, about the electivity of all judges, to the Program.

b) *Destruction of the Capitalist Courts*

There was no question in Lenin's mind about the necessity to completely destroy the capitalist state with all its organs, including the court system, since Marx had written to Kugelman in April 1871 : "I declare that the next attempt of the French Revolution must be : not, as in the past, to transfer the bureaucratic and military machinery from one hand to the other, but to break it up (*zerbrechen*) and that is the precondition of a real people's revolution on the continent ..." [1]

However, no French Revolution fulfilled Marx' prognosis to the end. This had to be done by the Bolshevist Revolution of 1917 in Russia. Lenin wrote : "Only the forceable overthrow of the bourgeoisie, confiscation of its property, destruction of the parliamentary, judicial, military, bureaucratic, administrative, municipal, etc. bourgeois state apparatus from top to bottom, including the banishment or internment of the most dangerous and persistent exploiters to a man, the setting of a strict supervision over them in order to fight the inescapable attempts toward resistence and preservation of capitalistic slaverny, only such measures are capable to insure the real subordination of the entire exploiters' class". [2]

The dictatorship of the proletariat and Soviet power presume the necessity of breaking up, smashing to pieces the bourgeois state apparatus (even a democratic one), including the courts, the civil and military bureaucracy, a.s.o. [3], according to Lenin. He saw the importance of the French Commune in its attempt to smash, destroy to the foundation the bourgeois official, judicial, military and police state apparatus, replacing it with a self-governing mass organization of workers, which did not know "the principle of separation of legislative and executive powers". [4]

Thus, Lenin wished the Russian courts together with the entire legal

---

[1] Lenin, *State and Revolution* (*op. cit.*), p. 33.
[2] Lenin, XXV, p. 314.
[3] Lenin, XXV, p. 309.
[4] Lenin, XXIV, p. 9.

system to go down in the ruins of the entire state machinery, after the Bolsheviks seized power. This was the path on which the French Commune of 1871 attempted to proceed, but did not reach the end of it. Its example had to be followed, according to Marx and Lenin.

Lenin understood, however, that "to destroy officialdom immediately, everywhere, completely—this cannot be thought of. That would be Utopia. But to *break up* at once the old bureaucratic machine and to start immediately the construction of a new one which will enable us to gradually reduce all officialdom to naught—this is no Utopia—it is the experience of the Commune, it is the direct and urgent task of the revolutionary proletariat". [1]

... "Overthrow the capitalists, crush with an iron hand of the armed workers, the resistance of these exploiters, break up the bureaucratic machine of the modern state—and you will have before you a machinery of the highest technical equipment freed of parasites, capable of being set into motion by the united workers themselves who hire their own technicians, managers, bookkeepers, and pay them all, as, indeed, every state official, with the usual workers' wage. Here is a concrete practical task, immediately realizable in relation to all truth, a task that frees the workers of exploitation and makes use of the experience (especially in the realm of the construction of the state) which the Commune began to reveal in practice".

To organize the whole national economy like the postal system, in such a way that the technicians, managers, bookkeepers, as well as all officials, should receive no higher wages than 'workingmen's wages' all under the control and leadership of the armed proletariat—that is our immediate aim. This is the kind of state and economical basis we need". [2] This, Lenin thought, was not Utopia. [3]

Also the Russian Revolution of 1905 had to serve as an example to this effect. Thus, the Novorossiysk Soviet declared at that time that since the population had completely lost confidence in the governmental judicial institutions, the Executive Committee had to work out and present, for confirmation to the Soviet, a draft on a people's court. During the armed insurrection in May and December 1905, a Revolutionary Tribunal was established in Presnya. [4] People reverted

---

[1] Lenin, *State and Revolution*, p. 42.

[2] *Op. cit.*, pp. 43-44.

[3] Still, it was a Utopia. Such state was never established under the Soviets. An attempt in this direction by Lenin under War Communism failed and Stalin called the principle of equal wages for all, despisingly *"Uravnilovka"*.

[4] A part of Moscow.

to the Petersburg Soviet of Workers' Deputies and the Riga Federative Committee even in civil cases, in 1905, and had no confidence in regular courts. [1]

Lenin declared about the tsarist court at the IIIrd Congress of Soviets in January 1918, "Soviet power acted by the way bequeathed by all proletarian revolutions—it pulled it down completely. Herewith we cleared the way for a real people's court (characterized) not as much by the power of repression, but more by the example of the masses, the authority of the working population, without formalities; the court as a means of exploitation we converted into an implement of education in the firm basis of socialist society. Let them vociferate that we turned it over for destruction at once without reforming it". [2] As soon as Soviet power was installed, the annhilation of the old court system began because "... only the Soviet organization of the State can right away break up and definitely liquidate the old bourgeois officials and court apparatus" [3] and "because the formation of the dictatorship of the proletariat itself is based not on law, but on ... the direct revolutionary movement of broad masses of the people, breaking the police and serf laws, creating revolutionary law and forcibly destroying the organs of people's suppression ..." [4]

B. The First Revolutionary Courts

Already previous to the issuance of the Decree No. 1 on Courts published on December 12, 1917, and the reception of it in far regions of the country, in Petrograd, Moscow and many cities of Central European and Asian Russia, new courts were formed. They had various names and their composition and the kind of procedures they employed differed to a great extent. [5] Let us give some examples.

The first court organized in Petrograd after the October Revolution and before the promulgation of the Decree No. 1 on Courts had its seat in the Vyborg Borough.

Thus, a temporary people's court was already organized "for the

---

[1] V.A. Ivanov, "Organization of Court and Prosecuting Body", in *40-let sovetskogo prava*, Leningrad, 1957, I, p. 562.

[2] Lenin, 26, p. 421.

[3] Lenin, XXIV, p. 14.

[4] Lenin, IX, p. 40.

[5] "The Anniversary of the Decree No. 1 on Courts", *Pravda*, Dec. 7, 1918.

fight against robbery, pillage, drunkenness, hooliganism, etc." by the Soviet of Vyborg Workers' and Soldiers' Deputies, according to a Decision of October 28, 1917, communicated to the Vyborg Borough Duma, which had a Bolshevist majority. This court did not receive definitely established status. In the documents of the court and of the Vyborg Borough Soviet it was sometimes called "Temporary Peoples' Court", "Temporary Revolutionary Court" "Military-Revolutionary Court" "People's Court" and "People's Revolutionary Court".

The first Decision of the Vyborg Borough Soviet provided for a court with five independent departments, manned by five justices each. But on 1 November, the Soviet changed its mind and a court with one department consisting of five members, representatives of the Borough Soviet Labor Union, the Plant and Factory Committees, from the Borough Duma and the Soviet Building Committee respectively was created. [1]

The worker Chakon was elected Chairman of the court. He was a member of the Borough Soviet. His background for this position was his active participation in the October Revolution (he led the disarmament of the Women's Brigade of the Provisional Government.)

The jurisdiction of this court extended to criminal cases and civil suits. The latter were very rare because of the troubled times.

However, criminal cases abounded. The court examined cases of theft, robbery, hooliganism and other criminal cases with the exception of counter-revolutionary and other very dangerous crimes which belonged to the competence of the Military-Revolutionary Committee. The local competence of the court extended only to the Vyborg Borough of Petrograd.

The preliminary investigation in criminal cases was entrusted to a commission consisting of a chairman and several members. But preliminary investigation belonged also to the duties of the Borough's Red Guard. Furthermore, home searches were also conducted by members of the Borough Soviet.

The court started criminal proceedings on the grounds of the results of the preliminary investigation or on the request of individual persons, institutions, public organizations or officials. In many cases Red Guardists brought to court arrested thieves, hooligans and other

---

[1] *Izvestia TsIK'a i Petrogradskogo Sovieta Rabochikh i soldatskikh deputatov*, Nov. 19, 1917.

criminals, without preliminary investigation. The court at once examined their cases.

The procedure in court was very simple. After the opening of the session, the court requested the public in the court hall to help the court in deciding the cases. If a preliminary examination had taken place proceedings were started by the reading of the minutes of the findings of the Preliminary Investigation Commission and then the accused and withnesses were interrogated. The citizens of the public had the right to direct questions to the accused and the witnesses.

No special organs of accusation and defense were used. Every citizen could take the floor as prosecutor or counsel of the accused. The only limitation concerned the number of prosecutors and defenders admitted : not more than two persons had the right to speak for the accusation and the same number of persons for the defense.

In many cases, nobody wanted to take over the functions of a prosecutor or counsel and the court had to proceed, even in serious criminal cases, without the participation of these organs of the administration of justice.

The right to appeal the decision or the verdict of the court was not limited. It was the Executive Commitee of the Borough Soviet,—a purely administrative and not a judicial body—which was competent to decide about the complaint. However, the court itself could reconsider the decisions and verdicts on the pretense of new evidence if submitted.

The court did not apply any laws in its decisions for the simple reason that it did not know them (not a single jurist belonged to the court's personnel). [1] The Court was guided only by its "revolutionary conscience" and the general policy proclaimed by the Communist Party", "keeping a hard class line", as I.A. Ushakov [2] remarks.

Penalties applied by the Court were : confinement in jail, forced labor under arrest and without arrest, fines, confiscation of property, revisition, public censure, etc. [3] Some of them were new, as for instance, forced labor without confinement.

Here is an example of a trial in the Vyborg Borough People's Court as related by *Izvestia.* [4]

---

[1] The tsarist laws were not yet abolished.

[2] I.A. Ushakov, The "Creations of the First People's Court in Petrograd", *S.G.P.* 1957, No. 1, p. 8.

[3] *Izvestia*, Nov. 9, 1917.

[4] *Izvestia, TsIKa i Petrogradskogo Soveta Rabochikh i Soldatskikh Deputatov*, Dec. 8, 1917.

Accused of theft is *"Vas'ka ryzhiy"* (Vas'ka-the Red Head)—
Vas'ka was not accused of a concrete case of theft when he was arrested.
Only a master key and seven trunk keys were found in his possession.
Vas'ka explained that one of the trunk keys was for his own trunk, the
second from the trunk of his mother, the third—of his brother and
so on. The accused admitted that he had committed thefts before the
Revolution, in bourgeois times, but emphatically denied thefts "after
the Revolution".

This explanation found no belief with the public in the court hall
which met them with fits of laughter. Although no other evidence
was produced, one of the justices suggested a punishment of forced
labor for Vas'ka. The suggestion was met with frenetic applause by
the public. Someone proposed the punishment should not be less
than a year. The defense asked for the reduction of the term, but the
public protested and Vas'ka was sentenced to one year of forced labor.
In accordance with the "legal consciousness" of the people.

The example of the Vyborg Borough was followed by other Boroughs
of Petrograd and revolutionary courts were created in the Spaskiy,
Narvskiy and some other Petrograd Boroughs.

Also the Saratov Soviet decided to form a People's Court consisting
of three justices : one representative of the Soviet, one of the Bureau of
The Labor Unions and the third—a person picked up from the
audience in the court.

A "Court of Public Conscience" was organized in Kronstadt.
Temporary Revolutionary Courts in Novgorod, Cherepovets and
Kuznetsk, in the Central regions of European Russia.

The Decree on Courts No. 1 was received in remote parts of Russia
not before the first months of 1918. [1] In the meantime, courts were
organized in West and Central Siberia.

All of the temporary courts had similar features : elected judges
without any juridical background, participation of the public in court
in the proceedings, use of the "revolutionary legal consciousness"
in place of laws, justice with a strong class character.

But some of these courts applied procedures which little resembled
orderly court procedures. For example, the newspaper *"Novaya
zhizn'"* [2] reported that in a People's Court of another Borough of

---

[1] It is interesting to note that the Samarkand Province Soviet wrote to the RSFSR
Commissar of Justice in the beginning of 1918 asking to clarify as to whether tsarist
courts created in 1886 should be still retained (*Materialy...* II, 67).

[2] November 8, 1917.

Petrograd the following procedure was used : "One of the justices reported the case and asked as to whether someone wanted to defend the accused; if the audience was indignant at the offence committed by the accused, it loudly expressed its indignation and in such cases nobody desired to defend the accused. After the guilt of the accused was established in this way, the court asked the audience about the punishment. The suggestions of the public were voted and the court decided in accordance with the suggestion of the majority.

"Revolutionary Courts" functioned also in villages.

The creation and the activity of the temporary courts was sharply criticized by the Petrograd City Duma (the majority of its members were strongly opposed to the October Revolution.) The Duma decided to ask the Committee of Public Safety to liquidate the activity of the newly formed courts. This decision was never made since the real power was in the hands of the Bolsheviks.

In conformance with the Decree No. 1 on Courts, the temporary courts in Petrograd were liquidated on December 11, 1917 and Local Courts formed.

Lenin saw in these spontaneous courts the realization of his principles, that justice should be administered by all the people, that every member of the proletariat is fit for the functions of a justice in line with his slogan that every proletarian is in a position to run the state. According to Lenin "the old, *incongruous*, savage, vile and detestable prejudice that only the so-called 'upper-classes' only the rich or graduates of the rich people's schools, can alledgedly control the state and be in charge of the building of the socialist society, must be destroyed".[1]

This was written by Lenin in December 25-28, 1917 in an article entitled "How to Organize the Competition". In this article he advanced the opinion that there are enough capable people among the proletariat to successfully compete with educated and rich people in the organization and control of the state and all its functions and the economic life of the country. He thought that the uneducated people have enough practical sense in order to take over this tremendous task. Although somewhere else [2] he admitted that "certainly the working population has no experience in administration, that does not scare us. ... (Because) previously, the entire human mind, all

---

[1] Lenin, XXII, p. 162.
[2] Speech at the closing of the IIIrd Congress of Soviets, January 18, 1918.

its genius created only with the purpose of supplying to a part of the people all the blessings of technology and culture and to deprive the other part of the most necessary education and development. Now, however, all the miracles of technique, all the achievements of culture will belong to the entire people, and from now on, never will the human mind and genius be used as a means of violence and exploitation". [1]

---

[1] Lenin, XXII, p. 225.

CHAPTER TWO

THE REGULAR SOVIET COURTS

A. THE DECREE NO. 1 ON COURTS

a) *The First Draft*

The creation of the "Revolutionary People's Courts" mentioned above was regarded by Lenin as the first realization of the take-over by the masses of the control of one of the functions of the State. In the spontaneous organization of these courts and their functioning Lenin saw the expression of the creative power of the people.

That is why the first draft of the Decree No. 1 on Courts, prepared by Stuchka, retained the main features in common with the courts established after the October Revolution and before the Local Courts were introduced by the Decree No. 1 on Courts.

Indeed, the first draft of this Decree provided for the abolition of all tsarist judicial institutions, including the justice of the peace; the elimination of the bar, the prosecution and the preliminary investigation magistracy; the newly installed local and revolutionary courts had to decide not by the codes of the overthrown governments but in accordance with the Decrees of the People's Commissars and their revolutionary conscience and legal consciousness. [1]

However, this draft was not adopted by the Council of People's Commissars. As we will see later, a corrective for the "creative mind" of the masses had to be introduced.

This failure to pass a more radical Decree on courts was explained later, [2] by the necessity to moderate the people's impetus in judicial affairs. Mal'kovich writes that the concessions made in the final draft were necessary in order to bring nearer the views of the "people's conscience" to the views of the government. Although the people's government "did not want to thrust its will upon the people, it strived in the direction of meeting the creative conscience of the people".

Stuchka declared (in the beginning of 1918) that "from the first day

---

[1] *Materialy Narodnogo komissariata yustitsii*, II, M. 1918, 103-104.

[2] See T. Mal'kovich, "On the History of the First Decrees on Courts", *S.G.P.* 1940, Nos. 8-9, p. 172.

of the Revolution, I had no doubt that only in the ruins of this temple
of the bourgeois justice will we achieve to create the building of the
Socialist justice, more modestic in external appearance, but infinitely
more solid according to its contents". [1]

The wholesale destruction of the entire judicial system based on
the democratic judicial reform of 1864 [2] found some opposition in the
Soviet Government.

The left Social-Revolutionary Steinberg, who was People's Commissar
of Justice from December 1917 to March 1918 in Lenin's unique
coalition government, thought on the contrary that the new courts
should be a final realization of the reform of 1864, distorted by the
reaction of the subsequent reigns. "We had to lay the foundations
of a democratic court not in an empty place", he wrote. [3]

P. Stuchka, who became People's Commissar of Justice after the
coalition with the left Social-Revolutionary was dissolved and was
the author of the Decree No. 1 on Courts, wrote that the advisability
of the suggestion to completely break up the old court system was
doubted by some, even very radical minded comrades, especially
among theoreticians ... They agreed to destroy the top level—the
Senate,—but opposed the liquidation of the lower courts. [4]

Especially the abolition of the institution of the judges of the peace
was challenged. "Even Marxists shuddered (from the thought of being
even one day without courts) ... But Voltaire wrote : first old laws
must be burned and then new ones written". Stuchka relates that some
of the "comrades were of the opinion that the old laws must be kept
until new ones are written, and new judges elected when the new
laws are in force. Other comrades argued about the question where
the abolition of courts should be started : at the top beginning with
the Senate, or the lower courts. Finally, after ten days of arguing
the opinion that all courts without any exception should be abolished
prevailed. [5]

The new Soviet Government, the Council of People's Commissars,
took up the question of new courts on November 15, 1917 and referred
it to the sessions of the body of November 16, 1917.

---

[1] P.I. Stuchka, *Izbrannyye proizvedeniya po merksistko-leninskoy teorii prava*, Riga,
1964, p. 229.

[2] See on the Reform, Samuel Kucherov, *Courts, Lawyers and Trials Under the Last
Three Tsars*, N.Y., 1953.

[3] I.N. Steinberg, "Fundamentals of the People's Court", *Znamya truda*, Feb. 23, 1918.

[4] P.I. Stuchka, *Proletarskaya revolutsija i pravo*, M. 1918, No. 1, p. 3.

[5] *Ibid.*

On November 16, it was decided to entrust A. Lunacharsky with the writing of a declaration to the draft of a decree concerning the revolutionary courts and the closing and liquidation of the old judicial institutions. The draft had to be presented to the Council on the morning of November 17, 1917.

Also, a commission for the drafting of the decree was formed, which included among others I. Stalin.

It is evident that Lunacharsky did not write a declaration at all, or he wrote a paper not acceptable to the majority of the Council, since the decree appeared without any declaration or preamble. [1]

The Decree on Courts was not discussed in the session of November 17. It was decided to transfer the draft for adoption to the TsIK., the legislative body at that time. However, the Council of People's Commissars deemed it unadvisable to wait until the bill would pass the Scilla and Charybdis of legislation, and the bill was discussed by the Council of People's Commissars on November 23, 1917, and passed on November 24, 1917, using the right of the Council "to pass decrees independently and then to present them to the V TSIK for confirmation in case of emergency". [2]

b) *Contents of Decree No. 1 on Courts*

1. *Local Courts*

The provisions of the Decree No. 1 on Courts were as follows : [3]

1. All tsarist courts, civil, criminal, military and naval, were abolished with the exception of the Courts of the Peace which were "suspended" replacing the existing justices of the peace, elected up to the present time not by direct voting, by local courts, composed

---

[1] Lunacharsky wrote an article, Revolution and the Court, in the *Pravda* of 1 Dec 1917, in which he attempted to vindicate the "breaking to pieces of the old court, the weapon of our enemies and our fathers" and the creation of a new law by quotations from Menger, Jellinek and Petrazhitsky, especially by the "Intuitive Law" theory of hte latter. Lunacharsky wrote in his article : "Down with the courts — mummies, the altars of the dead law; down with judges-bankers ready to continue to drink fresh blood in the tomb of the undivided domination of the capital. Long live the people creating in his court, boiling, fermenting as young wine, a new law-justice for all, the law of great brotherhood and egality of the toilers".

[2] Mal'kovich, *op. cit.*, pp. 170-171.

[3] *Sob. uz., RSFSR*, 1917, Item 50.

of a local judge and two next-in-turn assessors; local judges had to be elected by direct democratic elections in the future, and until such elections would be set temporarily by District and Village Soviets, or if such did not exist, by City and Provincial Soviets of Workers', Soldiers' and Peasants' Deputies. The same justices of the peace were not deprived of the right of being elected to local judges elected temporarily by Soviets and definitely in democratic elections.

In the same way, local courts had to be elected by regional soviets, and where the latter did not exist, by regional committees, for the decision in criminal cases;

2. The existing institutions of investigating magistrates, prosecutors, as well as the institution of sworn and private lawyers were divested. Up to the time when the entire court procedures were to be reorganized, the preliminary investigation in criminal cases was assigned to local judges personnally, but their arrest and indictment decisions had to be confirmed by the whole local court. Citizens of unblemished character of both sexes, in possession of their civil rights, were entitled to function as prosecutors and counsels for the defense;

3. Local Courts had to pronounce their decisions and verdicts in the name of the Russian Republic and were to be guided in their decisions and verdicts by the laws of the overthrown government, only as far as these laws were not abolished by the Revolution and did not contradict revolutionary consciousness and revolutionary legal consciousness and the programs of the Social-Democratic and Social-Revolutionary Parties;

4. In order to fight counterrevolution and take measures to preserve the Revolution and its achievements, as well as for decisions in cases of marauding, predatoriness, sabotage, and other abuses by traders, industrialists, officials and other persons, workers' and peasants' revolutionary tribunals were established benches of which consisted of a chairman and six assessors, sitting with them and elected by province or city soviets of workers' soldiers' and peasants' deputies; investigation in these cases had to be conducted by a special investigation commission;

5. All the previously existing investigating commissions were abolished and all the cases pending there transferred to the newly organized investigation commissions. The jurisdiction of the local courts extended in civil cases to include amounts in litigation up to 3,000 rubles, and in criminal cases punishment of up to two years in jail; decisions and verdicts of the local court could not be appealed

but cassation was admitted. The cassation instance was the assembly of local justices.

Thus, the entire court system with the judges, prosecutors, investigating magistrates and attorneys-at-law was abolished.

2. *Resistance of the Abolished Institutions*

The institutions discarded by the Decree No. 1 on Courts tried to resist or ignore the Decree.

In a special decision of November 23, 1917, the Ruling Senate prohibited the application of the Decree to judicial institutions. It was said in the decision : ... "It has come to the knowledge of the Senate that the persons who seized power shortly before the convention of the Constituant Assembly, which alone has to be the true representative of the sovereign will of the Russian people, made an attempt against the very existence of the Ruling Senate which stood watch over law order in Russia for more than two hundred years. These persons, in deciding to abrogate the Ruling Senate and all the courts. undermine the very foundations of the state structure and deprive the population of its last support—the legal defense of its personal and material rights. Criminal actions of persons who have named themselves "People's Commissars" during the last weeks, certify that they will not hesitate to apply violence to institutions and persons watching over the Russian state. Before violence will touch the oldest of the higher Russian institutions and will deprive the Ruling Senate of the possibility of raising its voice in the hour of greatest danger for the fatherland, the General Assembly of the Senate, convoked, according to Art. 14 of the By-laws of the Senate, not recognizing legal force to the orders of any arbitrary organization, decided to perform steadfastly, as long as possible, the duties assigned to it by law in the future up to the decision of the Constituant Assembly on the formation of power in the country, and to inform of this decision all subordinate places and persons. A copy of this decision is to be communicated to the Chief Prosecutor of the First Department of the Senate, in order to be printed in the Collection of Laws and Ordinances of the Government". [1]

After the building of the Senate was occupied by the Bolshevists, the Senate held a General Assembly in private quarters and decided on November 29, 1917 : "to acknowledge that the violance perpetrated

---

[1] *Russkiye vedomosti*, Nov. 24, 1917.

on the Ruling Senate, prevents it from the possibility of continuing normal sessions; in consequence the decisions of cases which have greatest state importance and concern the most vital interest of private persons cannot be passed; that is why it is necessary to take measures for the continuation of the Ruling Senate's activity in its full extent, at the first possibility". [1]

The General Assembly of the *Sudebnaya palata* (Court of Appeal) discussed the decision of the Senate of November 23 and decided to follow the decision of the Senate and to inform all the Circuit Courts of this. [2]

Although the justices of the peace were treated more liberally by the Decree No. 1 on Courts, still the General Assembly of the justices of the peace in Moscow discussed the Decree in its General Assembly of November 27, 1917 and decided that :

1. violence was committed not by a power, acknowledged by the entire people and possessing the right of sovereign and competent government, administrative or legislative authority;

2. activity of the justices of the peace must be continually based on laws promulgated by the Senate, according to the set order and compulsory regulations published by competent organs of local administration, according to laws in force, and

3. it recognizes that only forcible violence of the principles of independent court can compel the justices of the peace to suspend temporarily their activity. [3]

In Petrograd the provisions of the Decree were enforced by Representatives of the Investigation Commission of the Military-Revolutionary Committee already on November 29, 1917. This was made known to the Petrograd population by its representative in the following announcement : "Since the old judicial institutions, subject to closure, according to the Decree No. 1 on Courts of the Council of People's Commissars, arbitrarily continued their activity, I closed the following institutions on November 29 : the Ruling Senate, the Main Military Court, with the staff of military prosecutors and investigators and the Petrograd Court of Commerce ..." [4]

The Petrograd Circuit Court was closed on the night of November 30, 1917. The Commissar assigned to the job appeared with several armed

---

[1] *Ibid.*, November 30, 1917.

[2] *Ibid.*

[3] *Ibid.*, Nov. 28, 1917.

[4] *Dokumenty velikoy oktyabrskoy revolutsii*, M. 1938, I, p. 321.

soldiers at the Court and declared that on orders of the Workers' and Peasant's Government he takes over the control of the Court. He called a meeting of the lower employees and assigned duties to them. Then he summoned the justices and prosecutors of the court and required them to hand over to him the court documents and money. A part of those convoked showed up voluntarily, measures of coercion were applied to the others. [1]

The judiciary of the Moscow Circuit Court also decided in a General Assembly of November 11, 1917 to continue their activity exclusively applying also in the future legislative norms passed by decisions of the legally invested government and promulgated by the Ruling Senate ... [2] But since the building of the Circuit Court had been sacked, they decided to suspend sessions in the building, with the exception of the Administrative Department, the jurisdiction of wich covered cases related with the election to the Constituant Assembly.

The Moscow Judicial Institutions were closed on December 17, 1917 by a Commissar of the Kremlin with the help of some armed soldiers.

The overwhelming majority of justices and prosecutors, as well as a part of the lower employees of the judicial institutions in Russia, struck and refused to recognize the new government and its orders. The strike took on tremendous proportions and lasted a long time. So, for instance, among the 65 members of the judiciary of the Vitebsk Circuit Court, 5 persons remained for work as of the middle of 1918, and among 35 lawyers—only one. [3]

The reaction of the government was that all the employees of the Ministry of Justice up to the VIII grade, who did not show up for work were discharged without rights to pension by order of the People's Commissar of Justice of November 22, 1917.

Stalin defined this first period after the October Revolution as follows : "From the viewpoint of the internal situation, this period can be characterized as the period of demolition of the entire apparatus of the old bourgeois power". [4]

On the occasion of the Anniversary of the Decree No. 1 on Courts, Stuchka wrote "Themida is decrowned. This corrupt Goddess of

---

[1] M.V. Kozhevnikov, *Istoriya sovetskogo suda*, M. 1948, p. 17.
[2] *Russkiye vedomasti*, Nov. 12, 1917.
[3] *Izvestia*, Aug. 27, 1918.
[4] Stalin, *Works*, M. 1953-4, p. 384.

bourgeois justice is deposed and declared out of the proletarian law. The cruel sword was torn from her hands and her faked scales are confined to the museum of the Revolution. And the laws and Senate Rulings are burned on bonfires ... Down with the laws, long live revolutionary consciousness". [1]

The future abolition of the tsarist laws after the discarding of the judicial system was also based on Marx' teachings. In his speech before the Jury in 1848, Marx said, "This Code of Napoleon in my hands did not create the contemporary bourgeois structure (of society). The bourgeois structure, which came into being in the eighteenth century and developed further in the nineteenth, found in the Code only its juridical form. *It represents only a piece of paper if it ceases to correspond to public conditions.* (I.M.). You cannot use these old laws as a foundation of the new social development, since these old laws did not create the old legal structure. They are children of this legal structure and have to perish together with it. They unescapably change together with the changing life conditions".

Since, according to Marx, laws belong to the "superstructure" of society, whereas the economic relations build its foundations, the super-structure is bound to follow the fate of the foundation : it must be completely renewed in accordnace with the changed economic basis.

However, Marx's teaching was not fully applied as Stuchka and others desired it in the beginning of Soviet rule. The provision of the Decree No. 1 on Courts that old laws could be applied if not contradict-ing the programs of the two socialist parties was an obvious concession to more moderated circles, since the first Bolshevist government was a coalition with leftist Socialist-Revolutionaries. Although both programs differed in many questions, especially in rural policy, Stuchka explains, "these differences were essential, however, only at the continuation of capitalism which loses its accute character at the transition to socialism". [2]

The discarded capitalist laws had to be replaced by new laws and new administration of justice, since the proletariat already allegdly brings with it a new economic structure, much higher than the capitalist one and, "it is also the promoter of a new law, incomparably higher than the old one", according to D. Kurskiy, People's Commissar of Justice from March 1918 to 1928. "Such a law cannot be prepared

---

[1] *Pravda*, Dec. 7, 1918.
[2] P.I. Stuchka, "The Old and the New Courts", *Materialy...* II, p. 10.

beforehand", thinks Kursky. It would be then an utopia, a theoretical play. Every class creates its law in reality when it applies its power, when it "builds its world, according to its basic class interests on one side given concrete conditions on the other. No class, even one, coming to power by an abrupt overturn can create a new world at once". [1] "Thus", continues Kursky, "The revolutionary class brings with itself a new legal consciousness, a presentiment of new legal relations and forms being in deep conformity with new economic conditions of life created by its revolution. It brings a new judicial conscience, new notions of good and evil. The revolution itself is a great contraposition of the new law and the old one ... The creation of new civil and penal laws, new state structures, of new organs of power, including the judicial one, is the consolidation of the Revolution, the formulation and realization, of a new legal conscience, hidden in it, and erected by new class interests, i.e., by a new economic plan". [2]

3. *Class Courts*

According to Lenin, the court is an implement of the ruling class in order to oppress all other classes of the population. Thus, since the proletariat seized power in Russia in October 1917, the newly created courts were courts of the proletariat, an organ of the state with the purpose of oppressing other classes. "Our courts are class courts [directed] against the bourgeoisie" [3] writes Lenin, establishing herewith, the political character of the Soviet Courts. This character is retained by the Soviet court up to the present time.

In the first draft of his article, "The New Problems of Soviet Power" dictated on March 28, 1918, Lenin expressed again his views on the old and new courts.

Having asserted that the court in a capitalist society was an apparatus for the suppression and bourgeois exploitation and therefore it was necessary for the proletarian revolution not to reform it, but completely annhilate and to whip out down to the foundation the old court and its apparatus. "This necessary problem was solved by the October Revolution—Lenin continued—, and solved successfully. In the place of the old court it began to create a people's court, better a soviet, court constructed on the principle of the participation

---

[1] P.I. Kursky, "Revolution and the Court", *Materialy...* II, p. 15.
[2] *Op. cit.*, p. 16. Indeed, the RSFSR had to wait for its own codes up to 1922-23.
[3] Lenin, XXVI, p. 339.

of the working population and exploited classes—and only by them—in the administration of the state.

The new court must serve two scopes, according to Lenin. The first scope is to fight the exploiters striving to reinstall their supremacy. The second scope is to insure the carrying out of the strictest discipline and self-discipline of the working population.

The second scope is even more important than the first for Lenin.

But these scopes cannot be achieved without coercion and "the organ of the proletarian state which realizes such coercion—are the Soviet courts". [1]

That the class character of the Soviet court demands that it should be manned exclusively by representatives of the proletariat and the peansantry was clearly formulated by Lenin in his draft of the first Communist program, in 1919.

Article 1 of the draft reads : "On the way to Communism through the dictatorship of the proletariat the Communist Party, repudiating democratic slogans, completely does away also with such bourgeois organs of supremacy such as the old court system, and replaces these with workers' and peasants' *class* [italics supplied] courts... Having taken all power in his hands, the proletariat in the place of the formula : eligibility of judges brings forward the class slogan : "electability of judges from the working, only working population, and carries it out in the entire organization of the courts". [2]

Lenin's draft of Art. 1 was almost verbally incorporated into Art. II of the first program of the Russian Communist Party of 1919.

The first scope of the Soviet court as a class court was the fight against the bourgeoisie... "The new court is necessary, in the first place, for the struggle against exploiters, attempting to restore their supremacy" ... Lenin wrote. [3]

The Soviet court was from the beginning called upon to help, as an organ of the state, to realize the dictatorship of the proletariat, which was established after the October Revolution.

The revolutionary dictarorship of the proletariat is, according to Lenin, a power, acquired and sustained by violence exercised by the proletariat against the bourgeoisie, a power bound by any kind of law. And when the court does not ruthlessly suppress bourgeois tendency, Lenin did not hesitate to interfere in the administration of justice.

---

[1]   Lenin, 27, p. 191.

[2]   Lenin, XXII, p. 460.

[3]   *Ibid.*, p. 424.

4. *Eligibility of Judges and Assessors*

The eligibility of judges and assessors who had to replace the jury was proclamed. They had to be elected by direct democratic elections.

Temporary, however, up to the time when such elections could be conducted, the justices and assessors had to be appointed by local Soviets of Workers', Soldiers' and Peasants' Deputies.

This "temporary" lasted more than thirty years, up to 1948, as we will see later. In the meantime, judges of the courts and the assessors were elected by Executive Committees of Soviets, which is tantamount to appointment.

5. *No Separation of Powers*

The doctrine of separation of powers, one of the fundamental principles of democratic states, is repudiated in the Soviet Union. Lenin wrote that in communist states, representative institutions will remain, but parliamentarianism as a particular system, as delimitation of legislative and executive work ... will not. [1]

The Communist Program of 1919 repudiates the separation of power flatly. "Holding for the toiling masses the assurance — incomparably greater than was possible with bourgeois democracy and parliamentarianism — of conducting the elections and recall of deputies in a manner most easy and accessible to workers and peasants, soviet authority at the same time abrogates the negative sides of parliamentarianism, especially the separation of legislative and executive powers". [2] ... According to Vyshinsky, "under the bourgeois principle of so-called separation of powers into three or four powers, these powers are separated from, and practically dominate over society". [3]

Reviewing the doctrine of separation of powers and its history A. Ya Vyshinsky comes to the conclusion that complete separation of powers in reality was not achieved in any country. He is of the opinion that the executive had a dominant position over the other powers everywhere.

With regard to the U.S., Vyshinsky writes that, "The equalization of powers existing in the United States puts forward into first place the President (head of the executive authority and not responsible

---

[1] Lenin, 25, p. 396.
[2] Par. 5.
[3] A. Ya. Vyshinsky, *The Law of the Soviet State*, N.Y., 1948, p. 318.

to the Congress). Furthermore, the bourgeoisie insures itself against all sorts of undesirable laws by the Supreme Court (whose members are designated by the President, with the consent of the Senate). If a majority of the Supreme Court is hostile to the policy of the President, the latter can appoint an additional member of Judges to assure himself a majority in the Supreme Court". [1]

Evidently with regard to the U.S., Vyshinsky failed to make his point. The system of checks and balances, described by him, equalizes the three powers in a very high degree. Vyshinsky's assertion that the President "can appoint" additional members to the Supreme Court is not correct because the President needs the consent of the Senate to this effect. The unsuccessful attempt of Franklin D. Roosevelt in this direction is an excellent example of how efficiently the system of checks and balances works. Certainly, no measure can work 100 % constantly. That sometime the equilibrium of power deviates on one or another side are exceptions which only confirm the rule. The truth is that the doctrine of separation of powers cannot be applied in a totalitarian state, since all the powers are concentrated in the hands of a dictator or a party which exercises dictatorial power.

The Soviet State began its existence by enforcement of the dictatorship of the proletariat maintained it under the unrestricted rule of Stalin. His death did not change the totalitarian character of the Soviet State, and as long as this character prevails separation of powers will remain excluded there.

Indeed, Montesquieu and Locke built the doctrine of separation of power as a remedy against absolutism. The introduction of the doctrine into the Soviet State administration would mean a retreat from totalitarianism.

6. The Use of Old Laws

The local courts could apply the laws of the overthrown government as far as they were not abrogated by the Bolshevist revolution and did not contradict revolutionary conscience and revolutionary legal conscientiousness. In a note to Article 5 of the Decree No. 1 on Courts, it was clarified that abrogated are all the laws contradicting the Decrees of the Central Executive Committee of the Soviets and of the Workers' and Peasants' Government, as well as the program—

---

[1] *Ibid*, p. 316.

minimum of the Russian Social Democratic Workers' and the Social-Revolutionary Parties.

Hence, the Decree No. 1 on Courts strived to create a legal base for the decisions of the local courts, by a conditional permission of using laws of the previous governments. As we will see, not for a long time. Although again we are here faced with this arbitrary concept of "revolutionary conscience" and "revolutionary legal consciousness" as a criterion for the applicability of old laws, in this case, however, revolutionary conscience and legal consciousness did not replace law and make an action punishable without being forbidden by a legal instrument. The right of decision as to whether an old law may be applied under the new political and social conditions of life created by a revolution was confined to the conscience and consciousness of a court investing the court with legislative power for the case on hand.

7. *Jurisdiction, Appeal and Cassation*

Jurisdiction of the Local Courts extended to suits involving 3,000 rubles in civil cases and a punishment of not more than 2 years in jail in criminal cases.

Thus, the competence of the local court was approximately similar to that of the former justices of the peace. But what courts had to decide in other criminal cases and civil suits ?

The newspaper *"Petrogradsky golos"* reported on January 26, 1918 that "according to a decision of the Council of People's Commissars, civil suits valued from 3 to 10,000 rubles and criminal cases involving a punishment from 2 to 4 years in jail, were submitted for decision to the council of local judges. However, the study of the statistics of cases decided upon by the councils of local judges made by Kozhevnikov does not warrant the conclusion that these assemblies sat over cases as a court of first instance. Kozhevnikov is of the opinion that the figures he studied are convincing proof that the local courts or revolutionary tribunals decided upon cases exceeding their individual jurisdiction, as established by the Decree No. 1 on Courts.

It is also possible that some of these cases were decided upon by arbitration courts.

No appeal was admitted against the decisions of the local courts. However, a review in cassation by the council of local judges was possible, if the judgement provided a fine of more than 100 rubles, or imprisonment of more than 6 months.

8. *Preliminary Investigation, Prosecution*

Up to the time when the entire judicial procedure had to be re-organized, preliminary investigation was entrusted to the justices of the local courts personnally who had to try the case later. Arrests had to be confirmed by the concil of local judges.

Every citizen, man or woman, without criminal records, and in possession of civil rights had the right to take over the duties of a prosecutor or counsel in the preliminary investigation and in the sessions of the court.

9. *Arbitration Courts*

The Decree No. 1 on Courts provided that the parties could submit to arbitration their claims in all civil cases and all criminal cases that could be started only on complaint. The procedure in the arbitration courts was regulated by decree of the VTsIK of February 3, 1918. [1]

According to the Decree, all civil litigation except cases under the jurisdiction of special courts or other jurisdictions or laws concerning labor contracts and social security, as well as all criminal offenses punishable only on complaint of the plaintif or the victim (as in cases of personal offenses, etc.) could be submitted by the parties to the decision of an arbitration court.

The Decree provided that the arbitration court may consist of one arbitrator, and of an equal number of members chosen by both parties involved. Complaints on the decision of the arbitration court could be directed to the assemblies of local judges, according to rules established for cassation.

Kozhevnikov asserts that this form of court did find no wide use by the population. [2]

10. *Volost' Courts* [3]

The Decree No. 1 on Courts did not provide for an instance to decide cases above the competence of the local courts. Also, it did not create a court for the rural population. This last gap was filled in simply by an instruction of the Department of Local Administration of the People's Commissars of the Interior on the Organization of Soviet

---

[1] M.V. Kozhevnikov, *op. cit.* p. 33.

[2] *Ibid.,* p. 34.

[3] Volost' — a small rural district.

Power in Volost's of February 9, 1918. These rural courts were composed as follows : every village elected a representative. The assembly of these representatives elected two judges of the Volost' Court and one member of the Volost' Executive Committee took over the duties of a chairman of the Volost' Courts. These 3 persons formed the bench who had to decide the cases brought to it. According to the Instruction, the court had to be guided in its decision by conscious, customs and new legislation, but by no means by laws of the tsarist government.

Complaints against the decisions had to be directed to the Soviets of Peasants' Deputies through the Chairman of the Volost' Court, who had the role of a Raporteur of the case before the Soviet. [1]

The creation of a court by means of instructions of an administrative agency is a flagrant example of the dependence of the courts upon the administration. When the Local Courts were brought into existence, not by action of the legislative power — VTsIK — but by the Council of People's Commissars, that could be and was explained by the provision giving the right to the Council to act apart from the legislation in some cases and under some circumstances. But to install a court for the rural population, the majority of the Russian People, and to regulate its activity by instruction of a department of a commissariat is a direct violation of the rights of the legislature.

The dependence of the courts upon the administration was made even more flagrant by the fact that complaints against decisions of the Volost' court were decided not by a higher judicial instance (as it was in the case for the local courts and revolutionary tribunals) but by an administrative agency — the Volost' Soviets.

B. Decree No. 2 on Courts

An attempt was made to correct the obvious shortcomings of the Decree No. 1 on Courts by the Decree No. 2 on Courts. [2]

The Decree was discussed in the meetings of the Council of People's Commissars of January 16, and 30, 1918, but not published until March 7, 1918, because of some objections brought forward by some Party members and officials (especially P.I. Stuchka) of the People's

---

[1] *Vestnik Kommissariata vnutrennikh del*, 1918, No. 6, p. 16.

[2] *RSFSR, Sob. zak.*, 1918, Item 420 (The correct number of this item is 347. For the story of the editorial error, see John N. Hazard, *Settling Disputes in Soviet Society*, N.Y. 1960, Footnote 19, pp. 9-10.

Commissariat of Justice which, beginning with December 7, 1917, was in the hands of the left Socialist Revolutionaries represented by Commissar Steinberg. The accusation that Steinberg "pulled through" the Decree No. 2 on Courts brought forward by some critics of the Decree, is refuted by Golunsky and Karev. [1] The reason for the refutation is obvious : Lenin himself took part in the editing of the Decree and is responsible for it.

The Decree No. 2 on Courts filled the gap left by the Decree No. 1, by creating a Circuit Court for cases exceeding the jurisdiction of the Local Courts. These courts had civil and criminal departments, the number of which was established by the general assembly of the members of the court. The general assembly also elected the Chairman of the court and the individual departments.

The justices of the circuit courts were elected by city and province Soviets, which had also the right to recall them if their behavior was deemed not appropriate.

The bench in the civil department of the circuit courts consisted of three professional judges and four assessors, elected by city and province soviets, according to lists prepared by district and volost' soviets.

The bench in criminal cases was manned by a professional justice and twelve regular and two deputy assessors. The professional justice functioned as chairman of the bench.

In matters of jurisdiction, Art. 9 of the Decree also provided that in civil cases all the non-adversary proceedings, such as probate of testaments, adoption, matrimony, etc., i.e., all cases classified not according to the value involved, belonged to the competence of the local courts. However, cases of bankruptcy, involving more than 3,000 rubles, came under the jurisdiction of the circuit courts.

It must be emphasized that setting the jurisdiction of the local people's court and the circuit courts in relation to the punishment involved in the case, the Decrees on Courts Nos. 1 and 2 made it necessary to revert to the pre-revolutionary Criminal Code since, in the absence of Soviet Codes, only in this Code could the court find the information, enabling it to define as to whether it had the competence to sit over the case or not.

However, some local courts preferred to resolve the question of jurisdiction not beforehand, but during the trial and according to their socialist legal consciousness. Thus the local people's court in

---

[1]   S.A. Golunsky and D.C. Karev, *Sudoustroystvo SSSR*, M. 1946, p. 73.

Petrograd accepted any criminal case and established the jurisdiction during the procedure, whereas the Local People's Court in Moscow passed judgment on all cases, except murder, robbery and robbery with violence. [1]

The preliminary investigation of cases under the jurisdiction of the Circuit Court was entrusted to a special commission of three persons also "temporarily" elected by the Soviets until the time when direct elections would take place.

The defense had the right to participate in the procedures of the preliminary investigation. However, the Investigative Commissions could exclude the defense in the interests of the disclosure of truth.

The conclusive decision of the investigation commission had the force of an indictment. If the circuit court found the decision of the commission not founded enough, it had to return the case to the commission for the completion of the investigation, or assigned this job to a justice of the circuit court.

It must be emphasized that Art. 8 of the Decree regulated civil and criminal procedure in courts, according to the provisions of the Civil and Criminal Procedure Codes of 1864, as far as they were not abrogated by Decrees of the TsIK or the Council of People's Commissars, and did not contradict the legal consciousness of the working classes.

Should the court decline to apply an old law, it had to give the grounds for its decision. Thus, a steady foundation was given to the civil and criminal procedures.

The tendency to come as near as possible to the laws of 1864 may be seen in the new number of assessors in criminal cases (12) equal to that of jurors under the 1864 laws. Furthermore, although the assessors passed decisions together with the professional judge, in matters of the verdict of guilty or not guilty the professional judge (chairman) had only a consultative voice, so that in reality the 12 assessors functioned as jurors of the old time. The independence of the assessors from the professional judges was also strengthened by the most unusual provision that the assessors had the right to challenge their chairman in every stage of the proceedings, certainly a right which no jurors or assessors had at their disposal anywhere in the world.

Steinberg was in general inclined to promote in the new judicial legislature the revival of the laws of 1864. As we know, he wanted to lay the foundations of a democratic court not on an "empty place".

---

[1] D.I. Kursky, *Izbrannyye stat'i i rechi*, M. 1953, p. 64.

Thus, in his attempt to retain democratic principles in the administration of justice, Steinberg succeeded in making the criminal court with 12 assessors different from the court with jury only to a small extent, since in participating in the decision over the guilt or innocence of the accused, the professional judge had only a consultative voice. In this way the influence of the professional judge upon the assessors was reduced to a minimum in the most important matter in a criminal trial : the verdict of guilt or innocence.

Lenin's consent to a more moderate approach in matters of the creation of the new court system in the Decree No. 2 on Courts can perhaps be explained by the fact that Lenin's government was a coalition and he still had to make concessions to his government partners.

The Decree also provided for a cassation instance — the province courts, the members of which had to be elected by the general assembly of cricuit courts justices. The members of the province courts had to elect among them a chairman of the court and chairmen of the individual departments.

A peculiar judicial agency provided by the Decree No. 2 on Courts was the supreme judicial control whose members had to be elected by the general assembly of the province courts among themselves for one year. The scope of the supreme judicial control was to interpret contradictory decisions of the courts of cassation and issue directive decisions for these courts. In cases when the supreme judicial control established unsolvable contradictions between the law and the popular legal sense, it had to ask the legislature for a new law. Only the legislature was empowered to overturn a decision of the supreme judicial control.

The Decree No. 2 on Courts obviously decentralized the administration of justice and made it independent of the central government. However, the full dependence upon the local government remained.

C. DECREE NO. 3 ON COURTS [1]

The participation of the left Socialist-Revolutionary Party in the Soviet government ended with the insurrection staged by this party in July 1918. With Steinberg's resignation, the Commissariat of

---

[1] *Sob. uz., RSFSR*, 1918, Item 589.

Justice fell into the hands of a full-fledged Bolshevik. The result was that some provisions of the Decree No. 2 on Courts were not introduced and some others abrogated by subsequent legislation. Province courts and the Supreme Control in Moscow were never established and the Decree No. 3 on Courts published on July 20, 1918 did not contain any reference to the laws of 1864. Omitted also was the provision that the courts could use pre-revolutionary laws under special conditions. According to the Decree No. 3 on Courts the courts had to be directed in their decisions by the Decrees of the Workers' and Peasants' government and their revolutionary legal consciousness only.

Thus, in the Decree No. 1 on Courts, the condition for the use of pre-revolutionary laws was the absence of contradiction to the Soviet Decrees, the socialist law-consciousness and the Programs-inimum of the two socialist parties.

In the Decree No. 2 on Courts, this third condition was omitted and the Decree No. 3 on Courts dropped the reference to the old laws completely, although it did not yet forbid their use explicitly.

Among the other provisions of the Decree No. 3 on Courts, the more exact delimitation of the jurisdiction of the Local and Circuit Courts must be noted : The local courts had to decide misdemeanor and felony cases, with the exception of crimes against life, rape, robbery, banditism, counterfeiting of money, bribery and speculation, which were assigned to the competence of the circuit courts. The local courts had the right to inflict a punishment not higher than 5 years in jail. In civil cases their jurisdiction extended to suits involving not more than 10,000 rubles.

The Decree No. 3 on Courts officially abrogated the province courts and the supreme judicial control and established, in place of the latter, a provisional Cassation Court in Moscow, with two departments : Civil and Criminal. The Cassation Court had not only to decide on complaints in cassation against the decisions or the verdicts of the circuit courts, but also to supervise the activity of the Local and Circuit Courts.

With regard to the criminal and civil procedure, the Decree No. 1 on Courts provided for the publication of a special Decree on procedure which appeared much later. The Decree No. 2 on Courts permitted, as we have seen, the use of the Codes of Criminal and Civil Procedure of 1864. Since the Decree No. 3 on Courts did not mention the laws of 1864 anymore and did not regulate matters of procedure, a special

Instruction was published by the Commissariat of Justice on July 23, 1918 [1] containing rules of procedure.

Thus, again an instruction was issued with provisions, the adoption of which was the domain of the legislature and this time by the Commissariat of Justice; it was later included in the Codes of Procedure of the Republic.

The Commissariat of Justice certainly had no legal authority to issue instructions having the force of laws.

For instance, according to the Instruction, a kind of appeal on merits excluded in all the three Decrees on Courts, was permitted under the hide of special rules of cassation. Indeed, the Instruction provided that the assembly of local judges, the cassation instance for the decisions of the local courts, could not only quash the decision of the local court because of violations of procedure, but if it also found the decision evidently unjust, diminish or set aside the punishment, which is tantamount to a review on the substance of the case, i.e., to a review on appeal.

The Instruction also contained other provisions on civil and criminal procedure which evidently belonged to a Code of Procedure and not into a Commissariat' instruction. For instance, the instruction provided that in cities, all the organizations accepting Soviet power, i.e., political parties trade unions, workers' cooperatives, factory and plant committees, etc., took part in the composition of the lists of candidates to the functions of an assessor by including into the lists one candidate per fifty electors in their organizations. The lists had to be confirmed by corresponding executive committees of the local soviets.

In rural places, the candidates had to be appointed by the village community : one candidate for fifty electors in the community, and where there were less than fifty electors—one condidate for every village.

The candidates were definitely appointed by the executive committees to assessors for one year.

The Instruction provided, furthermore, provisions on the jurisdiction of courts, preliminary investigations, the starting of a suit or criminal case, preparatory actions of the courts, the order of taking decisions and passing verdicts, execution of verdicts, and deciding controversial procedure and review (cassation) procedure, etc.

The fact that the Instruction was published in the RSFSR Collection

---

[1] *Sob. uz., RSFSR*, 1918, Item 597.

of Laws gives to it also the formal importance of a law ... a "law" passed by an institution not having legislative power, since these powers belonged to the VTsIK (Art. 33 of the RSFSR Constitution of 1918) and to the Council of People's Commissars in matters of administration or in case of emergency (see Art. 38).

Thus, in a matter of months, three decrees on courts and two instructions were issued, but did not satisfy either public opinion or legal specialists. Demands for a simplification of the court system, for a single people's court became louder and louder. Already the First Conference of the Province and Regional Commissars of Justice, in April 1918, unanimously expressed itself for the creation of a single people's court for all cases, civil and criminal, in the near future. [1] With regard to this desire, the formation of the circuit courts (partly realized) and of the province courts (never realized), were thoroughly criticized.

D. The One and Single People's Court

The Statute on the One and Single People's Court was published on November 30, 1918. [2] It abrogated the people's circuit courts and the court of Cassation introduced by the Decree No. 2 on Courts, and established a uniform people's court for the entire Republic.

All civil and criminal cases, as well as the non-adversary cases in which the Court had to establish a fact or an occurrence on the request of a soviet agency, were under the jurisdiction of the court (Art. 4). A note to the article provided that cases of counter-revolution, sabotage discrediting soviet power and espionage are to be tried by the revolutionary tribunals on which it depends to recognize the case without political importance and to refer it to the people's courts.

The bench consisted of one permanent people's judge, or of one permanent judge and two to six assessors.

The single judge examined divorce cases and the non-adversary cases. A very important function of the judge was the checking of the legality of keeping people under arrest in places of confinement of his district, and if the arrest was illegal, the setting of the arrested person at liberty; [3] they had also to watch over the inquests carried

---

[1] *Materialy, op. cit.* I, 9.

[2] *Sob. uz., RSFSR,* 1918, Item 889.

[3] A kind of habeas corpus which with regard to persons arrested by order of the Revolutionary Tribunals or the CheKa — remained on paper only.

out by organs of the soviet militia, giving guiding instructions, confirming or changing measures of detention taken by the militia.

A bench of one permanent judge (chairman) and six assessors decided on crimes of attempts on human life, infliction of serious wounds or disability, rape, robbery, counterfeiting of money and documents, bribery and speculation with monopolized or rationed products of consumption. All criminal and all civil cases were submitted to a bench of one professional judge (chairman) and two assessors.

The reference to pre-revolutionary laws was explicitly prohibited by the Statute on the One and Single People's Court (Note to Art. 22). The Court, had to decide only according to its socialist legal consciousness if no decree of the new regime could be applied.

The court was also free to use, at its discretion, all evidence submitted.

Judges were selected by the general assembly of borough soviets in cities having borough soviets, or by the general assembly of the City soviets, from lists prepared by their executive committees. In districts, including the cities which had no city soviets, the judges were appointed by executive committees of the district soviets from lists of candidates including the candidates presented by the village and volost' executive committees of the soviets.

The permanent judges were subject to recall at any time by Soviets or their executive committees, which appointed them.

The Statute also introduced requirements for the election of the assessors : they had to be in possession of the *active and passive* right to vote and be elected to the soviets (Art. 14). Lists of candidates to be elected as assessors were prepared by workers' organizations, volosts' and village soviets for the district and were submitted for confirmation to the district executive committees.

In matters of evidence, the court was not bound by any rules and could admit or reject any evidence presented. The assessors and the permanent justices had the same rights in the proceedings before the the court : they could interrogate the accused, the witnesses, decide upon the questions of guilt and punishment. Decisions were taken by the majority of voters.

A cassation instance was established. It was the Council of People's Judges formed of a chairman, people's judges of the district, and assessors. The council also supervised the activity of the people's courts of its district.

The preliminary investigation in important criminal cases remained in the hands of a commission. The permanent judge, however, had to carry out the preliminary investigation in cases to be submitted to the decision of the bench of one permanent judge and two assessors.

Some changes in the Statutes of People's Courts were brought about again not by legislation but by a decision of the RSFSR Commissariat of Justice on September 16, 1920. [1]

The decision introduced special sessions of the people's courts in province and district cities. These special sessions decided on most important cases in the competence of the court. Also, Chambers on Permanent Duty were formed in the people's courts with the assignment to sit on cases which could be examined at once without investigation. If the Chamber was of the opinion that the investigation was not yet completed it could refer the case for an additional investigation to a regular Chamber of the court. The Chambers on Permanent Duty had the authority to speed up and simplify procedures in petty cases.

The program of the Russian Communist Party adopted at the VIIIth Congress [2] recapitulated the fundamental principles on which the soviet court system had to be banded : 1) election of judges by the working population; 2) participation of the largest masses of the proletariat and the poorest peasantry in the administration of justice; 3) creation of one and single people's court to replace the endless variety of former courts of varying structures; 4) abolition of the laws of the overthrown governments and the realization of the will of the proletariat by applying the decrees of the soviet power and in case of obscure or inperfect decrees, socialist legal consciousness of the judges elected by Soviets.

E. The Statute on People's Courts of October 21, 1920

Then, on October 21, 1920, a new Statute on the People's Court was published. [3]

The new Statute referred the competence to appoint people's judges to the province executive committee : people's judges selected by the city and district soviets were presented for confirmation to the province executive committees. In the absence of candidates presented, the province executive committee appointed judges

---

[1] *Sob. uz., RSFSR*, 1920, Item 541.

[2] March 1919.

[3] *Sob. uz., RSFSR*, 1920, Item 407.

according to its choice. Judges were also recalled upon decision of the soviets which selected them, but on approval of the province executive committee.

An important change took place in the preliminary investigation : the Investigating Commissions were abolished and the preliminary investigation entrusted to special investigating magistrates.

The examination of complaints against actions of people's judges and the supervision over the activity of the people's court was transferred to the presidium of the council of people's courts. The bench of the province council of people's courts was curtailed from five to three judges. No basic changes from the Statute of People's Courts of 1918 was made in the statute of 1920.

However, again not by means of legislation but by an administrative order of the Commissariat of Justice of November 6, 1920, [1] the class character of the court was intensified. The Commissariat found that it was necessary to increase the number of foremost workers among the assessors and ordered that in the lists of assessor candidates their membership in the Communist Party, participation in elections, organization, etc. should be indicated.

The approved assessors were assigned to various people's courts by the districts offices of justice of the Commissariat of Justice.

---

[1] *Sob. uz., RSFSR*, 1920, Item 542.

CHAPTER THREE

EXTRAORDINARY COURTS

A. REVOLUTIONARY TRIBUNALS

Besides the local courts, the Decree No. 1 on Courts established the workers' and peasants' revolutionary tribunals, for the fight against counterrevolutionary forces and in order to protect the Revolution and its achievements from these forces, as well as for the passing of judgments in cases of pillage, plunder, sabotage and abuses by traders, industrialists, officials and other persons.

The tribunal justices were appointed by province or city Soviets and the bench consisted of a chairman and six assessors serving in turn.

Special Commissions for the Investigation in these cases were attached to the same Soviets.

a) *Instructions of December 17, 1917*

Naturally, this was a too brief a formulation of the scope and functions of the revolutionary tribunals. Consequently, on December 19, 1917 Steinberg issued an Instruction to the revolutionary tribunals [1] regulating the activity of the revolutionary tribunals, which in its turn was more a real piece of legislation than a clarification.

The instruction contained a detailed list of cases put under the jurisdiction of the revolutionary tribunals : subject to the competence of the tribunals were persons a) who organize insurrections against the power of the workers' and peasants' government; who actively counteract the government or do not submit to it, or call other people to counteract it or not submit to it; b) who use their positions in state or public service in order to disturb or impede the regular work in agencies or enterprizes in which they are or were employed (sabotage, hiding or destruction of documents or property, etc.); c) who accumulate or curtail the production of products of mass consumption without real necessity; d) who by means of cornering, hiding, spoiling and destroying of products otherwise strive to produce scarcity of them on the market, in order to increase the price of them; e) who violate decrees,

---

[1] *Sob. uz., RSFSR,* 1917, Item 170.

orders, obligatory decisions and other published regulations of the workers' and peasants' government organs, if these decrees, decisions or regulations provide for the jurisdiction of the revolutionary tribunals in case of their violation; f) who take advantage of their administrative or public position in order to misuse the power entrusted to them by the revolutionary people.

Crimes against the people, committed by means of the press were put under the jurisdiction of a special press revolutionary tribunal to be established.

According to the Instruction, decisions of the revolutionary tribunals were final. However, in case of an obviously unjust sentence or violation of the order of procedure, the Commissariat of Justice assumed the right to reject the complaint or to ask the TsIK to order a final retrial of the case. Hence, to this effect, the Commissariat of Justice opened a Cassation Department at the Commissariat on January 25, 1918 for the examination of complaints against the decisions of the revolutionary tribunals.

Consequently Steinberg's Commissariat allocated itself the right of reviewing in cassation complaints against decisions of the revolutionary tribunals.

However, after Steinberg's departure, in March 1918, by April 2, 1918 the College of the Commissariat of Justice decided that the creation of the Department took place without decree or decision of the College and decided to dissolve the Department of Cassation and re-install the right of the College to give conclusions on complaints in cassation against decision of the revolutionary tribunals in the future, up to the time when a decree on the cassation procedure concerning the decisions of the revolutionary tribunals would be published.

The subject was again taken up and the College decided to establish a Cassation Desk at the Investigation Department of the Commissariat of Justice. The Desk distributed the cases among the members of the College. [1]

The instruction not only set details of the revolutionary tribunal's jurisdiction but also established a new kind of tribunal; The Press Revolutionary Tribunal.

It is important to note the punishments, the tribunal could inflict, according to Steinberg's instruction : 1) fine; 2) deprivation of liberty; 3) banishment from the capitals and other places or from the entire Russian Republic; 4) public censure; 5) declaration of being an enemy

---

[1] Kozhevnikov, *op. cit.*, p. 51-52.

of the people; 6) deprivation of all or some civil rights; 7) requisition or confiscation (partial or general) of property; 8) condemnation to obligatory public work.

As we see, the death penalty was not included into the program of punishments. This was another attempt of Steinberg to inhibit the flood of executions which, as he knew had to be and was ungeared after he left the Commissariat of Justice. It was, certainly, represented only as a temporary concession on the part of Lenin who was firmly convinced of the necessity of shedding blood in a revolution.

Another provision, introduced by Steinberg's instructions was the selection of assessors for the individual cases from the general lists of assessors for the session, by means of lot and not by picking by the executive committees of the Soviets, according to their reliability, as was the case in other courts.

As soon as the coalition with the left S-R was dissolved Lenin, in a letter adressed to the newly appointed Commissar of Justice wrote that "attention should be drawn to the practical results of the Commissariat's work in matters of the creation of a real revolutionary and fast working court mercilessly strict with regard to counter-revoultionaries, hooligans, do-nothings and disorganizers". [1]

When four members of the Investigation Commission were accused of taking bribes and were sentenced by the Revolutionary Tribunal to six months in jail only, Lenin wrote to the Party Committee on May 4, 1918 : "Please put on the agenda of the day the question of excluding from the Party members who participated as judges in the case (r.v.18) of bribery which was established and acknowledged (by the accused) who were sentenced to only one-half year in jail. In place of the execution of the bribers, to pronounce such a mockingly lenient sentence, *is a disgraceful action* (I.L.) for a communist and a revolutionary". [2]

The Council of People's Commissars examined the case in its session of May 4, 1918, noted the extraordinarily lenient character of the decision and charged the Commissariat of Justice with the working out of a law inflicting a high punishment as a minimum for the crime of bribery and any participation therein.

The case is of interest not only because it is a flagrant example of Lenin's interference in the administration of justice, but illustrates also his viewpoint on the death penalty.

---

[1] *Leninsky sbornik*, XXI, p. 219.

[2] *Ibid.*, p. 223.

In this respect, Lenin thought that, on the one side, arguments against the death penalty may be deemed valid only with regard to mass executions of the working population by exploiters in the interest of the preservation of exploitation without applying the death penalty to exploiters (i.e., to landowners and capitalists), but hardly any revolutionary government could do without it, in the other.

Two other sentences pronounced by the Revolutionary Tribunal provided indignation at the top of the Soviet government. The Petrograd Revolutionary Tribunal examined the case of the Countess Panin, former Minister of Education in Kerensky's Government, accused of having handed out to some persons 92,802 rubles of fiscal money "to be used as assigned".

The Tribunal decided to hold Countess Panin under arrest until the money would be returned and to punish her with public censure only, in consideration of her former educational activity. [1]

Another case was the trial of the wellknown blackguardist Purishkevich, former member of the Duma, and other members of the monarchist organization, created by Purishkevich. The same Revolutionary Tribunal sentenced Purishkevich to force labor in jail for four years, and released him on probation. The other members of the organization received even more lenient punishments.

In Lenin's opinion, without the right to inflict the death penalty, the Revolutionary Tribunal could not fulfill the task of suppression which he thought out for it.

In consequence, the Commissariat of Justice revised its Instructions of December 19, 1917, concerning the enumeration of punishments meted out by the revolutionary tribunals. In the decision of the College of the Commissariat of Justice of June 16, 1918, the revolutionary tribunals were freed of any limitation in applying penalties with the exception of crimes for which the law establishes a penalty of "not lower than".

Although not taking part in the government anywhere, the socialist-revolutionary continued to protest against capital punishment, in their press.

In answer to these recriminations, Lenin wrote "We are told that when the Dzerzhinsky's Commission [2] executes people—that is all right, but if the court says openly, before the entire people : he is a counterrevolutionary and deserves to be shot—that is wrong. Persons who run into such hypocrisy are politically dead ... No, a revolutionary

---

[1] *Sov. yust.*, 1937, No. 21, p. 48.
[2] The CheKa.

who does not want to be a hypocrite cannot repudiate the death penalty. There have been no revolution and periods of civil war without executions". [1]

In order to underline his indignation with the intelligentia protesting capital punishment, Lenin cites the incident with General Krasnov who surrendered to the workers in Petrograd. "The workers let him go," said Lenin. This was in the beginning of the Bolshevist Revolution in Petrograd. But now, "I would like to see the people's court which would not shoot Krasnov, as he himself shot down workers and peasants". [2] Also Stalin was of the opinion that such leniency undermines the strength of the Soviet power' [3]

The importance of the statements as a stimulation to the boundless use of the death penalty cannot be overestimated.

b) *Decree of May 17, 1918*

The next move in the history of the revolutionary tribunals was made by a Decree of the Council of People's Commissars of May 17, 1918. [4]

The Decree abolished revolutionary tribunals in small places. Revolutionary tribunals were left in the main cities, important railroad junctions, and industrial centers. The revolutionary tribunals were unified.

Discarded also were the special tribunals such as the Press Revulutionary Tribunal. The jurisdiction of the revolutionary tribunals was on the one hand curtailed by the transferring of all general crimes to the competence of the local courts, but on the other hand, enlarged by cases of pogroms, bribery, forgery, illegal use of Soviet documents, hooliganism and espionage. A college of prosecutors was established at revolutionary tribunals for the prosecution of cases coming before them.

c) *Revolutionary Tribunal Attached to the TsIK*

It was felt, however, that a small Revolutionary-Tribunal attached to the TsIK should be created "for the trial of the most important cases transferred from the jurisdiction of local revolutionary tribunals

---

[1] Lenin, 27, p. 478.

[2] Lenin, XXIII, p. 124.

[3] Lenin and Stalin, *Sbornik proizvedeniy k izucheniyu istorii VKP (b)* III, p. 525.

[4] *Sob. uz., RSFSR*, 1918, Item 471.

by decision of the Presidium of the TsIK, or the Council of People's Commissars, or the Commissariat of Justice. This Revolutionary Tribunal consisted of a chairman and six members elected for three months by the TsIK. The chairman and the members of the Tribunal could be recalled also before the end of their terms by the TsIK. It was this court which pronounced the first death sentence in the case of Admiral Shchastny, accused of having "maliciously prepared conditions for a counterrevolutionary overthrow of the Soviet Government". [1]

Also a cassation instance for the decisions of the revolutionary tribunals, was created in the form of a Special Department of Cassation of the TsIK, by Decree of June 11, 1918. [2] It consisted of a chairman appointed by the Council of People's Commissars and confirmed by the TsIK, and two permanent members : one delegated by the Commissariat of Justice and the other a representative (not member) of the TsIK. A member of the College of Prosecutors at the Revolutionary Tribunal attached to the TsIK, had the function as Raporteur for the Department of Cassation.

The grounds for appeals in cassation were : violation of rules of jurisdiction, of established rules of procedure or an obviously unjust sentence.

If the cassation was decided the case was remanded for retrial by a new bench of the Revolutionary Tribunal which pronounced the sentence, or to another Tribunal. The same action was taken when the sentence was reversed because the punishment did not correspond to the imputed action or an obviously innocent person was condemned.

The interference of the Cheka in the competence of the Revolutionary Tribunals discussed infra necessitated a delimitation of the rights of both institutions.

To this effect a decision of the TsIK of February 17, 1919 [3] provided that the right to pass sentences in all cases initiated by the Cheka, belong to the revolutionary tribunal.

A reorganization of the revolutionary tribunals with the purpose of facilitating speedy trial and the resolute suppression of crimes took place by the same decisions. The bench consisted of three judges elected for a month of service by the province executive committees. In cities with a population of more than 200,000, city revolutionary

---

[1] *Sov. yust.*, 1932, No. 33, p. 33.

[2] *Sob. uz.*, *RSFSR*, 1918, Item 545.

[3] *Sob. uz.*, *RSFSR*, 1919, Item 130.

tribunals were established, the members of which were appointed by city soviets.

The revolutionary tribunals had to pronounce a sentence within 48 hours after the end of the investigation. It had also the right to check the investigative actions of the CheKa : members of the revolutionary tribunal could visit the places of confinement in order to verify the legality of the arrests.

d) *Military Revolutionary Tribunals*

In September 1918, a Military Revolutionary Tribunal was created by the Revolutionary Military Council and attached to this body.

The Revolutionary Military Council adopted a Statute of the Military Revolutionary Tribunal on February 4, 1919, confirmed by the TsIK on November 20, 1919. [1] This Statute separated the military revolutionary tribunals from other revolutionary tribunals. A special revolutionary tribunal was established at the CheKa.

The centralization of the revolutionary tribunals was undertaken by the new Statute on Revolutionary Tribunals of March 18, 1920.'[2] The powers of the revolutionary tribunals were made more incisive by this Statute : the tribunals were empowered to abstain from the interrogation of witnesses when their testimony taken during the preliminary investigation was clear, and also to stop court proceedings at any stage when the court reached the opinion that the case was sufficiently clarified. Furthermore, the tribunals were entitled to bar the prosecution and the defense from the proceedings and exclude pleadings. They could also inflict any punishment within the framework of the existing Decrees. The purpose of the Statute was to unify the activity of organs fighting crime against the workers's and peasant's power and the order established by the Revolution for the unification of measures of extraordinary repression in such cases.

The administration of justice in the Army experienced a development similar to that of the civil administration of justice. After the October Revolution, military courts began to be set up, arbitrarily under different names, and without any system attached to Military Soviets of the units in various parts of the Red Army.

The Statute on Revolutionary Military Tribunals of February 4, 1919 set up the following system of revolutionary military tribunals :

---

[1] *Sob. uz., RSFSR,* 1919, Item 549.
[2] *Sob. uz., RSFSR,* 1920, Item 115.

revolutionary military tribunals of the armies; revolutionary military tribunals of the fronts, and the revolutionary military tribunal attached to the Revolutionary Military Council of the Republic. Every tribunal consisted of a chairman and two members appointed by the corresponding military soviet. The revolutionary military tribunals were not subordinate to the Commissariat of Justice and formed a special military judicial system.

According to the Statute of February 4, 1919, the revolutionary military tribunals had to decide upon cases of counterrevolutionary crimes and crimes committed in office by civil persons and upon all offenses charged to military personnel. In reality, they sat in justice over all other criminal offenses, since there were no regular courts at the front.

e) *Supreme Revolutionary Tribunal*

Its Statute prescribed the unification of the revolutionary judicial, military, military-transportation, as well as province branches of the tribunal under the Supreme Revolutionary Tribunal.

The Supreme Revolutionary Tribunal was thought of as a single cassation instance for all the tribunals, a supervisory body for them and a court of first instance for especially inportant cases.

Organs of the Supreme Revolutionary Tribunal were : 1) its Plenum —a supervisory and revision organ for all revolutionary tribunals of the Republic, and 2) colleges of cassation.

The tribunals had to be guided in its decisions "by the interests of the socialist republic, the defense from enemies of the socialist revolution and the interests of the class struggle for victory of the proletariat, according to ist communist, revolutionary and legal consciuosness". [1]

The procedure defined in the Statute was underdeveloped. It only provided that all the material collected by the preliminary investigation should be sent to the Chairman of the Tribunal who appointed a rapporteur and set a date for the trial. There were no provisions for the appearance of the accused before the Tribunal, of the examination of witnesses, of publicity of the trial, etc.

The decisions of the Supreme Revolutionary Tribunal were final and had to be executed within 24 hours.

---

[1] *Sob. uz., RSFSR,,* 1919, Item 131.

f) *Revolutionary Military Railroad Tribunals*

On March 18, 1920 [1] the Statute on Revolutionary Military Railroad Tribunals was adopted by the VTsIK, creating an independent system of revolutionary military railroad tribunals : the main Revolutionary Military Railroad Tribunal attached to the Commissariat of Railroads, and revolutionary military railroad tribunals attached to adminitrations of railroad lines.

g) *Statute of March 20, 1920*

The Statute of March 20, 1920 [2] on Revolutionary Tribunals abolished the Statute of February 4, 1919 on Revolutionary Military Tribunals and created the Supreme Tribunal of Cassation attached to the VTsIK. A link between the general and military administration of justice was established by making the Chairman of the Revolutionary Military Tribunal of the Republic a member of the Cassation Tribunal.

The jurisdiction of the revolutionary tribunals was not defined by an enumeration of offences under its competence, as it was the case in the previous statutes. Article 1 of the new Statute stated that the competence of the revolutionary tribunals extended to cases "submitted to the Tribunals by the CheKa, special departments and commissions for the fight against desertion and accepted by the tribunals for examination".

The decision of refusal or acceptance of a case was final and not subject to any appeal. In this way, the Investigation Commission of the Tribunals were *de facto* abolished.

h) *Statute of May 4, 1920* : *Decree of June 23, 1921*

A new Statute on Revolutionary Military Tribunals was published on May 4, 1920. [3]

The difference between the Statute of March 18, 1920 and that of May 4, 1920 was the order of appointing members of the Tribunal.

Thus, three tribunal systems, very loosely bound together, functioned at that time : the system of province revolutionary tribunals, headed by the Cassation Tribunal attached to the VTsIK, the system of revolutionary military tribunals, attached to the Revolutionary Military Council and the system of revolutionary military railroad

---

[1] *Sub. zak.*, *RSFSR*, 1920, Item 112.

[2] *Ibid.*, Item 115.

[3] *Sob. uz.*, *RSFSR*, 1920, Item 236.

tribunals under the Main Military Railroad Tribunal, attached to the Commissariat of Railroads.

A separate place in the system was occupied by the Supreme Revolutionary Tribunal, attached to the VTsIK.

Finally, the Decree of June 23, 1921 [1] united the three systems : The Revolutionary Military Tribunal of the Republic attached to the Revolutionary Military Council with the revolutionary military tribunals subordinate to it, except those who functioned at the front; the Main Revolutionary Military Railroad Tribunal, attached to the Commissariat of Railroads, with its entire net of tribunals, and the Supreme and Cassation Tribunals attached to the VTsIK, were united to one single Supreme Tribunal attached to the VTsIK. The functions of these unified tribunals were transferred to the Supreme Tribunal and to the local province revolutionary tribunals.

The Supreme Tribunal headed the entire system of tribunals. It had four colleges : 1) Cassation; 2) Judicial (court of first instance for cases handled previously by the Supreme Revolutionary Tribunal attached to the VTsIK) 3) Military and 4) Military Transportation. Province Branches of the Supreme Tribunal functioned in provinces.

The Plenum of the Supreme Tribunal formed by the Chairmen of the four Colleges, a rapporteur and the Representative of the VCheka exercised supervision, control and revision over all the tribunals and instructed the tribunals on all questions of principle.

Sentences and decisions of the Colleges could be suspended or reversed by the Plenum only in the way of supervision, *ex officio* (not in the way of an appeal or cassation).

At all province revolutionary tribunals, departments for the trial of cases of military offenses and important crimes committed in office were established. These Departments had the right of revolutionary military tribunals. They could apply the death penalty independently as to whether the province was declared under martial law or not.

Thus, all the revolutionary military railroad tribunals were abolished with the exception of one for every railroad and waterway district. Also all revolutionary military tribunals were closed, the existence of which became unnecessary upon the cessation of military operations. An exception was made for regions in which, although military actions were stopped, the immediate closing of revolutionary military tribunals was still deemed premature.

May the revolutionary tribunals be called real courts ?

---

[1] *Sob. uz.*, *RSFSR*, 1921, Item 294.

This question was correctly answered by Kursky himself, the People's Commissar of Justice, when he wrote : "The Revolutionary Tribunals are not courts in the real sense of the word, but special organizations for the fight against counterrevolution and, already now, when the local courts are developed, these organizations are freed more and more from the role of temporary courts, which is not peculiar to them, and are, although temporary, nevertheless absolutely indispensable organizations of the political struggle". [1]

The same opinion was given by Larin, a high ranking representative of the Commissariat of Justice, at the 4th Congress of Judicial Workers when he said : "We always looked upon the revolutionary tribunals as ... on a court of class dictatorship, as on a court of political struggle and not as on a court in the proper sense of the word ... The principle of suppression prevailed over that of justice". [2]

Indeed, a court which is at the same time an instrument of political struggle and suppression is not a "court" in the sense given to it in general. A court must have at least the theoretical possibility of being objective and impartial. The purpose of the revolutionary tribunals excluded these necessary features of a "court" *a priori* : They had not to render justice but fight counterrevolution and help to suppress the bourgeoisie by the proletariat. As an organ of the dictatorship of the proletariat they were called upon to help inforcing this dictatorship on the rest of the population.

That is why the revolutionary tribunals are discussed here under the rubrum of Extraordinary Courts.

B. The All-Russian Extraordinary Commission (VeCheKa)

a) *Its Purpose*

The Military-Revolutionary Committee [3] took the decision to create a Commission for the Fight Against the Counterrevolution, on November 21, 1917. The move to organize such a commission belonged to

---

[1] D.I. Kursky, "The Fundamentals of a Revolutionary Court", *Materialy*, I, p. 60.

[2] Quoted by N.V. Krylenko, *Sudoustroystvo*, p. 153.

[3] The Military-Revolutionary Committee, formed by the Bolsheviks in Petrograd on October 12, 1917, was instrumental in the overthrow of the Provisional Governm and the establishment of Soviet Power.

F.E.Dzerzhinsky. [1] In a special note to Dzerzhinsky, Lenin wrote :
"With regard to your report of today, is it possible to bring out such
a decree : On the Fight Against the Counterrevolution and Sabotage ? [2]

The All-Russian Extraordinary Commission on the Fight Against
Counterrevolution and Sabotage, attached to the Council of People's
Commissars, was created by Decree of the Council, on December 7,
1917. Its scope was the following : 1) "To be after and liquidate every
attempt of counterrevolution and sabotage in all Russia, regardless
by whom generated ; 2) To bring to trial by the Revolutionary Tribunal
all the counterrevolutionaries and saboteurs, and the working out
of measures to fight them; 3) The Commission conducts only the
preliminary investigations as far as it is necessary for the suppression
of the attempts". [3]

Thus, on paper, the activity of the Commission in judicial affairs was
limited to the preliminary investigation. The Premilinary Investigation
Commissions of the Revolutionary Tribunals and the Extraordinary
Commission had the same scope with regard to the same kind of crimes.

However, in reality, the Extraordinary Commission did not limit
itself to the preliminary investigation. It applied death and other
penalties on its own decision assuming judicial functions without
presenting the case to the revolutionary tribunals.

A basis for such an activity was seen by the Commission in Article 8 of
the Council of People's Commissars' Decree of February 21, 1918,
"The Socialist Fatherland is in Danger", providing : "Enemy's
agents, speculators, thugs, hooligans, counterrevolutionary agitators,
German spies are to be shot on the spot". [4]

Sofinov writes that this provision was an "immediate directive
of the Communist Party and the Soviet Government for all Soviet organs including the Extraordinary Commission". [5]

In accordance with this directive the Extraordinary Commission
declared in the press "to the knowledge of all city citizens", that
"up to the present time it was magnanimous in the fight against the

---

[1] The minutes of the evening session of the Military-Revolutionary Committee of
November 21, 1917, reads : "Discussed : the formation of a committee for the fight
against counterrevolution, M. Dzerzhinsky moves to organize such a committee. The
proposal is carried. (*Dokumenty velikoy proletarskoy revolutsii*, Vol. 1, p. 282).

[2] Lenin, 2, p. 336.

[3] *Pravda*, December 18, 1917.

[4] P.G. Sofinov, *Ocherki istorii Vserossiyskoy Chrezvychaynoy Komissii (1917-1922)*,
M. 1960, p. 34.

[5] *Ibid.*

people's enemies ... but now ... basing itself on the Decision of the Council of People's Commissars, it does not see any other measure for the fight against counterrevolutionaries, spies, speculators, thugs, hooligans, saboteurs and other parasites, than merciless destruction on the spot". [1]

Two days later, on February 25, Prince Eboli was arrested, accused of counterrevolutionary activity under the disguise of a member of the CheKa, and executed.

Sofinov asserts that it was the first death sentence pronounced and executed by the CheKa. "Previously, all the cases, after a preliminary investigation, were sent for decision to the Revolutionary Tribunal by the CheKa". [2]

Even, according to the opinion of some staunch Bolsheviks, as for instance, Krylenko, "The Extraordinary Commission was an institution terrible with regard to the repression it exercised in complete secrecy of its operations. Besides the carrying out of arrests, it misappropriated the right of preempting decisions on questions of life and death. These decisions were passed by commissions "of threeths" (*troyka*) or "fives" (*pyatyerka*) ... in absence of any norms establishing its jurisdiction as well as the method of investigation. ... An investigating organ according to its essence, it transformed also into a judicial institution" [3]

Edifying about the principles on which the activity of the CheKa was based is the instruction given by Latsis, Dzerzhinsky's Assistant, to the members of the Extraordinary Commission :

"We are destroying the bourgeoisie as a class. Do not look, during the investigation, for material, as to whether the accused acted against the Soviet power by word or deed. The first question you have to present to him is as to what class does he belong, what are his origin, education, training or profession. These questions have to decide about the fate of the accused". [4]

In an article in the Weekly of the VeCheKa, the members of the Extraordinary Commission were required to apply torture to the accused during the preliminary investigation. [5]

According to M.Ya. Latsis, a very active member of the CheKa,

[1] *Izvestia*, February 23, 1918.
[2] Sofinov, *op. cit.*, p. 36.
[3] N.V. Krylenko, *Sudoustroystvo RSFSR*, M. 1923, p. 97, 322.
[4] *Pravda*, December 25, 1918.
[5] *Yezhenedel'nik VeCheKa*, No. 3, October 6, 1918.

"only" 18, 380 persons were shot by the Commission during 1918 and
1919 for various crimes in 20 central provinces only.

It must be emphasized that Latsis explains that the figures he gives
is the official statistic and do not include the secret cases. He concludes
his book with the assertion that "Every citizen must be a member
of the Red Army and of the Extraordinary Commission, [1] and Lenin
declared "A good communist is a good CheKist (member of the CheKa).[2]

Certainly the figures given by Latsis are only a fragment of the real
number of the Commission's victims.

Still he is of the opinion that "if the Extraordinary Commission can
be accused of any thing, it is not of superfluous zeal in favor of executions, but of insufficient use of the highest measure of punishment.

The activity of the CheKa received an additional stimulus : the
introduction of the "red terror".

The immediate reason for the measure was provided by a series of
attempts against the life of high Soviet Officials : (V. Volodarsky
was killed on June 20, 1918, Uritsky, Chairman of the Petrograd
CheKa, on the morning of August 30) culminating by the shots of
Fanny Kaplan at Lenin, at 6 pm. of the same August 30, 1918. [3]

On September 5, 1918, the Council of People's Commissars adopted
a decision which served as a Directive to all Extraordinary Commissions :

"On the report of the Chairman of the Extraordinary Commission
for the Fight Against Counterrevolution on the activity of this Commission, the Council is of the opinion, that in the present situation,
the insurance of the rear by terror is a direct necessity". [4]

Sofinov relates that the Soviet Government directed the VeCheKa
to isolate class enemies in concentration camps and to shoot to death all
persons participating in white guardist organizations, conspiracies
and rebellions, publishing their names and the reasons for the measure
in the press. [5]

When already after Volodarsky's assasination Petrograd workers
demanded the introduction of the "red terror" and the Petrograd

---

[1]   Ya. Latsis, *Dva goda bor'by na vnutrennem fronte,* M. 1920, p. 75.

[2]   Lenin, 30, p. 450.

[3]   She shot three times : Lenin was greatly wounded by two projectiles which   were,
according to Sofinov, poisoned (S.G. Sofinov, *op. cit.,* p. 101).

[4]   Sofinov, *op. cit.,* p. 110.

[5]   *Ibid.*

leaders, Zinov'yev, Lashevich, Yevdokimov and others rejected the demand, Lenin denounced the leader's cowardice and wrote :

"I absolutely protest.

We are compromising ourselves : we threaten with mass terror even in decisions of the *Sovdep* (Council of People's Deputies), but when it comes to action, we hinder the completely correct revolution on initiative of the masses.

This is im-pos-sible !" [1]

Along with the death penalty the Commission inflicted punishments depriving persons of liberty. So during 1918 and the first seven months of 1919, a total of 86,893 persons were confined : 9,496 in concentration camps, 34,334 in jail, and 13,111 were held as hostages. [2]

b) *Its Relation to Revolutionary Tribunals*

Thus, parallel to the local courts and revolutionary tribunals created by the Decree No. 1 on Courts, judicial power was exercised by the Extraordinary Commissions in a great range of cases. Indeed, the jurisdiction of the extraordinary commission extended to a variety of cases such as : 1) sabotage; 2) counterrevolution; 3) speculation; 4) crimes committed in office; 5) banditry; 6) kulaks upheavals; 7) desertion; 8) hooliganism and 9) parasitism in general.

It must be noted that such criminal actions as sabotage, counter-revolution, speculation, hooliganism and parasitism were defined nowhere and left room to wide interpretation. An open act of counter-revolution, such as, for example, armed upheaval instigated by left socialist-revolutionary or rightist elements were deemed clearly counter-revolutionary actions from the viewpoint of Bolshevism. But along with open counterrevolutionaries secret ones were active, and certainly, the Extraordinary Commission was free to interpret any undesirable behavior as counterrevolutionary and widely used this freedom. Also the concepts of sabotage, speculation etc. are very vague and give way to an arbitrary definition. Let us keep in mind that the juris-diction of revolutionary tribunals extended also to counterrevolution and sabotage. After every investigation of a case the Extraordinary Commission had the choice of two alternatives : to send the case for decision to the Revolutionary Tribunal or to decide itself over the case.

The CheKa did not admit any restriction on its activity. It carried out arrests and executions without any legal authorization.

---

[1] Lenin, 35, p. 275.
[2] Latsis, *op. cit.*, p. 76.

From Lenin's viewpoint, the CheKa was the necessary medium of the dictatorship of the proletariat which, itself, was based on no legality whatsoever, but on naked force only. Lenin wrote that "the CheKa directly realizes the dictatorship of the proletariat and its help in this respect is invaluable. There is no other way for the liberation of the masses than suppression of the exploitaters by force. This is the job of the CheKa and in this is its service to the proletariat". [1]

As a matter of fact, Lenin himself used Dzerzhinsky, the Chairman of the Extraordinary Commission, as his hangman. For instance, Lenin telegraphed to Dzerzhinsky in December 1917 : "It is necessary to arrest immediately the board of directors of the Ural Works, located here (in Petrograd) and confiscate all the Ural Works". [2]

There is no doubt that Lenin shouldered and approved the ruthless doings of the Extraordinary Commissions. "When the revolutionary class is fighting the possessing classes, which is fighting back, it must suppress its resistance and we will suppress this resistance by all means they employed to suppress the proletariat, ... no other means have been invented up to the present time". [3]

When Steinberg, protested against the illegal activity of the CheKa and freed people arrested by Dzerzhinsky, Lenin always supported the latter against the former. When, for instance, by order of Steinberg and Karelin, (a high official of the Commissariat of Justice, also a left Socialist-revolutionary), members of the Association for the Defense of the Constituant Assembly arrested by Dzershinsky were set free, the Council of People's Commissars adopted the following resolution, introduced by Lenin and Stalin on 19 December 1917 : [4] "The Council of People's Commissars recognizes that any changes of the decisions of Dzerzhinsky's Commission ... are admissible only on complaint to the Council of People's Commissars, but not on the individual order of the Commissar of Justice ...".

Two days later, however, on December 21, 1917, a decision [5] of the Council of People's Commissars regulated the relations between the Commissariat of Justice and the CheKa. The Council decided that :

1. The All-Russian Extraordinary Commission, attached to the Council of People's Commissars, is created for the purpose of a merciless fight against the counterrevolution, sabotage and speculation;

---

[1]   Lenin, XXIII, p. 274.
[2]   Lenin, XXIX, p. 428.
[3]   Lenin, XXII, p. 110.
[4]   *Leninsky sbornik*, XXI, 113-114.
[5]   Drafted by Steinberg and edited by Lenin, *Leninsky sbornik*, XXI, 110-111.

2. The Commission has to transfer the results obtained by its investigation to the Investigation Commission of a Revolutionary Tribunal or drop the case;

3. Its work is carried out under the closest supervision of the Commissariats of Justice and Internal Affairs, as well as of the Presidium of the Petrograd Soviet; the work of the investigation commissars of the revolutionary tribunal [is carried out] under the closest supervision of the Commissariat of Justice and the Presidium of the Petrograd Soviet;

4. ....

5. ....

6. The Commission has to notify the Commissariats of Justice and Internal Affairs about all political arrests which have an outstanding importance;

7. Every arrest must be followed by an indictment or by liberation;

8. Conflicts not regulated by an agreement between the Commissariat of Justice, or of Internal Affairs or the Presidium of the Petrograd Soviet [on the one side] and the Commission [on the other] have to be presented to the Council of People's Commissars for a final decision, but without stopping the usual activities and the measures under competence of the Commission.

Certainly this decision seems to have had the purpose of eliminating the CheKa's abuses. It is evident however, that the decision remained only on paper and was never enforced against the CheKa.

Indeed, the CheKa, as Krylenko wrote in 1922, "defended its privileges with special persistence" and in 1922 he characterized its work as "the most scandalous form of punishment". [1]

About a month before the Red Terror was introduced (on November 4, 1917) Lenin, addressing the session of the Petrograd Soviet, said : "We are accused of employing terror, but we do not use the kind of terror French revolutionaries did who executed on the guillotine unarmed people, and I hope, we will not use it". [2]

With regard to Lenin's views on the enforcement of the dictatorship of the proletariat and the employment of armed force for the suppression of the possessing classes, his "hope" could not have been sincere, considering his most frank assertion of the necessity for terror. For instance, in 1921, when arguing with social-democrats and social-revolutionaries who were against terror, he said : "... we will say the

---

[1] N.V. Krylenko, "The Court Reform", *Sovetskoye pravo*, 1922, No. 3, p. 54.

[2] Lenin, XXII, 50.

severe but unquestionable truth that in countries which live through unprecedented crises, the following apart from old relations, the sharpening of class struggle after the imperialistic war of 1914-1918— this is going on in all countries of the world—it is impossible to dispense with terror, in spite of hypocrites and phrasemongers. Or the white-guardist bourgeois terror... in American, English (Ireland), Italian (Fascists), German, and other style terror, or the red proletarian terror. There is no middle way; there is no third way and such a way cannot exist". [1]

c) *Its Ramification*

After the All-Russian Extraordinary Commission was created in the capital, a wide net of branches was established in the provinces.

In March 1918, the VeCheKa decided to ask the local Soviets to organize local CheKas. In the same decision, it was asserted that henceforth the right to make all the arrests, searches, requisitions, confiscations, etc. connected with speculations, crimes in office, and news of the press, belongs exclusively to the CheKa. [2]

In May 1918, Border CheKas were set by all the Province CheKas located along the borders of the République. They were divided into circuit, district and station CheKas. The VeCheKa opened a Border Department at Headquarters in Petrograd.

Railroad departments were established at province CheKas for the fight of crimes on railroads in July 1918. Special post and telegraph desks were set within these departments for the handling of crimes committed in post and telegraph agencies. [3]

Although the functions of the CheKa were somehow defined by the Decree of September 5, its relations to other governmental agencies and especially to revolutionary tribunals occupied with the investigation and trial of political crimes, remained unclear.

The constant interference of the CheKa with the activity of the revolutionary tribunals brought a vigorous protest of the Congress of Chairmen of the Revolutionary Tribunals of April 12, 1919.

The Congress passed a resolution demanding the following legislation: 1. The immediate enactment by the legislature of a statute on the rights and powers of the CheKa; 2. The strict determination of conditions under which summary justice, apart from courts, is not only permissable, but obligatory; 3. To submit to the powers of judicial

---

[1] Lenin, XXVI, 33.

[2] *Vestnik NKVD*, 1918, No. 9-IV, p. 6.

[3] *Yezhenedel'nik NKVD*, 1918, Vol. 1, p. 9.

control of the revolutionary tribunals all the organs of the CheKa, from beginning to end, to the same extent as all other governmental agencies are submitted.

The Congress was of the opinion that the following instructions should be immediately given to the CheKas : 1. Forbidden to the CheKa are the conduct of parallel investigations in cases already transferred by the CheKa or generated outside the CheKa and being carried on by revolutionary tribunals or other courts; 2. The CheKas are not allowed to register without the consent of the revolutionary tribunal any person or persons as being under their jurisdiction in any way who are already taken under the jurisdiction of revolutionary tribunals or other courts, if there is no other accusation against these persons than those leveled by the courts; 3. The arbitrary transfer without the permission of the tribunals or other courts, of arrested persons, already under the jurisdiction of tribunals or other courts, to other places of detention, their release on bail or under other conditions, the repeated arrest of persons released by decision of investigating agencies or courts is forbidden to the CheKas; 4. The CheKas have no right to inflict administrative punishments in cases being transferred by them for judicial decision or already under court investigation; 5. The CheKa is forbidden to confine in jail persons for a defined time in cases investigated by the commissars if such a confinement was not provided in mandatory orders of the CheKa or other agency and the person was not arrested for the violation of such an order; 6. Furthermore, all the CheKas are informed that the investigation commissions of the revolutionary tribunals have the right to prosecute agents of the CheKa for crimes committed in office, like all other agents of the government and that in this respect members of the CheKa have no privileges. [1]

This decision of the Congress was prompted by the fact that the CheKa arbitrarily took the right not only of final decisions not subject to further appeal in cases under the jurisdiction of revolutionary tribunals, but also the function of supervision of the activity of judicial institutions by requiring for examination cases already processed by the tribunals, and the liquidation of cases in which a decision of the tribunals had not yet taken place as well as reviewed sentences already pronounced by the tribunals, or liquidated cases already under investigation by the tribunals.

The absence of exact legislative definition of the rights of the

---

[1] N.V. Krylenko, *Sudoustroystvo, RSFSR*, 1924, p. 99.

CheKa and their delimitation with regard to those of the tribunals and the absence of publicity of the CheKa's procedures were the cause of this "regretable" situation, according to the Congress.

In particular, the Congress accused the CheKa of having seized control over the places of detention with the consequence that cases occurred when the same accused was registered as under the jurisdiction of the tribunal and the CheKa at the same time; the CheKa independently set free or arrested persons already arrested or freed by the tribunals, transferred arrested persons to other places of detention without the knowledge or consent of the tribunals.

However, it must be kept in mind that, formally, according to the instructions of September 7, 1918, the CheKa had official right to take the final decision in all counterrevolutionary cases investigated by the Extraordinary Commission. Only some cases selected by a special council in which a representative of the Commissariat of Justice took part, were directed for final decision to a revolutionary tribunal or a people's court.

With regard to the crimes committed in office, the CheKa had to decide upon important cases only. The other cases had to be transferred to the competent courts.

The exclusive competence of the CheKa extended to the investigation of cases of speculation and the requisition of the proceeds of speculation. The people's courts decided upon the merits of these cases.

d) *Statute of the VeCheKa*

In order to further clarify the activity of the CheKa and its relation to the revolutionary tribunal a Statute of the VeCheKas was enacted on November 2, 1918. [1]

The local CheKas were entrusted with the direct fight against counterrevolution, speculation, and crimes committed in office. They were organized by the local soviets as a regular department of their executive committees and worked as such, but at the same time, their activity was centralized and subordinate to the CheKa.

The VeCheKa itself, being attached to the Council of People's Commissars, had to work in close contact with the Commissars of Internal Affairs and Justice. It was said in the Statute that the VeCheKa "is the central organ unifying the activity of all the CheKas and systematically conducting the direct fight against the counterrevolution, speculation, bribery, etc."

---

[1] *Sob. uz.*, 1918, Item 842.

This was all that the Statute said about the rights and powers of the CheKa!

The meaning of the sentence "in close contact with the Commissariats of Internal Affairs and Justice" remained unclear. The Setatut only provided to the effect that the Commissariats of Internal Affairs and Justice had to send their representatives to the VeCheKa and the Chairman of the VeCheKa was made a member of the College of the Commissariat of Internal Affairs.

As a result of the voluntarily created vagueness in the relations of the CheKa with other agencies the representatives of both Commissariats soon walked out of the Cheka and thus, as Krylenko puts it, the contact "was not only never established but the Commissariats remained in open opposition to the CheKa and under break of "diplomatic relations".

That the Bolshevist leadership desired to hold the rights of the CheKa as uncertain as possible, in order to facilitate its work of ruthless suppression, is obvious. Lenin did not desire any limitation to this work and the restrictions which had to be enacted under pressure of public opinion never materialized.

When Krylenko declared to Ya. M. Sverdlov about the Statute of November 2, 1918 that it is not a law, but "God knows what; why don't you want to say openly, what is the matter?" Sverdlov answered "Why? It is obvious to every one anyhow". [1]

Certainly, as we have seen, the revolutionary tribunals retained the right to chek the investigative actions of the CheKa to visit the place of detention, in order to examine their legality, according to the Decree of February 17, 1919, mentioned above. But also, these rights remained on paper only and in reality the CheKa acted independently: it investigated the crimes, sentenced and executed the accused.

The rights of the revolutionary tribunals with regard to the CheKa were formulated in the Decision of the TsIK of February 11, 1919 amending the Statute of the Revolutionary Tribunals of November 4, 1918. The Decision had also the purpose of regulating the relations between the CheKas and the revolutionary tribunals. It was said in the Decision that the right to sentence belongs to the revolutionary tribunal also in all the cases initiated by the CheKa and that the investigation of the CheKa had to be completed not later than within a month.

However, in the case of an armed action of counterrevolutionaries,

---

[1] N.V. Krylenko, *Sudoustroystvo*, p. 100.

banditry, etc, the CheKa retained the right of summary justice. This right of summary justice legally belonged to the CheKa also in places declared under martial law with regard to crimes enumerated in the declaration concerning the introduction of martial law. The Decree also confirmed the right of the Cheka to confine persons in concentration camps (a limit of time for the confinement was not indicated.)

With regard to the catastrophic food conditions, speculation was the subject of a special decision of the Council of People's Commissars of 23 September 1919. The Council decided to charge the CheKa with all measures for the fight against speculation, subordinating to it all the "organs conducting the struggle against speculation at the present time..." [1]

e) *Special Revolutionary Tribunal at the VeCheKa*

But duplication in the work of the revolutionary tribunals and the CheKa, especially in cases investigated by the CheKa, still existed. In order to eliminate this, another attempt was made by means of the Decree of the Council of People's Commissars of October 21, 1919 [2] establishing a special revolutionary tribunal at the VeCheKa. This tribunal was set for "the merciless fight against important speculation with rationed goods and products, with crimes committed in office by persons caught in misappropriations, forgery, illegal issuing of warrants, participation in any kind of speculation and bribery". The bench of the special Revolutionary Tribunal consisted of a Chairman and two members appointed by the College of the CheKa (one of them was appointed by agreement with the All Russian Council of Trade Unions) The sessions of the Special Revolutionary Tribunal were public and the sentences final, i.e., not subject to review in cassation. The Tribunal was not bound by any form of procedure.

It is evident that the creation of a special revolutionary tribunal of the VeCheKa meant a victory of the latter over the tribunals in the everlasting fight for competence.

In discussing the legislation of 1919 on revolutionary tribunals, especially the creation of the Special Revolutionary Tribunal of the VeCheKa and the creation of Revolutionary Military Tribunals, Krylenko wrote : "In other words, the judicial machine was going to

---

[1] Kozhevnikov, *op. cit.*, p. 89.
[2] *Sob. uz., RSFSR*, 1919, Item 594.

pieces, everyone could build courts according to his desire. They could not last anymore". [1]

The Decree on the Unification of all Revolutionary Tribunals of June 23, 1921, mentioned above, [2] brought some limitation in matters of setting punishments by the CheKa in cases under its trial power; the CheKa could set a punishment not over two years of confinement and only with regard to persons charged with belonging to anti-soviet parties, to evident white-guardist elements. All other cases processed by the CheKa had to be directed to special Chambers of the people's courts, or the revolutionary tribunals.

However, the CheKa retained the right to set any punishment, including death, in places under martial law, but restricted only to perpetrators of the following crimes: espionage, banditry, and participation in an open armed insurrection.

f) *The Death Penalty*

The civil war was liquidated by the victory of the Soviet government at the end of 1919. Hence, it was decided that the death penalty and the Red Terror could be abolished by a Decree of the VTsIK of January 17, 1920. [3] The CheKa and the tribunals, with exception stated below, lost their rights of applying the death penalty. The city province and supreme revolutionary tribunals could no longer set the highest penalty.

However, the limitation was not extended to revolutionary military tribunals.

It was said in the Decree that "only renewed attempts of the Entente to disturb the steady position of Soviet power and the mighty labor of workers and peasants in the establishment of socialist economy by armed intervention or material support of mutinying tsarist generals, can force the Soviet Government to revert again to terroristic methods". Thus, the Decree stated, responsibility for a possible return of the Soviet Government to the cruel method of the Red-Terror in the future, "lies completely and exclusively with the governments and the classes of the Entente and their friends ... the Russian landowners and capitalists".

Only three days later, however, on January 20, 1920, the Presidium

---

[1] Krylenko, *op. cit.*, p. 116.
[2] p. 54
[3] *Sob. uz.*, *RSFSR*, 1920, Item 22.

of the VTsIK decided that "in regions under the jurisdiction of Revolutionary Military Soviets of the front, the Province CheKa and the Province Revolutionary Tribunals should have the same rights possessed by its Revolutionary Military Tribunals", i.e., these CheKas and tribunals were not limited in the using of the death penalty. [1]

Soon other measures directed toward the simplification of the Tribunal System were taken. The Statute on Revolutionary Tribunals of March 18, 1920 [2] declared that : with the publication of this Statute, the Decree of the Presidium of the VTsIK of June 20, 1919 and the Decree on the Special Tribunal attached to the All-Russian Extraordinary Commission of October 21, 1919 were cancelled. All the existing extraordinary military courts and other agencies of an extraordinary character with judicial functions, as well as all revolutionary tribunals, established in another way or acting not on ground of the Statute, are abolished".

Still, the CheKa retained the right to confine to labor camps for not more than five years, persons who "violate labor discipline, the revolutionary order, as well as for furthering parasitic elements, if the investigation does not give enough grounds for a criminal proceeding". This right belonged to province CheKas with the approval of the VeCheKa.

The condition for the resuming of terrorism set in the decree of January 17, 1920, was provided by the Polish-Russian war of 1920.

On May 28, 1920 [3] a Decree of the TsIK conceded the rights of a revolutionary military tribunal to the VeCheKa and its organs with regard to crimes directed against the security of the Republic, i.e., also the right of applying the death penalty.

A Decree of June 20, 1920 [4] defined that the right of summary justice, including the death penalty, was retained by the CheKa in regions declared under martial law previous to this Decree, with regard to the following crimes : 1. Participation in a counterrevolutionary organization or in a conspiracy directed against the Soviet power ... ; 2. Treason against the State, espionage, concealing of traitors and spies ; 3. Concealing of weapons with a counterrevolutionary purpose ; 4. Counterfeiting money, forging of documents with a counterrevo-

---

[1] Kozhevnikov, *op. cit.*, p. 97.
[2] *Sob. uz., RSFSR*, 1920, Item 115.
[3] *Id.*, 1920, Item 370.
[4] *Id.*, 1920, Item 301.

lutionary purpose; 5. Participation in counterrevolutionary arsons and explosions; 6. Malicious damaging of railroad tracs, bridges and other structures, telegraph and telephone communications, stores of military armaments, products and forage; 7. Participation in a gang formed with the purpose of murder, robbery and pillage, as well as the sheltering of and complicity with such a gang; 8. Plunder and armed robbery; 9. Breaking into soviet and public stores with the purpose of illegal appropriation; 10. Illegal trade with cocaine.

In his book, "The Extraordinary Commission for the Fight Against the Revolution", [1] Latsis writes : "The Extraordinary Commission is not an investigation commission and not a court, and not a tribunal. It is a fighting organ, and active on the internal front of the civil war, using in its fight methods of investigative commissions, courts, tribunals and armed forces".

This definition must be corrected, however : The CheKa was an investigative organ, acting as a court, a tribunal and an executioner of its own judgments at the same time. This mixture of police, judicial and terroristic activity was carried on by the CheKa up to 1922, already when normal investigation and judicial organs created by the new Codes functioned. All the attempts to limit the activity of the CheKa to investigatory work, to delimit functions between the revolutionary tribunals and the CheKa, mentioned above, as well as abolition of the death penalty in the beginning of 1920' ... all these measures failed to eliminate the parallelism of work of the CheKa on the one side and the revolutionary tribunals and even the people's courts on the other.

How can this failure be explained ? The answer to this question is obvious. Lenin and his associates approved of the CheKas activity. Its ruthless terrorism was necessary in their opinion to maintain the dictatorship of the proletariat or, rather, of the Bolshevist Party. The enacted restrictions of this activity were small concessions on paper only to public opinion in the country and abroad. "Experience was to demonstrate that whatever actions the CheKa considered necessary in order to defend the dictatorship, including imprisonment and execution, would be approved by the Party leadership, notwithstanding any formal or legal limitations in its powers", wrote S. Wolin and R.M. Slusser. [2]

---

[1] *Chrezvychaynaya kommissiya po bor'be s kontzrevolyuvtsiyey*, M. 1921.

[2] *The Soviet Secret Police, Symposium*, edited by S. Wolin and R.M. Slusser, N.Y., 1957, p. 4.

There is no doubt that the limited legal power for the summary executions carried out by the CheKa was outrageously exceeded. Latsis himself admitted that this activity "was" a violation of the law and was a measure taken arbitrarily by the CheKa and authorized by nobody. "Life itself made this measure necessary", explains Latsis. [1]

The activity of the CheKa was critized not only by the Socialist-Revolutionaries and Mensheviks whose opposition to the regime was tolerated for a certain time, but also within the Bolshevist administrative apparatus. It was a period of Soviet rule when criticism was still admitted. For instance, the Second Congress of the Members of the Revolutionary Tribunal of April 26-28, 1920 passed a resolution on the subject of the relationship between the revolutionary tribunals and the CheKa, in order to eliminate the following shortcomings of the work of the CheKa : 1. Unnecessary deprivation of liberty with regard to accused persons taking place very often; 2. keeping these persons under arrest for too long a time without any move in their cases; 3. illegal actions committed by individuals and members of the CheKa during interrogations, arrests and beatings; 4. arrest of persons accused of actions not forbidden by law; 5. the faulty work of the CheKa apparatus which resulted in incomplete investigations which did not attain the result it was bound to achieve". [2]

The Civil War was ended and also peace between the RSFSR and Poland concluded on March 18, 1921. Thus, the main reason for the existence of the CheKa was eliminated. It seemed the time had come when "a kindergarten will be opened in the headquarters of the CheKa", according to Zinov'yev's prediction of 1918. [3] The existence of the CheKa could not be defended anymore in the face of the great discontent with its activity produced in Soviet society.

On the other hand there was no desire in the highest strata of the bureaucracy and the Party to discard completely an organization which rendered so many services to the dictatorship of the proletariat and could also be useful in the future. A compromise was chosen : The CheKa, together with its hated name, was abolished, but another organization was created in its place : The State Political Administration-G.P.U.

---

[1] M. Ya. Latsis, "Comrade Dzezzhinsky and VeCheKa, *Proletarskaya Revolutsiya*, 1926, No. 9, p. 85.

[2] Krylenko, *Sudoustroystvo, op. cit.*, p. 23.

[3] *Yezhenedel'nik sovetskoy yustitsti*, 1918, No. 27, p. 122; Wolin and Schlusser, *op. cit.*, p. 17.

C. The State Political Administration-GPU

The decision to liquidate the CheKa was taken by the IXth All-Russian Congress of Soviets in December 1921. A corresponding Decree was adopted by the VTsIK and the Council of People's Commissars on February 6, 1922. [1]

Besides the abolition of the CheKa, the Decree set the structure and the purpose of the new institution.

It was said in the Decree that to the Commissariat of the Interior was assigned the job of "a. suppression of open counterrevolutionary actions and banditry; b. taking of measures for the defense from and the fight against espionage; c. protection of the railroad and water lines; d. the political protection of the RSFSR borders; e. fight against smugglers and illicit crossing of the Republic's borders; and the fulfillment of special assignments of the TsIK or the Council of People's Commissars concerning the protection of the revolutionary order".

For the completion of this job, the State Political Administration (GPU) attached to the RSFSR Commissariat of the Interior, was established under the chairmanship of the Commissar of the Interior, or another person appointed by the Council of People's Commissars. Branches of the GPU named local political departments were attached to the Executive Committees of the Soviets in provinces and autonomous Republics. Special armed forces were put under the command of the GPU.

Some rules for the arrest and detention of political criminals were set in the Decree. It was provided that if measures of suppression had to be taken with regard to persons involved in counterrevolutionary crimes, banditry, espionage, plunder on railroad and water lines, smuggling and border crossing without permission, the State Political Administration, the political departments and their representatives in districts have the right of search, seizure and arrest under the following conditions : a) with regard to persons caught red-handed, searches, seizures and arrests may be carried out by agents of the state political administration or political departments without a special decision of the state political administration or the political departments and a special order, if the measure taken is approved by the Chairman of the state political administration or the political department; in all other cases, arrests as well as searches and seizures are permissible only on

---

[1] *Sob. uz., RSFSR*, 1922, Item 160.

the ground of a special decision of the state political administration or of a political department, signed by the chairman; b) the accusation must be made known to the arrested person not later than two weeks after the arrest; c) not later than two months after the arrest, the state political administration must free the arrested person or ask the permission of the Presidium of the VTsIK for the continuation of the confinement for a duration to be established by the Presidium, if special circumstances of the case make it necessary, or direct the case to the court transferring the arrested person to its disposal.

The Decree also prescribed that all cases of speculation, crimes committed in office and other crimes having a general immoral character and the subject of proceedings by the All-Russian Extraordinary Commission and its organs prior to the publication of the Decree, had to be transferred to the revolutionary tribunals and people's courts, respectively, according to their jurisdiction within two weeks, and in the future all offenses directed against the Soviet regime or violations of RSFSR laws had to be tried exclusively in court proceedings by revolutionary tribunals or by people's courts, in accordance with their respective competence.

Thus, the judicial activity of the CheKa was officially terminated together with its existence by the Decree.

However, it was resumed later by its heirs.

a) *The OGPU*

The creation of the Soviet Union in 1923 made necessary the establishment of a federal agency entrusted with the work of the GPU. The agreement creating the Soviet Union provided such an organization called The Federal State Political Administration (OGPU). The USSR constitution of 1924 (Art 61-63) entrusted the OGPU with the task of unifying the efforts of the union republics in the fight against the political or economic counterrevolution, espionage and banditry.

The OGPU was attached to the USSR Council of People's Commissars and had its representative at the USSR Supreme Court. It controlled its local organs with the help of representatives attached to the councils of people's commissars of the union republics.

The activity of the OGPU was regulated by a Statute adopted by the USSR TsIK on November 15, 1923. [1]

---

[1]   *Vestnik TsIK SNK i STO*, 1923, No. 8, Item 225.

According to this Statute, the Chairman of the OGPU and his Deputy were appointed by the Presidium of the TsIK and the Chairman or his Deputy were members of the USSR Council of People's Commissars with a consultative voice.

Also a College was attached to the Chairman of the OGPU which, on paper, had "the same rights as other Colleges of the USSR People's Commissariats".

The field of operation of the OGPU was defined in the Statute as follows : a) guidance of the work of state political administrations of the union republics and of the special departments subordinated to the military districts, as well as of transportation organs of the GPU at railroad and water lines on the territories of the corresponding union republics; b) direct guidance of special departments of the fronts and the army; organization of the protection of the USSR borders; direct operation on an all-union scale. Thus, no judicial activity was officially assigned to the GPU or OGPU. However, the Decision of TsIK and the Council of People's Commissars of 22 August 1932 [1] on the Fight Against Speculation empowered the OGPU ... to take measures for the uprooting of speculation "applying to speculation and secondhand dealers confinement in concentration camps of 5 to 10 years without the right of being amnestied".

Furthermore, from a law of 1934, [2] passed by the TsIK and establishing a USSR People's Commissariat of Internal Affairs, we learn that the OGPU had a Judicial College which was abolished by the said law (Art. 5). This Judicial College was very active from 1923 to 1934 and, as Soviet sources remark, "had the right to apply all measures of criminal repression, including death before a firing squad". [3]

It follows from these quotations that a judicial college of the GPU, organized under secret law or executive order, examined, as a court, cases investigated by the OGPU, and rendered sentences including the death penalty.

It is also possible that no special Judicial College was active at the OGPU, but that its regular College assumed judicial functions in appropriate cases. This follows from a statement by Rykov made

---

[1] *Sob. zak.*, *SSSR*, 1932, Item 375.

[2] *Sob. zak.*, *SSSR*, 1934, Item 283.

[3] S.S. Studenikin, V.A. Vlasov and I.I. Yevtikheyev, *Sovetskoye administrativnoye pravo*, M. 1950, p. 273.

to a British Labor Party member in 1927 : "According to the law of our state the Collegium of the GPU is competent in all cases where it is necessary to take energetic actions against the counterrevolution; in these cases it has all the rights of a revolutionary tribunal" [1]. Rykov speaks of the College of the OGPU which assumes judicial power from case to case. However, the 1934 law provides the abolition of the "Judicial" College of the OGPU.

The judicial functions of the GPU College is also mentioned in a decision of the USSR TsIK of March 14, 1933 [2] on "The Responsibility the Employees of State Agencies and Enterprises for Acts of Sabotage". Having established facts of participation of officials in counterrevolutionary wrecking activity, the decision continues : "in this connection, the USSR TsIK clarifies that the right of the College of the OGPU granted by a decision of the TsIK of November 15, 1923, of examination in judicial sessions of the College of cases of sabotage, arson, explosions, wrecking of machines and installations of state enterprises and of other forms of wrecking, and applying of all measures of repression according to the character of the crime committed, must be used with particular severity to employees of state agencies and enterprises guilty of such crimes".

There is no Decision of November 15, 1923, concerning GPU in the books, besides the establishment of this institution.

Thus, the decision of the TsIK refers to the judicial activity of the GPU College using all kinds of punishment, i.e., also the death penalty, and quotes as the source of this power a Decision on the GPU of 15 November 1923.

However, the Statute of November 15, 1923 contains nothing about a judicial power of the College. On the contrary, the statute provides that "the OGPU College will have the same rights as the other colleges of the Commissariats ". None of them had judicial power at that time.

Only one judicial decision of the OGPU College was made known in the press. It is the sentence pronounced in the case of a group of employees of the People's Commissariat of Agriculture of March 11, 1933 and which evidently prompted the Decision of the TsIK of March 14, 1933 cited above.

---

[1] Quoted by William Chamberlin, *Soviet Russia*, London, 1930, p. 389 and Simon Wolin, *op. cit.*, note 68 on p. 44.

[2] *Sob. post.*, USSR, 1933, Item 108.

In this case, the "Judicial College" of the OGPU sentenced 36 persons to death and 22 persons to 10 years and 22 persons to 8 years of confinement respectively. [1]

Moreover, the OGPU was entrusted with a special task of great economic importance : the management and use for economic purposes of forced labor camps. After 1930, all the criminals sentenced to confinement for a term of three years and over, became the prisoners of concentration camps in Siberia and the far North, administered by the OGPU. The Soviet government decided to use the forced labor of these inmates, numbered later in the millions, for the construction of canals and timber work.

According to the same law of 1934, the OGPU and its institutions were integrated into the USSR People's Commissariat of Internal Affairs (NKVD). The functions of the OGPU were taken over by a Department of the NKVD called Chief Administration of State Security (GUGB).

The new USSR People's Commissariat of Internal Affairs had, in the future to direct for trial to courts, cases investigated by it and its organs according to their jurisdiction.

When the OGPU was integrated into the NKVD this Commissariat took over, together with the other tasks of the OGPU, also the direction of the forced labor camps. The population of these camps was greatly increased by the purges of the thirties and then in 1941 when huge deportations of "anti-Soviet elements" from Latvia, Lithuania, Estonia and other Republics were carried out. Until Stalin's death in 1953, the population of the concentration camps increased highly, particularly as a result of the activity of the Special Board of the NKVD.

Inexperienced forced labor became an ingredient of the Soviet economy and the Secret police—one of the largest agencies of Soviet administration.

b) *The Special Board of the NKVD*

That Kozhevnikov sees in the transfer of the trial of cases investigated by the OGPU to the regular courts a sign of the strengthening

---

[1] *Izvestiya*, March 13, 1933; quoted by Gsovski, *Soviet Civil Law* I, 237, footnote 17; see also on this subject Gsovski in Gsovski and Grzibowski (General editors), *Government, Law and Courts in the Soviet Union and Eastern Europe*, N.Y., 1960, I, 571-572.

of the Soviet judicial system proves that the judicial activity of the OGPU, as previously that of the CheKa, was a violation of the official court system. [1]

However, not the "strengthening" of the court system was in mind of the Soviet Government when it abolished the Judicial College of the OGPU. Indeed, in place of the Judicial College of the OGPU, another even more formidable instrument of punitative power was established outside of the official judicial system by the same law of 1934 : the notorious Special Board of the NKVD.

According to the provision of Art. 8, the Special Board had the right "to apply exile, banishment, confinement in a corrective labor camp for a time up to five years as well as banishment outside the borders of the USSR". The Special Board was an administrative agency not bound by any code of procedure.

The composition of the Special Board was established in a decision of the USSR TsIK and USSR Council of People's Commissars of November 5, 1934. [2] According to the law, members of the Special Board were : a) a deputy of the USSR Commissar of the Interior; b) a representative of the USSR Commissariat of Internal Affairs; c) the Chief of the Main Administration of the Workers' and Peasants' Militia; d) the people's commissar of internal affairs of the republic on which territory the case was started.

A feeble link with the judicial system was created by Art. 3 of the Decision, providing that the presence of the USSR Prosecutor or his Deputy was mandatory in the sessions of the Special Board. The Prosecutor or his Deputy in case they did not agree with the decision of the Board or the direction of the case for decision to the Special Board, had the right to lodge a protest with the Presidium of the USSR TsIK. In this case, the decision of the Special Board was suspended until a ruling of the Presidium of the USSR TsIK was made.

During 19 years, a huge number of Soviet citizens were sentenced by a panel of officials without any guarantee of legality.

But it is evident that this "work" of the NKVD did not satisfy Stalin in the beginning. N.S. Khrushchev, in his famous speech before the XXth Congress of the Party on February 25, 1956, [3] cited the following telegram of Stalin and Zhdanov to members of the Polit-

---

[1] Kozhevnikov, *op. cit.*, p. 245.

[2] *Sob. zak.*, *SSSR*, 1935, Item 84.

[3] See Infra, p. 689 ff.

bureau of September 25, 1936. "We deem it absolutely necessary and urgent that comrade Yezhov be nominated to the post of People's Commissar of Internal Affairs. Yagoda [1] has definitely proved himself to be incapable of unmasking the Trotskyvite-Zinovievite bloc. The OGPU is 4 years behind in this matter..." [2]

The Plenary Session of the Party's Central Committee of February-March 1937 repeated the statement that "the People's Commissars of Internal Affairs" has fallen behind at least 4 years in the attempt to unmask these most inexorable enemies of the People.

An unprecedented mass-terror against "enemies of the people" was started. Since the so-called "exploiting classes" were already thoroughly liquidated many years ago, this time the action was directed against members of the Communist Party themselves, independently of their position in the Party and the government, the military and private citizens.

Hence, we have a continuity of judicial activity by administrative agencies outside of the courts applying and executing all kinds of punishment : The CheKa, the GPU, the OGPU and the Special Board.

---

[1] The People's Commissar of Internal Affairs of that time.

[2] Release and translation of the speech for the press by the State Department, on June 4, 1956, p. 16. Evidently Stalin and Zhdanov forgot that the OGPU did not exist any more since 1934.

CHAPTER FOUR

COURTS, 1922-1936

A. COURTS UNDER THE NEP

As it is well known Lenin had to retreat from the attempt to install Communism with one stroke in Russia after the collapse of the economy, and the Xth Congress decided to introduce a New Economic Policy known under the abbreviation of NEP.

With regard to the drastic repressive measures taken under War Communism and during the civil war Lenin said at the Xth Congress of the Russian Communist Party : "It would be the greatest mistake if we would come to the conclusion that only such measures and such relations are possible. This would, surely, mean the collapse of Soviet power and the dictatorship of the proletariat". [1]

The new economic policy required the publishing of codes. The time had come to exchange "socialist conscience and socialist law consciousness", for a more stable basis for judicial decisions and sentences-codes, although still in the beginning of 1922, Lenin wrote to D.I. Kursky, People's Commissar of Justice, "We do not acknowledge anything 'private', for us, everything in the economy is public and not private ... It follows that state interference in 'private-legal' relations must be intensified, the right of the state to cancel (private contracts) must be enlarged, not the *corpus juris romani*, but *our revolutionary legal consciousness* must be applied to civil relations ..." [2]

But the Civil Code had to take account of the reinstalled private trade and some other "capitalistic" features of the NEP.

The year 1922 is remarkable for the almost feverish legal legislation introduced by the Soviet government. The RSFSR Criminal Code was put in force as of February 1, 1922. The RSFSR Code of Criminal Procedure followed on August 1, 1922. On this date also the Statute on the Prosecutors and the Statute of the Legal Profession began to function.

---

[1] Lenin, XXVII, p. 143.
[2] Lenin, XXIV, p. 419.

The Labor Code and the Land Code were enacted on October 30, 1922, then the Code of Civil Procedure on October 31, 1922. On October 31, 1922 the new Statute of Judicial Structure was adopted and the Civil Code introduced as of January 1, 1923 followed by the Code of Civil Procedure on September 1, 1923.

Krylenko puts the question as to the reason for this sudden activity of the legislation in the legal field. He acknowledges that a great number of people are of the opinion that it was the NEP which caused the necessity of the shift to legality, that this legality had to show Russia in a good light to the West; that for that purpose "Russia needs exact juridical norms, legal order, legal life, legality and other good but empty words". [1]

Krylenko thought that such an opinion "is pure nonsense, deep cynicism, and even an offense of the Russian Revolution", although he admits that the NEP had a certain influence on the legislation. Still this legislation retained the previous anti-capitalistic structure of the Bolshevist state.

Certainly, Art. 1 of the Civil Code states that "civil rights are protected by law as far as they do not contradict its economic and social purpose", but Krylenko mixes up the facts of the legal legislation with its contents.

It cannot be denied that this legislation was not a surrender to capitalism, but a small concession only; that it retained the main features of the new order. But what is of great importance, it is the pure fact of this legislation, that it was understood that in spite of the glorification of "socialist consciousness" and "revolutionary law consciousness", administration of justice cannot be based on them, that a legal state needs legality and that this legality must be established, supported and observed by the administration and its organs.

a) *The Legal Reform of 1922*

The Statute on the Court Structure in the RSFSR adopted by the VTsIK in October 31, 1922 [2] provided for the following system of regular courts : a) the people's courts with one permanent judge and

---

[1] Krylenko, *Sudoustroystvo, op. cit.,* p. 159-160.
[2] *Sob. uz., RSFSR,* 1922, Item 902.

two assessors on the bench; b) the province or territorial or regional
courts and c) the Supreme Court of the RSFSR.

It is peculiar that the competence of the people's court and of
the province court as a court of first instance, was not defined in the
Statute. In Article 39e of the Statute it is said that the province court,
"in the quality of a court of first instance passes upon cases assigned
to it by law". Kozhevnikov, speaking of the competence of the province
court as court of the first instance, is of the opinion that in this capacity
the province court decided the most important civil and criminal cases
previously under the jurisdiction of the former people's court bench
consisting of one permanent judge and six assessors [1] and of the former
province revolutionary tribunal abolished by the reform of 1922. A
source for his opinion is not quoted by Kozhevnikov. Admitting that
his opinion is correct, it follows that the jurisdiction of the people's
courts extended to all other criminal and civil cases not under the
competence of the province court or the special courts.

Requirements were set for the selection of the people's judges:
Only persons with no criminal records and in possession of active
and passive elective rights to the soviets could be elected to the position
of a people's judge. The candidates also had to prove two years of
responsible work, of a political character, in a workers' and peasants'
public professional or political organization, or three years of practice
in the administration of justice in a position not lower than that of
a judicial investigator. People under a defamatory court sentence or
excluded from public organizations for derogatory activity or behavior
could not occupy the position of a people's judge.

The people's judges were elected and recalled by the province
executive committees. The fact that the judges were elected and recalled
by the province and not by the local executive committee as before
"insured the independence from local influences upon judges", according to Kozhevnikov. [2] One cannot agree with this opinion. As stated
above, soviet judicial elections up to 1948 were tantamount to appointments, and the appointment by the province executive committee
exposed the judges to the influence of the Party and administration
to the same extent as if they were "elected" i.e., appointed by local
agencies.

Requirements for the choice of assessors were not changed by the
Statute on Judicial Structure of 1922 : Any "working" citizen of either

---

[1] Kozhevnikov, *op. cit.*, p. 135.

[2] *Ibid.*, p. 128.

sex, with passive and active rights for election to the soviets could be called for assessor duties. Excluded, however, from elections were persons under a defamatory court sentence or excluded from public or professional organizations for defamatory actions or behavior.

Lists of candidates were compiled by special commissars of the local executive committees in such a way that 50 % of the assessors were workers, 35 % from the rural population and 15 % from the armed forces. According to this distribution the candidates were listed and their lists posted.

For a period of one week everyone had the right to oppose the candidates. On the other hand, if the opposed candidate was dropped from the list, he had the right to appeal to a higher organization above the one which crossed his name from the list. The decision of this organization was final. [1]

The list of the candidates were presented to the commission which was empowered to cross out the names of persons considered unsuitable for the job. Again the decision of the local Commission could be appealed to the province commission the decision of which was final.

In this way the Executive Committee retained the right of the final choice of the assessors.

At the individual sessions of the courts the assessors were not selected by lot but according to the alphabetical lists established by the commissions.

It is interesting to note that as of the beginning of 1923, only 10 % of the people's judges had a higher education (8.1 % of them were jurists), 17.5 % had graduated from secondary schools and the bulk of 72.5 % from primary schools only. About 60 % of the Judges were members of the RKP (B); their number increased to 68 % as of January 1, 1924. [2]

The province courts, besides the functions of a court of first instance, described above, were also a cassation instance for decisions of the people's courts and fulfilled administrative supervision functions with regard to the people's courts of their individual province. The councils of people's judges were abolished.

The appointment requirements for the Chairman of the province court and his two Deputies were increased in comparison with members of the people's court; they had to have three years practical experience

---

[1] Illiteracy was not a reason preventing the appointment of assessors according to a Decision of the RSFSR. Supreme Court Plenum of 1925.

[2] Kozhevnikov, *op. cit.*, p. 130.

in judicial work in the capacity of a people's judge or member of a revolutionary tribunal. A requirement of two years of the same work was attached to the position of a province court judge.

All the members of the province court were selected by the province executive committees for one year and confirmed by the People's Commissar of justice of the Union Republics who had the right to present other candidates for these positions. Also the recall of the members of the province courts needed the sanction of the people's commissar of justice. But if the people's commissar of justice did not approve the candidate for chairman and his deputies and no other candidates were presented, the Commissar had the right to appoint to these positions his own candidates.

Thus, the final decision on the filling in of judicial and assessorial vacancies remained in the hands of the administration.

The plenum of the province court, the quorum of which consisted of not less than one half of all members of the court (also the presence of the province prosecutor or his assistant was required), had to decide questions of disciplinary procedure against members of the people's court, investigation magistrates and other officials of the people's courts, as well as members of the province courts and its employees. The plenum decided also on questions of local delimination of people's courts jurisdiction and other important administrative affairs.

With the consent of the president, the decision of the plenum was set in force immediately. If the president did not agree with the decision the case was transferred for decision to the people's commissar of justice, or to the supreme court or the province executive committee, respectively, depending upon the character of the question on hand.

Another function of the plenum was the interpretation of laws on the request of the cassation department of the province court or the province prosecutor. Such requests could be made exclusively in connection with a certain pending case; the conclusions of the plenum were presented to the supreme court for final action.

The plenum of the province court could also be involved in the proceedings started by the province prosecutor in the way of supervision. If after a case was decided by the lower court and the sentence was already in force or the cassation department of the province court had confirmed the decision of the first instance, but the prosecutor had found irregularities in the proceedings, he had to inform the president of the province court of his findings and the latter could bring the case to the plenum of the province court which referred it with its conclusions to the supreme court, according to a law of June 10, 1923. [1]

The RSFSR Supreme Court consisted of a : Presidium; a Plenum; Cassation Colleges in Civil and Criminal Affairs; a Judicial College; Military and Military Transportation Colleges; and a Disciplinary College.

The Chairman, his Deputy and the Chairmen of the Judicial, Military and Military Transportation Colleges were directly appointed by the VTsIK's Presidium.

All other members of the Supreme Court were appointed on recommendation of the People's Commissar of Justice with the exception of the members of the Military and Military Transportation Colleges who were appointed by the VTsIK Presidium on recommendation of the Revolutionary Military Council of the Republic or the People's Commissar of Railroads (a positive resolution of the people's commissar was also necessary.)

The Reform of 1922 abrogated the Supreme Tribunal attached to the VTsIK and its local branches as well as the highest judicial control and their functions were transferred to the Supreme Courts of the Republics.

The functions of the Supreme Court including the RSFSR Supreme Court consisted of the following :

They exercised the supervision over all the courts of the republic, examined as court cassation complaints against the decisions of Province (territorial or regional) courts.

In the way of supervision cases already in force were decided by all the courts of the republic.

As courts of original jurisdiction the Supreme Courts examined cases of particular importance, according to jurisdiction established by law. The bench of the cassation colleges was comprised of three members of the Supreme Court. But the bench of the judicial college was manned by a member of the college and two assessors.

Sentences of the judicial college on criminal cases which acted as court of original jurisdiction were not subjected to complaints in cassation and could be rescinded or changed only by the plenum of the supreme court in the way of supervision. But the Presidium of the Supreme Court, the Prosecutor of the Supreme Court, the Prosecutor

---

[1] *Sob. uz., RSFSR*, 1923, Item 480.

of the Judicial College in criminal affairs and his assessors (the latter only if they directly took part in the trial) had the right to lodge complaints against the sentences of the college in criminal affairs.

However, the complaint was restricted only to the subject of incorrect application of law in setting the punishment.

Parallel to the system of regular courts special courts were established : 1) Military tribunals for crimes against the stability and power of the Red Army; 2) Military-Transportation tribunals for especially important crimes against the transportation system; 3) Special labor sessions of the people's court for crimes violating the Labor Code; 4) Land commission on land cases and 5) Central and local arbitration commissions attached to the council of labor and defense and province and economic conferences for the arbitration of cases of property rights of state organizations.

b) *Courts Renamed According to the New Administrative Territorial Division*

The Law of October 16, 1924 established a presidium of the province court to which administrative and disciplinary duties were assigned.

During 1924-25, a new administrative-territorial division was carried out in the RSFSR. In place of "volost'", "uyezd", "gubernya", = "selo" (village), "gorod" (city), "rayon" (district) and "oblast" (region) in some places "kray" (territory) were introduced. According to the new order, the province courts became oblast (regional) or kray (territorial) courts. The regions were larger than the former provinces and some of the first included several of the latter. The jurisdiction of the regional (territorial) courts and structure were the same as those of the former province courts.

B. Special Courts

The Military and Military-Transportation Tribunals functioned under the supervision and direction of the People's Commissariat of Justice and the RSFSR Supreme Court.

Front or District Military Tribunals were attached to Front or District Military Commissars. Army Corps had Corps Military Tribunals; Division departments of the District Military Tribunals functioned as individual divisions.

Military-transport tribunals were established in Petrograd, Khar'kov, Rostov-on-the-Don, Omsk, Tashkent and Smolensk.

The Military Tribunals had jurisdiction over crimes committed against the steadfastness and power of the Red Army.

Especially important crimes against transportation were put under the jurisdiction of the Military Transportation Tribunals. The members of these tribunals consisted of appointed members of the tribunals without the participation of assessors.

All the Military-transportation Tribunals were liquidated and their competence transferred to general courts by the Decree of the USSR TsIK of November 23, 1923. [1]

The Military-Transportation College of the USSR Supreme Court was abolished in 1927. [2]

The creation of the Soviet Union brought the necessity to revise the judicial system.

C. Basic Principles of Court Structure of 1924

The establishment of basic principles of court structure was in the competence of the federal legislation, according to the 1923 Constitution.

In fulfillment of this competence, the USSR TsIK adopted the Basic Principles of Court Structure of the USSR and Union Republics, on October 29, 1924. [3] The individual union republics had to build the judicial system in compliance with the Basic Principles' premises.

The scope of activity of soviet courts, as formulated in the Basic Principles of 1924 is : a) the protection of the achievements of the proletarian revolution, the workers' and peasants' power and public order established by it; b) the protection of the interests and rights of the working population and their associations; c) the strengthening of the public-working discipline, solidarity of the working population and their legal education; d) the realization of revolutionary legality and individual and property relations of the citizens.

---

[1] *Sob. uz., RSFSR*, 1924, Item 119.

[2] Kozhevnikov, *op. cit.*, p. 166.

[3] *Sob. zak., SSSR*, 1924, Item 203.

The individual court structure was not changed : the people's court functioned with a single permanent judge and two people's assessors as a rule; the regional courts retained its jurisdiction as a cassation instance and court of final instance for important civil and criminal cases, and the Supreme Court (in Autonomous Republics they were called higher courts) remained on the top of the ediface.

The requirements for the appointment of judges and the election of assessors remained the same; also the system of their appointment and election was retained. It must be underlined, however, that the principle of the participation of assessors on the benches of all the courts was not completely upheld; cassation benches were occupied by three permanent judges, without the participation of people's assessors.

D. The USSR Supreme Court

Already in the agreement on the formation of the Union of Soviet Socialist Republics, accepted by the first Congress of Soviets of the USSR on December 30, 1922, the creation of the USSR Supreme Court was provided. It was said in the agreement that "In order to consolidate revolutionary legality in the USSR territory - - a Supreme Court with the functions of supreme judicial control, attached to the Central Executive Committee (TsIK) of the Union of Soviet Socialist Republics, is established".

In compliance with this agreement, the USSR Constitution of 1923 [1] set up the USSR Supreme Court attached to the USSR Executive Committee.

The jurisdiction of the Supreme Court was extended to the following functions : a) interpretation of union laws for the supreme courts of the union-republics; b) execution and appeal to the USSR Central Executive Committee of decisions and sentences of the Supreme Courts of the union republics, on the initiative of the Prosecutor of the USSR Supreme Court, on the ground of the discrepancy with federal legislation or violation of interests of other republics; c) the giving of conclusions on demand of the USSR Central Executive Committee, with regard to the legality of decisions of the union republics from the viewpoint of the constitution; d) decision upon claims of the

---

[1]   *Sob. uz.*, *RSFSR*, 1923, Item 789.

union republics against each other; e) examination of cases on accusation of higher officials of the union of crimes committed in office.

The USSR Supreme Court functioned by its Plenum, or in its Civil and Criminal Judicial Military and Military-Transportation Colleges.

The initiative for the presentation of questions (paragraph a) above) belonged exclusively to the USSR TsIK, its Presidium, the Prosecutor of the USSR Supreme Court, Prosecutors of the Union Republics and of the OGPU.

To the competence of the Plenum belonged further, the formation of special benches for the examination of the most important criminal and civil cases, involving interests of two or more union republics as well as for trials of members of the Central Executive Committees and the USSR Council of People's Commissars. Such trials could take place exclusively on special decisions of the VTsIK or its Presidium for each individual case.

Also the central authority of the union republics could ask the Plenum of the Supreme Court to contact the TsIK Presidium about the suspension or abolition of unlawful decisions, actions, or orders of the central organs and individual Commissariats, with the exception of those generated by the TsIK and its Presidium. The Plenum of the Supreme Court had the right to undertake such action also on its own initiative.

Thus, the Supreme Court was invested with the right to examine the constitutionality of every law, decision or order (with the exception mentioned above) a right that could be compared with that of the Supreme Court of the USA. However, the USSR Supreme Court was not empowered to abrogate a law, a decision or an order of the administration violating the Constitution or the federal legislation; it had to ask the USSR TsIK or its Presidium for such an action. It was the Plenum of the Supreme Court that had the right to rescind decisions of all the courts, including those of its Colleges, and of all institutions having a judicial character, if it found them violating federal legislation. [1]

An Instruction to the USSR Supreme Court, passed by the TsIK on July 14, 1924 [2] regulated the details of the Supreme Court's functions, according to the 1923 Constitution and the Statute on the USSR Supreme Court as discussed above.

---

[1] Statute of the USSR Supreme Court of November 28, 1923, *Vestnik TsIK, SNK i STO*, 1923, Item 311.

[2] *Sob. zak., SSSR*, 1924, Item 25.

In compliance with the Basic Principles the VTsIK adopted a new Statute on Court Structure in the RSFSR on November 19, 1926. [1]

E. THE USSR BASIC PRINCIPLES OF COURT STRUCTURE OF 1926

No major changes in the structure and functions of courts were adopted by the 1926 Statute. Worth mentioning is the establishment at the province (territorial, regional) courts of an instruction and revision department which had to work on the preliminary development of the statistical material pertaining to the activity of the province court and the institutions subordinate to it, the working out of projects, circulars, letters and instructions issued by the province court, the preparation of accounts, on the work of the province court and agencies subordinate to it, the drawing up of revision data, following revisions and inquiries carried out by the province court. The direction of this department was entrusted to a member of the court by the plenum.

The new statute also regulated proceedings for the disciplinary prosecution of members of the judiciary.

The decisions of the plenum of the province or regional (territorial) court in the interpretation of law were obligatory for all the judicial institutions of the province, region (territory). The province court was charged not only with the supervision over the lower courts, but was also an organ of direct control with regard to all judicial institutions, investigation magistracy, notary publics, court marshalls, colleges of advocates and court interpreters of the province. The province court had the right in cases of non-agreement with the decisions of the plenum to appeal to the plenary of the Supreme Court. In the meantime, the courts had to submit to the decision of the plenum.

F. THE RSFSR STATUTE ON COURT STRUCTURE OF 1926

This law established the following judicial structure : 1) the people's court; 2) the province court (called main court in autonomous republics) or regional and kray (territorial) courts; 3) the RSFSR Supreme Court.

---

[1] *Sob. uz., RSFSR*, 1926, Item 624.

Besides these regular courts special courts functioned; a) military tribunals for military and important crimes committed by civil persons; b) land commissions for cases concerning the land tenure; c) arbitration commissions for the arbitration of claims of state agencies and employees to each other, consisting of a Supreme Commission attached to the RSFSR Economic Council and local commissions; d) special censors of the people's court were functionaries for decisions in labor litigation, in the main cities of the autonomous republics, territories, regions, provinces and industrial centers.

The Statute on Court Structure of 1926 did not introduce great changes as compared to the Statute on Court Structure of 1922. The requirements for the election of people's judges were eased in permitting the election of persons with experience in work also in state agencies other judicial ones. The people's judges could be elected not only by province executive committees but by city soviets as well.

Some changes were introduced also with regard to the people's assessors : according to the 1926 Statute persons excluded from public and professional organizations for disgraceful actions of behavior, were barred from the election to people's assessors during three years; the same restriction was applied to persons sentenced for criminal offences, with a duration up to the expunction of the criminal records. The assessors could be elected at general assemblies of workers at the places of work.

G. The RSFSR Supreme Court

The activity of the RSFSR Supreme Court was also regulated by the Statute of 1926. According to the Statute, the RSFSR Supreme Court sat as a court of first instance over civil and criminal cases of great state importance assigned to its jurisdiction by law, a cassation instance for decisions of the main courts [1] of the autonomous republics, regional (territory), province [2] and circuit courts, and had the immediate direction of the judicial practice and realized the highest judicial

---

[1] Courts of the second instance of the Autonomous Republics (corresponding to province, territorial and regional courts) were called "Main Courts".

[2] By a special law of 1928, the province and territorial (regional and main) courts became cassation instances for lower courts.

supervision over all judicial institutions, forming a single and one judicial policy in the RSFSR.

The Presidium of the RSFSR Supreme Court examined the questions of reprieves or change of sentences and decisions of the Supreme Court Colleges and of any court of the republic in the way of supervision. If a decision on a principle was necessary, the Presidium had to present it to the Plenum of the Supreme Court for confirmation. In other cases, the Presidium had the right to reprieve the sentence or decision of the lower court and return the case for a new examination.

On the initiative of the Chairman of the Supreme Court or its Prosecutor, the Presidium of the Supreme Court examined the question of presenting to the VTsIK or to the Economic Council for review of decisions of the Special Commission on land Arguments and decisions of the Higher Arbitration Commission, attached to the Economic Council. The decisions of the Presidium in the cases had to be confirmed by the Plenum. The Plenum of the RSFSR Supreme Court interpreted law on all questions of judicial practice in the field of the material and procedural law, on the initiative of the individual departments of the Supreme Court or its staff, the Presidium of the Supreme Court, the Prosecutor of the Republic or his Assistant, attached to the Supreme Court, as well as on the initiative of the plenum or the main courts of autonomous republics, and regional (territorial) province and circuit courts.

H. Special Courts

a) *Military Tribunals*

The structure and activity of the military tribunals were regulated in this period by the Statute on Military Tribunals of August 20, 1926 adopted by the TsIK and the RSFSR Council of People's Commissars, and the Statute on Temporary Members of the Military Tribunals of November 9, 1926, passed by the RSFSR Council of People's Commissars. [1]

The district, front and individual army military tribunals consisted of a chairman, deputy chairman and regular or temporary members. The bench was formed by the chairman (or his deputy) and two members (not people's assessors).

---

[1] *Sob. zak.*, *SSSR*, 1926, Item 413.

The general direction of the military tribunal's activity remained in the hands of the RSFSR Supreme Court through its Military College. The establishment of new military tribunals and the liquidation of old ones was carried out by the Military College of the USSR Supreme Court, in agreement with the commissariat of justice of the union republic involved.

The jurisdiction of the military tribunal remained the same as established in the 1924 Basic Principles of Judicial Structure of the USSR and in the Code of Military Crimes of 1924.

The competence of military tribunals extended also to all crimes committed by military or civil persons in places where, in consequence of extraordinary circumstances, no other court functioned.

The cassation instance for all the military tribunals was the Military College of the USSR Supreme Court.

The Statute of 1929 gave the USSR Supreme Court the right to initiate checking of the legality of decisions and orders passed by the federal and state agencies with regard to the USSR Constitution.

To this effect the USSR Supreme Court was charged 1) with giving its opinion to the Presidium of the TsIK, on demand, on the legality, from the wiewpoint of the USSR Constitution, and the federal legislation, of decisions of central executive committees of the union republics and their presidiums, as well as of the USSR Council of People's Commissars and the Council of Labor and Defense; 2) on demand of the Presidium of the USSR TsIK, of the presidium of the central executive committees of the union republicsor of the USSR Supreme Court itself, as well as on the initiative of the Prosecutor of the USSR Supreme Court, the suspension or cancelling of decisions of People's Commissars and other central institutions of the USSR, with the exception of decisions of the USSR TsIK and its Presidium, the USSR Council of People's Commissars and the Council of Labor and Defense, can be ordered on the grounds of non-conformity of these decisions with the USSR Constitution and federal legislation.

The USSR Supreme Court fulfilled the function of commenting on federal legislation on demand of the supreme courts of the union republics and on its own initiative.

Also the protest right against decisions of the plenums of the supreme courts of the union republics which contravened federal laws or violated the interests of other republics was retained by the USSR Supreme Court according to the 1929 Statute.

The VTsIK and the Council of People's Commissars criticized the work of the regular courts in a joint decision of March 26, 1928. [1] At that time the decision found that besides some other defects "the number of sentences had increased extraordinarily, especially of those providing imprisonment for a short period of time and that in many cases the indictment was groundless. The decision found it necessary "to apply severe measures of repression exclusively to class enemies and professional criminals and recidivists, such as bandits, incendiaries, horse thieves, embezzlers, bribers and thieves; the severe measures of repression with regard to these criminals must be supplemented by not less strict execution of sentences, while admitting the mitigation of the measures of social defense applied by the courts, and their release before serving full time only on exclusive circumstances and under the condition that the safety of society be assured with respect to them.

On the other hand, the decision denounced the exaggerated number of suspended sentences passed in place of acquittals and recognized the necessity to enlarge the use of the right of the court to acquit even when the commission of the crime was established, if the application of measures of social defense would obviously prove fruitless.

---

[1]   *Yezhenedel'nik sovetskoy yustitsii*, 1928, No. 14, pp. 417-419.

CHAPTER FIVE

INDUSTRIALIZATION, COLLECTIVIZATION AND THE COURTS

The NEP period ends in 1929 with the adoption of the First Five-Year Plan which started the huge industrialization effort in the USSR. The formidable collectivization process and the ruthless annhilation of the kulaks was conducted. However, the major support was given to the actions not by regular courts but by the special institutions of suppression : the military tribunals, the OGPU and the NKVD. These institutions also took over the bloody work of the purges in the thirties.

A. THE PEOPLE'S COURT

In the process of territorial redivision the circuits (okrug) were abolished by the law of June 23, 1930. [1] Hence, the Circuit Courts were dissolved and their civil and criminal jurisdiction transferred to the people's Courts with the exception of counterrevolutionary crimes under kray, regional or territorial courts. [2]

In this connection the same law introduced the following changes : *a*) sections of the people's court must be established in every rayon district (a smaller territorial division than the Circuit) [3] *b*) the people's judges are elected by the rayon executive committees and in cities, by City Soviets, for a duration established by Art. 16 of the Statute on Court Structure; *c*) sentences of the people's courts may be appealed in cassation with the following exceptions : 1. in civil cases if the suit for wages does not involve more than a month's wages and is not the terminal pay, as well as all other suits if they involve not more than 100 rubles; decisions on claims of alimony may be appealed on cassation notwithstanding the sum involved; 2. sentences in criminal cases if they involve forced labor lasting three months or less, or prohibition of a certain activity or trade, or public censure, warning or a fine of no more than 100 rubles.

---

[1]   *Sob. zak.*, *SSSR*, 1930, Item 400.
[2]   *Sob. zak.*, *SSSR*, 1930, Item 601.
[3]   City "rayons" correspond to city boroughs.

The competence of the territorial and regional courts was not changed. They were the cassation instance for cases decided by people's courts. The appeals on cassation were heard in cassation courts or during visiting sessions of the territorial or regional courts.

A judge of the local People's Court had to take part in the visiting session of the cassation court.

B. Territorial and Regional Courts; Oblast (Kray) Courts

The structure of the oblast (kray) courts was established by a decision of the VTsIK of October 10, 1930 [1] as follows : *a*) plenum; *b*) presidium; *c*) civil and criminal colleges; *d*) a united organization and instruction sector (this sector was abolished in 1934).

The cassation function of the territorial and regional oblast (kray) courts were already described above.

On July 10, 1934, [2] the TsIK passed a law on the jurisdiction over the cases investigated by the NKVD and its organs.

This law provided that cases of crimes against the state (counter-revolutionary and against the regime) investigated by the NKVD and its local organs, had to be examined by the USSR Supreme Courts, supreme courts of the union republics, territorial and regional oblast courts and the main courts of the autonomous republics, according to their individual cognizance.

For the trying of these cases, the law prescribed the formation of special colleges consisting of a chairman and two members. Assessors were excluded from these benches.

Accordingly, such special colleges were organized at territorial and regional Kray courts.

Another change in the Statute on Court Structure was made by a Decision of the VTsIK and the RSFSR Council of People's Commissars of July 20, 1934. It was decided that in places where by special orders oblast courts were established within a territory, the regional court will be charged with : 1) organization and guidance of all people's courts in the region; 2) examination of appeals in cassation and supervision of protests in cases decided by all the people's courts of the region; 3) examination as a court of first instance of all

---

[1]   *Sob. zak., SSSR*, 1930, Item 400.
[2]   *Sob. zak., RSFSR*, 1934, Item 627.

cases under the jurisdiction of the territorial court, the latter having the right to request any case from the regional court for its own examination; 4) guidance of institutions and organizations attached to the court (court marshalls, notary publics, the regional college of advocates); 5) guidance of public courts active in the region.

The general guidance of the regional courts belonged to the territorial court which retained also the examination of cases decided by the People's Courts with regard to which the decision of the plenum of the Regional Court was under protest. The RSFSR Supreme Court was the cassation and supervisory instance for decisions of the regional court acting as a court of first instance.

Among the changes in the structure and jurisdictions of the territorial (regional) courts the organization of Special Colleges charged with the examination of cases under the jurisdiction of these courts and investigated by the NKVD and its local organs must be underlined: in contradistinction to other colleges of the territorial (regional) courts they sat without the participation of people's assessors.

C. Changes in the USSR Supreme Court

In the period on hand, the USSR Supreme Court was entrusted with the supervision of an unified judicial policy and practice of the union republic courts and of a consistant fulfillment of federal laws. [1]

On the other hand the prosecution was separated from the USSR Supreme Court and made an independent USSR Agency [2] and the USSR Supreme Court was relieved of the burden of supervision of legality in the USSR in general.

In matters of jurisdiction the Law of July 10, 1934 [3] provided that cases of treason to the fatherland, espionage, terriorism, explosion and arson, investigated by the NKVD and its organs, had to be submitted for trial to the Military College of the USSR Court or to military tribunals, according to their individual jurisdiction.

Cases investigated by the same Commissariat and its organs, concerning crimes committed on railroads and waterways had to be examined by the Transport and Water College of the USSR Supreme Court

---

[1] Decision of the USSR TsIK Presidium of Sept. 13, 1933, confirmed by the TsIK on January 4, 1934 (*Sob. zak.*, *SSSR*, 1934, Item 17).

[2] *Sob. zak.*, *SSSR*, 1934, Item 26.

[3] *Sob. zak.*, *SSSR*, 1934, Item 284.

or by the railroad and water line courts, in accordance with individual competance.

D. Special Courts

a) Railroad Line Courts

From the beginning of soviet power great attention was paid to crimes committed on railroads.

The railroads were the main medium of food transport and supply. During the years of food scarcity crimes committed on railroads with regard to food transportation, and the work of the railroad in general often wrecked by railroad accidents and sabotage, were of great concern to the Soviet government. As described above the CheKa and GPU had to watch especially over this kind of crimes.

In order to strengthen the fight against crimes, endangering the normal work of transportation, to bring the examination of such crimes closer to the place of their commission and to accelerate their trial, as well as to attract to the fight against railroad crimes the proletarian masses, the USSR TsIK and the USSR Council of People's Commissars decided to organize Railroad Line Courts in November 27, 1930. [1]

In the RSFSR the railroad line courts were attached to the territorial regional courts at the seat of the Board of Direction of the lines.

They were composed of a judge of the territorial (regional) court as chairman and two assessors appointed from lists of employees of the line by the territorial (regional) executive committees.

The jurisdiction of the railroad line court extended to : a) malicious violation of labor discipline by persons employed in railroad transportation; b) malicious violation of and non-compliance with train rules resulting in the damage or destruction of the rolling stock or constructions of the line, or accidents involving personal damage; c) violation of and non-compliance with traffic rules although not resulting in the consequence enumerated in Par. b, but representing a direct threat to the order and safety of the traffic; d) crimes resulting in the accumulation of cars in places of unloading as well as idle standing and the hoarding of unneeded cars in parks; e) cases of low-grade repair of locomotives and putting in circulation deficiently

---

[1] Evidently with the exception of cases under the jurisdiction of the Military Tribunal.

repaired locomotives, cars, cisterns and other transportation equipment; *f*) cases of other crimes commited on railroad lines disrupting the normal work of transportation; *g*) all cases of revolutionary crimes connected with railroad line transportation. [1]

The competence of railroad line courts, included persons other than those working on railroads. The offenders had to be tried in railroad line courts at the place where the crime was committed.

Complaints against the decisions of the railroad line court had to be lodged with the Transportation Department of the USSR Supreme Court.

However, on August 27, 1933, [2] the USSR TsIK and the USSR Council of People's Commissars decided to transfer the railroad line courts from the systems of the People's Commissariats of justice of the union republic to the system of the USSR Supreme Court under the Transportation College of the USSR Supreme Court.

The Transportation College had to select the staff of the railroad line courts with the cooperation of the Political Department of the People's Commissariat of Railroads. The USSR Statute on the discipline of worker's and Employees' of Railroad Transportation of June 4, 1933 [3] was extended to all the staffs of the Transportation College of the USSR Supreme Court, and the Railroad Line Courts.

b) *Waterways Courts*

Waterways Courts were established by Decision of the USSR TsIK and the USSR Council of People's Commissars on June 7, 1934. [4]

The purpose of the decision was similar to that which prompted the installation on railroad line courts. The fight against violations of socialist legality, the protection of socialist property, and the strengthening of socialist discipline on water transportation lines.

The waterways courts were not concentrated in the system of the USSR Supreme Court as it was the case with the railroad line courts since 1932. Only a part of the waterways courts belonged to the USSR Supreme Court system under a newly formed college of Water Transportation. The other part was included into the court and commissariat net of the union republics.

---

[1]   Evidently with the exception of cases under the jurisdiction of the Military Tribunal.
[2]   *Sob. zak.*, 1933, Item 324.
[3]   *Sob. zak.*, 1933, Item 206b.
[4]   *Sob. zak.*, 1934, Item 251.

The waterways courts of the Basins of the Black and Caspian Seas and of Upper-Middle- and Lower Volga and of the Dnepr Rivers were directly subordinated to the USSR Supreme Court, whereas all other waterways courts of other basins were included into the court systems of the corresponding union republics.

A net of district waterways courts was organized at the main production and operation places of the basins. They were subordinated to the Basin Waterways Courts for offenses as those under the jurisdiction of the railroad line courts with the difference that the waterways courts tried cases of crimes committed on waterways and with regard to ships and their operation and traffic.

Also, the disciplinary provisions in force with regard to the staffs of the railroads were extended to the staffs of the water lines.

c) *Special Benches of the People's Courts*

On July 31, 1931, the People's Commissariat of justice issued an order [1] prescribing the organization of special benches of the people's courts for the trial of ship-wreck cases located in places according to a list attached to the order. Assessors for these benches had to be selected from members of waterways trade-unions.

Another special bench of the People's Court was entrusted with the examination of labor and production crimes.

These benches were introduced by decision of the VI Congress of the Leading Workers of the Administration of Justice, approved by the College of the People's Commissariat of Justice on February 21, 1932. [2]

The benches were organized at people's courts in the basic industrial regions. The most qualified judges, experienced in production and reliable, had to be assigned to these benches. Also the assessors had to be chosen from shock-workers, shock-specialists, business executives and professional workers.

The main purpose of the industrial and labor courts was to examine offenses directed against the industrial and financial plan committed by officials.

Hence, the jurisdiction of these courts extended to abuse of power, bureaucratism, bad management, negligence of leading and other employees of state and cooperative institutions and enterprises,

---

[1] Circular letter No. 79; *Sov. yust.*, 1931, No. 21, p. 36.

[2] *Ibid.*, 1932, No. 6-7, pp. 35-36.

resulting in the non-fulfillment or the tardy fulfillment of the assignment in capital construction, production, the improvement of production, lowering of its costs, and spoilage and the overage of labor efficiency, etc., as well as to all criminal and civil cases connected with the violation of legislation on the protection of labor committed by officials of institutions and enterprises.

The same decree ordered the formation of Special Cassation Colleges at regional courts on which examination of all labor and production cases had to be concentrated, in order to obtain unified decisions and practice in these cases.

d) *Village Courts*

We have seen that in 1928 conciliatory chambers were reorganized in village courts by decision of the TsIK of 29 Sept 1930. [1]

The village court consisted of the chairman, his deputy, judges (not less than 15) and assessors. The Chairman, his Deputy and judges were appointed by the village Soviet whereas the assessors were elected in general assemblies of the villages by citizens in possession of electoral rights and had to be confirmed in their position by the executive committees of the soviets.

The village courts were subordinate to the soviets on the one side but on the other side the people's court judge in whose district the village was located had the right in the way of supervision, to suspend and even set aside a decision of the village court in which he found substantial violations of law or interest of the working population. He could quash the proceedings or take the case for decision to his court. Otherwise, the decision of the village court was final.

The jurisdiction of the village courts covered cases of violations of public security and order and other petty criminal offences and civil claims in which not more than 50 rubles were involved. Claims generated by labor relations could not exceed 25 rubles.

Punishment inflicted by the village courts were : warning, public censure which could remain unpublished, or published or publicly declared at the village assembly, fines of not more than 10 rubles, obligation to make up for the material damage not exceeding 50 rubles, and fulfillment of public work during not more than 5 days.

---

[1] *Sob. zak.*, 1930, Item 531.

Two years later, the competence of the village courts were enlarged by a decision of the Presidium of the TsIK taken on May 4, 1932. [1]

The decision acknowledged the increased importance of village courts, the active participation of kolkhoz members in court work and aimed at the further development of the activity of the kolkhoz members and of poor and middle class masses of the village population.

The competence of village courts was extended to cases connected with the failure to carry out obligations with regard to state and public assignments by individuals, if according to the opinion of the village soviet it is more rational to apply methods of public influence to the top management of such economies, than to subject them to court or administrative responsibility; cases of larceny or damage to kolkhoz property if they were directed to village courts by elective organs or by the general assembly of the kolkhoz and of the extent of the damage done did not exceed 50 rubles; cases of petty larceny if committed for the first time, distribution of or damage to property if not exceeding 50 rubles; of property claims if their value does not exceed 75 rubles.

The people's court in whose district the productional comrades court operated had the supervision over its activity. If a people's court judge discovered a case under examination in the productional comrades court not under its jurisdiction, or a decision of this court in excess of its authority, or a substantial violation of law, he had to suspend the execution of the decision and transfer it to the people's court.

The productional comrades courts worked under the guidance of the All-Union Central Council of Trade Unions and the RSFSR Commissariat of Justice.

---

[1]   *Sob. zak.*, *SSSR*, 1932, Item 180.

CHAPTER SIX

FROM THE 1936 CONSTITUTION TO WORLD WAR II

A. Principles of Administration of Justice
in the 1936 Constitution

The Constitution contains a chapter on the administration of justice bringing forward democratic principles to govern this administration. These principles are : independence of the judiciary, participation of people's representatives (assessors) in the administration of justice, publicity, the right to counsel of the accused and the conduct of proceedings in the language of the union or autonomous republic at the place of trial.

According to the original provision of the Constitution, administration of justice, is carried out in the USSR by the Supreme Court, the Supreme Courts of the Union Republics, Territorial and Regional Courts, courts of the Autonomous Republics, Autonomous Regions, Circuit Courts, special courts of the USSR, created by resolutions of the USSR Supreme Soviet, and People's Courts.

In Kozhevnikov's words, "These principles make the Soviet Court the most democratic court in the world". [1]

In order to implement these principles, the USSR Supreme Soviet, accordings to Art 14, of the Constitution, provided that legislation in the judicial system on judicial procedure, criminal and civil codes belongs to the jurisdiction of the USSR, and adopted a law on the "Judicial Structure of the USSR, the Union and the Autonomous Republics", on August 16, 1938. [2]

B. The Basic Principles of Court Structure of the USSR

The purpose of the administration of justice, as defined in the law of 1938, was to secure exact and unflinching observance of Soviet law by all institutions, organizations, officials and citizens of the USSR. To

---

[1] Kozhevnikov, *op. cit.*, p. 294.
[2] *V.V.S.*, *SSSR*, 1938, No. 11.

this effect the administration of justice had to protect from any encroachment :

a) the public and state structure of the USSR as established by the USSR Constitution, the constitutions of the union and autonomous republics, the socialist system of economy and socialist property;

b) the political, labor, dwelling and other personal and property rights of the soviet citizens as guaranteed by the USSR Constitution and Constitutions of the union and autonomous republics;

c) the rights and interests, protected by law, of state organizations, enterprises, kolkhozes, cooperatives and other public organizations.

The law repeats the principles established by the USSR Constitution that the judges are independent and subject only to law; court proceedings are conducted in the local language, and the accused has the right to counsel and public trial if otherwise not provided by law; assessors participate in all cases examined in the USSR courts, with exceptions provided by law; the judges and assessors are elected and all citizens in possession of voting rights may serve in these capacities; one and the same court shall administer justice to all citizens independently of their social property or service status, nationality or race; the same criminal, civil, and procedural legislation must be applied in all courts of the USSR.

However, only people's court judges and assessors were elected according to the law. Justices of the territorial regional and circuit courts as well as those of the autonomous regions were appointed by territorial, regional, circuit and autonomous region soviets for a term of five years.

Also elections of people's courts judges and assessors had to take place by vote of the citizens of the district on ground of general "direct, and equal voting rights by secret ballot" as was provided for in the Constitution.

Another exception to assessors' participation in decisions of the people's court was made by the Ukase of the Presidium of the USSR Supreme Soviet of August 1940 [1] providing that cases of shirking work without valid reasons and the arbitrary leaving enterprises and institutions shall be examined by the people's court judge alone, without the participation of assessors.

In 1936-1938 during the so called great purges and latter up to Stalin's death and even in one case after his death [2], trials were carried

---

[1] *V.V.S.*, *SSSR*, 1940, No. 28.
[2] Trial and execution of Baria.

out and sentences pronounced and executed, of which the public was informed only *post-factum* or not at all".

a) *The People's Court*

The law of 1938 provided broad jurisdiction for the people's court. It extended : a) in criminal cases to crime against life, health, liberty and dignity of persons, as well as to cases of malicious non-payment of alimony, insults, hooliganism and libel; property, crimes committed in office; crimes against the administration; b) in civil cases to suits about property, claims generated by labor relations, alimony obligations, inheritance and to all other criminal and civil cases assigned to it by law.

A great burden on the people's court was the enforcement of the drastic Ukase of the Presidium of the Supreme Soviet [1] of June 26, 1940 on the prohibition of the arbitrary abandoning of work. This Ukase provided for confinement in jail for from two to four months of workers and employees of state, cooperative, and public enterprises who arbitrarily left work in these enterprises. The people's courts had to examine such cases within five days and execute the sentence at once.

Also the directors of enterprises and chiefs of institutions guilty of failing to subject to prosecution in court persons who arbitrarily abandoned work in enterprises and institutions or shirked work without valid reasons. The same responsibility was attached to directors and chiefs of enterprises and institutions hiring persons who arbitrarily left other enterprises or institutions.

Workers and employees of enterprises and institutions who shirked work without valid reason had to be punished by people's courts by forced labor at places of their work for up to six months and the loss of 25 % of their wages.

The people's court also had the duty to examine cases not under the jurisdiction of comrades courts which involved petty larceny committed at the premises of enterprises and institutions or hooliganism at enterprises, institutions and public places; the cases were presented to the court within two days after.

---

[1] *V.V.S.*, 1940, No. 20.

b) *Territorial, Regional and Circuit Courts and Courts of the Autonomous Regions*

According to the law of 1938, the territorial, regional and circuit courts, as well as the courts of the Autonomous Regions, fulfilled two functions : they were courts of first instance for a number of criminal and civil cases and they examined appeals in cassation and protests against decisions of the people's courts.

The jurisdiction was identical for all these courts.

As courts of original jurisdiction, the territorial, regional and circuit courts as well as the courts of the autonomous regions, tried cases of counterrevolutionary crimes, of especially dangerous crimes against the administrative order, of plundering of socialist property, of particularly important economic crimes and crimes committed in office, and examined civil suits between state and public institutions, enterprises and organizations.

In the quality of an appellate court, the territorial, regional, circuit courts, as well as the courts of the autonomous regions examined complaints and protests against sentences, decisions and interlocutory orders of people's courts.

The territorial, regional, circuit courts and courts of the autonomous regions were divided into two colleges : The criminal judicial college tried criminal cases and examined appeals and protests; the civil judicial college fulfilled the same functions in civil cases.

As a court of original jurisdiction the bench was manned by a chairman, a member of the criminal or civil college, and two assessors.

The appeals and protests were examined also by a bench of three members of the corresponding colleges. The former special colleges were abolished and their jurisdiction transferred to the criminal or civil colleges, respectively.

The territorial, regional and circuit courts as well as the courts of the autonomous regions, were freed of their administrative and supervisory functions with regard to people's courts. This function was taken over by special departments of the people's commissariats of justice of union republics attached to territorial and regional soviets.

No popular election were provided for justices of the territorial, regional and circuit courts as well as of courts of the autonomous regions, even on paper.

According to the law of 1938, they were elected not by executive committees of territorial regional, cricuit or autonomous regions, as before, but in sessions of the soviets themselves.

Some Soviet writers see in this change a democratization of procedure. [1] The reason for such an assertion is not clear. Whether selected by the executive committee of a soviet, or in plenary session of it, such an "election" is tantamount to an appointment. In both cases the justices are not elected by the people, but selected by an administrative body.

c) *Supreme Courts of the Union Republics*

The supreme court of a union republic is the highest judicial body of the republic. Its function is a judicial and a supervisory one.

The criminal and the civil judicial colleges tried cases and suits, as a court of first instance, assigned to them by law. In the way of supervision over the judicial activity of all the courts of the republic, the colleges examined protests against sentences, decisions and rulings in force and appeals in cassation against pending sentences, decisions and rulings of territorial, regional and other courts of the republics with the exception of special courts which were under the jurisdiction of the USSR Supreme Court as we shall see below.

Benches of the colleges of the supreme courts of the union republics, consisted of a member of the college as chairman and two assessors for cases examined as courts of first instance. In cassation cases the assessors were excluded and the bench was occupied by three justices of which one was the chairman.

Members of the supreme court of a union republic were elected by the supreme soviet of the republic.

d) *Supreme Courts of Autonomous Republics*

The supreme courts of the autonomous republics were organized in the same way as the supreme courts of the union republics; they had two judicial colleges : for criminal cases and civil suits and for carrying out the appellate activity.

The jurisdiction of the supreme court of an autonomous republic is identical with that of the territorial, regional and circuit courts and courts of autonomous regions (Art. 40 of the Law on Judicial Structure of the USSR, Union and Autonomous Republics covering the jurisdiction of autonomous republic supreme courts is identical

---

[1] So, for instance, Kozhevnikov, *op. cit.*, p. 314.

with Art. 32 listing the competence of the territorial, regional, circuit and autonomous regions courts).

It is elected by the Supreme Soviet of the Autonomous Republic for 5 years and functions as a court of first instance, and as an appellate court for sentences, decisions and private rulings of the People's Court. Also, the benches of the two colleges are manned by a member of the court (Chairman) and two assessors for cases and suits examined as a court of first instance, and by 3 members of the court for appeals and protest cases.

e) *The USSR Supreme Court*

According to the Law of 1938 the USSR Supreme Court is the highest judicial organ of the country and is elected by the USSR Supreme Soviet for five years. It supervised the judicial activity of all judicial organs of the USSR and the union republics. Its function extended to :

a) examination of protests of the USSR Prosecutor and the Chairman of the USSR Supreme Court against sentences, decisions and private rulings of courts, already in force :

b) examination of appeals and protests in cases examined by military tribunals and by railroad and waterway transportation courts.

The USSR Supreme Court had five colleges : *a*. a Judicial College on Criminal Cases; *b*. a Judicial College on Civil Suits; *c*. a Military College; *d*. a Railroad College and *e*. a Water Transportation College.

The judicial colleges examined cases and suits assigned to their competence by law as courts of first instance, appeals in cassation and protests against sentences, decisions and private rulings of the supreme courts of union republics.

The bench of the judicial colleges functioned also as a court of first instance and consisted of a member of the college and of two assessors.

The appellate functions of the Colleges were fulfilled by a bench of three judges without the participation of assessors.

The Military College sat as a court of first instance in cases assigned to it by law and heard protests and appeals against sentences and private rulings of military tribunals. Its trial benches when acting in the capacity of a court of first instance, consisted of a member of the Military Colleges (chairman) and two assessors except in cases provided for by the Criminal Code of Criminal Procedure when the bench consisted of three members of the court.

Also the bench examining appeals and protests was manned by three judges.

The Railroad and Water Transportation Colleges examined cases assigned to them by law and functioned as appellate courts for sentences and private rulings of the railroad and waterways courts. The benches were manned, in performance of the first activity, by a member of the college and two assessors, and the second by three justices.

For the examination of protests, against sentences, decisions and private rulings of the Colleges of the USSR Supreme Courts, lodged by the Chairman of the USSR Supreme Court, or the USSR Prosecutor, a Plenum of the USSR Supreme Court, consisting of the Chairman, his Deputy and all the members of the USSR Supreme Court is convoked. The participation of USSR Prosecutor in the Plenary Session is mandatory. Plenary Sessions have to take place not less than once in two months. The examination of protests takes place in the absence of the parties or accused involved and their lawyers.

The Plenum gives leading directives on questions of judicial practice on the basis of decisions taken by the USSR Supreme Court in judicial cases examined by the court.

The Chairman of the USSR Supreme Court may take over the chairmanship in any case under examination by a College of the USSR Supreme Court.

The Chairman of the USSR Supreme Court and RSFSR Prosecutor are entitled to obtain the record of any case from any court of the USSR or a union republic and to lodge a protest in this case, according to the procedure established by law.

C. The USSR Special Courts

The law of 1938 listed the following special courts :

1. Military tribunals; 2. Railroad line courts and 3. Waterways courts.

The chairmen, their deputies and members of the special courts were elected by the USSR Supreme Soviet for a term of five years. Assessors participated in the sessions of the special courts. They were elected by territorial and regional Soviets and by the supreme soviets of union and autonomous republics.

The benches of the special courts consisted of a member of the court and two assessors with the exception of some cases when the bench was manned by three members of the court (for instance when the military tribunals functioned as appellate courts). By decision of the TsIK and the USSR Council of People's Commissars of April

7, 1963, [1] the waterways courts were transferred from subordination to the RSFSR Supreme Court to the system of USSR Supreme Court.

a) The military tribunals were attached to military districts, fronts and naval fleets and *b*) to armies, air corps and other military units and militarized institutions.

The jurisdiction of the military tribunals extended to military crimes, as well as to other crimes assigned to them by law. [2]

The military tribunals attached to districts, fronts and naval fleets examined cases under their jurisdictions as courts of first instance, and decided on appeals and protests against sentences pronounced by military tribunals attached to armies, army corps and other military units or militarized institutions.

The railroad and waterways courts had no appellate functions. They had to decide upon cases of crimes intended to undermine labor discipline on transportation lines and other crimes disturbing the normal work of transportation, assigned by law to their jurisdiction.

---

[1] *Sob. zak.*, *USSR*, 1936, Item 36.

[2] For instance, according to the decision of the TsIK and the USSR Council of People's Commissars of July 10, 1934, (*Sob. zak.*, 1934, Item 284) "Cases of treason, espionage, terroristic acts, explosions, arson and other sabotage actions (Art. 68 and 69, Statute on State Crimes) shall be tried by the Military according to their respective jurisdictions".

CHAPTER SEVEN

FROM WORLD WAR II TO THE PRESENT TIME

During the Russian-German War of 1941-1945, the Soviet courts faced special tasks : they had to try crimes directly connected with the war operations and the crimes endangering the war effort of the rear. In order to achieve these goals some changes in the judicial jurisdictions were carried out.

A. SPECIAL COURTS

The Statute on Military Courts in places under Martial Law [1] and in regions of war operations reorganized the railroad and waterways courts into railroad and waterways military tribunals.

When the city of Moscow and a part of the USSR territory was declared under a state of emergency, Moscow's People's Courts, except one in every city borough, were transformed into Military Tribunals with benches occupied by three judges without assessors. The Moscow Military Tribunals also sat in visiting sessions in districts of the Moscow Region.

The competence of the Moscow Military Tribunal covered crimes enumerated in Art. 7 of the Law of June 22, 1941, except crimes committed by military persons and treason, espionage, diversion and terroristic actions ; voluntary desertion from work in enterprises of the military industry by workers and employees, according to the Ukase of the USSR Supreme Court Presidium of December 26, 1941.

The People's Courts in Moscow which were not converted into Military Tribunals examined civil suits.

The competence of the Military Courts of the NKVD was extended to the following cases formerly under the jurisdiction of the people's courts : robbery, murder, forcible escape from houses of detention, evasion from military service, resistance to authorities, illegal acquisition, sale and storage of arms, as well as plunder of arms. If these crimes were committed on railroads or waterways, the military tribunals of these lines were competent for the trial of these cases.

The territorial (regional) courts lost to the military tribunals of

---

[1] Martial Law was introduced by the Ukase of the USSR Sypreme Court Presidium of June 22, 1941 (*V.V.S.*, *SSSR*, 1941, No. 42).

the army and navy all the cases of crimes committed by military persons and the cases of treason, espionage, terroristic acts and sabotage.

The military authorities received the right to submit for examination to the military tribunals cases of speculation, malicious hooliganism and other criminal cases, if the military deemed it necessary with regard to the war.

The cases of evasion from paying taxes or of some other duties (especially on the military automobile, horse-carriage and ship transportation) in war time, were examined by military tribunals in places under martial law but in all other places by people's courts and, if committed under aggravating circumstances, by supreme courts of union republics where no regional division was introduced, and by territorial, regional and supreme courts (in autonomous republics) where they existed.

The military tribunals (in places under martial law) had the right to examine cases submitted to them within 24 hours after the indictment was served on the accused. The bench was composed of three regular justices.

Appeals in cassation against sentences of military tribunals in places under martial law were excluded and could be set aside or changed only by way of supervision.

Military circuit, front and army (fleet and flotilla) soviets, as well as front, army and circuit commanders had the right to suspend death sentences, but at the same time, had to communicate their opinion by telegraph to the Chairman of the Military College of the USSR Supreme Court and the Chief Military Prosecutor of the Red Army or the Chief Prosecutor of the Navy, respectively, for further direction in the case.

The same person had to be informed by telegraph of every death sentence pronounced by the military tribunal.

In case no answer was received from any of the persons listed above, about the suspension of the sentence, within 72 hours after the telegram was handed over, the sentence had to be executed.

Other sentences of the military tribunals were executed immediately.

We know that the right of supervision over the work of the military tribunals belonged to the Military College of the USSR Supreme Court. However, this right was extended to the Front and Circuit Military Tribunals since it was necessary to act fast if a sentence had to be protested.

By Ukase of April 15, 1943 [1], martial law was introduced on the rail-roads, mobilizing all the workers and employees of the railroads in their place of work, and subjecting them to military discipline and responsibility as in the case of military personnel. Offences committed by railroad workers and employees were examined by railroad military tribunals.

This Ukase was extended to workers and employees of water trans-portation on August 9, 1943.

The Ukase of August 6, 1943 confined, for the time of war, the right to military tribunals to examine civil claims connected with criminal cases in misappropriation of property and mercenary crimes in office under their jurisdiction. Claimants could be military formations and civil persons filing suits against accused military persons. [2]

In the beginning of the war, as stated above, some of the people's courts were converted into military tribunals and deprived of criminal jurisdiction.

However, as a result of this measure, the military tribunals were now swamped with petty criminal cases. Hence, the number of people's courts which retained their jurisdictions over criminal offences, to extent they had before the war, increased during 1942.

B. Constitutional Changes in Jurisdiction

The decentralization tendency expressed at the XX Congress of the Communist Party was made evident also in the legal field of administra-tion : the rights of the union Republics had to be enlarged also in this field.

On February 11, 1957 the USSR Supreme Soviet adopted a law introducing a change in the federal jurisdiction. [3]

The 1936 Constitution in establishing the extent of federal juris-diction provided "for the right of the federal power, as represented by its highest organs of state authority, to legislate" on the judicial system and juridicial procedure, criminal and civil codes. (Art. 14u).

The law of February 11, 1957 transferred this jurisdiction to the union republics, while reserving to federal power the establishment of fundamentals of legislation in court structure and procedure, and fundamentals of civil and criminal legislation.

---

[1] *V.V.S.*, 1943, No. 15.
[2] *V.V.S.*, 1943, No. 17.
[3] *V.V.S.*, *SSSR*, 1957, Item 85.

Thus, Art. 14 "u" of the 1936 Constitution was amended as follows : "on the establishment of fundamentals of the legislation on court structure and procedure, fundamentals of civil and criminal legislation".

a) *The USSR Supreme Court*

The next day, on February 12, 1957, the USSR Supreme Soviet confirmed a Statute of the USSR Supreme Court [1] which also authorized such powers of the union republics and restricted the supervision functions of the USSR Supreme Court over the union republic to "the limits set by law". The unrestricted supervision power of the USSR Supreme court over all the union republic courts provided by the original wording of Art 104 of the 1936 Constitution was thereby curtailed.

This supervision power, as we will see below, was in effect transferred to the supreme courts of the individual union republics.

Also Art. 105 of the Constitution was amended, providing that chairmen of the union republic supreme soviets become members of the USSR Supreme Cour *ex officio*. [2]

The limitation of the supervision rights of the USSR Supreme Court is also expressed in the fact that the USSR Supreme Court may no longer demand and obtain any case already final from any court in the USSR, in order to review it by way of supervision, as it could according to the old Statute of the USSR Supreme Court of August 16, 1938, included as Chapter VII in the Law on the Court Structure of the USSR and the Union and Autonomous Republics. Now, the USSR Supreme Court may review a case only if the sentence, decision or ruling of an union republic supreme court violates a federal law or is contrary to the interests of another union republic.

A change also affected the former right of the Military College of the USSR Supreme Court to examine some cases as a court of original jurisdiction, by a bench of three members of the College. At the present time, according to the general rule that two assessors must belong to benches of all courts acting as a court of original jurisdiction, the bench of the Military College, when acting as a court of original jurisdiction, must consist of a member of the Military College and two assessors.

An important addition to the functions of the Plenum of the USSR Supreme Court is the right to make representations to the Presidium

---

[1]   *V.V.S.*, *SSSR*, 1957, No. 4.

[2]   The text of Art. 104 and 105 of the 1936 Constitution were correspondingly amended.

of the USSR Supreme Soviet which is tantamount to legislative initiative concerning questions in need of solution by legislation, and to interpret USSR laws.

The USSR Supreme Court is responsible to the USSR Supreme Soviet for the general character of its activity. [1]

The structure of the USSR Supreme Court and its functions are as follows :

The USSR Supreme Court Staff is formed by the Chairman of the Court, his Deputies, Members of the Court elected by the USSR Supreme Soviet for a term of 5 years and assessors as well as of chairmen of the union republic supreme courts.

In its activity the USSR Supreme Court is guided by USSR, as well as by union republic, laws.

The activity of the Court is realized by :

a) a Plenum

b) a Judicial College in Civil Cases ;

c) a Judicial College in Criminal Cases ;

d) a Military College

To the Plenum belong the Chairman, his Deputies and the Members of the USSR Supreme Court. It is convoked by the Chairman of the USSR Supreme Court not less than once every three months.

The participation of the USSR General Prosecutor in the Plenum's sessions is mandatory.

The Plenum examines :

a) protests of the Chairman of the USSR Supreme Court and the USSR General Prosecutor against decisions, sentences and rulings of the USSR Supreme Court Colleges;

b) protests of the Chairman of the USSR Supreme Court and the USSR General Prosecutor against resolutions of the union republics supreme courts when they contradict federal legislation or violate interests of other republics;

c) generalization of judicial practice and judicial statistics, and issues guiding interpretations for the courts concerning the application of legislation in examining cases in court;

d) controversies between individual union republics.

The right of legislative initiative belonging to the Plenum was already mentioned above.

---

[1] Realization of the principle that courts, judges and assessors are responsible to the bodies which elect them and have to account to them.

The Judicial Colleges of the USSR Supreme Court examined civil and criminal cases of exclusive importance as courts of original jurisdiction. The Bench also in these cases consists of one member of the College and two assessors.

Cassation functions are reserved only to the Military College of the USSR Supreme Court which examines cassation complaints and protests against the sentences of the district and fleet military tribunals, in cases provided by law.

In the way of judicial supervision, the Judicial Colleges decide upon protests of the Chairman of the USSR Supreme Court and the USSR General Prosecutor and their Deputies against decisions and sentences contracting federal laws or violating interests of other union republics.

The Benches of Colleges consist of a Member of the College and two assessors when the Colleges act as courts of original jurisdiction, and of three Members of the College in all other cases.

Besides the general guidance of the USSR Supreme Court work, the Chairman of the Court presides over the sessions of the Plenum of the USSR Supreme Court and is entitled to assume the presidency over any session of the College. He also lodges protests with the USSR Supreme Court against decisions, sentences and rulings of the colleges of the USSR Supreme Court and the supreme courts of the union republics.

The Chairmen of the Colleges assume the guidance over the organizational and administrative work at their respective Colleges. The Chairman of the Military College is also charged with the organizational guidance over the work of the military tribunal.

The Statute on the USSR Supreme Court of 1957 has been extended and amended by the Ukase of the Presidium of the Supreme Soviet of September 30, 1967. [1]

1. The Supreme Courts of the Union Republics received the right to examine protests of the Chairman of the USSR Supreme Court and his Deputies against decisions, sentences and resolutions of the Union-Republic Supreme Courts in cases provided by the Statute on the USSR Supreme Court.

2. The Chairman of the USSR Supreme Court and his Deputies have the right to lodge protests with the presidiums of the union-republics supreme courts against decisions, sentences and resolutions of the union-republic supreme courts in accordance with the competence

---

[1] *V.V.S., SSSR*, 1967, Item 526.

of the presidiums and plenums established by the union-republic legislation.

Realizing the supervision of the judicial activity of the court organs of the union-republics, the USSR Supreme Court checks the applying by the court organs of the union-republics of the federal legislation, as well as the fulfillment of resolutions taken by the Plenum of the USSR Supreme Court.

A new function of the USSR Court is the examination of questions ensued from the application of treaties on legal aid concluded by the USSR with other countries.

Added to the functions of the USSR Supreme Court is also the hearing of accounts of the chairmen of the judicial colleges of the union-republics supreme courts on the judicial practice in applying federal legislation and the resolutions of the USSR Supreme Court Plenum.

An Art. 75 is added defining the competence of the USSR Supreme Court Chairmen's Deputies. They replaces the Chairman in his right to lodge protests against decisions, sentences and resolutions of the union-republic supreme courts, including the case of sentences and resolutions countradicting federal legislation or violating the interests of other republics.

b) *Abolition of the Transportation Courts*

The transportation courts were abolished by the Law of February 12, 1957 [1] "since an important reduction in the number of crimes disturbing the normal work of railroad and water transportation took place".

Abolished were the line and district transport courts of the railroad and water transportation systems.

All cases previously under the jurisdiction of the transportation courts were assigned to the people's courts, regional and territorial courts and supreme courts of the union and autonomous republics, according to their general jurisdiction.

C. The USSR Law on Court Structure of 1958

In the realization of the distribution of legislative functions introduced by the Law of 1957, the USSR Supreme Soviet adopted the Law on

---

[1]   *V.V.S., SSSR*, 1957, No. 4. Item 86.

the Basic Principles of Legislation on Court Structure of the USSR
and the Union and Autonomous Republics on December 25, 1958. [1]

The court system is divided into two categories : the USSR courts
and the republic courts.

To the first group belong the USSR Supreme Court and the Military
Tribunals.

The second group comprises the supreme courts of the union and
autonomous republics, the regional, territorial and city courts as well
as the courts of the autonomous regions and national districts and
district (city) people's courts.

The borough system of people's courts was replaced by a single
district or city people's court in the district or city.

D. CHANGES INTRODUCED BY THE LAW OF 1958

The provision of Art. 103 of the Constitution that all court cases
are tried with the participation of people's assessors except in cases
specially provided for by law, has been amended by the Law of 1958.

In all courts of original jurisdiction, with no exception, the participation of two assessors in the trial was made mandatory. In all higher
courts the bench consists of three members of the court, when it sits
not as a court of original jurisdiction.

Different electoral systems were adopted with regard to people's
judges and assessors : whereas the people's judges of the district (city)
people's courts were to be elected by citizens of the district (city) on
the basis of a general, equal and direct electoral system by secret
voting; the assessors of the district (city) people's courts are elected
at general assemblies of workers, employees and peasants, at the place
of their work or residence ; assessors of the military courts are elected
by their respective military units. The law of 1958 established special
provisions for the recall of judges and disciplinary procedures against
them.

Nothing has been changed in the electoral system of the other
courts : the USSR and union republic supreme courts are elected by
the USSR and the union republic supreme soviets respectively :
the supreme courts of the autonomous republics — by the respective
autonomous supreme soviets; territorial, regional, district, circuit
courts and the courts of the autonomous regions and national districts

---

[1] *V.V.S., SSSR*, 1959, No. 1.

are elected by the corresponding territorial, regional and district soviets, as before.

All the courts are responsible to the bodies which elected them (the USSR Supreme — to the USSR Supreme Soviet, etc.), whereas the judges of the district (city) people's courts, are directly accountable to their electors. The rendering of accounts has to take place systematically.

The eligibility of judges was changed by the law insofar as the required age was increased from 23 to 25. The term of service of judges is five years and not three as previously, whereas the assessors have to serve only two years instead of three. [1]

As a matter of decentralization, the supervision of courts has been entrusted to the union republics. Also the competence of the union republic supreme courts has been enlarged by the creation of plenum for these courts by the law of 1958.

The Law of 1958 also provided that the review of sentences already in force is examined on protests, in the individual Colleges of the Supreme Courts of the USSR and the union republics by a bench of three members of the corresponding court.

The provision of the Constitution that judges and people's assessors, in meting out justice, are independent and subordinated only to law, is repeated in the Law of 1958.

Also, the provisions of Arts. 110 and 111 of the Constitution on the language to be used in court, and the public examination of cases in all courts, unless otherwise provided by law, respectively, are contained in the Law of 1958, as well as the right of the accused to counsel.

An article of the Law is dedicated to the Colleges of advocates. A definition of the college of advocates is given in the article : "The Colleges of Advocates are voluntary associations of persons occupied with advocating activity regulated by a Statue confirmed by the Supreme Soviets of the individual union republics".

The Law states, further, that the public accusation and defense may be conducted by representatives of social organizations, in accordance with USSR and union republic legislation. This important innovation was inspired by the desire to involve wide masses of the population in the administration of justice. We shall deal with the provision later.

---

[1] The electoral system and the terms of service for judges and assessors was set by a special law of the same date (Law on the Change of the Electoral Order for People's Courts—Dec. 25, 1958, *V.V.S.*, 1959, No. 1).

The accusation, in cases provided by the USSR and union-republic legislation, may be supported in court also by the victims of the criminal actions.

The Law of 1958 has also formulated the scope of the administration of justice to protect from every encroachment :

a) the social and state structure as established by the USSR Constitution and the Constitution of the union and autonomous republics, the socialist structure of the economy and socialist property;

b) the political, labor, dwelling and other personal and property rights and interests of USSR citizens, as guaranteed by the USSR Constitution and the constitutions of the union and autonomous republics;

c) the rights and interests preserved by law of state institutions, enterprises, kolkhozes and cooperatives and other public organizations.

According to the Law, the administration of justice in the USSR has the scope to insure the exact and unflinching fulfillment of law by all the institutions, organizations, officials and citizens of the USSR.

All the court's activity has the goal to educate the USSR citizens in the spirit of devotion to the Fatherland and Communism, in the spirit of exact and unflinching fulfillment of Soviet laws, careful attitude toward socialist property, observance of labor discipline, honest attitude toward state and public duties, respect for the rights, honor and dignity of citizens and for rules of society and common life.

Thus, besides general principles, the Law of 1958 established what questions of court structure have to be decided not only by federal but also by republican legislation.

It must be underlined that also the Law of 1958 did not introduce educational requirements for the election to judicial positions. Indeed, Art. 29 provides that "Any USSR citizen in possession of electoral rights and who is 25 years of age as of the day of the election, may be elected a judge or people's assessor".

During their term of office in court, the people's assessors enjoy all the rights of a judge.

D.S. Karev does not seem happy about this fact, since, according to him, all objective premises exist for all judges to have a legal education. He underlines that 55.4 % of people's judges have a higher and 37 % a secondary legal education, so that "only a small number of judges have no legal education, although they are in possession of great practical experience in judicial work". [1]

---

[1] D. S. Karev, "The Further Improvement of the Soviet Court System", *S.G.P.*, 1959, No. 2, p. 67.

Prior to the Law of 1958, a system of borough people's courts existed in many republics. This system was abolished by the Law of 1958 and a single people's court for the district or city established.

The USSR Law on Court Structure of Dec. 25, 1958 and the RSFSR Law on Court Structure of Oct. 27, 1960 reduced the number of people's courts, amalgamating people's courts into single courts with several benches for the entire city. The number of people's courts was reduced from 4,500 to 2,375 in the RSFSR. [1]

The Law contains also provisions with regard to the composition of supreme courts at the union and autonomous republics and are more advantageously taken up in the discussion of the RSFSR Law on Court Structure.

In order to eliminate superfluous centralization in the guidance of the court institution's work and the strengthening of the role of Union Republics, the USSR Ministry of Justice was abrogated in 1956 as was the administrations of the Ministries of Justice of the Union Republics attached to Territorial and Regional Soviets.

In this connection, the functions of territorial and regional courts have been enlarged charging them with the supervision of people's courts activity.

Presidiums were created at the supreme courts of union and autonomous republics, territorial and regional courts and courts of the autonomous regions, They were empowered to examine cases in the way of court supervision.

Transportation and other special courts were abolished. Cases in their competence were transferred to general courts of union republics. At the present time, only general courts are in action and as special courts — Military Tribunals.

All the cases concerning crimes against the state, committed by private persons with the exception of cases of espionage, have been transferred from the jurisdiction of military tribunals to the competence of territorial, regional courts and supreme courts of the union and autonomous republics.

The Basic Principles provide that nobody can be declared guilty of committing a crime and criminally punished if not than by virtue of a court sentence. They do not apply anymore the principle of analogy in Criminal Law. Another innovation was the admission of the defense to the preliminary investigation.

---

[1] *S.G.P.*, 1961, No. 1, p. 25.

Besides that, the Basic Principles set a limited term of one year for protests against acquitting sentences already in force.

The age at which criminal responsibility of minors starts has been established at 16 years and only with regard to some crimes this responsibility begins with 14 years.

The courts got the right to suspend sentences transferring the convict to public organizations and workers' collectives on their request, for re-education and reform.

If a convict by an exemplary behavior — and honest attitude toward work has proven his reformation the court may permit conditional liberation before time or the replacement of the punishment by a more lenient one.

This provision is an important change from the previous practice, when the conditional liberation before time was granted by the prison administration according to the number of work days served by the prisoner. Now only the court can grant conditional liberation, after the prisoner has served not less than one-half, and the culprit of an especially dangerous crime such as against the state — after not less than two-thirds of his term.

The Basic Principles also provided terms after which previous convictions are dropped from the records. On request of public organizations the cancellation can be ordered by the court also before the expiration of the term. [1]

In compliance with the Basic Principles of Legislation on Court Structure of the USSR and Union and Autonomous Republics of Dec. 25, 1958, all the Union Republics have adopted Laws on the Court Structure of their individual Republics.

Let us take a look at the RSFSR Court Structure, as a sample of union republic legislation on this subject.

E. The RSFSR Court Structure

The Law on Court Structure of the RSFSR was adopted by the RSFSR Supreme Soviet on October 27, 1960. [2] All the general provisions of the Federal law of December 25, 1958 are taken over almost literally.

Also, the judges of the people's courts and the higher courts are

---

[1] We shall have to deal with many provisions of the Law in the corresponding parts of this book.

[2] *V.V.S., RSFSR*, 1960, No. 40.

elected in the manner prescribed by the USSR Law discussed above.

The jurisdiction of a district (city) people's court covers all criminal and civil cases as long as they are not under the competence of other courts, according to law.

The territorial, regional, city courts, as well as the courts of autonomous regions and national districts function as courts of original jurisdiction in cases assigned to them by law, and cassation courts in criminal and civil cases.

As cassation courts these courts examine :

a) complaints and protests against decisions, sentences and rulings of district (city) people's courts not yet in force;

b) protests against decisions, sentences and rulings of district (city) courts already in force.

These courts carry out revisions of people's courts and control all their activity.

They have presidiums, chairmen, deputy chairmen, members and people's assessors (for the sessions in cases of original jurisdiction) and are divided into : *a*) civil judicial and *b*) criminal judicial colleges.

The presidiums consist of the chairman of the court, his deputies and members in a number set by the executive committee of the corresponding Soviet.

Whereas the colleges examine civil and criminal cases as courts of original jurisdiction and cassation courts for complaints and protests against decisions, sentences and rulings of the people's courts not yet in force, the presidium deal with protests against decisions, sentences and rulings already in force of the people's courts, as well as protests against indictment resolutions of people's judges and against rulings of courts' colleges passed on complaints and protests.

The chairman of the territorial, regional and city courts and the courts of autonomous regions and national districts, besides purely administrative functions, lodge protests against decisions, sentences and rulings of district (city) people's courts not yet in force and indictment resolutions of people's judges, as well as against rulings of court colleges passed on complaints and protests.

a) *The RSFSR Supreme Court*

The RSFSR Supreme Court is the highest judicial organ of the RSFSR elected by the RSFSR Supreme Soviet for a tenure in office of five years. It exercises supervision over all the courts of the RSFSR and has the right of legislative initiative.

The RSFSR Supreme Court examines :

a) as a court of original jurisdiction, civil and criminal cases assigned to its competence by law : [1]

b) as a cassation instance, complaints and protests against decisions, sentences and rulings of supreme courts of autonomous republics, territorial, regional and city courts and courts of autonomous regions and national regions not yet in force :

c) cases on protests against decisions, sentences and rulings of all courts of the RSFSR already in force.

The RSFSR Supreme Court issues guiding interpretations of laws of the RSFSR to courts.

The RSFSR Supreme Court consists of a :

a) Judical College for Civil Cases ;

b) Judical College for Criminal Cases ;

c) Presidium of the RSFSR Supreme Court.

As courts of original jurisdiction the Court Colleges examine :

a) as courts of original jurisdiction, the civil and criminal cases assigned to the competence of the RSFSR Supreme Court by law, and as a cassation instance complaints and protests against decisions, sentences and rulings of supreme courts of autonomous republic, territorial, regional and city courts and courts of autonomous regions and national districts not yet in force ;

b) protests against decisions, sentences and rulings passed by all courts of the republic, as well as protests against resolutions of the presidiums of supreme courts of autonomous republics, territorial, regional and city courts of national region and national districts.

The Presidium of the RSFSR Supreme Court consisting of the Chairman of the Court, his deputies and a number of court members set by the Presidium of the RSFSR Supreme Soviet, has special functions : it examines protests against decisions, sentences and rulings of the Court College of the RSFSR Supreme Court, as well as against accusatory resolutions of the RSFSR Supreme Court judges.

---

[1] Criminal cases of special complexity or public importance, assigned to it on its own initiative or on the initiative of the RSFSR Prosecutor (Art 38 of the Code of Criminal Procedure). The law does not define the cases in the competence of the RSFSR Supreme Court. According to *Nauchno-praktcheskiy kommentariy k ugolovno-protsessual'nomu kodeksu RSFSR*, M. 1963, p. 103, ... the RSFSR Supreme Court examines cases : a) of special public importance and on demand of the public; b) when the accused have committed especially dangerous crimes in the territory of several republics, territories or regions; c) of particular complexity causing an incorrect solution by the lower court; d) when the consequences of the crime are particularly serious.

The participation of the RSFSR Prosecutor in the sessions of the Presidiums is mandatory.

Important functions are fulfilled by the Plenum (General Assembly) of the RSFSR Supreme Court, consisting of the Chairman of the Court, his Deputies and all members of the Court; the participation of the RSFSR Prosecutor in the sessions of the Plenum is mandatory, but also the RSFSR Minister of Justice takes part in the sessions.

These functions are :

a) to give direction, interpretation to courts with regard to the application of RSFSR legislation, in examing civil and criminal cases, on the bases of the generalization of judicial practice, statistics and decisions passed in cases, examined by the RSFSR Supreme Court, as well as on the bases of representations made by the RSFSR Minister of Justice and the RSFSR Prosecutor;

b) makes representations to the Presidium of the RSFSR Supreme Soviet on questions to be resolved by the legislation and interpretation of RSFSR laws;

c) hears the accounts of the Chairman of the Court Colleges on the activity of the RSFSR Supreme Court Colleges;

d) confirms the selection of members of Court Colleges of the RSFSR Supreme Court from among the members of the RSFSR Supreme Court;

The Chairman of the RSFSR Supreme Court, besides furnishing the general guidance over the Court and presiding in the sessions of the court, fulfills specific duties :

1) he lodges protests against decisions, sentences, rulings and resolutions of all RSFSR Courts, as well as against indicting resolutions of the judges;

2) suspends the execution of the protested decision, sentence, ruling, and resolution of any RSFSR Court;

3) calls together sessions of the RSFSR Supreme Court Plenum, presides at these sessions and presents questions for solution to the Plenums.

b) *The Supreme Court of an Autonomous Republic*

The supreme court of an autonomous republic is the highest court of this republic. It supervises the activity of all its courts, has the right of legislative initiative and is elected by the supreme soviet of the autonomous republic for a term of five years.

The structure of an autonomous republic's supreme court is like that of its namesake at the union-republic level : a chairman, members, and people's assessors of the court. Civil and criminal judicial colleges and a presidium manned by a chairman and members of the supreme court. The chairman is confirmed by the presidium of the autonomous republic's supreme soviet on recommendation of the chairman of the supreme soviet. There is no plenum, since the autonomous republic court does not fulfill functions provided for the plenums of supreme courts of union republics and on the federal level.

The judicial colleges as courts of original jurisdiction examine, respectively, civil and criminal cases assigned to them by law [1] as well well as complaints and protests against decisions, sentences and rulings of district (city) people's courts not yet final.

The organizational work of the colleges is fulfilled by the chairmen of the colleges, confirmed by the Plenum of the RSFSR Supreme Soviet on recommendation of the Chairman of the Supreme Court.

The presidium consists of the chairman, his deputies and members of the autonomous republic's supreme court, confirmed by the presidium of the autonomous republic's supreme soviet on recommendation of the chairman of the supreme court.

It examines protests against decisions, sentences and rulings of district (city) people's courts, indicting resolutions of people's judges already final, as well as against rulings of the judicial colleges passed on complaints or protests.

Also the chairman of an autonomous republics' supreme court has specific functions besides his administrative work and chairmanship in judicial colleges. He :

a) lodges protests against decisions, sentences and rulings of district (city) people's courts already final; against accusations, resolutions and rulings of the judicial colleges of the supreme court of the autonomous republic passed on complaints and protests;

b) convokes the court's presidium and presides at its sessions;

c) carries out the general organizational guidance of the court. [2]

---

[1] The jurisdiction of autonomous republic's supreme courts is similar to that of territorial, regional and national district courts.

[2] As to the slight differences between laws on the court structures of the individual union republics see *Zakonodatel'stvo o sudoustroystve soyuza SSSR i soyuznykh respublik*, M. 1961, pp. 10-16.

c) *Military Tribunals*

On the same day, December 25, 1958, the USSR Supreme Soviet adopted the Statute on Military Tribunals, a federal institution under federal law supervised and guided by the Military College of the USSR Supreme Court, according to the Statute of the USSR Supreme Court of 1957 mentioned above.

The members of the military tribunals are elected not by the USSR Supreme Soviet but by its Presidium.

Chairmen, their deputies and members of the tribunal may be elected only from among persons on active military service and not less than 25 years of age.

The assessors of the military tribunals are elected at general assemblies of the military units for service of 2 years. Every USSR citizen on active military service may be elected by open voting of his military unit. No age requirement exists.

The Statute narrowed [1] the jurisdiction of the military tribunals. Under its competence remained :

a) all crimes committed by military personnel;

b) all cases of espionage (involving civil and military persons) [2]

The first instance of the military tribunals comprises : military tribunals of armies, flotillas and formations. Their jurisdictions extend to crimes perpetrated by military persons up to the rank of (full) colonel inclusive. [3]

The second instance is formed by military tribunals of corps military groups, fleets and separate armies. They sit as courts of original jurisdiction in cases of crimes committed by military persons of a higher rank (starting with Colonel in the Army and Captain 1st grade in the Navy) and all crimes punishable by death in time of peace.

The Military College of the USSR Supreme Court examines, as a court of original jurisdiction, criminal cases of exceptional importance, crimes of persons with the rank of general (admiral), as well as of military persons having the position of a commissioner of formations (large units) and other persons with a similar rank.

---

[1] Dropped were the cases concerning operative members of state security organs and the Ministry of Internal Affairs, which are referred to the general courts.

[2] Thus, the military tribunal had jurisdiction over the cases provided by all paragraphs of the famous Art. 58 of the Old Criminal Code on counterrevolutionary crimes so widely applied during the cult of personality.

[3] In places where general courts are not functioning, the military courts are also competent for all criminal and civil cases involving civil persons.

The military courts of the second instance :

a) examine cassation and private cases, complaints and protests against sentences, decisions and rulings of military courts of first instance ;

b) examine, in the way of judicial supervision, protests of the Chairman of the USSR Supreme Court, the USSR General Prosecutor, their Deputies, the Chairman of the Military College of the USSR Supreme Court, the Chief Military Prosecutor, chairmen of military tribunals and military prosecutors of districts, military groups and fleets, against sentences, decisions and rulings of military tribunals of the first instance.

The Military College of the USSR Supreme Court decides upon :

a) cassation and private complaints and protests against sentences, decisions and rulings of the military courts of the second instance ;

b) in the way of judicial supervision, protests of the Chairman of the USSR Supreme Court, USSR General Prosecutor, their Deputies, the the Chairman of the Military College of the USSR Supreme Court and the Chief Military Prosecutor against sentences, decisions and rulings of the military court of second instance.

Besides his administrative functions the Chairman of the Military College of the USSR Supreme Court :

a) organizes the checking of the activities of the military tribunals ;

b) guides the study of the practice of the military tribunals for the purpose of generalization ;

c) prepares, in cooperation with the USSR Ministry of Defense, suggestions on the question of the organization of military tribunals ;

d) issues orders on the work of the military tribunals.

CHAPTER EIGHT

ADMINISTRATIVE COURTS

A. *Arbitrazh*

A Soviet definition of the term *Arbitrazh* reads as follows:
"In the USSR, *Arbitrazh* is a state organ which settles disputes concerning property between state, non-state [obshchestvennyy] and cooperative institutions, enterprises and organizations". [1]

In order to clarify our approach to the debatable subject of the legal character of this institution, let us first review its history.

a) *Arbitration Commissions*

According to Article 15 of Decree No. 2 on Courts, "court litigation between different state institutions is inadmissible". [2] During the period of War Communism, economic disputes between state agencies, enterprises, organizations and institutions were regulated through "administrative" channels. After the shift to NEP, state enterprises received greater freedom in their operations, which assumed a more contractual and commercial character, and the creation of a special institution to regulate such disputes became necessary. To this end, an Arbitration Commission was set up in 1922 under the auspices of the Supreme Council of the National Economy, with the power to resolve economic disputes between organs of enterprises and organizations subordinated to the Council or its branches. Confirming the principle already quoted, the statute of the Commission laid down that bodies subordinate to the Council were not entitled to submit their contractual disputes for decision to any organs, whether administrative or judicial, other than the Arbitration Commission. [3]

This was, of course, only a partial regulation of the question, since not all institutions and enterprises were subordinate to the Supreme Economic Council. On September 21, 1922, the All-Union Central

---

[1] *Entsiklopedicheskiy slovar' v dvukh tomakh*, Vol. 1, 1963, p. 63

[2] *Sob. uz., RSFSR*, 1918, Item 347.

[3] The statute of the Commission was not confirmed until 1926 (*Sob. zak., SSSR, 1926*, Item 90).

Executive Committee and the Council of People's Commissars of the RSFSR approved a Statute on the Procedure for Deciding Property Disputes between State Institutions and Organizations, [1] which provided for a Supreme Arbitration Commission attached to the Labor and Defense Council and for local commissions attached to the regional economic councils. Further commissions were established at the guberniya (province) economic conferences (soveshchaniya). The Supreme Arbitration Commission was composed of a chairman and two members, all of whom were appointed by the Labor Defense Council. The members of local commissions were appointed by the guberniya economic conferences, but the chairmen were appointed by the Labor and Defense Council on the recommendation of the People's Commissar of Justice. Appeal against a decision of a local arbitration commission could be lodged with the Supreme Arbitration Commission or the Labor and Defense Council if the dispute involved a sum of more than one thousand gold rubles.

b) *State Arbitration*

All these central and local arbitration commissions were dissolved by a decree of the Central Executive Committee and the Council of People's Commissars of March 4, 1931, [2] and on May 3 of the same year the Central Executive Committee approved the Statute on State Arbitration, [3] which marks the birth of state arbitration in the form that it has largely retained up to the present time. Its function, according to the Statute, was to resolve property disputes between institutions, enterprises and organizations of the socialized sector "in a manner such as to ensure contractual and planning discipline and self-sufficiency". However, before referring any dispute arising from contracts, transactions or other property matters to state arbitration, the parties had to take all measures to come to an agreement by themselves.

Excluded from examination by state arbitration were :

a) disputes between organs of the same *vedomstvo* ("a system of central or local organs and institutions charged with a single branch of state administration, subordinate to the same guidance") [4] and financed by state or local budgets ;

---

1 *Sob. uz., RSFSR*, 1922, Item 769.

2 *Sob. zak., SSSR*, 1931, Item 135.

3 *Ibid.*, 1931, Item 203.

4 *Yuridicheskiy slovar'*, Moscow, 1956, Vol. 1, p. 87.

b) disputes between institutions and enterprises of the same system (as under *a*), economic union or cooperative system not permitted by the appropriate higher organ;

c) disputes over operations of the State Bank if the latter was a party to the dispute;

d) disputes arising from contracts concerning railroad transportation;

e) disputes over taxes and other payments exacted according to indisputable procedure;

f) disputes over the contractual use of communal services; and

g) disputes falling under the jurisdiction of state arbitration organs attached to the Labor and Defense Council, to Economic Councils (Conferences) and to other bodies but involving sums less than 5,000, 3,000 and 1,000 rubles respectively.

The entire system was headed by the organ of state arbitration attached to the Labor and Defense Council, whose competence was limited to the examination of disputes between parties of which at least one was a central organ of all-union importance and to disputes between central organs of different union republics. The organs of state arbitration attached to the Economic Councils (Conferences) of the union republics had to settle disputes involving a central organ of the republic concerned or a republican organ of "enterprises of all-union importance" as well as disputes between kray and oblast' organs of different krays, oblasts and autonomous republics. Finally, there were the organs of state arbitration attached to the councils of people's commissars of autonomous republics and to the executive committees of krays and oblast's, including autonomous oblast's.

c) *Reorganization : The Decision of July 23, 1959*

On July 23, 1959, the Council of Ministers of the USSR passed a resolution stating that the Statute on State Arbitration of 1931 "is obsolete and does not contribute to a proper solution of economic disputes under the existing conditions of industry and construction administration". [1] The resolution further expressed the opinion that practical work of the organs of state arbitration did not correspond to the demands imposed by the national economy under changed conditions. When examining economic disputes, the organs of state

---

[1] *Sob. post., SSSR*, 1959, Item 105.

arbitration did not produce the desired effect of consolidating "planning and contractual discipline", especially in cases concerning the fulfillment of plans and the observance of laws relating to the quality and quantity of output. They also did not work as they should do to suppress undue manifestations of local interests, nor did they contribute sufficiently to the elimination of defects established in the work of enterprises and organizations. Furthermore, it was stated that a great number of groundless disputes were submitted to state arbitration as a result of the failure of enterprises and organizations to examine claims properly and to satisfy on their own account demands that were indisputable. In Article 1 of the resolution, the Council of Ministers stated that it considered the main function of state arbitration to lie in exerting "an active influence upon enterprises, organizations and institutions in matters concerning the improvement of their work, the fulfillment of economic plans and the consolidation of economic selfsufficiency".

The competence of the organs of state arbitration was extended to cover all disputes between state, cooperatives (with the exception of kolkhozes) and other public organizations which had hitherto come under the jurisdiction of the courts. A Decree of the Supreme Soviet Presidium of the USSR issued in 1959 promulgated this measure. [1] The Decree, which came into effect on January 1, 1960, also extended the competence of state arbitration organs attached to the Councils of Ministers of the USSR and the union and autonomous republics and to the executive committees of kray and oblast' soviets. In particular the state arbitration organ of the Council of Ministers of the USSR was given the right to suspend the execution of decisions taken by similar organs at union-republic level which violated national interests or the legitimate interests of other republics and to raise the question of reconsidering such decisions in due order.

On the other hand, the jurisdiction of republican and local organs of state arbitration was extended by assigning to the organ of state arbitration attached to the Council of Ministers of the USSR only the most important disputes involving enterprises, etc, of different union republics or of "all-union subordination", and as a rule only precontractual cases involving the sum of ten million rubles and regular disputes involving not less than 100,000 rubles. A further restriction imposed on the work of the all-union body was that even in the most

V.V.S., SSSR, 1959, Item 163.

important cases its jurisdiction was excluded when both parties to the dispute, even though of all-union subordination, were located in the same republic.

With regard to the blemishes mentioned above, the resolution of the Council of Ministers charged the organs of state arbitration to draw the attention of leaders of enterprises, etc, to essential defects in their work established during the examination of disputes. (A similar provision had been incorporated in the Statute of 1931, but the Council of Ministers evidently deemed it necessary to emphasize the point once more.)

An innovation was the granting of permission to refer individual complicated cases to the decision of private arbiters elected by the parties in order to "reinforce democratic principles in the resolution of economic disputes".

d) *The New Statute on State Arbitration at All-Union Level of 1960*

On August 17, 1960, the Council of Ministers of the USSR approved a statute relating to the work of the state arbitration organ attached to this Council. [1] This body is charged with settling the most important disputes. Its functions, as given in the Statute, are : 1) during the decision of economic disputes, to protect the property rights and legitimate interests of enterprises, etc.; 2) to promote collaboration among enterprises, etc., in matters concerning the fulfillment of economic plans and to suppress all tendencies toward the prevalence of local interests and narrow departmentalism; 3) during the settlement of disputes, to exercise an active influence upon enterprises, etc., in order that the latter should abide by the law and by resolutions and orders of the government in questions of economic structure, and to apply material sanctions for the "non-fulfillment of plans and assignments concerning the supply of products, the delivery of defective and incomplete products and other violations of state discipline and contractual obligations"; and 4) to cooperate in the realization of plans and assignments concerning the supply of products and other obligations as well as in the elimination of defects discovered in the work of enterprises, etc., during the examination of economic disputes.

The competence of the state arbitration organ attached to the Council of Ministers of the USSR covers :

---

[1] *Sob. post.*, *SSSR*, 1960, Item 127.

a) precontractual disputes involving more than ten million rubles;

b) precontractual disputes concerning the exploitation of spur tracks not in general use when the turnover of goods is greater than 100 railroad cars in 24 hours;

c) disputes over the fulfillment of contracts and other matters involving a sum of over 100,000 rubles;

d) disputes referred to state arbitration by the Council of Ministers of the USSR; and

e) disputes accepted for examination at the request of the union-republic councils of ministers.

The all-union body is also entitled to initiate proceedings concerning the violation by enterprises, etc., of "planning and contractual discipline and the rules of self-sufficiency". The forfeits and fines exacted in these cases (as laid down by current legislation) are assigned to the union budget or to the benefit of the enterprise, etc, in whose behalf the proceedings were initiated.

A dispute properly coming under the jurisdiction of all-union state arbitration organ may be submitted to private arbitration if the parties agree. Another function of this body is to approve special conditions governing the supply of particular kinds of products, technical equipment and consumer goods, as well as instructions concerning the procedure for accepting goods according to their quantity and quality.

Like a supreme court, this body is entitled to interpret the laws and regulations pertaining to the work of state arbitration; it can pronounce contracts violating legislation, governmental resolutions and orders, state plans and assignments to be totally or partially invalid, or bind the parties to amend the contracts accordingly. In order to ensure the necessary consistency in the settlement of disputes, it studies the work of state arbitration organs attached to *sovnarkhozes* and administrative systems, gives them instructions and publishes rules of procedure for the examination of disputes by state arbitration.

Like all other organs of state arbitration, this organ has to report to the body to which it is attached, viz., the Council of Ministers of the USSR, on the most important violations of state discipline and legislation concerning the quality, etc., of products put on the market, as well as on cases of the undue promotion of local interests and other violations of "socialist legality" in the economic activity of entrprises, organizations and institutions.

e) *Settlement of Disputes within the Same Organizational System*

We have already seen that disputes between organs of the same *vedomstvo* are not subject to state arbitration. In order to settle such disputes, arbitrations organs were set up within each *vedomstvo* or administrative system, and were known as *vedomstvennye*, or "departmental", arbitration organs. They functioned alongside the organs of state arbitration. They were only indirectly legalized by the resolution of the Council of People's Commissars of the USSR of December 8, 1931, which said that "the councils of people's commissars of the Union republics must charge the corresponding [organ of] state arbitration with the task of giving instruction to local and departmental [organs of] arbitration". [1]

When the country's system of economic management was reorganized in 1957 and economic regions were created, each under its *sovnarkhoz*, organs of departmental arbitration were also created and subordinated to the *sovnarkhozes* or to union-republic ministers. The sovnarkhoz statute of September 26, 1957, provided that the *sovnarkhozes* should approve and confirm the Statute on Departmental Arbitration and the procedure for examining disputes between enterprises, etc., subordinate to the same *sovnarkhoz*. [2]

The functions of departmental arbitration are similar to those of state arbitration. The sphere of competence is also in principle the same, except that it is confined to the *vedomstvo* concerned. In view of this, the question whether two systems of arbitration are necessary has been discussed in the Soviet press. Some writers suggested liquidating departmental arbitration and transferring its functions to the state arbitration system; other proposed authorizing those in charge of the *vedomstvo* to settle disputes arising within it. [3]

f) *The Present Structure*

In spite of these discussions, the structure of *arbitrazh* remained two-fold. The present structure, therefore, is as follows. The highest level of state arbitration is that of the Council of Ministers of the USSR; then come the councils of ministers of the union republics,

---

[1] *Sob. zak., SSSR*, 1931, Item 470.

[2] *Sob. post., SSSR*, 1957, Item 121.

[3] See R.F. Kallistratova, *Razresheniye sporov v gosudarstvennom arbitrazhe*, Moscow, 1961, p. 58.

and finally the local level, i.e., the executive committees of the kray and oblast' Soviets, the councils of ministers of the autonomous republics and the executive committees of the city soviets of Moscow and Leningrad. To each of these governmental bodies is attached a state arbitration organ.

It must be emphasized that this division is not a hierarchical one, i.e., each organ of state arbitration is subordinate only to the governmental body to which it is attached and not to the state arbitration organ at the next highest level. The same is true of the organs of departmental arbitration, which are individually attached to different economic and non-state administrative agencies and subordinate to them. The staffs of state arbitration organs consist of arbiters, formerly appointed individually by the Labor and Defense Council [1] and by the Economic Councils (Conferences) and now appointed respectively by the Council of Ministers of the USSR, the councils of ministers of the union republics and autonomous republics and kray and oblast' executive committees, which also appoint the staffs of their respective organs of departmental arbitration. In each case, the arbiters are headed by a chief arbiter appointed by the same agency.

The work of arbitration is under the general guidance of the chief arbiter and his deputies. Although the decisions of the state arbitration organs are final and there is no appeal against them, the chief arbiter has the right to suspend the execution of a decision within one month after it was taken and to submit the case for further consideration to another organ of state arbitration. Each dispute is dealt with by a bench comprising one representative from each party and an arbiter assigned by the chief arbiter. If the representatives of the parties cannot come to an agreement, the dispute is decided by the arbiter, who must be guided by the laws and rulings of both central and local authorities as well as by the general principles of Soviet economic policy.

g) *Precontractual Disputes : Differences over Contractual Conditions*

By the resolution of the Council of People's Commissars of the USSR of December 19, 1933, [2] the competence of state arbitration was extended to a sphere which in other countries is free from judicial or

---

[1] The Labor and Defense Council was abolished in 1937 and its functions relating to state arbitration transferred to the Council of People's Commissars.

[2] *Sob. zak., SSSR*, 1933, Item 445.

semijudicial interference, namely, to the settlement of differences arising from the conditions of contracts to be concluded and the request for the signing of a contract presented by one party to the other.

It is obvious that arbitration in such cases can be necessary only in a country where the economy is socialized, [1] In a capitalist state, no one can force an organization or private person to conclude a contract or dictate the conditions of a contract to be concluded. But when the entire economy belongs to one master, the state, and is directed by state plans, the acceptance of conditions for a contract providing for the production required by the plan can be enforced. The most important provisions concerning the state arbitration of precontractual disputes are contained in the above-mentioned resolution of December 19, 1933, and in those of the Council of Ministers of the USSR of April 21 [2] and May 22, 1959. [3]

As a rule, the draft of a contract within the framework of the plan is prepared by the seller or contractor, who directs two signed copies of it to the buyer or customer. The buyer or customer is bound to sign the contract within ten days after receipt of the draft and to return one copy to the seller or contractor. A peculiar point is that differences about the conditions of the contract do not suspend its signature. Objections to individual conditions of the contract may be formulated by the buyer or customer in a special document called "Record of the Differences", signed by both parties.

If the differences cannot be removed by the parties, they must be submitted for state arbitration within ten days by the seller-contractor. Differences about contractual conditions have to be scheduled for examination by the state arbitration organ within twenty-four hours after filing, and examined within four days. If one or both parties reside outside the city where the state arbitration organ charged with the case is located, the time necessary for the arrival of the parties' representatives and the presentation of explanations is added to the four days.

Such precontractual disputes are examined by the bench of state arbitration, consisting of one representative of each party and the arbiter. As stated, if the parties' representatives cannot reach an agree-

---

[1] Throughout this section, the kolkhozes are to be regarded as excepted from consideration.

[2] *Sbornik normativnykh aktov*, M. 1959, p. 50.

[3] *Sob. post., SSSR*, 1959, Item 68.

ment, the dispute is decided by the arbiter, whose decision is declared in the same session and delivered to the parties, together with the motives for his decision, in writing, within forty-eight hours after the communication of the decision.

h) *Compulsion to Enter a Contract*

It must be borne in mind that the conclusion of contractual relations between parties is prescribed by the plan, which determines the economic activities of all the participants in the country's economic life. Consequently, if the organs of state arbitration become aware that economic units do not enter a contract for the delivery of products provided for by the plan, they are obliged to start proceedings on their own initiative for the compulsion of one or both parties to conclude a contract, and, after the appropriate decision has been taken by state arbitration, to see that this decision is carried out. The usual reason for the initiation of such proceedings is the refusal of one of the parties to enter a contract. If proceedings are started by one of the parties, state arbitration has to consider whether a legal obligation to enter the contract exists for the reluctant party. As stated, such an obligation exists only if a corresponding assignment is provided by the plan. If the plan does not name the economic units obliged to sign a contract, the organ of state arbitration has to consider the expediency of creating direct contractual relations between the parties in order to improve the supply of goods. By way of precontractual supervision, the organs of state arbitration, at the request of the enterprises, etc., involved or on their own initiative, may declare invalid entire contracts or those parts of them that conflict with the law, with governmental decisions, state plans and assignments, and bind the parties to make the necessary amendments to contracts already concluded.

i) *Arbitral Procedure*

The procedure followed by state arbitration is laid down in the "Rules for Examination of Property Disputes by Organs of State Arbitration" of August 10, 1934, [1] which are still in force. Proceedings may be initiated (a) at the demand of the organization interested in the dispute, (b) at the request of the agency to which the state arbitra-

---

[1] *Arbitrazh v Sovetskom khozyaystve*, Moscow, 1948, pp. 199-210.

tion organ is attached, and (c) on the initiative of the state arbitration organ. In addition, the following four conditions must be met : (1) the case must fall within the competence of the arbitration organ petitioned; (2) measures for reaching a voluntary agreement must have been taken before recourse is had to arbitration; (3) provisions of limitation must be taken into consideration; and (4) there must be no previous decision in the case by an arbitration organ.

After having estalished that these conditions are met, the arbiter must study the materials of the case in advance of the session. The defendant has to file a brief with a detailed substantiation of his objections immediately after he has received a copy of the claim. Article 34 of the Rules of 1934 reads : "If an agreement cannot be reached by the parties or if the agreement reached contravenes revolutionary legislation or planning and contractual discipline, the dispute is resolved by the state arbiter". Article 43 confers on the arbiter the right to adjudicate beyond the claim presented by the parties "with the purpose of increasing the responsibility of economic organs for the fulfillment of plans and contracts and the prevention of further disputes in the case".

As stated, the arbiter must pronounce his decision immediately after the examination of the case in the presence of the parties. If the case is very complicated, the decision may be postponed, but not for longer than three days. The arbiter's decision comes into force on the day it is pronounced, if no other date is laid down in the decision. A date for the execution of the decision may be established in the decision. If the arbiter deems it necessary to fine the chief of an economic organization or its accountant for the irregular taking of stocks and keeping of accounts, or to deprive an expert of the right to present conclusions in the litigation, the decision must be presented to the chief arbiter for confirmation. Such a decision does not come into force without such confirmation.

The arbiter's duties include bringing to the attention of higher economic organs defects in relations between economic organs, negligence, abuses, etc., brought to light during the examination of the dispute. This duty is based on the function of "strengthening revolutionary legality, contractual and planning discipline and the principle of self-sufficiency". [1] In the case of particularly serious violations of law or of Party and governmental directives, *arbitrazh* notifies

---

[1] A similar significance with the private ruling issued by the regular courts.

the Committee for Party and State Control, and where necessary transfers the case to organs of the State Prosecutor's Office.

The arbiters further have to see that their decisions are carried out whenever the latter require economic organs to remove some defects in their mutual relations or signify negligence, abuses, etc., in these organs' work. If the decision is not complied with, the arbiter has to notify higher authority in order that the necessary measures may be taken. In the same way, he has to ensure that the organ of the state prosecutor's office to which a case has been referred has taken the necessary measures and to report any failure to do so to higher organs of the state prosecuting body.

j) *Re-examination of State Arbitration Decisions*

In state arbitration, as in civil and criminal procedure, there is no right of appeal (in the Western sense), nor even of cassation; as we have seen, the decision of a state arbitration organ is final. However, such decisions, like the decisions and sentences of the general courts, may be reviewed by way of supervision. In contradistinction to court procedure, this review may be initiated not only by the authorities, but also by the parties themselves. The supervision of both state and departmental arbitration is in the hands of the agencies to which the arbitration organ is attached, i.e., the Council of Ministers of the USSR, etc. Within each organ of state arbitration, the chief arbiter supervises the work of his own organ. Thus, the review of a state arbitration decision may be initiated by the parties or, ex officio, by the agency to which the arbitration organ is attached or by the chief arbiter of this organ. A petition for review by a discontented party must be adressed to the chief arbiter of the organ which pronounced the decision; it is he who then reviews the decision. The party has one month after pronouncement of the decision for filing its petition for review, which does not suspend execution of the decision. An ex-officio review may take place at any time. If the chief arbiter rejects a petition for review, the party is entitled to petition the agency to which the state arbitration organ is attached.

A further review ex officio may be initiated by a higher organ of state arbitration, which however, in contradistinction to the review of court sentences and decisions already in force, is not entitled to reverse or change the decision. If the higher arbitration organ considers the decision of a lower state arbitration organ or of the latter's chief arbiter to be incorrect, it makes representations to the agency to which the lower organ is attached. Thus, the review of any decision taken by a chief arbiter is carried out by the agency to which his arbitration organ is attached. This might be, for exemple, the executive committee of an oblast' soviet.

It must be agreed with R.F. Kallistratova that... it is not expedient to charge the executive organs of state and administration with the examination of complaints against state arbitration decisions and the taking of countermeasures for the elimination of mistakes committed by state arbitration [organs], including the reversal of [these organs'] decisions. [1]

Kallistratova is of the opinion that the exercise of this function by a governmental body conflicts with the strict delineation of spheres of competence between state organs according to the nature of their work. It is natural that an oblast' executive committee, for example, should not have personnel familair with the instructions issued by the organ of state arbitration attached to the Council of Ministers of the USSR. As a result, the decisions of such a body are drafted by the chief arbiter against whose original decision the complaint is being made.

A curious method of dealing with complaints against decisions of the chief arbiter was reported some years ago at a conference of the personnel of state arbitration of the Kazakh SSR. [2] At the executive committee of the Aktyubinsk Oblast' Soviet, complaints were prepared for decision by the executive committee's legal adviser, Dzharasov, who in turn invited the legal advisers of the organizations involved in the case to draft the decision to be taken by the executive committee. The parties'legal advisers were eager to do the job, but, of course, in the interest of their parties.

Thus, the legal provision that there is no appeal against the decisions of state arbitration is a fiction, since the decision can be reviewed by several authorities and even on the initiative of the parties involved. The only difference from a regular appeal is that a petition for review does not suspend execution of the decision. Even here, however,

---

[1] Kallistratova, *op. cit.*, p. 197. See also P. V. Loginov, *Notariat i arbitrazh v SSSR*, M. 1957, p. 9.

[2] *Sov. yust.*, 1958, No. 9, p. 62.

there is a remedy in that the chief arbiter has the right to suspend
execution of a decision until it is reviewed.

Having reviewed the structure and the functioning of arbitrazh,
we are now in a position to examine its legal character. On this question,
the opinions expressed in Soviet legal literature have undergone a
process of change, and three views have been put forward by three
groups of writers.

B. Is Arbitrazh a Court ?

Writing in 1936, Z. Shkundin declared that arbitrazh is an "economic
court" [1] but a special type of court, since the property disputes examined by it arise from, and in the course of, the one and undivided
socialist administration of property, [2] and because arbitrazh has
features which differentiate it from regular courts. [3] These peculiar
features are : the right to initiate proceedings on its own initiative;
the obligation to initiate proceedings on instructions from a higher
organ of arbitration; the duty of examining suits on orders from the
sovnarkhoz or of the executive committee of the soviet to which the
arbitration organ is attached; the obligation of the parties to discuss
the possibility of reaching an agreement before resorting to arbitration;
and the possibility of initiating proceedings not only by the organization
interested in the dispute but also by a higher organization. Some
twelve years later, Shkundin declared : "Arbitrazh is a special kind
of court... an economic court examining only economic disputes
between socialist organizations and enterprises". [4] Another article,
written jointly by Shkundin and V.N. Mozheiko, asserts :

The principles of the arbitral examination of disputes correspond
basically to the principles of our civil procedure, and the scope of
court procedure and the arbitral examination of disputes is identical,
as is also the policy pursued by the courts and the organs of arbitration. [5]

The article denies the possibility of a contraposition of court and

[1] *Sovetskoye gosudarstvo*, 1936, No. 3, p. 49.
[2] *Ibid.*, p. 50.
[3] *Ibid.*, p. 60.
[4] *Arbitrazh v Sovetskom khozyaystve*, p. 21.
[5] *Ibid.*, p. 57.

state arbitration because of the unity of the Soviet systems of economy and socialist law and also because of the similarity of scope of the courts and the arbitration organs.

Court and arbitration alike must protect public and socialist property by their decisions and educate a socialist attitude toward it; they must strengthen revolutionary legality in the sphere of contractual economic relations, and inculcate a socialist attitude toward duties in economic relations and toward the state, as well as principles of self-sufficiency and state discipline. Furthermore, a contraposition of court and arbitration is impossible because of the similarity of the methods which they employ... namely, the method of deciding disputes that arise by applying Soviet law to them. [1]

Mozheiko also comes to the conclusion that "arbitrazh has many features and peculiarities inherent in the courts", [2] and that "according to its scope and methods of work, arbitrazh has much in common with the court". [3] Similarly, M.S. Lipetsker asserts that "as regards the content and the nature of their work, the organs of arbitrazh can be placed on the same footing as the judicial organs". [4] A.A. Volin is of the opinion that state arbitration is by nature a kind of private court of arbitration (treteisky sud). [5]

In the United States, the conception of arbitrazh as a kind of court is put forward by Harold Berman, who writes :

Both precontract and contract disputes of a commercial nature are, with certain exceptions, adjudicated by a special system of courts called the State Board of Arbitration (Gosarbitrazh)... They are rather "economic courts" whose jurisdictions are independent of the will of the parties, whose procedures, though informal by American standards, are similar to those of the regular courts, and whose decisions are governed by the Civil Code and by relevant statutes. [6]

Thus, the group of people who define the organs of arbitration as special courts base their assertion on the similarity of scope, competence activity and role in the fulfillment of state economic, organizational, cultural and educational functions which exists between the courts and the organs of arbitration.

---

[1] *Ibid.*, p. 20.

[2] *SGP*, 1947, No. 6, p. 23.

[3] *Ibid.*, p. 20.

[4] *Trudy Voyenno-yuridichesky akademii*, 1948, No. 8, p. 66.

[5] *Kommunist*, 1959, No. 3, p. 59.

[6] Harold V. J. Berman, "Commercial Contracts in Soviet Law", *California Law Review*, Berkeley, Cal., 1947, No. 35, pp. 204-5.

Practical conclusions have been drawn from these assertions by Soviet writers. It has been suggested to amend the Code of Civil Procedure in order to make it fully applicable to arbitration and even to transfer the functions of arbitrazh to the regular courts. Thus, Shkundin, having declared that a number of fundamental provisions of the Code of Civil Procedure can be applied to arbitral procedure and that only a few specific provisions pertain to the latter, comes to the conclusion that "the unification of court and arbitral procedure, their coordination in a single code of procedure, is practically expedient and will contribute to the improvement of decisions in disputes between enterprises of the socialist economy". [1] A. Rogovin, writing on "The Unification of the Norms of Court and Arbitral Procedures" demands that all provisions of the Code of Civil Procedure be applied to arbitration. This would eliminate the special provisions applied to arbitral procedure and introduce features of regular procedure such as appeals in cassation. [2]

M. Rivkin flatly denies the necessity of arbitrazh. He argues :

Since the courts and the organs of arbitration alike watch over socialist legality [to ensure] that it shall not be violated in the process of deciding property disputes within the socialist economy and that socialist property shall be preserved, the existence of two parallel systems, the court and arbitrazh, cannot be justified. [3]

Such a situation, he says, can only lead to a victimization of socialist legality. Rivkin strongly objects to certain fundamental features of the practice of arbitration. A court decision, he says, can be appealed against and the appeal examined by a higher court, whereas a complaint against the decision of a state arbitration organ is examined by the chief arbiter of the same organ. He cannot assume "an objective attitude on the part of the chief arbiter toward the review of decisions made by the organ of which he is the chief". [4]

Rivkin is shocked to discover that when looking through arbitrazh decisions over a period of five years he could find no reference to law. In one case, it was said that "in his decision the arbiter proceeded from the importance of the parties' economic interests, not from the degree of legality and stability of the bank transaction of sale and

---

[1] *Sov. yust.*, 1937, No. 4, p. 28.

[2] *Ibid.*, 1937, No. 17, p. 12.

[3] *Ibid.*, 1937, No. 5, p. 18.

[4] *Ibid.*, p. 19.

purchase as considered from a narrow legal viewpoint". Thus, by placing himself above parties, the contract and the law and by taking the view that only matters of economic importance and state interests were relevant, the arbiter freed himself of all responsibility. [1]

The American writer Kazimierz Grzybowski considers that not observance of the law and the contract but compliance with the plan primarily guides the arbiter in his decision. "Adjusting conflicting interests,... decisions of the economic arbitrator can be made exclusively in terms of economic policy and without reference to abstract rules of law". [2] Grzybowski points out that this view has been sharply rejected by Soviet writers. Mozheiko and Shkundin, for example, declared:

Arbiters who imagine that an arbitral decision can be taken in spite of the law because a decision not corresponding to law is allegedly "economically" expedient must be blamed and punished. State arbitration has no right to deviate from the law even by one step. [3]

If arbitrazh insists on remaining by a contract or by inidividual provisions in it, it must bring it into alignment with the law. "The law of a socialist state", they say, "is the highest expediency. A contraposition of socialsit legality and so-called 'economic expediency' is completely inadmissible".

Rivkin totally rejects assertions that the parallel existence of regular courts and arbitrazh is justified because the court defends socialist property from violations by individual persons while arbitrazh protects it from violations by enterprises and institutions, and that the court cannot investigate disputes within the socialized sector. The court, he says, examines disputes not only of a civil but also of a criminal character, of individual citizens among themselves and with enterprises of the socialist sector. The court must, and can, have sufficient knowledge of the work of economic organizations, of economic plans and contracts, to settle disputes between enterprises. [4]

Another writer, L. Lensky, also strongly denounced the arbitral habit of being guided by "economic expediency" rather than by law, the reviewing of decisions by the arbiters who themselves made them and other features of arbitral procedure which, according to him,

---

[1] *Ibid.*

[2] Kazimierz Grzybowski, *Soviet Legal Institutions, Doctrines and Social Functions*, Ann Arbor, 1962, pp. 99-100.

[3] *Arbitrazh v sovetskom khozyaystve*, *op. cit.*, pp. 10-11.

[4] *Sov. yust.*, 1937, No. 5, p. 18.

undermine the principles of legality advocated by Lenin and Stalin. He came to the conclusion :

It is not expedient to permit the existence of an organ outside the courts which ignores their decisions, works virtually behind closed doors, cannot fight real barratry, and creates a system tolerating the disregard of law. We vote for the liquidation of the organs of state arbitration and the transfer of cases examined by them to the jurisdiction of the courts. [1]

Analysing the specific forms of procedure observed by arbitrazh, A. Farbstein comes to the conclusion that almost all of them have counterparts in the Code of Civil Procedure, so that the Code could be easily amended for the purpose of applying it to arbitration. Hence he sees no reason for the separate existence of arbitrazh : "There is no ground for the further existence of state arbitration as an organ outside the general system of courts of the USSR. The only possibility that can be entertained is special economic sessions of courts". [2]

A.G. Goikhbarg, one of the creators of the RSFSR Civil Code of 1922, was of the opinion that the arbitration commissions functioning at that time were a kind of court and should be merged with the general courts. His view is reproduced by John N. Hazard as follows :

The special tribunal had been created because it was thought that such disputes should be heard by a body authorized to decide each case on the basis of expediency rather than law... He [Goikhbarg] found also that there was added reason for union in that the arbitration commission was in its decisions applying the rules on contract law to disputes between agencies. It was being as legal as the courts.

The Fifth Congress of the Communist Party, in its resolution in response to Goikhbarg's jurisdictional proposals, accepted his view that the arbitration tribunals should no longer be independent but should be brought immediately within the general court system. [3]

According to Hazard, "Goikhbarg's colleagues had frequently expressed their desire to reduce the number of special courts, and now it was his turn to revert to Kursky's old theme of a unity-court system". [4]

---

[1] *Ibid.*, 1937, No. 11, p. 38.

[2] *Ibid.*, 1937, No. 13, p. 13.

[3] John N. Hazard, *Settling Disputes in Soviet Society*, N. Y., 1960, pp. 431-32.

[4] *Ibid.*, p. 431.

a) *Or an Organ of State Administration ?*

The second group—the majority of Soviet writers at the present time—is of the opinion that arbitrazh is not a court but an administrative unit. P.P. Yakimov writes :

Soviet arbitrazh is a system of organs of state and public government of an administrative character, which, by examining and settling economic disputes and applying means of coercion, contributes to the strengthening of planning and contractual discipline, self-sufficiency and socialist legality in the work and relations of socialist enterprises, institutions and organizations for the fulfillment of the plan of the national economy. [1]

This conclusion is derived from the following premises : (1) the organs of state and departmental arbitration have no judicial functions; and (2) the constitutional basis for the existence of arbitrazh is Article 68 of the Soviet Constitution, which establishes the right of the Council of Ministers of the USSR to set up in case of need special organs in matters of economic, cultural and defensive structure.

Both premises are incorrect—the first because the arbitration commissions were created as a judicial institution by the Statute on Court Structure of the RSFSR of October 30, 1922. [2] Article 2 of this statute, enumerating judicial institutions designed for the examination of special types of cases demanding special knowledge and skill, lists under 'd' "local and central arbitration commissions".

That arbitrazh was conceived as a special judicial institution by the legislators also follows from statements made by Krylenko, the leading jurist of that time. At the first all-Russian arbitrazh congress, held in 1932 (and so after the dissolution of the arbitration commissions and the publication of the 1931 Statute on State Arbitration), Krylenko declared that "different natures of arbitral and judicial cases, different methods for their examination and different principles of material and procedural law cannot exist with us". He insisted on the unity of Soviet law and on the identical nature of arbitral and judicial cases, asserting that "the principles governing the settlement of disputes in the court system must be elevated to [the level of] the principles governing the settlement of disputes by state arbitration". He maintained that in Soviet society there could be no difference between the nature

---

[1] *Uckenyye zapiski Sverdlovskogo yuridicheskogo instituta*, Sverdlovsk, 1957, No. 5, pp. 247-48.

[2] *Sob. zak., RSFSR*, 1923, Item 292.

of cases coming up for arbitration and that of those submitted to the courts, no difference in the methods of passing judgment on them and no difference in the principles of substantive or procedural law. [1]

In the Regulations on Procedure in Arbitration Commissions of March 14, 1923, it was stated that "procedure in the arbitration commissions and the Supreme Arbitration Commission is similar to the rules of procedure in the regular courts, with the exception derived from the peculiarities of cases coming under the jurisdiction of arbitration commissions". [2] The "judicial bench" comprised a chairman and two members of the arbitration commission. One member of the bench had to be a jurist and another an economist.

The main function of arbitrazh is the settlement of economic disputes—a typical judicial activity.

The second premise is incorrect since the Statute on State Arbitration was promulgated in 1931, five years before the Constitution of 1936.

Kleinman bases his denial of the judicial character of arbitrazh on the assertions that (1) the sphere of competence of courts is not the same as that of organs of arbitration; the courts protect not only the interests of economic organizations but also the political, labor, housing and other personal and property rights of citizens; and (2) the methods of administering justice are different. [3]

Kleinman's arguments are not convincing. The competence of any special court, as for example the military or railroad courts, is limited in comparison with that of general courts. As for the methods employed, in almost any civil suit the bench attempts to reach an agreement between the parties before formally deciding the dispute, and the impartial decision of the court is in essence an act of arbitration. In its turn, the decision of the arbiter is similar to that of a court according to its form and its consequences : if not complied with by the losing party, it can be enforced. That the responsible representatives of the parties to the dispute are members of the bench is irrelevant, because the purpose of their participation is to reach a voluntary agreement is not reached, the arbiter makes his decision without their participation.

According to Kleinman, the Soviet Constitution charges only the courts with the dispensation of justice. [4]

---

[1] *Sovetskoye gosudarstvo*, 1932, No. 7/8, p. 39.

[2] *Sob. post., RSFSR*, 1923, Entry No. 292.

[3] *Arbitrazh v SSSR*, M. 1960, pp. 41-42.

[4] *Ibid.*, p. 42.

A.A. Dobrovolsky admits that the arbitration commissions, "according to the nature of their work, were put on the same footing as the judicial organs, and, in contradistinction to the regular courts, were considered as special courts". [1] He denies, however, that arbitrazh is a kind of court of arbitration, as asserted by Volin, and in support of his view quotes the resolution of the Council of Ministers of the USSR of July 23, 1959, entitling the parties to especially complicated disputes to submit such disputes to private arbitration :

If arbitrazh were a court of arbitration, there would be no necessity for a provision permitting the examination of a dispute, by way of exception, by a private court of arbitration especially organized by agreement of the parties and elected ad hoc for the case in hand.

It is evident that no support for Dobrovolsky's view can be found in this provision, the purpose of which, as given in the resolution, was to "reinforce democratic principles in the resolution of economic disputes". The democratization consists in the substitution of a private for the state court of arbitration and in the replacement of the arbiter appointed by the state with three arbiters elected by the parties and applying, not the special provision of state arbitral procedure, but the norms of the Code of Civil Procedure. The resolution, therefore, hardly supports the claim that arbitrazh is not a kind of arbitration court.

Dobrovolsky goes on to point to peculiarities in arbitral procedure that are unknown to the Code of Civil Procedure, and these lead him to side with those writers who define arbitrazh as an "administrative organ of economic management and state government". [2] The activities of state, sovnarkhoz and departmental arbitrazh are of an administrative, not judicial, nature", he concludes". [3]

These peculiarities are also taken by other writers in the group as a basis for relegating arbitrazh to the administrative state organs. [4]

b) *Or Neither Regular Court nor Administrative Agency ?*

A third group of jurists defines arbitrazh neither as a judicial nor as an administrative or governmental institution, but as an organ

---

[1] *Ibid.*, p. 25.

[2] *Ibid.*, p. 45.

[3] *Ibid.*, p. 47.

[4] See writers listed in Kallistratova, *op. cit.*, p. 16.

sui generis in the Soviet state system. [1] Let us review the arguments of R.F. Kallistratova, an eminent representative of the third group.

Kallistratova rejects the classification of state arbitration as a judicial institution because of "the normative material in accordance with which it functions and because of its practical application, which testify to the numerous and essential differences between arbitrazh and judicial organs", and also because "according to the Constitution arbitrazh is not considered a judicial organ". [2] Evidently she here has in mind Article 102, which enumerates the courts dispensing justice in the USSR. However, only regular courts are listed in this article of the Constitution, because only regular courts enjoy the rights and privileges granted in Section IX of the Constitution. [3] The list contained in Article 102 is not, therefore, exhaustive. For instance, comrades' courts are also not mentioned therein, but no one would deny that the comrades' courts are courts, and fulfill judicial functions. It may be added that Article 1 of the Fundamental Principles of Court Structure of the USSR, Union and Autonomous Republics of 1958 only repeats the list given in Article 102 of the 1936 Constitution and so is equally incomplete.

Kallistratova observes that "arbiters are not elected, but appointed by the administration, and there are no people's assessors on the bench in arbitrazh proceedings". To this it may be replied that judges were appointed and not elected in the USSR for many years, and there is a score of courts which even now function without the participation of people's assessors—for example, all the courts of appeal.

Kallistratova further remarks that "the organs of arbitrazh are structurally bound to the organs of state government". Here it may be pointed out that the railroad courts, which functioned from 1930 to 1935, belonged to the system of people's commissariats of justice of the Union republics and still were considered courts and not administrative organs.

Finally, Kallistratova maintains that "the responsible representatives of the parties involved in the dispute submitted for arbitration take part in the decision concerning the merits of the case. "This, however, is not correct : the parties' representatives participate in the

---

[1] For writers listed in this group, see *Uchenyye zapiski Sverdlovskogo yuridicheskogo instituta*, 1957, No. 5, p. 237, Footnote 2.

[2] *Op. cit.*, p. 14.

[3] See R. Maurach, *Handbuch der Sowjetverfassung*, Munich, 1955, p. 276 (Comment No. 3 to Article 102).

examination of the dispute only so far as an agreement can be reached. It is the arbiter alone who decides.

Much more convincing is what Kallistratova has to say in rejection of the theory that arbitrazh is an organ of the government. Despite some administrative functions, she argues, arbitrazh is not a normal governmental organ : it has no right to issue orders in the sphere of economic planing, organization and administration, and has no administrative organs subordinate to it. She also rightly points out contradictions in the arguments of her opponents. Yakimov, for instance, asserts that the principles of court procedure are inapplicable to state arbitration, but convincingly demonstrates the use in arbitral procedure of the controversial principle and of the principle of evidence valuation on the basis of inner conviction. [1] Her conclusion is as follows :

In fact, state arbitration has at the same time features of both judicial and administrative institutions, and consequently assumes a place peculiar to itself in the system of the Soviet state apparatus, which differs considerably from [that of] both administrative and judicial organs. [2]

Strogovich wrote : "Court procedure is used sometimes also in the actions of administrative organs. So, state arbitration—not a court, but an administrative organ and its examination of a case is not court procedure—but the examination itself in Arbitrazh is near to court procedure". [3]

Also according to Loeber, "Arbitrazh", is an administrative agency though it acts, to a considerable extent, in a judicial manner". [4]

Taking into consideration everything that has been said about the legal position of state and departmental arbitration, the present writer is of the opinion that these organs may be defined as administrative courts—"administrative" because their functions are limited to settling disputes between socialized enterprises, organizations and institutions and because they employ special norms of procedure along with provisions of the Code of Civil Procedure, and "courts" because they were intended as such by the legislators and because their main

---

[1] Kallistratova, *op. cit.*, pp. 16-17.

[2] *Ibid.*, p. 17.

[3] M. Strogovich, "Development of the Court Structure and Procedural Legislation", *Sov. yust.* 1961, No. 22, p. 5.

[4] Dietrich A. Loeber, "Plan and Contract Performance in the Post War in the Practice of USSR State Arbitrazh, in *Law in the Soviet Union*, Urbana, Ill., 1965, pp. 131-32.

purpose is the fulfillment of judicial functions. The intention of the legislators and the judicial activities confer the status of courts upon the organs of state and departmental arbitration, despite all deviations from normal courts procedure and despite their administrative functions. Arbitrazh—is an administrative court.

Besides Gosarbitrazh which is a government agency with compulsory jurisdiction, there are optional arbitration courts, such as the Maritime Arbitration Commission of the all-Union Chamber of Commerce in Moscow to which disputes relating to maritime claims may be referred, and the Foreign Trade Arbitration Commission of the same Chamber arbitrarily examining disputes arising in foreign trade.

The tendency to transfer disputes of agencies, institutions, enterprises and organizations to private arbitration courts must be noted.

So the Deputy of the Chief Arbiter of State Arbitration attached to the USSR Council of Ministers, A. Volin [1], commended the possibility to submit property disputes between enterprises, institutions and organizations to private arbitration. He wrote that the private arbitration court is one of the new forms of public independent activity applied on the guidance of the national economy; according to him,

"State arbitration attached to the USSR Council of Ministers, in its instructions, draw the attention of the entire staff of Arbitrazh to its most important duty of clarifying the political and public essense and importance of private arbitration court and extending help to economic organs for the submitting of disputes to this court".

CONCLUSIONS

We have discussed the question of the legal nature of arbitrazh at some length because this question has a direct bearing upon the work and the importance of Arbitrazh.

Indeed, if the organs of arbitration are courts, their main task must be the preservation of legality. Any court, whether general or special, must be particularly concerned with the correct application of the law. Considerations of "expediency" cannot serve as a basis for a court's decisions, and those Soviet writers who denounce arbiters who are guided in their decisions by such considerations are certainly

---

[1] A. Volin, "The Activity of Arbitrazh in the Light of the Decisions of the XXII Congress", *Sov. yust.*, 1961, No. 24, pp. 5-6.

right. *Pacta sunt servanda* and arbitration organs deciding the question of the violation or non-violation of a contract must be guided by the provisions of the law of contracts and not by other considerations.

When the Supreme Court of the USSR ruled in 1963 that "no violations of legality whatsoever can be justified by reliance on the notion that they are necessary in order to consolidate the fight against crime", [1] it evidently wanted to ban all violations of law in all branches of Soviet justice. And when it continued that "every criminal case, regardless of the nature and seriousness of the crime and of the official of social position of the accused, must be decided in strict accordance with the requirements of criminal and procedural law", it meant that the decision should not be influenced by the position of the person to be sentenced. It wanted to exclude from the influence on sentence formation every consideration violating law, including consideration of plan fulfillment in detriment of a contract.

In analogy to this ruling, it may be concluded that the law must also in the decisions of arbitrazh take precedence over "economic expediency". Decisions guided by considerations other than law are violations of the law, regardless of the branch of judicial administration in which they occur, and arbitrazh, whether it be considered an administrative court, an administrative unit or an institution *sui generis*, metes justice and so is bound above all to the observance of the law.

As we have seen, however, the Statute on State Arbitration of 1931 lays down that when deciding disputes, organs of state arbitration "must be guided by the laws and rulings of both central and local authorities as well as by the general principles of Soviet economic policy" (Article 8) and that they must proceed from the necessity of "strict compliance with planning and contractual discipline" (Article 9). On the other hand, the rules for arbitral procedure of 1934 charge the organs of state arbitration with "the further strengthening of legality". Thus, the arbiter must not seldom find himself in a dilemma, being confronted with the obligation, on the one hand, to apply the law unflinchingly and, on the other, to observe the interests of plan fulfillment. Sometimes the fulfillment of the contract is no longer in the interests of the plan, and then the arbiter decides, not according to the law, but with regard to expediency. The interests of the plan prevail, and the law is violated. Such violations of the law hardly, speaking generally, contribute to the "strengthening

---

[1] Ruling No. 2 of March 18, 1963, *Byuleten' Verkhovnogo Suda SSRS*, 1963, No. 3.

of legality", but they are particularly reprehensible when committed by a court—an institution which is called upon to enforce the law and preserve legality.

Writing in 1961, Kallistratova maintained :

At the present time, no one still proposes to liquidate arbitrazh and to replace it by the court, because the arbitral form of deciding disputes has sustained the challenge of time and has been consolidated; in the main, those defects which provided the grounds for suggesting its liquidation have been overcome in arbitral practice. [1]

Kallistratova does not, however, substantiate her claim. There is no evidence that the practice of applying expediency in the place of law has been abandoned.

There is also no evidence to show that the defects authoritatively indicated in the resolution of the Council of Ministers of 1959 have been removed. This much may be concluded from a discussion published by the journal Sovetskaya yustitsiya in 1963. The discussion was opened by I. Gorbunov, who wrote an article entitled "When Disputes are Conducted to the Detriment of the State", in which he pointed out many faults in the work of the arbitral system. [2] According to the editors of the journal, Gorbunov's article found a wide response among jurists and economists. Many readers reported defects in the work both of the arbitral system and of enterprises obliged to resort to it for the settlement of disputes, and a number of suggestions were made for improving this situation. These comments and suggestions were summarized in a later issue. [3]

With regard to "strengthening legality", the transfer of the activities of arbitrazh to the general courts suggested by Lensky, Rivkin and others seems to be well founded. Mozheiko and Shkundin rightly emphasized that strict observance of the law is the most expedient method of resolving disputes. Indeed, the plan should be adapted to the law, and not the law broken in favour of the plan. All this, of course, remains little more than *pia desiderata* so long as the Soviet Union continues to be a totalitarian state in which the interests of the state prevail over everything else, including the law. Admittedly, the new Party Program claims that "justice in the USSR is exercised in full conformity with the law. It is based on truly democratic lines". [4]

---

[1] Kallistratova, *op. cit.*, p. 15.

[2] *Sov. yust.*, 1963, No. 2. pp. 6-8.

[3] *Ibid.*, 1963, No. 12, pp. 9-11.

[4] *Programma Kommunisticheskoy Partii Sovetskogo Soyuza*, M. 1961, p. 96.

But the main "democratic foundation" of law is its supremacy over the state; and this is not the case in the USSR. [1]

---

[1] Harold Berman (*Justice in the USSR : An Interpretation of Law*, rev. ed., Cambridge, Mass, 1963, p. 87) quotes the answer he received from Deputy Procurator General of the USSR, P. I. Kudryavtsev, to the question, "Suppose the law conflicts with the interests of the state : which prevails"? The answer was : "The interests of the state".

CHAPTER NINE

SOCIAL COURTS

A. FROM STATE TO SOCIAL COURTS

According to Engels and Lenin, the State withers away. Under communism the state and its coercive power will not be necessary anymore since the communist society will administer itself using no measures of coercion but persuasion.

"We set ourselves the ultimate aim of destroying the state" wrote Lenin, "i.e. every organized and systematic violence, every use of violence against every man in general. We do not expect the advent of an order of society in which the principle of subordination of minority to majority will not be observed. But striving for Socialism, we are convinced that it will develop into Communism; that side by side with this there will vanish all need for force, for the *subjection* of one man to another, and of one part of the population to another, since people will grow *accustomed* to observing the elementary conditions of social existence *without force and without subjection*". [1]

During the transition period from socialism to communism in preparation of the complete transfer of administration from the state to society, administration of justice must be partially entrusted to social organizations.

To this effect the people must be trained in the administration of the state and justice.

Indeed, one of Lenin's basic ideas about the administration of the state, including the administration of justice, was the attraction of the mass of the population to this activity. "Our goal" wrote Lenin, "is the attraction of the poor as one way to the practical participation in the administration..." [2]

The democratic principle of organization, according to Lenin, consisted in the creation of a situation when... "every representative of the masses, every citizen is put into a condition of giving him the possibility to participate in the discussion of state laws, the election of his representatives, as well as in the realization of the laws in life".

---

[1] V. I. Lenin, *State and Revolution*, N. Y., 1932, *op. cit.*, p. 68.

[2] Lenin, 27, p. 243.

Elsewhere he wrote that it is necessary "to educate the wide mases of workers and peasants in matters of independence and speedy businesslike participation in the supervision of the observation of legality". [1]

At the XXIst Congress of the USSR Communist Party of 1959, the transfer of some state functions to social organizations was discussed. By taking over a part of its functions "the public would help the state enormously and contribute to its strengthening and the development of socialist democracy". [2]

These functions were the preservation of public order and the fulfillment of regulations concerning socialist common life. As Khrushchev who referring to Lenin was the promoter of the movement in 1959 put it at the same Congress : "Things are moving toward the fulfillment of functions of preservation of public order and security by social organizations parallel to such state institutions as the military and courts". [3]

At a meeting of the electors of the Kalininskiy Electoral District on February 24, 1959, N.S. Khrushchev said : "The direction toward the gradual shift of a series of state organs functions to social organizations, outlined by the XXIth Party Congress... is prepared by life itself, by the entire development movement of the Socialist Soviet State". [4]

It was said in the resolution of the XXI Congress that "the transfer of individual functions from state to social organs will not weaken the role of the socialist state in the building of communism, but will widen and strengthen the political foundation of socialist society and insure the further development of socialist democracy". [5]

The XXII Congress of the Soviet Union Communist Party (October 1961) took up Lenin's idea and considered the attraction of the entire adult population to the task of administration of the state and society as a practical goal. In the report of the Central Committee of the USSR Communist Party to the XXII Congress, Khrushchev even gave out the opinion that "we are now near the goal, set by V.I. Lenin, to attract

---

[1] *Ibid.*, 33, p. 155.

[2] Editorial, *S.G.P.*, 1959, No. 4, p. 13.

[3] N. S. Khrushchev, *O kontrol'nykh tsifrakh razvitiya narodnogo khozyaystva*, 1959-1965, M. 1959, p. 120.

[4] N. S. Khrushchev, *Rech'na sobranii izbiratel'nogo okruga goroda Moskvy, 24 fevralya 1959 goda*. M. 1959, p. 7.

[5] Editorial *S.G.P.*, 1959, No. 2, p. 6.

all the citizens, without exception, to the fulfillment of state functions". [1]

On the way to this goal, the socialist legislator passed three laws : the law on the Statute of comrades' courts; the law of 1961 against parasites, transferring judicial power over certain offences from the state to society; and the law of 1960 on the formation of people's brigades.

Only the first two laws concern the administration of justice and will be discussed in detail below.

The police activities of the people's brigades are directed to the maintenance and protection of public order and thus depart from the theme of this book. [2]

The Basic Principles of Penal Legislation of the USSR and the Union Republics of 1958 and the RSFSR Criminal Code of 1960 contain provisions referring some petty offences, under certain conditions, to the competence of comrades' courts.

In its ruling of June 19, 1959, "On the Practice and Application of Criminal Punishments by Courts", the Plenum of the USSR Supreme Court instructed the Courts to transfer more extensively cases of law violations presenting no serious danger, to the competence of the public, in accordance with Art. 7[2] of the Basic Principles of Penal Legislation of the USSR and the Union Republics, quashing such cases in criminal procedure.

B. Comrades' Courts

The comrades' courts have a long history in the Soviet Administration of Justice.

Let us examine the development of these courts.

It has already been emphasized that Lenin wanted the greatest participation of the people in the administration of the state, and hence, of the administration of justice. The comrades' courts established in Lenin's time were certainly one of the expressions of this desire.

a) *Historical Development*

1. *Legislation under Lenin*

The first mention of Comrades' Courts is to be found in an Order of

---

[1] N. S. Khrushchev, *Otchet Ts, K. PKSS XXII s"edzu*, M. 1961 pp. 101-102.
[2] Their scope is to help the militia in the insuring of public order.

the Field General Staff of the Commander in Chief to the Petrograd Military District, signed by Antonov-Ovseenko, Commander in Chief. It was ordered there : "To establish, in the name of the workers' and peasants' power, public comrades' courts in all the companies, squadrons and batteries in the District, entrusted to me, for the examination of offenses humiliating the name of a citizen-warrier". [1]

The RSFSR Council of People's Commissars headed by Lenin, signed the Decree on Workers Disciplinary Comrades' Courts on November 14, 1919. [2] It was said in its preamble that the Decree was prompted by the "especially precarious military, food, and fuel situation of the Soviet Republic". Its scope was indicated as the increasing of labor discipline and work efficiency, "to the highest limit;" also the "expedient utilization of all productive forces in the country" was one of the goals to be reached by the Decree.

Previous to the Decree, the Program of the Party adopted at the VIII Congress of the RKP (b) in March 1919 gave a positive valuation in its court section to the organization of the court system and the realization of court policy, which gives the possibility to apply comrades' courts in practice. [3]

As follows from the title, the stress in the Decree was on the enforcement of work discipline.

The bench of the court consisted of a representative of the union, a delegate of the local or central plant direction and a worker occupied at the plant belonging to the union and elected in the workers' assembly of the plant.

The worker's disciplinary comrades' courts were attached to local branches of production trade-unions.

The courts had the right to set the following punishments : 1)rebuke, with its being made known in the enterprise or the organization; 2) temporary deprivation of active and passive electoral rights in elections to federal organizations, not longer than for six months; 3) temporary shift to a lower position for not longer than one month; 4) assignment to public necessary work, remunerated according to the rate assigned to this work and, in case of stubborn non-compliance with comradely discipline and repeated punishments-firing from the enterprise and transfer to a concentration camp.

---

[1] N. V. Krylenko, *Sudoustroystvo RSFSR*, M. 1924, pp. 35-36.

[2] *Sob. uz.*, 1919, Item 537.

[3] *KPSS v rezolyutsiyakh i resheniyakh s"ezdov, konferentsiy i plenumov TsK*, Part I, M. 1954, p. 419.

The right of appeal in cassation against the decision was awarded to the parties involved.

The appeal in cassation had to be directed to the province comrades' disciplinary court, attached to the province department of labor. This higher court was organized in the following manner : one representative of the province department of labor; of the province council of trade-unions and of the province council of the people's economy, respectively. Decisions of this court were final and executed immediately.

It is peculiar that the jurisdiction of the workers' disciplinary comrades' court was not established in the Statute. It must be assumed that it extended to any offense committed at work or related to work. It was a time when neither the competence of the court was directly delineated nor the laws directing their activity were established.

"The workers' comrades' courts, as Rudzutak declared in his report to the Vth All-Russian Conference of Trade-Unions on November 4, 1920 have this purpose : "In the task of labor organization... the disciplinary courts, to which not much attention has been paid up to the present time, must be transformed into a real meaning for the fight against the violations of proletarian labor discipline". [1]

Also Lenin emphasized that "We have forgotten the disciplinary courts and productional democracy... without disciplinary courts... is only twaddle". [2]

Speaking of Rudzutak's report before the VIIIth Congress of Soviets on December 20, 1920, Lenin said that he was not aware as to whether a Decree on disciplinary courts, which he himself signed on November 14, 1919, existed or not; when he got acquaited with Rudzutak's report. Lenin namely declared : "When I read Rudzutak's theses about the disciplinary courts I thought : certainly there must be already a decree on them. It turned out there was one : The Statute on Workers' Disciplinary Comrades' Courts, published on November 14, 1919". [3]

"In this court", Lenin continued, "the main role belongs to the trade-unions. As to whether these courts are good, how successfully and constantly they work—I do not know." [4]

In the Decision of the Plenum of the Soviet Union Communist

[1] Lenin, 32, p. 21.
[2] *Ibid.*
[3] *Ibid.*, p. 22.
[4] *Ibid.*

Party Central Committee of January 12, 1922, On the Role and Scopes of Trade-Unions in Conditions of the New Economic Policy, drafted personally by Lenin, it was said, "In particular the disciplinary courts must steadfastly heighten the discipline of labor and the cultural forms of the fight for it and the increase of productivity, not interfering, however, with the function of the People's Courts in general and the administration's functions". [1]

This scope of increasing labor discipline and productivity of work up to the highest limit was already formulated previously in the Statute on Disciplinary Comrades' Courts of April 5, 1921 [2] which amended the Statute of 14 November 1919.

In the name of the court the word "workers" was dropped, evidently since the competence of the court was extended to include besides the workers, also employees as well as administrative-technical and higher federal personnel (Art.1). The scope remained, however, the same : To increase labor discipline and productivity of work up to the highest limits... literally repeated from the Decision of the Central Committee of January 12, 1921.

In contradistinction to the law of 1919, the Statue of 1921 contained a list of offenses put under its jurisdiction. This list may be divided into two parts : offenses concerning production of work, and those pertaining to general behavior.

To the first category belonged late showing up for work, leaving the place of work ahead of time, without good reason, actions detracting others from work or impeding it, shirking work, careless fulfillment of work duties, in particular the production of poor quality goods, damaging material or machines, non-reaching of norms of work efficiency, violation of norms of work protection, non-compliance with rules of cleanliness and safety, performing of outside work during work time.

In the second group were included : hooliganism, indecent behavior and rudeness during the work, disobedience to orders of superiors, rudeness and lack of attention with regard to visitors, violations of tariff rules, connivance and lack of administrative ability with regard to a rational use of the labor force, petty thefts connected with work if they have not an organized and systematic character, petty abuses committed during the distribution of items of first necessity such

---

[1]   Lenin, 33, p. 166.
[2]   *Sob. uz., RSFSR*, 1921, Item 142.

as food, violation of established rules of internal order and other actions not provided by this statue.

The second part of the last sentence means that the long list is still not an exhaustive one and that the court has leave to bring also other actions not defined in the statue under its jurisdiction.

This permission to decide about offences, not provided in the statue is a counter part to the famous provision of the 1923 Soviet Criminal Code extending the jurisdiction of the court to "analogous" crimes not listed in the Code.

A great variety of punishments could be applied by the disciplinary comrades' courts according to the Statue of 1921.

It begins with a simple remark and ends with concentration camp for a period of time not over six months. In between are the rebukes, lowering of the remuneration for work, working off on overtime of the time lost in regular work, shift to a lower position for a period of time not longer than three months, prohibition of the occupation of an elective or responsible position in the given enterprise for a period of time not longer than six months, firing with or without deprivation of electoral rights in federal enterprises or organizations for a period of time, up to six months.

Again the court had the right to set also other punishments not provided in the Statue, but not heavier than those listed in it.

Although the Statute provided that, in setting the punishment, the court should keep in mind the "role of the disciplinary comrades' courts as a disciplinary-productional institution", the list of offenses in the competence and punishments applied, are obviously beyond the jurisdiction of a usual disciplinary court.

The disciplinary comrades' courts remained attached to trade-unions: the local courts... to district offices of trade-unions and the province comrades' courts to province councils of trade-unions.

Also the composition of the bench remained the same. The chairmen were appointed by the district office and the province council of trade-unions for the local and province courts, respectively. The other two members of the bench were elected : one by the directive organ of the group or local plant administration and the other-in general assemblies of union members of the enterprise or institutions involved in the case.

The provincial disciplinary comrades' courts functioned as an appellate instance for the decisions of the local desciplinary comrades' courts. It must be emphasized that with regard to sentences of comrades' courts, the general rule of excluding appeal and admitting cassation only of court decisions was abandoned : the complaint against the sentence of the first instance to the second is a full fledged appeal. The sentence is reviewed in its formal legality and merit with the repeating of the entire procedure in the court of second instance. We will see that this practice was not retained in the subsequent statute of comrades' courts.

Members of the bench of the provincial disciplinary comrades' courts were : a chairman, elected by the provincial council, and two members of which one was appointed by the province Council of People's Economy and the other was a member of the district disciplinary comrades court, serving in turn.

Another peculiarity was the attendance at the session of a member of the province council of people's judges with a consultative voice.

His presence can be explained by the necessity of having a jurist (although far not all judges were such, as we know) participate in the discussion of the case in the second instance.

Appeal had to be filed within three days after the pronunciation of the decision of the local court. The decision of the province disciplinary comrades' court was final and subject to immediate execution.

2. Further Legislation on Comrades' Courts

During the twenties the Comrades' Courts lost, together with their designation as disciplinary, their predominantly disciplinary character and enlarged their competence over petty offenses of a general character. [1]

Indeed, the Decision of the VTsIK and Council of People's Commissars "On Comrades' Courts at Factory and Plant Enterprises", "State and Public Institutions and Enterprises", of December 30, 1929 [2], resembles very little the Statutes of 1919 and 1921.

The Comrades' Courts were no longer attached to trade-unions, but to individual factories, plants and institutions and organized by regular courts. Their composition was quite different from the composition

---

[1] See the laws "On Comrades Courts at Factory & Plant Enterprises at State and Public Institutions" of Aug. 17, 1928 (*Sob. uz.*, RSFSR, 1928, Item 707); "On the Realization of the Experiment on the Enlargement or Rights and Duties of Lower Organs of Justice in the Experimental-Demonstrative Disputes" of Aug. 26, 1929 (*Sob. uz.*, RSFSR, 1929, Item 662).

[2] *Sob. uz.*, RSFSR, 1930, Item 52.

of the disciplinary comrades' courts : the bench consisted of a chairman and two members, all three elected by general assemblies of the conferences of workers and employees for six months of service. The general assemblies or conferences had the right to revoke the members of the comrades' courts any time.

The competence of the comrades' courts was extended to such offenses as insults inflicted orally, in writing or by action; spreading of false defamatory information without corporal injury; theft of money not over 25 rubles from workers and employees at enterprises or workers' dormitories; theft of material or work implements belonging to the enterprise valued not over 15 rubles.

Also civil suits involving not more than 25 rubles were brought under the competence of comrades' courts, with the exception of allimony and claims arising from work relations. The plaintiff could be any private person or public organization, but the defendant had to be a worker or employee of the enterprise or institution to which the court was attached.

Also in this decision the competence of the comrades's courts was not exhaustively established. It was said in the decision that "also other petty cases reflecting the daily negative sides of life", deriving from mischief, drunkenness, violation of dormitory rules, etc., come under the jurisdiction of the comrades' courts.

It is peculiar that included in the list of offenses examined by the comrades' courts was also the "accustoming of children to the use of alcohol by the grown-up persons". Evidently, the provision must have been prompted by the frequency of such use.

But the jurisdiction of comrades' courts at that time covered also some work discipline violation, such as showing up late for work, showing up for work not sober, incorrect handling of machines, etc. However, these offenses could be submitted to the comrades' courts only by the administration of the enterprise or institution itself or on the initiative or demand of public organizations or workers, if the administration did not object to the examination of the case by the comrades' court.

However, not more than one and one-half year later, the Decision of 1929 was superseded by a new Decision of the VTsIK and the RSFSR Council of People's Commissars "On Productional Comrades' Courts at Factories and Plants, State and Public Institutions and Enterprises of February 20, 1931. [1]

---

[1] *Sob. uz., RSFSR*, 1931, Item 160.

The scope of this Decision was again the attraction of large masses of workers and employees into the fight against the violation of labor discipline and disorganization of production at enterprises tending toward "remnants of the old life, such as drunkenness, etc, which undermine labor discipline".

Thus, also this Decision is an attempt to counter and prevent in the first place irregularities in the work of labor and employees in production.

This scope of the Decision is expressed in the renaming of the Comrades' courts into productional comrades' courts at factories, plants and state and public enterprises with not less than 100 workers and employees.

There was not much change in the jurisdiction of the productional comrades' courts, as compared with that of their predecessors. It extended to the violation of labor discipline on the one side and to improper and criminal behavior at work on the other. Repeated late showing up for work in a state of drunkenness or never sober, shifting from one enterprise to another without valid reasons, systematically negligent handling of socialist property as well as production of wastes over the allowed limit were the violations of labor discipline submitted for examination to the production comrades' courts.

The list of offenses of a general character under the jurisdiction of productional comrades' courts remained the same : insults, dissemination of false defamatory information, beating without producing corporal injury and hooliganism not requiring criminal prosecution.

A change was made with regard to theft. The value limit of the stolen goods established as within the competence of the court was increased from 15 to 50 rubles. In the same way, property disputes in which not more than 50 rubles were involved (the preceding limit was 15 rubles) could be examined by the court.

Restored was also the provision that other behavior not listed in the Decision, not conforming with requirements of a socialistic collective and reflecting "negative sides of life" could be examined by productional comrades' courts.

Disputes arising between subordinate persons and their superiors in an institution and between workers and a member of the administrative and technical personnel about relations resulting from work in the given institution or enterprise as well as suits concerning alimony and remuneration for work were also excluded from the competence of the productional comrades' courts in this Decision. [1]

Furthermore, the Decision contained a new limitation with regard to persons entitled to resort to the productional comrades' courts. These courts could only examine cases in which the parties were workers or employees of the same enterprize or institution or members of their families as well as persons although not workers at the given enterprize or institution, but living on the factory's or plant's premises.

Also when the parties were workers or employees of a different enterprize or institution in the same city or district, where productional comrades' courts were established, then the case could be examined by the court of the enterprise or institution where the defendant or the person involved with the offense were workers. Incidentally, when claims were directed against individual workers or employees by workers or employees of the same enterprise or institution, as well as by the administration of a public organization, both of the given enterprise or institution and also others, located in the territory of the city or the district, were competent to decide.

The composition of the bench remained the same : a chairman and two members serving in turn, and elected from among workers and employees at the enterprise at general assemblies for one year of service, subject to recall if they do not live up to the confidence put in them.

A peculiarity was the right of local factory and plant committees to challenge the election of individual court members. The court was not bound by any procedural rules.

The punitive right of the productional comrades' courts was limited to the following measures :

a) warning ;

b) public rebuff, published or not published in the wall newspaper or the general press ;

c) fine, not exceeding 10 rubles to the benefit of public organizations ;

d) obligation to make good the inflicted material damage, if it did not exceed 50 rubles ;

e) raising the question before the administration about the dismissal of the delinquent ;

f) raising the question before the trade-union about the exclusion of the culprit from the trade-union for a definite term.

---

[1] Specifically, labor disputes are settled by a labor dispute board, manned by an equal number of representatives of trade-unions and management at enterprises, institutions and organizations.

The most significant innovation was the finality of the decisions of the productional court, subject to immediate execution. No appeal or cassation was provided.

However, the People's Court had a kind of supervision over the activity of the productional comrades' court. If the people's judge discovered that the productional comrades' court decided over a case outside of its competence or exceeded its jurisdiction or in its decision substantially violated the law, he had the right to suspend the execution of the decision and take over the case for his own examination.

In this manner a kind of review of certain cases, reminiscent of the review of decisions and sentences already in force of general courts, was possible.

However, a return to the old pattern was realized in the sense that the direction of activities of the productional comrades' courts was entrusted to the All-Union Council of Trade-Unions along with RSFSR People's Commissariat of Justice. The local organs of these institutions realized the direction of the individual productional comrades' courts. Whereas, according to the Statute of 1929, both the supervision and the direction were in the hands of the RSFSR People's Commissariat of Justice.

Furthermore, in the Statute of 1929, in place of the People's judge the prosecuting body had to decide as to whether the comrades' courts had exceeded its jurisdiction or violated the law in its decision. It is this body which had the right to suspend the execution of the decision, which was also final, and to submit the case for examination to a regular court.

3. Comrades' Courts at Housing Units

In virtue of the Decision of the VTsIK and the RSFSR Council of People's Commissars of June 30, 1931, [1] comrades' courts were established at housing and house renting associations, as well as at housing trusts.

The scope of these comrades' courts was the attraction of wide masses of the population into independent action in the fight against the thriftless attitude toward the use of state, municipal or cooperative buildings and the settlement of housing disputes.

To this effect, comrades' courts were attached to housing and house-renting and cooperative associations, as well as housing trusts, inhabited by not less than one hundred persons.

---

[1] *Sob. uz., RSFSR*, 1931, Item 295.

The comrades' courts, numbering 10-25 members, were elected in general assemblies of the inhabitants who were in possession of electoral rights.

The bench of the court, consisting of a chairman and two members, serving in turn, had to decide on various kinds of disputes arising between the inhabitants of individual houses about the use of their common apartments and facilities.

However, besides these specific jurisdictions, the competence of these comrades' courts extended to some offenses of a general character, also examined by other comrades' courts, such as insults, thefts involving not more than 50 rubles, hooliganism, acts of arbitrary actions involving a damage of not more than 50 rubles and committed for the first time.

Similar to the other comrades' courts, disputes between the inhabitants and the management were excluded from the competence of the comrades' courts at housing units, as well as actions involving offenses also were outside the competence of comrades' courts.

The list of punishments meted out by the comrades' courts at housing units were similar to those set by other comrades' courts : warning rebuke, fine not over 10 rubles, obligation to make good the inflicted damage if it did not exceed 50 rubles.

Decisions of the court were final and subject to immediate execution.

Also in the case of these courts, if a people's court judge found a case in the files of the comrades' courts which was not within its competence, or discovered in the decision were substantial law violations or an excess of competence, he suspended the execution of the decision and took the case over for examination by the people's court.

4. *The Downfall of the Comrades' Courts*

Thirty years passed between the publication of the Statutes of 1931 and 1961. In the interval of time, the activity of the comrades' court came virtually to a standstill.

"Various reasons have been advanced by Soviet authors to explain the decline of the Comrades' Courts of the 1930's : the built-in weakness of the legislation, the absence of a single statute for all comrades' courts, the unclear and conflicting supervisory responsibilities for these bodies among state administrative agencies, the ambiguity in their relationship to the judiciary, the domination of their competence

resulting from the expansion of the scope of criminal law, the centralization of law enforcement in all-union hands", writes Albert Boiter. [1]

Certainly, all these reasons had affected the work of the comrades'
courts. But the main reason which brought the temporary uselessness
of the comrades' courts was the change in the economic life and the
political climate of the 30's.

Ideed, it was the time of forced industrialization and collectivation
under Stalin's iron fist.

Industrialization required from workers a strictness of labor discipline in order to insure the amount of necessary work and its quality,
which comrades' courts could not enforce. To this effect, a "court of
their own peers" was not sufficient. Hence, criminal punishments
were set for the violation of labor discipline which were steadily
increased. Already, a special law "On the Fight Against
Shirking Work" of April 27, 1920 [2] sent to concentration camps
workers who shirked work less than 3 days and did not compensate
the loss by working overtime or on holidays. And shirking work more
than 3 days within one month made the worker responsible before a
disciplinary court under the accusation of sabotage. But the Ukase
of the Presidium of the USSR Supreme Soviet of June 26, 1940 [3]
provided that shirking work without "valid" reasons is punishable
by the people's court with corrective labor up to six months and the
loss of up to 25 % of wages at the place of work.

The same law sent to jail for 2-4 months workers and employees who
arbitrarily left work.

With regard to the preservation of state property, the law of August
7, 1932 [4] introduced the death penalty for its violation. As Berman
and Spindler put it : "prior to Stalin's death many of the offences
that are now subject to the sanctions of Comrades' Courts were
severly punishable as crimes in the regular courts". [5]

Furthermore, in the thirties, the worst period of Stalin's dictatorship,
there was certainly no place for such liberal notion as the people's
participation in the administration of justice although advocated
by Lenin himself. It is only natural that Vyshinsky, Stalin's henchman

---

[1] Albert Boiter, "Comradly Justice : How Durable is it ?" *Problems of Communism*,
March-April 1965, p. 86.

[2] *Sob. uz., RSFSR.* 1920, Item 172.

[3] *V.V.S., SSSR*, 1940, July 5th.

[4] *Sob. zak., SSSR*, 1932, Item 360.

[5] H. Berman and J. W. Spindler, "Soviet Comrades' Courts", (38) *Wash. Law
Review*, 1936, No. 4, p. 845.

in the administration of justice, disclosed in a speech addressed to
the Ukrainian prosecutors that "the old twaddle about the mobilization
of social active workers, of aid groups... all that must be put aside,
something new is needed at the present time". [1] These words were
interpreted by local authorities, according to A. Vinberg, G. Kocharev
and G. Minkovskiy as a directive of the USSR Prosecutor "to remove
public participation from the activity of strengthening the Soviet
legal order". [2]

If the interpretation is correct, these assertions Vyshinsky made in
1936 in the atmosphere of the starting "great trials" is still a departure
from his own opinion expressed only two years before. In 1934, namely,
he published a monograph on the "Marx-Lenin Teaching on Courts
and the Soviet Judicial System", in which he quoted Lenin's words
that... "courts under the condition of participation in them of the
widest masses of the working and exploited population will be achieved,
in conformance with the Soviet power and in democratic forms, that
the desire of discipline and self-discipline should not remain a desire
only". [3]

It goes without saying that in citing Lenin, Vyshinsky wanted to
express his adherence to the same opinion. The comrades' courts
were just the courts, set within the scope of promoting and preserving
labor discipline, in order to attract wide masses of the population to
the task of meting out justice. To call this Lenin's cherished principle
"old twaddle" is a serious offence against Lenism, which can be
explained only by the new requirements of the "cult of personality"
period.

5. Revival of the Comrades' Courts

But, *tempora mutantur*. Stalin died in 1953 and with him the
so-called "cult of personality". The XXI and XXII Congresses of
the Soviet Union Communist Party revived the interest in public
participation in the administration of justice. The Statute of 1961
brought new life and increased importance to the comrades' courts.

---

[1] A. Ya. Vyshinsky, "Up the Banner of Socialist Legality", *Sots. zak.*, 1936,
No. 11, p. 7.

[2] A. Vinberg, G. Kocharev and G. Minkovsky, "Against Vyshinsky's Vicious Theories in Soviet Criminal Procedure", *Sots. zak.*, 1962, No. 3, p. 18.

[3] Lenin XXII 425; A. Ya. Vyshinsky, *Marksistsko-leninskoye ucheniye o sude i
sovetskaya sudebnaya sistema*, M. 1934, p. 33.

It was Khrushchev who initiated the return to an increased public participation in the administration of justice. Already at the XXth Congress of the USSR Communist Party (1956) Khrushchev declared that the creation of such conditions are necessary that persons violating norms of behavior and principles of Soviet morals should feel the blame of their actions by the entire society. [1]

At the XXI Congress of the Soviet Union Communist Party, in 1959, Khrushchev declared that more attention should be paid to comrades' courts. When the Soviet comrades' courts will actively function and society itself will single out persons for the protection of public order, then it will be much easier to fight violations. It will be possible to identify such a violator not only when he already committed the misdemeanor or the crime, but when he will produce signs of deviation from the norms of social behavior, which might bring him to anti-social actions. People may in good time influence him in order to suppress his evil inclinations... The main thing is that this is prophylactic treatment, educational work. [2]

Thus, Khrushchev underlined the preventive character of comrades' courts. He thought that the jurisdiction of these courts should extend not only to questions of behavior on the job but also to apparent incorrect and immoral conduct of everyday life.

Khrushchev was persuaded that "the Soviet public can cope with the violators of socialist legal order. Our social organization has no less possibilities, means and power to this effect than the organs of military courts and prosecutors". [3]

In his report to the XXIth Congress Khrushchev declared that comrades' courts have to examine not only productional questions but also problems of conditions of life and morals, facts of irregular behavior of members of the collectives, permitting themselves deviations from norms of the social order. [4]

According to the accepted Soviet patterns, also Khrushchev explained, "the deviations" by bourgeois survival and influence. Khrushchev turned against those Soviet officials who underestimate the

---

[1] *XX S"ezd Kommunisticheskoy partii Sovetskogo Soyuza, Stenografichesky otchet*, M. 1956, p. 95.

[2] *Vneocherednoy XXI S"ezd Kommunisticheskoy partii Sovetskogo Soyuzd. Stenograficheskiy otchet*, M. 1959, p. 104.

[3] N. S. Khrushchev, *O kontrol'nykh tsifrakh razvitiya narodnogo khozyaystva SSSR, na 1959-1965 gg*, M. 1959, p. 211.

[4] *Ibid.*, p. 122.

end of bourgeois influence on Soviet young people. "We cannot ignore the possibility of bourgeois influence and must struggle against it, against the penetration of foreign opinions and customs into Soviet surroundings, especially in the midst of young people". [1]

Upon Khrushchev's report, the XXIst Congress of the USSR Communist Party passed the following resolution : "In matters of compliance with rules of socialist common life, the people's militia, comrades' courts and other similar organizations are called upon to play an increasingly important role in fulfilling the functions of public order and the preservation of citizens' rights, as well as the preservation of actions detrimental to society, alongside state institutions". [2]

Khrushchev said at the electoral meeting of the Kalininskiy Electoral District of February 24, 1959 that the attraction of great masses of the working population into the process of production will be a "preparatory step" of the further development of Soviet socialist democracy to the highest goal, when, according to V.I. Lenin's definition—all persons will learn to rule and will nearly independently control all the affairs of society. [3]

Thus, the XXI Congress, on Khrushchev's initiative, returned to the path indicated by Lenin : the takeover by social organizations of some functions of the state, especially of the judicial ones. On this path, the people have to be educated according to Lenin, in a manner that every man will learn how to control independently all the affairs of society, so that the state may wither away.

The people's squads, the comrades' courts and the anti-parasite legislation are the products of the movement on this path. When the replacement of the judicial by social institutions will be achieved, the remnants of bourgeois mentality will disappear and Soviet citizens will allegedly commit no crime not because out of fear of punishment but in compliance with communist morals.

Thus, the principal scopes of comrades' courts are of a prophylactic and educational character : the preparation for the future paradisiacal conditions.

---

[1] *Ibid.*, p. 63-64.

[2] *Resolutsiya XXI S'ezda Kommunisticheskoy partii Sovetskogo Soyuza po dokladu N.S. Khrushcheva O kontrol'nykh tsifrakh narodnogo khozyaystva SSSR, na 1959-1965 gody*, M. 1959, p. 29.

[3] N. S. Khrushchev, *Rech' na sobranii izbirateley Kalininskogo izbiratel'nogo okruga*, M. 1959, p. 71.

Thus K.S. Yudel'son defines comrades' courts in the practical text-book on comrades' courts as follows : "Comrades' courts represent elective social organs, called to contribute actively to the education of citizens in the spirit of communist attitude toward socialist property, compliance with rules of socialist-communist life, development of a sense of collectivism and comradely mutual help, consideration, dign-ity and honor..." [1]

6. *The Statute of 1961*

On July 3, 1961, the Presidium of the RSFSR Supreme Soviet confirmed the Statute on Comrades' Courts. [2]

At the same time, the resolution of the RSFSR VTsIK and the Sovnarkom on the Organization of Comrades' Courts at Housing and Housing-Renting Cooperative Associations and House Trusts was abrogated. Thus, the Statute of 1961 extended to all kinds of comrades' courts.

This Statute extensively describes the essence and scope of comrades' courts. These courts, according to the Statute, are elective public organs, called to contribute actively to the education of citizens in the spirit of communist attitude toward work, socialist property, compliance with rules of socialist common life, development of feelings of collectivism and comradely mutual help, and respect of citizens' dignity and honor.

The main scope of comrades' courts' activity is the prevention of law violations and offences damaging society, education of people by means of persuasion and social influence, and creation of conditions intolerant of any antisocial activity.

Thus, the educational and prophylactic and not the punitive scope of the comrades' courts is stressed by the Statute.

The Statute returns to the purely elective principle. The comrades' courts are elected in a general assembly of the workers and employees of the enterprises, institutions and organizations at which they function. The number of workers and employees of these enterprises, institutions or organizations must be not under 50 persons.

There is nothing peculiar in the nomination procedure of the candidates to members of the comrades' courts. It is the usual procedure followed in the elections in the Soviet Union : candidates are proposed

---

[1] K. S. Yudel'son, *Prakticheskoye posobiye dlya tovarishcheskikh sudov*, M. 1961, p. 12.
[2] *V.V.S., RSFSR*, 1961, Item 371.

by communist cells or with their approval and one candidate for every position appears on the ballot and is elected in the general assembly by majority of votes for a period of two years.

The elected members of the comrades' courts chose among them the chairman, his deputy and a secretary.

The comrades' courts function at enterprises, institutions, organizations, secondary and special institutions of learning, kolkhozes, houses serviced by housing operation offices, house administrations or such united by street committees, as well as in rural populated places and settlements.

Members of comrades' courts, as the members of regular courts, have to render account about their activity to the electorate and may be recalled before their time if their activity is deemed unsatisfactory and replaced by other members.

A case can be initiated before a comrades' court : 1) on representation of a factory, plant and local committee of trade-unions; voluntary people's squads for the protection of the public order; street, house, district, block committees and other public organizations and citizens' assemblies; 2) on representation of executive committees of local Soviets and permanent commission of Soviets; 3) on communications of state organs, chiefs of enterprises, institutions, organizations and boards of kolkhozes; 4) on the bases of materials presented by courts, provinces, as well as by an inquest organ with permission of a prosecutor; 5) on a declaration of citizens; 6) on the initiative of the comrades' courts itself.

The decrease of the punitive character of the comrades' courts as compared with the foregoing statutes is clearly expressed in the enumeration of punishments inflicted by the comrades' court according to the new Statute. Forced labor, concentration camps, firing from the job, disappeared from the list of punishments in the new statute. The punishments are limited to : 1) the obligation of public excuses before the victim or the collective; 2) the expression of comradely warning; 3) the expression of a social rebuke; 4) the expression of a social reproof, published or not published in the press; 5) fines, not exceeding ten rubles if the offence is not combined with the violation of labor discipline; 6) raising the question before the management of the enterprise, institution or organization about the application of the following two measures, in accordance with the labor legislation in force : [1] the transfer of the culprit to work at a remunerated lower rate or to a lower position.

Since the Statute of 1961 which also cover the activities of the housing comrades' courts the following specific punishment may be meted out by the court : the eviction of the culprit from his apartment if a common life with others is made impossible or because of his predatory treatment of the apartment, or malicious non-payment of the rent.

As a general provision, 8), the court may, besides the punitive measures under 1-7, oblige the culprit to compensate the damage-caused by the illegal action up to the amount of 50 rubles. [2]

Another liberalizing provision of the Statute not known to the previous Statutes is that the court may, after the public examination of the case, abstain from any punitive measures described above, if the culprit will frankly repent and present his excuses to the collective or the victim and will voluntarily compensate the damage.

Also, the Statute of 1961 extended the competence of the comrades' courts to decide on cases of shirking from work without excuse or reason, being late for work, or leaving work before the proper time; poor completion of work, or idle standing as a consequence of an unscrupulous attitude toward one's duties; non-compliance with rules on security technique and other regulations of labor protection, except cases involving criminal responsibility; damage to the equipment, tools or material as a result of carelessness.

The extent of comrades' court jurisdiction in disciplinary cases was greatly enlarged by the Presidium of the USSR Supreme Soviet of April 15, 1956 by the Decision "On the Abolition of Court Responsibility of Workers and Employers for Arbitrary Leaving of Enterprises and Institutions and for Shirking From Work Without Valid Reasons". [3]

All these cases, not more criminally punishable, were referred to the comrades' courts.

The second group of offenses pertains to the behavior of the culprit: unworth behavior in state of drunkness at work and public places, as well as with regard to women and parents; non-fulfillment of educational duties toward children; insults, the dissemination of expressions disgracing members of the collective if these actions are

---

[1] This means that the curtailing of remuneration and the assignment to a lower position must not contradict provisions of the Code of Labor.

[2] The measures 1-8 are enumerated in Art. 15 of the Statute.

[3] *V.V.S., SSSR*, 1956, Item 203. This was the abrogation of the labor law of June 26, 1940, mentioned above, with its drastic criminal punishments.

committed for the first time, and ribaldry; damage to trees and other green plants; damage to habitable and unhabitable places, and communal equipment if the losses were not substantial; violation of the internal order in apartments and dormitories; disputes of tenants about the use of subsidiary locations, out-buildings, the payment of communal services and the order of use of land plots between joint owners of housing; property disputes between members of the same collective involving not more than 50 rubles, when the parties agree to submit the case to the comrades' court; other anti-social actions not involving criminal responsibility; administrative and other petty offenses if organs of the militia, prosecuting body or the court deem it necessary to submit such cases to the examination of the comrades' courts.

Article 5, Paragraph 9 of the 1961 Statute confers the right to the comrades' court to examine "other anti-social actions which do not involve criminal responsibilty".

Excluded from the competence of comrades' courts are criminal and civil cases in which sentences or decisions have been already pronounced by other courts.

In taking its decision, the comrades' court must be guided by legislation in force, by the Statute and its sense of social duty. [1]

But that is not all. The bench of the comrades' court has also to consider the opinion of the people present at a session in taking its decision, which sessions ordinarily take place at the plant, factory, apartment office, etc., where the culprit is working or leaving, although no provision on this is included in the Statute. The bench must, in the development of its decision, explain, according to the comments to the Statute in the *Sovetskaya justitsiya*, how it arrived at a milder or stronger decision in comparison to that demanded by the speaker in the audience, since the decision must be a product of the entire collective represented by the comrades' court. [2] Since the assembly participates in the examination and discussion of the offence and the offender, the court has to take into consideration the opinions given by the persons who engaged in the discussion. For, under the provision of Art. 11 of the Statute, persons "attending the session may, with the permission of the court, ask questions and speak on the merits of the case examined by the court".

---

[1] The sense of social duty replaces the revolutionary and socialist consciousness of Soviet first-period legislation, in those cases.

[2] *Sov. yust.*, 1961, No. 21, p. 20.

It must be emphasized that those speaking in court are not public prosecutors or counsels sent to sessions of the regular courts by collectives. The comrades' court, itself, is an organ of the collective and every member of the collective has the right to come forward and express his opinion on the case.

It is peculiar that the number of judges on the bench is not exactly established by the Statute. Article II provides that "a case is examined publicly by no less than three members of the comrades' court". "Usually there are three of them : a chairman and two members of the court", writes Yudel'son. [1] It is not said in the Statute who sets the number of judges on the bench, but it may certainly occur that this number is an even one, and since decisions are taken by a majority of votes of judges participating in the examination, an equal split of the voices is possible. What then ? Yudel'son thinks that "in case of an equal split, the decision must be in favor of the accused. Thus, for instance, if two members of the court think that the law violation took place and the remaining two deny it, the difference in opinion must be interpreted in the sense that the charged violation is not established. [2]

Berman and Spindler in their comment on the Statute do not take a position on the question.

The Statute provides a particular remedy against the decision of the comrades' court, which is in principle final : if the decision contradicts the circumstances of the case or the legislation in force, the corresponding factory-plant-or local committee of the trade union or the executive committee of the local soviet has the right to ask the comrades' court to examine the case a second time (Art. 18).

Thus, the provision of Art. 18 is a major change from the previous Statutes, since the referral of the judgment as to whether the decision of the comrades' court contradicts the circumstances of the case or the legislation in force means a decision on the merits of the sentence by institutions [3] having nothing to do with the administration of justice and have no staff trained for the taking of such a decision.

We have seen that, according to the previous statutes, the people's

---

[1] K. S. Yudel'son, *Polozheniye o tovarishcheskikh sudakh*, M. 1962, p. 158-159.

[2] Yudel'son, *op. cit.*, p. 163. This is an analogy to the provision of tsarist law that if jurors equally divided their twelve voices, the verdict was pronounced in favor of the accused.

[3] As we know, the decision permitting the review of a social sentence belonged to the functions of the people's judges or the prosecuting body according to foregoing Statutes on Comrades' Courts.

judges [1] or the prosecuting body were in charge of such functions. However, the prosecuting body may use its right of general supervision also with regard to comrades' courts.

Furthermore, the decision on the retrail of the case may be passed by two different organizations: factory, plant and local committees of trade unions or the executive committee of the local Soviet. What happens if a trade union committee refuses to remand the case, may the executive committee take a contradictory decision and vice-versa? The wording of Art. 18 seems to admit such a possibility, since both institutions enjoy the same right on an equal footing. [2]

Still, there is also another way to bring the case to a retrial. If, namely, a sentence of the comrades' court imposing damages, a fine or another material exaction is not fulfilled at time, the chairman of the comrades' court has to direct the case to a people's judge for execution, since the comrades' court has no means to enforce the sentence. The people's judge has then to check the material of the case and the legality of the sentence. If he is satisfied he issues a writ of execution which is carried out by the marshall of the court.

But, if in the opinion of the people's judge, the decision of the comrades' court is illegal, he rejects the petition for a writ of execution in a resolution substantiated by reasons made known to the comrades' court and the corresponding trade-union committee or executive committee of the local Soviet for the decision on the re-examination of the case (Art. 19).

In this way, a judicial review of a decision imposing material sanctions takes place if the offender does not submit voluntarily to the decision of the comrades' court.

Furthermore, if according to Art. 5 (6) of the Statute, the comrades' court decides to suggest the transfer of the offender to a position remunerated at a lower rate or to a lower position, this has to be done according to regulations in force.

As Bilinsky remarks, this means that the lowering of remuneration or position may be done only in accordance with the labor legislation in force, which gives the right to the offender to protest such actions to the people's court which will have to review the decision of the

---

[1] In their comments to Art. 18 of the 1961 Statute, Berman & Spindler correctly remark that "finality" in Soviet legal parlance does not connote irrevocability, but only means that there is no right of appeal to a higher agency of the same type".

[2] Berman and Spindler do not discuss the eventuality. Also Soviet writers do not take a position on the question.

comrades' court, providing another case of judicial review of a comrades' court's decision. [1]

Also the supervision of the comrades' court is divided between the two institutions, however, with regard to different comrade's courts. The factory, plant and local committees of trade-unions carry out the supervision of comrades' courts at enterprises, institutions, organizations, higher and secondary special institutions of learning, whereas the supervision of comrades' courts at kolkhozes, housing and rural inhabited places is in the hands of the executive committees of local Soviets.

The Statute contains no provision on the supervision of comrades' courts activities as did the previous statutes.

"The main thing in the work of Comrades' courts... reads Art. 1 of the 1961 Statute... is the prevention of law violations and acts damaging to society, education of people by persuasion and social influence, creation of conditions of intolerance to any anti-social action..." [2]

In the 1961 program of the USSR Communist Party it is said that "the activity of social organization must be extended in matters of strengthening of public order, especially to people's volunteer squads and comrades' courts. [3]

b) *Village Social Courts*

The creation of new courts was extended to the rural areas. On 29 September 1930, the Presidium of the Central Executive Committee decided to organize village courts. [4]

The scope of these courts established by a federal law was the realization of the well-known principles of bringing the court nearer to the population and the attraction into court work of wide working masses, but also the alleviation of people's courts of the examination of petty criminal and civil cases.

Village courts were established on the territory of village (or units corresponding to them) Soviets. They were composed of a chairman and

---

[1] Andreas Bilinsky, "Kameradschaftsgerichte in der UdSSR", *Osteuropa-Recht*, 1962, No. 4, p. 322.

[2] K. S. Yudel'son, in *Prakticheskoye posobiye dlya tovarishcheskikh sudov*, M. 1961 p. 12.

[3] *Programma i ustav KPSS*, M. 1964, p. 183.

[4] *Sob. zak., SSSR*, 1930, Item 531.

his deputies elected by the plenum of the village or its counterpart council from among its members and confirmed by the district executive committee, and people's assessors, elected in general assemblies of village citizens who were in possession of electoral rights according to the Constitution and confirmed by the plenum of the village council.

The jurisdiction of the village court extended to cases of :

a) violations of public security and order, rules preserving public health, hooliganism; slander, insults inflicted orally, in writing or by actions, beatings without causing corporal injury;

b) property disputes involving not more than 50 rubles, claims for payment of established alimony for the maintenance of children, cases of indisputable claims for alimony not connected with the establishment of paternity, as well as cases of distribution of land and the right to its working use;

c) labor disputes over work involving not more than 25 rubles, over the payment of overtime and over professional clothing.

The punitive power of village courts included : *a*) warning, public rebuke with publication of it in the press or announcement at the village assembly, or without them; *b*) fines not exceeding 10 rubles used for general cultural measures of local importance, or for the needs of individual local and public organizations; *c*) forced labor not longer than for 5 days.

A peculiar provision was that if the court established that an agreement concluded by the parties before the examination of the case by the courts considerably violated the interests of a working person involved in the case, it had to examine the case on its merits and pronounce a decision ignoring the concluded agreement. This provision tended to protect from exploitation persons not experienced in legal matters.

The decisions of village courts were final and not subject to appeal, but could be set aside in the way of court supervision by the people's court, which carried out supervision over the village courts. The supervision of its activity belonged to the people's court and the prosecuting body.

It is obvious that the village courts, according to their scope (the alleviation of the burden of people's courts), composition (people's assessors), jurisdiction (cases of alimony claims), excluded by previous Statutes on Comrades' Courts, are general courts and not comrades' courts at all (The word "comrades" is not mentioned a single time in the Decision). Furthermore, the decision charges the central executive of the Union Republics to organize at village soviets, village courts for the examination of civil and criminal cases, the character of which is defined by stated provisions. [1]

However, something very strange occurred. The VTsIK and the RSFSR Council of People's Commissars, in fulfillment of the TsIK's decision of Sept. 29, 1930, passed a Decision [2] on Oct. 10, 1930, differing in principle from the federal law.

In place of general village courts, village social courts were installed in the RSFSR.

The social character of the court is not only underlined in its name, but also in its provisions. Although, for example, the chairman of the court and his deputies are elected by the village Soviet to which the court is attached, and the "social judges" (not people's assessors) are elected at general assemblies of citizens in possession of electoral rights according to the RSFSR Constitution, in the same way as provided in the federal law, candidates for the election to social judges are nominated by the local organization of trade-unions, groups of laborers, the poorest population, delegate assemblies of female workers and peasants, committees of peasant's mutual aid societies, as well as by other organizations and individual citizens in possession of electoral rights.

With regard to alimony claims, also spouses were entitled to sue one another for alimony before the village courts.

The jurisdiction of the RSFSR Village Social Courts was enlarged to include disputes concerning land in which the parties are individual households or citizens without limit of the amount involved in the dispute if the dispute did not originate during the organization of land exploitation. These disputes were settled by the village soviet and district executive committees.

A special provision of the RSFSR law excluded from the competence of the village social courts, land disputes in which at least one party was a land society, agricultural collective, state institution or enterprise, cooperative or other public organization and referred these disputes to the jurisdiction of people's courts.

Thus, the village social courts were a kind of comrades' courts for the rural population.

This discrepancy between the federal law which installed village

---

[1] These provisions were mentioned above.

[2] *Sob. uz., RSFSR*, 1930, Item 629.

courts and the RSFSR legisleation which set up village social courts has not been commented on by soviet or American writers. [1] The village social courts were abrogated when the Statute on Courts of 1961 was promulgated.

C. Pro and Contra

Every court has prophylactic and educational scopes. Every sentence serves to prevent the criminal from repeating and other people from committing the action for which a just punishment is set. By meting out justice every court educates people in the sense of compliance with and obediance to law.

But a court is essentially and first of all a place where justice is meted out. The prophylactic and educational effects are duly correlatives of the sentence. The more just the sentence, the greater its prophylactic and educational influence.

Also comrades' courts are called upon to examine offenses or claims of citizens and to decide upon them. They fulfill, thus, the main function of every court, despite some dissimilarities with the work of other courts. Also these prophylactic and educational values are in direct relation to the quality of the decisions.

In order to mete out justice adequately a court must be put in condition to do so. Since the comrades' court has to be guided in its decisions by law, the members of the court have to know the substantive law to apply, and the preservation of which is the first duty of the comrades' courts as is true of any courts. Whereas in a regular court, one person on the bench is (or should be) a jurist, all three (or more) persons on the bench of the comrades' court are lay judges, for they are elected from working members and employees of plants, factories, housing or organizations, kolkhozes etc, which very seldom have, as it may be assumed, jurists on their staffs.

But, also procedural laws are applied by the comrades' courts, although efforts have been made to simplify the procedure as far as possible and provide the comrades' courts with a social and not judicial character. For instance, the offender is not called "an accused",

---

[1] See for instance, Harold J. Berman, "Soviet Comrades' Courts", *Wash. Law Review* (38) Winter 1963, No. 4, or Albert Baxter, "Comradely Justice, How Durable is It ?" *Problems of Communism*, March-April 1965.

the public has not to stand up when the members of the bench appear in the hall, the decision is not pronounced in the name of the republic, etc. Still, in matters of witnesses and experts, interrogation and evaluation of evidence, etc, as in civil suits, the comrades' courts have to observe the norms of civil procedure.

A deviation from the rules of criminal procedure is the carrying out of a kind of preliminary investigation by one of the members of the future bench (Art. 10) if the case requires a check of the prosecution material. Thus, investigative functions are combined with judicial ones. Usually, the material of the case prepared for the court session is submitted to all members of the court bench.

The tendency of avoiding similarity with regular courts in comrades' courts is underlined by K.P. Gorshenin, who argues against the composition of the bench of comrades' courts by three members of the court. For Gorshenin it reminds too much of the state people's court where the chairman sits in the center flanked by two people's assessors. "And why not four or five should compose the bench of a comrades' court. Why adher to form established long ago and create psychologically a situation of state court activity", asks Gorshenin. [1]

He would also like to restrict the activity of the comrades' court members to one year, in order to attract more and more people to the functions of comrades' court members.

Certainly, why not four or five members on the bench of comrades' courts ? But why not three ? To argue against this number because the bench of regular courts consists of three members is not convincing. When Rakhunov pleads for the increase of the number of people's assessors on the bench that is undisputable because as more assessors the less the possibility of being influenced by the professional judge. But, on the bench of comrades' courts sit only lay judges. Usually an odd number of judges is put on the bench, in order to create a majority for the sentence. *"Tres faciunt collegium"*—asserted the Romans.

With regard to the term of service of members of comrades' courts, a two year term is preferable because of the possibility of training and acquiring a certain experience on the job.

---

[1] K. P. Gorshenin, "Participation of the Public in the Fight against Law Breaking, Further Development of Soviet Democracy", in *Sovetskaya obshchestvennost'na strage sotsialisticheskoy zakonnosti*, M. 1960, p. 148.

Gorkin sees the educational influence of comrades' courts as the main value of their activity. [1]

The call for legality is clearly heard in the Statute on Comrades' Courts. So Article 14 of the Statute is categorical to this effect. It reads : "The comrades' court, in the examination of the case and its decision, is guided by legislation in force, the present Statute and the sense of social duty."

In his commentary to Art. 14, Yudel'son remarks that "Examining cases of law violations the members of the court must be guided first of all by corresponding laws; the same is true for decisions about property disputes among citizens". [2]

An abnormal situation is created every time lay judges are called upon to decide legal questions. We have emphasized it with regard to people's assessors. [3] But the assessors have at least the guidance of the professional judge whereas the bench of the comrades' courts consists of laymen only. It is true that the legal questions with which the comrades' courts deal, and only in a part of cases of their jurisdiction, are often uncomplicated, but still recrimination of the Soviet legal press against the adequacy of the elected members of the comrades' court for the performance of their duties are comprehensible.

But not always the lack of juridical knowledge is denounced. Savitsky and Keyserov, for instance, wrote that the authority of the comrades' courts and the prosecuting of its decisions depends greatly upon the fact, how far the collective esteems the members of the court and trusts them. Therefore, the local trade-union committees must select and recommend to the general assembly for election to membership of comrades' courts persons really worthy and esteemed : shock workers of production, activists, members of squads of communist work". [4]

An effort in the right direction is made to instruct members of comrades' courts in legal matters, which resembles measures taken with regard to people's assessors in this respect. At many factories and plants, seminars for members of the comrades' courts are organized.

---

[1] A. F. Gorkin, "On the Problems of Soviet Court in the Period of Intensive Construction of Communism", in *Sovetskaya obshehestvennost'na strazhe sotsialisticheskoy zakonnosti*, M. 1960, p. 92.

[2] Yudel'son, *op. cit.*, p. 166.

[3] See pp. 336-372 of this book.

[4] M. Savistky and N. M. Keizerov, "The Development of Legal Forms of Comrades' Courts Organization and Activity", *S.G.P.*, 1961, No. 4, p. 46.

Prominent in this action is the People's University in Sverdlovsk which organized courses for the members of comrades' courts lasting an entire year. The initiative of the Sverdlovsk Legal Institute, named after A. Ya Vyshinsky, must attract attention.

In order to disseminate knowledge of legal matters among the population, and social organizations active in the legal field, the University has organized a public university of legal knowledge with three special faculties : 1) the faculty of soviet structure; 2) the faculty for commanders of voluntary people's squads and 3) a faculty for chairmen of comrades' courts. Furthermore, a series of lectures, open to everyone, is being delivered.

No tuition is required. The students, however, must punctually attend lectures and pass examinations. A certificate of graduation is provided at the end of the one-year course.

The program of the faculty of chairmen of comrades' courts consists of lectures (60 hours) and discussions on labor laws, and basic principles of criminal, civil and administrative law. The scope of the teaching is not only to make the students acquainted with the basic principle of these institutes, but essentially to clarify the most important provisions and the applications of them in deciding the various categories of cases now under the jurisdiction of comrades' courts.

Besides questions of substantive law, 16 hours are dedicated to the procedure employed in comrades' courts.

It is also projected to arrange for moot sessions of comrades' courts under the chairmanship of one of the students, and discuss the results. [1]

V. Moroshinin reports on a discussion in which chairmen and members of the comrades' courts, party workers of local soviets, professors of the Public University of Legal Knowledge at the Sverdlovsk Legal Institute and members of the courts, prosecuting body and the bar, took part. [2]

However, the members of the comrades' courts are elected for one year only, so that the end of their judical activity corresponds with the end of the course, and they leave the court just at the moment they seem to be best prepared for the activity there. The decision to give access to a possibly greater number of people to the administration of justice caused the reduction of a two-year service as a member

---

[1] N. Semenov, and V. Yakushev, "The Public University of Legal Knowledge", *Sov. yust.*, 1960, No. 4, p. 15-16, A. Belinsky, *op. cit.*, p. 323.

[2] Moroshinin, "It was an Interesting Encounter", *Sov. yust.*, 1962, No. 3, p. 22.

of the comrades' court, provided in the 1954 draft of the Statute of 1961. [1] The curtailment of two-year term to a one-year term seems most unfortunate for the task of legal instruction to the court members.

An attempt toward the improvement of work of the comrades' court is the creation of councils of chairmen of comrades' courts.

The scope of these councils is to assist the executive committees of the city Soviet and the trade-union committees to insure control of activities of comrades' courts; the organization of chairmen and members of comrades' courts assemblies for discussion of questions pertaining to the application of the Statute on Comrades' Courts and exchange of experiences in the work of these courts.

This project also provides for the organization of seminars and moot court sessions.

The project was generated in the port of Makhachkala in which 130 comrades' courts are at work, and approved by the local administration.

The council received the right to check the work of the individual courts at enterprises, institutions and organizations, as well as street committees, and to inform the executive committee about its findings.

The council of chairmen of comrades' courts is an organization elected by the general assembly of all the members of the comrades' courts of the city for one year, and works under the immediate guidance of the executive committee and the trade-union organs and is accountable to them.

Legal assistence to the council is provided by the people's court. [2]

Another interesting undertaking is the Public Councils in the Comrades' Court's Work. [3] These councils have been established in all districts of Moscow. They consist of 15 to 30 members. Among these members are many jurists : prosecutors, advocates and justices (about 25 % - 35 %) and representatives of trade-unions. They were formed by executive committees of district soviets, without an active participation of the trade-unions.

The scope of the councils is to help the executive committees in the guidance of comrades' courts and the organization of the legal education of the members of the comrades' courts and the information on the legislation in force.

---

[1] On the same ground the duration of the service of the people's assessors was shortened from three to two years.

[2] Yu. Istomin, "The Council of Comrades' Courts Chairmen", *Sov. yust.*, 1962, No. 4, p. 25.

[3] See M. Postnikov, A. Selivanov, "To Perfection the Guidance of Comrades' Courts, *Sov. yust.*, 1965, No. 8, p. 8 ff.

On assignment of the executive committees, the councils examine complaints against the work of the comrades' courts in a session in which the chairman of the given comrades' court and the plaintiff participate. The council takes a decision on the case which is presented to the executive committee. Also the authors underline that the work of comrades' courts has many defects in all its stages, beginning with the preparation of the case up to the pronouncing of the decision.

Some jurists are of the opinion that the public councils on the work of comrades' courts are completely superfluous since the district soviet have commissions on socialist legality. Others oppose this opinion arguing that the work of the public councils on comrades' courts, if transferred to the commissions of socialist legality would take all the time of the latter, not leaving a possibility for other work which the commissions on socialist legality are charged.

Certainly, in all cases of disciplinary violations, relations between apartment tenants etc, only a minimum of legal notion is required from the comrades' courts.

On the other hand, it cannot be denied that a court of his own peers held at his place of work of the delinquent, in the presence of his comrades at work can have a substantially preventive and educational value with regard to first time culprits. For a sensitive person to be tried in the presence of his companions of every day work must be much more embarassing than in a criminal court, before an occasional and strange public.

"In contemporary conditions when hooliganism, spongers, thieves and other criminals still exist, we cannot and must not weaken the legal impact on these people. Manners of social influence must complement but not replace the work of the militia, prosecuting body, court and other state organs. The work of comrades' courts should only supplement but not replace the activity of the regular organs of administration of justice". [1]

Grishayev sees in the comrades' courts a program of public independent activity directed toward the strengthening of soviet legality and legal order and at the same time an insurance of the individual's security and preservation of his rights.

---

[1] N. Zhogin and V. Kudryavtsev, "Law and Morals in Our Society", *Pravda*, Sept. 21, 1966.

Also he emphasizes the preventive and educational importance of comrades' courts. [1]

Answering the questions as to whether the institution of comrades' courts is a just one, Albert Boiter thinks that "one might perhaps say that as long as one disregards such bourgeois prejudices as the right to privacy or non-conformity, and assuming a stable climate of legality (which is hardly the case today) there is nothing inherently wicked or unjust in it. Indeed the attempt to bring the comrades' courts in lines with the existing law codes might even be described as a step in the right direction". [2]

Other American writers are even more constrained in their appraisal of comrades' courts. Thus, according to Fainsod, "The support of comrades' court in which culprits were judged by fellow workers without the possibility of judicial appeal from their verdicts marked a definite retreat from legality", [3] although he admits that the educational effect of comrades' courts is heightened to the extent that "the sentences imposed appear to derive not from management but from workers themselves". [4] And, for instance, Azrael, asserts that "the strengthening of 'public organizations'... forms the basis of Soviet claims of achieving a transition from 'punitive' to 'prophylactic' coercion... what is involved in 'prophylasos' is not a relaxation of pressure but a fundamental assault on all aspects of privacy including those which are formally prescribed by law. In sum, the 'public organizations' do not represent 'democratization' in any meaningful sense, but rather a simultaneous effort on the regime's part to increase its ideological legitimacy".

According to him, comrades' courts "have been turned into agencies of political control..."; Khrushchev's speech at the XXIth Congress "constituted an authorization to invade the realm of politics...". This is made clear to the author by an editorial of the *Sovetskaya Rossiya* which stated that 'the basic task of the comrades' courts is the struggle for the purity of Communist morality and against manifestations of alien bourgeois ideology". [5]

---

[1]   P. Grishayev, "Against the Anti-Communist Libel of the Soviet Law", *Sots. zak.*, 1963, No. 6, p. 71.

[2]   Albert Boiter, "Comradely Justice : How Durable is it ? Problems of Communism", March-April 1965, p. 91.

[3]   Merle Fainsod, "How Russia is Ruled", Cambridge, 1963, p. 125.

[4]   *Op. cit.*, p. 521.

[5]   Yeremy R. Azraell, "Is Coercion withering Away ?" *Problems of Communism*, 1962, No. 6, pp. 12 and 13.

Lipson, on one side admits that in part "the claim is justified that the non-courts [1] in the Soviet Union... bring the processes of justice closer to the people and at the same time induces the people to take part in the process of justice", "When a court hold session" he writes, "in the little Red Corner of an apartment house or the club-room of a trade-union local, many attend who otherwise probably would not, and the responses of the audience frequently interact (not always in the interest of justice) with the proceedings 'on stage'. The speeches made by members of the audience toward the end of the trial in a comrades' court, while some of them appear to reflect the instructions of the local *aktiv*, do convey a sense of popular morality — channeled into a stage established, though nominally unofficial, sanction". But on the other side, "Nonetheless, it is clear", he continues, "that the 'popularization' of justice tends to bring an even larger portion of life under the eye of a watchful regime. The non-courts do not, as is sometimes asserted, merely relieve the official courts from that portion of their caseload, that can be handled with less formal procedures and less drastic sanction". [2]

Berman and Spindler [3] summarize the dangers threatening the comrades' court in four points; 1) party abuse; 2) degradation of law; 3) dulling of the sense of legality and 4) invasion of privacy. [4]

With regard to the first danger the authors think that the party agencies, whether at a higher or lower level, may exert pressure on the comrades' courts to condemn persons for acts which neither immoral, nor illegal, such as criticizing party politics or party leaders.

The second danger of lowering the prestige of law is reduced to a temporary phenomenon since in the distant time, the legal system will die out.

The third danger consists, according to them, in the very use of standards and procedure borrowed from the judicial system in a manner that threatened their integrity. The Comrades' Courts, are in effect, parasites upon the regular legal system, deriving their nourishment from legal institutions, which yet disturb these institutions and which

---

[1] Lipson does not draw a difference between comrades' courts and courts procee-dings against parasites.

[2] Leon Lipson, Hosts and Pests, "The Fight Against Parasites", *Problems of Communism*, March-April 1965, pp. 980-981.

[3] Harold J. Berman and J. W. Spindler, "Soviet Comrades' Courts", *Washington Law Review*, 38, pp. 843-910 (1963).

[4] *Ibid.*, pp. 845-846.

may ultimately supplant them. The danger is that people who participate in these quasi-judicial proceedings will identify their work with law, and that their sense of such basic legal principles as the right to counsel, the presumption of innocence, the precise formulation of issues and the like will thereby become dulled".

The last danger underlined by Bergman and Spindler is invasion of privacy labelled as "perhaps the most serious danger", since it could provide the possibility "to pry into the personal affairs of Soviet citizens and will be an instrument for imposing conformity of thought and behavior in all phases of life". Caused by a wide interpretation of the provision of Art. 5 (9) of the 1961 Statute extending the jurisdiction of comrades' courts also to "other anti-social acts not entailing criminal liability", the authors fear that under this provision matters of political opinion, of personal relations, of religious faith or worship and other matters of personal nature may fall. [1]

The importance of Art. 5 (9) is greater than the invasion into privacy.

The transfer to the competence of the comrades' courts of action although socially dangerous but not punished by the Criminal Code and defined in the Statute creates a special category of actions, anti-social but not criminal. According to the Soviet legislation these actions are too insignificant to provide criminal responsibility; they are anti-social and must be punished by social measures of suppression.

The provision of Art. 96 of the 1960 RSFSR Criminal Code can serve as an example of such a shift from penal to social punishment. Art. 96 provides namely, that cases of petty misappropriation of state or public property are to be punished by measures of social coercion.

Also the general provision of Art. 51 of the same code which along with some cases listed in this and other articles of the code permits the liberation of a person from any penal responsibility if offenses have been committed for the first time, and if according to the character of the offense and the personality of the offender, he can be reformed without applying a punishment, but with the help of measures of social coercion, is an expression of the same idea.

The measure to punish petty offenses not by criminal but by social coercion is an excellent one.

Still every action indifferently as to whether it is punishable by state or social coercion, must be defined in advance by a law, regulation, order, etc if the rule of *nullum crimen, nulla poena sine lege*, should not be violated.

---

[1] Harold J. Berman and J. W. Spindler, *op. cit.*, p. 905.

If the comrades' court itself decides as to whether an action although not punishable according to law, is still punishable because a similar action is punishable, it applies the ignominious analogy banished from the criminal code by the Basic Principles of Criminal Legislation of the USSR and the Union-Republics of 1958. The consequences of the application of analogy can be much more serious

D. CONCLUSIONS

Causes which prompted the creation of comrades' courts and their revival, after a period of stagnation, were of a various character.

As we have seen the primary purpose of comrades' courts as thought out by Lenin, was the enforcement of labor discipline. Already then it was thought that a court of their own peers would have a greater prophylactic and educational influence on workers than the regular courts. With their return, the jurisdiction of these courts was also extended to petty offenses of a general character, not provided by criminal codes, to violations of moral standards with regard to relations to women, children, drunkenness, etc.

In 1930, by the creation of village courts, the federal legislation wanted to alleviate the burden of regular courts by the exemption from their jurisdiction of petty cases; the union republics gave to the village courts the form of comrades' courts.

Gradually comrades' courts were extended to almost all fields of Soviet life. According to Art. 2 of the 1961 Statute on Comrades' Courts these courts exist at enterprises, institutions. organizations, higher and secondary and special institutions of learning, kolkhozes, apartment houses and in villages and settlements. In large enterprises, separate comrades' courts may be installed at shops, and at individual brigades in large kolkhozes.

The punitive power of these courts has been reduced in connection with the general trend of weakening general punishments reflected in the new criminal codes of the Union Republics. The scopes of the comrades' courts are to be achieved not by punishment, but by persuasion.

And, through all their existence, the comrades' courts main purpose was to prevent law violations and foster education of Soviet citizens in the spirit of compliance with moral standards.

"Comrades' courts" reads Art. 1 of the 1961 Statute, "are called upon for cooperation in citizens' education in the spirit of communist relation to work, socialist property, the observance of rules of socialist common life, respect of dignity and honor of citizens. The main thing in the work of comrades' courts is the prevention of law violations and actions, damaging to society, the education of people by persuasion and social influence, the creation of conditions of intolerance to any anti-social actions..."

It seems to the present author that there is no possibility to assess from here, as to whether the comrades' courts are reaching the goals set for them and fulfill the scopes expected of them. The Soviet writers while praising the work of the comrades' courts, in general also criticize sometimes the lack of juridical knowledge of their members, the supervision of their activity and other details.

For instance, G. Kazin writes that "the noble work of comrades' courts contributes to the strengthening of productional discipline, the education of the working population in the spirit of strict compliance with Soviet law and the ethical principles of the moral code of the constructors of communism". [1] At the same time, Kazin reports that the Standing Commission of Socialist Legality of the Moscow City Soviet, having examined the work of comrades' courts in two precincts of Moscow found that the professional organs poorly guide the comrades' courts and extend not enough help to them.

N. Prusakov, Deputy Chairman of the RSFSR Supreme Court, underlines that there are many difficulties in the work of the comrades' courts. Also he accuses the trade-unions and the local soviets of not paying enough attention to their activity. This is also the fault of the administrative organs, of the general court, and the prosecuting body. In the RSFSR alone, 150,000 comrades' courts with 5 to 15 members each, are active. "Unfortunately, one cannot say" writes Prusakov, "that this army of public workers work faultlessly. It happens, casually selected persons *"sluchaynyye lyudi"*, without authority are elected to comrades' courts. The members of the courts rarely render account to their electors. Those who do not justify the confidence put in them are not recalled before term. In the place of a collective, wise commaradely examination of cases some courts create superfluous long-drawn-out proceedings, bringing nervousness into the work and sometimes create real squabbles". [2]

The poor work of comrades' courts at enterprises is to be

[1] G. Kazin, "The Court of Comrades", *Pravda*, May 13, 1963.

[2] N. Prusakov, "In the Name of the Comrades", *Izvestia*, Feb. 10, 1967.

explained, also according to Stavtsev, by the fact that trade-union organs, and especially the Factory, Plant and Local Committees, do not adequately direct the work of comrades' courts, do not extend daily help to them, do not require economic leaders the bringing to comrades' courts of violators and by this do not use in the proper degree comrades' courts as a great force of social influence upon violators of labor discipline, insuring the compliance to rules of socialist morals. [1]

But the great number of comrades' courts [2] and the steady widening of their jurisdiction, testify to the fact that the Party and government are satisfied with the institution of comrades' courts. A sign to this effect is the amendments of 1963 to the 1961 Statute, providing that comrades' courts may be installed if the number of members of the collective is less than fifty, and instituting the extension of competence to petty cases of hooliganism, theft, etc.

Another sign of the trust of the Soviet legislator in the comrades' court is the provision of Art. 51 of the new RSFSR Criminal Code discussed above.

On ground of his personal observations, Harold Berman writes, "The comrades' courts that I have seen in action have impressed me by the good spirit with which they act and with what they are received. Especially important is the fact that these powers are very limited and that these limits are enforced by the courts and the legal system". [3]

It must suffice for the American writer who has not had the opportunity to observe personally the activity of comrades' courts, to examine as to whether the comrades' courts, as shaped by the legislation in force at the present time, are able to reach the goals set for them.

Let us take a look at the criticisms presented by American writers mentioned above.

There is no much ground to see in comrades' courts "agencies of political control, realizing an effort to increase political legitimacy". It would be too farfetched.

That the Party intends to increase its pressure by influencing the

---

[1] A. I. Stavtsev, "The Problems of the Comrades' Courts of Enterprises and Institutions in the Education of Communist Attitude Toward Labor and Rules of Socialist Common Life", *Vsesoyuznyy juridicheskiy institut Uchenyye zapiski*, M. 1961, No. 11, p. 64.

[2] According to Kazin there were 197,000 comrades' courts in the RSFSR only in 1963. However, in the article mentioned above, writing in 1967 he gives the figure 150,000 for the RSFSR, with 5-15 court members in every court.

[3] Harold J. Berman, "The Dilemma of Soviet Law Reform", *Harvard Law Review*, 1963, No. 5, p. 947.

petty cases devoid of any political character submitted to the comrades' courts is hardly probable. It seems unwarranted to ascribe special political goals to the increase of all social organizations participating in the administration of justice, without making a difference between the comrades' courts and courts for parasites. [1]

The people's assessors are, for instance, also a form of public activity in court, not as an organization but as individual citizens. Their participation is, even very imperfect, still a "democratization" of court procedure. This is true also for comrades' court devoid of formalism not appropriate to the cases under jurisdiction of these courts. [2]

Lipson, who also does not differentiate between comrades' and parasite courts, sees political implications in the popularization of justice bringing "an even larger portion of life under the eye of a watchful regime". What "larger portion of life", which were previously not apparent to the eye of the regime, are now being disclosed in comrades' courts, is not clear.

Berman and Spindler admit the possibility of Party abuse with regard to comrades' courts, but they are right when they assert that "it cannot simply be assumed, however, that because such abuse is possible it is therefore inevitable". [3]

Indeed, the influence of the Communist Party is everlasting and omnipotent in the Soviet Union. It permeates every aspect of Soviet life, not exempting the administration of justice in its regular, special or social forms. But there is no evidence that the comrades' courts are a particularly favorite channel of Party influence and evidently there was no need to create and develop these courts in order to strengthen Party influence. The comrades' courts deal with petty cases devoid of any political interest.

But there is another more real danger threatening the objectivity and justice of the comrades' courts' decision : it is the pressure of the public's opinion present at the session in the court room.

Certainly, the pressure of public opinion is expressed in the press before the trial takes place also with regard to a regular court. However, this pressure is more distant, less immediate, than the influence produced by a public in a court room, entitled to the expression of their opinion on the case on hand and which opinion must be considered

---

[1]   For them, see below, pp. 198 ff.

[2]   For criticism of Arzael's views see Berman and Spindler, *op. cit.*, p. 894.

[3]   Berman and Spindler, *op. cit.*, p. 845-846.

by the comrades' court in taking its decision. "Public opinion" is prearranged by the Party in political cases! But in some cases when the Party does not care to interfere, the pressure of biased public can be exercised in a session hall of a comrades' court.

The danger of lowering the prestige of law threatening the comrades' courts alluded to by Berman and Spindler is eliminated, according to them, by the tendency to subject the decisions of comrades' courts to legal supervision and the insistance on the conformity with legal principle.

It must be kept in mind that Art. 14 of the 1961 Statute prescribes that the comrades' courts be guided in the first place by law in making their decisions, so that the presence of legality remains emphasized.

However, in the very quasi-judicial character of the comrades' courts, a further even more serious danger for the comrades' court, is seen by the authors. In spite of absence of legal safeguards such as the right to counsel, presumption of innocence, etc., the impression may be produced that the proceedings are correct in reaching decisions in general.

But again, the authors themselves see countervailing factors also against this danger in the attempt to maintain a sharp distinction between the role of the comrades' courts and of the regular courts. [1]

But, furthermore, the "limited safeguards seem to be not so negligible; the material of the case is checked by the tribunal in advance. It may demand information and documents from officials and others. The charges must be brought to the notice of the person charged. He has the right to produce documents and information and to call witnesses. He may challenge the tribunal. The trial is public. There is a right to be heard. The tribunal is bound by the 1961 Statute and by prevailing legislation". [2]

To this list of guarantees must be added the hearing of experts, if their testimony should be required. [3]

It must be also said that the 1961 Statute nowhere excludes the presence and activity of counsel. As we know, every one attending the session has the right to speak on the merits of the case, with the permission of the courts. Why should a counsel be excluded from this right?

The danger of the invasion of privacy and the extension of the jurisdiction of comrades' courts to "other anti-social acts and embracing

---

[1] *Op .cit.*, p. 846.

[2] *Op. cit.*, p. 902.

[3] Yudel'son, *op. cit.*, p. 158.

criminal legality", i.e., to such matters as religion, sexual promiscuity, etc., stressed by Berman and Spindler is indeed serious. But also this "danger" is purely theoretical. Since the functions of the comrades' courts according to the 1961 Statute, and certainly not before, such cases have not been reported. But if they occurred, they would have been certainly widely publicized for anti-Soviet propaganda purposes.

The analysis of the pros and cons does not lead Berman and Spindler to a definite conclusion. Weighing the dangers against "the safeguards that limit them and the positive advantages of the comrades' courts in deterring crime and strengthening group morals" they do not find a difinite answer to the question as to whether the comrades' courts do in fact serve to discourage anti-social behavior at an early stage and to exert a healthy influence upon persons who have started on the path of serious misconduct... and strengthen the inner unity of the neighborhood, factory, university or other social organization of which they are part. [1]

"The creation of comrades' courts created a new court instance which, although it does not belong to the system of regular courts, in reality is a regular court instance", writes Andreas Bilinsky. [2]

This definition is correct. The comrades' courts are, according to their jurisdictions, courts for petty cases relieving the People's courts of the great burden of these cases, as it is stated in the USSR Law of 1930 creating the village courts.

They may be compared with the courts of the justices of the peace in tsarist Russia, which also did not belong to the general system of courts, but formed a separate court instance.

Certainly the structure of comrades' courts and that of the courts of justices of the peace is quite different : The comrades' courts is an elected body of three lay judges whereas the justices of the peace, according to the Law of 1864, although elected, were in their great majority, jurists, especially in cities, and acted as single judges.

There is a great affinity of purposes between the two institutions. The aims of the legislator of 1864 in creating the justices of the peace, as formulated by the State Council, were : "The duty of the justice of the peace, is the examination of petty cases occurring almost daily among

---

[1] *Ibid.*, p. 907.

[2] Andreas Bilinsky, "Comrades' Courts in the Soviet Union", *Osteurop-Recht*, 1962, No. 4, p. 323.

the majority of the population, a considerable part of which has no knowledge of laws, cannot endure formalism, respects natural equity only, and seeks first of all a rapid decision in accordance with its notion of justice. The main goal of the justice of the peace is to satisfy this elementary need of administration of justice according to conscience". [1]

It is interesting to note that the tsarist State Council emphasized the duty of the justice of the peace to be guided in his decisions more by his sense of justice than by statute law. This was especially made evident in the creation by the State Council of an appelate instance for the decisions of justices of the peace : namely the Conference of the Justices of the Peace, and not of a regular court. The regular court was excluded from the appeals procedure because, according to the State Council, the examination of one and the same case by the justice of the peace and ordinary court is inconvenient : the first is subordinated to conscience and the second to law and thus a decision of a justice of the peace could be overruled by a sentence of an ordinary court which is bound by the formalism of the statutory law. [2]

Thus, the State Council deliberately retreated from the principle of strict legality with regard to petty cases, referring them to the sense of justice of the justices of the peace.

But, in this respect, Soviet legalislation is more legalistic than the tsarist State Council : Article 14 of the 1961 Statute puts in the first place the legislation in force as a guide for the examination of and the decision over a case by the comrades' courts.

Furthermore, there is no doubt that the institution of justices of the peace, the nearest and the most accessible instance of administration of justice pursued the same prophylactic and educational goals as the comrades' courts.

Also, a simplified procedure was applied by the justices of the peace and is used by comrades' courts, and the simplification of the procedure was never regarded as dulling the people's sense of basic legal principles.

Certainly, the comrades' courts differ, if not by their basic purposes and goals, still by their structure from the courts of the justices of the peace.

Although not excluding the possibility of political influence by

---

[1] *Zhurnal Soyedinennogo Departamenta Gosudarstvennogo Soveta*, No. 65 (1864), p. 300.

[2] *Ibid.*

the Party and hence, deviations from the right path, which is possible
and latent in every aspect of administration of justice in the Soviet
Union, at any time, but not greater with respect to comrades' courts
than elsewhere, the basic defect of comrades' courts is the lack of
knowledge of legal matters of their members, since they have to apply
material and procedural law in a great many of the cases submitted
to them.

As in the case of people's assessors, measures are taken for the
alleviation of this defect.

However, the prophylactic and educational value of comrades'
courts cannot be denied in the opinion of the present writer.

This scope is best realized by the system of comrades' courts sessions
at places of work or residence of the delinquent. Indeed, it is a great
difference for the impact on the conscience and morals of a first time
delinquent if he is judged by his own work colleagues or cohabitants
in the presense of the rest of them, at the place of his work or residence,
or by people completely foreign to him, before a casual audience
without any relation to him, in an official courtroom. "Punish me
with any fine, but let me not be submitted to such a shame", beseeched
a kolkhoz woman, when she heard that her case would be brought
before a comrades' court.

The Soviet Community on the Watch over Socialist Legality reports
also the case of N. who understanding that his case would be referred to
a comrades' court by the prosecutor in order to produce a more lenient
sentence for him, asked the prosecutor to present the case to a people's
court. "It is easier for me to submit to a stronger punishment set by
a people's court, than to endure a public reprimand and a sentence
pronounced by the entire collective". [1]

Gorshenin reports the following case : arrested by members of a
people's brigade, a slightly drunk citizen beseeched : "Arrest me,
convict me, send me where ever you like, but do not refer my case to
the collective where I work". "His own comrades, the society of the
collective, in which the violator of law works is more frightful to him
than the state court or an administrative organ", remarks Gorshenin. [2]

It must be admitted that many persons submitted to such an ordeal

---

[1] *Sovetskaya obshchestvennost' na strazhe sotsialisticheskoy zakonnosti*, M. 1960, p. 221;
Belinsky, *op. cit.*, p. 327.

[2] K. P. Gorshenin, "Participation of the Public in the Fight Against Law Breaking
is the Further Development of Soviet Democracy", in *Sovetskaya obshchestvennost' na
strage sotsialisticheskoy zakonnosti*, M. 1960, p. 152.

as the court of ones own peers will abstain from the opportunity of a repetition and many in the audience will be prevented from playing the main role in such a performance.

The comrades' courts are a step from strict legality. But, this step is not dangerous because they deal with petty cases, a great number of which concern moral and not law violation.

However, in the Soviet Union, this step is considered as directed toward the paradisical conditions of the future when, under communism, legal coercion will not be necessary and people will act rightously not from fear of punishment but directed by rules of communist morality, as Lenin taught, which is, of course, pure utopia.

CHAPTER TEN

COURTS AND PARASITES

A. ANTI-PARASITE LAWS

b) *Lenin and Khrushchev on Parasites*

On May 22, 1918, Lenin wrote to Petrograd workers : "Who does not work, he shall not eat. [1] This is comprehensible to every toiler ... In this simple, most simple and most evident truth lies the basis of socialism, the incredible source of its strength, the indestructable guarantee of its final victory". [2]

It was also Lenin who gave the definition of a parasite. According to him "the rich and the rogues are two sides of the same medal, two main categories of parasites reared by capitalism, the main enemies of socialism; these enemines must be taken under special supervision of the entire population, short shrift must be made of them, merciless, on the occasion of the slightest violation of rules and laws of socialist society. Every weakness, every hesitation, every sentimentalizing would be a most serious crime against socialism". [3] Lenin demanded that the resistance "of the spongers preserving capitalist customs "should be broken with an iron fist". [4]

The rich were disposed of already in the beginning of Bolshevist rule. The second category of parasites came under fire much later.

Khrushchev led the violent propaganda against parasites, taking up Lenin's theme, and he declared at the XXII Congress of the Soviet Communist Party in 1961; "We must strictly realize the principle 'he who does not work, neither shall he eat'. At the same time it is necessary to close all and any kind of loop-holes through which the anti-socialist elements rob society, derive an annual income and lead a parasitical life". [5]

---

[1] The sentence is taken from the Bible : "The charge we give you on our visit is that the man who refuses to work must starve" (2 Thessalonians, 3, 10).

[2] Lenin, 27, p. 355-6.

[3] Lenin, 26, p. 372.

[4] Lenin, 28, p. 79.

[5] N.S. Khrushchev, *Programma Kommunisticheskoy partii sovetskogo soyuza, Doklad na XXII s"ezde*, M. 1961, p. 123.

In his indignation against parasites, Khrushchev brought forward a peculiar legal theory which is fortunately not followed by the Soviet codes.

In his speech at the XIV Congress of the Komsomal, Khrushchev, said : "Some people argue that if someone committed a theft, but is not exposed, he cannot be punished, although it is known that he is a thief, but such a morality is inherent to bourgeois society. There they say : 'not caught—not a thief'. No, we need other principles".

Khrushchev asserted that the Soviet man has the right to make responsible those people who do not work but live at the expense of society, "to make a thief responsible not only when he reaches into your pocket, but when a person does not work, but lives in clover. You see, he robs society because he lives on your work, he robs you. It is not necessary to wait until he is caught redhanded and only then to make him responsible before a court. Society can and must present its own requirements to spongers : 'you live in a house which we built, wear clothes and foot-wear produced by our own hands. But what did you do for the betterment of life of the people with whom you live" ? [1]

Khrushchev returned to the same argumentation in his address to the Conference of Workers of the RSFSR Industry and Construction on April 24, 1963 : "Radical measures are necessary against spongers and parasites. They must be punished according to the most stringent provisions of the law. Parasites must be fought not only in the case when they are caught red-handed removing from your pocket, from a store-room, or elsewhere. No, this must be understood more extensively".

He requested his audience to look closely at some people who live in grand style, but do not themselves work anywhere. If a person, Khrushchev again asserted, does not work, does not produce any value but lives in easy circumstances it means that he lives on the work of other people, he robs those who work, and the fact that he has not been caught yet is to explain only by the thief's dexterity. "Thus, do not wait until someone will catch them, expose the parasites yourselves and fight them", he exhorted his audience. [2]

Khrushchev argued that if a citizen does not work, society must

---

[1] *Pravda*, April 21, 1962.
[2] *Sots. zak.*, 1963, No. 9, p. 11.

ask him, why does he not work, on what does he live ? He does not nurish himself with air and water only, but by products which are created by the work of the Soviet people. A toiler has the right to say to a sponger : "I am working, my brother is working, every man capable of working is working. Why don't you work but rather devour that which is created by the work of our society ? If you do not work, but eat, it means that you live at the expense of others, it means that you rob society. The question is only which form the theft takes. [1]

Lenin's formula was introduced into Par. 1, Art. 12, of the 1936 Constitution which makes work "a duty and a matter of honor for every able-bodied citizen, in accordance with the principle 'he who does not work, neither shall he eat' ".

In order to give the Soviet Citizens the possibility of fulfilling his duty to work, Ar. 118 of the 1936 Constitution guarantees the right to employment and payment for working accordance with its quantity and quality.

Thus, work in the Soviet Union is a duty and not a freely chosen activity of the Soviet citizen.

The second paragraph of Art. 12 of the 1936 Constitution sets another socialist principle : "from each according to his ability—to each according to his work".

One's work is put into relation to that which one can require from the state for his work. In consequences those who can, but do not work shall not eat either, or have a claim against the state.

Those men are called spongers and parasites in the Soviet Union.

b) *The First Anti-Parasite Laws*

The first law "On the Strengthening of the Fight Against Anti-Social and Parasitic Elements" was adopted in the Uzbek SSR on May 27, 1957. The Turkman SSR followed suit two days later. Similar laws were passed by the Latvian SSR on October 12, 1957; The Tadzkih SSR on January 21, 1958; the Azerbaydzhan SSR on June 18, 1958; the Kirghiz SSR on January 15, 1959 and the Georgian SSR on Sept. 5, 1960.

Thus, between 1957 and 1961 nine Russian republics out of the fifteen of the federations adopted a law against parasites. Conspicuous was the absence among them of the two greatest union republics : the RSFSR and the Ukranian SSR.

---

[1] Quoted by A.S. Shlyapochnikov, *Tuneyadtsev k otvetu*, M. 1964, p. 8.

The anti-parasite laws of 1957-1960 were met with great suspicion even by Soviet writers and the Soviet Press. For instance, Harold Berman relates that "the principal draftman of the 1958 Fundamental Principles of Criminal Procedure told him in 1959 that in his opinion the anti-parasite laws contravene the provisions of the Fundamental Principles that "no person may be subjected to a criminal penalty except by sentence of a court"; he said that he expected the anti-parasite laws to be repealed".

The laws of 1957-1960 were directed against two categories of parasites; 1) those who seem to have work or a position, but in reality pick up their livlihood from unearned income, and 2) those who, being of age and able-bodied, do not work either for the state or in the family. Also vagrants and beggars belong to this category.

The fight against parasites had to be conducted by means of public influence and state coercion.

At general assemblies of public organizations or kolkhozes it could be decided according to these laws, after hearings, that the person accused of parasitism of the first category should receive a warning and if the warning did not induce the accused to change his way of life during the time set by the assembly, to ban him to a place assigned by the government for a period of up to five years, with the obligation to work at the place of new residence. Such a decision had to be confirmed by the executive committee of the district or city Soviet.

The decision concerning parasites of the second category had to be taken by an assembly of their neighbours.

It is evident, these laws introduced a kind of "ostracism",—banishment vote,—criticized already in old Greece where it was first applied because it proceeded without a proper investigation, court trial and other guarantee of a fair procedure and, thus, opened the door to every kind of abuse and injustice.

"It must be noted", writes Shlyapochnikov, "that in practice the application (of the laws against parasites) turned up cases of violations of legality as a result of noncompliance with the requirement for the passing of right and just decisions. A number of public sentences providing banishment and confirmed by executive committees of Soviets were set aside on protests by the prosecuting body". [1]

Shlyapochnikov cited a statistic of the application of the first law

---

[1] A.S. Shlyapochnikov, "Legislation and Society in the Fight Against Parasitic Elements", *S.G.P.*, 1961, No. 8, p. 65.

against the parasites of May 25, 1957. Among all the persons whose behavior was discussed by general assemblies of citizens in the Uzbek SSR, in the period of 1957-1960, 25% were sentenced to banishment. The rest received warnings. He underlines that discussions took place more often in villages and small towns. In big cities such as Tashkent and Samarkand, "the law was used rarely and, thus, was not used in full for the fight against malicious parasitical elements to be found in the big cities of the Republic". [1]

Still, Shlyapochnikov explains, the passing of laws against the parasites by the remaining union republics, by "the insistent demand of toilers for a decisive fight against anti-social and parasitical elements "up to the complete eradication of this phenomenon on our society". [2]

Following this appeal, the Presidium of the RSFSR passed an antiparasite law on May 4, 1961. Similar laws were passed by the Belorussian SSR on May 15, 1961, the Lithuanian SSR on May 27, 1961; the Moldavian SSR on May 29, 1961; the Estonian on June 8, 1961 and the Ukrainian SSR on June 12, 1961.

The Uzbek, Turkmen, Azerbeydzhan and Georgian SSR amended their former laws according to the legislation of 1961.

The RSFSR law against the parasites served as pattern with insignificant deviations, for legislation of the other union republics. Let us discuss it in some detail.

c) *The RSFSR Law Against Parasites*

The Presidium of the RSFSR Supreme Soviet adopted an Ukase "On the Strengthening of the Fight Against Persons Avoiding Socially Useful Work and Leading an Anti-Social Parasitical Way of Life, on May 4, 1961. [3]

In its preamble, the Ukase lists the kind of people against whom it is directed: they are persons who stubbornly decline to do honest work, apparently take a job but in reality live on an income not produced by work, and enrich themselves at the expense, of the state, the total population, or, in general, being able to work, do not work anywhere, indulge in prohibited trade, private enterprise activity, speculation, begging, draw-income not derived from work, but from

---

[1] *Ibid.*

[2] *Ibid.*

[3] *V.V.S., RSFSR*, 1961, Item 273.

the exploitation of personal automobiles, use of hired work and receiving income, not based on work, from cottages and land lots, erecting houses and cottages by means obtained not by work and using for this purpose construction materials acquired illegally, and performing other anti-social actions. In kolkhozes, such persons enjoing privileges granted to kolkhozniks avoid honest work, produce home-brewed vodka, head a parasitic way of life, undermine discipline, and inflict by this behavior damage upon the cooperative economy.

The Ukase asserts that such a parasitical life of these persons is, as a rule, accompanied by drunkeness, moral dissoluteness and violation of rules of socialist common life which have a negative effect on other unstable members of society.

The scope of the Ukase is to fight parasitical elements up to the "total uprooting of this disgraceful phenemenon in our society, by building around these persons an atmosphere of intolerance and general condemnation".

Consequently, Article 1 of the law provides that able-bodied citizens who are of age and who do not wish to fulfill their most important constitutional duty to work honestly according to their capacities, who avoid socially useful work, receive unearned income from the exploitation of land plots, automobiles, dwelling space [1] or commit other anti-social actions, which permit them to lead a parasitic way of life, are subject to banishment to a locality especially assigned therefor, for the duration of two to five years with confiscation of

---

[1] The ideologic and administrative fight against personal housing started in 1960. The Decision of the USSR Council of Ministers of December 30, 1960 forbid the assignment of plots for the construction of personal houses in cities and the granting of loans for the construction of personal houses in cities was halted (*Sob. post.*, 1961, Item 2). The decision of the same body of September 18, 1961 revoked the assignment of garden plots for personal use by workers and employers (*Sob. post.*, 1961, Item 113). The confiscation of personal houses built on unearned income has been ordered by a special ukase of the Presidium of the RSFSR Supreme Soviet "On the Gratuitious Confiscation of Houses and other Buildings erected or Acquired by Citizens on Unearned Income", of July 26, 1962 (*V.V.S.*, *RSFSR*, 1962, Item 464). Peculiar is the difference made by the Supreme Court with regard to the rent of automobiles and personal houses. The money provided from the rent of a personal car has been declared an unearned income already in 1942 (Decision of the USSR Supreme Court of January 10, 1942, No. 1367 in the Polyakov Case). However, the rent of a personal house has been legalized by the law on Bases of Civil Legislation of the USSR and the Union Republics of December 8, 1961 (*V.V.S.*, *SSSR*, 1961, Item 525) which gave the right to the union republics (Article 25) to establish the rules and conditions pertaining to the rent of personal houses : See also Samuel Kucherov, "Property in the Soviet Union", *American Journal of Comparative Law*, 1962, No. 3, p. 384-392.

property acquired by non-earned income, and mandatory work at the place of resettlement by decision of the district (city) people's court.

The same measures of repression may be inflicted, pursuant to a decision both of a district (city) people's court, or a public sentence passed by a collective of toilers at enterprises, shops, institutions, organizations, kolkhozes and kolkhoz brigades, on persons taking work at enterprises, state and public institutions, or who are members of kolkhozes, only for the purpose of outward show, who enjoying the privileges and advantages of workers, kolkhozniks and employees, in reality undermine work discipline and are engaged in private enterprise actions, live on unearned income or commit other anti-social actions, allowing them to lead a parasitic way of life.

It must be emphasized that the failure to work is punishable only when it leads to a parasitic way of life. That means that not working in itself, if not resulting in a parasitic way of life, is not punishable under soviet law. Only the avoiding of socially useful work connected with anti-social actions, which permit a parasitic way of life, are sanctioned by law. [1]

Not producing socially useful work is, as we have seen, a violation of Article 12 of the Constitution. The Law of May 4, 1961, provides, under certain conditions a sanction for this violation.

Other offenses enumarated in Article 1 of the anti-parasite law, such as indulging in prohibited trade; the same action combined with the use of hired work; private enterprise; speculation, [2] systematic vagrancy and begging, home brewing; illegal acquisition of construction materials, under some aggravating circumstances, come also under the provisions of Articles 162, part 1 and 2, 153, 154, 209, 158, 208 and 170 respectively, of the RSFSR Criminal Code.

However, the punishments provided by the Law of May 4, 1961 are not criminal in nature. Their real character will be discussed later.

---

[1]   See also A.S. Shlyapochnikov, *Bor'ba s tuneyadtsami*, M. 1962, p. 29.

[2]   It is interesting to note that speculation with personal houses could not be punished under the old RSFSR Criminal Code, since its Article 107 defined speculation as "buying up and reselling of agricultural products of mass consumption by private persons with the purpose of profit taking". It is not clear if also Article 154 of the New Criminal Code, defining speculation as the "buying up and resale of goods and/or other items for the purpose of making profit" may be applied to speculation with personal houses and dachas.

So we see the Ukase goes much beyond the formation of an atmosphere of intolerance. It provides very sensible punishments.

As to the elements of the offense, the parasites are, thus, divided into two categories : those who do not work at all or indulge in the illegal activity described above, and those who nominally take a job but in reality draw their income from the same illegal activity.

In cases of the first category the district (city) people's court is competent to banish [1] the culprit to specially designated places for the duration of from two to five year, with confiscation of the property acquired not by work and to mandatory work at the place of resettlement.

However, the delinquents of the second category are subjected to the same punishment but upon decision of the district (city) people's court *or* upon public sentence passed by collectives of toilers at enterprises, shops, institutions, organizations, kolkhozes and kolkhoz brigades.

For culprits of both cotegories the decision sending them to special places of resettlement can be taken only if a warning issued before the trial by state organs or public organizations has not the effect of inducing them to take the path of an honest working life during the time set in the warning.

The decision of the district (city) people's court with regard to a person avoiding useful work and leading a parasitical way of life is final and cannot be appealed.

A public sentence of eviction, however, is subject to confirmation by the executive committee of the local district (city) soviet, the decision of which is also final.

Still, it must be kept in mind, that any court decision even if already in force may be reviewed in the way of judicial supervision. Decisions of the People's Courts in case of parasitism are no exception to this rule. Also decisions of the public bodies confirmed by executive committes, are subject to the general supervision right of the prosecuting body and may be reviewed on protest of the prosecutor.

---

[1] The Russian word employed by the Ukase is "vyseleniye" (eviction, expulsion). Although Lipson correctly translates "vyseleniye" by "exile", not literally but according to its meaning, he errs when he thinks that the Soviet legislature avoided using the word "vysylka" (exile, banishment) because of its "harsh connection with tsarist and previous Soviet history" (L. Lipson, *The Future...* op. cit., p. 3 and Footnote 5) Tsarist legislation used the word "ssylka" (exile, banishment) and not "vysylka". That "vyseleniye" is tantamount to exile or banishment in this case follows from the reference to Art. 186 of the RSFSR Criminal Code by the Ukase which employs the word "ssylka",

The identification of persons leading an anti-social and parasitical life and all circumstances pertaining to it, is made by the militia and the prosecuting body according to the material in their possession, on the initiative of the state and public organizations and individual citizens. After the checking is completed, the material is submitted for examination, with the approval of the prosecutor, to the district (city) people's court or the collective of toilers according to the decision of the prosecuting body.

If, during the checking of the material, signs of criminal offenses are established in the behavior of a person leading a parasitical life, the case is transmitted to the prosecuting body for regular prosecution.

The eviction sentence is executed by the militia.

If, upon arrival at the place of re-settlement, the parasite continues to avoid work, he may be sentenced, on representation of the militia, by the people's court to corrective labor with the loss of 10 percent of remuneration. Should he also flinch from corrective work, the people's court may replace corrective work by imprisonment, according to article 28 of the RSFSR Criminal Code. [1]

Escape from the place of re-settlement or on the way to it is punishable criminally according to Art. 186 of the RSFSR Criminal Code. [2]

The Ukase also provides that if a banished person proves his reformation by exemplary behavior and honest attitude toward work, he may be released before his time after not less than one half of the time set for the banishment has passed, by decision of the district (city) people's court of the place of banishment on demand of public organizations and with the acquiescence of the executive committee of the district (city) Soviet of the place of his former residence.

d) *Laws of 1957-1960 and 1961 Compared*

The comparison of laws directed against spongers and parasites by nine union republics in 1957-1960 and the legislation of 1961 and thereafter discloses important changes.

The most important innovation is the jurisdiction over the parasite cases.

Certainly, the 1957-1960 legislation was passed during the trend to enlarge the participation of the people in the administration of justices, as preached by Lenin and emphasized by the XXI Congress

---

[1] Every three days of flinching from corrective work is replaced by one day in jail.

[2] Imprisonment for up to one year.

of the USSR Communist Party. As Lipson puts it : "Had the 1957 drafts come after rather than two years before the XXI Congress, we should have little trouble fitting the anti-parasite measures into the trend of what the Soviet literature now calls the expansion of the role of the public in the administration of justice". [1]

But the most significant fact is that just two years after the XXIst Congress the RSFSR anti-parasite law, and following the pattern set by the law all the other union-republic legislation on the subject, removed from the competence of the "people" a whole category of the parasite offenses, transferring the jurisdiction to the people's courts. And with regard to the second category of parasites, these lows left to the discretion of the prosecuting body the decision, as to whether to submit the case to the people's court or the assembly of workers and employees.

Thus, with regard to the employment of the principle of people's competence in matters of the administration of justice the law of 1961 is a retreat as compared with the initial laws on parasites.

On the other hand, along with banishment which is a heavy punishment in itself, the new laws prescribed the confiscation of the property acquired by other means than work, a punishment not provided for by the old legislation.

It is evident that the legislator thought it appropriate to restrict the competence of social groups to impose such punishment as banishment and confiscation of property. Certainly, the confiscation of property may be applied also by the public sentence, but it must be assumed that in important cases the prosecuting body refers the trial to the court and not to the assembly of workers, or employees.

"The study of the practice of applying the legislation of the union republics in the strengthening of the fight against persons avoiding socially useful work and leading an anti-social parasitic way of life", writes Shlyapochnikov, "shows that public decisions about the warning of parasitic elements or the banishment of the malicious ones among them, who do not react to warnings is a rare phenomenon. The material about such persons is mostly examined by people's courts". [2]

Lipson also thinks that "even the few sham workers who were

---

[1] L. Lipson, "Commentaries to The Future Belongs to the Parasites", *Problems of Communism*, May-June, 1963, p. 4.

[2] A.S. Shlyapochnikov, "Questions of Strengthening of State-Legal and Social Influence in the Fight with Parasitic Elements", *S.G.P.*, 1963, p. 47.

tried were usually brought not to the workers' public meetings, but to the people's court". [1]

An essential, very important feature of the anti-parasite law is the prerequisite of a warning issued by the court or the general assembly, setting a certain period of time in which the parasite may change his way of life and avoid trial. This limits the application of the law to persons maliciously persisting in illegal behavior.

While restricting the jurisdiction of workers and employers assemblies, the new laws enlarged the number of assemblies competent to decide banishment : the former laws conferred this right to assemblies of citizens of the place of residence of the parasite, whereas the new assemblies of workers and employees at enterprises, shops, institutions, organizations, kolkhoz brigades may pass decisions upon him. The old laws also provided for the confirmation by the executive committee of the district soviet to make the assembly's Decision, valid.

Finally, the new laws apply penal sentences in case the banished person avoids mandatory work also at the place of banishment or escapes on the way to or from it which was not provided for by the previous laws.

The 1961 program of the Communist Party of the Soviet Union sets the goal "to insure the strict compliance with socialist legality, the eradication of every violation of law and order, the liquidation of criminality and the elimination of all causes generating it". [2]

In order to achieve this goal the 1961 Criminal Codes of the union republics introduced a new coercion : "social pressure", which had to replace penal punishment of petty criminal offenses committed for the time. Also the sanctions of the Law of May 4, 1961 are measures of social pressure as will be shown below.

It is evident from the Rulings of the USSR Supreme Court, mentioned below, that the laws of 1961 have extended to persons brought to responsibility according to them all the safe-guards granted to those accused in criminal cases regardless of the fact that the court is engaged in the setting of a non-criminal punishment. [3]

---

[1] L. Lipson, Hosts and Pests, "The Fight Against Parasites", *Problems of Communism*, March-April, 1965, p. 78.

[2] *Programma i ustav kommunisticheskoy partii Sovetskogo soyuza*, M. 1964, p. 170.

[3] Lipson seems to be of another opinion when he writes about the Law of May 4, 1961 "The parasite who held no job was placed under the exclusive jurisdiction of a people's court which, however, was supposed to try the case not criminally and, thus,

Those safeguards are : in the first place the establishment of the objective truth regarding the violation of law imputed to the person brought to responsibility. Consequently, the inquest, conducted by the militia for both categories of parasites, must be as complete and thorough as in criminal cases in general.

Another guaranty is the confirmation of the inquest by the prosecuting body and the decision, as to whether the case should be directed for trial to the regular court or to the general assembly at the place of work of the accused. Furthermore, the confirmation by the executive committee of the local soviet of the banishing sentences and the admission of counsel on desire of the person envolved.

The right of the prosecuting body to protest the sentence of the people's court, as well as the decision of the general assembly, is also a guarantee against possible abuses. Finally the participation of counsel is deemed necessary every time when a prosecutor, official or public, takes part in the proceedings.

On the other hand, criminal proceedings must not be applied to cases of parasitism mechanically, [1] since the proceedings have not a criminal character.

Still as a matter of fact also the application of the new law against the parasites gives ground to legitimate criticism. This become especially evident from the two rulings of the Plenum of the USSR Supreme Court of September 12, 1961 [2] and March 18, 1963. [3]

e) *Basic Rulings in Parasite Cases*

In its rulings of September 12, 1961 the Plenum of the USSR Supreme Court established in particular that courts rendering decisions banishing persons avoiding socially useful work while evidently giving them insufficuent time for obtaining the work specified in the warning, thus, not fulfilling their obligations of giving additional time to the suspect for reformation, underestimate the importance

---

without such safeguards as were contained in the Code of Criminal Procedure (L. Lipson, Hosts and Pests, "The Fight Against Parasites", *Problems of Communism*, March-April 1965, p. 76).

[1] Shlyapochnikov reports a parasite case in which a people's court decided to banish the person brought to responsibilty but suspended the sentence for three years. The sentence was reversed A.S. Shlyapochnikov, *Bor'ba s tuneyadtsami-vsenarodnoye delo*, M. 1962, p. 48.

[2] Ruling No. 6, *Bulleten' Verkhovnogo Suda SSSR*, 1961, No. 5, pp. 8-11.

[3] Ruling No. 3, *op. cit.*, 1963, No. 3, pp. 10-13.

of the warning provisions of the legislation on the fight with parasitic elements, and pronounce decisions banishing persons who, although having transgressed the term set in the warning, started to work before the court session. In some cases the court, without checking the material and submitting it to an exhaustive examination, decided upon the banishment of persons not able to work, in spite of the direct provision of the law. Individual courts adopted a simplified procedure for the examination of the material on persons leading an anti-social parasitic way of life. They do not analyze the submitted evidence during the trial and do not summon and interrogate witnesses even when it is necessary; in some individual cases, the courts examing the evidence concerning persons leading a parasitic way of life, do not hear explanations from the accused themselves.

In the session of March 18, 1963 the Plenum of the USSR Supreme Court found that in spite of the foregoing ruling, the courts in many cases still wrongly applied the Law of May 4, 1961.

The Plenum of the USSR Supreme Court emphasized that measures of administrative pressure are applied by courts not only to those persons who, being able-bodied, stubbornly refuse to do socially useful work and continue to lead a parasitic way of life, despite educational measures and the help to obtain work extended to them, but also to those persons to whom such measures cannot be applied : in some cases administrative measures were taken by courts with regard to persons, who only temporarily did not work and were guilty of facts showing their anti-social parasitic attitude.

Furthermore, individual courts underestimated the prophylactic value of the useful work and leading an anti-social parasitic way of life, and erroneously show the courts' purpose only in the punishment of the persons brought to responsibilty, which resulted in flagrant violations of legality.

In spite of the former ruling of the Plenum of the USSR Supreme Courts, courts, remarks the Plenum, do not use their rights to give the suspects necessary additional time for obtaining a job and changing their behavior. The reasons causing an interruption in the working activity of such persons are not always taken into consideration which also produces the rendering of unwarranted banishment sentences.

The Plenum denounced also administrative measures which are taken with regard to disabled persons, in particular those who have reached the age of retirement, are invalid or temporarily disabled, to women with infant children; to persons with sicknesses, preventing them from work and needing special treatment, as well as to persons who exercise a trade not forbidden by law and, accordingly, possessing a license to this effect.

Furthermore, the Plenum maintained that the courts do not react to illegal actions of officials who without foundation bring to responsibility individual citizens, withdraw their passports, labor booklets, and other documents necessary for obtaining work, make illegal arrests and detain citizens when there is no evidence that the person brought to responsibilty will fail to appear in court.

Also the setting of terms of banishment by the courts, was criticized by the Plenum because the courts do not always take into consideration the family status of the law violator, the reasons which caused his anti-social behavior, and the possibilty of his reformation and rehabilitation. As a result, in setting the term of benishment, courts take a lenient attitude toward malicious antisocial elements and at the same time unfoundedly prolong terms of banishment not required for the reformation of these persons.

Finally, the Plenum stressed the educational value of the parasite trials underestimated by courts and the necessity of these trials in house sessions outside the court. [1]

All these defects in the work of the district (city) people's courts in trials of parasites, are explained by the Plenum of the USSR Supreme Court in the main by the underestimation of the necessity of strict compliance with legality in the examination of these cases, as well as by the poor control of the work of people's courts by the supreme, territorial and regional courts.

The ruling of the Plenum of USSR Supreme Court charges the courts to eliminate all the defects cited above. It admonished them to examine the parasite case in a procedure which guarantees the taking of a correct and motivated decision : in particular the suspected persons must have the possibilty to get acquainted with the files, to present demands for the collection of additional material, including documents and the summoning of witnesses; all the collected evidence must be thoroughly exhausted and the declaration of all the summoned persons heard and checked during the trial; after the deposition of the witnesses and the analysis of all the evidence presented, the right to give additional explanation to the court must be granted to the persons under accusation; when a prosecutor takes part in the trial

---

[1]   Usually at plants, kolkhozes, etc.

or the person brought to responsibilty petitions for defense counsel, counsel must be admitted to the case; the sentence passed by the courts must be thoroughly supported by reasons and contain con-concrete facts certifying the anti-social, parasitic way of life of the person to whom measures of pressure are applied.

In spite of the detailed criticism of the USSR Supreme Court, the defective work in parasite, cases has not been eliminated, judging by the case of Josef Brodsky. This case is cited below *in extenso* because it shows clearly how an accusation can be framed and supported by the partiallity of the judge, the ignorance of the assessors, and the influence of "public opinion", in violation of the rulings of the USSR Supreme Court cited above.

B. The Brodsky Case

a) *The Framing*

In order to gain a complete understanding of the methods applied for the framing of the Brodsky case we cite excerpts from a note on the case written by some literary men of Moscow and Leningrad and clandestinely forwarded to and printed in the Russian newspaper "*Russkaya mysl'* " in Paris. [1]

In 1962 two men, Shakhmatov and Umansky, were arrested, [2] tried and sentenced in Leningrad. They were accused of evil influence upon young men and girls preaching to them the yoga philosophy, anarchic individualism, etc. Among the young men under the influence of Shachmatov and Umansky was Josef Brodsky, born in 1940.

However, Brodsky broke his connection with the two men in 1961, almost one year before their arrest, of his own will, so that the KGB [3] did not involve him in the prosecution of the two men. However, two Brodsky diaries from the time when he was 16-17 years old were confiscated. The prosecuting magistrate discovered a couple of anti-soviet statements in the diaries, but thought that these unhealthy boyish sentiments had been overcome by Brodsky and did not subject him to criminal responsibility.

In the subsequent years, Brodsky worked very hard on poetic creations and literary self-education; he studied the Polish and English

---

[1]   May 5, 1964.

[2]   These two names will figure prominently in the Brodsky trial.

[3]   Committee on Public Safety.

languages and persistently worked on poetic translations. His translations and original poetry were highly praised by such demanding masters of poetry as A. Akhmatova, K. Chukovsky, S. Marshak, and appeared in collections of poetry such as "Dawn over Cuba", "Yugoslav Poetry", "Polish Poetry".

On 29 November 1963, a feulleton "Literary Drane" (*okololiteraturnyy truten'*) appeared in the *"Vecherniy Leningrad"* containing several slanderous accusations. Poetry ascribed to him which he never wrote, [1] two quotations from Brodsky's verses were distorted beyond recognition; it was asserted that he left the Literary Association to which, as a matter of fact, he had never belonged; he was pictured as a dissolute, cynical sponger, but in reality Brodsky, in contradistinction to many of his coevals does not drink, or smoke, does not tolerate foul language, is very moderate in his way of life and completely absorbed in his literary work.

The feuilleton was signed by Lerner, Medvedev and Ionia, but the main organizer of the case against Brodsky is Lerner. He is a former Captain of the State Security, dismissed from this institution in 1955. At the time of the trial, he dedicated all his activity to the headquarters of the People's Brigade. Working in the Brigade, Lerner used methods and ways censored by the XXth and XXIInd Congresses of the KPSS. He extorts political denunciations from people occasionally arrested by Brigade members on the ground of having nothing to do with politics, he searches them, takes away their documents, intimidates and blackmails them, recruits them to be informers, and creates false material evidence.

When the editors of "Vecherniy Leningrad" received letters in defense of Brodsky, Lerner started to intimidate the authors of the letters, informing their employers that they defend "a political criminal".

All that was told orally and in writing by many persons, including members of the Leningrad Branch of the Association of Writers, Ye. Vechtomova and R. Grachev. But not only did Lerner remain unpunished, but he succeeded to persuade A. Prokof'yev, Secretary of the Leningrad Branch of the Association of Writers, that it is necessary to expel Brodsky from Leningrad, and that for this purpose all means are good, including falsification and direct illegality.

---

[1] The real author of the poetry reported about it to the Commission on the Work with Young Authors.

On December 13, 1963, Prokof'yev reported on Brodsky at a closed session of the Secretariat and Party Office of the Leningrad Branch of the Association of Writers. None of the writers personally acquainted with Brodsky and his work were invited to this session. Neither were these invited writers belonging to the People's Brigade informed about Lerner's activity who had attempted several times to expose Brodsky. On Prokof'yev's insistance, who by his authority strengthened Lerner's insinuations, on the ground of the same slanderous feuilleton, the Secretariate of the Leningrad Branch of the Association of Writers took the official decision demanding "the bringing of Brodsky to court" as a sponger.

Also Ye. Voyevodin, Secretary of the Commission on the Work With Young Writers acted as Lerner's accomplice. He prepared a report allegedly in the name of the Commission, although none of the members of the Commission, including its Chariman, D. Granin, knew anything about it.

In this report, full of rude abuses, it was asserted that Brodsky has nothing to do with literature, writes anti-socialistic and pornographic verses, etc. These notorious lies were decidedly denouced by members of the Commission who were really acquainted with Brodsky and his work.

Brodsky was, from childhood, subjected to a nervous illness of a chronic character and is registered at a mental hospital. All these persecutions put him again in the hospital, named after Kashchenko, in Mocsow, in January 1964. When he returned to Leningrad he was arrested in the street, on 13 February, as a "sponger avoiding trial", although he never recieved a summons of the court.

In spite of the prosecutor's protest against the illegal arrest, Brodsky remained in custody before and during the trial.

b) *The Trial* [1]

Brodsky was tried in the sessions of the Dzerzhinsky District People's Court on February 18 and March 13, 1964. The bench consisted of the Judge Savel'yeva and two assessors. A public prosecutor and counsel for the defense participated in the trial.

---

[1] A verbatim report of the trial was brought to the West from the Soviet Union and printed in the Russian periodical *Vozdushnyye puti*, New York, 1965, pp. 279-303; translations of excerpts from the verbatim report appeared in *Encounter*, London, September 1964, pp. 85-91 and in the *New Leader*, New York, August 31, 1964. The following translation is by the present author.

1. *The First Session of February 18, 1964*

Judge :   What is your profession ?

Brodsky :   I write verses. Translate. I think...

Judge :   Cut out "I think". Stand correctly. Do not lean against the wall. Face the Court. Answer the court correctly.

To Brodsky :   Do you have steady work ?

Bodsky :   I thought that it is steady work.

Judge :   Answer exactly.

Brodsky :   I wrote verses. I thought they will be printed. I think...,

Judge :   We are not interested in "I think". Answer, why did you not work ?

Bordsky :   I worked. I wrote verses.

Judge :   This does not interest us. We are interested in knowing what organization you were connected with.

Brodsky :   I had contracts with a publishing house.

Judge :   Your contracts, dated when ? In what amount ? These contracts with a publishing house sufficed for a livelihood ?

Brodsky :   I do not know exactly. All my contracts are with my counsel.

Judge :   I am asking you.

Brodsky :   Two books with my translations appeared in Moscow (enumerates).

Judge :   What is the length of your working period ?

Brodsky :   Approximately...

Judge :   We are not interested in "approximately".

Brodsky :   Five years.

Judge :   Where did you work ?

Brodsky :   At a plant. With geological groups.

Judge :   How long did you work at the plant ?

Brodsky :   One year.

Judge :   In what capacity ?

Brodsky :   As a milling-machine operator.

Judge :   And in general, what is your speciality ?

Brodsky :   I am a poet, a poet translator.

Judge :   And who has acknowledged that you are a poet ? Who ranked you among poets ?

Brodsky :   None. And who numbered me among mankind ?

Judge :   And did you study to become a poet ? Did you try to graduate from an instition of higher learning... where someone is prepared, trained ?

Brodsky :   I did not think that this (poetical inspiration) is acquired by learning.

Judge :   And by what.

Brodsky :   I think this (embarrassed)... I think it comes from God.

Judge :   Do you have demands to present to the Court.

Brodsky :   I would like to know why I was arrested.

Judge : This is a question, not a demand.

Brodsky :   Then, I have no demand.

Judge :   Has the defense questions ?

Counsel :   Yes. Citizen Brodsky, what you earn you bring to your family ?

Brodsky :   Yes.

Counsel :   Your parents also earn ?

Brodsky :   They are pensioned.

Counsel :   You live together as a family ?

Brodsky :   Yes.

Counsel :   Consequently, your income was a part of the family budget ?

Judge :   (to the counsel) You do not pose questions, you generalize. You help him to answer. Do not generalize, but question.

Counsel :   Are you registered in a mental dispensary ?

Brodsky :   Yes.

Counsel :   Did you undergo stationing in-hospital treatment ?

Brodsky :   Yes. From the end of December 1963 to January 5 of this year at the hospital named after Kashchenko in Moscow.

Counsel :   Don't you think that your disease did prevent you from working for a long time at the same place ?

Brodsky :   Maybe. Certainly. However, I do not know. No, I do not know.

Counsel :   Did you translate poetry for the collection of Cuban posts ?

Brodsky :   Yes.

Counsel :   Did you translate the Spanish "Comancero" ?

Brodsky :   Yes.

Counsel :   Were you connected with the translation Section of the Assn. of Writers ?

Brodsky :   Yes.

Counsel :   I ask the court to take notice of the characteristics (of the accused), by the Office of the Translator Section—the list of published poetry—copies of contracts— The Telegram : "Please speed the signing of the contracts"—I ask the submitting of the Citizen Brodsky to a medical examination in order to establish the state of his health and as to whether it impeded regular work. Furthermore, I ask for the immediate release of Brodsky from custody. I am of the opinion that he committed no crime and that his arrest is illegal. He has a steady residence and can appear in court at any time.

The Judge addressing the person who made notes for the verbatim report quoted here : "Stop taking notes at once, or you will be taken out."

The court withdraws for deliberation and when it returns the following decision is read :

"To submit Brodsky to a forensic mental test with the aim to provide an answer to the question, as to whether he suffers from a mental disease and whether this desease prevents the sending of Brodsky to a remote place for forced labor. In view of the history of Brodsky's illness inducing him to avoid hospitalization, to ask the 18th Militia Precinct to deliver him for the forensic-mental test".

According to the opinion of counsel, Z. N. Toporova, the Judge Savel'yeva was bound to release Brodsky from custody that he could himself go to the assigned hospital for the test next day. But Savel'yeva left him under arrest and he was brought to the hospital under police escort.

2. *The Second Session of March 13, 1964*

The second trial took place in the Hall of the Constructors' Club. The same judge presided.

The session opened with the reading of the test's results : "Psychopathic features of character have been established. But Brodsky is able to work. Consequently administrative measures may be applied to him".

It is established that, both previously to the first court session, and to the second, Brodsky had no opportunity to get acquainted with the files of his case. He is led away (evidently he is still under arrest), in order to give him this possibility. Brought back to the courtroom, he declares that poetry listed on pages 141, 143, 155, 200 and 234 of the files, attributed to him, are not by him. Furthermore, he asks the court not to put on record his diary which he wrote in 1956 when he was 16 years old.

Judge : With regard to the so-called poetry—we will take into consideration, but in particular, there is no ground to eliminate the diary. Citizen Brodsky, from 1956 you changed your place of work 13 times. You worked at a plant one year and then ceased to work for one-half year. In the summer you were with several new groups, and after that you did not work for 4 months. Explain to the court why you didn't work in the intervals but led a parasitic life ?

Brodsky : I worked in the intervals. I was occupied with that on which I work at the present time : I wrote poetry.

Judge : It means, you wrote your so-called poetry. But what is useful in your changing your place of work so many times ?

Brodsky : I began when I was 15. Everything was interesting to me. I changed work so many times because I wanted to know as much as possible about life and people.

Judge : And in what useful way did you serve your fatherland ?

Brodsky : I wrote poetry. This is my work. I am persuaded... I believe that what I wrote will serve the people, and not only now, but future generations.

A Voice from the Public : Ain't he something ! He thinks too much of himself.

Another Voice : He is a poet. He must think so.

Judge : Thus, you think that your so-called verses are useful to men ?

Brodsky : Why do you speak about my "so-called" verses ?

Judge : We qualify your verses "so-called" because we have no concept of them.

Sorokin : (the public prosecutor) You say that you are very inquisitive. Why then, did you not want to serve in the Soviet Army ?

Brodsky : I decline to answer such questions.

Judge : Answer.

Brodsky : I was excused from military service and not because I did not want to serve. These are different things. I was excused twice. The first time because my father was sick, the second time by reasons of my illness.

Sorokin (public prosecutor) : Can one live on the money you earn ?

Brodsky :   One can. In jail I had to sign everyday that 40 kopeks were spent on me, but I earned more than 40k daily.

Sorokin :   But one has to have clothes, footwear.

Brodsky :   I have one suit—an old one, but I do not need another.

Counsel :   Was your poetry appraised by specialists ?

Brodsky :   Yes, by Chukovskiy and Marshak [1] who spoke very well about my translations, much better than I deserve.

Counsel :   Were you connected with the Translation Section of the Association of Writers ?

Brodsky :   Yes. I contributed to the almanac the first time in the Russian language and then I read translations from the Polish.

Judge :   (to the counsel) You must ask him about his useful work and you ask about his appearance in the press.

Counsel :   His translations are just his useful work.

Judge :   (to Brodsky) ... Explain how your participation in our great progressive movement toward communism should be appraised.

Brodsky :   Construction of communism is not only work on a machine-tool or tilling of the soil. It is also intellectual work which (interrupted by the Judge).

Judge :   Stop grandiloquence. Tell the court better how you intend to construct your toiling activity in the future.

Brodsky :   I wanted to write poetry and make translations. But if this contradicts some generally accepted norms, I shall take some steady work but will write verse anyhow.

Assessor Tyaglyy :   With us every man works. But you remained idle for such a long time ?

Brodsky :   You do not count my work as a work, I wrote poetry, I think it is work.

Judge :   Did you draw conclusions from the article in the press ?

Brodsky :   Lerner's article was mendacious. That is the only conclusion. I drew.

Judge :   It means that you drew no other conclusion.

Brodsky :   In my opinion I am not a man leading a parasitic life.

Counsel :   You said that the article "Okololiteraturnyy truten" [1], published in the Vecherniy Leningrad is not correct. Why ?

Brodsky :   Only the first and the family name are correct there. Even the age is false. Even the verses are not mine. There, persons are named as my friends whom I hardly know, even do not know at all. How can I then appreciate the article as correct and draw conclusions from it?

Sorokin :   How could you make translations from the Serbian independently without using the work of other people?

Brodsky :   Your question is put ignorantly. The contract assumes an interlinear translation sometimes, I know Polish, less Serbian, but these are kindred languages and with the aid of an interlineary I could complete the translation.

a) Witnesses for the Defense [2]

In the procedure, "witnesses" or experts were not separated into groups : those for the accusation and those for the defense, but their

---

[1]   Both very eminent Soviet writers, poets and translators.

[2]   The persons who testified in favor or against Brodsky were called "witnesses."

hearing was mixed up. For a better understanding of thier testimonies they are divided here into the two groups.

Grudnina : I guided the work of beginning poets more than eleven years. During seven years I was a member of the Commission on the Work with Young Authors. At the present time, I guide poets of the senior classes at the place of Pioneers and at the Circle of Young Literary Men of the Svetlana plant. On demand of publishing houses, I have collected and edited four symposiums of young poets which contained more than 200 authors. In this way, I know from experience the work of almost all young poets of the city.

The work of Brodsky as a young poet is known to me from his verses of 1959 and 1960. These were not yet perfect poetry but with vivid boons and images. I did not include them in the collection, but I hold the author to be capable. I did not meet Brodsky until the fall of 1963. After the publication of the article "Biliterary Drone" in the Vecherniy Leningrad, I invited Brodsky to my apartment for a conversation since young people beseeched me with demands to interfere in the case of a slandered person. To my question, with what he is occupied in the present time, he answered that he has studied languages and worked on artistic translations for about 18 months. I took his manuscripts for examination. As a professional poet and specialist in literature, according to my education, I assert that Brodsky's translations are on a high professional level. Brodsky has the specific, not often encountered, talent for an artistic translation of poetry. He submitted to me a work of 368 lines of verses; furthermore, I read 120 lines of his translations of poetry printed in Moscow publications. In accordance with my personnal experience of artistic translations, I know that such an amount of work requires from the author not less than six months on concentrated work time, not including time for steps necessary for the publication and conferences with specialists. The time to be spent on all these steps cannot be evaluated as one knows. Estimating Brodsky's work already done, at the lowest publisher's rates, he has already earned 350 rubles of the new money and the question is only when all that will be printed. Besides contracts for translations, Brodsky submitted to me contracts for radio and television work, which is already completed, but not yet paid in full.

From conversations with Brodsky and with people who know him, I am aware that he lives very frugally, stints himself in clothes and food, sits at his work most of the time. The money he gets for his work he adds to the family budget.

Counsel : Is it necessary for artistic translations to know the works of the author in general ?

Grudnina : Yes, for good translations such as those of Brodsky's it is necessary to know the works of the author and to grasp his voice.

Counsel : Is interlinear work used by translators ?

Grudnina : Yes, everywhere. One of the most eminent translators in Leningrad, A. Gitovich, translates from Old Chinese with the help of interlinear translations.

Assessor Lebedeva : Is it possible for self-taught person to learn a language ?

the trial. There are not witnesses in the sense of American law, since they did not testify about things they have seen. Some of them may be named experts, according to American qualification.

Grudnina : In addition to those languages I learned in the University, I learned two languages by the self-taught method.

Counsel : If Brodsky does not know Serbian can he still make a highly artistic translation ?

Grudnina : Yes, certainly.

Counsel : Don't you think that an interlinear translation means the use of foreign work ?

Grudnina : Certainly not. (*Bozhe sokhrani*)

Judge : Then what is your opinion about Brodsky ?

Grudnina : My opinion is that as a poet he is very talented and by a head higher than many, who are regarded as professional translators.

Judge : And why does he work alone and does not join any literary associations ?

Grudnina : In 1958, he asked to be admitted to my literary association, but I heard about him as a hysterical young man and did not accept him. Pushed him away with my own hands; this was a mistake and I regret it very much. Now I shall take him into my association and shall work with him, if he wants it.

Assessor Tyaglyy : Did you personally see at any time how he works on verses or does he use foreign work ?

Grudnina : I did not see how Brodsky sits and writes, but I did not see either how Sholokhov sits at his desk and writes. But that does not mean that...

Judge : (interrupting) It is improper to compare Sholokhov with Brodsky.

Counsel : I want to ask you, witness. Brodsky's production for 1963 is the following : verses in the book "The Dawn over Cuba", translations of Galchinskiy's poetry (not yet published), verses in the book "Yugoslavian Poets", songs of Ganeso and publications in *Koster*, (camp or bon fire). Can it be evaluated as serious work ?

Grudnina : Yes, certainly. This is a year filled with work. But money this work can bring—not now, but some years later. It is not correct to define the work of a young author by the amount of remuneration received at the present time. A young author can fail, a new long work may be necessary. There is such a joke : The difference between a sponger and a young poet consists of that, that the sponger does no work, but eats, but a young poet, ... works, but does not eat.

Judge : We do not like your assertion : in our country every man receives according to his work, that is why it cannot be that he works much, but receives little. In our country where such a concern is shown about young poets, you say that they starve. Why did you say, that young poets do not eat ?

Grudnina : I did not say that. I warned that it is a joke which has some truth in it. Young poets have very uneven income.

Judge : Well, that depends upon them. It is not necessary to clarify that for us. All right, you clarified that your words were a joke. Let us accept this clarification.

Witness Etkind, Member of the Association of Writers and Teachers of the Institution named after Hertsen :

In accordance with my publicly-literary work connected with the education of beginning translators, I often have to read and hear translations of young literary men. About one year ago I happened to get acquainted with the works of Josef Brodsky. These were translations of poetry of a remarkable Polish Poet Galchinsky, which was not yet translated here in a great amount. I was very much impressed by the clarity of poetical images, musicality, passion and energy of the verses. I was also struck by the fact that Brodsky learned the Polish language independently,

without foreign help. He read Gal'chinskiy's poetry in Polish with the same enthu-
siasm with which he read his own Russian translations. I understood that I have
to do with a man endowed with ability and—what is not less important—with
capacity for work and assiduity. Translations which I had the opportunity to
read later, fortified me in this opinion. These are, for instance, translations of the
Cuban poet Ferrandez, published in the book, "Dawn over Cuba", and excerpts
from modern Yugoslavian poets printed in his collection of the State Literary
Publishing House. I conversed extensively with Brodsky and was amazed by his
knowledge in the fields of American, English and Polish literatures. The translations of verses is a most difficult work requiring assiduity, knowledge and talent.
On this path the literary man can expect numerous failures, but the material
income is a thing of the future. One can translate verses during several years and
not earn a single ruble. Such work requires selfless love of poetry and of the work
itself. The study of languages, history, culture of a living people all that cannot
be mastered at once. My knowledge of Brodsky convinces me that he has, as a
poet-translator, a great future before him. This is not my opinion only. The Office
of the Translator Section, after having taken cognizance that the publishing house
had dissolved the contract concluded with Brodsky, unanimously decided to
petition the Director of the publishing house to attract Brodsky to the work and
to restore contractual relations with him. I know for certain that this opinion is
shared by such autorities in the field of poetical translations as Marshak and
Chukovsky, who...

Judge :   (interrupting) Speak only for yourself!

Etkind :   It is necessary to give Brodsky the opportunity to work as a poet-translator.
To do that far from a big city, without the necessary books and a literary environment—is very difficult, almost impossible; in my opinion, a great future awaits
him in this field. I must say that I was very astonished when I saw the poster
"Trial of the sponger Brodsky".

Judge :   But you knew this connection.

Etkind :   I knew, but I never thought that the court would accept such connection.
Thanks to his technique of making verses, he could easily turn out hack-work,
translate hundreds of lines if he would take work easy, lightly. The fact that he
earned little does not prove that he did not work.

Another witness for the defense was Admoni, professor of the Institute named after Hertsen, linguist and translator.

Admoni :   When I heard that Brodsky was brought to court on an accusation of being
a sponger, I held it is my duty to present my opinion to the court. I think to have
the right to do it because during 30 years I worked with young people in my capacity
of teacher at institutions of higher learning and because I occupy myself with
translations for a long time. I am barely acquainted with Brodsky. We greet each
other, but it seems to me we did not exchange even two sentences. However, during
the last year approximately, or somewhat longer, I intently watched his translation work as featured in his appearances at parties and in publications. And on
the ground of these translations from Galchinskiy, Ferrandez and others, I can
say, taking full responsibility, that the translations required extraordinary work

on the part of the author. They testify of the great mastery and culture of the translator. But miracles do not take place. Either mastery or culture do not occur by themselves. Steady and persistent work is needed to this effect. Even if the translator works with interlineary help, he must, in order to produce a valuable translation, get a notion of the language from which he translates, a feeling of the structure of the language, must know the life and culture of the people, etc. But Brodsky, besides that, also learned the languages themselves. That is why it is clear that Brodsky works intensely and persistently. And when I heard, only heard today, that he, in general, graduated only after seven classes, it became clear to me that he had to perform a really gigantic task to acquire the mastery and culture he possesses. Mayakovky's words about poetical work "You use for one necessary word thousands of tons of wordy ore" may be applied to the work of a poet-translator. The Ukase according to which Brodsky is brought to responsibility is directed against those who work little, but not against those who earn little. Spongers are those who work little. That is why the Brodsky accusation of sponging is absurd. You cannot accuse a man of sponging who works assiduously and much, not thinking of great income, ready to stint oneself on everything, only in order to create valuable artistic work.

Judge : What did you say that it is not necessary to try those who earn little ?

Admoni : I said, the essence of the Ukase is, that one must try those who work little, but not those who earn little.

Judge : What do you want to say by that ? Did you read the Ukase of May 4th ? Communism is created only by the work of millions.

Assessor Tyaglyy : Where did Brodsky read his translations and in what language did he read them ?

Admoni : (with a smile) He read in Russian. He translates from a foreign language into Russian.

Judge : If a simple man asks you, you must explain to him, but not smile.

Admoni : And I explained that he translated from Polish and Serbian into Russian.

Judge : Adress the court and not the public.

Admoni : I beg your pardon. It is a professional habit, to speak to the audience.

b) Witnesses for the Accusation

Smirnov : I am not acquainted with Brodsky, but wish to say that if all the citizens would assume Brodsky's attitude toward the accumulation of material values, we could not build communism for a long time. The mood is a dangerous weapon for its owner. Every one said that he is clever—almost a genius. But nobody said what a man he is. Brought up in an intelligent family, he has only a seven-year education. May those present here say, would they like to have a son with a seven-year education ? He did not join the Army because he was the only bread-winner of the family. But, what a bread-winner is he ? It was said here—talented translator, but why does nobody say that he has much confusion in his mind ? And anti-Sovietic lines.

Brodsky : That is not true.

Smirnov : He has to change many of his thoughts. I call in question the certificate about his nervous disease, given by the mental dispensary. It is these illustrious friends who set all the bells ringing : "Save the young man". But he must be treated by forced labor, and nobody will help him, no illustrious friends. I personally do not know him. Know about him from the press. And I am acquainted with the certificates. I question the medical certificate which freed him from military service. I am not a medical man, but I question it.

Brodsky : When I was freed (from military service) as an only bread-winner, my father was sick, he was in bed after an infection, but I worked and earned. Then I was ill. What are the sources of your knowledge about me in order to speak so about me ?

Smirnov : I got acquainted with your personal diaries.

Brodsky : On what ground ? ...

Judge : I overrule the question.

Smirnov : I read his verses.

Counsel : There are some verses not belonging to Brodsky in the files. But how do you know that the verses you read really are by him, since you speak of non-published verses ?

Smirnov : I know, and that is all...

Witness Logunov : (Deputy Director of the Economic Department of Ermitazh) I am not acquainted with Brodsky personally. The first time I saw him was here, in court. It is no longer possible to live as Brodsky lives. I could not envy parents who have such a son. I worked with writers. Moved in their circles. I compare Brodsky to Oleg Shestinskiy. Oleg travelled with the propaganda brigades, he graduated from Leningrad State University and from the University in Sofia. And also he worked in a mine. I wanted to come forward with assertion that if all cultural skill would be employed Brodsky's poetry would be real poetry. Brodsky must start his life anew.

Counsel : It is still necessary that withnesses speak on facts. But they...

Judge : You can evaluate testimonies of witnesses later.

Witness Denisov (tube layer) : I am not acquainted with Brodsky personally. I know about him from our press. I appear as a citizen and representative of society. After I read the article in the newspaper I became indignant at Brodsky's work. I wanted to look into his book, and went to the Library. There are no books by him there. I asked acquaintances as to whether they know him. They do not know him. I am a worker. I changed my work twice only during my life. And Brodsky ? Brodsky's testimony that he knows many specialties does not satisfy me. No specialty can be learned in such a short time. It was said that Brodsky represents something as a poet. Then why was he not a member of any association ? He does not agree with dialectic materialism ? Yet, Engels is of the opinion that work creates the man. But Brodsky is not satisfied with this formula. He is of a different opinion. Maybe he is very talented, then why does he not find a way in our literature ? Why does he not work ? I would like to suggest the opinion that I, as a worker, am not satisfied with his working activity.

Witness Nikolayev : (retired) I personally am not acquainted with Brodsky. I would like to say that I knew about him during three years by the pernicious influence he exercises upon his coevals. I am a father. I was convinced by an example of my own how hard it is to have a son who does not work. I saw Brodsky's verses several times with my son. A poem 42 chapters and separate verses. I know Brodsky from Umansky's case. There is a proverb : "Tell me who your friends are... (and I will tell you who you are). I know Umansky personally. He is an inveterate anti-soviet man. In listening to Brodsky I recognized my son. My son also told me that he is a genius. He, like Brodsky, does not want to work. Persons such as Brodsky and Umansky exercise a pernicious influence on their coevals. I wonder about Brodskys, parents. Obviously, they echoed him. They sang with him in unison... According to the form of his poetry, it is evident that Brodsky is able to versify. But no, his verses brought nothing but harm. Brodsky is not a simple sponger. He is a militant sponger! Action must be taken against such persons, like Brodsky, without mercy. (Applause)

Assessor Tyaglyy :   You are of the opinion that Brodsky's verses influenced your son?

Nikolayev :   Yes.

Judge :   Had a bad influence?

Nikolayev :   Yes.

Counsel :   How do you know that it was Brodsky's verses?

Nikolayev :   There was a folder and an inscription on the folder... Josef Brodsky.

Counsel :   Your son was acquanted with Umansky?

Nikolayev :   Yes.

Counsel :   Then why do you think that it is Brodsky and not Umansky who had a pernicious influence on your son?

Nikolayev :   Brodsky and those with him. Brodsky's verses are shameful and anti-Sovietic.

Brodsky :   Name my anti-sovietic verses. Cite at least one line from them.

Judge :   I shall allow no quotation!

Brodsky :   But I would like to know of the verses he is talking about. Maybe they are not mine.

Nikolayev :   If I had known that I shall appear in court I would have made a photo and brought it.

Witness Romasheva :   (teacher of Marxism-Leninism at the school named after Mukhina) I personally am not acquainted with Brodsky, but his so-called activity is known to me. Pushkin said that a talent—it is work, in the first place—work. And Brodsky? Does he really work? Does he really work on his verses in order to make them comprehensible to the people? I am astonished that my colleagues create such a halo around him. You see it can occur only in the Soviet Union that the court so benevolently speaks with a writer, so comradely advises him to study. I, as a secretary of the Party organization of the school named after Mukhina, can say that he badly influences young people.

Counsel :   Did you at any time see Brodsky?

Romasheva :   Never. But his so-called activity permits me to judge him.

Judge :   Can you bring forward some facts?

Romasheva :   As an educator of young people I know the opinions of them about Brodsky's verses.

Counsel :   And you yourself are acquainted with Brodsky's verses?

Romasheva :   I am acquainted. It is a h-hhorror! I hold impossible to repeat them. They are horrible!

Judge :   Witness Voyevodin, do you know Brodsky personally?

Witness Voyevodin :   (A member of the Association of Writers) No. I work in the Assn. for only six months. I am personally not acquainted with him. He comes seldom to the association, only to translators' evenings. He obviously understands how his verses will be received and does not attend other associations. I read his epigrams. You would have blushed reading them, comrades Judges. There was mention here of Brodsky's talent. A talent is measured only by popular recognition and this recognition is lacking and cannot occur. A folder with Brodsky's poetry was handed over to the Assn. of Writers. The verses are on three themes : The first theme is aloofness from the world, the second is pornography, and the third dislike of the fatherland of the people there when Brodsky speaks of a "foreign" fatherland. Wait a moment, I shall recall... "monotonous is the Russian crowd". May these shaking verses remain on his conscience. A poet Brodsky does not exist ! A translator may be is there, but a poet there is not ! I completely support the assertion of the comrade who spoke about his son who was perniciously influenced by Brodsky. Brodsky tears young people away from work, world and life. In that is a big anti-social role of Brodsky.

Judge : Did you discuss Brodsky's talent in the Commission ?

Voyevodin : There was only one short session at which Brodsky was mentioned, but the talk did develop into a wide discussion. I repeat Brodsky limited himself to half-pornographic epigrams and seldom visited the Association. My friend, poet Kuklin, once expressed his indignation at Brodsky's verses aloud, from the platform.

Counsel : The opinion you wrote about Brodsky was shared by the entire Commission ?

Voyevodin : We did not submit the report for approval to Elkind because he was of another opinion.

Counsel : And to other members of the Commission, the content of your report was known ?

Voyevodin : No, the report is not known to all members of the Commission.

Brodsky : And how does it come that you had my verses and my diary ?

Judge : I overrule the question.

(Here ends the interrogation of witnesses.)

Judge : Citizen Brodsky, you worked occasionally ? Why ?

Brodsky : I said already. I worked all the time as a member of a staff and then wrote verses (with despair). This is work—to write verses !

Judge : But your earnings were very small. You said you earned 250 rubles in a year, but the information of the militia is that it was only 100 rubles.

Counsel : At the previous session, it was decided that the militia should check the information about the earnings, but this was not done.

Judge : A contract—which was sent to you by the publishing house is filed here. But it is only a piece of paper signed by no one.

(A note is sent to the Judge from the public that contracts are signed first by the author and then by the officials of the publishing house.)

Judge : Please do not send me more notes.

c) Summing-up by the Public Procesutor

Sorokin : Our great people is building communism. A remarkable quality is developing in the Soviet man—the enjoyment of socially useful work. Only that society is thriving where idleness does not exist. Brodsky is far away from patriotism. He has forgotten the main principle, "he who does not work shall not eat". And Brodsky has led the life of a sponger for too many years. In 1951, he left school and took up work in a plant. He was 15 years old. He quit work the same year.

(The public prosecutor then cites Brodsky's statement of service and the intervals between work and explains them by idleness.)

Sorokin : (continues) We checked that Brodsky received only 37 rubles for work. But he asserts that it was—150.

Brodsky : This is a payment on account. Only a payment on account. A part of that I shall receive later !

Judge : Shut up Brodsky !

Sorokin : There where Brodsky worked he embarrassed everybody by his lack of discipline and desire to work. The article in the "Vecherniy Leningrad" met with great response. Especially many letters came from young people. They sharply condammed Brodsky's behavior (reads letters). Young people think that he has no place in Leningrad. That he must be severely punished. He lacks completely the sense of conscience and duty. Every man thinks it a pleasure to serve in the army. But he avoided it. Brodsky's father sent his son for a test to the dispensary and he brought from there a certificate which the credulous military commission accepted. Already before the summons to the military commissariat Brodsky wrote to his friend Shakhmatov. "A date with the Commissariat of Defense is forthcoming. Your desk will be a safe refuge for my iambi." He belonged to a group whose satiric laughter met the word "work" and listened with respect to its "Führer" Umansky. Brodsky is united to him by the hate of work and the Soviet literature. Sets of pornographic words and concepts met there with particular success. This is the stinking place from where Brodsky appeared. There was mention of Brodsky's gifts. But who says it ? Persons like Brodsky and Shakhmatov.

A shout from the public : "Who ? Chukovsky and Marshak are alike to Shakhmatov ?"
(Members of the people's brigade expel the shouter from the hall.)

Sorokin (continues) : Brodsky is defended by rogues, spongers, ... lice and bugs. Brodsky is not a poet, but a person who attempts to versify. He forgot that in our country a person must work, create values : at benches breed a producing not verses. Brodsky must be forced to work by coercion. He must be exiled from the Hero-City. He is a sponger, cad, rogue, a man with filthy ideas. Brodsky's admirers sputter. But Nekrasov said :

> "A Poet you may not be
> But a citizen you are obliged to be !"

We sit in court today not over a poet, but a sponger. Why was a man who hates our fatherland defended here ? The moral make-up of the persons who defended him must be checked. He wrote in his verses : "I love a foreign fatherland". There is an entry in his diaries : "I thought about the exit across the red line for a long time already". "In my coroded head constructive thoughts are ripening." He wrote also this : "The town hall in Stockholm inspires me more than the Kremlin in Prague". He called Marx "an old glutton, with a wreath of fir cones". In a letter he wrote : "I spit on Moscow". That is the value of Brodsky and of all who defend him.

(Then a letter of a girl is cited who writes with disrespect of Lenin. What relation the letter has to Brodsky is completely unclear. It is not written by him and not addressed to him).

At that moment the Judge addresses me (the stenographer)

Judge : Stop taking notes.
I : Comrade Judge, I beg to be permitted to take notes.
Judge : No.
I : I am a journalist, member of the association of writers. I am writing about the
    education of young people. I beg permission to take notes.
Judge : I do not know what you are writing. Stop it !

(Sorokin is continuing his speech, then speaks the advocate. I can give an account of her speech only citing the theses, since I was not permitted to take notes).

d) Theses of the Defense

The public prosecutor used material, which are not in the files, which are brought forward in the case for the first time and about which Brodsky was not interrogated and gave no explanation.

The identity of the materials from the special case tried in 1961 [1] was not checked by us and that, cited by the public prosecutor, we cannot check. If he speaks about the Brodsky diaries, they date from the year 1956. It is a youthful diary. [2] The public prosecutor quotes as a public opinion letters of readers to the editors of "Vecherniy Leningrad". The authors of the letters do not know Brodsky, did not read his verses and judge by a newspaper article which is biased and incorrect concerning many facts. The public prosecutor not only offends Brodsky calling him "cad", "sponger", "anti-Soviet element", but also persons who stood up for him : Marshak and Chukovsky, respected witnesses.

Conclusion : Not in possession of objective evidence, the public prosecutor uses forbidden methods.

What material is at the disposal of the prosecution?

1. The information about the working activity of Brodsky from 1956 to 1962. In 1956 he was 16 years old : he could in general study and live at the expense of his parents up to 18 years. The frequent change in work is an influence of a psychopathic feature of character reflected in the incapability to find his place of life at once. Interruptions in particular are explained by seasonal work on expeditions. There is no reason to speak about avoiding work until 1962. (The

---

[1] The Umansky and Shakhmatov case.
[2] Brodsky was 16 years old at the time.

advocate speaks about his respect of assessors, but regrets that there is no person among them competent on questions of literary work). When a minor is accused ... there is without fail a teacher among the assessors; if a physician is in the dock, a physician necessarily sits as an assessor. Why then this just and rational custom is forgotten when literature is invaded.

2. Brodsky does not work regularly since 1962. However, contracts with publishing houses from November 1962 and September 1963, information given by the television studio, the periodical, "*Koster*" also the published book of translations from Yugoslav poets—testify to his creative work. There is a report, signed by Ye. Voyevodin, which is sharply negative, with inadmissible accusations of anti-Soviet activity, a report reminding of the worst times of the cult of personality. It was explained that the report was not discussed in the commission, is not known by its members, is the opinion of the prosaic Voyevodin. There are opinions of such persons, foremost masters of translation, such as Chukovsky and Marshak, of the witness V. Admoni, eminent specialist on literature, linguist and translator,—expert on translated literature, member of the board of the Translators' Section and member of the commission on the work with young poets ... all of them value Brodsky's work very higly and speak about the great expenditure of work for the publications of his writings of 1963. *Conclusion*: Voyevodin's report cannot refute the opinion of these persons.

3. No one of the witnesses does know Brodsky, and did not read his verses; the witnesses testify on the ground of documents unchecked and received by them in an incomprehensible way, and express their opinion by pronouncing accusatory speeches.

No other material is at the disposal of the accusation.

(The advocate requests the court not to consider the following)

I. The material of the special case, examined in 1961, quashed with regard to Brodsky.

If Brodsky would have then or later, committed an anti-Soviet crime, written anti-Soviet verses, this would have been then the subject of an investigation by the security organs.

Brodsky was closely acquianted with Shakhmatov and Umansky and stood under their influence. But, fortunately, he freed himself from their influence a long time ago. However, the public prosecutor read entrances of those years, presenting them without relation to time and space, by which he aroused the public against Brodsky.

Many young people belonging to Umansky's group, thanks to the interference of rational grown-ups, were returned to the normal life. The same thing happened also to Brodsky during the last two years. He began to work much and creatively. But at this point he was arrested.

II. The question of the quality of Brodsky's verses.

We do not know as yet what verses from those in the files are by him, because according to his statement there are a number of verses which are not written by him.

To establish as to whether these verses are decadent, pessimistic or lyrical is the work of authoritative experts in literature and translation. This question can be resolved neither by court nor the parties to the trial themselves.

Our problem is to establish as to whether Brodsky is a sponger, living on unearned income and leading a parasitic way of life.

Brodsky is a poet-translator, who invests his work in the translalations of poets of brotherly countries of people's democracies, in the fight for peace. He is not a drunkard, not an amoral person, not a grabber. He is reproached for having earned too little, thus, for having not worked. (The advocate informs about the specifics of literary work, the order of remuneration. Speaks about the huge amount of work spent for translation, about the necessity of studying foreign languages and the creations of the author under translation. About the fact that not all the presented work is accepted and remunerated).

The system of advance payment. The figures produced in the case, are not correct. According to Brodsky they are higher. It was necessary to check that. The sums are unimportant. Then—on what did Brodsky live? Brodsky lived with his parents, who during the time of his formation as a poet supported him.

He had no means of existence from unearned sources. He lived poorly, in order to have the possibility to occupy himself with his beloved work.

e) Conclusions of the Defense

Brodsky's responsibility is not established. Brodsky is not a sponger and measures of administrative pressure cannot be applied to him. The importance of the Ukase of May 4, 1961 is very great. It is a means of clearing the city from real spongers, and parasites. The unfounded bringing to responsibility discredits the Ukase. The ruling of the USSR Supreme Court of March 10, 1963 obliges the court to adopt a critical attitude toward the presented material, not to permit the sentencing of those who work, to observe the rights of those brought to responsibility to get acquainted with the files and to present evidence of their innocence. Brodsky was groundlessly arrested on February 13, 1964 and deprived of the possibility to present all the evidence of his innocence. However, the evidence presented and that which has been said in court suffice for the conclusion that Brodsky is not a sponger.

f) Conversations During the Recess

(The following opinions given by the public in the hall were overheard by the stenographer during the recess before the sentence was read ... they are characteristic of the atmosphere of the trial).

—Writers :   They should all be exterminated (at our hands).
—Intellectuals :   They thrust themselves upon us.
—But does the intelligentsia not work ? They also work.
—And you did not see how it works ? Profits from the work of others !
—I also shall get myself an interlinear and shall translate verses !
—But do you know what an interlinear is ? Do you know how a poet works with an interlinear ?
—Imagine !—Important things !
—I know Brodsky ; he is a regular guy and a good poet.
—He is an anti-Soviet man. Did you hear what the prosecutor said ?
—And did you hear what the advocate said ?
—The advocate spoke for money, but the prosecutor... gratis. It means that he is right.
—Certainly, the advocates want just a little more money. For them there is no difference what to say if only the money can be pocketed.
—It is nonsense, what you are saying.
—You are calling names. I'll call a member of the brigade at once ! Did you hear what quotations were made ?
—He wrote it a long time ago.
—So what, if a long time ago.
—I am a teacher. If I would not believe in education, what a teacher I would be.
—We do not need such teachers like you.
—We are sending our children—and what are they taught ?
—But Brodsky did not even get a chance to exonerate himself.
—Enough, we heard enough of your Brodsky.
—And you, you who made notes, why did you make them ?
—I am a journalist. I am writing on education and want to write about that.
—And what is to write about it ? Every thing is clear. You all stick together. Your notes should be taken from you.
—Try it !

—And what will happen ?

—Try and you will see.

—So you threaten. Hallo, *druzhinnik* (member of the people's brigade). There is somebody threatening !

—He is a *druzhinnik* and not a policeman in order to grab you for every word.

—Hallo, *druzhinnik*, you are called a policeman here ! You should be all exiled from Leningrad, you would learn what a pound of evil costs !

—Comrades, what are you discussing. He will be acquitted ! You heard what the advocate said.

g) The Sentence

The following sentence was read by the court.

Brodsky is systematically not fulfilling the duty of a Soviet man to produce material values and personal security, which is seen from the frequent change of work. He was warned by the organs of the MGB in 1961 and 1962 by the militia. He promised to take steady work, but he did not draw the consequences and continued not working, but wrote and read his decadent verses at parties. As can be seen from the report of the Commission for the Work with Young Writers, Brodsky is not a poet. He was condemned by the readers of the newspaper "Vecherniy Leningrad", That is why the court is applying the Ukase of May 4, 1961 (sentencing) Brodsky to be exiled to remote localitites for five years with the application of mandatory work.

h) The Aftermath

After the sentence Brodsky remained under arrest of the militia and then in the *"Kresty"*, prison in Leningrad, up to March 22 when he was transported in a train car together with thieves and murderers to a kolkhoz in Konosheskiy District, Arkhangelsk Region and worked there as a manure transporter.

Victor Zarza relates in the Manchester Guardian [1] that during the trial such eminent Soviet writers as Samuel Marshak, Korney Chukovsky, as well as the composer Dmitry Shostakovich had sent telegrams to the court to plead for Brodsky and that "many other writers, less well known, took part in the fight to save Brodsky".

A protest against the sentence was sent to the Soviet leadership by a number of prominent writers, artists and composers including those mentioned above. This was reported in a letter which reached the West by underground channels.

---

[1] May 13, 1964, p. 1 and 12.

It was said in the letter, writes Zarza, that the proceedings have been received as revival of the methods used during the Stalin cult of personality and completely alien to the principle of socialist legality.

As it is stated in the report forwarded to *"Russkaya Mysl'"* in Paris, Brodsky was sentenced :

1. in spite of the fact that after 1961, when the authorities did not deem it possible to condemn him in the Shakhmatov and Umansky case, with whom he previously broke relations himself, he persistently worked during the subsequent years and achieved success in literay work;

2. in spite of the fact that telegrams of K. Chukovsky, S. Marshak and D. Shostakovich, who intently followed the creations of the young poet, were filed in the case. Not a single one of them were read in court;

3. in spite that defense witnesses, men like Etkind and Grudnina, well known literary figures, gave positive and well-founded characteristics of Brodsky's work and asserted orally and in writing that accusations against Brodsky were either groundless or false;

4. in spite of the fact that all the witnesses of the accusation frankly admitted that they neither knew Brodsky nor his verses and base their opinion only on the feuilleton of the *"Vecherniy Leningrad"*;

5. in spite of the fact that the public prosecutor constructed his speech partly on the quotations from an old childish diary not explaining why any quotations from old diaries can support an accusation of parasitism.

Thus, in reality the sentence was based on a feuilleton, not read in court, material in the report on Brodsky by the KGB and Voyevodin and the defamatory feuilleton by Lerner.

To this the following must be added :

Besides these evident procedural and material violations, and the obvious prejudice against Brodsky, the court falsely applied the Ukase of May 4, 1961 to Brodsky.

The sentence is based on the assertion that Brodsky did not work and did not produce "material values" (the producing of spiritual values is, evidently, not "the obligation of a Soviet man", according to the court).

But even assuming that writing poetry and making translations is not "working" in the sense of the Ukase of May 4, 1961, which of course, is wrong, still the bare fact of not working is not punished by any Soviet law. Not working is punishable according to the Ukase only when it is related to a livlihood supported by an unearned income which is characterized by the law as parasitic way of life.

It remained uncontested, however, that Brodsky had no unearned income "allowing him to lead a parasitic way of life", as the law reads. It was also not proven by the prosecution that his income from work, although small, was insufficient for a very modest life, within his family, which in reality he led.

However, in the Ruling of 1963, cited above, the Presidium of the USSR Supreme Court denounced courts which banish without having established "facts, certifying an anti-Soviet, parasitic existence" of the accused. A life is parasitic, let us not forget, only when it is supported by unearned income. The sentence violates law and the rulings of the USSR Supreme Court.

It is therefore peculiar that the prosecution body, which protested unsuccessfully Brodsky's arrest, did not protest the sentence at once, after it was pronounced.

The sentence found a defender in the person of A.B. Chakovsky, Editor of *Literaturnoya gazeta*.

In an interview given in New York by him to George Feifer, Chakovsky said : "Brodsky is what we call 'podonok' [scum, riff-raff] a plain and simple 'podonok'. He was tried in open court under the established procedures of our law; he defended himself; judges heard all the relevant testimony from literary experts and Leningrad public opinion—and they came to the conclusion he should be banished from the city and given some honest work—it is simply amusing that you can work up so much self-righteous indignation about the so-called 'Brodsky case' when here [in the United States] bombs are thrown into churches, young girls are killed and the killers are allowed to go free ...". [1]

On July 7, the Washington Post reported from Yugoslavia that the Soviet poet Turkov told a Congress of the Pen Club in Bled that the Brodsky case was under review by the USSR Supreme Court.

According to the information of the same paper from Moscow of April 7 1966, "The Soviet poet Joseph Brodsky has been freed from prison (?) and will publish a new book of poems, informed sources reported today".

The Soviet poet Yevtushenko, answering a question about Brodsky's whereabouts at a reading of Yevtushenko's poetries in Princeton

---

[1] *The New York Times*, December 20, 1964, Sect. 6, p. 22.

in November 1966 said : "I do not know exactly but evidently he is in Moscow. A short time ago we appeared together at an evening and he was received with an ovation by the public". [1]

The American Poet Stanley Kunitz, who visited the USSR in Spring 1967 met Brodsky in Moscow. Kunitz reproduces Brodsky's words as follows : "My exile was supposed to last for five years.... They sent me to Arkhangelsk to work in the fields, as an agricultural laborer.

In September 1965, after one year and nine month, my sentence was commuted. It was a fruitful experience, and, really I enjoyed it. The peasant in whose house I lived, treated me as a son. I did not encounter any anti-Semitism. The local officials and indeed the whole community were good to me. I think of these people with love. They were happy to have a poet in their midst, and they tried in all possible ways to help me, so that I could write. It was one of my most productive periods". [2]

Kunitz conversed with Brodsky with the help of an interpreter. Maybe the translation of the Russian word used by Brodsky into "commuted" is not exact. But if the translation is correct, it would mean that the banishment was shortened not as a result of a legal procedure—the review of the sentence—but in the way of a pardon.

The sincerity of Brodsky's declaration, that he "enjoyed" his banishment is questionable. Speaking to a foreigner who would repeat his words in the press abroad, Brodsky was hardly free to tell the truth.

The mitigation of the puishment after twenty-one month of time served does not change anything in the illegality of the evidently biased sentence.

C. The Anti-Parasite Law Amended

Important changes were brought into the RSFSR Law of 1961 by the Ukase of the Presidium of the RSFSR Supreme Soviet of September 20, 1965, [3] in force since October 5, 1965.

---

[1] *Novoye Russkoye Slovo* (N.Y.), November 22, 1966.

[2] Stanley Kunitz, "The Other Country Inside Russia", in *The New York Times Magazine*, August 20, 1967, p. 40.

[3] *V.V.S., RSFSR*, 1965, Item 932.

The definition of persons subjected to the law (parasites) is limited in paragraph 2 of the preamble to persons being of age and able-bodied who do not desire "to fulfill their most important constitutional duty of working honestly according to their capacity and lead an anti-social, parasitic way of life".

Thus, dropped from the list are persons who are engaged in forbidden businesses, employ hired labor, etc. [1]

Furthermore, amendments to paragraphs 1,2,3,5 and 6 of the 1961 law restrict the banishment for 2 to 5 years to special places assigned to this purpose only with regard to those parasites who live in the city of Moscow, the Moscow Region and the city of Leningrad, on decision of the District (City) People's Court.

Parasites residing in all other places are assigned to work, on decision of the District (City) Executive Committees of local Soviets at enterprises (constructions) situated in the district of their steady residence or other places in the limits of the given region, territory or autonomous republic.

Eliminated is the banishment jurisdiction of assemblies of collectives of toilers at enterprises, shops, intitutions, organizations, kolkhozes and kolkhoz brigades.

According to Berry and Berman [2] the amendment of 1965 "makes it difficult if not impossible to repeat the 1964 fiasco which resulted in the exile of Iosif Brodsky ... if the amendment is followed".

Yes, "if the amendment is followed".

But the real trouble with Soviet administration of justice is not the imperfection of laws, but their violation when desired by the Party. The Brodsky case was framed, tried and executed, under the flagrant violation of laws of Criminal Procedure and the law of 1961. Why should another similar case not be staged if the Party deems it necessary, in violation of the 1961 law as amended in 1965 ? The authors themselves state that the amendment makes it "difficult, if not impossible". What difficulties ever prevented the Soviet Communist Party from violating the law by organs of administration of justice ?

---

[1] See Law of 1961, *V.V.S.*, 1961, Item 273.

[2] Donald D. Berry and Harold J. Berman, "The Soviet Legal Profession", *Harvard Law Review*, 1968, No. 1, p. 38.

D. Political Importance of the Anti-Parasite Laws

"Khrushchev has replaced the Stalinist dualism of law and terror by a new dualism of law and social pressure" wrote Berman. [1] "One is free from arbitrary arrest by the secret police, but one is not free of the social pressure of the collective ... whether it be the innocuous pressure of the factory, one's co-workers, or the local Party organization. The new dualism still stands in the shadow of the old".

Leon Lipson is somewhat of the same opinion. "... the abolition of the special Board" he stated, "may be thought by some of the party leaders to have left a gap that ought to be filled. The Anti-Parasite collectives could well have considered a device, less odious because newer and more public than the Special Board, for separating from the community those elements who presented a 'social danger' but whose behavior need not be classified as criminal action warranting regular criminal prosecution". [2]

For Frederich-Christian Schroeder, the legislation against parasites stands not only in the shadow of Stalinist terror but generates an administration similar to the work of the Special Board of the NKVD. Schroeder sees the similarity in the banishment sentence of five years, in the uncertainty of the corpus delicti, and the exclusion of an appeal. Conspicuous to Schroeder is also the resemblance of the MVD role in Stalin's times with supervising rights of the Ministry of Internal Affairs over the local authorities participating in the proceedings against the parasites.

However, the most shocking resemblence Schroeder sees in the fact that the right of banishment exercised by the Special Board of the NKVD "developed from the right of arrest of the CheKa with regard to Parasites"! The first decree, basically, conferring the right of taking in custody had the purpose of fighting violators of work discipline, the revolutionary order and the parasitic elements of the population and to confine them in forced labor concentration camps for a period of up to five years, when, during the investigation, reasons for a criminal responsibility were not established. [3]

Schroeder also relates the anti-parasitic laws directly to the pre-

---

[1] Harold J. Berman, "The Dilemma of Soviet Law Reform", *Harvard Law Review*, 1963, No. 5, p. 950.

[2] Leon Lipson, "The Future Belongs to the Parasites", *op. cit.*, p. 4.

[3] Friedrich-Christian Schroeder, "Social Courts and Administrative Justice", *Osteuropa-Recht*, 1962, No. 4, p. 296.

revolutionary legislation going back as far as the 18th and 19th centuries. He quotes an Ukase of 1760 conferring upon landowners the right to hand over to the authorities, for banishment to Siberia, their serfs for "dissoluteness and evil actions". This right was established by the Ukases of 1765 and 1766, and extended to punishment for "bad behavior" in general.

But the real source of the anti-parasitic legislation Schroeder discovers in the Regulation of May 15, 1808 concerning the peasants belonging to the imperial family. According to this Regulation the general assembly of peasants could vote by a majority the recruiting or banishment of a member of the community who in consequence of a lack of zeal or bad behavior is not in position to pay taxes. The ruling uses even the expression "social sentence", writes Schroeder in italics. [1]

The connection between the banishment of the modern anti-parasite legislation and the banishment because of reprehensible way of life on the basis of a commune's sentences of the 18th and 19th centuries Schroeder holds close and surprising. Firstly, it is expressed in the term of the banishment: five years in both legislations. Secondly, in the similarity of the element of the crime : "dissolute way of life" and "the non-payment of taxes because of negligence" in the old Russian legislation and "parasitic way of life" in the new one. But first of all ... the resamblence lies in the procedure in which the measure is taken : vote of the commune or of another smaller group, and in the absence of an appeal against the banishment sentence. [2]

Having established the source of anti-parasitic laws in the Russian legislation of the 18th and 19th centuries, Schroeder comes to the somehow surprising conclusion that "although one cannot speak of a direct continuity because of the long interval between both and becasue of the changed circumstances, the legal institute so deeply rooted in the past, must be still vivid through literature and history". [3]

---

[1] The expression "obschestvennyy prigovor" is in no way specific for the ruling quoted by Schroeder. The "mir" or the peasants' commune was called by documents and the peasants themselves "obschestvo" (society) and the word "prigovor" when not used by a court but by the peasant assembly, meant any decision. The technical expression used by the peasants' assemblies was "mir prigovoril" which meant the taking of any decision of the assembly.

[2] Schroeder, op. cit., p. 303.

[3] Ibid., p. 304.

R. Beermann [1] even prolonged Schroeder's list of old Russian enactments concerning all kinds of banishments by peasants, landlords, officials etc. in prerevolutionary Russia. He claims that "the historical and sociological aspects of this practice (banishment) are worth tracing—because it suports the controversial theory of historical continuity in Soviet law, which claims that a considerable part of the law is derived from pre-revolutionary legal institutions, despite official Soviet pronouncements, Marxist legal theory and the abrogating decrees of Soviet authorities" [2]

Reaching as far back as the 18th century for the sources of the parasite laws, Schroeder and Beermann overlook the law of August 14, 1881 on "Measures for the Preservation of State Order and Public Tranquillity". [3] This law empowered the province and city administration of provinces declared to be "in a state of reinforced or extraordinary protection", to *banish* administratively persons to various localities of the Empire under the open supervision of the police for a term not exceeding *five years*. (Article 24).

The state of reinforced or extraordinary protection was first introduced into several provinces was then subsequently extended to other provinces so that in 1901 almost all of Russia was in a state of reinforced or extraordinary protection.

In his secret report to the Committee of Ministers of December 4, 1904, A.A. Lopukhin, Director of the Department of Police, asserted that banishment was impartially applied to "those who are really dangerous for the state and to "those who only express independent opinions, and to the latter was more than to the former". He emphasized that during the last years administrative banishment was inflicted upon young people who participated in student disorders which had no political character, upon workers for strikes which were

---

[1] R. Beermann, "Soviet and Russian Anti-Parasite Laws", *Soviet Studies*, 1964, No. 4, p. 424.

[2] In support of the continuity theory Beermann quotes Gsovski and Grzybowski. But just these two authors assert the discontinuity of prerevolutionary law in Soviet legislation (*Government, Law and Courts in the Soviet Union and Eastern Europe*, The Hague and New York, 1960, I, p. 473). When a total discontinuity of the application of tsarist law, although ordered already by first Soviet legislation in the legal field, was practically difficult because of the absence of new codes until 1922-23, the idea that Soviet Legislation of the fifties and sixties of the 20th century was inspired by samples of tsarist laws of the 17th and 18th centuries is evidently unfounded.

[3] *Svod ustanovleniy o preduprezhdenii i presechenii prestupleniy*, St. Petersburg, 1890, Article 1, Note 1.

quite peaceful and pursued exclusively economic ends, and, futher-more, upon peasants who, after long arguments about the land with landlords, occupy it arbitrarily. Persons who committed public offen-ces, the investigation of which would present too much trouble for the public, and even those persons who merely insulted officials, were also benished. "Using administrative banishment for twenty years" Lopukhin wrote, "the administration got so accustomed to it that registration of banishments exists only for those persons who were put under open supervision of the police". [1] Evidently, this law could be better identified as a source for the parasite laws since the banishment on grounds of parasite laws is also an administrative measure, according to Soviet authors.

Schroeder's and Beermann's comparison with tsarist legislation is farfetched and not convincing. It is at least very doubtful as to whether the Soviet leaders were inspired by the Ukase of 1760 or 1808 when they introduced the anti-parasite laws.

Certainly, administrative banishment was used in Russia for a long time before the 1917 Revolution and may be Stalin used the same method of elimination of political foes by banishment to Siberia which he experienced himself on his own person on basis of the 1881 law. But only the banishment measures and term of five years for its duration used by the Special Board and the Law of May 1961 were similar to the provision of the law of 1881. The reasons for the admi-nistrative banishment and the conditions under which it was carried out in Tsarist Russia have little in common with Soviet administra-tive banishment. Stalin's victims were sentenced to forced labor in concentration camps, under appalling conditions, whereas the tsar's subjects administratively banished to Siberia, were free there and not compelled to any work.

The similarity of the banishment by administration or by decision of peasants' communes of the tsarist legislation and the banishment voted by an organization or other group according to the Law of May 4, 1961, is confined to the method of punishment itself and the duration of the banishment. The actions punished by banishment are, however, in both cases completely different. And after all, it was not the Rus-

---

[1] Lopukhin's report was first published in Geneva in 1905 under the title *Dokladnaya zapiska direktora departamenta politsii rassmotrennaya v Komitete ministrov*, with an introduction by N. Lenin. Quoted from *Tsarizm v bor'be s revolutsiyey*, edited by A.K. Drezen, M. 1936, pp. 30-31. See also Samuel Kucherov, *Courts, Lawyers and Trials Under the Last Three Tsars*, N.Y., 1953, pp. 202-205.

sians who invented the banishment by government or a people's decision : it was applied in old Rome (for instance, Ovid was banished to the present Dobryja (Rumania) and the Greeks practiced ostracism a long time before the Russians. European countries which possessed remote unpopulated territories or colonies used to send there their criminals, political or other, as for instance, France to Cayenne and Great Britain to Australia.

It seems to the present author futile to search for the continuity up to the present time of measures taken at the time of serfdom, under completely different social and political conditions. The similarity of methods of punishment does not prove anything. All methods of punishment applied in the Soviet Union were used before in tsarist Russia and elsewhere and do not serve as proof for the continuity of Soviet laws from tsarist legislation and in other counrtries previously. The duration of five years is a term applied in the Soviet Union not only to banishment; the first economic plans were conceived also for five years of duration.

It is true that the dualism of penal coercion and social pressure ascertained by Berman remains. But to say that Stalin's terror is replaced by social-pressure so that the present dualism stays in the shadow of the former, is an exaggeration.

Also Lipson's suspicion is not convincing. The anti-parasite legislation of 1961 cannot fill in the gap formed by the abolition of the Special Board. As a replacement for the Special Board activity, the anti-parsite laws are too weak.

However, both authors are right in so far as the anti-parasite legislation, especially that of 1951-1959, presented the possibility of interference and abuses of justice maybe more than any other legislation, and not only by the omnipotent and omnipresent Party, but by public organizations, collectives, neighbours, etc. The lack of exact definition of parasitism, as contradistinct from work and especially the general provision about "other anti-social actions", contribute in a large extent to this possibility.

But the anti-parasite legislation is at least appropriate to settle accounts with political foes of the regime, since, if a political element is established by the inquest the case must be presented to the prosecution body for criminal prosecution. Par example, in the Brodsky case, Brodsky was first cleared by the MGB and only after that prosecuted according to the anti-parasite law.

But in other fields, the Law of 4 May 1961 serve as tool for the elimination of undesirable elements. Still its application cannot be compared with the activity of the Special Board and cannot serve as a replacement to it.

The "shadow of Stalin's terror" does not approximate it. Judging by the rulings discussed above, the USSR Supreme Court is endeavoring to inculcate the people's court with the strict compliance with the law in parasite cases. Certainly, not always with success, as exemplified by Brodsky's case.

E. The Legal Nature of Anti-Parasite Laws

There is unanimous consent among Soviet writers about the administrative, not penal character of the anti-parasitic laws.

V.F. Kirichenko, for instance, writes that the punishments of banishment and confiscation of property acquired not by work, provided by the Law of May 4, 1961, are measures of administrative and not criminal repression. He brings forward four arguments for his assertion.

Firstly, criminal punishemnt may be applied only to a person who committed a crime. Since the actions enumerated in the Law of May 4, 1916 are not crimes, but anti-social offenses, they cannot be repressed by criminal punishments.

Secondly, according to Part 2, Art. 3 of the Basic Principles of Penal Legislation of the USSR and the Union Republics and Art. 3 of the RSFSR Criminal Code, [1] criminal punishment may be applied only by a sentence of a court, but, on grounds of the anti-parasite laws, also collectives may pronounce sentences of banishment and confiscation.

Thirdly, punishment provided by the law at hand does not produce criminal records of the punished person.

Fourthly, the order of liberation from punishment before the term has run out provided by the anti-parasite sentence differs substantially from the conditions of liberation from punishment before expiration of the term provided by Art. 53 of the RSFSR Criminal Code.

Indeed, Article 6 of the Law of May 4, 1961 provides that if a person

---

[1] Article 3 of the RSFSR Criminal Code : Only a person guilty of crime, e.g., who has committed deliberately or carelessly an action dangerous to the public and provided by criminal law, is subject to penal responsibility and punishment.

proves his reformation by an honest attitude toward work during the banishment he may be freed before the end of his term, if one-half has been served, on petition of a public organization of the people's court but on consent of the executive committtee of the local soviet at the place of his former residence, whereas Article 53 of the RSFSR Criminal Code gives the right to the court to free conditionally a person condemned ... to banishment ... if he has already served not less than one-half of his term. [1]

Also Shlyapochnikov is of the opinion that "the measures of state coercion provided by them (the anti-parasite laws) with regard to parasitic elements are considered as measures of administrative pressure. These measures are qualitatively different from those of a penal punishment". Also Shlyapochnikov evokes the same differences as Kirichenko that criminal punishment is applied only by courts and punishments are mainly not made a matter of record.

In a discussion of the Law of May 4, 1961 at a common session of the Criminal Law and Procedure Section and the Sector for the Study and Prevention of Criminality of the Institute of State and Law of the USSR Academy of Sciences, Strogovich, however, emphasized that the procedure of applying the Ukase of May 4, 1961 is not a criminal, not a civil one, but as concerns the cases examined by a court, it nears an administrative procedure. [2]

Perlov remarked that according to the Ukase, sponging and parasitism are not penal crimes, and the measures applied are not criminal punishments. But when, in case of a violation of the sentence (at the place of banishment), corrective measures are invoked or in the case of avoiding corrective work they are replaced by confinement, the order of this replacement must be carried out according to the norms of the RSFSR Criminal and Criminal Procedure Codes (Articles 368 and 169 of the Code of Criminal Procedure). [2,3]

Recognizing that "Soviet jurists characterize violation of the anti-parasite law as an administrative offense", Berman, however, finds that these offenses differ from other administrative offenses on four counts.

---

[1] V.F. Kirichenko, "Legal Questions of the Fight Against Persons Avoiding Socially Useful Work and Leading an Anti-Social Parasitic Life", *S.G.P.*, 1961, No. 8, pp. 128, 129.

[2] These articles regulate the juridiction of courts for decisions on questions about the fulfillment of sentences.

[3] *S.G.P.*, 1961, No. 8, pp. 132-133.

First, because it imposes responsibility not for a specific action or omission, but for *any* "anti-social act" resulting in the leading of a parasitic way of life. The gist of the offense, according to Berman, is not the mere failure to work (which is in itself not prohibited in Soviet law), but "the status of constituting an anti-social parasitic element".

Secondly, the "administrative measure" of *vysileniye* (resettlement)[1] applied by the anti-parasite law is very similar in character to the criminal sentence of banishment (vysylka) and exile (ssylka) and "is much more severe than the administrative measures in quality. Escape from the place of resettlement is expressly made a crime under the provisions of the Criminal Code dealing with escape from the place of exile".

Thirdly, another application of the Criminal Code is prescribed when persons avoid work in the place of banishment. In such an event, the parasite may be sentenced by the local people's court, on representation by the militia, to corrective work with confiscation of 10% of the pay, and when the parasite avoids also corrective work the court may replace corrective work by confinement according to Article 28 of the RSFSR Criminal Code.

Fourthly, Berman remarks that in contrast to other administrative violations, "it can be tried in court" which in this sense is said to be acting administratively rather than judicially"[2]

As stated in the beginning of this chapter also, the parasite laws, especially those of 1957-1960, as enacted in the first nine republics, were an expression of the trend to bring the population nearer to the process of shifting from regular courts to people's courts, a development which has to be completed with the withering-away of the State, law and regular courts under communism.

However, it was evidently found very soon that it was premature to entrust the decision of such importance as the banishment of people for the duration of two to five years, to casual assemblies of citizens at plants, factories kolkhozes and apartment houses, thus opening the doors to every sort of abuse. That is why the new laws of 1961 restricted

---

[1] It seems to me that the translation is not correct : The word *Vysileniye* means eviction, expulsion; the forced separation from a residence and does not suggest resettlement in another place, although Smirnitsky's dictionary under 2 attributes to the verb "vyselit'" the sense of a transfer from one residence to another.

[2] Harold J. Berman, *Soviet Criminal Law and Procedure, RSFSR Codes*, Cambridge, Mass., 1966, pp. 9, 10.

the jurisdiction of citizens' assemblies to one category of parasite only, encountered very seldom, and also for this category the prosecuting body has to decide as to whether to direct the case to the citizen's assembly or to the people's court, competent for deciding all other parasite cases. In this way, the development from regular courts to people's courts certainly experienced a setback.

As in the case of comrades' courts, also the parasite laws have, in the first place, a preventive and educational character. That is why the warning which has to precede the trial is so much stressed by Soviet writers and the USSR Suprmee Court.

At the XXII Party Congress, L.F. Il'yichev said that "one should not be carried away by administrative punishment and forget that the main scope of the legislation on spongers is re-education by means of persuasion and warning. A formal, soulless approach in this matter is not permissible". [1]

But together with the preventive and educational purpose, a punitative measure is applied which is much stronger than those in use by comrades' courts. But it must be kept in mind that the jurisdiction of comrades' courts is limited to petty offenses, although comrades' courts are enabled to mete out very sizeable punishments, such as eviction from apartments, demotion at factories, etc. But anti-parasite laws extend to such serious offenses from the Soviet viewpoint, as methodical flinching from work, the misuse of property rights, the employment of hired work, speculation and private enterprise which actively violate some basic principles of communism.

Analyzing the essence of anti-parasite laws the majority of Soviet and American writers come to the conculusion that the punishment of banishment is not a penal but an administrative measure, although neither the assembly or the people's court are administrative instances (the Executive Committee of the local Soviet only confirms the decision of the assembly). Also the plenum of the USSR Supreme Court names the measures appled by courts, on the basis of the law of May 4, 1961, "administrative" as we have seen.

This conclusion is reached by the method of exclusion : since it is not a penal measure because it differs from a criminal punishment in many instances ... it is an administrative measure (since punitative measures other than criminal or administrative are not known).

---

[1] *XXII' S'ezd KPSS i voprosy ideologicheskoy raboty*, M. 1962, p. 51.

Those who do not quite agree with the definition of administrative measure for the provisions of the anti-parasite laws, such as Berman or Strogovich, do not find another definition for them. As we have seen, Berman stresses only the difference between them and administrative measures and thinks that they resemble very much to criminal provisions but still are not such.

Strogovich emphasizes that the parasite trial is neither a criminal nor a civilian proceding, but only "approaches" the administrative one.

It is peculiar, that Shlyapochnikov, who is of the opinion that even the warning of anti-parasite law, if carried out by the court, is not a measure of social pressure but an administrative measure [1] as in the case of warning issued by an assembly of citizens, writes elsewhere : "It would be expedient to provide in statutes of comrades' courts of the union republics for the right of these courts to examine materials about pressure (warning with the setting of a term for the change of the previous way of life and to petition the executive committee of the district of city soviet to banish malicious spongers)". [2]

Thus, according to Shlyapochnikov, the comrades' courts should issue the warning or banishment, according to the Law of May 4, 1961. Since all decisions and sentences of the comrades' courts are undoubtedly the exercise of social pressure and not criminal or administrative punishment, also the banishment would fall into the category of social pressure. But from the point of view of a social institution exercising administration of justice, there is no difference between an assembly of citizens having jurisdiction according to the anti-parasite law, and the comrades' courts. Hence the conclusion is that also banishment pronounced by these assemblies are also measures of social pressure. [3]

---

[1] A.S. Slyapochnikov, *Bor'ba s tuneyadtsami-vsenarodnoye delo*, M. 1962, p. 41.

[2] A.S. Slyapochnikov, "Questions of the Strengthening of State Legal and Social Pressure in the Fight with Parasitic Elements", *S.G.P.*, 1963, No. 9, p. 48.

[3] As a matter of fact, some comrades' courts examine cases of a parasitic way of life. Slyapochnikov himself who commends such practice, reports about a parasite cases where a comrade court issued a warning (A.S. Slyapochnikov, "Soviet legislation and Society in the Fight with Parasitic Element", *S.G.P.*, 1961, No. 8, p. 69). Also Yudel'son recognizes the competence of comrades' courts in parasite cases, according to Art. 5/10 of the Statue on comrades' courts : *Polozheniye O tovarishcheskikh sudakh*, M. 1962, pp. 118-124. It is evident however, that a banishment sentence cannot be pronounced by a comrade' court, since the Law of May 4, 1961 names expressly only two instances empowered for such a sentence : the people's court and the citizens' assemblies.

It cannot be said, in the author's opinion, that one and the same measure provided by the same law ... warning ... is a measure of social pressure when taken by a citizen's assembly and an administrative one [1] if applied by the people's court.

The Soviet legislator, inspired by the decision of the XXI Congress of the Party on comrades' courts, parasites and people's brigades, introduced a third kind of coercion— *"obshchestvennoye vozdeystviye"* or social pressure. All measures provided by the comrades' courts are not criminal and not administrative but measures of social pressure. The warning of the anti-parasite law, if initiated by the plant or other assembly, is undoubtedly a measure of social pressure. Why should the banishment pronounced by the same assembly be somthing else than a measure of social pressure? Its severity is not a basis for the change of its character.

With regard to people's courts, it was said, in order to support the version of an administrative and penal measure, that the courts act in parasite cases as an administrative arm and not judicial instance. Also court warnings are administrative measures according to this opinion.

In the opinion of the present writer the warning and banishment of the Law of May 4, 1961 are not administrative measures also when pronounced by people's courts, and these courts are not acting as an administrative instance in parasite cases. Both measure are "social pressure".

The transfer of certain cases not covered by the criminal code to the competence of social bodies by the soviet legislator created a new jursidiction. The jursidiction of social bodies. These bodies act not as criminal or administrative instances but as social entities. The cases they judge are neither criminal nor administrative offenses, but violations of the social morality, of the way of life considered obligatory within Soviet society, and are punishable by measures of social pressure, independantly of whether the sentence is pronounced by the social body or the court. The court acts only in place of the social body in certain cases. If it can be asserted that a judicial instance sets an administrative punishment—why should it not be admitted that the court applies a measure of social pressure in parasite cases?

That the banishment provided by the anti-parasite laws is a measure

---

[1]   This distinction is made for instance by Shlypochnikov : *Bor'ba s tuneyadstami-vsenarodnoye delo*, M. 1963, p. 41.

of social pressure cannot be denied and is not denied as far as we know. The introduction of the people's court jursidiction for a certain category of cases by the laws of 1961, was only a guarantee for the fairness of the procedure. It did not produce a change in the character of the punishment.

It is evident that among all the laws introducing the participation of the people in the administration of justice, the anti-parasite laws are the most controversial, and dangerous because of the importance of the punishement they carry. Still it should not have the sinister character the American writers see in it, if applied with the observance of legal guarrantees prescribed by the law itself and required by the Soviet writers and the USSR Supreme Court. Certainly also this law is open to abuses and undue pressure of the Party, but not more than any other Soviet law.

Although Berman is right when he writes : "Some Western students of the Soviet scene, have, in my opinion, exaggerated the evils of this kind of new Social justice", [1] still the danger of injustice provided by the application of the antiparasite Law as exemplified by the Brodsky case, is great.

Lipson remarks that "Soviet commentators sometimes treat the parasite laws like a nuclear weapon maintained more in order to make threats credible than to be regularly invoked. Mere enactment and dissemination of the anti-parasitic decrees, somehow [2] have driven the great majority of persons into regular work". [3]

But, nuclear weapons, even when not employed, still represent a great danger.

---

[1] Berman, "The Dilemma of Soviet Law Reform", *Harvard Law Review*, 1963, No. 5, p. 947.

[2] Lipson refers to I.D. Perlov, *Sovetskaya obshehestvennost'v borbe s tuneyadstsami*, M. 1962, p. 12.

[3] Leon Lipson, Hosts and Pests, The Fight Against Parasites, *Problems of Communism*, April 1965, p. 79.

PART TWO

MEN OF LAW

CHAPTER ELEVEN

LEGAL EDUCATION

A. LEGAL EDUCATION UNDER THE TSARS

a) *Birth of the Russian Universities*

The first idea to create an institution of higher learning in Russia was born at the time of the shaping of a new Russia by Peter the Great.

In 1724, Peter I approved a report by Blumentrast, providing the establishment of an "University attached to the Academy of Sciences". Already after the death of Peter I, the professorial staff of the university arrived from abroad in Petersburg in 1725 and 1726.

However, there was a complete lack of native professors for university teaching and there were also no adequately prepared students for the hearing of lectures in institutions of higher learning.

Not until in 1738 was the attempt made to start regular teaching at the university. In 1742 the twelve professors of the university had twelve students. According to M. V. Lomonosov, there was nothing similar to a university at the Academy of Sciences.

Thus, this attempt ended in complete failure.[1]

The first real Russian University was opened for all classes of the population in Moscow in 1755 according to a project worked out by Lomonosov—the Russian peasant-genius and I. Shuvalov—the eminent statesman, and confirmed by Empress Elisabeth I, on January 12 and April 26, 1755, respectively.

The famous "Peasant from Arkhangel'sk", whom Pushkin characterized as "our first university", wrote to Shuvalov : "My only desire consists in the getting the university into operation from which numberless of Lomonosovs may descend". Lomonosov believed that "Russia is able to produce her own Platos and Newtons 'alert' in thinking".

Lomonosov's desire was fulfilled. The Russian universities educated

---

[1] In 1738 there were two students at this "university" of whom neither knew a foreign language, whereas the professors did not understand Russian.

a great number of scientists, statesmen and public figures, of which Russia can be proud.

Two secondary schools (*gimnazii*) were attached to the university in which pupils were prepared for study in the university.

Among two others, the university had also a faculty of law (law school).

The three professors of the faculty of law taught : 1) general jurisprudence, natural law and law of nations as well as the legislation of the old and new Roman Empire; 2) the domestic state laws; 3) politics, "which showed the relation, union and actions of states and rulers, as they are and were during the past centuries and in the present time", according to the program devised by Lomonosov and confirmed by the Senate. [1]

b) *University Statutes of 1804, 1835, 1863 and 1884*

Up to the end of the 18th Century the faculty of law of the Moscow University remained the sole source of legal education in Russia.

The history of the pre-revolutionary universities and their faculties were tightly bound to the internal policy of the individual tsars.

Thus, the liberal tendencies of Alexander I rule were reflected in the University Statutes of 1804. [2]

Still, the University suffered in the beginning under the initial handicaps : absence of Russians fit for professorial activity and the lack of students adequately prepared for study at a university.

Two remedies were thought out in order to eliminate this situation. Russian students were sent to foreign universities for undergraduate and graduate studies and the curriculum of the *gimnazii* was reorganized into secondary schools, and reinforced by Latin, Greek and other subjects, according to the German model.

Also, the Russian Universities were thought to resemble German ones.

The University Statutes of 1804 granted them autonomy. The president of the university (*rector*), the deans of the departments (*dekany*), a board and a council all were elected by the professorial staff, which itself was also elected. The board had a "permanent assessor" appointed by the school district curator whose prupose was "to supervise the keeping of order and preservation of law".

---

[1]   A.F. Shebanov, *Yuridicheskiye vysshiye uchebnyye zavedeniya*, M. 1963, p. 10.

[2]   *Polnoye sobraniye zakonov*, St. Petersburg, 1830, Nos. 1497-1500.

The council, consisting of the professors, confirmed the programs of the individual lectures and schedules of examination. At that time "the main purpose of the organization of universities was their unification, with a system of secondary school", writes Milyukov. [1]

To this effect a pedagogical institute had to be attached to every university.

New universities were opened in Derpt, Kazan' and Khar'kov at the beginning of the 19th century under Alexander I in relation with the reorganization of the entire school system and they were regulated by the Statute of 1804.

At the faculties of law of the universities, called departments of moral and political sciences, the following subjects were taught : laws, and the law of nations, diplomacy and national economy; speculative and practical philosophy; dogmatic and moral theology, interpretation of the gospel and church history.

The reaction which characterized the reign of Nicholas I and its three basic principles of autocracy, orthodoxy and nationality were extended also to education.

Indeed, the Minister of Education, Count S.S. Uvarov, gave the following formulation to the basic educational purposes : "In the middle of the speedy downfall of religious and civil institutions in Europe, at the time of the exposure of destructive notions everywhere, it is necessary to strengthen the fatherland on solid foundations, to find principles on which welfare is based, forces which represent distinctive characteristics of Russia exclusively owned by her; to collect in one whole the sacred remains of her nationality and to fasten on them the anchor of our salvation. Fortunately, Russia has enough warmth of faith in the salutary principles, without which she cannot prosper, gain strength, live ... A Russian, devoted to his fatherland, would not agree to the loss of one dogma of our orthodoxy, any more than he would agree to the theft of even one pearl of the Monarch's crown. Autocarcy is the main condition of Russia's political existence. Besides these two national principles there is also a third one, not less important, not less powerful : nationality ... These are the main principles which had to be incorporated in the system of education". [2]

Consequently, the new statutes on universities of 1835 and the order

---

[1] P.N. Milyukov, "The University", *Entsiklopedicheskiy Slovar' Brokhauza i Efrona*, St. Petersburg, 1902, V. 68, p. 790.

[2] Quoted by P.N. Milyukov, *op. cit.*, p. 791.

of the Minister of Education of 1849 abolished the autonomy of the universities, and put them under the supervision of the school district curators. The university president was not any more elected but appointed by the government and not from among the staff of the university. Also the deans of the departments were appointed by the Ministry of Education and could be dismissed at any thime by the Minister. Furthermore the professional staff was not elected but appointed. Censorship over teaching was introduced. The professors had to present an exact program of their lectures and the chairman of the department was obliged to see to it that there was nothing covert in the content of the program which contradicted the teaching of the Orthodox Church or the form of government and the spirit of state institutions; they had to attend lectures and report to the university president the smallest deviation from the program, although completely harmless. [1]

The children of the lower classes, the so-called "cook's children", were not admitted to universities.

The program of the faculties of law came directly under the influence of the reaction. The teaching of philosophy [2] and constitutional law of European countries "shaken to the roots by internal and pernicious riots" [3] were abrogated.

These measures led to decay and stagnation in higher education. "There is little wonder", writes Milyukov, "that a professor of history was prevented from speaking about the downfall of paganism and the establishment of Christianity; a professor of Russian history did not dare to mention "veche" [4] and the heresies of the XVth century, and a jurist could not speak on English state institutions. [5]

Only one university, in Kiev, was added, under Nicholas I, in 1834. It was transformed from a lyceum to replace the Vil'na University closed after the Polish Insurrection of 1830.

The great epoch of liberal reforms of Alexander II produced the most liberal university statute in tsarist Russia, in 1863. [6] Extensive

---

[1] Milyukov, *op. cit.*, p. 792.

[2] "Because of the pernicious development of this science by German scientists" as stated by the Minister of Education in 1850.

[3] *Ibid.*

[4] Public assemblies in the old republics of Novgorod and Pskov in the 1st period of Russian history.

[5] Milyukov, *op. cit.*, p. 792.

[6] *Polnoye sobraniye zakonov*, St. Petersburg, 1866, V. 38, No. 39752.

rights for the election of the professorial staff, the president, the chairmen of the departments as well as for the division into departments were granted.

Two universities were added to the list of institutions of higher education : in Odessa and Warsaw, in 1865 and 1869 respectively, and a third university was projected for Tomsk. [1]

The curriculum was enlarged with new disciplines added.

The admission of students from every class of the population in unrestricted number was permitted. Education in a secondary school was not required as a prerequisite of admission to a university : home education sufficed for the admission to entry examinations. The program of 1850 was abolished.

The Statute of 1863 returned full autonomy to university life. The power of administration belonged to the council of the university which was elected by the professorial staff among them. It elected the president, the department chairmen who had to be confirmed by the Minister of Education, and all other administrative personnel. Although the sanction of the curator was needed for the establishment of rules of admission and behavior of students, the council had the independent right to distribute subjects to the individual faculties and confirmed the order of their teaching.

Still, the Statutes of 1863 did not provide for the free selection of subjects by students. They were bound to the program.

Also, women remained barred from the universities by the Statute of 1863, notwitstanding the fact that the coucils of the universities of St. Petersburg, Kiev, Khar'kov and Kazan' declared themselves in favor of the admission of women to the universities.

Although the Statute of 1863 attempted to form the university and the teaching in them according to the model of the German autonomous universities, the corporative organization of the students was not taken over. Also the freedom of teaching and learning of the German professors and students was not reflected in the Statute of 1863 : the first and the second remained bound to a definite program and curriculum.

But the pendulum of history again swung from the left to the right and remained there under the reactionary regimes of the last two tsars, Alexander III and Nicholas II, up to the Revolution of 1917.

---

[1] Opened in 1888 under Alexander III.

The University Statute of 1884 [1] put an end to any academic free-dom. The electability of the administration and the teaching personnel were abrogated and the universities came under strict control of the Minister of Education and the District Curator.

c) *Priviliged Law Schools*

But not only the universities, their professors and administration were under supervision of the government : also the students' life was submitted to strict regulation.

According to the "Rules for Registered and Non-Registered Stu-dents" of 1885, married students and females were not admitted to the University; marriage was forbidden to students during their registration at the university; a police certificate attesting to irre-proachable behavior was required for admission; students were for-bidden to form corporations and societies, they had no right to file petitions or requests signed by several persons, to formulate any requests in the name of students; every assembly or meeting of students were prohibited as well as the delivery of public speeches, and the col-lection of money.

The freedom of selection of the university by the student for his studies was abrogated. Every graduate from a *gimnasiya* was admitted only to the university of his school district.

The subjects were divided into two groups : the subjects in which the student had to pass an examination during the four years of study and the topics in which he had to prove his knowledge at the state examinations for graduation.

Along with law faculties of universities, special law schools as independent institutions imparted legal education to young people. The *Aleksandrovskiy Litsey*, founded in 1810, was a combination of a high school (somewhat like the French "lycée") and a law school. The first six forms provided for a secondary education; in the last three grades, law was taught according to a university program.

The *Aleksandrovskiy Litsey* [2] located in *Tsarskoye Selo*, the summer residence of the Tsars, near the palace, was a pet creation of Alexander I and under his personal sponsorship. Only children of the nobility were admitted to the Lyceum and graduation from it provided special privileges in civil and military service.

---

[1]   *Polnoye sobraniye zakonov*, St. Petersburg, 1887, V. 24, No. 2404.
[2]   Pushkin's *alma mater*.

Another privileged institution for higher legal learning was the School of Jurisprudence (*Uchilishche pravovedeniya*) in St. Petersburg. Only children of the hereditary nobility were admitted to this school. The system of education was the same as that for other lyceums : high school teaching in the lower grades and legal subjects at the higher three forms. The graduates were obliged to serve in the system of the Ministry of Justice at least six years.

The *Nikolayevskiy Litsey* was founded in Moscow, in 1868 and had eight forms of secondary school similar to *gimnasia* and three forms of law school. However, in contradistinction to the *Aleksandrovskiy Litsey*, the law school of the *Nikolayevskiy Litsey* was not an independant institution with its own professors : the students of the *Nikolayevskiy Litsey* attended lectures at the law faculty of the Moscow University and had to take their examinations there.

The students of the *Nikolayevskiy Litsey*, like those of the Aleksandrovskiy, lived at the lyceum. Tutors — one for every fifteen students — had to supervise the mental and physical develpoment of their students.

Another law school was the *Demidovskiy Litsey* in Yaroslav. It was organized into a real law school with a program similar to a legal faculty of a university in 1874.

The pendulum swung again to the left when Nicholas II was forced to liberalize somehow his regime after the Revolution of 1905.

The Ukase of the tsar of August 27, 1905 "On Provisional Rules" with regard to the universities abrogated the most conspicuous provisions of the Statute of 1884. In particular the elective rights with regard to the professorial staff and the administration of universities was restored.

The "liquidation" of the 1905 revolution brought with it the strengthening of the reactionary elements in the universities. But no other changes in the Statute took place up to 1917.

The programs of the law faculties differed according to the individual statutes.
In the following diagrams the various curriculi are listed.

1755	1804	1835	1863	1884
1. Natural law and the law of nations, and laws of the old and new Roman Empire;	1. Laws of the most eminent peoples of the past and present;	1. Roman legislation and its history;	1. Roman law (history dogmatic, and Byzantine law);	1. Roman law;
2. Russian jurisprudence and domestic state laws;	2. Civil laws and criminal laws and procedures of the Russian Empire;	2. Civil laws : general, extraordinary and local;	2. History of the most important foreign legislation, old and new;	2. Civil law and procedure;
3. Politics : interrelations, unions and actions of states and rulers as they were in the past centuries and are now.	3. Natural, political laws and the law of nations;	3. Police and criminal law;	3. Civil law, social structure and procedure;	3. Criminal law and procedure;
	4. Diplomacy and national economy;	4. Encyclopaedic jurisprudence and Russian state laws (fundamentals on classes and institutions);	4. Criminal law and court structure and procedure;	4. State law;
	5. Speculative and pratical philosophy;	5. Notions of international jurisprudence;	5. State law/Theory of state law of the most important foreign existing countries; Russian state law;	5. History of Russian law;
	6. Dogmatic and moral theology;	6. Laws of welfare, public service and decency;	6. History of Russian Law;	6. International law;
	7. Interpretation of the gospel and church history.	7. Laws on state taxes and finance;	7. History of Slavic legislation;	7. Police law;
		8. Canon law.	8. International law;	8. Finance law;
			9. Police law; doctrine of security or laws of decency. Doctrine of welfare or laws of public service;	9. Commercial law and procedure;
			10. Finance laws (theory of finances : Russian finance law);	10. Canon law;
			11. Canonical jurisprudence;	11. National economy and statistics;
			12. National economy and statistics;	12. Encyclopaedic law and history of philosophy;
			13. Encyclopaedia of law (encyclopedia of public and legal sciences, history and philosophy of law)	13. Theology, dogmatic and moral : is an obligatory topic for all faculties, according to the last four programs.
				14. Foreign language : French or German.

The present writer studied at the law faculty of the University in Kiev (The St. Vladimir University) from 1911 to 1915 and passed the state examinations in October-November 1915. The program of the faculty of law was the same as listed in the table, p. 258, under the Statute of 1884.

Among the subjects taught during the four years, a middle term examination had to be taken in Roman Law, History of Russian Law, Police Law, State Law, Canon Law, National Economy, Statistics and Encyclopaedic law. Also, an examination in a foreign language (French or German) had to be passed *pro forma* only.

The State examination for graduation at the end of the four years of attendance, which lasted six weeks, had to be passed in System of Roman Law, Civil Law, Civil Procedure, Criminal Law, Criminal Procedure, International Law and Finance Law.

All examinations of both groups of subjects were exclusivley oral.

Teaching techniques developed slowly at the institution of higher learning, yet it was adapted to the requirements of the epoch. Already in the second half of the 19th century, teaching by lecture was supplemented by work in seminars.

Seminars on civil, criminal and international law, as well as in civil and criminal procedures existed at the law faculty of the University in Kiev already before the revolution.

In order to bring theory and practice closer togehter, the seminars on civil and criminal procedures were headed by members of the Court of Appeal.

d) *The Students and the Liberation Movement*

It must be kept in mind that the Russian intelligentia was actively engaged in the fight against autocracy since the Decembrists up to the Revolution of 1917.

The Russian students were in the first ranks of this fight, and the tsarist government considered them enemies number one.

It can be said that, among the students, those studying on the faculty of law were the most active. I.V. Veretennikov, in his book of reminiscences of Lenin's youth, relates that, when asked why he chose the faculty of law for his studies, Lenin answered, "Now is such a time that one must study the legal sciences and national economy. Maybe I would have chosen different sciences at another time". [1]

---

[1] Quoted by A.F. Shebanov, *op. cit.*, p. 30.

The students fought with demonstrations, meetings, dissemination of illegal literature, anti-governmental propaganda and organization of strikes at plants and factories. The government answered with whipping the demonstrators by Cossacks, closing of universities and administrative banishment of the most active students to Siberia.

In 1900, 183 students of the Kiev and 28 of the Petersburg Universities were forcibly drafted into military service for having "caused disorder in a crowd".

The revolutionary activity in the institutions of higher learning reached its peak during the "first Russian Revolution" of 1905. Students assembled in illegal gatherings and opened the doors of their institutions to public meetings.

In the period of the "liquidation of the Revolution" (1907-1911), the institutions of higher learning functioned in an atmosphere of ruthless reaction. The government dismissed hundreds of liberal professors and instructors, arrested and banished to Siberia thousands of students. In 1911, one hundred professors at the Moscow University resigned in protest against repressive measures taken by the government against the management of the University. [1]

The Soviet writer Shebanov comes to the conclusion that "the better part of students and professors took part in the revolutionary movement; a great number of progressively-minded jurists graduated from the university and this despite the fact that the whole teaching was subordinate to the strengthening of the belief of students in the stability of the autocratic regime".[2] Still this did not prevent him from writing that "the greater part of the professors and students were reactionary inclined".

With regard to students this assertion is not correct. The overwhelming majority of Russian students were liberally-minded in contradistinction to their colleagues in Germany and France at that time. This was a natural consequence of the authoritative regime in tsarist Russia.

Very disputable is further Shebanov's assertion that the majority of students and professors saw the purpose of the faculty of law in the preparation of officials for the legal and bureaucratic apparatuses. [3] Certainly, students were prepared for a legal career at the faculty

---

[1] See *Narodnoye obrazovaniye v SSSR*, M. 1957, p. 384.

[2] *Op. cit.*, p. 31.

[3] *Ibid.*

of law of the universities. So are students of the Soviet universities. But in Shebanov's assertion the implication is reflected that the education of tsarist universities was especially utilitarian. This is not so.

Russian youth of the 19th and the beginning of the 20th centuries was very idealistically minded which was perfectly reflected in its fight against the government, led not for the bettering of their own situations, but for the general ideals of liberty, equality, and justice.

Comparing the Russian young people with Germans, Alexander Hertsen wrote about the Germans, "I think that the situation of a people whose young generation is not youthful is a great misfortune". And about the Russians : "General questions, civic exaltation saved us ; not only they but also the strongly developed scientific and artistic interest. They are as a burning paper, burned out tallow spots.

We (Hertsen was a student of the Moscow University at that time) watched step by step every event, every word, of the General LaFayette and General Lamarc : we not only knew all the details about the public of that time, but fervently loved them, of course the liberal ones ..." [1]

The leading educators of the time, such as for instance, Pirogov, were against extreme specialization at the universtiy.

In answer to the question, what is the scope of teaching in the universities, Wagner states : "The university must not prepare screws and nuts of the state machinery ... it must educate persons—citizens, with humanitarian ideals and spiritual interests ..." [2]

An overwhelming number of students belonged to the intelligentsia. Webster defines "intelligentsia" as "the people regarded as, or regarding themselves as the intellectual or learned class." [3]

But the Russian intelligentsia of the 19th and beginning of the 20th century was much more than that. Not every intelletcual or learned person was a member of the intelligentsia, and to belong to it a formal degree or diploma was not necessary. "The Russian intelligentsia", writes Berdyayev, "is a most particular spiritual and social formation. Intelligentsia is not a social class and its existance produces obstacles for Marxist explanation. The intelligentsia was an idealistic class, a

---

[1] Quoted by V. Wagner, "The University", *Entsiklopedicheskiy slovar' Granata,* 7th Ed., Vol. 42, p. 338.

[2] *Ibid.,* p. 339.

[3] *Webster's New Twentieth Century Dictionary of the English Language,* Cleveland & New York, 1962, p. 954.

class of people completely carried away by ideas and ready in the name of these ideas to go to jail, forced labor, or execution". [1]

Those ideas were liberation from autocracy and the freedom of the Russian people. The intelligentsia of pre-revolutionary time was a specifically Russian phenomenon, not repeated at any time or in any country, the Soviet Union included.

The father of the Russian intelligentsia was Radishchev, who published the first revolutionary book in 1790; "The Trip from Petersburg to Moscow". In the dedication of the book, he wrote : "I looked around me and my soul became stung by the suffering of humanity." And the soul of the Russian intelligentsia remained stung by the suffering of the Russian people, up to 1917.

Beginning with the Decembrists, the Russian intelligentsia fought with all possible means for the rights and welfare of the Russian people, not retreating before any sacrifices.

Men of the forties, sixties, seventies and eighties, and of the beginning of the 20th Century : cadets, menshevists, social revolutionaries and bolshevists ... all of them fought differently, according to their individual convictions, but all of them were inspired by a common goal : the freedom and welfare of the Russian people.

The great majority of the Russian intelligentsia acquired its freedom loving ideas in or from the universities. There social barriers were smoothed out.

In his recollection of the Moscow University, Hertsen states, "Young forces in Russia flew in from all sides, from all levels of the population, into the University as in a common reservoir; in its halls they were purified of all prejudices caught at home, were brought to one and the same level, fraternized and flew out again to all sides of Russia, to all levels of the population ... The mixed youth, arriving from above, below, the south or the north was speedily melted into a compact mass of comradeship". [2]

Russian students, the most progressive in the world at that time—sensitively reacted to all occurances of political life and stood immutably in the first row of the liberation movement.

Words of acknowledgement of the successful activity of the pre-revolutionary Russian university are said by the eminent Soviet educator Yelyutin : "The fruitful activity of the foremost Russian

---

[1] N. Berdyayev, *Russkaya ideya*, Paris, 1946, p. 28.

[2] Alexander Hertsen, *Byloye i dumy*, Leningrad, 1947, pp. 57-58.

scientists who worked at the pre-revolutionary Russian higher schools in spite of all unfavorable circumstances deserve our thankful attention. They were able to enrich the treasury of human knowledge with outstanding achievements." [1]

Still, Yelyutin is of the opinion that a reserved caste spirit dominated in pre-revolutionary higher schools: it was difficult to democratic *elements to open a way* for themselves". [2]

This opinion is not correct in general. With the exception of special law schools for the nobility, the atmosphere was very democratic at the law faculties of the universties, similar to that at all other faculties. Here is what Hertsen says on this subject:

"Up to 1848, the structure of our universities was purely democratic. The doors were open to everyone who could pass the entrance examinations and was not a serf, or a peasant not released from his commune. Nicholas [Emperor Nicholas I] distorted all of that, limited the admission of students, increased the tuition required from paying students and permitted only poor students from the nobility to be freed from it. Social differences had not the offensive influence in Russia which we meet in English schools and barracks; I do not speak of English Universities: they exist only for aristocrats and the rich. A student who would entertain the thought of boasting of his *blue blood* or wealth would be *separated from 'water and light'* and fagged out by comrades". [3]

Under Alexander the II democracy was completely reinstalled in the general higher institutions of learning, and in spite of the reactionary character of the last reigns democracy prevailed in the relations of students among themselves.

B. LEGAL EDUCATION AFTER THE OCTOBER REVOLUTION

a) *Initial Development*

Regular Legal Education. Having smashed the court system and all organs of the administration of justice as they existed under the tsars, the Soviets replaced them by new ones adapted to the concepts of Marxism-Leninism in the field of administration of justice.

---

[1] V.P. Yelyutin, *Vysshaya shkola strany sotsializma*, M. 1959, p. 8.

[2] *Ibid.*, p. 11.

[3] Hertsen, *op. cit.*, pp. 57-58.

To this effect also the legal education had to be reorganized.

"*In the past*", wrote Lenin, "the entire human mind, all its genius created only with the purpose to extend to some people all the blessings of technology and culture, and to deprive the others of the indispensible enlightenment and development. But now all the wonders of technology, of all the achievements of culture will belong to all the people, and henceforth, the human mind and genius will never be transformed into means of violence and exploitation." [1]

The first enactment of Lenin's governmnt with regard to institutions of higher learning were the "Rules for Admission to the Institutions of Higher Learning of August 2, 1918". [2] According to this Decree, admission was open to toilers and their children, learning was free of cost and scholarships were established for students.

Lenin wrote in the assignment of August 12, 1918 to the Commissariat of Education, "to prepare at once a number of decisions and steps, in order that, if the number of candidates for the admission to institutions of higher learning exceeds the usual number of vacancies, measures for the possibility to study for all desiring to do so should be taken, and no privilege not only legal, but also factual, should be granted to the possessing classes. Unconditionally must be admitted in the first place, persons belonging to the proletariat and the poorest peasantry, and scholarships in extending number will be granted to them". [3]

But opening widely the door of institutions of higher learning to all persons Lenin was faced with the same problem which was raised before the creation of the first Russian universtiy : the lack of people prepared to assimilate teaching in these institutions.

Thus, it was also Lenin who initiated the creation of workers faculties (*rabfak*) at which workers could be taught in subjects of secondary schools necessary for the attendance at universities.

The "*rabfaks*" were attached to faculties of institutions of higher learning and their students enjoyed all the privileges granted to regular students of these institutions (scholarship, social security, etc.). [4]

The number of workers faculties grew steadily. There were 1025 of them around 1932-33.

---

[1] Lenin, 26, p. 436.

[2] *Sob. uz., RSFSR*, 1918, Item 632.

[3] Lenin, "On the Admission to Institutions of Higher Learning of the RSFSR", 28, p. 31.

[4] *Sob. uz., RSFSR*, 1919, Item 443.

But at the end of the thirties, beginning of the forties, the *"rabfaks"* were liquidated in connection with the development of the secondary education in the USSR.

In the task of reorganization of the higher education, the Bolshevists encountered also the same obstacles which stood in the way of the organization of universities in Russia at the end of the 18th and the beginning of the 19th centuries : the lack of professors able or willing to teach their disciplines now from the Marxist viewpoint besides the absence of candidates adequately prepared for higher education among workers and the poorest peasants who had to be admitted in the first place.

With regard to the old professorial staff, a purge was carried out with help of the Decree of the Council of People's Commissars of October 1, 1918 "On some Changes in the Staff and Organization of State Scientists :" professors and instructors who worked in an individual university more than 10 years or had more than 15 years of teaching activity, had to pass a competition. "As a result of the competition", writes Shebanov, "the reactionary part of the teachers was eliminated, the teaching staff was replenished by candidates from among the young people ..." [1]

Another handicap to the reconstruction of education was the complete lack of textbooks written from the Marxist viewpoint.

This prompted Lenin to write in a foreword to the book of V.I. Stepanov on "Electrification" in 1922 : "If all our Marxist men of letters, in place of spending their energies on newspapers and periodicals, political jabber, boring everyone, would set down to work on such textbooks on all, without exceptions, social questions, we would not go through such a disgrace that almost five years after the proletariat captured political power in his, the proletariat's, state schools and universities, old bourgeois scientists teach young people the old bourgeois trash ..." [2]

The reshaping of legal education was more radical : the faculties of law were abolished and replaced by "faculties of public sciences" by decision on the "Statutes of the Faculty of Public Sciences" of the RSFSR People's Commissariat of Education of March 1919.

According to this Statute, the following subjects were taught at the Legal-Political Departmnet of the faculty of public sciences :

---

[1] A.F. Shebanov, *op. cit.*, p. 36.
[2] Lenin, 33, pp. 217-218.

history of law and state, evolution of political and juridical thought, public law of the Soviet Republic, social law, criminal sociology and politics, labor law and social policy, history of international relations and international law, social hygiene and sanitation.

At first glance, it is conspicuous that such basic subjects of legal education as criminal and civil laws and criminal and civil procedure were not taught to future judges, prosecutors, investigating magistrates and advocates. The explanation for this is, however, very simple : there was no criminal, civil or procedural law to be taught in the RSFSR between 1917 and 1922 : the tsarist laws were abrogated and new codes published only in 1922/1923.

Beginning with the fall of 1921, the institutions of higher learning in the RSFSR became segregated : admission to children of the former bourgeoisie was denied. The method of Nicholas I of excluding "cooks children" from higher education was applied by the Bolshevists to young people not of proletarian descent.

The great majority of students were recruited from the pupils of the *rabfaks*, workers and peasants who graduated from the workers' faculties.

The faculties of social sciences were gradually liquidated in the twenties at individual universities. For instance, in Saratov and Rostov, and the faculty of social sciences was transformed into two faculties in 1924 : of soviet law and of ethnology at Moscow University. A faculty of Soviet law was organized at the Leningrad University in 1926.

The first "Statute on Institutions of Higher Learning" was published on September 2, 1921. [1] But a program of studies frimly based on Marxism was published only in 1925 : all the students had to study the program of the VKP (b), national economy and historiacl materialism.

The program of the faculty of Soviet law provided the study of the following legal subjects : the basis of the Soviet Constitution, criminal law, economic law, land law, administrative law, family law, court structure, criminal procedure, cooperative and trade union movement.

The next step taken by the legislation in the field of university organization was the decision of the USSR TsIK of September 19,

---

[1] *Sob. uz., RSFSR*, 1921, Item 486.

1932 "On Study Programs of Universities and Technikums" [1] A strict study plan and an exact time-table were established.

The Decision of the TsIK and the Council of People's Commissars of March 5, 1935, [2] "On Measures for the Development and Improvement of Legal Education" had direct and important bearing on legal education. As indicated by its title, the scope of the Decision was to improve the deficient preparation of the organs of the administration of justice for their jobs.

At that time, legal education was given at law institutes in Moscow, Leningrad, Saratov, Kazan', Sverdlovsk and Minsk, and in the faculties of law in Baku, Tbilisi and Yerevan. Two law institutes were added to the list in 1935 : in Khar'kov and Tashkent.

It is evident that up to this point, the opportunity for a legal education was inadequate. The functions of judges, prosecutors, and investigating magistrates and lawyers were fulfilled by persons lacking a regular legal education in the majority of cases.

It must be emphasized already here that despite a strong development of legal education in the future, the requirement of a legal education as it will be shown in the pages of this book, is still not mandatory for all agents of the administration of justice in the Soviet Union up to the present time.

b) *Legal Education and the Withering Away of State and Law*

The program of legal learning in the institutions of higher education was deeply affected by the Soviet theories of state and law prevailing at the end of the twenties and the beginning of the thirties. [3]

Marx and especially Engels expressed the opinion that the state will wither away after the proletariat had come into possession of the means of production.

Engels wrote in Anti-During : "When there shall be no social classes which it is necessary to hold in subjection ... when there shall be neither the dominance of one class over another nor a struggle for

---

[1] *Sob. uz., RSFSR*, 1932, Item 400.

[2] *Sob. uz., RSFSR*, 1935, Item 99.

[3] No attempt is made here to give a complete picture of Soviet legal theory of that time. This theory is discussed only as far as it affected the program of legal education. For a detailed discussion see "The Communist Theory of Law by Hans Kelsen, N.Y., 1955; The Soviet Legal Theory by Rudolf Schlesinger, London, 1951. The appropriate texts are translated by W. Babb in Soviet Legal Philosophy, Cambridge, Mass, 1957, with an introduction by John N. Hazard, in which the texts are commented.

existence based on the contemporary anarchy of production, and when the clashes and the violence caused thereby shall have been done away with ... then, there will no longer be anyone to crush and to hold in restraint and then the need for the state authority which now performs this function will vanish. The first measure in which the state will come forward as the true representative of all society ... the turning of the means of production into social property will be the last independent action *qua* state. Little by little, it will become unneccessary for state authority to intervene in social relationships and such intermeddling will automatically cease. The government of persons comes to an end, and the management of things and direction of production processes take its place. The state is not abolished ... *it withers away*".

Since, according to Marx-Engels-Lenin, the State is an organ of suppression of one class by the other—by the bourgeoisie of the proletariat in capitalist states—the state is not necessary any more after the proletariat has taken power and suppressed the bourgeoisie "Once the majority of people itself suppresses its oppressors a 'special force' for suppression is no longer necessary. In this sense, the state begins to wither away" Lenin wrote. [1]

However, the states "whither away", as Engels stated, only "little by little". Marx set the economic term when it will completely disappear in his critique of the "Gotha Programme", in his letter to Drake of May 15, 1875. Marx wrote "In a higher phase of Communist Society when the enslaving subordination of individuals in the division of labor has disappeared and with it also the antagonism between physical and mental labor; when labor has become not only a means of living, but itself the first necessity of life; when, along with all-round development of individuals, the productive forces too have grown and all the springs of social wealth are flowing more freely—it is only at that stage that it will be possible to pass completely beyond the narrow horizon of bourgeois rights, and for society to inscribe on its banners; from each according to his ability, to each according to his needs! [2] Lenin underlines that when all that will take place, how rapidly this development will go forward, is completely uncertain. According to Lenin "the question of length of time, or the concrete forms of withering away must be left open since the material for the solution of such questions is not available." [3]

---

[1] Lenin, *State and Revolution*, International publishers, N.Y., 1932, p. 37.

[2] *Ibid.*, pp. 78-79.

[3] *Ibid.*, p. 79.

Not knowing when State and law will wither away completely, Lenin following Marx, sets the condition necessary to this effect. Only in a communist society, when the resistance of the capitalists has been completely broken, when the capitalists have disappeared, when there are no classes (i.e., there is no difference between the members of society in their relation to the social means of production) *only then* "the state ceases to exist" and *it becomes possible to speak of freedom.* [1]

But still, under Socialism, Lenin continued, "Bourgeois rights with *respect to distribution* of articles of *consumption* inevitably pressuppose, of course, the existence of a *bourgeois state*, for rights are nothing without an apparatus capable of *enforcing* the observance of the rights."

Consequently, for a certain time, not only bourgeois rights, but even the bourgeois state remains under Communism (in its first socialist stage) without the bourgeoisie. [2]

In the first stage of Communism as it is called by Marx, or Socialism as defined generally by Lenin, as long as the conditions set by Marx are still not fulfilled, "the existence of a narrow horizon of bourgeois rights (laws) in a "semistate" — as identified by Lenin — is still unavoidable". A form of state is still necessary which, while maintaining public ownership of the means of production, would preserve equality of labor and equality in the distribution of products. [3]

Thus, it is established that according to the founding fathers Marx, Engels, and Lenin, after the revolution in which it cises power, the proletariat establishes the dictatorship of the proletariat and its ownership of land and all means of production. However, the State is not abolished, together with the capitalistic laws and administrative apparatus. A semi-state (Lenin) and law with a "narrow bourgeois horizon" (Marx) remain, but they begin to wither away as soon as the means of production are nationalized (Engels). How long this process of withering away will last is uncertain (Lenin). But in any case it is not completed before the higher stage of communism is reached, i.e., when everyone receives not according to his work, as under socialism, but according to his needs (Marx, Lenin). Then state and law have withered away—disappear ...

"Law withers away together with the state during the first phase

---

[1] *Ibid.*, p. 73.

[2] *Ibid.*, pp. 81-82.

[3] *Ibid.*, p. 78.

of Communism or Socialism; people will gradually become accustomed to the observance of the elementary rules of social life that have been known for centuries and repeated for thousands of years in all school books. They will become accustomed to observing them without force, without compulsion, without subordination, without the special apparatus for compulsion which is called the state. [1] Thus, law will also gradually become unnecessary, since people will get accustomed to observing by themselves the rules of life protected previously by law.

But it is only developed communism (in its second stage) which will render the state (and law) "absolutely unnecessary".

It is this theory of state and law of Marx-Engels-Lenin which had to be observed by the first legal theoreticians.

c) *Pashukanis and Legal Education*

The theory of state and law taught by E.B. Pashukanis, the Soviet legal philospoher, Vice-President of the Academy and Director of the Institute of Soviet Constitution and Law, had a decisive influence on the programs of higher legal education in the twenties and the first half of the thirties.

Pashukanis was the creator of the so-called "commodity exchange" theory; the source of law was the market where the commodities were exchanged. Law had a bourgeois character because it reached its highest development under capitalism. He wrote : "Only bourgeois-capitalist society creates all the conditions essential to the attainment of complete definiteness by the juridical element in social relationships". [2]

Thus, he denied the possibility of a system of socialist law. He wrote : "The point is that the transition period—when the dictatorship of the proletariat has achieved the revolutionary transition from capitalism to communism—cannot be regarded as a special and complete social-economic integration, and it is therefore not possible to create for it a special and complete system of law or to seek out any special for of law, and proletarian law". [3]

Pashukanis was comforted in this opinion by the teaching of Marx and Lenin that bourgeois law and state remain under socialism in the

---

[1] Lenin, *op. cit.*, pp. 73-74.
[2] *Soviet legal philosophy, op. cit.*, pp. 119-120.
[3] *Ibid.*, p. 331.

first stage of communism as shown above. It was clear for him that "Marx conceived of the transition to expanded communism, not as a transition to new forms of law, but as the dying out of the juridical form in general—as liberation from this heritage of the bourgeois epoch which was destined to outlive the bourgeois itself".

H. Kelsen concludes that "it follows from Pashukanis' identification of law with capitalist economy not only that there can be no law in the communist society of the future, but also that there can be no proletarian socialist law in the transition period of the proletariat dictatorship [1] since "The dying out of the categories of bourgeois law will in these conditions signify the dying out of law in general". That is to say, the gradual disappearance of the juridical element in human relations, as Pashukanis wrote. [2] But if law reached its highest point of development under capitalism it cannot develop further into a proletarian or socialist law. The consequence is for Pashukanis that the law, as a concomitant of capitalism, must be abandoned in general. [3]

According to him, since law was a reflection of economic relations, only private law is real law. Civil law must be replaced by economic law; hence, public law is not a legal subject at all.

Taking into consideration that the quintessence of private law (i.e., of all law) is the old Roman formula—*do ut des*—it means the exchange of goods, Pashukanis asserted that criminal law is also based on an exchange : the criminal produces the crime and is paid by punishment. He writes : "Crime can be regarded as a special variety of turnover in which the exchange—that is to say, the continual relationships—is established ex post facto : that is to say, after the willful action of one of the parts of the ratio between the crime and the requital, is nothing more than the same exchange ratio". [4]

In support of his reasoning Pashukanis quotes the idea of Aristotle who also thought that punishment comes out as an equivalent of the damage sustained by the injured party, as a consequence of a contract concluded against one's will with the state. However naive the concep-

---

1 H. Kelsen, *The Communist Theory of Law*, N.Y., 1955, p. 106.

2 *Soviet Legal Philosophy*, op. cit., p. 122.

3 Another Soviet scholar, an adept of Pashukanis and his theory of the impossibility of the creating of a socialist system of Law, P.I. Stukhka, wrote : "We have read Speranskys who is creating the statutes. But when shall we have read Voltaires making a bonfire of statutes". *Ibid.*, p. 330.

4 *Soviet Legal Philosophy*, op. cit., p. 208.

tion may appear at a first glance, states Pashukanis "there is latent in them far more of a fear for the form of law than in the eclectic theories of contemporary jurists". [1]

Thus, Pashukanis brought forward the following assertions.

1. The state law and moral are forms of the bourgeois society and cannot accommodate socialist teaching;

2. every law reflects commodity relations and is organizationally bound to them;

3. consequently state and law started to wither away from the beginning of the establishment of the dictatorship of the proletariate.

This practically meant the negation of the possibility for the proletariate to use the revolutionary socialist law as an implement of the state for the establishment of socialist structure and was called by Krylenko "nothing else as a counterrevolutionary Trotskist assertion about the non-socialist character of our state and law reproducing in the sector of the state and law theory the negation of the possibility of the construction of socialism in one country". [2]

In general, Krylenko thought that "To the distortions belongs first of all the 'theory'-widely circulating among legal writers.—[3] that the withering away of the state of the dictatorship of the proletariate starts already with the moment of the formation".

Another authority on law of the time, A.G. Goykhberg, asserted that religion and law are the idealogies of the oppression of classes ... "And if we have to struggle bitterly against religion idealogy now, we will have to fight the legal ideology even on a greater extent ... A much more difficult and, perhaps, much more urgent task, than the antireligious propaganda is the anti-law propaganda". [4]

Reisner, a legal philosopher of the twenties, did not know, as to whether "we need law, and to what extent we need it, and whether it is necessary to guild the proletarian dictatoship and the class interest with enigmatic juridical symbols and formulas for no reason at all". [5]

---

[1] *Ibid.*, p. 208. Hans Kelsen calls this Pashikanis view on criminal law "absurd". H. Kelsen, *The Communist theory of Law*, N.Y., 1955, p. 100.

[2] N.V. Krylenko, "To the Situation on the Theoretical Legal Front", *Problemy ugolovnoy politiki*, M. 1937, Issue IV, p. 6. But how is it with Engels' assertion that when the proletariat has seized the means of production etc., "the state withers away"? The sentence is used not in the future but in the present tense.

[3] A.G. Goykhberg, "Some Remarks on Law", *Sovetskoye pravo*, 1924, No. 1, p. 3.

[4] *Ibid.*, p. 7.

[5] M.A. Reisner, "Pravo, nashe pravo, inostrannoye pravo, obshcheye pravo", M. 1925 p. 29.

The "little-by-little" withering away of bourgeois law under socialism and the impossibility of replacing it with a system of socialist law asserted by Pashukanis led inadvertently to the conclusion that studying law in general is a useless occupation. "Students discussed whether or not it was worhtwhile to continue studying law", as Schlesinger puts it. [1]

Pashukanis' teaching had a direct bearing on the program of legal education. "Pashukanis influence was such", Hazard writes, "that courses on civil law in the law schools were abandoned. Courses on economic planning, called in Pashukanis' parlance "economic law", as in Germany, replaced them. A few hours only were devoted at the end of a full year's courses to those aspects of civil law which Pashukanis interpreted as a vestige of the past."

Textbooks on civil law likewise were replaced by textbooks entitled "economic law".

A similar atrophying of criminal law was anticipated with the substitution of "general principles" to guide the judges instead of precise articles defining types of crimes and setting specific penalties. This work in cirminal law was pressed generally by the then Commissar of Justice, Nikolai Krylenko, "who was closely associated with Pashukanis—at that time". [2]

Krylenko, departing from Pashukanis' idea that punishment of the crime is an expression of an equivalent transition of goods owners, suggested the structure of the criminal code in a way to exclude from it the concept of guilt and setting of punishment in accordance with the gravity of the crime and the guilt of the criminal.

Adversary procedure was for him also an expression of the competition between two owners of goods and he thought a maximal limitation of the procedural guarantees inherent to the adversary procedure. All that in order to eliminate bourgeois law from the Soviet system. [3]

d) Statutes and Laws Strengthened

The Soviet state did not follow the pattern predicted by Marx, Engels and Lenin. It did not start to wither away although "the means

---

[1] R. Schlesinger, *Soviet Legal Theory*, London, 1954, p. 202.

[2] J.N. Hazard, *Introduction to Soviet Legal Philosophy, op. cit.*, p. XXXI.

[3] See M.S. Shrogovich, "To the Question of Putting Individual Legal Problems in the Works of P.I. Stuchka", N.V. Krylenko and Ye. B. Pashukanis, in *Voprosy obshchey teorii prava*, M. 1960, pp. 392-398.

of production were turned over to social property, the bourgeoisie crushed and the classes allegedly done away with, as claimed by communists, and there no longer was anyone "to crush and hold in restraint". It did not only become unnecessary for state authority to intervene in social relationships and "such intermeddling" did not only "cease automatically", or "even little by little", but state authority and its interference in all aspects of Soviet life grew boundlessly until the soviet state developed into the Leviathan of our time. The government of persons "did not only come to an end" and was to be "replaced by the direction of production processes", but the "government of persons" degenerated into the government of one person, under the dictatorship of Stalin.

Certainly, in order to carry out industrialization and collectivization inside, Stalin had no use for a withering-state, as conceived by Marx-Engels-Lenin.

Consequently, Stalin asserted that the state will wither away after it has realized the peak of its development and strength and that Engels' formula does not apply to a state which alone achieved socialism and is encircled by capitalistic states. This was declared by Stalin in his report to the XVIIIth Congress of the Communist Party on March 10, 1939. [1]

Naturally, Pashukanis 'and his followers' theory of state and law did not fit the concept of "withering away", as formulated by Stalin.

But already before that, Stalin's mouthpiece in legal affairs and the most influential figure in the field of the theory and practice on the administration of justice in the thirties, A. Ya. Vyshinsky, undertook the task of destroying Pashukanis' theory by declaring his teaching fallacious and he and Krylenko as provocateurs and traitors to the fatherland. [2]

"In asserting that law is nothing but a form of capitalist relationships and that law can develop only in the conditions of capitalism when law supposedly attains its highest development, the wreckers who have busying themselves on our legal front were striving toward a single objective : to prove that law is not necessary to the Soviet-state—and that law is superfluous as a survival of capitalism in the conditions of socialism. In reducing Soviet law to bourgeois law and

---

[1] I.V. Stalin, *Voprosy leninizma*, M. 1947, p. 603.

[2] Both paid with their lives for the unfitness of their theories for the requirements of Stalinist rule.

affirming that there is no ground for the further development of law under socialism the wreckers aimed at liquidating soviet law and the source of soviet law. This is the basic significance of their activity as provocateurs and wreckers. Proceeding along this path they outdid themselves in discovering all sorts of motives, concepts and 'theories' which could facilitate the achievement of the criminal purpose". [1]

Accusing Pashukanis, Vyshinsky goes so far as to compare his theory to the "treasonable" acitivities of Bukharin and Tukhachevsky, the accused in the well-known trials of the thirties. [2] He said "the treason of Tukhachevsky and that of a whole series of other persons, —proceeded along the same line of provocateur activity pursued by Bukharin, Pashukanis and company, operating in the field of theory". [3]

After the condemnation of Pashukanis, the subjects eliminated before were restored to the program of higher legal education. Since the importance of socialist state and law was established, the study of them was, naturally, enlarged. Courses of soviet state, administration and financial laws were reinstated.

The number of legal institutes was enlarged so that about 1940, ten legal institutes were functioning. The legal institutes formed under the guidance of the individual people's commissariats of justice of the union republics were put under the jurisdiction of the USSR People's Commissariat of Justice in 1940, one of them teaching through correspondence courses.

Also the number of legal faculties at universities increased : up to 1938, there were three legal faculties at the universities of Kiev, Tbilisi and Yerevan, but in 1939 the University of L'vov and in 1940 the University of Tartu, Vil'nyus and Kovnas with their legal faculties joined the family of the soviet union universities.

All the legal institutes previously under the administration of the people's commissariats of education of the individual union republics were transferred to the jursidiction of the USSR People's Commissariat of Justice in 1940. On the other hand, the "cult of personality" had an evil influence on the teaching of those legal subjects on which Stalin was allegedly an expert. For instance, accor-

---

[1] A.Ye. Vyshinsky, "The Fundamental Tasks of Science of Soviet Socialist Law", Address of the I Congress of Problems of the Sciences of Soviet State and Law (1938), *Soviet Legal Philosophy, op. cit.*, pp. 328-329.

[2] Also Pashukanis was posthumously rehabilitated, as well as Bukharin and Tukhachevsky after the liquidation of the cult of personality.

[3] *Ibid.*, p. 311.

ding to Stalin it was he and not Lenin, who developed the doctrine
of a socialist state, since Lenin had only defended Marx's and Engels'
state theory from the attacks of the international opportunism and
did not have time enough to develop it further on the basis of the
experience of the Soviet country. [1]

Soviet legal scholars did not dare to touch on any part of Stalin's
teaching. For instance, a very modest attempt of some state law
specialists to build their course on soviet state law slightly differently
from the pattern on which Stalin's 1936 Constitution was formed,
produced the most acerbic attacks and was declared almost a hostile
sortie. Criticism of a specialist of kolkhoz law because he had only
reproduced the text of the Exemplary Statute on Agricultural Cooperatives (*Artel's*) without making any scientific generalizations, was
rejected on the ground that "Stalin's Statute on the Agricultural
Artel's is the highest expression of science and his text is just science". [2]

Thus, there was nothing else to do for scholars in the field of legal
science handled by Stalin, than to quote him with expression of
highest admiration of his wisdom.

The Reference book "Culture, Science, Art in USSR" [3] underlines the negative influence of the cult of Stalin's personality on the
development of the legal science creating conditions for a slightly
nihilistic attitude toward law and its authority.

According to the reference book, the decisions of the XXth and
XXIInd Congress of the USSR Communist Party have radically
changed the conditions for juridical science development.

C. LEGAL EDUCATION DURING AND AFTER WORLD WAR II

a) *During the War*

World War II greatly affected legal education. A number of law
schools and universities in regions occupied by Germans had to close
if they were not evacuated at time.

---

[1] This was rectified by A.I. Mikoyan in an address at the XXIIth Congress of the
Party : "The truth is that just V.I. Lenin, and not someone else, who not only restored
and vindicated the Marxian doctrine on the State but also developed the theory of the
Socialist State, starting from the experience of the Soviet State", *S.G.P.*, 1962, No. 4,
pp. 4-5.

[2] See the editorial in *S.G.P.*, 1962, No. 4, p. 5.

[3] *Kultura, Nauka, Iskusstvo SSSR*, M. 1965, p. 140.

The legal institutes in Khar'kov and Minsk and the legal faculties in the universities of L'vov, Tartu and Riga ceased functioning temporarily. The Moscow Legal Institute was transferred to Alma-Ata and united with the local legal institute. The legal institute in Leningrad was evacuated first to Balashov (Saratov Region) and then to Dzhambul (Kazakh SSSR) in 1942.

The Moscow University was displaced to Ashkhabad and later to Sverdlovsk. The Leningrad University found a temporary home in Saratov. The Kiev University and the other Ukrainian universities were united in an Ukrainians University located in Kzyl-Orda (Kazakh SSR) and new quarters were asigned to the Rostov University in Osh (Kirgiz SSR).

From 5900 in 1940, the number of students of law in institutions of higher education shrank to 2732 in 1941 and 960 in 1942. Registration of post-graduate students (for the "aspirantura") ceased almost completely.

During their retreat from the USSR the Germans destroyed a number of institutions of higher learning. Thus all the buildings and dwelling houses of the Donetz Industrial Institute were demolished. The main structure of the Kiev University with its laboratories, museums and library including 1,500,000 books were blown up. Also razed were the buildings of the higher institutions of learning in Voronezh, Stalingrad, Khar'kov, Dnepropetrovsk, Odessa, Rostov-na-Donu and other cities. [1]

However, already beginning with 1943, the institutions of legal education started their return home. At the end of 1944, all the evacuated institutions of higher learning were restored to their legitimate residences and activities. In 1943, 4192 students of law were registered; in 1945-6550 more than before the war.

In the 40-ies a program calculated for five years of study was established for legal faculties of all universities.

In the first four years, 4,100 instruction hours in 33 subjects per year were given. During the first year the program was extended to 5,300 instruction hours. The first four years were dedicated to the study of Soviet Law (73% of the instruction laws). For the remaining 27%, 18% was occupied with purely political topics and the remaining 15% was for labor, history, logic, foreign language, etc.

Thus, for instance, in the 4th and 5th years, the students had to

---

[1] *Narodnoye obrazovaniye v SSSR, op. cit.,* p. 390.

specialize in one of the following groups of subjects : state laws, international law, criminal law and civil law. During the fifth year of study, besides the completion and defense of a diploma paper, the student had to pass three state examinations : on fundamentals of Marxism-Leninism, theory of state and law, and according to the group of subjects chosen by the student, on state law, or international law, or criminal procedure, or civil law and civil procedure. [1]

b) *Post War Period* : *Critism by the Central Committee*

On 5 October 1946, the Central Committee of the USSR Communist Party adopted a resolution "On the Broadening and Imrpoving of Legal Education in the Country" which contained a devastating criticism of the status of legal education in the USSR and a number of measures for its improvement.

The Central Committee emphasized that legal education is conducted inadequately, the training of jursits for the work in international relations and in Soviet institutions (organs) is not organized : the legal institutes and legal faculties of the universities are not yet media for the preparation of highly qualified jurists; in many legal institutes there is not a sufficient number of qualified teachers in jurisprudence so that the level of legal education is still low; the secondary legal schools of the ministry of justice admit also persons lacking basic secondary education, a significant part of jurists graduating from these schools are poorly trained for the work in court and prosecuting organs ; serious training and retraining of court and prosecution workers is not carried out.

According to the Central Committee, one of the major causes of the unsatisfactory organization of legal education in the country is the neglect of scientific work in the field of jurisprudence : the All-Union Institute of Legal Sciences [2] of the Ministry of Justice and the Institute of Law of the USSR Academy of Sciences did not prepare and publish serious scientific works in the field of jurisprudence, especially on the theory of state and law, soviet state law, international law and the history of the social state. Also textbooks on the most fields of legal science, such as theory of state and law, soviet state law, international

---

[1] Shebanov, *op. cit.*, p. 68.

[2] According to European terminology, jurisprudence is a science. In the United States jurisprudence is generally not considered a science, although Webster defines jurisprudence as a "science of Law".

public law, general history of political doctrines, have not been written and put in circulation.

Furthermore, the Central Committee stated that collections of articles and periodicals published by the institutes contain erroneous theses, capable of confusing the legal staffs; scientific criticism is lacking in the field of jurisprudence; scientific staffs are trained extremely slowly and not sufficiently. The number of graduated law students has decreased threefold as compared with 1940.

The Central Committee was dissatisfied with the teaching in secondary schools where interest for the study of legal sciences is not inculcated in the pupils and the study of legal science in institutions of higher learning is in this way impeded; the teaching of courses on the USSR Constitution is unsatisfactory: there is no textbook on this course and the students do not acquire general knowledge on state and law in the secondary law schools.

As a remedy to these defects, the Central Committee decided: to consider as the most important task of the Ministries of Justice and Higher Education, the raising of the training level of the legal staffs in the country and in the first place that of the court and prosecution workers.

In order to broaden and improve legal education in the country plans were made:

1. to increase to 2,000 the number of students admitted to the first courses of the university and to 3500 students—to the first courses of the legal institutes, beginning with 1947.

2. to establish legal faculties at the universities of Rostov, Tomsk, Khar'kov, Odessa, as well as at the Belorusskiy and Sredneaziatskiy State Universtities, in 1947-49.

3. to work out a new study plan for the legal faculties of the universities providing the training of a broad type for jurists and specialization in the field of international legal relations and soviet state structure and administration.

The Central Committee made not only instutional changes, but also gave personnel assignments in these institutions, with preparation as of 1, 1947 and publication, as of 1 September 1947, of textbooks. Thus, "the USSR Ministry of Higher Education (com. Kaftanov), the All-Union Institute of Legal Sciences (com. Golyakov), the Law Institute of the USSR Academy of Sciences (com. Traynin)" had to insure the preparation of textbooks on the "Theory of State and Law", "Soviet State Law", "International Public Law", "General

History of State and Law", "History of State and Law in the USSR", "History of Political Doctrines", and the OGIZ [1] (Com. Grachev) had to publish them.

The Ministries of Higher Education and Justice were ordered to increase admission for post graduate studies on legal sciences by up to 150 students in the 1946-7 academic year and by up to 200-in the 1947-48 academic year, thus insuring the training of post-graduate students first of all, in the theory of state and law, Soviet state law and international law.

Another important topic stressed in the decision is the retraining of the court and prosecution staffs. To this effect, the Central Committee ordered the USSR Minister of Justice, Rychkov:

1 To organize, beginning with 1947, one-year higher courses for jurists to perfect the retraining of the leading personnel of the republic, territorial and regional organs of the prosecuting body, as well as of the supreme, territorial and regional courts;

2 to organize nine-month courses for the retraining of people's judges, district prosecutors and investigating magistrates in Moscow, Leningrad, Khar'kov, Tashkent, Minsk, Sverdlovsk and Baku, in order to raise their juristic qualifications; graduates from secondary schools were admitted to these courses;

3 to admit, due to the necessity of raising the level of the training of jurists graduating from two-year legal schools, to these schools only persons in possession of a completed secondary school education, not younger than 23 years of age with experience in Party, Soviet or social work;

4 To assign groups of qualified teachers in theory of state and law and Soviet state law through the USSR Ministry of Higher Education, for the improvement of the preparation of jurists in the Tartu, Riga, Vil'nyus, and L'vov universities, during the 1946-47 academic year.

The editorial boards of the Soviet periodicals S.G.P. and *Sots. zak.* were admonished to carry out a detailed criticism of defects and mistakes in the field of jurisprudence and legal education. [2]

It may be assumed with certainty that the request of work and books on the subject of state and law, especially stressed by the Central Committee, is the result of changing viewpoints on the topic described above, among the leading soviet jurists, in the twenties and

---

[1]   State United Publishing Houses.
[2]   *Sots. zak.*, 1946, No. 11-12, pp. 13-14.

beginning of the thirties. There was no time to fill the gap before and during World War II.

Following the Central Committee, strong criticism was also voiced by the periodical *Sotsialistichiskaya zakonnost'*. In an editorial [1] it was declared that not enough attention was paid to the training of the young scientific staff. But even those few who completed post-graduate education and defended their dissertions remained in Moscow and Leningrad and were not directed to those law institutes and faculties where the need in pedagogical staffs was felt most. As a result, the Moscow and Leningrad Institutes are provided with teachers with high qualifications, whereas the Minskiy, Kazanskiy, Tashkentskiy, and Alms-Atinskiy Institutes almost completely lack doctors and professors in the legal sciences.

The editorial further complained that the retraining of legal workers who have an insufficient legal education but work in organs of the administration of justice were carried out very poorly by the USSR Ministry of Justice. This retraining is especially necessary since a great number of legal practitioners have no adequate legal education and those who graduated from secondary law schools and even higher institutions of learning, forgot what they had learned in the intervening time.

Among almost 10,000 legal practitioners only 700 had to be retrained in three-month courses in 1946.

In order to broaden the retraining of legal practitioners, higher one-year courses for the perfecting of jurists had to be opened in Moscow in 1947 in which judges and prosecutors could be retrained. Two hundred judges and prosecutors had to be admitted to these courses.

Non-credit courses, in place of the existing three-month courses, for the retraining of people's judges, regional prosecutors and regional investigating magistrates had to be opened in Moscow, Leningrad, Khar'kov, Minsk, Sverdlovsk, and Baku. Those practical workers who had a secondary education had to be admitted as students. The number of students to be admitted in 1947 was set at 850 by the USSR Ministry of Justice.

Especially strong criticism is expressed by the Editorial against the method in which education in the secondary law schools is being handled.

---

[1]   1947, No. 11, p. 15 ff.

Only few of the teachers in these schools had academic degrees or titles. In cities where law institutes are located, teachers from these institutes are lecturing in schools, but in other places, practical workers from the organs of the Ministry of Justice were assigned to teaching positions.

With great emphasis the editorial declares that "the decisive link in legal education must be the higher institutions of learning—the law faculties of the universities and the law institutes. To wager on the middle link—the law schools, not to mention the law courses— would be erroneous and should not be done under conditions of the increased request for the activity of legal practitioner.

The conclusion of the editorial is that "legal education is organized inadequately in our country". [1]

c) *After the Central Committee's Criticism*

The criticism raised in such a high place as the Central Committee of the Soviet Communist Party could not remain without effect and the measures ordered by the Central Committee were carried out.

According to Zaitsev and Poltorak, [2] 2000 students graduated from law institutes and university law departments in 1947. Between 1947 and 1955, 15,000 legal practitioners acquired a higher legal education in evening schools and through correspondence courses.

Furthermore, Karev reported that already in 1941, 20,900 persons with higher legal education worked in the administration of justice, and that the number of such persons increased to 56,500 as of 1956 in 1957-8, there were 12,000 graduates of secondary law schools in the administration of justice. According to him, more than 36,000 students were enrolled in institutions of higher learning in 1948. [3]

1. Programs

Already in November 1946, by a decision of the USSR Council of Ministers, the courses in the law faculties were adapted to a five-year study period and in them (since 1947) the unified program of all law faculties of the universities, approved by the USSR Ministry of Higher Education on July 15, 1948, introduced, among others,

---

[1] *Ibid.*, p. 17.

[2] Zaitsev and Poltorak, *op. cit.*, p. 52.

[3] P.S. Karev, *Sots. zak.*, 1959, No. 2, pp. 17-18.

such topics as theory and history of state and law; Soviet state structure and administration; and international law.

In the program of law institutes, special seminars on the theory of state and law were introduced. The course of state law of foreign countries was divided into two individual courses : "State Law of Bourgeois Countries" and "State Law of People's Democracies". [1]

Besides the theoretical study, the students of law of universities and institutions were obliged to perform practical work at courts, prosecution bodies and at administrative organs, according to the specialization chosen by them.

"An examination of a 1959 curriculum on jurisprudence", writes N. DeWitt, "indicated that the basic structure had remained about the same". [2]

New faculties of law were opened at the universities of Rostov and Odessa in 1947, at the Tomsk, Perm' and Middleasian Universities in 1948, at the Irkutsk and Tadzhik Universities in 1949 and at the Turkmen University in 1950.

However, the number of professors among the teaching personnel of the law faculties was not yet adequate. Shebanov remarks that "there were no professors at all for the teaching in a number of special fields. Among 125 law departments existing in 1953, at law institutes and of faculties of universities, only 39 were headed by professors". [3]

The slow growth of scientific qualifications of the law—teaching personnel Shebanov attributed to the insufficient development of research work. Although some scientific and important work was published, still only 45 of such publications appeared in 1948-50. Among them not more than 5 were published in the filed of"Theory of State and Law", "Soviet State Law" and "International Law", but on the history of state and law of the USSR and the history of political doctrines—not a single book was published. [4]

---

[1] Shebanov, *op. cit.*, pp. 71-72.

[2] N. De Witt, *Education and Professional Employment in the USSR*, Washington D.C., 1961, p. 282.

[3] Shebanov, *op. cit.*, p. 75.

[4] *Ibid.*, p. 76.

2. Decision of the Central Committee of the Soviet Union's Communist Party and the USSR, Council of Ministers of August 30, 1954

Another milestone in the development of the legal education in the Soviet Union is the decision of the Central Committee of the Soviet Communist Party and the USSR Council of Ministers of August 30, 1954 on the improvement of the training, the distribution and use of specialists with higher and secondary special education (Order of the USSR Minister of Higher Education of September 9, 1954, No. 975) .[1]

The decision started with the statement that "some successes in the work of higher and secondary special institutions have been achieved during the last years; in 1954 the number of graduates in all kinds of learning (including teaching by correspondence and evening courses) has increased 56% as compared with 1940" Nevertheless, this statement is followed by a strong criticism.

"However, serious defects exist in matters of training, distribution and use of specialists ...

The Ministry of Higher Education and other Ministries and administrations do not display the necessary care for the improvement of the scientific level of lectures, practical training of students and a correct organization of their work day. The students are overburdened with obligatory studies and a great number of tests and examinations, some courses duplicate one and the same study material and suffer from too great attention to details. Higher and secondary institutions of learning, textbooks and equipment and teaching are lacking ...

The higher institutions of learning are not sufficiently provided with highly qualified professorial and teaching staffs ..."

A special reproach is directed at local Party, Soviet and Komsomol organizations : "They do not educate students enough in the spirit of consciousness, discipline and high regard to duty toward the state and readiness to work whereever required by state interests, after graduation".

Gureyev and Klochkov report that the number of graduates with a higher legal education declined from 1956 to 1963. During this period the number of graduates from the regular legal departments of the institutions of higher learning and legal schools was reduced over 50%.

---

[1] *Vysshaya shkola*, M. 1957, pp. 10-15.

At the same time also the instruction of students in evening and correspondance courses was not adequate. Many persons registered at these courses did not work in the field "for the further advancement of jurisprudence and the bettering of legal education", in the future specialities and did not display interest in them. In this connection the elimination of a great number of correspondence course students took place. For example, in the All-Union Law Institute for Teaching by Correspondence where one-third of all students are taught by correspondence, a great number of the students were eliminated. About 60% of students of this Institute were not connected with practical legal work in the 1963/64 academic year. Persons graduating from evening and correspondence departments of law faculties and institutes were not distributed according to the plan; that is why many of them after graduation continue to work in positions not requiring legal training.

Consequently, declare the authors of the editorial, there is not enough qualified legal staff, especially at local Soviets, in the government apparatus and the economy. Many officials of the local Soviets and governmental organs directly responsible for the legal aspect of decisions, do not possess the required minimal legal knowledge.

Especially defective was the situation with regard to the training of legal staffs for the Siberian Regions, the Far East, Kazakhstan, Central Asia and the Ukraine. For instance, the Irkutsk State University graduated only 34 jurists in 1964, when the organs for the preservation of public order, prosecution and social security of this region alone required a much greater munber of specialists with a higher legal education. Moreover, it must be considered that this university is obliged to prepare legal staffs not only for the Irkutsk Region but also for the Buryat ASSR, Yakut ASSR, Khabarovsk Territory and the Chita, Amur and Kamchatka Regions.

The authors are shocked by the small number of law students registered at some universities. Not more than 25 students were registered at the universities of Kiev, Voronezh, Kishinev, Far Eastern, Tashkent, Tbilisi, Tortu and some others. Facilties for legal training are not fully used at universities for the training and development of jurists with higher legal education. On the other hand, cases are known where legal staffs are trained at pedagogical and even agricultural institutions of higher learning.

Gureyev and Klochkov also point out significant defects in the teaching and educational work of the law faculties and institutes. Subjects not connected with the future practical activity of the students are included in the obligatory curriculum on the one hand, but on the other, topics, the study of which has a great practical value (the labor reform law, fundamentals of the study and prevention of crimes) are absent from the curriculum. The lists of faculty subjects and special courses not seldom has a casual character.

Furthermore, teaching methods are criticized by the authors. Individual lectures, seminars and practical exercises on legal subjects are carried out not on a high theoretical legal level, without relation to the work of the administration of justice and governmental organs. Court, prosecuting, and state administrative workers seldom participate in the teaching process. Teachers of a number of institutions of higher learning in law do not posess the necessary pratical experience, even in such subjects as criminalistics, criminal law, criminal procedure, civil procedure, administrative law, and some of them never worked at organs for the administration of justice. The authors assert that among the ten teachers of the department of criminal law of the Leningrad State University, only four have practical experience, and among the four teachers of criminalistisc ... only one. All lectures on the tactics of investigating, methods of investigation and the majority of practical exercises are carried out at that department by teachers who had no practical experience in their subjects.

The same situation exists at the Department of Criminal and Civil procedure at the Leningrad State University. Often, persons not in the possession of the necessary qualifications, practical knowledge and vocation for research and pedagogical work are admitted to graduate studies at law research institutes and institutions of higher learning. As a result of the poor scientific guidance of the graduate student work, many among them do not defend their dissertations on the established date.

Defects in the training of graduate students and their distribution in the country result in a lack of staffs at a number of institutions of higher learning and scientific institutions of the union republics. [1]

It is interesting to note that in contradiction to Gureyev and Klochkov, the Decision of the USSR Council of Ministers of May 25, 1955 [2] established that "the number of graduates in jurisprudence from

---

[1] P.P. Gureyev, V.V. Klochkov, For the Further Heigtening of Soviet Jurisprudence and the Improvement of Legal Education, (Editorial), *S.G.P.*, 1964, No. 8.

[2] *Vysshaya shkola, op. cit.*, p. 16.

institutions of higher learning exceeds the need for them of ministries and administration. This fact, which was true in previous years, shows that substantial defects existed until now in matters of planning the training and distribution of young specialists", reads the Decision.

But, on the other hand, the same Decision introduced measures for the bringing of order into the training of specialists with secondary higher legal education. To this effect it was decided : to set at 600 the number of students admitted to legal institutes every academic year; to charge the USSR Ministry of Justice with the provision of law faculties of state universities and law institutes with the necessary practical legal experience and the USSR Ministry of Higher Education with the publication of textbooks for the teaching of law.

3. *The Law of December 24, 1958*

Guided by Lenin's principles, the XXth Congress of the USSR Communist Party (1956) acknowledged the necessity for education to prepare students for practical work and liquidate "the separation between the school and life", to ensure an intricate connection of education with socially useful work. To educate the upcoming generation in the spirit of communist attitude toward work. [1]

On December 24, 1958, the USSR Supreme Soviet adopted a law "on the Strengthening of the Bond Between School and Life and on the Further Development of the System of Education in the USSR". [2]

The Law strived first to eliminate defects still "pertaining to the educational systems and its functioning, such as that of education being out of touch with life and poor preparation of the graduates for practical activity". Consequently, the purpose of the Law was the narrowing of the gap between intellectual and physical work which had the proportion of a "precipice" in the old society. For centuries culture was a forbidden fruit for millions of simple people. The old society allegedly constructed its schools in a manner to make them, in essence, inaccessible to wide masses of toilers.

According to the Law, education has to be guided more effectively towards the practical life and to give to the working population the possibility to better fulfill their work.

It was also Lenin's opinion already in 1897 that intellectual workers must have experience in physical work and that industrial and agri-

---

[1] *Sovetskaya shkola na sovremennom etape*, M. 1961, p. 16.

[2] *V.V.S., SSSR*, 1959, Item 5.

cultural workers must have a certain degree of education. He wrote :
"It is impossible to imagine the ideal of the future society without
the combinations of education with productive work of the young
generation : either training and education without productive work,
or productive work without parallel training and education cannot
bring up to the degree which is demanded by the contemporary level
of technology and scientific knowlegde ... In order to combine the
general work in production with general education, it is, evidently,
necessary to charge everyone to take part in the productional work". [1]

The alienation from life was considered one of the major defects
of Soviet schools in the fifties. Yelyutin complained that not a few
persons were admitted to institutions of higher learning who had no
experience in practical and physical work whatsoever, although they
had some knowledge acquired from books. In the process of teaching,
the higher institutions of learning did not pay due attention to the
mastering by students of practical experience, accumulated at factories, plants, sovkhozes, kolkhozes, scientific and other institutions. [2]

To this effect, secondary and higher education must be combined
with practical work and great importance must be assumed by teachers
by correspondence and in evening courses.

The preamble of the Law closes with the assertion of the necessity
"to prepare children, already with the first years of education; they
must participate in socially useful work in the future. Starting with
the age of 15-16, young people must be drawn into socially useful
work and it is necessary to combine all further teaching with productive work in the national economy".

According to the principle of increased practical work for students,
the Law provided that the recruitment of students in the universities and the combination of learning with (practical) work in them,
must be organized in such a manner that students acquire the skill
in the process of study to work in their specialty, and the specialists
in the humanities, economists, philosophers, jurists, etc. besides all
that, should gain a certain experience in socially useful work.

The reconstruction of higher and secondary education had to be
carried out within three to five years, beginning with the 1959/60
academic years.

The principles mentioned above were applied also to legal education.

---

[1]   Lenin, 2, pp. 440-441.

[2]   Yelyutin, *op. cit.*, p. 64.

In order to inculcate the students with the practical skill prescribed by the Law, the students at law faculties were subjected to practical training divided into three stages : during the first and second years of study, the students attend sessions of the local soviets, courts, etc. At the end of the third year, when the students have already mastered the basic theoretical subjects, they carry out practical work at people's courts, district prosecution bodies, local organs of government and administration which lasts 12 weeks. Finally, when they have mastered all the special topics, students during the ninth semester (fifth year) must undergo 22 weeks of practical training which, if possible, must have the character of probation [1] at the organs and institutions of the administration of justice to which the young specialist is intended to be directed after his graduation. [2]

The reform of education of 1958 had the main purpose to change essentially the way to form the working intelligentia. "In a society in which a distinction between intellectual and physical work is latent, a high level of education may be achieved only by intellectual work", it is asserted in a symposium edited by I.A. Kairov. [3] But socialism allegedly liquidates this distinction, gradually reasing the dividing line in the cultural and educational level in various strata of the population and creates a new type of toiler prepared for intellectual as well as physical work.

Critics of the reform in the West argued that the requirement of socially useful work in production for students will lower the quality of education and reduce the number of intellectuals in the Soviet Union.

Beginning with 1959, all union republics have centers of legal education : regular, evening courses and teaching by correspondence, at the law faculties of their universities in their capitals. As a result, all universities, with the exception of the Far East University, train jurists with and without separation from work.

However, it must be emphasized that the number of law graduates, as it will be shown below, declined between 1956 and 1963.

---

[1] "*stazhirovka*".

[2] Shebanov, *op. cit.*, p. 131-132.

[3] *Sovetskaya shkola na sovremennom etape*, edited by I.A. Kairov, M. 1961, p. 25.

D. Legal Education Without Separation from Production

A very important role of the legal education was and is played by teaching by correspondence "learning without separation from production", as defined by administration and literature, the"university at home" called by students, and teaching in evening courses.

a) *Teaching by Correspondence*

The first attempt to introduce this form of teaching was made by the opening of an Office of Teaching by Correspondence at the University of Moscow in 1927. The program was calculated for four years of teaching.

In 1931, theBureau of Teaching by Correspondence was transformed into Central Courses of Soviet Law Teaching by Correspondence, attached to the Moscow Institute of Soviet Law.

The by-laws of these Courses, approved by the College of the People's Commissariat of Justice on December 25, 1931, established the duration of learning at $3^1/_2$ years with a program basically similar to that of the faculties of law at universities.

The course had two departments : a court-prosecution-investigating and a reformation-labor department.

The prupose of the first department was to prepare for responsible work in courts and the prosecution body and the second department had to train the leading personnel of places of detention.

Attached to the courses was also a department for the retraining, by correspondence, of court and prosecution workers within two academic years.

Then, by Decision of the same College of Octobe 21, 1933, the Central Courses were renamed into the Central Institute of Soviet Law Teaching by Correspondence.

Finally, the USSR Council of People's Commissars transformed by Decision of March 29, 1937, the Central Institute into the All-Union Law Institute for Teaching by Correspondence. All branches and departments and consultation units of regular law institutes teaching by correspondence were put under the direction of the All-Union Law Institute for Teaching by Correspondence.

The by-laws of the All-Union Institute for Teaching by Correspondence were approved by the All-Union Committee for Higher Education, attached to the USSR Council of People's Commissars, on April 5, 1939.

Previously an important regulation of teaching by correspondence was provided by the Decision of the USSR Council of People's Commissars On the Higher Teaching by Correspondence [1] of August 29, 1938.

The Decision underlines that, although the organization of teaching by correspondence has justified itself by its great importance for the training of specialists without their separation from work, still there is a number of substantial defects in the system of higher teaching by correspondence.

These are : 1) the lack of necessary guidance on the part of people's commissariats and the administration which leads to a planless development of the net of institutions teaching by correspondence; 2) the lack of one and the same rules for admittance and duration of learning, as well as of a teaching regime; 3) failure to provide students learning by correspondence with textbooks, systematic training aids and programs.

In order to improve teaching by correspondence, the USSR Council of People's Commissars decided :

1. to charge the All-Union Committee on Affairs of the Higher Institue of Learning, attached to the USSR Council of People's Commissars, with the general guidance of higher teaching by correspondence;

2. to charge the People's Commissariat's Administration with guidance and inspection in respect to all questions of training and retraining by correspondence of staffs with higher and secondary qualification in independent institutions, as well as in the departments for teaching by correspondence of regular institutions of higher learning;

3. to establish the following organizational forms of higher institutions of teaching by correspondence :

a) departments of teaching by correspondence in regular higher institutions of learning;

b) institutes of teaching by correspondence.

From the other decisions of the Council of People's Commissars it must be inferred that the Council prohibited the continuous admission of students to courses by correspondence and ordered the admission to take place once a year, at the admission time established for the regular institutions of higher learning.

The Council also charged the All-Union Committee on the Affairs

---

[1] *Sob. post.*, *SSSR*, 1938, Item 228.

of the Higher Institutions of Learning, with the working out, together with the People's Commissariats, of plans and programs of teaching on the basis of programs confirmed for regular institutions of higher learning and of the system of dividing the teaching into courses for the departments and institutions teaching by correspondence and to approve them within three months.

Furthermore, the Council prohibited the taking of written examinations in institutions of teaching by correspondence. An obligatory oral examination was introduced with regard to all subjects of the academic plan.

Additional leave was granted to those students who successfully fulfilled the academic plans. The basic leave for holding examination, attending lectures and visiting consultation units was established at 20-30 days. Transportation to the session both ways is to be paid by the enterprise and institution employing the students.

Another paid leave of one month for the taking of the State examinations was provided.

The Committee and the People's Commissariats were charged with the publication of methodical textbooks and other material contributing to independent work by the students.

Those who graduated from the institution of teaching by correspondence after having fulfilled the full course of study and passed the state examination receive regular diplomas and are directed for work first of all to those enterprises in which they had worked during their studies.

The Decision does not permit the requirement of tuition-paying in the system of teaching by correspondence.

Undoubtedly, all these measures must have contributed to the improvement of teaching in the institutions of learning by correspondence and the increase of the number of students there.

A trend to transform branches of the All-Union Law Institute for Teaching by Correspondence in cities where regular institutions of higher learning were located into departments of teaching by correspondence of these institutions, developed in the fifties and had also a salutary influence on the quality of teaching at the departments since the professorial staff of the regular universities was used to this effect.

In a number of cities without regular institutions of higher learning, new branchrs of the All-Union Law Institute for Teaching by Correspondence were opened.

The measures taken for the improvement of legal education in general, following the Decision of the Central Committee of USSR Communist Party of Oct. 5, 1946 also influenced the teaching by correspondence. They produced a new program for the Departments of teaching by correspondence by the law institutes.

This program provided for a five-year course for the students learning by correspondence with the same subjects and examination prescribed for regular students. Also, the passing of the State Examination in six basic subjects was required for graduation.

Shebanov remarks that "these measures permitted the improvement to some extent of the teaching by correspondence and an increase of the number of jurists with higher educational training without separation from work". [1]

The sweeping reforms of education of December 24, 1958 also emphasized the importance of learning by correspondence. In the preamble to the Law, it was said that "the training of specialists in higher and secondary institutions of learning by correspondence and in evening courses acquires particular importance". According to the Law, the system of teaching by correspondence and in evening courses must function in such a manner that people engaged in useful to society work, could have the possibility to work at their own will for the acquisition of higher or secondary special education or for the improvement of their qualifications during the time not taken up with work.

To this effect the Law established the necessity of the improvement and broadening of the teaching by correspondence and in evening courses by strengthening the institutions of higher learning on the basis of the regular institutions of higher learning ... [2]

Also the establishment of special privileges for students of senior courses of institutions of higher learning studying without separation from work [3] was prescribed by the Law.

Students of institutions of higher learning received paid leave of 20-30-40 days for the completion of special work and the passing of examinations, beginning with the third academic year. During the last year, an additional 30 days of leave ofr the passing of state examinations were granted.

The pay during these leaves is the average of their regular remune-

---

[1] Shebanov, *op. cit.*, p. 74.

[2] Art. 29.

[3] Art. 41.

ration. However, not more than 100 rubles monthly for students of institutions of higher learning could be paid out.

Besides these study leaves, students who prepare for state examinations have the right of one day's leave weekly during ten months preceeding the examinations. The pay during this leave is 50% of the regular remuneration, but not less than the established minimum.

Furthermore, the student may, if desired, obtain additional leave without pay of one to two days weekly.

The right for study leave belongs to every regular employee and worker. However, trade unions in practice recognize this right also for temporary and seasonal workers who in general have no claim to a regular leave.

The study leave must be granted without relation to the duration of the occupation of the employee or worker at the enterprise or institution.

Once a year, the employer is obliged to refund to the student, learning without separation from work, 50% of the transportation costs of a round trip to the institution teaching by correspondence for the purpose of taking examinations or performing special work.

The employer particpates to the same extent also in the costs of the trip to submit to the state examinations.

The time necessary for the trip is added to the leave but not payed for by the employer.

All these privileges are awarded only to those students who successfully complete the assigned work in time, and pass the examinations. [1]

In 1958, Khrushchev stated : "The development of our institutions of higher learning must proceed along the lines of teaching by correspondence and in evening courses ... It is necessary to achieve that people engaged in useful work in society should have more opportunities to be taught or aspire to art, painting and humanities at institutions of learning in their free time". [2]

The study in the system of teaching by correspondence is organized in a manner to make the students work independently on the teaching material. Study programs with methodical instructions are sent to help with his work. During the teaching and examining sessions, he attends "review" [3] and "directive" [4] lectures.

---

[1] See V.S. Korotkov, "Learning Without Separation from Production", in *Slovar' pravovykh znaniy*, M. 1965, pp. 267-268, *Sob. post., SSSR*, 1959, Items 90 and 157 E.

[2] *Pravda*, November 16, 1958.

[3] *Obzornyye*.

[4] *Ustanovochnyye*.

Review lectures are delivered to students studying by correspondence, as a rule, before examinations. They contain a review of the newest literature, legislation and other informative literature.

The "directive" lectures are more important since they touch upon the main problems pertaining to the subjects the student intends to study and give directives for his future independent work. These lectures are delivered before the student starts the study of the subject. [1]

"Practically", wrote Shebanov, "there is no city or other inhabited place in the USSR, where it is impossible to get a higher legal education without separation from work. At the present time, 4.5 times as many students are getting legal education by correspondence or in evening courses than at institutions of higher learning during day time. There were more than 30,000 law students studying by correspondence and 6,000 in evening courses in 1963". [2]

Admitted to the teaching without separation from productive work are persons qualified according to the rules of admission without limitation of age.

Rules for admission to the study by correspondence were in some respects not similar to the general rules. Universities and institutions teaching law by correspondence, as well as their study consultation units, extend their work to a certain territory and, as a rule, only students living and working within the zone assigned to the institution may enroll for study by correspondence at that institution.

b) *Evening Courses*

Another opportunity for legal studies without separation from production is provided by evening courses at universities and institutions teaching law.

They are of comparatively recent origin. In the period of 1954-1959, law faculties of universities and the legal institues organized evening courses. The rules of admission to the program and the duration of learning were the same as for the regular law faculties, legal institutes and the teaching by correspondence.

In comparison with the latter the evening courses give to the students

---

[1] Shebanov, *op. cit.*, p. 134.
[2] *Ibid.*, pp. 105 and 108.

the important privilege of personal contact with the teaching personnel, permitting educational improvement without absence from the usual job.

The teaching by correspondence and in evening courses is now integrated with the regular teaching into one system of higher legal education.

An important broadening of the systems of teaching by correspondence and in evening courses in the future development of higher education in general is predicted by Yelyutin. That is why he thinks it necessary to reorganize the systems with the purpose of providing it with a staff of qualified instructors and professors able to cope with the theoretical requirements of modern science and technology. The number of them must insure normal study, i.e., the number of students attended by one instructor or professor must be reduced. [1]

The programs of teaching by correspondence and in evening courses is basically the same as at regular courses of institutions of law. However, it is also adapted to the special needs of students not studying at the institutions or at special hours. The necessity of a more independent study of literature by their students, their unusual age and social position are taken into account.

The schedule of subjects taught is the same as in regular courses, thus giving the possibility to students to shift from learning by correspondence or in evening courses ot regular courses and vice versa. The study program is longer by one year than that in regular courses.

E. SECONDARY LEGAL EDUCATION IN THE USSR

It must be emphasized that, parallel to the higher legal education, also secondary legal education could be obtained in the USSR between 1935 and 1956.

In 1935, secondary law schools were organized by the USSR People's Commissariat of Justice. The purpose was to prepare judges and prosecutors for their activity.

In the beginning, the law schools provided a one-year law course, but in 1939, the course was extended to two years, and the status of secondary special schools was granted to law schools.

To the schools were admitted persons of 23-25 years of age. They

---

[1] Yelyutin, *Vysshaya shkola strany sotsializma*, M. 1959, p. 68.

were located in cities with law teaching institutions, the personnel of which taught in the law schools. There were 18 of these schools as of 1953 in which 1700 persons with secondary legal education graduated yearly. [1]

Shebanov is of the opinion that the "law schools played a positive role permitting the training of workers for the organs of the administration of justice and prosecution with secondary legal qualification in a short period of time. But—Shebanov continued—the problems of and specifications for court and prosecution work required that the workers of these organs be in possession of a higher legal education. That is why the graduates of these schools, on assuming work, have as a rule, to register with institutions of higher learning teaching by correspondence and study for another 5-6 years." [2]

It is no wonder that, due to these circumstances a part of law schools were closed in 1954 and the rest liquidated in 1956.

F. THE CONTEMPORARY SYSTEM OF LEGAL EDUCATION

a) *The Higher Institutions of Legal Learning*

The integrated system of higher learning of law consist of law faculties of universities and law institutes. In these institutions law is taught in regular day courses, by correspondence and in evening courses.

According to Shebanov, law is taught at 25 law faculties of state universities and 4 law institutes of which one is teaching by correspondence only.

A law faculty exists at every university located in the capital of union-republics, viz, in Moscow, Kiev, Minsk, Tashkent, Alma-Ata, Tbilisi, Baku, Vil'nyus, Kishinev, Riga, Frunze, Dushanbe, Yerevan, Ashkhabad and Tartu.

Law faculties function also at universites and in cultural and industrial centers, such as Leningrad, Voronzeh, Kazan', Rostov-na Donu, Perm', Tomsk, Irkutsk, Vladivostok, L'vov and Odessa.

The law institutes are located in Saratov, Sverdlovsk, Khar'kov and the All-Union Law Institute Teaching by Correspondence—in Moscow.

---

[1] Shebanov, *op. cit.*, p. 78.
[2] *Ibid.*

About the number of law students Shebanov reports that there were approximately 44,000 of them in the academic year 1962-63, as compared with 12,500 students at the law faculties of tsarist universities in 1914.

As we have seen above, [1] among this number 30,000 studied by correspondence and 6,000 at evening courses, so that the number of students attending regular day courses was about 8,000; i.e., 50% lower than at tsarist universities, which did not practice teaching by correspondence or at evening courses.

Yelyutin writes that 50% of all students in institutions of higher learning are women. [2] The total number ov law students in 1959 is calculated by Yelyutin at 36,500, including 24,00 studying without separation from production. [3]

It must be emphasized that for a long time admission to higher institutions of learning was not granted according to the academic merits of the candidate under the Soviets.

Prolitarization of the admission to and, hence, of the higher education, was ordered by Lenin under his instructions to the people's commissariat of Education of August 2, 1918 mentioned above. [4] Not only were persons of proletariat or peasant origin "inconditionally admitted", which means without regard to qualifications, but the youth belonging to other classes of society, i.e., the former bourgeoisie and intelligentia, were excluded from admission to the institutions of higher learning for a long time.

Thus, as DeWitt puts it : [5] "Academic admission criteria were virtually in total disuse in the USSR from the time of the Revolution until about 1935 ... the Party, Komsomal and trade-union organizations decided who should be admitted ... In general, during this period, the only qualification tests ... apart from working class origin ... were liberal and 'political understanding' ... These two tests alone were applied to applicants who either "bona fide" proletarians or who masqueraded as such either by obtaining forged documents or by taking 'proletarian' employment positions".

---

[1] See p. 295.
[2] Yelyutin, *op. cit.*, p. 16.
[3] *Ibid.*, p. 25.
[4] P. 264.
[5] N. De Witt, *op. cit.*, p. 246.

Regular entry examinations on subjects began as late as 1934, and in 1936 all institutions of higher learning required entry examinations for admission.

The class limitations for admission were abolished gradually; in 1928—for children of scientific workers, literay workers and sculptors; in 1931—for children of engineers and technical workers; in 1932—for children of bookkeepers and distribution specialists and technicians in socialized enterprises; in 1935—all restrictions pertaining to the origin of applicants were lifted.

b) *Admission*

According to the rules of admission to institutions of higher learning [1] admitted to regular day courses are citizens of both sexes in possession of a completed secondary education and not older than 35 years, who successfully passed the entry examinations. The admission is competitive; accepted are persons who have the best marks from recognized secondary schools and at the entry examinations.

The emphasis on practice, established by the law of 1958, is reflected in the rules of admission by the requirement of two years of practical work before admission to the study of law in an institution of higher learning. [2]

'Thus", writes Shebanov, previous participation in socially useful work is a mandatory prerequisite for persons seeking admission to law institutions of higher learning. Any young man or girl graduating from a secondary school and desiring to become a jurist, must know that the way to legal higher education lies through particpation in social production". [3]

The entry-examinations have the following topics : Russian language and literature (oral and in writing), or the language in which the teaching is conducted, and history of the USSR (oral). The students of day courses have to pass also a test in a foreign language ... English, French or German.

Admitted are, in the first place, those who received the highest marks at the entry examination. Privileged for the admission to law

---

[1] *Pravila priyema v vysshiye uchebnyye zavedeniya SSSR na 1963g*; Bull. MV SSO 1963, No. 4.

[2] Persons demobilized from the Army or Navy if they had 2 years of active service are admitted.

[3] Shebanov, *op. cit.*, p. 111.

studies are those candidates who receive the best marks in the Russian language and literature or history of the USSR.

No tuition is exacted. More than 80% of students of law faculties and all successful students of the law institutes receive scholarships. Students not residents of the city in which the institute is located live in dormitories and have to pay a small amount (about 3-5% of the scholarship) for rent and service, including the use of linen. The amount of the scholarship is increased 25% for students who pass all the examinations with the mark "excellent". Individual more important scholarships named for V.I. Lenin, M.I. Kalinin and F.E. Dzerzhinsky are awarded to the most successful students.

Food and non-alcoholic beverages may be obtained by students at lower prices in the refectories of the institutions of higher learning.

c) *The Program*

The contemporary program of subjects taught to law students was established by the Ministry of Secondary and Higher Education in 1959, [1] and divided into two groups : the first consists of social and economic topics such as national economy, history of the Soviet Communist Party, dialectic and historical materialism. Furthermore, study of Marxist-Leninist ethics, aesthetics and scientific atheism is recommended.

About 15% of obligatory study time is to be dedicated to the study of these topics.

The second group of subjects includes various fields of Soviet legal science.

The topics of the second group are divided into Soviet law, international law, state law of other socialist and bourgeois countries and some subsidiary topics such as forensic medicine and psychiatry, court statistics, fundamentals of bookkeeping and bookkeeping expertise. Furthermore, logic, fundamentals of Roman Law, literature and one foreign language (English, French or German) are taught to law students.

Topics pertaining to the Soviet law system are :

1. History of State and Law of the USSR (including the History of State and Law of Foreign Countrues;

2. History of Political Doctrines;

3. Soviet State Law;

---

[1]   Quoted by Shebanov, *op. cit.*, pp. 118 ff.

4. Soviet Administrative Law;

5. Soviet Land Law;

6. Soviet Finance Law;

7. Soviet Civil Law;

8. Soviet Family Law;

9. Soviet Labor Law;

10. Kolkhoz Law;

11. Soviet Criminal Law;

12. Soviet Criminal Procedure;

13. Soviet Civil Procedure;

14. Organization of Courts and the Prosecuting Body in the USSR and Union-Republics;

15. Prosecution Supervision;

There is one single program for all universities teaching law. It is calculated for 5 academic years or 10 semesters.

Also special courses in some individual subjects are offered to students during the last two years of study.

The subjects are taught by lectures in seminars and practical exercises, consultations and study papers.

The program of law institutes differs in some respects from the university program. The study at law institutes lasts only 4 years and 4 months. Roman Law is not taught. Family law is studied together with civil law and the foreign language is studied to a lesser extent than at the universities.

On the other hand, more hours are allocated to the study of civil and criminal law and civil and criminal procedure. Also less time is devoted to secondary and special courses. The law institutes provide the students more with practical knowledge than a scientific insight into the subjects at hand which is taken care of by the universities.

In all institutions of higher learning, independently of the form of teaching law, regular, in evening classes or by correspondence, the passing of the state examinations is necessary for graduation.

The final test is given in five subjects: 1) history of the Soviet Union Communist Party; 2) theory of state and law; 3) Soviet civil law; 4) Soviet criminal law and 5) depending upon the work completed by the candidate during study, Soviet state and administrative law, or Soviet criminal procedure, or Soviet civil procedure.

The productional, i.e., practical work is assigned to the student in conformity with the legal activity he intends to carry out after graduation. According to the Decision of the USSR Council of Ministers of August 4, 1959 [1] the practical work has to last one year during the studies for those who have been admitted after two years of productional work.

Graduation from a faculty of law of a university or a law institute does not confer an academic degree upon the graduate.

G. Post-Graduate Studies (Aspirantura)

a) *Regular Post-Graduate Studies*

The award of academie degrees was introduced in 1934. Two degrees may be acquired in law studies : "Candidate of legal science" and "Doctor of legal science".

Post-graduate studies leading to the degree of candidate of legal sciences may be conducted in two kinds of legal studies practiced in the Soviet Union, i.e., with separation from productional work at evening courses and by correspondence courses.

To post-graduate studies are admitted Soviet citizens not older than 35 years who have completed higher education, showed aptitude for scientific research work and completed two years of legal work after the graduation from an institution of higher learning. However, the council of the higher institution of learning of whih the candidate requests permission to study can decide to admit him to entrance examinations immediately after graduation.

Graduates from institutions of higher learning teaching by correspondence or in evening courses, not older than 45 years and having done two years of legal work, may be admitted to post-graduate studies immediately after graduation.

The passing of competive examinations is a mandatory preerquisite for admission to post-graduate studies. The examinations are : in the elected specialty (one of the law discipline), the history of the Communist Party of the Soviet Union and in one of the European language (English, French or German, Spanish or Italian).

If the applicant has no scientific publications to his credit he must present a paper before the examination on a question in the field of his specialization.

After his admission the aspirant has to study not longer than three years when he is taught by correspondence or at evening courses ...

---

[1] *Sob. post.*, *SSSR*, 1959, Item 115, Art. 2 g.

not longer than four years under the supervision of a professor or doctor of law assigned to him by the council of the institution, according to an individual plan of study prepared by the council of the institution of higher learning. During the study period the aspirant must again pass examinations on dialectics and historical materialism, a foreign language and the discipline in which he specializes. He has also to acquire an amount of pedagogical practice to the extent prescribed by the department to which he is attached.

Then, a term is established for the presentation of a candidate's dissertation and its defense in public.

b) *Post-Graduate Studies for Special Purposes* [1]

In the case when a republic has not the possibilty to prepare scientific-pedagogical and scientific staffs in its universties it sends appropriate aspirants to institutions of higher learning of another republic or its aspirants are prepared by correspondence courses by institutions of higher learning of other republics.

Such aspirants, as assigned by their republics, are admitted to postgraduate study without competition after having passed the regular examinations.

Having obtained the degree of candidate of legal sciences, they return to their respective republics for pedagogical or scientific work.

Post-graduate studies lasting up to one year are reserved for instructors and other personnel of institutions of higher learning, and for school teachers.

To be admitted these aspirants must pass the regular examinations and be in possession of experience in pedagogical or scientific work.

H. ACADEMIC DEGREES AND TITLES

According to Art. 29 of the Statute "The dissertation has to represent new scientific or practical conclusions and recommendations, reflect the capability of the aspirant for independent research work, deep theoretical knowledge in the discipline on hand and special erudition in the problems discussed in the dissertation. [2]

---

[1] *Tselevaya aspirantura.*

[2] Statute on the Post-Graduate Education at the Higher Institutions of Learning and Research Institutions. *Byulleten' Ministerskva vysshego i srednego spetsial'nogo obrazovaniya,* M. 1962, No. 9.

The Degree of Candidate of Legal Sciences is awarded by the council of the institution of higher learning at which the aspirant completed his post-graduate studies, after the defense of his dissertation by the candidate in a public session of the council. Official opponents usually criticize the dissertation, and the council decides by secret vote.

If the Degree of Candidate of Legal Sciences to some extent may be compared with the Master's Degree in the United States, there is no comparison between the American Ph. D. and the Doctor Degree in the Soviet Union.

Already in tsarist Russia the Doctor Degree was conferred on professors who had a number of years of teaching experience and a well-established scientific reputation in the field of their specialty; the doctorate was strictly a specialty. Thus, there were doctors of criminal law, civil law, etc.

In the Soviet Union the Degree of Doctor of Laws is awarded to a professor in recognition of his important merits in the field of legal science and practice. The doctoral dissertation, published in the form of a monograph, represent usually the summing-up of exhaustive and profound research work of the author in a number of articles and monographs. "It is like the completion of a distinct period in the development of the creative biography of the candidate", Shebanov writes. [1]

The Instructions on the Order of Conferring Scientific Degrees and Academic Titles requires of a doctoral dissertation that it be on an important scientific problem, representing a significant contribution to science and practice.

The degree of Candidate of Legal Sciences or the Doctorate are technically awarded by the higher Attestation Commission attached to the USSR Ministry of Higher and Secondary Special Education. The candidate and doctoral dissertation must be openly defended before a special testing board with official opponents.

Post-graduate studies (*aspirantura*) may not be conducted at all legal system of higher learning : only a few of them are selected for the offering of these courses.

The title of a professor is conferred by the same Commission, upon motion of the council of a higher institution of learning to doctors of sciences who published scientific works, especially after the dissertation, and elected through competition to chairmanships or profes-

---

[1] Shebanov, *op. cit.*, p. 151.

sorships of a department of the institution, after one year of work in this position.

I. Administration of the Legal Institutions of Higher Learning

From the beginning of the Soviet State to 1932, the administration of education was decentralized and the higher control put in the hands of the Training Section of Cadres of the *Gosplan* (State Planning Committee of the USSR Council of Ministers). After 1932 the All-Union Committee of Higher and Technical Education of the TsIK exercised centralized guidance and control.

Then, the All-Union Committee on Higher Schools of the USSR was formed by Decision of the TsIK and the Council of USSR People's Commissars of May 21, 1936. [1] Article 2 of the Decision extended to the Committee the guidance of all institutions of higher learning in the country, independently of the jursidiction under which the institution was functioning, with the exception of military institutions of learning and the Institute under the jurisdiction of the All-Union Committee on Art's Affairs.

The Committee was charged to examine the expense estimates of the maintenance of the institutions of higher learning of the people's commissariats of the republics; the establishment of the number and types of institutions of higher learning; the confirmation of teaching plans and programs; the establishment of the admission contingent of students; the examination of the dissertation plans of students graduated from the institutions of higher learning among the USSR and union republics; confirmation of the direction of institutions of higher learning and the confirmation of the titles of professor and candidate for teachers of the institutions of higher learning.

Thus, the Committee exercised higher guidance and supervision over the activity of the institutions of higher learning which were under the immediate administration of the individual union-republic people's commissariats according to the specialty of the institution. Hence, the legal institution of higher learning was under the direct supervision and administration of the People's Commissariats of Justice of the USSR and of the individual union-republics.

---

[1] *Sob. zak.*, *SSSR*, 1936, Item 250.

The All-Union Ministry of Higher Education assumed the higher guidance of and the supervision over the institutions of higher learning between 1946 and 1953 and the Main Administration of Higher Education of the USSR Ministry of Culture from 1953 to 1954. The Main Administration in Higher Education was replaced in that task by the All-Union Ministry of Education in 1954, renamed Union Republic Ministry of Higher Education. [1]

In connection with the educational reform of 1958, a change was also introduced into the adminstration of the institutions of higher learning. The USSR Council of Ministers adopted a Decision "On the Reconstruction of the Guidance of Higher and Secondary Institutions of Learning", on June 27, 1959. [2]

It was decided to transfer the institutions of higher learning from the federal subordination into the competence of councils of ministers of union republics within two months. (Article 1)

The Decision charged the councils of ministers of the union-republics with the study of the needs of the republics as to staffs, the selection and confirmation of the leading, scientific and pedagogic personnel of the institutions of learning, the organization of the teaching methodology, educational and research work, as well as with providing for the material, technical, financial and constructional needs of the institutions subordinate to them.

The Decision also established that plans for the admission to institutions of higher learning of the republic and of the institutions of the young specialists with higher education have to be confirmed by the councils of ministers of union-republics, on agreement with the USSR

Furthermore, the council considered it expedient to transform the USSR Ministry of Higher Education into the Union-Republic Ministry of Higher and Secondary Special Education of the USSR.

The competence of the new Ministry is also regulated in the same decision.

It has :

1. to develop the basic elements pertaining to the long-term planning of the development of the higher and secondary special education;

2. to draw conclusions with regard to propositions by union-

---

[1] See Nicholas De Witt, *op. cit.*, Footnote 72, p. 40.

[2] *Sob. post.*, *SSSR*, 1959, Item 79.

republic councils of ministers about the location of institutions of higher learning in the republics and economic districts of the Soviet Union;

3. to extend scientific and methodical aid to republics concerning the establishment of research work at institutions of higher learning and the coordination of higher learning and the coordination of research work plans;

4. to extend scientific and methodical aid to republics, to confirm teaching plans of programs in agreement with them on regulations of porductional teaching, as well as rules of admission to higher and secondary special institutions of learning;

5. to coordinate, between republics, plans for the publication of textbooks and production of teaching aids for institutions of higher learning and the Technicum;

6. to work out regulations and instructions on the training of scientific and pedagogical staffs and the attestation of scientific and pedagogical personnel;

7. to extend aid to the republics in the task of establishing teaching of social sciences at higher and secondary special institutions of learning;

8. to realize international communication concerning questions of higher and secondary special education.

The immediate supervision and guidance of the higher institutions of learning is in the hands of ministries or chief administrations of the union republics under which authority the individual institution of higher learning is placed according to their specialty : "The Ministries and administration guide the teaching, educational, methodical work of the higher institution of learning placed under their authority on the basis of general regulations worked out and confirmed by the USSR Ministry of Higher and Secondary Special Education". [1]

The *Polozheniye* (Statute) provided also that the Rector (President) of the institution of higher learning guided all the activities of the institution. He is appointed by the ministry or administration controlling the institution, from the most qualified members of the scientific and pedagogical staff and in possession of an academic title or academic degree and experience in practical work.

The functions of the president, enumerated in Article 44 of the

---

[1] Article 6 of the *"Polozheniye o vysshich uchebnykh zavedeniyakh"* confirmed by the USSR Council of Ministers on March 28, 1961, *Sob. post., SSSR,* 1961, Item 40.

Statute, extended to question of the inner academic and administra-
strative life of the institution.

The purely administrative and economic functions belong to the
Prorector (Deputy President), the next in the administrative hierarchy of the institution.

An insitution of higher learning has usually several faculties. The
term "faculty" is generally understood to mean the teaching staff
of a university or college in the United States. In Europe, including
pre-and post-revolutionary Russia, a faculty is a division of a university or other institution of higher learning at which a certain
branch of science or humanities is taught. [1]

The Statute defines a faculty as "an adminsitrative, teaching and
scientific division of an institution of higher learning, realizing the
training of students and post-graduate students in one of several
related specialties ... as well as the guidance of the research work
of the departments" (Article 34).

The *Dekan* (Chariman) is the head of a faculty which is subdivided
into *kafedry* (Departments) which are the basic structural units of the
pedagogical and scientific system. A department headed by a chairman
comprises the professors, lecturers, senior instructors, instructors,
senior and junior scientific workers and post-graduate students.

J. APPRAISAL

a) *Lack of Autonomy*

The absence of autonomy in the institution of higher learning in
the Soviet Union is a natural expression of the character of the power
system which controls them.

The institutions of higher learning are deprived of the right to select
their administrative and professorial staffs which are appointed and
confirmed by the Ministry supervising the institutions; the teaching
programs, which are established for the entire counrty identically,
the number of students to be admitted, the budget and, in general,
all important problems of their scientific, pedagogical and admini-

---

[1] However, in some American Universities, the word "faculty" is also applied in
the European sense, as for instance, the Faculty of Social Science of the Columbia
University.

strative activity, are decided and regulated centrally outside of the institutions.

Certainly, the administrative system of education in the USSR reflects its totalitarian regime, and character in the field of education even more completely than it was under the tsars. Indeed, the Russian universities enjoyed complete autonomy according to the Statutes of 1804 and 1863, although a restricted one even under the reactionary regimes of Nicholas I, Alexander III and Nicholas II.

b) *The Scope of Education*

According to Khrushchev's definition of the scope of Soviet education, "the mission of the soviet school is to prepare versatile educated people who have a good knowledge of the sciences and at the same time, are capable of systematic work, to educate the youth in striving to be useful to society and participate actively in the production of values necessary to society". [1]

The real scope of education in the Soviet Union is not to educate students in their own interest, according to their individual capacities and inclinations, but the primary objective is to train persons who can render the best services to the state, adapt themselves to the needs and demands of the state at a given time. The admission quotas are set in accordance with these needs and demands, and after graduation, the specialist has to serve during three years thereafter where ever the state sends him and in the capacity needed by the state.

Indeed, also regulated is scientific work in compliance with the general economic plan and the staffs for the fulfillment of the plan are educated accordingly. To this effect students are trained in specialties needed by the plan.

One of the means to influence the student in the choice of the specialty is the distribution of stipends. These stipends are of various amounts in relation to the importance of the specialty for the Soviet State. [2]

That is why Soviet institutions of higher education do not provide general education. The State has no use for generally educated per-

---

[1] N. S. Khrushchev, *Vospitat' aktivnykh i soznatel'nych stroiteley kommunisticheskogo obshchestva.* Speech of April 18, 1958, at the XIII Congress of Komsomol, M. 1958, p. 14.

[2] See Rainer Lucas, "Legal Education in the Soviet Union", *Juristenzeitung*, 1962, No. 1, pp. 21-22.

sons. All the programs are designed to train in a definite specialty required by the state.

Consequently, in their research work, neither the students nor their teachers are free to select the field and the direction of the work; all that must be approved from above. Thus, this applies to the dissemination of the results obtained by the research work.

c) *Quality of Education*

With regard to the quality of legal education, a difference must be made as to how the education was obtained : at ragular day courses with separation from productional work or without separation from it, i.e., by correspondence or at evening courses.

The teaching by correspondence, intensively developed in the Soviet Union, is a very efficient device for the mass-production of specialists. The student has the great privilege of remaining at home, he does not need to leave his family in order to travel to sometimes remote cities, and what is very important, he retains his permanent job and income, promoting his education and acquiring a higher specialty at the same time.

Also with regard to the State this kind of education seems to be preferred since it is less expensive and production is not diminished by the separation from work of the student.

However, in reality the state sacrifices the quality of education for the quantity of production, which is in the end effect, not advantageous : the future specialist will be less qualified for his job than his colleague who graduated in the regular way. This lack of the best qualifications will certainly have a detrimental influence on production or the job to which the expert will be assigned.

Indeed, the quality of education obtained by lectures and the personal contact with teachers in seminars cannot be compared with learning by correspondence and with the help of rare conferences provided at scientific information units; even when teaching by correspondence is conducted by regular institutes of higher learning and their qualified staffs, the results must be less than those obtained by regular teaching.

The tremendous development of the education by correspondence [1] makes the teaching task extremely difficult and its success even more questionable.

---

[1]   V.P. Yelyutin, "The Higher School Today", *Molodoy Kommunist*, 1960, No. 1, p. 3.

Yelyutin relates that an institution of higher learning teaching by correspondence has thousands, and sometimes, tens of thousands of students and does not have at its disposal the necessary teaching and material base to cope with such a number of students. [1]

According to *Narodnoye Khozyaystvo* the following numbers of law students was registered in all institutions of higher learning in the USSR : in the academic year of 1950-51 : 45,400; in 1958-59 : 36,200; in 1960 : 40,300; in 1963-64 : 50,200; in 1964-65 : 56,300; in 1965-66 : 60,000; 1966-67 : 64,400; 1967-68 : 67,100. [2]

In spite of all measures taken, legal education in the Soviet Union is still not adequate in order to cover the needs of legally educated persons. Complaints do not disappear from the pages of the press, up to the present time.

So, for instance, V. Kolmakov, complains in the pages of *Izvestia* about the ignorance of laws of the population. The reason is that law is not sufficiently taught to the population. The law universities have a small number of students and do not contribute to the dissemination of legal knowledge among the populace; the legal periodicals have an insignificant circulation and are read by legal specialists only; they do not propagate legal knowledge. Legal literature is not to be found in places and other libraries of massive use. Kolmakov is of the opinion that life requires new forms of legal propaganda. Its importance and necessity are evident. [3]

Pakalov points out the ignorance of law on the part of newly appointed administrations at plants and factories which leads to a frequent violation of the Labor Code. He suggests that every newly appointed employee with executive rights should pass an examination on elementary law knowledge. [4]

In an article in *Izvestia*, V. Terebilov, Deputy Chairman of the USSR Supreme Court, reports that legal agencies and other state institutions are feeling an acute need of legal experts with higher

---

[1] Writing in 1960, he reported that among the 470,000 students admitted to the institutions of higher learning in 1959, there were 270,000 to be taught by correspondence and in evening courses and that about one million of toilers were being educated without separation from production.

[2] *Narodnoye Khozyaystvo SSSR v 1964*, M. 1965, p. 679 and 1967, p. 789. The difference of registered students between 1951 and 1958 reported above and the slow increase afterward must be noted.

[3] V. Kolmakov, "To Know and Fulfill the Law", August 2, 1967.

[4] A. Pakalov, "How Important is the Knowledge of Law", *Pravda*, August 8, 1967.

education. However, the USSR Ministry of Higher and Secondary Education and the corresponding union-republic ministries do not care very much about it. He is of the opinion that it is not only necessary to create institutes for the perfection of jurists but also to reinstate secondary legal education. The government has charged the Legal Commission attached to the USSR Council of Ministers and the Gosplan, as well as the USSR Minister of Finance to prepare suggestions related to the introduction of secondary legal education and a list of positions requiring legally educated staffs.

A prospective plan for the publication of legal textbooks was approved in 1965, but the publication lags very much in comparison with the plan. The prospects for 1967-1968 are even more unfavorable. [1]

But if general legal education in the Soviet Union is wanting, a striking phenomenon is the absence of the requirement of higher legal education for judges. There is no country in the West, including former tsarist Russia, where professional judges are not in possession of such an education.

The lack of such a requirement can be explained only by the fact that it would contradict the principle established by Marx and Lenin, and upheld by Khrushchev and the Party, of the widest possible participation of the masses in the administration of justice.

Marx thought that the bourgeoisie had "a deadly fear" to let the poor and the "socially and politically unfortunate masses" take part in the administration of justice and build up a wall of qualification and educational requirements in order to prevent it. [2]

It is certain, however, that by tearing down the educational requirements especially for judges, the Soviets dealt a severe blow to their administration of justice.

---

[1] V. Terebilov, "Science and Staffs", *Izvestia*, August 20, 1967.

[2] Quoted by L. Mamut and A. Ugryumov, "Karl Marx on Court and Justice", *Sov. yust.*, 1958, No. 4, p. 36.

CHAPTER TWELVE

JUDGES

A. JUDGES IN TSARIST RUSSIA (1864-1917)

The Judicial Reform of 1864 strived to create the greatest possible independence of the judiciary from the administration.

The guarantees of independence were the following: 1) judicial power was separated from the executive and legislative ones; 2) the justices were appointed for life, by the tsar, to the Senate (The Supreme Court) by individual Ukases and to the courts of appeal and the circuit courts on recommendation of the Minister of Justice.

The nomination of candidates to the position of a judge took place in the general assembly of the court in which the opening occurred. Thus, they were nominated by their own peers.

However, justices of the peace were elected. It is interesting to note that the *"Mirovyye sud'i"* ("Peacemaking Judges", as the justices of the peace were called in Russia), were the first elective judges in Europe; 3) the supervision of the activity of all courts and their members in the whole Empire was exercised by a judicial institution : the Judicial Department of the Senate; the courts of appeal directed the activity of the circuit courts and judges of their respective districts.

A higher legal education was obligatory for all judges (with the exception of justices of the peace).

Lazarenko, who compared the provisions of the 1864 laws concerning the position of the Russian judge with those of other European countries, came to the conclusion that the Statutes of Judicial Institutions, of 1864 guaranteed to the Russian judges, a more independent position than that of their colleagues abroad (except England). [1]

This opinion is corroborated by Zavadsky who in his work on the irremovability of the judge and his independence, [2] asserted that the

---

[1]   A.N. Lazarenko, "Survey of the Basic Features of the Judicial System in Russia and the Main Mid-European Countries," in *Sudebnyye ustavy 20-noyabrya 1964, za pyat'desyat let,* Petrograd 1914, I, Footnote, p. 410.

[2]   A.V. Zavadsky, *Nesamenyayemost' sud'i i ego nezavisimost',* Kazan', 1903, p. 47.

Statutes of Judicial Institution of 1864 created for the Russian judge "a position unique in Europe".

Cardonne [1] wonders that Alexander II introduced the eligibility of judges to Russia, since he must have been aware of the fact that "an elective judiciary has brought most detestable results in the United States of America, where judges too often become servile instruments of political passions".

Anyhow, in Russia, the institution of the justices of the peace had a tremendous success with the population and was hihgly praised by the administration under Alexander II. [2]

However, Vyshinsky wrote that "Bourgeois historians represent the institution of justices of the peace as having stirred the sympathy and love of the population without distinction of classes. All the hypocrisy and falsity of such an assertion hardly needs to be proved". [3]

B. THE SOVIET JUDICIARY

a) *Initial Legislation*

The Decree No. 1 on Courts which abrogated the tsarist judiciary made an exception for the justices of the peace; they were not abolished but "suspended" and retained the right to be elected to the local courts by the local soviets and later in popular elections "if they consented to it". (Article 2).

The privileged treatment was applied to former justices of the peace because it was a liberal institution and also it was desired to have experienced jurists in the local courts.

Since also two people's assessors, introduced by the Decree, and representating the people sat on the bench together with the professional judge, it was assumed that the former bourgeois judges could be held in check by the representatives of the people.

In principle, the electoral system was introduced for the judiciary by the Decree No. 1 on Courts. However, justices of the local courts "temporary" up to the time when such election could take place, had to be appointed by the local soviets of workers', soldiers' and peasants deputies.

---

[1] C. de Cardonne, *L'empereur Alexandre II, vingt-six ans de règne*, Paris, 1893, p. 515.

[2] See Samuel Kucherov, *Courts, Lawyers and Trials, op. cit.*, pp. 87-91.

[3] A.Ye. Vyshinsky, *Sud i Procuratura*, M. 1937, pp. 16-18 passim.

The "temporary" measure—the appointment of judges by the administration remained in force thirty-one years, up to the Electoral Law of 1948.

No legal education was required of the justices of the local courts. Every citizen in possession of civil rights could be elected a justice of the court.

The Decree No. 2 on Courts introduced a circuit court into the court system for cases exceeding the jurisdiction of the local courts.

The members of the circuit courts were appointed (the "election" by an administrative agency is tantamount to appointment) by city and province soviets, whereas the chairman of the court and the chairman of the departments were selected by the general assemblies of these courts.

The Statute on the One and Single People's Court of November 30, 1918 introduced for the first time in soviet legilsation requirements for the appointment of judges.

The candidate had : 1) to have the right to vote for or be elected to the soviets of workers' and peasants deputies; 2) to have political experience in the work of proletarian organizations, such as the Party, trade-unions, workers' cooperatives, factory and plant committees, or soviet agencies; 3) to have a theoretical and practical preparation for the position of a soviet judge. [1]

The candidate had to meet unconditionally the first and at least one of the last two requirements.

Thus, political and legal experiences were put on the same footing and only one of them was a prerequisite for the appointment.

Judges were selected by the general assemblies of borough soviets in cities having such soviets, or by general assemblies of the city soviets from lists of candidates prepared by their respective executive committees.

In districts, including the cities which did not have soviets, the judges were appointed by executive committees of the district soviets, from lists of candidates prepared by their Executive Committees, including those presented by village and *volost'* executive committees.

The judges were subject to recall at any time by the soviets or executive committees which had appointed them.

A change in the appointment system of judges was brought about by the new statute on the People's Courts of October 21, 1920.

---

[1] The extent of the "preparedness" was not specified.

The competence to appoint was transferred to the province executive committees : people's judges nominated by the city and district soviets were presented for confirmation and appointment to the
province executive committees. From amorg the presented candidates, the province executive committees appointed judges according
to their choice. Judges could be recalled also upon decision of the
soviets which selected them, but with the approval of the province
executive committee.

The Judicial Reform of 1922 provided no changes in the qualification requirements of candidates to the position of a judge.

The system of selection and recall by the province executive committee also remained the same.

The recall or the transfer within the province could take place
on the initiative of the province excutive committee or of the people's
commissariat of justice. In the first case, the province executive
committee had to inform the people's commissariat of justice of the
reasons for the recall.

The judges were appointed for one year of service.

The fact that the judges were elected and recalled by the province
executive committees and not by local executive committees "insured
the independence from local influences upon judges", according to
Kozhevnikov. [1]

It cannot be agreed with this opinion since, as said, "election"
of judges up to 1948, carried out by administrative agencies, was
tantamount to appointment. The judges do not escape the influence
of the local party and administrative authorities because they are
confirmed and appointed by a higher administrative instance since
the list of candidates for the choice of the appointing agencies are
prepared and presented by the local authority.

Important is the status of legal education of the judiciary which
progressed very slowly. Kozhevnikov reports to this effect that, only
10% of the people's judges had a higher education (8.1%—a legal
one); 1-5% graduated from secondary school and 72.5% from primary
schools as of the beginning of 1923. [2]

Thus, 72.5% of the judges who had to handle the new codes and
decide on the liberty and life of thousands of people were in possession
of a primary school education only.

---

[1]   M.V. Kozhevnikov, *Istoriya sovetskogo suda, 1917-1947*, M. 1948, p. 128.
[2]   *Ibid.*, p. 130.

There were some changes in the appointment requirement for the justices of the Province Courts created by the Judicial Reform of 1922. The candidates had to have worked previously not less than two years in a position of a People's Judge or a member of a Revolutionary Tribunal. An exception from this rule could be made only with the agreement of the People's Commissariat of Justice.

The chairman of the province court and his deputies, in addition to the requirements existing for the appointment of court members, had to have not less than three years of practical court work in the position of a people's judge or of a member of a revolutionary tribunal.

All these functionaries of the province courts were selected by the province executive committees for one year of service and had to be approved by the people's commissariat of justice. The re-election of the same candidate for a further term was permitted. The commissariat of justice also had the right to present candidates for appointment.

The recall and transfer of judges of the province courts to other positions could be made only with the permission of the People's Commissariat of Justice (with the exception of the release from functions as a consequence of a court decision or a disciplinary procedure).

b) *The RSFSR Statute on Court Structure of 1926*

It is peculiar that the RSFSR Statute on Court Structure of November 19, 1926 brought a relaxation and not an intensification of the requirements for the appointment of judges: persons with experience in work in other than the legal field, could also be candidates for judicial appointments.

Furthermore, persons convicted for defaming crimes or excluded from public organizations for defamatory actions could be elected to people's judge positions if they were rehabilitated. The selection of people's judges could take place not only by province executive committees, but by city soviets as well.

The decision on "revolutionary legality" of June 25, 1932 [1] forbade the dismissal of people's judges or transfer in a manner other than by decision of territorial (regional) executive committees.

This measure was thought of as a means of strengthening legality at a time when continual violations of legality became the major characteristic feature of the cult of personality period.

---

[1] *Sob. zak.*, 1932, Item 298.

C. The 1936 Constitution

According to the original wording of Article 104 of the Constitution, the Supreme Court of the USSR is the highest judicial organ charged with the supervision of the judicial activity of all judicial organs of the USSR and of the union republics.

The justices of the USSR Supreme Court and the supreme courts of the union and autonomous republics are elected by their supreme soviets respectively, for five years of service.

The justices of the territorial, regional and autonomous region courts are elected by territorial, regional and autonomous region soviets respectively also for a term of five years.

a) *Independence of Judges*

Article 112 of the Constitution declared that the judges are independent and subject only to law.

Certainly, the independence is on paper only. Implemented it would contradict the basic foundations of the Soviet State, Soviet power, the rule of the Communist Party and the character of the Soviet court as a political institution.

The Soviet judge is an official of the Soviet state like all other officials and since the law to which he is subject stands not over the state, the judge has to submit to the direction of those who control Soviet power. It is they who prescribe to the judge the sentence when it is deemed appropriate to the interests of the state.

The judge is also a member of the Party in the great majority of cases. His allegiance to the Party also must take precedence over his sense of justice. As a member of the Party he has to follow the prescribed line. The establishment of judicial independence by the Constitution is a striking example of the gulf between written law and reality.

In his commetns to Article 112 of the Constitution, Maurach [1] remarks that no word was said in the two preceeding Constitutions (1918 and 1924) about the independence of the judges. The judge was not permitted to forget that he is an official of the state and the executor of its will who may not invoke independence in his actions; but as of 1936, the Soviet judge was so trained and accustomed to

---

[1] R. Maurach, *Handbuch der Sovjetverfassung*, Munchen, 1955, p. 307.

his position of an obedient organ of the state that there was no danger to grant him independence on paper.

Certainly, judicial independence recognized by the Constitution did not protect the Soviet judge from the most effective interference of the Party and government in the judicial work.

The limitations upon the independence of the judiciary are acknowledged by some Soviet authorites.

Thus, for instance, writing at the time of the cult of personality, Karev stated that "the independence of the Soviet judges cannot be understood in the sense of independence from the socialist state. The court is an organ of the State and an organ cannot be independent from the entity to which it belongs. The Soviet court cannot serve other purposes than the socialist society; it cannot implement another policy than that of the Communist Party and the Soviet government; it cannot realize any other will than that of the Soviet people". [1]

Also Polyansky is of the opinion that the provision of Article 112 of the Constitution does not mean the independence of the Soviet judge from the political directives of Party and the leading Soviet organs. He thinks that no court stands outisde of politics, irrespective as to whether it is a bourgeois or socialist court, since the court is an organ through which the dominent class realizes its predominance. [2]

From the principle of the independence of judges, the bourgeois literature derives the demand of the independence of judges from politics. But, in reality, according to Polyansky, "it is suggested to the people that the judges allegedly free from politics, are impartial servants of Themis who weight the citizen's actions on scales of justice and equates not only 'not looking at the faces' of those whom she tries, but also of those who hand out the scales to her. In reality, the picture of a judge outside of politics pertains to bourgeois mythology in the same way as the image of Themis herself belongs to Greek mythology. [3]

Polyansky came to the conclusion that the judge, in deciding an individual case, must be directed not only by his inner conviction with regard to the evidence and the mitigating and aggravating

---

[1]   D.S. Karev, *Sudoustroystvo*, M. 1948, p. 84.

[2]   N.N. Polyansky and I.D. Perlov, "Independence of judges", in *Entsiklopedicheskiy slovar' pravovykh znaniy*, M. 1965, p. 252.

[3]   Polyansky, "Soviet Criminal Court as a Medium of the Party and Soviet Power", *Vestnik moskovskogo universiteta, seriya obshchestvennykh nauk*, M. 1950, No. 11, p. 136.

circumstances, but he is bound also to follow the general directives issued by leading Soviet and Party organs about the importance of this or that crime or circumstances under which they are perpetrated when he chooses the punitive measure. [1]

With regard to the independence of bourgeois judges, Vyshinsky wrote "never was there, in history, a court more dependent and more slavishly worshipful of the interests, the will and even the whim not only of the bourgeoisie or the nobility as classes, but also the whim of individuals having power on this earth, than the court of any exploiting state.

Bourgeois justice is a justice prostituted, corrupt by exploiters' gold, tied to them by the flesh and blood of common interests ...

That is why there can be no word of any principles of 'independence' or 'irremovability' in the bourgeois court system, however hard the bourgeois theorists may try to prove it". [2]

But Vyshinsky denies also the independence of judges also in a proletarian state, their independence from the proletarian state, workers' class and from the state's general policy.

Doing so he negated the possibility of existence of an impartial court policy as devoted to justice only, as distinct from the general policy, the existence of judges who as members of the state apparatus would differ from other official because of a special inviolability or immunity, liberating them from responsibility before their state, their government and their class. This is quite natural, according to Vyshinsky because the court is a state institution; its activity is a part of state activity. Considering these assertions of the leading jurists of that time, how is the provision of Article 112 of the 1936 USSR Constitution, that "judges are independent and submit only to law", to be understood? Is not this provision in flagrant contradiction to what Vyshinsky wrote only two years previous to the adoption of the Constitution?

Indeed, neither the RSFSR Constitution of 1918, nor the Federal Constitution of 1924 contained provisions regarding the judges' independence. Was it a change in the Party's viewpoint on judges?

Certainly not. The judge remained an official of the state, bound to follow the genral policy of the State as indicated by the Communist

---

[1] *Ibid.*, p. 137.

[2] A.Ye. Vyshinsky, Marxist-Leninist Doctrine on Court and the Judicial System, *Ocherki po sudoustroystvu SSSR*, V. 2, M. 1934, p. 43.

Party. As a member of the Party he receives instruction directly from the Party. He is obliged to follow the general line in every individual trial.

But later Vyshinsky, on paper, did not recognize any limitation of judicial independence. He flatly declared that "only the socialist court, the court of the socialist worker—peasant state expressing the will of the entire toiling people of the Soviet Union, is truly independent in the authentic and direct sense of the word. Soviet judges are independent, in as much as the Soviet court, being subordinated only to the law, which sets forth the will of the entire people, is independent of all influences and inducements whatsoever, in deciding specific court matters. In arriving at their sentences and decisions, judges are subordinate only to demands of the law, and rely upon their inner judicial convictions, formed upon consideration of all the circumstances of the case. In this sense, the Soviet court, the court of the people, the court of the toiling masses is a genuinely independent court". [1]

Because "the decision of criminal and civil cases according to law, and socialist consciousness is possible only in conditions insuring the judge from any pressure or influence". [2]

And this was written in 1938 and 1940, respectively!

When I. D. Perlov, writing in 1965, declares that Soviet judges "examine and decide upon civil and criminal cases ... under conditions excluding any outside influence; no organization, institutions, organs or officials have the right to influence judges in their decisions about individual [3] cases" and a 1966 editorial also asserts that "meting out justice judges are independent and submit only to law, decide cases in court on ground of law in conformity with socialist legal consciousness, to conditions excluding foreign influence whatsoever ..." [4] they may hope that after the liquidation of Stalin's era, Article 112 will acquire real significance. However, some trials mentioned in this book which took place after Stalin's death do not meet this expectation.

The principle established in Article 112 of the Constitution has been reaffirmed in the Law on the Court Structure of the USSR and Union and Autonomous Republics of August 16, 1938, in Article 10 of the

---

[1] Vyshinsky, *The Law of the Soviet State, op. cit.*, p. 514.

[2] Vyshinsky, *Sudoustroystvo*, M. 1940, p. 86.

[3] I.D. Perlov, "The Independence of Judges", *Entsiklopedicheskiy slovar' pravovykh znaniy*, M. 1965, p. 252.

[4] Editorial "The Moral Make-up of a Legal Worker", *Sov. yust.*, 1966, No. 15, p. 11.

Basic Principles of Penal Legislation, in Article 9 of the Basic Principles of Criminal and Civil Procedures respectively, and the Basic
Principles of Court Structure of the USSR and the Union Republics of
1958.

Besides the behind-the-scenes-influence and pressure exercised in
individual cases by the Party and the Soviet hierarchy, official directives influence the judicial work.

For instance, according to its Statute of June 15, 1939 [1] the USSR
People's Commissariat (since 1946 Ministry) of Justice had the right
to "issue orders and instructions concerning the organization and
bettering of court work", which is an evident method of soviet influence
on judicial activity.

"The bourgeois jurist would be certainly greatly astonished", writes
Polyansky, "if he would get acquainted with the directives, the court
and prosecutors, receive from the guiding organs. The bourgeois
jurist is of the opinion that his business is to know laws and interpret
them with the help of purely juridical in their form interpretation of
the Cassation Court or the Ministry of Justice directives. However,
among the directives recieved by the Soviet courts was a great number
of those which draw the courts into the very midst of political and
economic life." [2]

Abuses of this right of directives have been commented on in the
Soviet legal press.

So A. Volin, Chairman of the USSR Supreme Court, at that time,
wrote : "Some Ministries of Justice of the Union Republics, their
administrations and Supreme Courts of the Union Republics, sometimes give instructions to courts concerning judicial practice which
exceed their competence. These directions and elucidations contain
instructions establishing criminal responsibility for these or those
actions, not mentioned in the law, qualification of crimes, a.s.o.
Also direct interpretations of the law are given in these directives.
Such instructions being illegal lead in practice to violations of legality
in court. It must be understood that judicial interpretation or leading
instructions concerning judicial practice cannot be the subject of
administrative guidance of courts and are, according to the law, in the
competence of the Plenum of the USSR Supreme Court". [3]

---

[1] *Sob. post.*, *SSSR*, 1939, p. 301.

[2] Polyansky, *Sovetskiy ugolovnyy sud*, *op. cit.*, p. 132.

[3] A. Volin, "To Observe Strict Legality in the Court Work", *Sots. zak.*, 1950, No. 1,
p. 12.

Also Polyansky cites cases when the USSR Ministry of Justice presented its interpretation of law.

For example in the Order No. 29 of March 25, 1940, the USSR Minister of Justice drew the attention of the supreme court of a union-republic to the illegality of the practice permitting to counsels the participation in the sessions of the supreme court examining protests against sentences already in force. [1]

The Soviet legislation did not create guarantees of this alleged independence and the guarantee of independence given to the tsarist judges and in the form of the separation of powers as we have seen above has been repudiated by Soviet authors. Also the irremovability of judges as a guarantee of independence has been rejected by Lenin and Soviet writers. Only the supervision over court activity has been entrusted to a judicial institution—the USSR Supreme Court—although supervision over legality in genral has been charged to the prosecuting body.

b) *Electiveness vs. Irremovability*

The irremovability of judges is a guarantee of the judicial independence according to Western writers.

But according to Lenin, irremovability of the judiciary is not a guarrantee of its independence from the administration. "Irremovability of judges", he wrote, "about which bourgeois liberals in general, and our Russian in particular, fuss so much is merely a partitioning of the remnants of the middle age privileges between ... proponents of serfdom and the bourgeoisie. In reality, irremovability cannot be realized completely and it would be nonsensical to defend it with regard to unfit, negligent and bad judges".

Lenin goes on explaining why the bourgeoisie is defending the principle of irremovability of the judiciary. "Since the appointment of judges was the privilege of feudalism and absolutism in the middle ages, the bourgeoisie which is now freely admitted to judicial positions 'defends' itself against feudalism by the principle of irremovability since appointed judges necessarily belong to the bourgeoisie because the majority of educated judges are by birth bourgeois. Defending itself in this way from feudals, the bourgeoisie, at the same time, defends itself from democracy by insisting on the appointing of judges". [2]

---

[1] Polyansky, "The Soviet Criminal Court", *op. cit.*, Footnote 1 on p. 138.

[2] Lenin, XXX, p. 195.

Lenin denies that irremovability does guarantee judicial independence also because judges belonging to the bourgeoisie are anyhow under the unescapable influence of their class and cannot avoid solidarity of interests with their class.

Finally, irremovability according to him prevents the replacement of bourgeois judges with representatives of the working population and peasants. [1]

Thus, in Lenin's opinion the election of judges by the people is preferable to the appointment of them for life.

Consequently, the principle of electiveness of judges was established already by the Decree No. 1 on Courts.

Vyshinsky thought that irremovability of judges is "nowhere developed completely. In any capitalist state the administration finds grounds to remove any judge whose activity does not conform with the views of the directing capitalist group ... How remote the appointment of judges by administrative authority is from meeting the needs of true democracy needs no demonstration". [2]

But also as to the electoral system for judges in capitalist countries "the vices of the capitalist system in the election of judges in the USA are so conspicuous that even observers who are whole-heartedly on the side of bourgeois ideology cannot remain silent". And Vyshinsky quotes James Bryce in support of his opinion who wrote that "in the United States the party organizations which nominate candidates for the bench can use their influence to reward partisans or to place in power persons whom they intend to use for their own purposes". [3]

c) *Judicial Independence Guaranties in Soviet Legislation*

Let us look into the guaranties of judicial independence given by Soviet legislation.

The first guaranty is the elegibility by popular elections provided by the Constitution (Art. 109), although, for people's court justices only. Justices of all other courts, as we have seen above, were and are elected (appointed) by administrative and legislative bodies.

Although the election of people's court judges had to take place by vote of the citizens of the district on the basis of general direct and equal suffrage, according to the Decree No. 1 on Courts elections did

---

[1] Lenin, *ibid.*

[2] Vyshinsky, *The Law of the Soviet State, op. cit.*, p. 513.

[3] James Bryce, *Modern Democracies*, 1921, V. II, p. 386.

not start until 1948. Thus, de facto, also the judges of the people's court were appointed by the local authorities during 31 years.

What was the reason of this prolonged delay?

Kozhevnikov explains the reluctance of the authorities to conduct elections on the basis of general, direct, equal suffrage by secret ballot during 1918-1935 by the circumstances of the class struggle and the necessity of eliminating from the participation in the elections of hostile elements. That is why the principle of "election of toilers among toilers" was established. [1]

But after the elective principle was repeated to no avail in the Constitution of 1936 and the Law on Court Structure of 1938, another 12 and 10 years, respectively, passed and the provision of popular election of judges remained, nevertheless, on paper only, although "hostile elements" were thoroughly eliminated. Did not Stalin himself declare in 1939 that "the peculiarity of the Soviet society of the present time is that in contradistinction to any capitalist society the Soviet society has no more antagonistic hostile classes; the exploiting classes are liquidated and the workers, peasants and intelligentsia which compose the Soviet society live and work on bases of friendly cooperation". [2]

Thus, the hostile elements" no longer existed within the Soviet Union in 1939.

It is also not clear why it was deemed possible to conduct elections to the Supreme Soviets but not to courts, and why only the people's courts judiciary was declared elective but that not of the other courts.

Evidently Maurach is not right. [3] True it is that in 1936 the judges were still considered not adequately politically trained and indoctrinated in order to be chosen directly by the people even with the aid of a Soviet-brand electoral system.

The second guaranty of the judicial independence is that the judges can lose their positions only on recall by their electorate or by virtue of court decision or sentence already in force.

Already the Decree No. 2 on Courts provided that the judges could be recalled by the Soviets which appointed them.

---

[1] N.V. Kozhevnikov, *op. cit.*, p. 295.
[2] Stalin, *Voprosy leninizma*, M. 1952, p. 629.
[3] See Supra p. 318-319.

D. Criminal and Disciplinary Responsibility

The third guarantee for judges independence is the special opening of the criminal and disciplinary procedures for judges.

The opening of a criminal procedure against judges and their suspension can have place only on decision of a union republic prosecutor confirmed later by the presidium of a union-republic supreme soviet.

With regard to a member of the USSR Supreme Court and justices of special courts, the opening of a criminal procedure may take place only on sanction of the Presidium of the USSR Supreme Court.

The disciplinary responsibility of judges was regulated by two Ukases of the USSR Supreme Soviet Presidium of July 29, 1940 [1] and July 15, 1948. [2]

There is a substantial difference between these two enactments.

The Law of 1940 conferred the right to set disciplinary punishments : reproof, reprimand and reprimand with warning to individual judicial and administrative officials. Thus, the USSR People's Commissar of Justice could set all three punishments with regard to all judges in the USSR.

To the people's commissars of justice of the union-republics belonged the right to impose all the punitative measures mentioned above, on all judges of the union and autonomous republics.

The people's commissars of justice of the autonomous republics had the right to impose only the first two punishments to judges of the autonomous republics.

Finally, the chairmen of circuit regional, territorial and special courts, as well as of the Supreme Courts of the USSR and the union and autonomous republics were empowered to set the punishments of reproof and reprimand on judges of the respective courts.

A complaint against the decision to a higher instance was permissible.

The law of 1948, however, established a special disciplinary college, attached to regional and territorial courts, military tribunals of military circuits and fleets as well as to the Supreme Courts of the USSR and union and autonomous republics, consisting of a chairman of the individual court and two court members appointed by the chairman.

---

[1]   *V.V.S.*, *SSSR*, 1940, No. 28.

[2]   *V.V.S.*, *SSSR*, 1948, No. 31.

The college decided cases of violations of labor discipline, dere-
lictions in judicial work committed by negligence, or in discipline
of the judge.

Punishments were : reproof, reprimand and severe reprimand. If
the disciplinary college was of the opinion that the accused judge
did not conform to his position, it informed the ministry of justice
and its union republic for the initiating of recall proceedings. If the
disciplinary college found in the actions of the inculpated judge indications of a criminal offence, it raised the question of criminal prosecution and informed the person who instigated disciplinary proceedings and the ministries of justice of the union-republic and the USSR.

The decisions of the disciplinary college were final and could be
reviewed only in the way of supervision by the disciplinary college
of the higher court, on the initiative of the chairman of this court,
of the Minister of Justice of the USSR and union or autonomous
republics.

E. Electoral Laws

The popular elections of judges promised already by the Decree
No. 1 on Courts, of 1917, and later in all laws on the judicial structure
and the 1936 Constitution was introduced by the Ukase of the RSFSR
Supreme Court Presidium on 28 September 1948. [1]

On paper it was a liberal law. It provided that lists of electors
have to be established by executive committees of soviets in cities,
and include all citizens of both sexes 18 years of age and in possession
of electoral rights, living in the territory under the administration
of the individual soviets, independently of their race, nationality,
religion, education, permanent residence, social origin, property,
qualification and past activity.

Not registered had to remain persons, deprived of electoral rights
by court sentence during the time set for the deprivation in the sentence, as well as persons recognized as insane by due process of law.
The passive electoral age was 23 years. No educational or professional
requirement for the candidate was set in the law of 1948. The judges
were elected for three years of service.

The right to nominate candidates for the election of judges and
assessors was granted to public and labor organizations, communist

---

[1] *V.V.S.*, *SSSR*, 1948, No. 39.

party organizations, youth organizations and cultural associations, as well as to the general assemblies of workers and employees at enterpizes and institutions, military persons at military centers, general assemblies of peasants at kolkhozes and villages and workers and employees of sovkhozes (Article 26).

With regard to the first judicial election of 1948, wrote V. A. Ivanov, "the elections were a real triumph of socialist democracy". [1]

Certainly, 99.87% of all electors cast votes in the RSFSR judicial elections of 1948; for judicial candidates—99.62% of the electoral and for assessors—99.87%. The elected belonged to 45 nationalities and 40% of them were women. All that according to Soviet statistics. [2]

Certainly, a "triumph", but of Soviet-brand of democracy.

Two features of these elections as in the case of all other elections in the Soviet Union, deprive them of "democracy" as understood in all non-socialist counrties : the appearance of only one candidate on the ballot and the absence of secrecy.

Let us look first at the process of candidate nomination.

The Communist Party and its organization occupy the first place on the list of institutions admitted to nominate candidates for the election. In reality it is the party and its organization which directly nominate the great majority of candidates.

However, also other organizations and establishments listed in Article 26 of the electoral law as having the right of nomination are under the control and influence of the Party. No candidate is nominated by these organizations without the approval of the Party operating through the medium of its cells at the organization and establishments.

According to law, *all* (italics provided) the nominated candidates must be registered.

Now, it seems, that the electors should have the right to choose between the candidates, the persons they prefer, in the process of voting. This follows literally from Article 32 of the Law which prescribes the "obligatory inclusion of all registered candidates into the ballot" and Article 43 provides that the voter "leaves the names of those

---

[1] V.A. Ivanov, "The Organization of the Courts and the Prosecuting Body" in *40-let sovetskogo prava*, M. 1957, II, p. 580.

[2] *Ibid.*

candidates to people's judges and people's assessors on the ballot for whom he votes, crossing out the names of all others".

But in reality, in flagrant violation of the Law, only one name of a candidate appears on the ballot. As Hazard puts it : "To this day, there had appeared on the ballot only one name for each place". [1]

The voter has the choice to vote for the candidate imposed on him or reject him by crossing his name out. This last action has not much sense since it must be repeated by more than 50% of the voters in order to eliminate the candidate and occurs very seldom, under the conditions of Soviet life. The insertion, however, of another name than that printed on the ballot is not admitted and invalidates the ballot.

An explantion for this illegal procedure is given by Soviet writers. So, in their textbooks on Constitutional Law, Lepeshkin, Kim, Mishin and Romanov write that "our society is welded by moral and political unity and has no competitive political forces" so that a choice between several candidates is not necessary. In reality, the *representatives* (italics provided) of the organizations, which have nominated candidates agree between them on a single candidate whose name appears then on the ballot. [2] Thus, the final selection of the candidate to be a judge or an assessor is made not by electors but by representatives of the nominating organizations, on the initiative or with the approval of the Party.

The nomination of candidates and the voting procedure take place according to some pattern established by the electoral law to the Supreme Soviets by all elections in the Soviet Union. The voting procedure as described by Maurach is the following : [3]

All the voters are registered by the Electoral Commission on numerated lists. When the voter appears for voting, his name is checked against the lists and he receives a ballot and an envelope into which he has to insert the ballot, marked by him, and drop the envelope into the ballot box.

Now, Maurach asserts that the envelope handed out to the voter is marked with the same number under which the voter is registered

---

[1] John N. Hazard, *The Soviet System of Government*, Chicago, 1960, p. 51.

[2] A.I. Lepeshkin, A.I. Kim, N.G. Mishin, P.I. Romanov, *Kurs sovetskogo gosudarstvennogo prava*, M. 1961, II, p. 357.

[3] Maurach, *op. cit.*, Notes to Art. 140 of the Constitution, pp. 412-414.

on the lists. In this way, the Electoral Commission can establish as to how the individual elector did vote. [1]

It is evident that such a procedure makes illusive the alleged secrecy of the voting process.

In this way was realized the promise of popular judicial elections.

In reality, the judicial elections were and are tantamount to appointment in the USSR. But Stalin wrote : "for us, workers' representatives, it is necessary that the people should not be only voting, but also ruling". [2] And Kalenov asserts that "the decision of the question as to whether a citizen deserves to be a people's judge or assessor and administer justice in the name of the RSFSR belongs not to an official, but to the people ...". [3]

F. EDUCATIONAL REQUIREMENTS

A peculiar feature of the Constitution and of the Basic Principles of 1938 is the complete absence of educational or practical requirements for the appointment of judges.

Indeed, whereas the Constitution is silent on this subject the Basic Principles of 1938 provide a provision "that all Soviet citizens in possession of electoral rights can be judges and assessors".

Until 1936, excluded from voting were persons who employed hired labor and former members of the tsarists police and the imperial family.

Not only did the electoral law contain no educational requirements, but a special ukase of the Presidium of the USSR Supreme Soviet of September 1948 [4] provided that all citizens of the USSR who enjoy voting rights, can be elected judges and assessors if they have reached the age of 23 and do not have criminal records. But also, according to the RSFSP Law of 1960, every citizen if he is 25 years of age and in possession of electoral rights can be elected to the position of a judge, i.e., whether he has a legal education or not.

Remarking that the law does not require a legal education or socialist public-political activity from the candidates, Kopylovskaya

---

[1] Maurach, *op. cit.* Footnote C to Art. 140 of the Constitution, p. 414.

[2] I.V. Stalin, *Sochineniya*, IV, p. 37.

[3] Yu. A. Kalenov, *Nauchno-prakticheskiy kommenteriy k zakonu o sudoustroystve RSFSR*, M. 1962, p. 21.

[4] *V.V.S., SSSR*, 1948, No. 38.

in her comment to Article 29 of the Law, asserts that "as shown in practice, elected judges and assessors as a rule are persons with legal education and a definite practice in public-political work. " She also asserts that 95.8% of the judges elected in the RSFSR in 1960 had legal education and that in higher courts the percentage is even higher. [1]

That this information is not correct with regard to assessors follows from what is said on the educational level of assessors in this book.

But Kopylovskaya's assertion on the extent of legal education of judges seems also more than improbable, according to the general stand of legal education in the Soviet Union.

V. Kulikov, Deputy Chairman of the USSR Supreme Court writing in December 1967 relates that 7,592 elected people's judges were checked of whom 84.1% had a higher legal education, as compared with about 10% with higher education in 1923.

Of them, 75.9% are working in the capacity of judges for five years and more.

Among the judges, 31.2% are women.

All the Soviet judges are themselves former workers, kolhozniks, employees or belong to working families.

He emphasises the improvement of the quality of judicial work. So, according to him, 5,656, or 75.5% of all sentences in criminal cases remained unchanged, in 1966. [2]

A new Statute on the Election of People's Judges and Assessors was enacted in the RSFSR on October 29, 1951, [3] and amended on October 4, 1954. No substantial changes as compared with the Statute of 1948 were introduced.

The USSR Law of 1958 on Court Structure [4] made no change in the system of selection or election of justices for courts. Only the age requirement of the candidates was increased from 23 to 25. [5]

---

[1] M.A. Kopylovskaya, Comments to Art. 29 in *Nauchno-prakticheskiy kommentariy k osnovam zakonodatel'stva o sudoustroystve soyuza SSSR, soyuznukh i avtonomnykh respublik*, M. 1961, p. 67.

[2] *Izvestia*, December 7, 1967.

[3] *V.V.S., SSSR*, 1951, No. 44.

[4] *Ibid.*, 1954, No. 1.

[5] Since the Basic Principles of Court Structure of 1938 did not set an age requirement for the candidates to judgeship, a special law of September 1948 filled the gap providing that this age should not be under 23 (*V.V.S., SSSR*. 1948, No. 38).

But a special law on "The Change of the Electoral Order of People's Courts" of the date provided that : [1]

The people's judges of the district (city) Courts are elected by the citizens of the district (city) on ground of general, equal and direct voting right by secret ballot for the term of five years.

Article 109 of the Constitution was correspondingly amended.

All other courts judges were selected in the previous order : the justices of the regional, territorial, city courts and those of the autonomous regions and districts are selected by corresponding soviets for five years of service.

The Supreme Courts Justices of the autonomous republics, union republics and the USSR are chosen by the corresponding supreme soviets for five years of service.

The Statute on Military Tribunals of December 25, 1958 [2] provided that the chairman, their deputies and the members of the Military Tribunals are elected by the Presidium of the USSR Supreme Soviet for five years of service.

The provision of Article 103 of the Constitution that all cases are tried in court with the participation of assessors, except in cases especially provided for by law, has been applied by the Law of 1958 with regard to trials in all courts of original jurisdiction.

The recall of judges before the expiration of term can be carried out only by those who elected them.

The courts have to give account about their activity to their electors.

The electoral order of judges has been changed in 1965. Whereas according to the old order the electors of a rayon or borough voted for candidates to people's judges of the entire rayon or bourough (10-15 positions in a large rayon or borough) electoral districts are established for every single judge's position, within the rayon, or the borough, so that electors vote for a candidate to the individual position of a judge in the people's court.

Reporting about the change in the electoral order of judges to the people's court, V. Shubin [3] writes : "now into the electorial bulletin

---

1   *V.V.S.*, *SSSR*, 1959, No. 1.

2   *V.V.S.*, *SSSR*, 1959 No. 1.

3   "In the Name of the Republic", *Izvestia*, December 11, 1965.

will be included names of *candidates* (italics provided) of only one electoral district". [1]

The use of the plural for "candidates" should not induce the reader to think that a change has been produced also in the Soviet electoral system according to which to every elective position, may it be the Supreme Soviet, courts or other agencies, the name of only one candidate appears on the electoral bulletin, although according to law, names of all candidates must be included into the bulletin. No changes in this regard have been made.

Commenting on the new electoral order for judges of the people's court, M. Yesenbayev and N. Klochkov write : "In conditions of unity of the Soviet society, there is no necessity to nominate several candidates in a given electoral district ... Therefore, as a rule, the name of only one candidate will be included into the electoral bulletin". [2]

Strogovich is of the opinion that there is no ground to have a different system for the election of people's judges and the justices of other courts. All the judges should be chosen, in general, direct, equal and in secret election. "This modus is more democaratic than the contemporary one". [3] The same order should be also observed with regard to people's assessors. [4]

Certainly, Strogovich is right : election even of the Soviet brand is still better than old system of appointment by an administrative agency.

G. Law on Court Structures of the USSR of 1958 Corresponding RSFSR Laws of 1960

The Law on the Court Structure in the RSFSR of October 27, 1960 adopted in accordance with the USSR Law on Basic Principles of Court Structure of 1958 [5] and the statute on the election of the Dis-

---

[1] Shubin, *op. cit.*

[2] *Kazakhstanskaya Pravda*, December 7, 1965.

[3] M.S. Strogovich, "Socialist Democracy of the Soviet Administration of Justice" in *Demokraticheskiye osnovy sovetskogo demokraticheskogo pravosudiya*, M. 1965, p. 9.

[4] According to the order in force, assessors are elected only to people's courts, whereas they are appointed to other courts, as judges, by regional soviets without an electoral campaign and not secretly.

[5] *V.V.S., SSSR*, 1958, No. 1.

trict People's Judges of October 28, 1960 [1] established some innova-
tions with regard to judges.

First of all the elcetion of judges was separated from that of the
assessors.

The time of service increased from three to five years for judges.

According to the law of 1948, persons deprived of electoral rights
by a court sentence could not take part in the election for the duration
of the deprivation. Since the suspension of the use of electoral rights
as a punishment has been abrogated, only persons declared insane
by a court sentence are excluded from voting.

The extension of the judicial tenure permits the acquisition of more
experience on the job, and the control of that of the assessors insures
the attraction of a larger number of persons to the administration of
justice which was the goal set by Lenin.

The order of nomination of candidates remained the same.

The laws of 1960 also retained the former appointing order of all
other judges.

H. Some Criticisms

N. Chetunova accuses individual judges of indifference toward
human fate, hard-heartedness, idleness of thought, disrespect of law,
low level of legal and general spiritual culture, i.e., of all that which
is the general cause of all the defects in the work of the administration
of justice, and, consequently of the numbers of reversed sentences
by the USSR Supreme Court because of groundlessness of the accusation and the failure to prove it, and gullible attitude toward slander and
perjury. [2]

Kisilev reproaches the judges that they lead the trial sometimes
so that the attendance involuntary has the impression of two forces
opposed to each other and engaged in an interesting fight : the chairman and the prosecutor, on one side and the counsel and the accused,
on the other.

Formally maintaining the egality of the parties, the judge, even
not so seldom, takes a different attitude not toward the parties, but
with regard to the evidence : evidences against the accused are inter-

---

preted as persuasive, and those for him are evaluated with a readiness, sometimes not realized, as deficient when this is not the case.

Kisilev is of the opinion that especially strict requirements should be presented to the judge and to the leading of the trial by him : a polished procedural ability; deepness of legal knowledge; the capacity of statesmanship; thinking; genuine intellectuality ... [1]

Rakhunov calls to end the system of evaluation of the judges' work according to the number of sentences thrown out or remanded, or visiting sessions carried out and the comparison of average data about the measures of punishment applied by the judge. This system does not provide a correct evaluation of the judges' activity.

He also points out the falacity of assessors selection by some judges who pick up for the particpation in a case those assessors who are known to him from the examination of other cases, or because they can be convoked without detriment to production and not strictly in turn, as prescribed by law. Such a method of assessor selection is practiced by judges not seldom, according to Rakhunov. He protests against the fact that there is no law or instruction which provides by whom and how the lists of assessors' turn is established and by whom confirmed.

Thus, the existing practice of assessors' appointing for an individual case gives to the judge the possibility of the choice of assessors who as he knows it beforehand would be inclined to share his opinion. [2]

Perlov complains that there are judges who grant even unsubstantiated requests to the prosecution and decline well-founded motions of the defense. "It is clear that the public in the court hall draws the conclusion about the judge's lack of objectivity". [3]

---

1 Ya. Kisilev, "When the Trial is Going On", *ibid.*, June 14, 1967.
2 Rakhunov, "Man and Law", *ibid.*, April 12, 1967.
3 N. Perlov, "The Alphabet of the Law", *Izvestia*, January 12, 1967.

CHAPTER THIRTEEN

PEOPLE'S ASSESSORS

The Decree No. 1 on Courts of December 24, 1917 which liquidated the entire tsarist system of administration of justice and all its organs also abrogated the jury and replaced it as a form of people's participation in the meting-out of justice by people's assessors.

The main difference between the jurors and the assessors is that the jurors decide only on the guilt or innocence of the accused whereas assessors are members of the bench participating together with the professional judge in the decisions of all questions under the competence of the court arising before and during the court session including the setting of the punishment.

A. The Abrogated Jury

Tsar Alexander II of Russia is called the "Liberator" not only because he abolished serfdom, but also because he freed the Russian people from the fetters of the old courts and the inquisitorial criminal procedure. [1] The judicial Refrom of 1864—a masterpiece of legislation in its field—introduced into the administration of justice a court structure and criminal procedure based on democratic principles. [2] It also established the court with jury.

The discussion of the necessity and timeliness of the introduction of the jury into adminstration of justice in Russia is of great interest because it yields the elements for the comparison of the two institutions the jury and the people's assessors.

Count D. N. Bludov, one of the outstanding Russian jurists of his time, and Chief of the Second Division of His Majesty's Own Chancery, wrote : "The expediency of creating juries at the present time is very doubtful. ... The majority of the people is not only deprived of juri-

---

[1] On Courts and criminal procedure before the 1864 Reform, see Samuel Kucherov, "Administration of Justice under Nicholas I of Russia", *The American Slavic and East European Review*, 1952, No. 2.

[2] On the Judicial Reform of 1864, see Samuel Kucherov, *Courts, Lawyers and Trials Under the Last Three Tsars*, N.Y. 1953.

dical knowledge but lacks the most elementary education : when the notions of right, duty and law are so underdeveloped and unclear that the violation of the rights of others ... especially of property rights ... is considered by many as a most normal act; other crimes are envisaged as an expression of boldness and criminals are regarded as nothing but unlucky persons ... Without contesting the advantages of the court with jury, especially in criminal cases, we are, however, of the opinion that decisions in cases involving crimes and misdemeanors have to rest, for the time being, with the judges". [1]

It is interesting to note that objections against introducing the jury to Russia were raised outside Russia with a very peculiar argumentation. Herbert Spenser, namely, wrote in 1850 : "That justice can be well administered only in proportion as man becomes just, is a fact too generally overlooked. 'If they had but trial by jury' says someone, moralizing on Russians. But they can't have it. It would not exist among them. Even if established, it would not work. They lack that substratum of honesty and truthfulness—on which alone it can stand. To be of use this like any other institution must be born of the popular character. It is not trial by jury that produces justice, but it is sentiment of justice that produces trials by jury, the organ through which it is to act, and this organ will be inert unless the sentiment is there". [2]

When the introduction of the jury was decided by the State Council, the legislative body of that time, Bludov's objections were refuted and some wise and thought-out reasons for the establishment of the institution of the jury were expressed which derseve an extended quotation : [3]

The State Council was perfectly aware of the fact that the main objection against the introduction of the jury in Russia was that the people were not sufficiently educated for entering into the consideration of questions demanding logical thinking and adequate education. However, it considered this objections as unconvincing. Of course, educated people have a beneficial influence upon the quality of institutions in which they participate, but on the other hand, people are developed and perfected by good institutions, the State

---

[1] Quoted by G. Dzhanshiyev, *Epokha vilikikh reform*, M. 1900, pp. 81-82.

[2] Herbert Spenser, *Social Statics; or the Conditions Essential to Human Happiness Specified, and the First of them Developed*, N.Y. 1875, p. 289.

[3] *Sudebnyye ustavy 20 noyabrya 1864 goda s izlozheniyem razsuzhdeniy na koikh oni osnovany*, St. Petersburg, 1867, III, pp. 95-99 passim.

Council argued, and in this respect a well-organized court is more important than any other institution, because it teaches the people the notion of justice and lawfulness without which no order or prosperity is possible; the insufficient education of the people is not only a poor argument for the inopportuneness of establishing jury courts, but, on the contrary, leads to the opposite conclusion : such people must be particularly defended in court; they need judges from their own milieu who would fully understand their frame of mind and mode of action; the degree of punishment should be determined exclusively by judges enjoying legal training, but no special juridical knowledge is needed for a conscientious answer to the question as to whether the accused is guilty or innocent of a crime : a person with sound comprehension, even if poorly educated, may give a correct answer to this question.

Moreover, the State Council considered the introduction of the court with jury in Russia even more necessary than in other countries, since the historical life of the people had nowhere created such a sharp difference between various strata of the population as in Russia. The morals, the conceptions of life of professional judges, belonging generally to higher classes of society differ considerably from those of an accused from a lower class; the law requires from a person who has to decide upon the question of guilt or innocence an answer based only on complete internal conviction, unconstrained by any formal evidence, and it is clear that the jury, elected usually from the same class of the population to which the accused belongs may better evaluate the fact than a judge who is alien to the milieu in which the crime has been committed; special knowledge of local morals, customs and mode of life sometimes throw light on circumstances which may seem to a scholar unclear and without connection with the crime.

a) *The Russian Jury in Action*

The rights and duties of the Russian jury were similar to those in all countries : the main duty was to pronounce a verdict of guilty or innocent. In order to facilitate this action, written questions were submitted to the jury by the bench, consisting of three permanent judges, one of them chairman of the court. The questions referred to the guilt of and imputability to the accused of the elements of the criminal act (in England and the United States the jury does not answer those specific questions, but expresses its opinion on the whole content of the indictment).

The decision of the jury concerning every question put to it required, in Russia, only an absolute plurality and the verdict was in favor of the accused in case of an equal division of votes (in the United States and England unanimity is required, in the old German jury court a 2/3 majority was necessary).

According to the verdict of the jury, the bench decided upon the measures of punishment, or acquittal.

There was no appeal against the verdict of the jurors, but the prosecutor and the accused had a right to apply for cassation to the Criminal Department of the Ruling Senate (no appeal or cassation of an acquitting verdict in England and United States).

The competence of the jury was limited "to cases of crimes or misdemeanors for which the law prescribed punishment involving deprivation of, or restriction in, civil rights". [1]

Political crimes were excepted from the jurisdiction of the jury in Russia, despite the favorable recommendation of the State Chancery. This high administrative agency advanced two remarkable considerations for the entrusting also of political cases to the jury. It argued that the discussion of the factual part of criminal cases by representatives of the people and not by regular judges is a real guarrantee of equity for the accused. Therefore, it is impossible to deprive the accused of this guarantee in cases of crimes against the state ... the gravest accusation ... without committing an injustice, especially because the state which prosecutes the case is, at the same time, the entity offended or harmed by the accused, and the sentence pronounced by regular judges, no matter how impartial or independent they may be, will never enjoy the confidence of society.

The second argument was that in order to deprive the accused of the sympathy of society it is necessary to let him be condemned by society itself in the person of its representatives, the jurors; convictions pronounced by the jury in cases of offenses against the state would have such a moral power that the influence of law on society would increase, even if convictions by jury prove to be less frequent than convictions by regular judges. [2]

In the beginning the activity of the jury was highly commended by the government itself. In his report to the Tsar on the activity of

---

[1] I. Ya. Foynitsky, *Kurs ugolovnogo sudoproizvodstva*, St. Petersburg, 1896, Vol. I, p. 43.

[2] *Zhurnal grazhdanskogo i ugolovnogo prava*, 1890, No. 8, pp. 235-236.

the new courts, in 1866, the Minister of Justice, D. N. Zamyatin, gave the following characterization of the work of the jury. "The Jurors, who often belonged mainly to the peasantry, fully met the expectations reposed in them. They had to solve difficult problems which would embarrass even experienced people accustomed to a correct handling of criminal cases. All these problems were solved by the jury, in most cases, correctly and adequately, thanks to the amazing attention with which the jurors considered the case submitted to them". [1]

Fourteen years later, the Ruling Senate expressed its opinion on the educational value of the Russian jury in these words : "The masses of the people who in the past had a very obscure notion of the significance of law courts and their functioning very often were unable even to distinguish the punishable from the permissible, as a consequence of their ignorance, the jurors who were called from the masses very soon became familiar with the moral concepts and ideas which are inherent in every developed society by listening to the speeches of the prosecution and the defense, and they learned to discern white from balck in the usual conditions of their every-day lives. They became conscious of the ideal interest pursued by the criminal court. They learned to respect the personality of their fellowmen, and, thanks to the acquired knowledge and experience, they brought light into the darkness of their environment which till then was not acquainted with any other element of right except force and wealth". [2]

Then, the work of the jury was examined in 1894 by a special commission appointed by the Ministry of Justice. The commission consisted of all Chief Chairmen of the Sudebnaya Palata (Court of Appeals). The commission decided that there was no ground for the widespread opinion accusing the jury of handling down an exaggerated number of acquittals. It found that the court with jury corresponded perfectly to its aims and that it had an ennobling influence on the people's sense of equity. [3] The majority of the Commission came to the conclusion that "not only does the work of this kind of court correspond to its aim, but it is the most perfect court which may be imagined for the trial of the major share of important cases. [4]

---

[1]   *Zhurnal ministerstva justitsii*, 1867, No. 2, p. 144.

[2]   Quoted by N.P. Timofeyev, *Sud prisyazhnykh v Rossii*, Moscow, 1881, pp. 11-12.

[3]   A.F. Koni, "Court With Jury" in *Entsiklopedicheskiy slovar' Brokgauza i Efrona*, St. Petersburg, 1901, Vol. 63, p. 6.

[4]   A.F. Koni, "Court Statutes of 1864-1914" in *Zhurnal ministerstva justitsii*, 1914, No. 9, p. 136.

b) *Jury Criticized and Praised*

The formation of the commission was caused by the continued attacks against the jury conducted by the reactionaries and their press. For instance, the famous reactionary Katkov, in a vicious article, called the jury a "court of the street" [1]. This prompted Lenin to come to the defense of the court with jury. He wrote :

"The reactionary press called the jury court a 'street court' and started persecuting it .... The government told the representatives of society that it considers them to be (people from the) street, from the populace, who have no right to take part in ... legislation and in government, who must be expelled from the sanctuary, where trial and justice are meted out to Russian citizens ...

The court of the street is valuable precisely because it breathes life into the bureaucratic formality which saturates our government in institutions through and through ... Aided by its flair, under the pressure of practical experience in social life and of the growth of political consciences, the street "is able" to grasp the truth toward which our official, academic judiciary, shackled by pedantry, is so laboriously and timidly groping ... That is why the reactionary publicists and the reactionary government hate ... and cannot help hating—the court of the street". [2]

But praising the court with jury, Lenin at the same time, reproached the Russian jury system of being not democratic enough, because of property or income qualifications required from jurors, so that, in this way, manual workers were almost excluded from the jury, which often produces the predominance of a very reactionary bourgeoisie in the jury. "This evil" thought Lenin", must be cured by development of democracy ... and not at all by a mean abdication of democracy", [3] it means abrogation of the jury.

However, when the time came for Lenin to rule over Russia he chose another form of people's representation in court, not the jury. The reason for this decision will be discussed later.

Also Marx denounced the property qualification. He asserted that "a man who is required to be a juror only because of his property

---

[1] *Moskovskiye vedomosti*, 1883, No. 39.
[2] Lenin, IV, pp. 83-84, passim.
[3] *Ibid.*, XXX, p. 194.

qualifications ... has a conscience qualified by property ... The point is that the consicence of the privileged is a privileged consicence". [1]

On the other hand, supporters of the jury system could be found even in the most reactionary camp. On the occasion of the 50th jubilee of the 1864 Statutes, I. G. Shcheglovitov, Minister of Justice at that time and one of the most outstanding figures among tsarist reactionaries wrote : "Yes, now, after fifty years of its existence, one may say that the jury in Russia has justified itself in spite of some darksides [2] ... The dark sides notwithstanding, the jury has won the general esteem and confidence of the wide masses of the people. That is why we must defend this institution from changes which could injure its substance". [3]

The fifty-three years of the jury's activity in Russia brilliantly proved all the futility of the objections presented against the introduction of this institution in Russia and of the criticism formulated against its functioning after it was introduced. The bold experiment of turning over jurisdiction concerning the most important and complicated criminal cases to a people emancipated from serfdom "almost yesterday" proved a success. This was a fact which the tsarist government had to acknowledge through the mouth of its Minister of Justice.

That this "court of the street" had a consience free from political, religious and social prejudice was proved frequently. The cases of Vera Zasulich [4] and Mendel Beilis [5] may serve as striking examples of how this court was able to resist the greatest pressure exercised by a government of an autocratic state.

---

[1] K. Marx and F. Engels, *op. cit.*, VIII, p. 558.

[2] The "darksides" were certainly in the opinion of the Minister, the acquittals of Vera Zasulich and M. Beilis.

[3] I.G. Shcheglovitov, "New attempts to change the Court of Jury in Western Europe" in *Sudebnyye ustavy 20-go noyabrya 1964, za 50 let.*,Petrograd, 1914, II, pp. 163-164.

[4] Vera Zasulich fired a shot at Gen. Trepov in 1878, avenging an offense committed by the Gen. the flogging of a revolutionary. She was acquitted. See Samuel Kucherov, "The Case of Vera Zasulich", *The Russian Review*, 1950, No. 2, pp. 86-96.

[5] Beilis, a Jew was acquitted of an accusation of ritual murder by a jury consisting of 5 simple peasants and 7 small officials in spite of a tremendous pressure for a verdict of guilty exercised by Shcheglovitov. See S. Kucherov, *Courts, Lawyers and Trials...*, *op. cit.*, pp. 243-269.

B. Schoeffen — Assessors

a) *Assessors Replace Jurors*

It must be said that in general a tendency toward the replacement of jurors by assessors developed in Europe at the end of the 19th century. Especially strong was the propaganda against the jury and for the "Schoeffen", as the assessors are called in Germany.

The Schoeffen, an institution of the old Germanic legal system, was reintroduced into the Reich's Code of Criminal Procedure of 1877 and limited to petty criminal cases.

The fight against the jury lasted in Germany until the first quarter of the 20th century. The main attack against the jury was led by Schwarze, and supported by such authorities as Jhering and Binding. The rise of Prussian nationalism after the victory of 1870-71 and the Kulturkampf contributed to the idealization of such old Germanic institutions as the Schoeffen to the detriment of the court with jury as taken over from revolutionary France.

However, the jury found also defenders among eminent German jurists. Mittermeier thought that the jury possesses the elements for the improvement of criminal procedure in Germany, [1] and Kohler refuted the main accusations against the jury and denounced the "desire to replace the court with jury by a special kind of court with Schoeffen, ..." [2]

The jurors had to cede their place to Schoeffen in 1924 during the Weimar Republic which were eliminated in their turn in 1935 by Hitler as the last remainder of public participation in the administration of justice.

In the West German Republic both institutions, the Schoeffen and the Jury, were reintroduced by "Gesetz zur Wiederherstellung der Reichseinheit auf dem Gebiet der Gerichtsverfassung der buergerlichen Rechtpflege, des Strafverfahrens und des Kostenrechts" of September 12, 1950. [3]

The courts with Schoeffen for petty cases consist, at the present time, of one permanent judge as chairman and two Schoeffen. [4] The courts with jury for the examination of serious criminal offenses is

---

[1] C. Mittermeier, *Erfahrungen über die Wirksamkeit der Schwurgerichte in Europa and Amerika*, Erlangen, 1864, p. 490.

[2] J. Kohler, *Moderne Rechtsprobleme*, Leipzig, 1913, pp. 70-74.

[3] *Bundesgesetzblatt*, 1950, No. 40.

[4] *Ibid.*, Art. 29.

composed of three professional judges of which one is the chairman and six jurors. [1] But the great innovation is that the jurors decide the questions of guilt and punishment together with the permanent judges [2] having, hence, the same functions as the Schoeffen.

In Italy, the Positive (Anthropologic) School of Lombroso and Ferri denounced the jurors because it wanted specialists to judge the criminals, and the jurors obviously lacked the ability to decide to what category of criminals, according to the anthropological theory, they belonged. [3] Thus, Lombroso recommended the replacement of all jurors and professional judges by commissions of experts.

The French sociologist and jurist Gabriel de Tarde accused the jury of ignorance, naivety, fickleness, inconsistency and partiality. He wanted the jury to be substituted by professional judges. [4]

The laws concerning the jury were amended in France in 1932 : the jury had to participate with the bench in setting the punishment. The Vichy government of General Petain reduced the number of jurors from 12 to 6 on November 2, 1941. They had to decide on the question of guilt and innocence together with the bench. Without changing the name the jurors were virtually transformed into assessors.

The use of the jury in civil cases was not accepted in Europe; with the exception of Great Britain, where, as well as in the United States, it functions in civil cases upto the present time.

b) *Soviet Peoples Assessors*

No reasons for the change from jury to assessors was given in Russia. The jury went simply down in the wholesale abolition of the entire court system. The Decree No. 1 on Courts provided that the benches of the newly formed local courts are manned in criminal and civil cases by professional permanent judges and two people's assessors next in turn on a roster. Assessors were called to every session of the court according to special lists established by judges and approved by the local soviets of workers', soldiers' and peasants' deputies. This type of election for judges and assessors was declared temporary and judges and assessors were henceforth to be elected by direct demo-cratic voting.

Six assessors took part in the sessions of the revolutionary tribunals

---

[1]   Art. 81.

[2]   Art. 82.

[3]   Enrico Ferri, *Sociologia Criminale*, Turin, 1892, p. 672.

[4]   Gabriel de Tarde, *La philosophie pénale*, Lyon, 1820, p. 434 and footnote 1.

also created by the Decree No. 1 on Courts. However, the bench of the Revolutionary Tribunal attached to the VTsIK established on May 29, 1918 [1], consisted only of six members without assessors. Also the bench of the Special Revolutionary Tribunal residing at the Cheka, set up on Oct. 21, 1919, [2] was manned by professional judges only.

As we have seen, the Decree No. 2 on Courts, passed by the Council of People's Commissars on January 30, 1918 [3] represented in particular an attempt to bring the institute of assessors as near as possible to the abrogated jury.

First of all, in the discussion of the question of guilt or innocence of the accused, the professional judges were given only a consultative voice so that this question was solved *de facto* by the assessors. Then, the assessors had the right to challenge the professional judges at any time during the trial. Finally the assessors for the session were chosen not individually by the judges and confirmed by the local soviet, but by lot and the assessors were entitled to choose the chariman of the bench and recall him any time.

Furthermore, the Decree No. 2 on courts established a court for the examination of cases beyond the jurisdiction of the Local Courts, created by the Decree No. 1 on Courts : the circuit court. In the civil department of this court the bench was manned by 3 professional judges and 4 assessors. However, in the criminal department which had to handle the most serious criminal cases as had the former court with jury, the trial bench was composed of 3 professional judges and 12 assessors with 2 deputy assessors, exactly as in the court with jury which was alos attached to the tsarist circuit court.

However, the coalition with the left Social-Revolutionaries was dissolved after their insurrection of July 6, 1918, and Steinberg left the government. He was succeeded by a full-fledged Bolshevist.

Scarcely 6 months after the liquidation of Steinberg's attempt by the Statute on the Single and One People's Court of Nov. 30, 1918; [4] the number of the assessors was reduced to two or six, according to the crime committed; the chairman, the single professional judge, participated in the decision of the guilt or innocence and all other privileges of the assessors granted by the Decree No. 2 on Courts were abrogated. If the bench was composed of one professional judge and

---

1 *Sob. uz., RSFSR*, 1918, Item 520.
2 *Ibid.*, 1919, Item 504.
3 *Sob. uz., RSFSR*, 1918, Item 347 E.
4 *Sob. uz., RSFSR*, No. 851918; Item 889.

two assessors, the judges were the chariman ipso iure, whereas on the bench with one professional judge and six assessors its chairman was elected by all seven members of the bench.

The participation of lay judges in civil cases is a complete innovation for the country.

c) *Choice of Assessors*

The assessors were chosen by the executive committee of the local soviets from lists prepared by workers organizations, by volost' and village soviets.

The Basic Principles of Court Structure of Oct. 29, 1924 [1] established the rule that all benches of the courts of original jurisdiction should be manned by one professional judge and two assessors. In military courts, people's assessors were selected from among military persons, independently of their rank. [2]

The RSFSR Statute on Court Structure of Nov. 19, 1926 [3] provided that every citizen in possession of electoral rights according to the RSFSR Constitution may be a people's assessor. Lists of people's assessors, two hundred assessors from every district of the people's courts, were compiled yearly. A special commission distributed the assessors between the individual courts.

The USSR Constitution of 1936 established another system for assessors' elections. The assessors for the people's courts had to be elected by the population by means of general, direct, equal and secret ballot.

We know also that the democratic principle of the elections of judges and assessors declared already in the Decree No. 1 on Courts for future realization, put on the books in the 1936 Constitution and repeated in the Law on Court Structure of the SSSR, Union and Autonomous Republics of 1938, remained only on paper until the promulgation of the Statute on Elections to the RSFSR People's Courts of Sept. 25, 1948. [4]

In the meantime, an Edict of the USSR Commissar of Justice of Oct. 1938, No. 82, prescribed, with regard to the election of assessors, the application of previous regulations, i.e., their election by District Soviets. [5]

---

[1] *Sob. zak.*, 1924, Item 203.

[2] *Sob. zak., SSSR.*, 1926, Item 413.

[3] *Sob. uz., RSFSR*, 1926, Item 624.

[4] *V.V.S., SSSR*, 1948, No. 39.

[5] See V. Gsovski, *The Soviet Civil Law*, Ann Arbor, 1948, I, p. 259, Footnote 62.

But also, after 1948, the elections of assessors as was the case for judges was conducted according to the Soviet brand of democracy : only one candidate, recommended or approved by the Party, appeared on the ballot for every place.

The provisions of Art. II of the Law of 1938 was amended by an Ukase of the Presidium of the USSR Supreme Soviet of Sept. 16, 1948, approved by the Law of March 14, 1949 [1] and reads as follows : "Any USSR citizen, who is in possesion of electorial rights and has reached the age of 23 on the day of the election may be elected as a judge or people's assessor. Barred from the election as a judge or people's assessor are persons with criminal records".

The Law of 1938 established the following system of assessors' elections to higher courts : for the military tribunals, line courts of railroad and water transportation, the assessors were elected by territorial and regional soviets and supreme soviets of union and autonomous republics; these soviets elected assessors also for the territorial, regional and circuit courts as well as for the courts of the autonomous regions; the election of assessors of the USSR union and autonomous republics supreme courts, were carried out by the supreme soviets respectively in open sessions orally. Thus, only assessors for the people's courts had to be elected by the population, by general direct, secret and equal ballot, according to the Constitution and the Law of 1938.

But also the "democratic" elections of assessors for the people's courts, started in 1948, was abolished by the Basic Principles of Legislation on the Court Structure of USSR, Union and Autonomous Republics of Dec. 25, 1958. [2] According to this law, the people's court assessors are namely no longer elected by the population but in general assemblies of workers, employees and peasants at the place of their work or residence; assessors of military courts — at their respective military units. The assessors have to serve two weeks yearly (about one day in a month).

The nomination of candidates for assessor duties are made openly in the general assemblies. Everyone has the right to suggest candidates and speak for and against them.

The voting takes place separately on every candidacy suggested. Only persons older than 18 years have the right to participate in the

---

[1] *V.V.S., SSSR*, 1949, No. 12.

[2] *V.V.S., SSSR*, 1959, No. 41.

ballot. Elected are candidates, who receive a plurality of votes in comparison with other candidates, however, not less than one-half of votes of electors present at the general assembly.

The same law raised the obligatory age of an assessor from 23 to 25. Another requirement for an assessor is USSR citizenship and the possession of electoral rights.

The system for the elections of assessors to all other courts has not been changed.

G. Z. Anashkin reports on the class composition of people's assessors elected in the period after the Second World War. According to him, among the 359,491 elected assessors in the RSFSR, there were : industrial, construction, transportation and agricultural workers— 86,082 (24%); members of kolkhozes—97.593 (27.2%); members of handicraft cooperatives—9,064 (2.5%); trade and public nourishment workers—10,995 (3.1%); engineers and agriculturists 23,067 (6.4%); scientists—3,973 (1.1%); the remainder was made up of military persons, students, pensioners, housewives and persons with other occupations (35.7%). [1]

It is evident that among these assessors 99% had no legal education whatsoever (perhaps with the exception of the 1.1% made up of scientists). Consequently, it is unclear how it can be asserted in the Commentary to the 1958 Basic Principles of Legislation of Court Structure of the USSR and Union and Autonomous Republics, edited by Yu. A. Lalenova, that "... as a rule, elected, as assessors are citizens who have legal education and experience in public and political work, although no such qualifcations are required by law". [2] If we admit that among "persons with other occupations" there is a small percentage of jurists, this is still far short of any "routine" elections of jurists as assessors.

It is evident that such a rule cannot exist because it would contredict one of the fundamental principles of soviet administration of justice, already established by Lenin, namely, the attraction into this administration of the widest cricles of the population, "all the people". That is why no requirement of a legal education can be set for assessors. On the contrary, it may be said that, "as a rule", the assessors of the

---

[1] G.Z. Anashkin, *Narodnyye zasedateli v sovetskom sude*, M. 1960, p. 8.
[2] *Kommentariy k osnovam zakonodatel'stva o sudoustroystve soyuza SSR, soyuznykn i avtonomnykn respublik*, M. 1961, p. 67.

People's Courts have no, or a very limited, idea of legal matters.

Just because the people's assessors are legal ignoramuses efforts are made to acquaint them with an elementary notion of legal matters, especially of their rights and duties in trials and civil suits. Guides for the assessors are printed and lectures delivered. The legal periodical *Sovetskaya yustitsiya* published an instructive discussion for the assessors in its pages in 1958.

M. Ponedelkov reports [1] that since the activity of the people's assessors in the examination of concrete cases depends very much upon the extent of their knowledge of the legislation in force and the problem posed to the courts, in many courts steady work for the bettering of their legal knowledge is carried out. Besides teaching seminars in a number of cities, popular universities of legal science were organized in which special departments for the instruction of people's assessors are functioning.

However, V. Savitsky complains that, although much is done for the improvement of the knowledge of people's assessors, still this is not done well enough: the subject of the lectures for people's assessors and the time of delivery is poorly chosen, the classrooms are inadequate, etc. The resulting attendance is very low. For instance, in the Kiev Borough of Moscow, which has thousands of assessors, at most two hundred attended the lectures.

The opportunity of study is not offered to assessors everywhere. F. Vorobyov, a people's assessor, complained in a letter to *Izvestia* that not a single lesson was given to the assessors of the Navy Court in Odessa during the entire year of 1964. [2]

The necessity to train assessors in legal matters is generally recognized in the Soviet Union. In the Conference of Leningrad Jurists in March 1964 [3] it was emphasized that in the majority of people's courts no adequate attention is paid to the legal training of assessors, or to the improvement of their qualifications. Questions of court practice and faults committed during trials are not discussed with them.

Also the fact that assessors take their places on the bench without knowing the essence of the case they have to examine was criticized.

---

[1] *Sov. yust.*, 1964, No. 7, p. 23.

[2] M. Savitsky, "According to Law, According to Conscience", *Izvestia*, Feb. 12, 1965.

[3] *Sov. yust.*, 1964, No. 9, p. 18.

This occurs because, as a rule, they are summoned to court on the same day on which the trial has to take place and simply have no time to study the files.

One of the assessors, a certain A. Afonin, [1] pointed out the necessity of a skillful and systematic organization of assessor training in order that they may better use their rights, participate more actively in the examination of cases and apply Soviet law more correctly.

Afonin recommends special attention to the training of assessors temporarily replacing judges : He thinks appropriate textbooks should be published for assessors. [2]

C. COUNCILS OF PEOPLE'S ASSESSORS

A new institution with the scope to direct their activity outside the court was created by the assessors themselves, namely, the councils of people's assessors. The councils help the courts in taking prophylactic measures against criminality.

The assessors take part in the work for the establishment and elimination of sources and conditions of criminal activity and of other law violations, as well as of causes contributing to them. To this effect, the assessors check the behavior of persons under suspended sentences and others serving sentences not connected with deprivation of liberty and assigned to the supervision of public organizations and workers' collectives; extend help to comrades' courts, watch over the correct and timely enforcement of court decisions as well as of the private rulings of the courts; deliver lectures and reports and so forth.

In order to regulate all outside court assessors' activities, the councils of assessors were started on the initiative of active assessors and judges in a number of territories and autonomous republics of the RSFSR. The councils were attached to district (city) courts, after the court election of 1960.

---

[1] *Sov. yust.*, 1958, No. 7, pp. 60-61.

[2] Elementary notion of assessors' rights, duties and activity is given in S.V. Baksheyev, *Narodnyye zasedateli v sovetskom sude*, M. 1951; G.Z. Anashkin, *Narodnyye zasedateli v sovetskom sude*, M. 1960; *Posobiye dlya narodnykh zasedateley*, Moscow, 1955. According to V. Kulikov, 565,000 people's assessors participated in the administration of justice in 1967. From them, 210,722 were workers and 70,661 kolkhozniks and 40 %— women. (*Izvestia*, December 7, 1967.)

The number of assessors taking part in the work of the councils depends upon the size of the activity of the court to which they are attached. The council's work is usually directed by the chariman of the court.

The activity of the council is distributed between sections, the number of which corresponds to the fields of work of the council. Every section is headed by a judge.

Examples of the activity of the councils follow : The Council of People's Assessors of the Vyborg District, Leningrad Region, attached to the Vyborg City People's Court was elected in the Assessor's General Assembly on April 25, 1963. It consists of 15 core members. Three sections of the Council were organized to supervise the behavior of persons under suspended sentences and assigned to worker's collectives for reeducation; to extend help to the 65 Comrades' Courts of the District; to check the fulfillment of alimony sentences and decisions for compensation of damage inflicted on the state. All the 103 assessors of the Vyborg City Court joined one of the three sections according to their choices and participated in the work of the sections.

Later the Council widened its activity to the checking of the fulfillment of private rulings of the City Court and formed a new section for the propaganda of Soviet Law. The new section planned intensive work in its field, in 1964.

The judges of the City Court participated in the sessions of the Coucil and the sections and helped planning and directing thair activity. [1]

In the Perm' Region councils of people's assessors were attached not only to people's courts, but also to the frequent outside sessions of the courts, since local groups of assessors particpate in the outside court sessions which cover the Districts of the Region.

Two methods of council organization are used in the Region : in some councils, as for instance, in the council attached to the Nyvin City Court, all the assessors are included in the council. But in the majority of the councils, the sections are headed by a judge and manned by a relatively small number of assessors to an extent prepared for their activity. The remaining assessors are employed by the Council for individual assignments.

In the field of checking the behavior of persons under a suspended

---

[1] See A. Agapov-Ivanov, "The Council of People's Assessors in Action", *Sov. yust.*, 1964, No. 2, pp. 20-21.

sentence, an assessor is attached to every such person. If necessary, the assessor has to take measures in order to eliminate the reasons, preventing the convict from bettering his behavior. These measures are the calling of the convicted person to a session of the council in which his behavior is discussed. Other measures are representation made to party and trade-union organizations about the inadequate work performed by the worker's collective toward the reeducation of the person assigned to its care.

The assessors have to give an account of their activity to the Council. [1]

There is also a Council of People's Assessors attached to the Regional Court of Tula. The membership is eleven persons. Also this Council checks the fulfillment of private rulings of the Regional Court, the behavior of persons under suspended sentences and punishments not involving deprivation of liberty. The activity of the Council is planned in advance for every three months. Active help is extended to the Council by the members of the Regional Court.

Members of the Council make themselves extensively acquainted with the work of councils attached to district people's courts of the Region. In this way, the experience of all the councils in the Region are collected and discribed in directive letters addressed to all councils attached to the District people's court of the Region. [2]

Yu. V. Yurburgsky reports that many assessors and judges are constantly looking for new forms of work for the councils. They strive to achieve a better contact with workers' collectives in charge of the reeducation of criminals in order to attract them into the fight against criminality. Thus, for example, in Smolensk, enlarged sessions of the councils are convoked directly at enterprizes and organizations. The councils of the Bauman Borough People's Court in Moscow check the work of marshals, the information of visitors, the work of the Chancellery, etc.

"The initiative of the People's assessors merits every support, and the dissemination of new forms of assessor activities contribute to their wide employment in the prophylactic work against criminality", [3] Yurburgsky asserts.

---

[1] Ponedelkov, *Sov. yust.*, 1964, No. 7, pp. 22-24.

[2] V. Lavrova and G. Kirsh, "Council of People's Assessors, attached to the Regional Court", *Sov. yust.*, 1964, No. 11, p. 11.

[3] Yu. V. Yurburgsky, "New Features of the People's Assessors Organization", *S.G.P.*, 1963, No. 10, pp. 129-131.

It is evident that the work of the Councils of people's assessors, which was started by private initiative can be useful in many ways, must be officially legalized and organized by laws establishing their purpose and defining the duties and rights of their members. [1]

The RSFSR Supreme Court declared in 1964 that Councils of people's assessors have been created already at all courts. With regard to the specificity of the cases, sections of the councils are formed : on the check of the behavior of persons under a suspended sentence and conditionally released from jail; the fulfillment of private rulings and decisions of the court, particularly those concerning the executors into property; on the extention of help to comrades' courts; on legal propaganda, etc.

The Supreme Court listed a number of assessors' councils, attached to various courts performing very useful work.

However, the Supreme Court also points out the fact that "the generalization of the prophylactic work experience shows that the courts do not yet pay enough attention to the work with people's assessors". [2]

The periodical "Sovetskaya yustitsiya" received many letters of assessors complaining about the defects of their work's organization. The periodical summarized these complaints. [3]

Unanimous were the assessors in their demand of a better and wider organization of the exchange of experience of their courts and prophylactic work. Positive examples of this work should be popularized by people's judges so that the assessors should not be put in the position of "discoverers" every time and expend effort and time for the "invention" of effective and perfect forms and methods of work known a long time before.

They recommend to enlarge the practice of business meetings, assemblies, conferences of assessors of various districts and regions. The system of teaching the assessors should be perfected : 1) constantly functioning seminars and 2) short courses for the newly elected assessors should be created.

Also the systems of people's universities of legal sciences should be more extended in general.

---

[1] At the Scientific and Methodical Conference of the USSR Supreme Court in 1960 it was suggested that the Basic Principles of Court Structure of the USSR and the Union Republics of 1958 should be amended by "Article 32a" providing for the setting of Councils of People's Assessors (*Sots. zak.*, 1966, No. 9, p. 14).

[2] *Bulleten' Verkhovnogo suda RSFSR*, 1964, No. 8.

[3] *Sov. yust.*, 1967, No. 7, pp. 15-16.

D. Suggestions of Changes

Suggestions to enact changes in the Status of people's assessors have been made when the Basic Principles of Court Structure of 1958 were in preparation.

Rakhunov thought that the time was ripe for some changes in the forms of the administration of justice. According to him, in cases of crimes against the state, murder, robbery and similar serious offenses, the number of people's asessors should be increased, for instance, to six; this should be an important guarantee for justice, truth and equity of the sentence and will permit to attract to the administration of justice a greater number of people.

And then Rakhunov made the crucial proposition that "the decision of the question of the guilt of the accused should be referred to the competence of the people's assessors with regard to some crimes". [1]

Rakhunov was rebuked for his suggestions, "meaning the reception of bourgeois law", by Karev.

The latter, however, brings no valid argument against the essence of the suggestions by Rakhunov. He simply asserts that Rakhunov's proposition of the division of the functions of the assessors and permanent judges means an attempt "to cast suspicion upon the principles of Soviet court organization according to which there is no artificial barrier between the permanent judges and the people's assessors ...". [2]

Several years later, after the new Code of Criminal Procedure was published without taking account of Rakhunov's suggestions, Karev came back to them in order to state (again without supporting arguments) that "we hold as erroneous R.D. Rakhunov's proposal to increase the number of people's assessors in cases involving the most important crimes and to deprive them, as in bourgeois courts, of the right to set the punishment and to exclude the elected people's judge (the chariman in the case) from the right to partake in the decision on the guilt or innocence of the accused together with the people's assessors". Karev brands Rakhunov's proposal as an attempt to restore the court with jury in the USSR. [3]

---

[1] R.D. Rakhunov, "Some questions of Criminal Procedure", *Izvestia*, March 27, 1957.

[2] D.S. Karev, "The Further Perfecting of the Soviet Court System", *S.G.P.*, 1959, No. 2, p. 68.

[3] *Sots. zak.*, 1962, No. 2, p. 58.

However, in spite of criticism, Rakhunov renewed his proposal, this time in *Pravda*.

"It seems expedient" Rakhunov wrote, "to further perfect the institution of people's assessors ... People's assessors are neither in a position of subordination to a higher court, nor in another way dependant upon it.

"The examination of the most important criminal offenses", he continued, "with the participation of only two assessors does not insure, under present conditions, the complete independence of the court and the achievement of truth. It is another matter when the bench consist of 7-9 persons, including a permanent judge. Let us call to mind that in the first years of Soviet power [1], 6-12 people's assessors also participated in the court's functions. Such an enlargement of the bench would increase also the educational importance of sentences which, even to a greater extent, would rely on the wisdom and common sense of the people and heighten the moral weight, the power and authoritativeness of the sentences not only in the eyes of the public, but also of the higher courts". [2]

It is interesting to note that Rakhunov's last article is also directed against some other forms of public particpation in the administration of justice so widely extended in the Soviet Union at the present time.

The publication of the article by the organ of the Communist Party suggests the presumption that the Party does not completely disagree with its contents.

Strogovich took position on both questions of increasing the numbers of assessors and to refer to them the question of the guilt separating the professional judges from the solution of this question and leaving to his exclusive competence the setting of the punishment.

With regard to the first question Strogovich shares Rakhunov's opinion and thinks that it is a rational proposal to increase the number of assessors siting in court on most important crimes, because it gives a greater opportunity to attract citizens into the participation of meeting justice, as well as will increase the assessor's activity, independence in the decisions of cases; if in more complicated cases, for example, six assessors will participate in the place of two ... their independence from the judge will be greater.

With regard to the second proposal Strogovich thinks that there

---

[1] He had evidently in mind the Decree No. 2 on Courts.

[2] R.D. Rakhunov, "Legality and Justice", *Pravda*, September 22, 1965.

is no reason to keep the assessors "away from the decision about the punishment of the accused ... In the question of the amount of this punishment the assessors have a deciding voice ... the decision is their's, not only an opinion. In the same way there is no ground to keep the judge away from the decision about the guilt. [1]

Certainly, the assessors have the majority of voices for the decision of both questions of the guilt and punishment of the accused. But Strogovich avoids taking into consideration subjugation of the assessors by the judge. The increase of their number to six or more would, naturally, reduce the possibility of this subjugation.

Both questions were discussed at the Scientific and Methodical Conference at the USSR Supreme Court in 1966.

The Raporteur, V. Zaychuk, was of the opinion that the number of people's assessors should vary according to the character of the crime.

Strogovich objected. He was of the opinion that the number of assessors should be increased numerically in *general*; he reminded that their number was greater (up to twelve) between 1918 and 1922, when the assessors were highly praised by Lenin, that the decreasing of the number to two was carried out on grounds of economic considerations, according to P. Stuchka.

"But at the present time", thought Strogovich, "during the shift from socialism to communism, in the period of the steady increase of democratization of our society, there are all reasons for the increase of the number of people's assessors in trials. This will heighten the quality of court examination, strengthen the independence of people's assessors and heighten the authority of courts in the eyes of the working population". [2] This time, Strogovich remained silent about the question of the separation of the functions of assessors and judges.

For the increase in the number of people's assessors spoke G. Shafir, G. Anashkin, T. Gersaliya and others.

Kuryleyev expressed opinions on the people's assessors in general that deserve to be quoted extensively. He said that "the people's assessors are passive at the present time during the trial. This is to be explained by the fact that the professional judge has the legal knowledge and is a person of authority. The people's assessors—are

---

[1] M. Strogovich, "The Development of Legislation on Court Structure and Court Procedure", *Sov. yust.*, 1961, No. 22, p. 4.

[2] *Sots. zak.*, 1966, No. 9, p. 15.

not jurists; they cannot argue the doubts which sometimes arise in their minds; this is the reason for their passivity, their submission to the will of the people's judge.

Then, Kuryleyev discussed the crucial question of the separation of the functions of the judge and the people's assessors.

In his opinion, this separation and the increase of the number of people's assessors are two faces of the same question, the positive solution of which "will contribute to the strenthening of their independence".

He admits that this division of functions will complicate the procedure. However, the complication of the procedure will improve the quality of the examination. The guiding of the people's assessors will be carried out openly, which will ameliorate the quality of their work. Also the requirements presented to the prosecutor will be hightened. Although the increase of the number of people's assessors may bring some detrimental effect to the nation's economy, still this can be avoided by the method of assigning of petty cases to the jurisdiction of one judge. [1]

However, opposition was voiced to the suggestion to increase the number of people's assessors and to separate their functions from that of the professional judge.

So Arsenyev argued that although the people's assessors do not represent a perfect particpation of the population in the administration of justice which must be improved, still not by the increase of their number. Admitting that the separation of people's assessors from the judge and the assignment of the question as to whether the guilt is proven, could increase their activity, still it may not be forgotten that it is a complicated job, not less difficult than that of qualification of the crime and the setting of the measure of punishment. "And it would be a mistake to award to the people's assessors the monopoly of deciding the question of the guilt".

The improvement of the people's assessor's work could be reached by other means. For instance, a check of what happens in the conference chamber could be achieved by installing there a stenographer who would lay down a verbatim report of the discussion in the chamber, as it is done in Poland. [2]

Arsen'yev's objections were shared by V. Shubin and G. Min'kovsky.

---

[1] *Ibid.*

[2] *Ibid.*, pp. 15-16.

The question was revived in 1967 with several articles in the *Literaturnaya gazeta*.

Chetunova described the situation of an assessor forced to take part in the decision of legal questions for which he is not prepared. She cites the following words of an assessor :

"To decide not only questions of guilt or innocence, but in contradistinction to the jurors, *all* (I.Ch.) questions, rising in the trial together with a professional judge puts me, as an assessor, before a dilemma insoluble in reality : or it is necessary to attempt resolving most complicated problems undoubtedly requiring special knowledge, or, not having this special knowledge, to completely rely upon the knowledge of the presiding judge and countersign a sentence, for the equity of which you, personally, cannot guarantee".

From this situation Chetunova makes the only possible conclusion. "It seems to me", she writes, "that the most important task for the people's assessors must be the right to decide about the guilt or innocence of a person in the same manner as Koni [1] advised [the jury] to do in the Vera Zasulich case : [decide] according to your deep convictions, based on everything you heard and saw [during the trial], and restricted by nothing, except the voice of your conscience ...

In the contradictory position of the assessor lies the reason for his passivity in the trial".

In Chetunova's opinion, the assessor can bring a real benefit to the case only solving the questions of guilt or innocence, of intent and the necessity or inappropriateness of indulgence in the setting of the punishment.

The legal questions should be referred to the professional judges.

Another assessor called Chetunova's attention to the necessity of increasing the number of assessors in the trial, in any case, He thought it wrong to refer to the judgment of two persons the fate of a human being, his honor, freedom, sometimes the question of his life or death.

But Chetunova not only gave the opinion of assessors and her own on the question at hand, but asked also for the viewpoint of such an authority as G. Z. Anashkin, Chairman of the Judicial College on Criminal Affairs of the USSR Supreme Court.

According to Chetunova, Anashkin said that the necessity for an increased number of assessors in important cases deserves attention

---

[1] Koni, one of the most outstanding Russian jurists was the Chairman in the Vera Zasulich trial.

without any doubt. This thought is confidently gaining its way. Precisely to what number? This question must be solved, evidently in accordance with special research available in the USSR and abroad. It is clear, however, already now that this number must be different in various cases. "It seems to me", Anashkin said, "that per example, in such cases as uncontroversial litigation as exacting of fines or alimony—the participation of even two assessors is an unnecessary formality. On the other hand, in cases when the death penalty is applicable, 5-7 or maybe more assessors are required".

With regard to the question of the division of functions, between the people's assessors and the professional judge, Anaskin was of the opinion that the question requires not only serious discussion but also a practical check. According to him, "logic seems to suggest that the complete transfer to the responsibility of a great number of assessors of the decision of such questions as guilt or innocence, the character of intent and the presence of mitigating or aggravating circumstances, must really heighten the activity of people's assessors, increase the exactness of the court toward the collected evidence and increase the cultural level of court investigation".

Anashkin thought that following the example of the introducing of new forms and methods of industrial guidance at the present time, it would be good to introduce, after thorough investigation, a new form of assessor's activity, it means, thus, of the entire court.

He suggested that as a test, such a reform should be introduced in some cities or districts. The test must be thoroughly studied, all the negative and positive aspects of the new practice evaluated and then decided as to whether the new form should be adopted in general.

Chetunova interviewed on the discussed question also Rakhunov and Strogovich who, according to her, opposed the suggestion of letting the judge alone decide over the measure of punishment. They thought "it was not good to keep the assessors from the decision on the question of punishment. Let the people's assessors decide it together with the chairman". [1]

The meaning of the objection is obvious : Rakhunov and Strogovich both advocating an increased number of assessors, want them to participate also in the setting of the punishment believing that they will have a salutary influence also on the resolving of this question.

---

[1] N. Chetunova, "The Court Retired for Deliberation", *Literaturnaya gaseta*, March 29, 1967.

Rakhunov formulated his objection in the same newspaper, two weeks later.

"I think", he wrote, "that the rights of people's assessors should not be curtailed in any way. It would be wrong to deprive them of their right to participate also in the setting of the punishment as N. Chetunova suggests".

Without any ground is also the fear that the reorganization will result in the belittling of the role of the judge. As his duty belongs the guidance of the trial session, the direction of the [court] investigation, the decision about solicitations, the examination of declarations, the formulation of questions, participation in the setting of the punishment and the passing of the sentence. [1]

Thus, Strogovich and Rakhunov agree with the exclusive jurisdiction of assessors an the question of guilt and innocence, but want also to retain their participation in the setting of the punishment.

Also Kisilev thinks that the increase in the number of assessors wil contribute to the equitable solution of the case; the judge, he argues, may be without realizing it, subjects the assessors to his influence. "The replacing of two assessors ... by 6 ... he writes, is not only a quantitative change, but also the beginning of the functioning of law of the transition from quantity to quality : six persons soldiered together by the similarity of their positions, feeling their firmness, realizing that they were elected in such a great number just for the purpose, that they, and only they, exert decisive influence on the sentence : six different characters which cannot be subjected to the ascendency of one man—they insure the authentic democracy of our court". [2]

Perlov suggested the participation of people's assessors in the examination of critical cases in the cassation instances. [3]

---

[1]   R.D. Rakhunov, "Man and Law", *ibid.*, April 12, 1967.

[2]   Ya. Kisilev, "When the Trial is Going On...", *Ibid.*, June 14, 1967. Suggestions for the increase of the number of assessors also was made by F. Burlatsky, "Questions of State in the KPSU Program Project (*Kommunist*, 1961, No. 13, p. 47) and by T. Dobrovol'skaya "Organization and Activity of the Soviet Court in the Period of the Extensive Building of Communism" (*S.G.P.*, 1963, No. 1, p. 96).

[3]   I.D. Perlov, "The Problems of the Further Development of Democratic Foundations of Criminal Procedure in the Light of the Soviet Union Communist Party's Program", *S.G.P.*, 1962, No. 4, p. 90.

E. COMPARISON AND APPRAISAL

When legally untrained elements are attracted to court work in order to decide the guilt or innocence of the accused in a criminal trial, the fact that the jurors are not legally trained is irrelevant because they need not present their opinion in legal questions as it was so convincingly stated by the tsarist State Council. Their purpose is to decide according to their personal viewpoint and their conscience as to whether the accused committed the incriminated action or not.

It must be underlined that the Russian jury was not obliged to pronounce a verdict of guilty even if the accused was undeniably proven to be the perpetrator of the criminal action charged to him, or confessed it and there were no legal grounds for his impunity. [1] When the jury felt that, according to the conscience of the majority of its members, the accused should not be punished for his action, it exercised a kind of right of pardon, which the American and English juries do not have. The French jury also had it.

As an illustration of this attention is directed to the case of the old provincial priest Kudryavtsev, who admitted having embezzled 10,000 rubles of church money. He was defended by one of the best, perhaps *the* best, forensic orator in Russia, F.N. Plevako. The counsel did not "defend" his client. He did not pose a single question to the witnesses, did not present a single request. But in his summing up which lasted one and one-half minutes, he appealed to the jury for pardon. This is what he said : "During thirty years one year after the other, you, gentlement of the jury, came to the priest Kudryavtsev for confession, and also as many times he absolved your sins. Now, once in thirty years, the repentent sinner comes to you for pardon with words of sorrow, repentence and entreaty. Won't you also absolve his sin" ? The jury, consisting of local small merchants and shopkeepers, returned a verdict of acquittal after one minute of deliberation.

The Russian jury assumed also the task of mitigating the punishment prescribed by law when, according to their conscience, it was too severe. The tsarist criminal Code of 1848 was not changed by the Judicial Reform of 1864. The punishments provided by the Code were too harsh

---

[1] The Ruling Senate first recognized this right of the jury, then denied it and even prohibited to the defense council to plead for an acquittal if the guilt was proven but then again reversed its opinion on this subject, coming back to its initial position. See S. Kucherov, *Courts, Lawyers and Trials...*, pp. 66-68.

in many instances, according to more advanced concepts, but the judges were prevented by law from prescribing a punishment under the lower limit, if they desired so. But not the jurors. If the inevitable punishment seemed too harsh to the jury, it simply acquitted the accused when there were no other means to mitigate the punishment. But sometimes the jury reverted to other means to this effect when the law presented a suitable opportunity. For instance, the theft of an amount over three hundred rubles was punishable much more severely than a theft under 300 rubles. In order to mitigate the punishment the jury answered the question as to whether the accused is guilty of the theft of a wallet containing six hundred rubles : "Yes, but less than three hundred rubles"—a logically nonsensical answer, but producing the desired effect of mitigation of punishment.

However, the situation is radically changed if "the man from the street" has to decide upon legal questions for which he is not prepared, as must the Soviet assessor, or the German Schoeffen. He inevitably has to rely on the opinion of the professional judge and is under his influence with regard to their solution.

These legal questions arise before the Soviet assessor already before the trial itself. In a preparatory session, the court (a professional judge and two assessors) has to decide on the indictment of the accused as suggested by the investigating magistrate. To this effect it has to check : has the preliminary investigation been carried out completely and correctly ? is the accusation well founded ? is a *corpus delicti* to be found in the action of the accused ? were the rules prescribed by law for the carrying out of the preliminary investigation followed ? are all circumstances of the case which speak against, but also for the suspect, which increase or attenuate his guilt, thoroughly investigated ? is the provision of the Criminal Code according to which the suspect is inculpated by the investigating magistrate and the prosecutor correctly chosen ?

How can "the man from the street" have his own opinion on all these questions and decide as to whether the case must be quashed, the preliminary investigation supplemented or the indictment pronounced ?

It must be also taken into consideration that he has a very short period of time, if any, to study the files of the case, which sometimes are very voluminous, before the preparatory or the trial session of the court.

Also during the trial issues of law are constantly raised by the prosecutor and the defense counsel for the solution of which the assessors are not trained but on which they have to vote.

In the chamber for deliberation, the assessors are again faced by questions of law, such as the legal qualification of the action, the application of this or that provision of the Criminal Code, etc., which lie outside of their real competence. Naturally they follow the opinion of the professional judge, although the assessors have to vote on every question first; it is psychologically quite understandable and inescapable that the assessors are awed also on other questions by the authority of the professional judge, the man who is trained in the job in which they are involved, but completely incompetent. It is evident that the infleunce of the professional on his two colleagues extends besides the purely legal problems also to the crucial question of guilt or innocence. [1] It can be assumed with great certainty that the overwhelming number of decisions of the court with assessors of the Soviet Union also are taken along the lines suggested by the professional judges.

In its decision of March 18, 1963 "On the Strict Completion of Law in the Examination of Criminal Cases by Courts" [2] the USSR Supreme Court remarked even that colleaguality required by law, is not always observed despite the provision of Article 9 of the Basic Principles of Criminal Procedure of the USSR and the Union Republics, providing equal rights, of the people's assessors and the presiding judge; the opinion of the assessors is not sufficiently taken into consideration concerning questions raised during the examination of the case, and sometimes the passing of the sentence.

"Although Soviet lay judges can under their law outvote a professional judge", Hazard writes, "the outside world has been informed of only a very few cases in which this has happened. These cases have been recounted by former Soviet lawyers who have fled to the West, and one is reported in the Soviet official reports. Generally the lay judges are believed to be quite docile in accepting the proposals of the professional judge. They rarely ask questions at the trial or show any independence of view. Nevertheless, they provide the oppor-

---

[1] The present writer, during the time of probation as a Referendar in Germany, took part in sessions of the German Court with Schoeffen and can testify that more than 90 % of the decisions were taken according to the opinion of the professional judges.

[2] Decision No. 2, *Bulleten' Verkhovnogo Suda, SSSR*, 1963, No. 3, p. 5.

tunity to the general public to share in the decision and as such may help the Soviet leaders to maintain popular support for the regime.

It is not entirely accurate,—he continues—to say that the Soviet lay judges represent the general public. While very few of them are members of the Communist Party, they are selected by institutions in each district, such as factories, farms, universities, retail stores, and army units. The Communist Party shares in the selection by these institutions, and the nominations are unopposed. In consequence, the panels from which the lay judges are called for service are not cross sections of the entire population as are the panels form which jurors are selected in the United States". [1]

How far the subordination of the assessors goes can be seen from the case related by V. Savitsky. [2]

Retired to the chamber for deliberation on the forthcoming sentence, the bench of the Supreme Court of the Azerbaydzhan SSR had no doubt about the guilt of the accused in the case. However, opinions diverged about the extent of the punishment : the two assessors were for a milder, the professional judge for a stronger punishment. But in the sentence, read by the judge, the stronger punishment was set.

On protest of the Deputy of the General Prosecutor of the USSR, the case was transferred to the Suprme Court of the USSR in which the following was established :

During the deliberation the two assessors declined to sign the sentence which contained the stronger punishment suggested by the professional judge. However the judge explained to them that "according to law, only one assessor can have a dissenting opinion, but that both of them must sign the sentence together with the chairman, in any case". After this "explanation" both assessors signed the sentence which reflected the opinion of the professional judge only.

It is very significant that the periodical, *Sovetskaya yustitsiya*, found it necessary to draw special attention to the fact that professional judges illegally influence their lay colleagues in order to produce a sentence or decision agreeable to them. In the Editorial on "The election to people's assessors" it is said : "... from letters received

---

[1] John N. Hazard, *The Soviet System of Government* [9th Edition], Chicago and London, 1968, pp. 176-177. Also Perlov stated that some judges ignore the rights of People's Assessors who enjoy equal rights with the professional judge. (N. Perlov, "The Alphabet of the Law", *Izvestia*, January 12, 1967.)

[2] *Izvestia*, February 12, 1965.

by the editorial board of the periodical, follows, that individual judges, in violation of the prescriptions of law, attempt to ignore the opinion of the assessors during the passing of the sentence or decision, or to thrust on them their viewpoint on the problems under solution". [1]

Such cases of disregard of the opinion of the people's assessors are evidently not a rarity, since in their book "Particpation of the Public in the Soviet Criminal Procedure", Galperin and Poloskov cite a case of setting aside the sentence of the Karelofinish Supreme Court by the RSFSR Supreme Court because the professional judge set the highest punishment provided by the law, although both people's assessors voted for a more lenient punishment of one year in prison. [2]

The ignorance of legal matters is certainly the main cause for the lack of independence and great passivity of the assessors during the trial. George Feifer depicts in this way the assessors in a trial at which he was present in Moscow : "Both assessors were factory workers ... one of them struggled conscientiously to follow the deluge of testimony throughout. The other one gave up : he grinned stupidly at the defendants nearest him, whispered to the soldiers standing guard at his table, stared for hours out of the double windows and after lunch, cradled his head on his hands and dozed. He never asked a question during the month and a half of the trial". [3]

Also, Yu. Feofanov writes [4] about the "silence" of the assessors : "not accidentally two non-jurists sat beside the chairman—people's assessors. The voice of every one of them is equal to the judge's voice. But sometimes they are for one reason or another silent in the deliberation chamber, and as a result an unjust sentence is pronounced".

Of the same opinion is O. Chaykovskaya, who wrote that during a trial when a member of the Komsomol was accused of the murder of a militia man and sentenced to death, the assessors did not open their mouths. In the author's opinion, they sat through all 8 days of the trial completely convinced that they could not grasp the legal matters of the case and have no aptitude to judge. "In other words", declared Chaykovskaya, "they came to court without any idea about our court system, about the character of the institution of people's assessors itself. Court examination without a juror is unthink-

---

[1]   Editorial, *Sov. yust.*, 1963, No. 3, p. 2.

[2]   T.M. Galperin and F.A. Poloskin, *Uchastiye obshchestvennosti v sovetskom ugolovnom protsesse*, M. 1961, p. 75.

[3]   George Feifer, *Justice in Moscow*, N.Y., 1964, p. 301.

[4]   *Izvestia*, January 12, 1963.

able. But a court without assessors (or a court with assessors who only nod assent) is impossible to the same extent". [1]

Especially precarious, even tragic, must be the position of the assessors who replaced professional judges, according to Article 19 of the Basic Principles of Court Structure of the USSR, the Union and Autonomous Republics of 1938. [2]

According to this provision, namely, when the professional judge is on vacation or temporarily not able to perform his duties, the judge is replaced in all his functions by an assessor. This assessor has to receive visitors and citizens who come to court with their requests and grievances, give the necessary information and explanations, accept briefs in civil cases, and other documents in cirminal cases not requiring a preliminary investigation : he must prepare and assign cases for trial, take over the chairmanship in the preparatory and the trial sessions of the court, the bench consisting then of three assessors; the assessor—deputy judge—has to direct the work of the marshalls and the chancelory.

Thus, in this case, the people's assessor fulfilled all the competent and responsibile duties of a professional judge ... a situation without parallel in the legislation of any non-communist country. No wonder that the provision of Article 19 was not taken over in the text of the law of 1958 which replaced the law of 1938.

However, the practice of temporarily replacing judges by assessors still exists : the replacement is every time ordered by the executive committee of the local soviet for every case.

Indeed, this disastrous practice of appointing people's assessors to deputy judges has evidently not been abandoned. In 1965, a booklet was published in the popular series, "Prochti, tovarishch" (Read it, Comrade) by the Publication House "Znaniye" (Knowlegde) under the title "Imenem respubliki" (In the name of the Republic). Notes of an assessor in which the author, I.K. Nedolya, a people's assessor, relates his experience as a deputy judge of the People's Court. Unfortunately, the present author could not locate the booklet and the quotations from it are taken from the review of the work : "Juridical ignorance" by A. Polyak, in Izvestia. [3]

The impossible stituation in which he was put prompted I.K.

---

[1] "Not in vain there are three of them", ibid., May 15, 1963.
[2] V.V.S., 1938, No. 11.
[3] July 1, 1965.

Nedolya, a noted writer, to publish his experience by describing a case in which he functioned as a deputy of the judge who went on leave. When he, who had no legal education or training, was reluctant to carry on the functions of the judge, he was told by other judges of the court: "You will cope with it. Within two or three months (after which the session had to take place) you will acquaint yourself perfectly with the direction of the court session".

Judges explained to the assessor that the job of a judge is much simpler than it seems, that it is not obligatory for a judge to be a jurist and know the laws, and if something goes wrong, it does not matter, the higher appellate court will straighten it out!

Thus, the hero of the story was made to preside over the trial of the following case: A young lad failed to re-enter his train at a small station and remained there without any identification papers, ticket or money. In despair, he finally decided to take the bicycle of a drunken man which lay about the highway to use it for the return to his home and then send the bicycle back to its owner.

All the evidence in the case confirmed the assertions of the lad and the two assessors thought that there was no reason to jail him. "I was completely of their opinion", relates the deputy judge, "but, today, I am the judge ... and I began to explain to the assessors that maybe the accused is a recidivist ... that if he should have identification papers we could pass another sentence, ... and I suggested the highest punishment which provided for the confinement of the accused in a colony. We argued a long time, until I persuaded the assessors to share my oponion and sign a sentence, sending the accused to a colony".

The episode should illustrate the fact that, according to Nedolya, sentences are always passed, in conformity with the opinion of the judge.

The author's experience as a deputy judge concerns also another interesting point. He is, namely, convinced that the court takes its decision according to the conclusions of the investigation organs and only sometimes on the basis of the results of the trial. He relates that "with regard to the circumstances known in this or that case before the trial, I looked up beforehand the corresponding provisions in the Code and prepared a draft of the future sentences".

A. Polyak wrote an annihilating review of the booklet in which he contended that the author is a complete ignoramus of legal matters and displays utter disrespect for soviet law.

I. Nedolya was offended by Polyak's review and expressed his dissatisfaction in a letter to the editor of *Izvestia*. The letter itself was not published by the newspaper, but O. Chaykovskaya, in an article, defended Polyak and expressed criticism of Nedolya's work also on her own. [1]

With regard to the assertion of the author, quoted above, that he was told by judges that "you will cope with it" and so on, Chaykovskaya states that she cannot imagine, herself, "that somewhere in our country there can exist such a court and jurists can pronounce such 'wise' speeches. I want to ask you : is it possible to admit that the chair of the residing judge in court should be occupied by a person who decides the case by overriding the conviction of the assessors" ?, Chaykovskaya exclaims emphatically.

The answer to Chaykovskaya's question is : "Unfortunately, yes, it happens". One is forced to ask whether Chaykovskaya read the issue of *Izvestia*, the newspaper to which she is such a distinguished contributor, of February 12, 1965, and the article by Savitsky mentioned above; and whether she is not acquainted with Article 19 of the Basic Principles of 1938? Chaykovskaya is indignant because the author justifies the appointment of a fresh assessor to the duties of a people's judge by the fact that the regular judge was on leave and that somebody had to replace him. "Imagine" she writes, "that a surgeon is on leave and his place is taken by a nurse who courageously seizes the knife, prompted by love of the diseased and the acute desire to help him. Perhaps the diseased would prefer to wait ...".

Certainly, Chaykovskaya is right and her example is excellent, but the reproach is directed not to the proper address : it should be levelled at those who in reality appoint such deputy judges and at the system which permits such appointments and not at the author of the booklet, whose great merit is to have turned the attention to the facts described in his work. Certainly, Nedolya is ignorant of the basic legal provisions governing the job to which he was appointed and which he reluctantly accepted. But not this is the most important thing. The appointment of persons such as Nedolya, as deputy judges is an inadmissible gesture. The mere possibility of such an appointment disgraces the Soviet administration of justice !

Lenin preached the largest possible participation of the people in the administration of justice. He was of the opinion that "We have

---

[1] O. Chaykovskaya, "This Strange Book", *Izvestia*, July 29, 1965.

to mete out justice ourselves. Citizens must participate to a man in court work and the administration of the country". [1] He thought that, in order that rational decisions be rendered, judges are necessary who are not reduced to the position of simple officials. "The participation of representatives of the public and public opinion are necessary in the discussion of the case". [2]

But on the other hand, he had a very poor opinion of the performance of people's representatives united with professional judges on one bench and deciding over questions of guilt and law. Having in mind the prerevolutionary court with class representatives, [3] Lenin wrote : "As it is well known, these class representatives, integrated in one college with judges-officials, are dumb extras playing a pitiful role of witnesses [to court procedure] signing to everything the officials of the court might deem to decide". [4] Did he not realize that people's assessors functioning according to the same principle, will be also "dumb extras" in court ?

Not a better opinion of the *Schoeffen* had Vyshinsky and preferred the jury to them. He rebuked Chel'tsov-Bebutov because the latter saw an analogy in organizational matter between the Soviet court with people's assessors and the court with Schoeffen. "In our opinion wrote Vyshinsky, the comparison of a Soviet court with a bourgeois court, although with a Schoeffen one, is wrong in principle and absolutely inadmissible. You cannot separate the form of a court from its contents, as you cannot do it with regard to any phenomenon. The separation of the jury from the bench is ... one of the guarantees of the 'independence' of the jurors from the state judges. The court with the Schoeffen destroys this guarantee, submitting the Schoeffen to the authority of the professional judges who lead, and subjugate them by their experience and state authority. Not by any chance, therefore, prefers the bourgeoisie to replace the court with jury with the Schoeffen court, presenting more advantages and convenience from the viewpoint of influence in the direction of its own state policy". [5]

It is evident, that, the subjugation of lay judges, by professional

---

[1] Lenin, 27, p. III.

[2] *Ibid.*, 4, p. 367.

[3] For the court with class representatives, see Samuel Kucherov, *Courts...*, *op. cit.*, pp. 86-87.

[4] Lenin, IV, p. 83.

[5] A. Ye. Vyshinsky, "Essays on the Court Structure in the USSR", in *Marksistsko-Leninskoye ucheniye o sude i sovetskaya sudebnaya sistema*, M. 1934, Vol. II, p. 47.

ones is inherent to the system of letting both the lay and professional judges decide over the questions of guilt and punishment, independently as to whether the system functions in a bourgeois or Soviet state.

At the XXIInd Congress of the Soviet Union Communist Party, the Central Committee of the Party posed the practical problem of involving the entire adult population in the administration of the state and, hence, of justice since the administration of justice is a part of the administration of the state. At the same Congress, N. S. Khrushchev declared in the report of the Central Committee of the Party to the Congress : "We must remark, with great satisfaction, that we are now near the realization of the aim indicated by Lenin, of the involvement of all citizens without exception, in the fulfillment of state functions'. [1]

Public participation in the regular courts' work [2] is necessary and is undoubtedly a progressive feature of this work. The public representatives bring fresh air into the bureaucratic administration, human feeling of compassion which must be excluded from the heart of a professional judge who is guided by and applies only the law. As correctly remarked by O. Chaykovskaya : "However conscientious and just a professional judge may be, his capacity for compassion may be deadening. He has seen too much suffering and is accustomed to it. He can hardly be accused of it—you cannot denounce a surgeon because he is not afraid of blood and does not flinch from the sight of a ripped-up belly. The surgeon works among bloody wounds, a judge among moral deformities and moral pains. They get accustomed, —there is nothing to do about it". [3]

"Assessors are necessary" continues Chaykovskaya, "not only because one mind is good but three are better. They bring to court their life experience, arguments and doubts which are so necessary in court. Appearing in court they must firmly know that they are not 'ersatz' judges but the best first-rate judges, that they are not 'poor relatives' of the court, but its masters, because the court cannot consist of one judge. It is not in vain that there are three of them".

In a fulminant editorial entitled "Questions of Law and Justice in

---

[1]　N.S. Khrushchev, *Otchet TsIKa KPSS XX s'ezdu*, M. 1961, pp. 101-102.

[2]　I have in mind the jury, but not the assessors, and the public prosecutors or counsels.

[3]　Chaykovskaya, "Not in vain there are three of them", *op. cit.*

a Distorted Mirror", of the *"Sotsialisticheskaya zakonnost'* " against the writings of Chaykovskaya to which we will have to return in this book, the latter was accused of distrust of professional judges who "allegedly live in the atmosphere of crime", [1] in the article "Not in vain there are three of them".

In Izvestia, I. Perlov came to the defense of Chaykovskaya. [2] Analyzing the Chaykovskaya's assertion, Perlov exclaims "Where is there distrust of professional judges? Where is there contraposition of judges and people's assessors?" [2]

Only the institution of the jury is capable of bringing in the refreshing atmosphere of conscientiousness, compassion and humanity. It spares the professional judge the crucial question of guilt or innocence, leaving to him the case for all the legal aspects.

Certainly, the competence of the assessors is much wider than that of the pre-revolutionary jurors since they participate in the preparatory and the trial work of all the regular civil and criminal courts of orginial jurisdiction in the Soviet Union. The assessors have the same right of decision in the same range of questions as the professional judge. But it is precisely these rights and duties they involve which deprive them of their public character and of the possibility to decide as laymen, and not as judges. As judges, they are bound by law to administer the law, which they do not know how to handle, in which they are not trained. And, thus, they inadvertantly but surely submit to the influence of the professional judge, losing the public feature which they were called to represent in the administration of justice. They cannot, as the jurors could and did, decide according to their conscience and sense of equity only, they cannot absolve an accused who pleaded guilty, if no legal reasons for his acquittal exist, they cannot artificially mitigate the punishment which they feel is too harsh when no legal means can be applied to this effect.

Writing much later on the German Schoeffen, Vyshinsky remarked : "In Germany the Schoeffengericht supplanted the court with jurors as early as 1924, signifying that it is easier for permanent judges in this court to exercise influence on the assessors, to subordinate and depersonalize them, than where there are juries". [3]

---

[1] *Sots. zak.*, 1965, No. 1, p. 96.

[2] I. Perlov, "Why Reproach the Mirror", *Izvestia*, February 14, 1965.

[3] A. Vyshinsky, *The Law of the Soviet State*, translated from the Russian by Hugh W. Babb, New York, 1948, p. 510.

But why did Lenin choose the people's assessors — the form of court be so bitterly criticized — and not the jury of which he had such a high opinion, for the people's participation in court work? He could have simply abolished the property qualifications for the jurors ... the only defect of the jury system according to him and Marx.

Was Lenin not moved by the same consideration expressed by Vyshinsky with regard to Schoeffen in choosing assessors to replace the jury? Was he not of the opinion that the establishment and operation of the dictatorship of the proletariat cannot afford the functioning of a free jury? There is a high degree of probability that Lenin preferred assessors to jurors because the former are much easier to be influenced by the permanent judge and through him by the Party, than the latter? If this was the reason, the choice was correct.

The United States' Constitution is also based on the "government by the people. But Thomas Jefferson defined this principle as the introduction of the people into all departments of government *"only as far as they are capable of exercizing it,"* [1] and wisely asserted that "they [the people] are not qualified to judge questions of law but they are very capable of judging questions of fact. In the form of the jury they determine all matters of facts leaving to the permanent judge to decide the law resulting from these facts". [2]

---

[1] Stress provided.
[2] Quoted by Thomas Fleming, *The Man of Monticello*, New York, William Morrow & Co, 1969, p. 269.

CHAPTER FOURTEEN

INVESTIGATIVE ORGANS

A. Preliminary Investigation

a) *Under the Tsars*

The preliminary investigation was conducted by the police up to the Ukase of the Tsar of June 8, 1860, which ordered the preliminary investigation to be entrusted to special officials in the provinces, subordinate to the Ministry of Justice.

Together with the Ukase a Statute on the investigating magistrates and instructions for the magistrates and the police was published. However, not the entire investigating procedure was taken from the hands of the police. The police retained the "inquest" (*doznaniye*), the collection of information for "the establishment of the occurrences connected with the crime or felony which really took place" (Art. 2 and 3 of the Instructions to the Police).

According to the Statute on the Investigating Magistrates, they had the same status as the district judges. They were appointed by the Ministry of Justice on nomination by the governor of the province involved in agreement with the province prosecutor.

The separation of the preliminary investigation from the police inquest as instituted by the Ukase of June 8, 1860, was a forerunner of the general separation of the judicial power from the legislative and executive branches of the government carried out by the judicial Reform of 1864. That is why the Basic Principles of the Judicial Reform published on September 29, 1862 retained the structure of the investigating magistracy of 1860, and the Reform of November 20, 1864 itself had only to coordinate the carrying-out of the preliminary investigation with the judicial examination in court during the trial, as introduced by the new Code of Criminal Procedure of 1864.

The Reform of 1864 not only retained the judicial status of the investigating magistrate, but he was also appointed in the same way as the other members of the judiciary : he was nominated by the general assembly of the circuit court and appointed by the Minister of Justice.

The rights of the suspects were guaranteed to a comparatively high degree during the preliminary investigation. Although counsel was excluded from the preliminary investigation the suspect could be present at all action undertaken by the investigation. If a witness was interrogated in his absence the minutes of the interrogation had to be read to him. The suspect had the right to refute testimonies made against him and ask the investigator to put new questions to the witness, and the allegation of the suspect against the testimony of the witness had to be investigated, if they were of substantial importance to the case. Copies of all documents pertaining to the investigation had to be handed over to the suspect on his request, free of charge, and after the completion of the investigation, the investigating magistrate was bound to ask the suspect as to whether he wished to present anything else in his defense. Every measure of suppression taken by the investigating magistrate could be appealed to the court by the suspect.

The investigating magistrate acted under the supervision of the prosecuing body. The prosecutor had the right to be present at all action of the investigating magistrate, who was bound to fulfill all the founded requests of the prosecutor with regard to the investigation of the crime and the collection of evidence. The prosecuting body had to be informed of the arrest of the suspected person by the investigating magistrate, and the prosecuting body could demand, in certain cases, that the arrest should be replaced by another more lenient measure of suppression, and this demand was mandatory for the investigating magistrate.

However, if the investigating magistrate held the arrest of the suspected not necessary and the prosecuting body insisted on the arrest, the investigating magistrate could request the court for a decision over the controversy. This provision of Art. 285 of the Code of Criminal Procedure was an example of the independence of the investigating magistrate from the prosecution.

On the other hand, the prosecutor could require the supplementation of the preliminary investigation in the direction indicated by him, although, according to the investigating magistrate, the investigation was closed.

b) *Under Soviet Power Till 1923*

The tsarist institution of the investigating magistracy was abolished together with the other institutions of the administration of justice by the Decree No. 1 on Courts.

With regard to the preliminary investigation, Art. 3 of the Decree No. 1 on Courts provided that "until the reorganization of the whole system of judicial procedure" the preliminary investigation in criminal cases was to be carried out by local judges individually, but arrest orders and indictments had to be confirmed by the general assembly of the local judges. Evidently, the combining of the jurisdiction of the investigator and the deciding judge in one person was thought to be a temporary measure.

The Decree No. 2 on Courts established an Investigating Commission of three persons appointed by the local Soviets "until direct elections would be set for the preliminary investigation of criminal cases beyond the jurisdiction of the local courts".

With regard to cases under the jurisdiction of the local courts, nothing was changed in the system of the preliminary investigation established by the Decree No. 1 on Courts.

It must be emphasized that counsel was admitted to the preliminary investigation at that time with the exception of cases where the investigation commission thought the presence of counsel to be against the interest of truth finding.

The final decision of the Commission transferring the case to the court was tantamount to the indictment. If the circuit court found the decision not well founded it returned the files to the commission for additional investigation, or charged one of the judges with such an investigation.

Complaints against the decisions of the commission were lodged with the circuit court.

The Decree No. 3 on Courts brought a slight change in the rules concerning the preliminary investigation, namely the preliminary investigation of more important cases still under the jurisdiction of the local courts could be entrusted to the commissions formed by Decree No. 2 on Courts. However, the preliminary investigation in all other cases in the competence of the local courts remained in the hands of individual judges of these courts. The final decision with regard to the direction of the cases investigated by the commission remained with the local courts.

The competence of the investigating commissions were enlarged by the Statute on the People's Court of November 30, 1918. The people's judge replaced the local judge, and the judiciary retained its investigating duties only in cases under the jurisdiction of a bench with one judge and two assessors.

Parallel to the regular investigating institutions, the All-Russian Extraordinary Commission for the Fight Against Counterrevolution and Sabotage, as we have seen above, carried out investigatory functions with regard to specific crimes.

The new Statute on the People's Court of October 21, 1920, introduced important changes in the preliminary investigation. The dual system of investigation by a judge and an investigating commission was abandoned and the position of a special investigating magistrate created.

A.N. Gusev writes that according to the first Decrees on Courts, the preliminary investigation was, as a rule, carired out collectively. He felt that experience suggested that individual investigation proved most workable and sucessful. [1] This is not quite correct.

We have seen that Decree No. 1 on Courts retained the traditional system of an individual investigator as applied also in tsarist Russia. The Decree No. 2 introduced an investigation commission alongside the individual investigation entrusted to the judge in general criminal cases. But the military revolutionary tribunal had individual investigating magistrates already since 1918.

Counsel was excluded from the preliminary investigation by the Statute of 1920.

The Statute on the Court Structure of the RSFSR of November 11, 1922, in force as of January 1, 1923, defined also the structure of the body of investigators called people's investigators. The investigating magistrates did not form a centralized body. They were attached to, a) investigating districts; b) criminal departments of province courts; c) the RSFSR Supreme Court, and d) the Prosecution Department of the People's Commissariat of Justice, in order to carry out urgent investigations in the most important cases.

The investigators of the investigating district were named "People's Investigators". Those attached to provinces were the "Senior Investigators" and those functioning at the RSFSR Supreme Court and the Prosecuting Department of the People's Commissariat of Justice had the title of "Investigators of Most Important Cases".

By a decision of the VTsIK and the RSFSR Council of People's

---

[1] A.N. Gusev, "The Procedural Position of the Investigating Magistrate in Soviet Criminal Procedure" in *Voprosy sudoproizvodstva i sudoustroystva v novom zakonodatel'stve soyuza SSSR*, M. 1959, p. 302.

Commissars of 1928, the investigating magistrates previously attached to the courts were incorporated into the prosecuting body. [1]

Relations of the investigating magistracy with the courts, the prosecuting body, the inquest organs and other authorities were regulated by the old RSFSR Code of Criminal Procedure. [2] This Code also established rules for the conduct of the preliminary investigation.

The investigating activity of the CheKa, the GPU and Special Board have been discussed above.

B. INQUEST AND PRELIMINARY INVESTIGATION
ACCORDING TO THE RSFSR CODES OF CRIMINAL PROCEDURE

a) *The Inquest and its Organs*

The Soviet investigation into a criminal offense is divided by the old and new Codes of Criminal Procedure into two parts : the inquest, and the preliminary investigation.

Article 108 of the old Code of Criminal Procedure enumerated the cases requiring a preliminary investigation and Article 101 defined the competence of the inquest organs in cases where a preliminary investigation is not obligatory.

The inquest differs from the preliminary investigation first of all by the authority carryiing out the two actions.

The inquest was conducted by the militia or some special organs of the GPU, by organs of the Technical Trade and Labor Inspection in cases under their competence and by state agencies and officials with regard to illegal actions of officials subordinated to them (Article 97 of the old Code).

Organs of the inquest in the Armed Forces were commanders of individual units and formations, as well as chiefs of military establishments and institutions.

The new RSFSR Code of Criminal Procedure, in conjunction with Article 29 of the USSR Basic Principles of Criminal Procedures of 1950, increased the number of inquest organs. According to Article 117 of the Code, organs of inquest are : a) the militia; b) commanders

---

[1] *Sob. uz.*, *RSFSR*, 1928, Item 733.

[2] *Sob. uz.*, *RSFSR*, 1922, Item 902 : Here quoted as in the revised edition of February 15, 1923, *ibid.*, 1923, Item 106.

of military units, formations and heads of military institutions with regard to all criminal offenses committed, by military men subordinate to them, as well as by reservists during training meetings; in cases of criminal offenses by workers and employees of the armed forces in connection with the fulfillment of their duties or committed on the area of a unit, formation or institution; c) organs of state security in cases under their jurisdiction; [1] d) heads of correctional work institutions in cases of violation of work regulations by employees of the institution, as well as in cases of crimes committed on the premises of the correctional work institutions; e) organs of state fire supervision in cases of fires and violations of fire-prevention regulations; f) organs of border protection in cases of violations of state borders; g) captains of sea vessels on long voyages and heads of working stations in periods when transportation to the station was lacking.

This enumeration is exhaustive. No other persons or institutions have the right to inquest.

Although the competence of every inquest organ is strictly defined, some of them extend their jurisdiction to all cases of criminal offenses (as for instance the military organs). Others are limited to a certain field such as the fire agencies.

Every member of the agency or institution entrusted with the carrying-out of an inquest may be assigned to the job, whereas the preliminary investigation, as we shall see later, may be conducted only by an investigating magistrate.

The duties of the inquest organs as formulated by Article 118 of the Code of Criminal Procedure is the taking of operational investigation and all other measures provided by the Code of Criminal Procedure in order to discover crimes and their perpetrators.

These organs are also charged with the taking of apppropriate measures for the prevention and suppression of crimes.

The law enumrates the ways in which the inquest organs (also the investigating magistrate and the prosecution) aid the court establishing the commission of a crime; 1) oral and written declarations of citizens; 2) statements by trade-unions and Komsomal organizations, people's brigades for the preservation of public order, comrade's

---

[1] The inquest in cases under the jurisdiction of state security may be entrusted to any organ of state security, whereas the preliminary investigation may be conducted only by an investigating magistrate of the organs of state security in cases under their competence.

courts and other public organizations; 3) statements by institutions, enterprises, organizations and officials; 4) articles, notes and letters published by the press; 5) surrendering of perpetrators; 6) the direct discovery of signs of a crime by inquest organs, the investigating magistrates, prosecutors or courts.

However, a criminal case may be opened only if sufficient evidence pointing to signs of an existing crime is discovered.

The opening of a criminal case does not require the complete certainty of a committed crime, which may be achieved in the further stages of the inquest or preliminary investigation.

What evidence is "sufficient" for the opening of a criminal case is not defined by law. According to the Scientific-Practical Commentary to the RSFSR Code of Criminal Procedure "Evidence is sufficient for the opening of a criminal case if, according to its character, it indicates a concrete penal action or inaction". [1]

The law obliges the prosecutor, the investigating magistrate, the inquest organ and the judge to accept statements and communications about any crime committed or in preparation and take measures concerning them not later than after three days from the reicept of the statement or communication and, in exceptional cases, not later than after ten days.

In connection with any statement or communication recieved, additional information and material may be requested, but without initiation of the investigative actions provided by the Code of Criminal Procedure.

Once in possession of the statement or communication, and of the additional material, one of the three following decisions must be taken : 1) the opening of a criminal case; 2) denial of the opening of a criminal case; or 3) reference of the statement or communication to the competent inquest organ, investigating magistrate or court.

A criminal case may not be opened and an open case quashed if : 1) no crime has been committed; 2) no corpus delicti has been established; 3) the action is under prescription; 4) the action falls under amnesty, eliminating the application of punishment for the action or pardoning individual persons; 5) the action is committed by persons who, at the time of the action, did not yet reach the age at which criminal responsibility is admissible according to law.

---

[1] *Nauchno-prakticheskiy kommentariy..., op. cit.*, p. 241.

The activity of the inquest differs concerning the question whether or not the committed crime legally requires a preliminary investigation.

Thus, if the inquest organ discovers a crime or is informed of it in cases where the law prescribes a preliminary investigation, the organs open a criminal case and performs the necessary and urgent investigative actions in conformity with the provisions of the law of criminal procedure, in order to establish and consolidate the indices of the crime : by inspection, security measures, seizures, examinations, arrests and interrogations of the suspects, victims and witnesses.

The organ of inquest has to inform the prosecutor without any delay of the discovery of the crime and the initiation of the inquest.

After the urgent investigative actions are completed the inquest organ must transfer the case to the investigating magistrate without waiting for the directives of the prosecutor and the expiration of the term of ten days for the completion of the inquest prescribed by Art. 121 of the Code of Criminal Procedure, if a preliminary investigation is mandatory in the case.

After the case has been transferred to the investigating magistrate, organs of the inquest must carry out investigative actions only on request of the investigating magistrate.

If a case was transferred to the investigating magistrate by an organ of inquest in which the inquest has not succeeded in discovering the culprit of the crime, the organs continue to take investigative measures for the establishment of the perpetrators. They must inform the investigating magistrate of the results of their actions (Art. 119).

It must be assumed that the actions to be taken by the inquest organs are enumerated exhaustively in Art. 119, so that they are not empowered to take other measures, as for instance, to inlist the services of an expert. [1]

In cases not requiring a preliminary investigation, the inquest organs institute criminal proceedings and take all the measures provided by the law of criminal procedure for the establishment of circumstances to be proved in the criminal case.

In carrying out the inquest in cases not requiring a mandatory preliminary investigation the inquest organ has to follow the rules for the preliminary investigation provided by the Code of Criminal

---

[1]   *Nauchno-prakticheskiy kommentariy, op. cit.*, p. 261.

Procedure with the following exceptions : 1) there is no participation of defense counsel in the inquest; 2) although the victim, the civil plaintiff, the civil defendant and their representatives must be informed of the completion of the inquests and the transfer of the case to the prosecutor, the materials of the inquest are not presented to them for examination; 3) the provision of Art. 127 [1] of the Code of Criminal Procedure is not applied to the inquest organs. If the inquest organ disagrees with the instructions of the prosecutor he has the right to appeal to a higher prosecuting instance while not stopping the execution of the given instructions.

Shafir is certainly right when he asserts that no difference in principle exists between the inquest and the preliminary investigation and that there is no ground to completely exclude the defense from the inquest. [2]

The material collected by the inquest in cases not requiring a preliminary investigation form the basis for the examination in court. The inquest organs have one month to complete this kind of inquest.

When the inquest is completed, the inquest organ has to decide whether to quash the case or issue an accusatory resolution. Both decisions must be presented to the prosecutor.

There is also a possibility to suspend the inquest : 1) if the accused has fled or his residence cannot be established for some other reasons; 2) in case when a mental or other serious disease of the accused is certified by a physician working in a medical institution; 3) when the identity of the person to be accused is not established (Article 124 in conjunction with Article 195).

b) *The Preliminary Investigation and the Investigating Magistracy*

The official charged with the preliminary investigation is the investigating magistrate. Only he has the right to carry out preliminary investigations.

There are several kinds of investigating magistrates.

The investigating magistrates of the prosecuting body are inte-

---

[1] Article 127 provides that if the investigating magistrate does not agree with the directive of the prosecutor he has the right to appeal to a higher prosecuting instance. The decision of the prosecutor is then reversed or another investigating magistrate assigned to the case.

[2] G.M. Shafir, "The Right to Defense in the Soviet Criminal Procedure and the Possibility of its Widening", *S.G.P.*, 1967, No. 2, p. 47.

grated into this body by Article 50 of the Statute on Prosecution Supervision in the USSR of 1955 which provided that the Investigating Magistrates for Especially Important Cases are attached to the USSR General Prosecutor and the Prosecutors of the Union Republics. Senior investigating magistrates function at prosecuting bodies of the autonomous republics, territories, regions and autonomous regions.

The circuit, city and district prosecuting bodies have senior investigating magistrates. There are also investigating magistrates appointed and attached to the military prosecutors. A special investigation magistracy functions at the organs of state security.

As in the case of the prosecutors, the investigating magistrates must be in possession of a higher legal education. However, persons without higher legal education may be appointed to positions of investigating magistrates in special cases only with the permission of the USSR General Prosecutor.

Graduates of institutions of higher legal learning may be appointed to investigating magistrate's positions only after the completion of one year of probation in the capacity of an investigating magistrate of a district (city) prosecuting body or an assistant to a district (city) prosecutor.

On August 30, 1962, an Ukase of the Presidium of the RSFSR Supreme Soviet [1] renamed the Ministry of Internal Affairs into the Ministry for the Protection of Public Order and on April 6, 1963, the Presidium of the USSR Supreme Soviet passed an Ukase [2] on the Granting of Rights of Preliminary Investigation to organs of the Ministries for the Protection of Public Order at the Union Republics.

In the Ukase of 1962 it was said that parallel to the investigating magistrates of the prosecuting body and state security, the preliminary investigation is carried out also by organs for the protection of public order. The investigating magistrates of the organs for the protection of public order are guided in their work by norms of the criminal procedural legislation provided for preliminary investigation.

Thus, parallel to the investigating magistrates of the prosecuting body and of the organs of state security, a third body of investigating magistrates, that is of the Ministries for the Protection of Public Order, was created.

---

[1] V.V.S., RSFSR, 1962, Item 535.
[2] V.V.S., SSSR, 1963, Item 181.

It must be said that already in 1957, at the time when the coming legal legislation was discussed in the press, voices for the unification of the inquiry and the preliminary investigation in one body were raised.

Thus, for instance, M.V. Barsukov, reported on an opinion that, considering the increased level of juridical knowledge of the militia members, the preliminary investigation should be concentrated in the hands of this institution. Barsukov himself objected against the order putting the preliminary investigation under the jurisdiction of the prosecuting body. He thought that two reasons speak against this order : firstly, the prosecutor, in guiding the preliminary investigation, i.e., being responsible for it, loses the necessary independence as an organ exercising the supervision over the investigation ; secondly, appearing in court and maintaining the accusation in the trial, the prosecutor who guided the investigation is in such a degree bound by its qualities and defects, that "it must be doubted as to whether he may claim the necessary objectivity and courage in his conclusions including, let us say, the dropping of the accusation in case of the lack of necessary evidence".

Hence, Barsukov thought that the prosecuting body may exercise its functions of supervision over the preliminary investigation in the best way only when the investigation magistracy is separated from the prosecuting body. [1]

On the other hand, the Deputy to the USSR Supreme Soviet, G.K. Pusepa, recommended that the investigation be unified in the hands of a single investigating organ, abolishing the parallel work of the investigating organs of the prosecuting body and the militia. [2]

I.D. Perlov and M. Yu. Raginsky also came to the conclusion regarding the necessity of the creation of a single investigating apparatus for the carrying out the preliminary investigation in all criminal cases, except those investigated by the Committee of State Security, and the establishment of a single order for the investigation in all cases under a single procedural regime. [3]

---

[1] M.V. Barsukov, "For the Further Perfection of Militias' Organization and Activity", *S.G.P.*, 1957, No. 2, p. 42.

[2] *Pravda*, Feb. 11, 1957. In the Union Republics of Uzbek and Turkmen, the inquiry and preliminary investigations are united in one investigation procedure.

[3] I.D. Perlov and M. Yu. Roginsky, "The Ripe Questions of Inquest and Preliminary Investigations", *S.G.P.*, 1957, No. 4, p. 119.

It must be said that neither the Basic Principles of Court Structure of the USSR and the Union Republic of 1958, nor the new Codes of Criminal Procedure took into account the unification suggestions. The New Codes of Criminal Procedure of the Union Republics retain the old order of inquest and preliminary investigation according to the crime committed. On the contrary, the USSR law of 1963 created a new investigating body in the place of unification : the investigation magistracy of the Ministry for the Protection of Public Order.

The Law itself conferred only equal rights with the investigating magistracy of the prosecuting body to the investigating magistracy of the organs for the protection of public order. A delimination of the competence of the two magistracies was not given in the law.

The creation of a new investigation body made it necessary to amend the Code of Criminal Procedure of the Union Republics. This was carried out in the RSFSR by the Ukases of April 15, 1963 [1] and December 14, 1965. [2]

With regard to the delimitation of competence between the various bodies of investigating magistrates no clear-cut provisions were established by the Ukases; however, both extended the competence of the investigating magistrate of the organs for the protection of public order. In the following, the law of 1965 will be discussed in detail as far as it establishes the competence of the new body of investigation magistrates.

The law of April 15, 1963 assigned to the competence of the investigating magistrates of the organs for the protection of public order cases discovered by the militia in the process of its inquesting operations and during the carrying out of its functions of protecting the public order. The jurisdiction of the investigating magistrates of the prosecuting body extended to more important offenses such as crimes committed in office, economic and especially grave crimes, as well as to offences committed by minors.

Still the delimitation between the competence of both the investigation bodies proved inadequate in practice, as K.I. Nikitin, [3] Section Chief in the Department of Administrative Organs of the Central Committee of the USSR Communist Party, asserts.

---

[1] *V.V.S., RSFSR*, 1963, Item 288.

[2] *Sov. yust.*, 1966, No. 3, pp. 29-30.

[3] K.I. Nikitin, "On the Further Perfection of the Investigation Apparatus Activity", *S.G.P.*, 1966, No. 4, pp. 27-28.

According to him, the most frequent conflict of jurisdictions happened in cases of misappropriation of state property. This is for the reason that the RSFSR Code of Criminal Procedure provides that in every case where misappropriation of state property is investigated by organs for the protection of public order, the participation in the crime of even one person who is in office necessitates the transfer of the case for investigation to the investigation magistrates of the prosecuting body. The same is true if during the investigation it was established that the misappropriation was made on an especially large scale or the case was instigated not as a result of investigative operations of the militia, but in consequence of audit materials or other official documents.

It happened often that the legal reasons for the transfer of the preliminary investigation were established in the end of a prolonged investigation by the investigation magistrate of the organs for the protection of public order, but the investigating magistrate of the prosecuting body, after the case was transferred to him, had to repeat the investigating actions from the beginning.

c) *The Law of December 14, 1965*

The law of December 14, 1965 was a further attempt toward the elimination of the conflict in the jurisdiction of the different investigating bodies. In respect to competence delimitation, Article 126 of the RSFSR Code of Criminal Procedure provided that the preliminary investigation of most important cases, such as economic crimes and crimes committed in office, are investigated, besides in the investigating magistracy of the prosecuting body, *also* [1] by investigating magistrates of the organs of state security.

> All cases of crimes perpetrated by minors are carried out by investigating magistrates of the prosecuting body, whereas in cases of crimes provided by Articles 64-70 of the RSFSR Criminal Code (treason against the fatherland, espionage, terroristic activity, terroristic actions against a representative of a foreign country, destruction of state buildings, railroads, etc., sabotage, anti-soviet agitation or propaganda), etc. are investigated, besides in the investigating magistracy of the prosecuting body, *also* [2] by investigating magistrates of the organs of state security.

Furthermore, the law provides that in cases of violations of Articles 88 (violation of rules of currency operation), 92 (misappropriation

---

[1] Italics provided.
[2] Italics provided.

of state or public property committed by appropriation or embezzlement, or by misuse of an official position) and 93 (misappropriation of state property of an especially big size) of the RSFSR Criminal Code, the preliminary investigation is carried out by the organ which instigated the criminal proceeding. If during the investigation of such cases, crimes committed in office (Articles 170-175 of the Criminal Code and under the investigation jurisdiction of the prosecuting body) related to the crimes under investigation are discovered, they continue to be investigated by the same organ. Thus, an exception to the exclusive competence of the magistrate of the prosecuting body in favor of the organs for the protection of public order was created and the transfer of such cases eliminated.

Finally, according to the same law, in cases of crimes provided by Articles 88[1] (failure to provide information of a state crime), 88[2] (concealment of state crimes), 181-185 (giving false testimony; refusal or evasion of a witness or the victim to testify or of an expert of presenting his conclusions; the inducement of a witness or the victim to fail to give testimony or of the expert to present his conclusions or the bribing of these persons), 184 (the divulgation of data of the preliminary investigation or the inquest), 185 (embezzlement, alienation or concealment of property under distraint or arrest), 189 (concealement of crimes), 190 (failure to give information of crimes)—of the RSFSR Criminal Code, the preliminary investigation is carried out by the organs to whose investigation jurisdiction the crime belongs.

A new provision (Article 127[1]) has been introduced into the RSFSR Code of Criminal Procedure which regulates the competence of the chief of investigating department of the organs for the protection of the public order. This official is supposed to control the timeliness of the investigating magistrate's actions, take measures for the most complete all-sided and objective carrying out of the preliminary investigation.

He has the right to check the criminal cases, give instructions to the investigating magistrate connected with the preliminary investigation as to the arraignment of the suspect, qualification of the crime and the extent of the accusation, the direction of the case, the carrying out of individual investigation actions, transfer the case from one investigating magistrate to another, assign the investigation of the case to several magistrates, as well as participate in the preliminary investigation in person, enjoying the rights of an investigating magistrate.

However, he may not reverse decisions of the investigating magistrate. This right belongs only to the prosecutors, according to Article 19 of the USSR Statute on the Prosecutorial Supervision of 1955.

Instructions of the chief of the investigating department are given in writing and are binding on the investigation magistrate.

The investigating magistrate has the right to complain to the prosecutor against the instructions of the chief of the investigating department; his complaint, however, does not suspend the execution of the instructions.

On the other hand, the chief of the investigating department has to submit to the instructions of the prosecutor given in conformity with the Code of Criminal Procedure, and his complaint to a higher prosecutor does not suspend the execution of instructions received from the prosecutor.

In this way, the prosecuting body retained its supervision position over the preliminary investigation in charge of both kinds of investigating magistrates.

The creation of a new body of investigating magistrates seems not to have improved the quality of the preliminary investigations and the work of the investigating magistrates. An editorial of *Sotsialisticheskaya zakonnost'* [1] remarks that the work of the investigating apparatus has many defects; many dangerous crimes remain undiscovered and the criminals unpunished; because of the poor quality of the investigation, it becomes unduly prolonged in many criminal cases; a great number of cases are remanded by prosecutors and courts for an additional investigation; the organs of preliminary investigation have not overcome violations of socialist legality.

The analysis of the practice brings the editorial to the conclusion that the activity of the investigating magistrates of the organs for the protection of the public order show essential defects. In many cases the investigating magistrates of this body do not investigate systematically, do not work intensively in the beginning, do not appoint experts in the proper time; the chiefs of the investigation department do not adequately guide the work of their subordinates; up to the present time, cases occur where organs for the protection of the public order do not initiate investigation of cases of theft, open theft and other dangerous crimes at the proper time, prevent,

---

[1] 1966, No. 4, p. 9.

without proper reasons, criminal proceedings from getting started, quash groundlessly unresolved cases.

The causes of this situation the editorial sees in the poor professional qualification of many investigating magistrates, inadequate level of guidance and help extended to them by the USSR prosecuting body, prosecutors and ministries for the protection of public order of Union Republics, as well as a weak supervision over the unflinching observance of legality during crime investigation.

N. Zhogin, Deputy of the General Prosecutor of the USSR, recommends that in connection with the organization of an investigation magistracy of the Ministries of Public Order Protection, new forms of interaction between the investigation magistrates of the prosecution body and their colleagues from the Ministry of Public Order Protection should be established. According to him, this interaction must take place in the form of organization of brigades for the common investigation of the most complicated cases, and the delimination of districts in which both kinds of magistrates have to investigate, to the limits of their respective competence, law violations and develop measures for their prevention. [1]

Evidently prompted by such defects, the Central Committee of the Soviet Communist Party and the Council of Ministries of the USSR passed a resolution "On measures for the Improvement of the Work of the Investigating Apparatus of the Organs of the Prosecuting Body and the Public Order Protection", on December 10, 1965. [2]

The Resolution identifies the main task of members of the investigating apparatus in the speedy and complete disclosure of each crime and the timely bringing of the culprits to a legal accounting; the investigating magistrate is strictly obliged to be guided by Lenin's principle that "not a single crime should remain undisclosed"; the investigating magistrate must observe socialist legality and actively contribute to the discovery and elimination of causes generating violations of laws.

In the first place the Resolution deemed it necessary to improve the professional training of the investigating magistrates. To this

---

[1] N. Zhogin, "The Investigating Magistrate and the Preliminary Investigation", *Izvestia*, September 20, 1964.

[2] The full text of the Resolution is not available in the United States. Identical official abstracts of the Resolution have been published in *S.G.P.*, 1966, No. 4, p. 20; *Sob. zak.*, 1966, No. 3, p. 2 and *Izvestia*, February 19, 1966.

effect the creation of an Institute for the Perfection of Investigating Magistrates, pertaining to the prosecuting body and the organs for the protection of public order and the increase of the number of students to be admitted to the Sverdlovsk, Khar'kov and Saratov Legal Institutes was decided upon. Also the quality of the retraining of investigating magistrates work be improved and the education through coorespondence and at evening courses effectively used; the experience of the best investigating magistrates was to be generalized and persistently dissiminated.

The Resolution pays attention to the creation of necessary conditions for the successful fulfillment of their duties by investigating magistrates; the salaries of individual categories of investigating magistrates was to be put in good order, the most distinguished of them encouraged.

It expects an improvement of the investigating work from the use of better technical equipment by the investigating organs and the inculcation of sceintific methods of crime investigation into the investigation practice, as well as the improvement of the organs of forensic expert work and the methodical guidance of criminalistic expert institutions.

The Resolution also requests Party and Soviet organizations, the USSR Prosecuting Body, the Ministries for the Protection of Public Order of the Union Republics to improve the investigating apparatus' activity and the political education of the investigating magistrates, to pay more attention to the professional skill of the investigating staff, to regulate their appointment and discharge; the prosecuting organs must increase their supervision activity during the investigation of criminal cases in order that no law violator may escape legal punishment and that no citizen be made answerable to it without sufficient reason.

It follows from the Resolution that deficiencies in the investigating work are largely attributed by the administration to the lack of professional training of the investigating magistrates; this is es pecially true of the new magistrates of the organs for the portection of public order. [1]

Certainly, the new Institute in Leningrad and the increasing number of students admitted to legal education in Sverdlovsk, Khar'kov

---

[1] Nikitin, *op. cit.*, p. 23 reports that about 50 % of them have no higher juridical education and in the same condition also are some investigating magistrates of the prosecuting body.

and Saratov [1] will be of help for the improvement of the professional training of the investigating magistrates. It is, however, more effective not to admit, in general, persons without higher legal education to positions of professional judges, prosecutors, investigating magistrates or lawyers, i.e., of persons directly involved in the meting out of justice, rather than to make them train and retrain when they are already performing their functions to the detriment of their cocitizens.

Rakhunov remarked that the evaluation of the work of an investigating magistrate depends upon the average number of cases the investigating magistrate completes and presents to the court. The more cases, the better the magistrate. The cases quashed by him because of lack of evidence are not taken into consideration. [2]

It is evident that this system contributes to the striving of the magistrate to accumulate as much accusing material as possible without regard to its value.

Thus, such a system is detrimental to justice.

Rakhunov also emphasizes that the fight for the observation of legality regarding the investigative organs requires the decisive realization in practice of the presumption of innocence. "The assumption of innocence is not a factor in the USSR, but the expression of legality in criminal procedure and the guarantee of an objective and all-sided examination of the case. In practice it means that conviction can take place only if the accusatory evidence is complete and absolute. Every doubt must be interpreted to the advantage of the accused". [3]

The structural complexity of the investigating organs, the division of their work between three different investigating bodies and the militia, producing overlapping competence, conflicts and unnecessary protraction cannot evidently contribute to the improvement of the preliminary investigation and the inquest.

It is peculiar that the laws of 1963 and 1965 extended greatly the competence of the investigating organs of the Ministries for the Protection of Public Order, which are the least prepared for such activities.

---

[1] Their number will be doubled during the next five years.

[2] R.D. Rakhunov, "Soviet Justice and its Role in the Strengthening of Legality", *Kommunist*, 1956, No. 7, pp. 48-49.

[3] *Ibid.*, pp. 46-47. That the investigative organs do not share Rakhunov's opinion sometimes, even after the publication of the new Codes of Criminal Procedure, is made evident in the Filimonov case. See below, pp. 441-446.

C. Rights and Duties of the Investigating Magistrate

The investigating magistrate carries out the preliminary investigation independently and with full responsibility, with the exception of cases when he is bound by law to request the sanction of the prosecutor.

If the investigating magistrate does not agree with the instructions of the prosecutor concerning the arraignment, the qualification of the crime and the extent of the accusation, the direction of the case to the court for indictment or the quashing of the case, he has the right to submit the case to a prosecutor in a higher echelon with a written statement of his objections. In this case the prosecutor reverses the instructions of the posecutor subordinate to him, or refers the case to another investigating magistrate.

It must be emphasized that the investigating magistrate's right of appeal is limited to the instructions of the prosecutor involving the subjects enumerated above. Although he may appeal also other instructions of the prosecutor, his appeal does not suspend the fulfillment of the instructions.

The exception from the obligation of the investigating magistrate to follow all the instructions of the porsecutor supervising the case is an important extension of the investigating magistrate's independence, accorded by the Basic Principles of Criminal Procedure and unknown to previous legislation.

Complaints about any action of the investigating magistrate can be filed with the prosecutor by the accused and other persons involved in the investigation, within seven days after the action becomes known to the complainant, but complaints against the measure of suppression, the slowness of the investigation or illegal actions of the investigating magistrate may be lodged any time. The prosecutor has three days for a decision on the complaint, but the appealed action of the investigating magistrate is not suspended during this time.

Resolutions of the investigating magistrate taken in conformity with law in criminal cases are subject to mandatory fulfillment by all institutions, enterprises, organizations, officials and citizens. He has the right to arrest and interrogate the person suspected of committing the crime.

However, the law prescribes definite rules for the arrest of the suspect. The investigating magistrate and the organ of inquest may arrest the suspect when the punishment to be expected for the crime consists in deprivation of liberty and only in the presence of one of the following reasons : 1) the suspect has been caught during the completion of a crime or immediately thereafter; 2) eye-witnesses or the victim points to the person as the perpetrator of the crime; 3) obvious signs of the crime are discovered on the person, his clothes or in his apartment.

The existence of other reasons vindicating the assumption that the suspect is the perpetrator of the crime may lead to his arrest only if he attempts to escape or has no steady residence, or his person cannot be identified.

The investigating magistrate has to notify the prosecutor within 24 hours of every arrest of a person suspected of having committed a crime. The prosecutor, on his part, has to sanction the arrest or set the suspect at liberty within 48 hour after the reception of the notification of the arrest.

D. Procedure of the Preliminary Investigation

a) *First Part*

The preliminary investigation begins immediately after the opening of the criminal case which is done by the investigating magistrate himself or by the organ of inquest who referred the case to him for a mandatory preliminary investigation. The rules for the opening of a criminal case are the same as quoted above.

The preliminary investigation is divided into two parts.

In the first part evidence is collected. This action is started by the inquest or the investigating magistrate.

A peculiarity of the RSFSR Code of Criminal Procedure is the provision obliging the investigating magistrate to make extensive use of public help for the identification of the crime and the discovery of its perpetrators as well as for the establishment and removal of causes and conditions contributing to the commission of the crime (Art. 128).

Undoubtedly, the provision of Art. 128 is an expression of the general tendency to attract the public as much as possible into all phases of the process of administration of justice, required by Lenin and reflected in such institutions as comrade's courts, neighbors' court, people's assessors, public prosecutors and defenders.

Certainly, public help may be very useful in the preliminary investigation. It may take the form of information about planned or committed crimes, the identification of victims, witnesses, the finding of a corpus delicti and other material evidence, as well as the apprehending of persons involved in the crime.

The attraction of the public into the participation in the discovery of the crime is not only an effective means for betterment of the quality of investigations, the improvement of the fight against criminality, but according to diverse writers also a means to heighten the educational role of court proceedings and the education of citizens in a spirit of an uncompromising attitude towards law violators. [1]

If enough evidence is collected in order to justify the accusation in a criminal action the investigating magistrate takes resolution substantiated by reasons, arraigning the suspected person in the capacity of an accused.

The arraignment-accusatory resolution—*obvinitel'noye zaklyucheniye*—has to take place after an evaluation of the whole body of facts and evidence already collected. The resolution ends the first part of the preliminary investigation which is not yet completed. The arraignment signifies only that, according to the conviction of the investigating magistrate, there is enough evidence to involve the definite person in the criminal case in the capacity of an accused.

The resolution of the investigating magistrate must be made known to the accused who is summoned to the office of the investigating magistrate if he is at liberty, or brought there if he is in jail. An accused who without legal reason ignores the summons is brought to the office forcibly.

The investigating magistrate declares his resolution to the accused and explains to him the essence of the accusation. In doing so the investigating magistrate is bound to explain to the accused his rights during the preliminary investigation. [2] The presentation of the accusation must be carried out not later than 48 hours after the arraignment resolution has been taken by the investigating magistrate.

If the arraigned person is an official [3] the investigating magistrate

---

[1] *Nauchno-prakticheskiy kommentariy...*, op. cit., p. 277.

[2] These rights are (Art. 46) to know of what he is accused and give explanations connected with the accusation; to submit evidence; to present requests; to get acquainted with all the materials of the preliminary investigation after it is completed and to have a defense counsel at that time.

[3] According to the note to Art. 170 of the RSFSR Criminal Code, an official is a person who steadily or temporarily fulfills the functions of a representative of the authority or occupies steadily or temporarily, a position in state or public institutions,

has the right to suspend him from carrying out his duties. The suspension takes place by a resolution substantiated with reason of the investigating magistrate which must be confirmed by the prosecutor, in order to be valid. [1]

The investigating magistrate must interrogate the accused in his capacity as such immediately after the communication of the arraignment resolution : before the resolution the suspect is questioned as a witness.

The law established definite rules for the questioning of the accused by the investigating magistrate. It forbids the interrogation during night time, [2] with the exception of cases which cannot be postponed. The questioning must be carried-out at the place of the preliminary investigation, but the investigating magistrate has the right to question the accused at the place of his residence.

At the beginning of the interrogation the investigating magistrate must ask the accused, as to whether he pleads guilty with regard to the accusation and then request the accused to testify about the essence of the accusation. The investigating magistrate listens to the deposition of the accused and then, if necessary, puts questions to him.

Commenting on the rules of interrogation the Scientific Practical Commentar to the RSFSR Code of Criminal Procedure emphasizes that "absolutely inadmissible are 'methods' based on the use of violence, threats, false promises, unfounded arrest etc". [3]

The old Code of Criminal Procedure also provided that the investigating magistrate has not the right to obtain statements or confession of the accused by means of coercion, threat and other similar measures. (Article 136).

And the old Criminal Code (Article 115) punished the illegal arrest or bringing up of a person, by deprivation of liberty for a term of up to one year, wheras the compulsion to provide evidence by illegal measure on the part of the interrogating person—up to five years.

---

organs, or enterprises, connected with carrying out of organizational, executive or administrative-economic duties, or fulfilling such duties in the institution, organ, or enterprise mentioned above in virtue of a special authorization. Thus, workers, employees, kolkhozniks, who do not fulfill such duties or functions of representatives of authority, cannot be suspended by the investigating magistrate.

[1] This resolution may be appealed by the accused, his counsel or the agency employing him to the prosecutor who confirmed the resolution or to a higher prosecutor.

[2] Night time is, according to Article 34[15] of the RSFSR Code of Criminal Procedure, between 10 pm. and 6 am. local time.

[3] *Nauchno-prakticheskiy kommentariy...*, *op. cit.*, p. 306.

What was considered as "illegal measures of coercion" is explained in the Commentary to the Criminal Code (Edition of 1927) as follows : "Such illegal measures are threats and every kind of oppression, all kinds of contrivances, such as promises, indulgences and the slackening of the strictness of the jail regime, etc.

However, if the organ conducting the investigation resorts to physical coercion, and particularly—to torture, he is responsible for exceeding his authority coupled with violance and is subject to the punishment provided by Article 110 of the Code. [1]

But in spite of these provisions, rules of interrogation were flagrantly violated in many thousands of cases during the "cult of personality" which is no longer a secret.

It may be assumed that they are being better observed after Stalin's death.

b) *Second Part*

Let us return to the investigating procedure. The questioning of the accused may be referred to organs of inquest by the investigating magistrate.

After the arraignment is pronounced the preliminary investigation is continued in its second part. The investigating magistrate collects additional evidence, interrogates the accused and wtinesses, if necessary, or other experts, and so on, until he becomes completely convinced of the guilt of the accused and proceeds to the final act of the preliminary investigation : the accusatory conclusion or, if according to his opinion, the accused is innocent, the quashing of the procedure.

When the investigating magistrate deems the preliminary investigation completed and the collected evidence sufficient for the formulation of an accusatory conclusion, he has to inform the victim about it, the civil plaintiff and the civil defendent or their representatives and to explain to them at the same time that they have the right to get acquainted with the material of the case (the civil defendent only with that part of the material concerning the civil claim against him).

The persons enumerated above have the right to present requests for additional investigating actions. If the investigating magistrate rejects their request in part or totally he has to take a written resolu-

---

[1] Article 110[2] provided a punishment of six months of strict isolation, which could be increased up to the death penalty in exclusive cases.

tion to this effect and inform the person who presented the request about the resolution, which can be appealed to the prosecutor.

The next step to be taken by the investigating magistrate is to notify the accused that the preliminary investigation in his case is completed and that he has the right to get acquainted with the entire file personally or with the help of counsel, as well as to present requests about the supplementation of the preliminary investigation.

If the accused has not expressed the desire for counsel, all the materials of the case are submitted to him. If he requests to participate with his counsel in getting acquainted with the material, and also if a defense counsel particpates in the case already from the time of the arraignment [1] the investigating magistrate has to present the entire material to the accused and his counsel. The presentation has to be postponed until the arrival of counsel but not longer than five days. If the counsel elected by the accused is prevented from showing up within the five days, the investigating magistrate has to take measures for calling upon another counsel. On request of the accused, the investigating magistrate has the right to make the files seperately accessible to the accused and his counsel.

If several accused are involved in the case, all the materials are submitted to every one of the accused.

The accused and his counsel have the right to submit oral and written requests for the supplementation of the preliminary investigation. [2]

If the investigating magistrate rejects the request in part or totally, he has to take a written resolution substantiated by reasons to this effect which may be appealed to the prosecutor.

After the completion of the supplemental actions, the investigating magistrate has to present again all the materials of the case to the accused and his counsel.

The law prescribes that the accusatory conclusions of the investigating magistrate should have a descriptive and a conclusive part. In the descriptive part, the investigating magistrate has to depict the essense of the case : the place and time of the crime by which means it was committed, its reasons and motives, consequences and other

---

[1] It must be recalled that the defense counsel may formally participate in the preliminary investigation only from the time when the completion of the preliminary investigation has been signified to the accused, with the exception of some cases.

[2] For the rights of the defense counsel during the preliminary investigation, See pp. 587-592.

essential cricumstances; information about the victim; the evidence which confirms the commission of a crime and the culpability of the accused; circumstances which aggravate or attenuate his responsibility; arguments brought forward by the accused for his defense and the results of the checking of these arguments ...

In the conclusive part information about the person of the accused are given and the presented accusation formulated with reference to the appropriate articles of the Criminal Code providing for the given crime.

With the signing of the accusatory resolution, the preliminary investigation on the part of the investigating magistrate is completed :[1] he has to submit his files to the prosecutor immediately.

The legal term for the completion of the preliminary investigation is not longer than two months. This period of time counts from the opening of the case until the submitting of the investigation material to the prosecutor, or the suspension or quashing of the case.

The period of two months may be, however, extended but not longer than for another two months by the prosecutors of an autonomous republic, territory, region, autonomous region and national district, the military prosecutors of a military district and the navy. Another extension of the term may be granted only by the Prosecutor of the RSFSR, the Chief Military Prosecutor or the Chief Prosecutor of the USSR, in exceptional cases.

If the case is returned for a supplementary investigation by the court, or the preliminary investigation previously suspended or quashed is continued, the term for the completion of the investigation is set by the prosecutor in charge of the supervision of the case within the limit of one month after the re-opening of the procedure. A still further extension takes place according to the general rule given above.

If an extension of legal term is needed, the investigating magistrate has to take a resolution to this effect substantiated with reasons and submit it to the corresponding prosecutor prior to the lapsing of the legal term.

A preliminary investigation may be suspended under the same provision as the inquest.

---

[1] If the prosecutor or the courts do not require a supplementation of the preliminary investigation, which also can be entrusted to another investigating magistrate.

c) *Extent and Thoroughness*

With regard to the extent and thoroughness of the preliminary investigation, Vyshinsky thought that not the same scale of investigation should be applied to every case.

Vyshinsky repudiated both viewpoints on the scope of the preliminary investigation emitted in the theory of the criminal procedure: one demands, namely, the court investigation to check the results of the preliminary investigation from the beginning to the end. This means that the preliminary investigation is bound to exhaust all the material of the case and the court investigation to check and take a decision or pass a sentence on confirming the results of the checking.

The other theory charges the investigating magistrate only with the answer to its basic question, as to whether the collected evidence permits the presentation of the accusation to the accused, and, consequently, the preliminary investigation and the court investigation are not two independent procedures related one to the other by the controlling functions of the court, but the preliminary investigation is just a "preliminary" action which establishes only the basic questions the detailed working out of which is not in the competence of the preliminary investigation and is, and must be, performed during the trial.

According to Vyshinsky not every case requires the same detailed preliminary investigation. All depends on the character of the case. A thorough and exhaustive investigation is necesaary in political cases. "In such a case [1] all possibility must be used in order to prove the guilt of every accused and of all of them collectively, the responsibility of every one for all and the responsibility of all for every one".

But in many cases, it suffices, when the investigating magistrate "raises the most important questions only in order that the rest should be worked out in court. [2] The court investigation is not the repetition of the preliminary investigation, not simply the checking of that which was established by the preliminary investigation. The court investigation — according to Vyshinsky — is a creative process during

---

[1] Vyshinsky has in mind the case of the Anti-soviet Trotskivite Center in which allegedly "The enemy of the people Trotsky and the Trotskivite Center traded parts of our fatherland : Sokol'nikov promised *Primor'ye* and *Priamur'ye* to Japan and Radek the Ukraine to Germany". The 17 persons on trial were accused of organization of terroristic acts, sabotage, especially dangerous crimes against the state (*diversiya*), or in connection with some representatives of foreign countries.

[2] Vyshinsky, "For the High Quality of Work", *Sots. zak.*, 1957, No. 2, p. 50.

which one can very often raise a series of new questions, even not noticed in the course of the preliminary investigation". [1]

It is evident that a difference in the thoroughness and extension of the preliminary investigation in political and other cases violates the principle of the preliminary and court investigations.

The investigation magistrate is bound to investigate all the circumstances important for the case, without distinction to its political or general character. He has to do it completely, objectively and thoroughly. If he comes to the conclusion of trustworthiness of the accusatory material collected by him, and formulates the accusatory conclusions which he presents to the prosecuting body for confirmation and direction to court, he must describe the facts established by him concretely and clearly, and give the evidence, confirmating the facts.

Every assertion must follow from the material and be confirmed by them. His conclusions are not "the raising of questions" to be answered by the court investigation.

Certainly, the court investigation is not a bare repetition and checking of the preliminary investigation. New evidence and new circumstances can be presented. But if the court cannot check them during the trial, it returns the case to the investigation magistrate for an additional investigation. Indeed, the accusatory conclusions of the investigating magistrate are only suggestions which the court can accept or reject. But these suggestions are the basis for the investigation carried out by the court and must be as conscientious and well-founded as possible without difference as to whether they are presented in a political or in an general criminal case.

d) *Does the Investigating Magistrate Fulfill Accusatory Functions?*

This question has been widely debated in soviet legal literature.

The Basic Principles of Criminal Procedure of the USSR and Union Republics of 1958 reads :

"The scope of the Soviet criminal procedure is the fast and complete disclosure of crimes, the exposure of the perpetrators and the assurance of the correct application of the law, in order that everyone who commits a crime should be submitted to a just punishment and no innocent should be arraigned and convicted". [2]

---

[1]   *Ibid.*

[2]   *V.V.S., SSSR*, 1959, No. 1.

This task is common to the preliminary investigation and the courts. But the investigating magistrate collects the evidence, checks and subjects it to a preliminary valuation. The court supplements the findings of the investigating magistrate, definitely valuates them during the trial and pronounces the sentence. As said above, the investigating magistrate only creates the premises for a court's decision.

Nevertheless the investigating magistrate is convinced of the rightness of his "accusatory conclusions", but not the court which has to re-examine all the results of the investigating magistrate's work on the grounds of a new investigation carried out during the trial, and only the material of the re-examination may be used by the court for the formulation of its ultimate conviction as expressed in the sentence.

In conducting the preliminary investigation, the law prescribes for the investigating magistrate, as well as to the court, the prosecutor and the person in charge of the inquest, with regard to their functions, to take all the measures provided by law, for a thorough, complete and *objective* (italics provided) investigation into the aspects of the case, to expose circumstances both inculpating and vindicating the accused, as well as aggravating or mitigating his guilt. [1]

Strogovich recognizes three aspects of the activity of investigating magistrates : criminal prosecutional, defensive and deciding. The last two functions appear only after the arraignment. These three functions combined in the activity of the investigating magistrates are then "divided between the prosecutor, defense counsel and the court in the trial", Strogovich writes. [2]

Chel'tsov discernes only two functions of the investigating magistrate : the prosecutional and defensive, [3] and thinks that since the entire preliminary investigating activity is subjected to the guidance of the prosecutor, [4] the preliminary investigation assumes the character of a prosecutional investigation. [5]

"Since the investigatigating apparatus and the prosecuting body are a single and one organization in the Soviet Union ... we have the right to conclude that in the state of the preliminary investigation

---

[1] Art. 14 of *Osnovy ugolovnogo sudoproizvodestva.*

[2] M.S. Strogovich, *Kurs sovetskogo ugolovnogo protsessa*, M. 1958, pp. 126-127.

[3] M.A. Chel'tsov, *Sovetskiy ugolognyy protsess*, M. 1948. p. 369.

[4] *Ibid.*, M. 1951, p. 235.

[5] *Ibid.*, p. 234.

we have no delimitation between the prosecuting and investigating functions", writes N.N. Polyansky. [1]

On the other hand, S.A. Golunsky emphatically denies the combination of prosecution and defense in the activity of the preliminary investigator.

According to him, a combination of functions could be spoken of "only in the case if various functions should be fulfilled by the investigating magistrate in different procedural forms or in individual periods of his activity. But it is well known that this is not the case. During the fulfillment of one and the same action, for instance, interrogation of a witness, or inspecting the locality of the criminal act, etc, the investigating magistrate at the same time clarifies facts which will serve for the accusation of the suspect or for the aggravation of his responsibilty and also those which will contribute to his acquittal or mitigation of his guilt. Furthermore, the investigating magistrate in the moment when he carries out this or that action, often does not know himself what value this or that fact established by him will have in the final count". [2]

Citing all these opinions, R.D. Rakhunov agrees with Golunsky that such conflicting functions as accusation and defense cannot be combined in the investigating magistrate's activity. [3] He thinks that "the functions of an investigating magistrate may be defined as an activity directed toward the disclosing of the crime, the discovery and exposure of persons guilty of its perpetration". This activity is not one-sided, i.e., accusatory or defensive, but consists in the all-sided, complete and objective investigation of all circumstances of the case, the result of which is the transfer of the case to the court, if the investigating magistrate comes to the conclusion as to the probability of the accusation, or quashing of the case if the fact of the crime is not established; the guilt of the accused is not proven, or other reasons excluding penal responsibiblity are present". [4]

Also Gusev rejects Strogovich's threefold scheme, as "far-fetched

---

[1] N.N. Polyansky, "To the Question of Controversy in the Stage of Preliminary Investigation", *Sots. zak.*, 1938, p. 72.

[2] S.A. Golunsky, "Questions of the law of evidence in the Basic Principles of Criminal Procedure of the USSR and the Union Republics, *Voprosy sudoproizvodstva i sudoustroystva v novom zakonodstel'stve SSSR.*, M. 1959, p. 126.

[3] R.D. Rakhunov, *Uchastiniki ugolovno-protsessual'noy deyatel'nosti po sovetskomu pravu*, M. 1961, p. 126.

[4] *Ibid.*, p. 130.

and impracticable". He argues that since the functions of prosecution and defense are carried out after the preliminary investigation is opend, the question arises what functions are fulfilled by the investigating magistrate before the arraignment. To answer this question, Strogovich is forced to introduce a fourth function, "the investigating activity", and herewith destroys his own three fold structure. [1]

It must be agreed with Rakhunov that during the preliminary investigation the investigating magistrate does not act now as an accusor, now as a defender. He has to act objectively, as prescribed by Art. 14 of the Basic Principles of Criminal Procedure, cited above. "The Preliminary Investigation", writes Rakhunov, "similar to the court investigation, is the examination of questions posed to the investigating magistrate and the court, respectively ... The investigating magistrate does not transform himself, each time supplying different methods in connection with new functions. He solves contradictions, correctly, looks into contrasts made apparent as a result of his investigating activity, which permits him to come to correct conclusions". [2]

Rakhunov is also right when he rejects the opinion of some writers that arraigning or choosing the measure of suppression, the investigating magistrate acts as an accuser, an accusatory organ. [3]

The arraignment or the arrest of the suspect is not an expression of accusation. The person arraigned is only suspected of being the perpetrator of the crime. The preliminary investigation is still being conducted further against and for him, the investigating magistrate has not yet formed a definite opinion in the case.

But when the preliminary investigation is completed, the investigating magistrate has to take a decision about the accusatory conclusion, if he has not quashed the case. This is undoubtedly an accusatory action, taken by the investigating magistrate on the grounds of his conviction of the accused's guilt, won as the result of the preliminary investigation. These conclusions, if approved by the prosecutor and the court, form the indictment, the accusation against which the accused has to defend himself in the trial.

Although a preliminary accusation is subjected to verification in the trial, the accusatory conclusions are an important act of the

---

[1] A.N. Gusev, "The Procedural Position of the Investigating Magistrate in the Soviet Criminal Procedure". in *Voprosy Sudoproizvodstva i sudoustroystva v novom zakonadatel'stve Soyuza SSSR*, M. 1959, pp. 314-315.

[2] *Ibid.*, p. 128.

[3] *Ibid.*, pp. 125-126.

accusation. Forming these conclusions, the investigating magistrate fulfills an accusatory function at the end of the preliminary investigation which he has to conduct objectively and during which "there is no accusor', as Rakhunov puts it.

Thus, during the preliminary investigation the investigating magistrate does not fulfill either an accusatory or a defensive function. He simply collects all the available evidence against and for the accused.

CHAPTER FIFTEEN

THE PROSECUTING BODY [1]

A. HISTORICAL DEVELOPMENT

a) *Prosecution before 1864*

The prosecuting body in Russia was created by Peter the Great in 1794. [2] A General Prosecutor and his Assistant, named Chief Prosecutor, were attached to the Senate. Also positions of prosecutors subordinate to the General Prosecutor were created at lower courts.

The Prosecutors had the duty of watching over the work of all the state's agencies, judicial and non-judicial, "including the Senate itself", in order to keep order in their affairs, to protect the people from attempts against their rights on the part of officials, as well as to prosecute in court all persons guilty of not observing or violating the law or the imperial ukases.

A detailed regulation of rights and duties of the prosecuting body was contained in the "Position of the General Prosecutor" of April 27, 1722. [3] According to Peter's desire the General Prosecutor was "the eye of the Emperor" and the prosecutors the "eyes of the General Prosecutor".

The special attention of the prosecuting body was directed toward the protection of fiscal interests. Consequently, the prosecutors were charged with the supervision over all persons and places handling the income of the State, especially the levy of taxes, dues, etc.

Upon Peter's death, under the reign of Catherine II and his other successors, the importance of the prosecuting body dwindled and reaffirmed in the reign of his daughter Elizabeth. It gained even more importance under Katherine II. The influence of the General Prosecutor was enhanced by his participation in the Commission for

---

[1] The Russian word *"prokuror"* is translated into English "prosecutor" or "procurator" by American experts on Soviet Law. For instance Prof. N. Hazard of Columbia University uses the word "prosecutor" whereas Prof. H. Berman of Harvard University — "procurator". The present author employs "prosecutor" for *prokuror* and "prosecuting body" for *"prokuratura"*.

[2] *Polnoye sobraniye zakonov*, N. 3877.

[3] *Ibid.*, N. 3779.

the Creation of the new Criminal Code as the only representative of the Empress instructed as to her views and desires. The General Prosecutor gradually became the leading figure in the State economy, finance and internal affairs. [1] He was, thus, the *de facto* head of the state mechanism and a rapporteur to the Empress on all questions of popular needs and welfare. [2]

The position of the prosecuting body was reduced under Alexander I. After the creation of the State Council and the Ministries [3] its activity was limited to the supervision of the administration of justice and the legality of the worker of state agencies.

b) *The Prosecuting Body and the Judicial Reform of 1864*

In the Journal of the Joint Departments of the State Council in which the basic principles of the Judicial Reform of 1964 were formulated, the following was said about the prosecutors : "The prosecutors are organs of the government for the protection of law and on this ground the essence of their duties is : the finding out and prosecution of every violation of the legal order and the requesting of orders for its reestablishment; presentation to the court of preliminary conclusions with regard to cases subjected to their particular supervision, according to the Codes of Criminal and Civil Procedure; supervision over the exact and uniform application of law and the requests for the clarification and supplementation of laws if misunderstandings of problems were generated in the administration of justice". [4]

The Judicial Statutes of 1864 assigned to the prosecuting body a threefold activity : law protection, accusation and execution of judgments.

The Minister of Justice in his quality of Prosecutor General headed the Prosecuting Body.

Also in court, the prosecutor had to be on watch over the law. To this

---

[1] See F.I. Gredinger, "Prosecutor's supervision during the fifty years after its reform according to the Judicial Statutes of Emperor Alexander II", in *Sudebnyye ustavy 20-go noyabrya 1864 g. Op. cit.*, p. 203.

[2] *Ibid.*, p. 204.

[3] Harold Berman writes : "In 1802 the Prosecutor General was transformed into the Minister of Justice". *Justice in the USSR*, N.Y., 1963, p. 290.

The new law created Minister of Justice also assumed the title of a Prosecutor General according to the Statutes of Judicial Structure of 1864.

[4] *Zhurnal soyedinennogo departamenta gosudarstvennogo soveta*, St. Petersburg, 1864, pp. 327-28.

effect he had to be present also at some civil suits. In criminal cases
the court had to hear the opinion of the prosecutor in all questions of
procedure such as jurisdiction, etc., with the exception of criminal
cases initiated by private complaint.

The prosecutor represented the state accusation in court. But, also
in this position he had to be impartial, and supervise the strict adherence
to the law. In this respect his position of a party in a controversial
and accusatory procedure was more limited in comparison with that
of counsel : the law required that the prosecutor drop the accusation
if he came to the conclusion during the trial that the accusation could
not be maintained.

The prosecutor had also to insure the execution of all decisions and
sentences of the courts.

Prosecutors were attached to the circuit courts, courts of appeal and
the Criminal Department of Cassation of the Senate (where the prosecutor was called Chief-Prosecutor). Thus, the prosecuting body was an
agency of the Ministry of Justice at that time.

c) *Prosecuting Body and Investigating Magistracy*

The prosecutor had the right to be present at all actions of the
investigating magistrate who was bound to fulfill all the founded
requests of the prosecutor with regard to the investigation of the crime
and the collection of evidence.

The prosecuting body had to be informed of the arrest of a suspected
person by the investigating magistrate, and the prosecuting body
could demand that the arrest should be replaced by another more
lenient measure of suppression.

This demand was mandatory for the investigating magistrate. However, if the investigating magistrate held the arrest of the suspected
person not necessary, but the prosecutor insisted on the arrest, the
investigating magistrate could request the court for a decision in the
controversy. This provision of Article 285 of the tsarist Code of Criminal
Procedure is an example of the independence of the investigating
magistrate in comparison with the subordinate position of the investigating magistrate in the Soviet Union, especially after 1928, as we will
see later.

But on the other hand, the tsarist prosecuting body also could
require the supplementation of the preliminary investigation in the
direction indicated by him, although according to the investigating
magistrate the preliminary investigation was closed.

But if the supervision duties of the Soviet prosecutor had some resemblance with those of the prosecutor of the time before 1864, there is a flagrant similarity between the position of the prosecutor in the criminal procedure and during the trial in the Soviet Union and in tsarist Russia after the Judicial Reform of 1864.

Also in prerevolutionary Russia the inquest and preliminary investigation were carried out under the supervision of the prosecutor, who was notified by the inquest organs about every committed crime [1] and he could require the suplementation of the preliminary investigation. [2]

However, in the Soviet Union, after the completion of the preliminary investigation, it is the investigating magistrate who write the accusatory conclusion, and the prosecutor approves it, whereas the prosecutor formulated the action in a document called "the accusatory act" (*obvinitel'nyy act*), in tsarist Russia. Both papers, the accusatory resolution of the Soviet investigating magistrate and the accusatory act of the tsarist prosecutor form the foundation of the indictment pronounced in both cases by the court (in the Soviet Union by the judge or in a preparatory session of the trial court and in tsarist Russia by the Chamber of Accusation, a body of 5 judges attached to the Circuit Court). It must be stressed that the accusatory conclusions and the accusatory act are only *preliminary* expressions of the accusation formed on ground of the results of the preliminary investigation. The final accusation directed by the state against the accused was and is formulated in the summing up of the prosecutor in the trial both in tsarist Russia and the Soviet Union, respectively.

The subsequent tsarist legislation did not change the position of the prosecutor in the administration of justice. It only enlarged his supervisory and executive functions in the quality of a member of several administrative boards.

B. The Prosecuting Body under the Soviets

a). *Prosecution — a Free Lance Activity*

The tsarist prosecuting body was abolished together with the other judicial institutions by the Decree No. 1 on Courts of November 24,

---

[1]   *Uchrezhdeniye sudebnykh ustavovleniy*, Article 250, 251.

[2]   *Ustav ugolovnogo sudoproizvodstva*, Articles 285, 286, 311, 312, and 512.

1917. The same Decree regulated anew the prosecuting activity providing that "all untainted citizens of both sexes, in possession of civil rights, are admitted to the role of prosecutors (in court) and during the preliminary investigations".

In the Decree of December 19, 1917 on the Structure and Functioning of the Revolutionary Tribunals, it was again said in Article 7a that all citizens of both sexes enjoying political rights and chosen by the parties have the right to participate in the trial in the capacity of prosecutors or defenders.

However, Article 7b of the Decree provided for the creation of a college attached to the revolutionary tribunals, of persons dedicated to the work of "defenders of rights" (*pravozastupnik*) in the capacity of a prosecutor or counsel. Anyone willing to bring help to the revolutionary administration of justice and in possession of a recommendation of a Soviet was free to join the college. From the list of members of the college the revolutionary tribunal could choose a public prosecutor for each trial, according to Article 8. Thus, this Decree did not prescribe a mandatory selection of the prosecutors from the lists of defenders of rights, since any person in possession of civil rights was qualified to do the job.

The Decree No. 2 on Courts of March 7, 1918 established colleges attached to the soviets, of persons who dedicated themselves to the defense of rights (*pravozastupnichestvo*) in the form of public prosecutors or public defenders also in regular courts. Members of these colleges (*pravozastupniki*) were elected or recalled by the soviets and only these members had the right to be remunerated for their activity in court. Again, the court or the parties could invite for public prosecution a member of this college, or another person, since beside the members of the college also other persons, who were not remunerated, had the right to take part in court procedures as prosecutors or counsels.

b) *Statute of November 30, 1918 and Further Legislation up to the Adoptation of the Code of Criminal Procedure*

Prosecution remained a free-lance activity up to the adoption of the Statute on the people's courts of November 30, 1918.

This Decree provided that in order to help the courts better to clarify all circumstances related to the accused or to the parties in a civil suit, a college of defenders, prosecutors and representatives of the parties in civil litigation was created and attached to city district and province executive committees of Soviets.

The members of the colleges were appointed by executive committees to which the college was attached, in the same way as all other officials. The members of the college as officials of the Soviet Republic, received the same wages as the people's court judges. The court selected the prosecutor from among the members of the college for individual cases.

The Statute on People's Courts of October 21, 1920 attached the prosecutors to the local department of justice. Their number was established by these departments. They were appointed (the law uses here plainly the word *"naznachayutsa"* and not *"izbirayutsa"*—elected —as in the previous Decrees) and recalled by the province executive committees of the soviets on nomination by the Department of Justice from among persons satisfying the requirements of Article 12 of the Law for the appointment of judges. [1]

However, also special representatives of soviet institutions and those unions which initiated the criminal proceedings retained the right to appear in court in the capacity of prosecutors.

The RSFSR Council of People's Commissars adopted an Instruction on the Organisation of the Prosecution and Defense in Court, on November 23, 1920. [2] It provided that public prosecutors could be persons capable of appearing in public meetings and satisfying the requirements of Art. 12 of the Statute on People's Court's. Persons not belonging to the Russian Communist Party had to be, in any case, thoroughly acquainted with the soviet apparatus and the work in professional organizations.

The participation of a prosecutor was necessary when the importance and complexity of the case, as well as the controversial nature of the evidence collected against the accused required an all-sided elucidation of all circumstances of the case or contenious proceedings.

In case of insufficiency of the number of soviet prosecutors, and sometimes together with them, the court admitted as public prosecutors representatives of soviet institutions and professional organizations, which initiated criminal proceedings.

The Statute of 1920 separated the prosecution from the defense

---

[1] The requirements were : 1. possession of active and passive election rights to the Soviets; 2. political experience in work or proletarian organizations, the Party tradeunions, cooperatives, plant and factory committees, and soviet institutions; 3. practical or theoretical training for the position of a people's judge.

[2] *Sob. uz., RSFSR*, 1920, Item 543.

which was recruited by the court in another manner than in the case of the prosecution.

But, Soviet administration of justice still lacked a steady organization which could fulfill the task of a prosecuting body.

c) *Statute of 1922*

Such a Body was created in 1922 in connection with the adoption of a Code of Criminal Procedure and the role which the Code assigned to the prosecution. It was thought as a centralized body.

The close connection between the Code of Criminal Procedure and the Statute on the Prosecuting Body was exemplified by the fact that when the effective date of the Code of Criminal Procedure was postponed from the 1st of July 1922 to the 1st of August 1922 by a special Decree of the VTsIK of July 8, 1922 [1] also the functioning of the Statute on the Prosecuting Body was delayed until August 1, 1922 by the same Decree.

It must be said that the setting of a centralized Prosecuting Body sponsored by Lenin met with strong opposition in the VTsIK. Members of the VTsIK argued not only against the retaining of the old name of "Prosecuting Body", but were opposed to the establishment of such a body in general, Vyshinsky relates. It was said that a centralized Prosecuting Body is tantamount to the organization "of a second juridical state parallel to the economic state", with more rights than the other state since it will supervise all economic and other organizations and make them answerable.

But the most vivid discontent was produced by the draft of the Statute (prepared by Krylenko) providing centralization of the Prosecuting Body.

Osinsky, Member of the VTsIK, asserted that the independence of the Prosecuting Body from the Province Executive Committees of the Soviet and their right to supervise their decisions "is a stab into the heart of the principle of the dictatorship of the proletariat".

Against the argument that the subordination of the prosecutor to the local executive committees would put the former under the influence of the latter, Osinsky asserted that "such an influence is completely inevitable and necessary, because it means adaptation to the necessities of life".

---

[1] *Sob. uz.*, 1922, Item 539.

Another member of the VTsIK, Nikitin, was of the opinion that the adoption of the draft would "bind hand and foot of the province executive committees, and kill any local initiative and independent action". [1]

Kamenov, Rykov and Zinov'yev spoke against the draft. They thought that a unified legality not only cannot exist in the Soviet country, but that it is impossible to establish such legality and, consequently, the creation of the prosecuting body will result in dual power locally.

The bill on the creation of the prosecuting body was discussed at the session of the Politbureau where Kamenev, Rykov and Zinov'yev argued against Lenin's proposal.

In result of the contradictory opinions, the Politbureau decided to submit the project about the prosecuting body to the Communist Fraction of the VTsIK with the provision that if the Fraction joins the majority of the Politbureau, the bill will be submitted to the VTsIK's Plenary Session unanimously, but if the Fraction shares the opinion of the minority, the Politbureau must meet again together with representatives of the Fraction according to the by-law for the taking of a final decision.

At the session of the Fraction, Lenin's letter to Stalin "On the Double Subordination and Legality" was read and Kamenov sharply criticized Lenin's proposal.

The Fraction did not accept the viewpoint of the Politbureau's majority and the question was again referred to the Politbureau where Lenin's proposal was accepted. [2]

The opposition in the VTsIK was so strong that the Commission of the VTsIK examining the draft rejected the protest right of the prosecuting body against decisions of the executive committee and other local agencies as illegal, so that Lenin had to interfere personally in favor of a centralized structure of the prosecuting body and its supervision rights.

In his opinion expressed in the letter to Stalin, mentioned above, the dependence of the prosecuting body from the executive committees of the soviets would create a "double subordination" : to them and the

---

[1] See Vyshinsky, *Sovetskaya Prokuratura i eye zadachi*, M. 1934, pp. 26-27.

[2] See R.A. Rudenko, "On the Problem of the Further Strengthening of Socialist Legality in the Light of the Sessions of the XXIst Congress of the USSR Communist Party", in *Sovetskaya obshchestvennost' na strazhe sotsialsticheskoy zakonnosti*, M. 1960, pp. 67-8.

higher instance within the body up to the corresponding people's commissariat; legality must be uniform in the whole country, subordination, however, of the body, called to supervise legality, to local agencies would create a "Kaluga" and a "Ryazan'" legality. He emphasized that the prosecutor must be responsible "that not a single decision of any local power should be in divergence with law". [1]

As for the scope of the prosecutor's activity, Lenin thought that the prosecutor has the right and the duty to do one thing : to watch for the establishment of a real uniform comprehension of legality in the entire Republic unencumbered by any local differences and in spite of any, whatsoever, local influences. The right and duty of the prosecutor is to refer the case to the court. [2]

Lenin thought that the decision of the Commission of the TsIk is not only an enormous mistake in principle, not only basiscally wrong in applying the principle of "double" subordination, but undermines any work for the establishment of legality.

He pointed out the calamity of local influences. "There is no doubt", he wrote, "that we live in a sea of lawlessness, and that local influence is one of the greatest, if not *the* greatest, enemy of the establishment of legality and culture. Hardly someone did not hear that the purge of the party, revealed that the squaring of accounts was the predominant fact in the local checking commission during the purge of the party". "Scarcely can someone deny that it is easier for our party to find ten reliable communists, enough legally educated and capable to withstand purely local influence than to find hundreds of them." [3]

Against the supporters of a double subordination, Lenin argued that the "depriving the prosecuting body of the right to lodge protest against any decision of local authorities is wrong not only in principle and disturbs our basic scope—the introduction of an unflinching legality, but also expresses the interests and prejudices of the local bureaucracy and local influence, i.e., the worst partition between the toilers and the local and central Soviet power, as well as the central power of the Workers' Communist Party". [4]

---

[1]   Lenin, 33, p. 328.
[2]   *Ibid.*, p. 327.
[3]   *Ibid.*, p. 328.
[4]   *Ibid.*

d) *Centralization*

The Statute on the Prosecuting Body was adopted by the VTsIK on May 28, 1922. [1] The prosecuting body was created as an agency within the People's Commissariat of Justice. This meant only a step on the way toward the strict centralization of the body since the prosecutors were previously attached to and appointed by the local executive committees of the soviets. [2]

The Statuts, as stated in its introductory sentences, was adopted for the purpose of supervision of obedience to the law and in the interests of a regular fight against criminality.

The activity of the Prosecuting Body had to be dedicated to these two purposes. Hence, the prosecutors had the duty : 1) of watching, in the name of the state, over the legality of actions of all organs of authority, economic institutions, public and private organizations and individual persons, initiating criminal proceedings against violators of the law, and lodging protests against illegal decisions; 2) of direct supervision over the activity of the investigating authorities in the field of crime detection, as well as over the activity of the organs of the state political administration; 3) of supporting the accusation in court; 4) of supervision over the legality of detention of persons under arrest.

The Prosecuting Body was headed by the People's Commissar of Justice in his capacity of the Prosecutor of the Republic. He had under his direction the Department of Prosecutors of the Commissariat of Justice.

The Prosecutor of the Republic had assistant prosecutors attached to him and appointed by the Presidium of the VTsIK upon nomination by the Prosecutor of the Republic. One of the assistants fulfilled the duties of a Prosecutor of the Supreme Tribunal of the VTsIK.

Immediately subordinate to the Prosecutor of the Republic and appointed by him, were prosecutors in every province and region; candidates for such appointment were selected from among officials of the center, as well as from among persons nominated by local authorities.

Assistant prosecutors were attached to the province prosecutors. They were appointed and discharged by the prosecutor of the republic

---

[1] *Sob. uz.*, 1922, Item 424.

[2] For the centralization of the prosecuting body and the instances passed by the draft of the Code and Lenin's role with regard to its acceptance, see Glenn C. Morgan, *Soviet Administrative Legality*, Stanford, 1962, pp. 38-42.

upon nomination by the corresponding province or regional prosecutors.

Military prosecutors were attached to revolutionary military tribunals and military transportation tribunals. They were directly subordinate to the assistant prosecutor of the republic in charge of the Supreme Tribunal of the VTsIK. Also the Military Prosecutors were appointed, discharged or transferred by the Prosecutor of the Republic.

Centralization was also emphasized in the Basic Principle of Court Structure of 1924 providing that the Prosecuting Body should be centralized and subordinate to the prosecutor of the republic only. The intention of this legislation was to free completely the prosecution from the influence of the local authorities.

According to Article 46 of the 1924 Constitution, a prosecutor and Deputy were attached to the USSR Supreme Court, but their activity was limited to the USSR Supreme Court; it means that they had to present conclusions on all questions submitted for decision to the Supreme Court, maintain the accusation in cases when the Supreme Court acted as a court of first instance and lodge protests against the decisions of the Plenum of the USSR Supreme Court to the Presidium of the TsIK if the Prosecutor did not agree with them. They had no directive power with regard to the prosecuting bodies in the country. Their activity was regulated by the "Statute on the USSR Supreme Court and the Prosecuting Body of the USSR Supreme Court" of July 24, 1929. [1]

The principle of centralization was somehow lessened with regard to prosecutors of the autonomous republics. Their appointment and discharge were entrusted to the TsIK of the corresponding republic. Prosecutors of the autonomous republics were invested with the same rights within their respective republics, as the prosecutors of the republics, with the exception of questions of federal legislation, with regard to which the prosecuting body of the autonomous republic was subordinated to the Prosecutor of the RSFSR.

The prosecution body of the autonomous republics was organized and worked on the same principle as the province prosecution.

Another reorganization of the USSR Prosecuting body by Decision of the TsIK and the USSR Council of People's Commissars "On the Establishment of the Prosecuting Body of the USSR" of June 22, 1933 [2] was also a step forward in the centralization process of this body.

---

[1] *Sob. zak., SSSR*, 1929, Item 845.

[2] *Sob. zak., SSSR*, 1933, Item 239.

The newly created Prosecutor of the USSR had the "general direction of the activity of the prosecuting bodies of the republics". His other rights and duties were the supervision over the conformity of orders and decisions of all the agencies of the USSR and the republics and of the local authorities, with the Constitution and the decisions of the USSR Government. The USSR Prosecutor had the right to initiate criminal proceedings and maintain the accusation in all the judicial institutions in the territory of the USSR. His rights extended to the supervision of the legality and correctness of the activity of the GPU, militia, criminal investigation and corrective-labor institutions.

The Law of 1933 regulated, however, only the functions of the USSR Prosecuting Body. Rules for the activity of the local prosecution bodies were provided by the Statute on Court Structure of the individual union republics.

According to these laws, the prosecuting bodies of the individual republics still remained in the system of the respective commissariats of justice.

The local Statutes on court structure were superceded by the USSR Law of 1938 on the Court Structure of the USSR and the Union and Autonomous Republics. [1] But, this law had no provisions on the prosecuting body. The Law of July 20, 1936 eliminated the double subordination of the prosecutor who was previously still subordinate to the USSR Prosecuting Body and to the respective commissariats of justice of the union republics.

This Law put all the prosecutors of the country under the USSR Prosecutor.

The final centralization of the prosecuting body as an independent institution was achieved by the 1936 Constitution of the USSR.

e) *The 1936 Constitution and the Prosecuting Body*

The USSR Constitution of 1936 established a unique position for the prosecuting body in the administrative system. Article 117 of the Constitution provides that "the organs of the Prosecuting Body fulfill their functions independently from any whatsoever local organ submitting to the USSR Prosecutor only".

Article 113 of the USSR Constitution defines the scope and the extent of prosecutive supervision : the scope is the supervision over the exact

---

[1] *V.V.S., SSSR*, 1938, No. 11.

fulfillment of law; it extends to the compliance with law by all ministries and all institutions subordinate to them, as well as to all officials and the USSR citizens.

The USSR Prosecutor is appointed by the USSR Supreme Soviet for a period of seven years and is responsible only to it. It is the USSR Prosecutor who appoints the republic, territorial and regional prosecutors, as well as the prosecutors of autonomous republics and autonomous regions, for a term of five years. The circuit, district and city prosecutors are appointed by prosecutors of the union republics and confirmed by the USSR Prosecutor; their term in office is also five years.

Thus, the Prosecuting Body was taken out from the People's Commissariat of Justice by the Constitution and established as a separate federal organ completely independent from local and federal administration, in order to watch over the legality of actions of all local and federal agencies, institutions and private persons.

However, this freedom from outside interference to the prosecutors activity did not extend to Party pressures. Certainly, the Prosecuting Body was and remained subjected to its universal influence. That is why the body called to watch over the legality of actions of other agencies and institutions in the USSR itself participated in violation of legality as, for instance, the trials of the thirties staged on orders of the Party dominated by Stalin, and closed its eyes on all the abuses of power during the "cult of personality".

Complete centralization of the prosecuting body system, freeing it from local pressures, made it even more accessible to interference from above.

f) Decentralization

The principle of strict centralization of the prosecuting body in the Soviet Union was not maintained when the general trend toward decentralization of the administration was inaugurated after Stalin's death.

Already on August 14, 1954, an Ukase of the Presidium of the USSR Supreme Soviet [1] decentralized court supervision. This was achieved by the creation of the presidiums of supreme, territorial and regional courts of the union and autonomous republics to which the examin-

---

[1]   V.V.S., SSSR, 1954, Item 360.

ation right of protests lodged in the way of supervision by presidiums was referred.

Since no presidiums were installed at the military tribunals, the protest right belonged to the chairman of the military tribunals and military prosecutors of districts, fleets and fronts. Jurisdiction for the examination of the protests lay with the district (fleet, front) tribunals.

g) *The Statute on the Prosecutor's Supervision of 1955*

1. Centralized Structure

The shape it retained up to the present time was given to the prosecuting body by the Ukase of the Presidium of the Supreme Court on the Statute of the Prosecuting Body of May 24, 1955. [1]

A chapter of the Statute of 1955 is dedicated to the structure of the prosecuting body, the rules of appointment and service of the prosecutors.

The structure of the prosecuting body is a centralized hierarchy. The USSR General Prosecutor, elected by the USSR Supreme Soviet for a term of seven years (the longest tenure in office for an elected official) heads a staff of prosecutors subordinate to him and to prosecutors on higher echelons. Directly under the USSR General Prosecutor are the prosecutors of the union republics. They head the prosecuting body of their respective republics but are appointed by the USSR General Prosecutors for a term of five years. Also the prosecutors of the autonomous republics, territorial and regional, are appointed by the USSR Prosecutor for a tenure in office of five years.

The next in the hierarchy downward are the circuit, district and city prosecutors who have also a tenure in office of five years, but are appointed by the prosecutors of the union republics and confirmed by the USSR General Prosecutor.

Investigating magistrates for especially important cases are attached to the USSR General Prosecutor and the prosecutors of the union republics.

All the prosecutors enumerated above have deputies and assistants.

An important innovation in the Statute is the requirement of higher legal education for the appointment to the position of a prosecutor and investigating magistrate. The candidate must be not less than 25 years of ago.

---

[1] *V.V.S., SSSR*, 1955, Item 222.

Thus, higher legal education was made mandatory only with regad to the prosecuting body and the investigating magistracy.

The Law of 1955 reiterated the duty of the prosecuting body of supervising the legality of action of all federal and local agencies, institutions, organizations, officials and private persons in the USSR. Provisions to this effect are contained in four chapters of the Law : 1) supervision over the compliance with law by institutions, organizations, officials and citizens of the USSR; 2) supervision over the activity and compliance with law by organs of inquest and preliminary investigation; 3) supervision over the legality and roundness of sentences, decisions, rulings and resolutions of court organs; and 4) supervision over the observance of legality in places of detention.

Article 2 of the Law of 1955 specifies the activity of the prosecuting body: it must be directed toward the strengthening of the socialist legality in the USSR and the protection from every attempt against the socialist structure and socialist property of the state; against the political labor and property rights and interests of citizens guaranteed by law; against the rights and lawful interests of institutions, enterprises, kolkhozes, cooperatives and other public organizations.

According to the Statute, the organs of the Prosecuting Body form a united and centralized system, headed by the General Prosecutor [1] of the USSR with the subordination of prosecutors in a lower position to prosecutors in a higher one. The organs of the prosecuting body, already provided in Art. 117 of the Constitution, function independently of any local authority what-so-ever, subordinate only to the General Prosecutor of the USSR, who is responsible and accountable to the USSR Supreme Soviet. [2]

2. *Duties of the Prosecuting Body*

a) General Supervision

In the performance of the general supervision duty the prosecuting body has the right to request the surrender of all documents, decisions, etc. records of every criminal case and civil litigation.

---

[1] A law of Feb. 25, 1947, (*V.V.S., SSSR* 1947, No. 8) changed the title of the Prosecutor of the USSR (Arts. 113-117 of the 1936 Constitution) into General Prosecutor of the USSR.

[2] For the hierarchical structure, see articles 38-49 of the Statute.

Article 10 of the Statute enumerates the agencies and institutions and persons under the general supervision of the prosecuting body. It has to watch over the exact conformity of enactments published by ministries, departments, institutions and enterprises subordinate to them, as well as by executive and administrative organs of local soviets of worker's deputies, cooperative and other public organizations —with the Constitutions and laws of the USSR, union and autonomous republics, resolutions of the Councils of ministers of the USSR, union and autonomous republics; over the exact fulfillment of law by officials and private persons.

The question as to which agencies, organizations and persons the general supervision power of the prosecuting body extends is exhaustively enumerated in Art. 10 of the Statute of 1955, and in Art. 113 of the USSR Constitution which extends the higher supervision of the prosecuting body to "all Ministers and institutions subordinate to them, as well as to all officials and citizens of the USSR".

It follows from the provisions of Art. 113 of the Constitution and Art. 10 of the Statute of 1955 that the general supervision power of the prosecuting body is limited to the executive power and does not extend to the legislative; thus, the prosecution has to check the compliance with law but not the law itself. Consequently, the prosecuting body may not check as to whether a law passed by the Supreme Soviet of the USSR, union and autonomous republics are conformable to the Constitution of the USSR, the union and autonomous republics, respectively.

Furthermore, it follows from the enumeration in Art. 113 of the Constitution and Art. 10 of the Statute that the highest executive powers—the USSR Council of Ministers and the union and autonomous republics—are also excluded from the supervision.

The question was made debatable on the one side by the fact that some legislation antedating the Constitution gave the prosecuting body an unlimited right of supervision even more over the laws passed by the legislature. Thus, in the RSFSR Statute on the Court Structure of 1922, it was said that : "The State Prosecuting body is charged with the realization of supervision in the name of the State over the legality of action of all organs of power, economic institutions and public and private organizations..." (Art. 78).

On the other hand, the exclusion of the legislature and the highest executive organs from the supervision was not stated in the Law.

With regard to new institutions created after 1955, as for instance, the *sovnazkhozy* (Councils of the People's Economy of 1957) one must agree with Berezovskaya [1] that they are submitted to the general supervision of the prosecuting body.

It seems to the present writer that Article 10 enumerates the agencies, institutions, organizations and persons under the general supervision of the Prosecuting Body—exhaustively. [2] Indeed not mentioned in the list are the legislative bodies and the councils of ministers of the USSR, union and autonomous republics, the bodies in charge of passing the laws and resolutions the conformity with which is the object of supervision by the prosecuting body.

It is certain that the Soviet legislator never intended to give the prosecuting body the right to check the conformity of laws enacted by the USSR Supreme Soviets with the Constitution, similar to that assumed by the U.S.A. Courts with regard to laws enacted by the Congress. The question of the extent of prosecutive supervision right to the highest institution of the Union is answered in this sense by Soviet writers at the present time. As Tadevosyan [3] puts it : "It is clear that the right to watch over the conformity with law of enactments published the highest and local organs of state power, as well as by highest executive and administrative organs of state power of the USSR union and autonomous republics, has not been conferred on the Prosecuting Body". [4]

In the general supervision duty of the prosecutor is also included the examination of complaints filed with his office by private citizens for instance against actions of the militia (police). He has to insure the protection of legitimate rights of citizens and the redress of violated rights.

---

[1] S.G. Berezovskaya, *Prokurorskiy nadzor za zakonnost'yu pravovykh aktov*, M. 1959, p. 34.

[2] Quoted are the Ukases of the Presidiums of the Supreme Soviets of the USSR, Union and Autonomous Republics which evidently belong on the list.

[3] V.S. Tadevosyan, *Prokurorskiy nadzor v SSSR*, M. 1956, p. 125.

[4] See on this question, Morgan, *op. cit.*, pp. 142-148.

If the prosecutor establishes a law violation on the part of private citizens or officials, he may initiate criminal, disciplinary or administrative proceedings against the violator or the violators.

According to the Statute of 1955 (Art. 25), the prosecuting body has also the right to protest against sentences, decisions, rulings, and resolutions of courts already in force. This right belongs to the USSR General Prosecutor and his deputies with regard to sentences, decisions, rulings and resolutions of any court of the USSR, union or autonomous republics; to a prosecutor of a union republic and his deputies with regard to sentences, decisions, rulings and resolutions of courts of a union republic and its autonomous republics, with the exception of the decisions of the plenum of the supreme court of the republic; to a prosecutor of an autonomous republic with regard to sentences, decisions, rulings and resoulutions of people's courts of the autonomous republic, as well as of rulings of the judicial colleges, territorial, regional, and autonomous republic courts, respectively, acting as a court of second instance; to a territorial, regional or autonomous region prosecutor with regard to sentences, decisions and rulings and resolutions of people's courts, as well as rulings of judicial colleges of territorial, regional and autonomous republics courts, respectively; to the chief military prosecutor and the chief transportation court prosecutor with regard to sentences and rulings of any military tribunal or transportation court, respectively; to the chief military prosecutor of a military district (fleet) with regard to sentences, and rulings of any military (navy) tribunal on a lower level.

In the performance of its general supervision duty, the prosecution body has to watch that all enactments issued by ministries' "systems of central organs and institutions controlling a single branch of state government and subordinated to a single leadership (*vedomstva*)", agencies and enterprises, subordinate to them, as well as by executive and administrative organs of local soviets of toilers' deputies, cooperatives and other public organizations- be in compliance with the constitutions and the laws of the USSR, the union and autonomous republics; to watch over the exact compliance with law by officials and citizens of the USSR.

The general supervision includes the examination of grievances of private persons about the violation of laws. As a result of the examination, the prosecutor may initiate criminal proceedings or take measures for the start of administrative or disciplinary proceedings.

b) The Prosecution Body in Action

In order to realize its extended supervisory power, the prosecution body has the right to require the submission of : orders, instructions, decisions, rulings, resolutions and other exactments, issued by ministries, systems of administration units—*vedomstva* [1]—by institutions and enterprises, as well as by executive and administrative organs of local soviets of toilers' deputies, cooperative and other public organizations and officials—for checking of compliance of these enactments with the law.

Also to request from the leaders of all the agencies, institutions, organizations, etc. mentioned above, the presentation of documents and information needed by the prosecuting body and to check on the spot the fulfillment of law in connection with the grievances filed by citizens and other information about violations of law.

In order to exercise his general supervisory right the prosecutor :

1. receives and examines all the most important acts issued by organs under his supervision, in order to check their legality, paying special attention to the legality of compulsory decisions promulgated by executive committees of local Soviets and the correctness of the provided punishments, because these acts concern the interests of the widest masses of the population ;

2. personally takes part in the sessions of the executive committees and soviets ; his presence gives the possibility to the prosecuting body of watching over the exact compliance with Soviet laws in the process of everyday work of the local organs of power and their executive committees ;

3. supervises the checking of appropriate compliance with the law in force by leading organs and their officials with regard to organizations subordinate to them. [2]

The general supervision of legality in the entire country by a single institution confers to it all the power to insure the uniform appliance

---

[1] "A System of central and local organs and institutions administering a branch of State government and subordinate to a single leadership" (*Yuridicheskiy slovar'*..., M. 1956, I, p. 87).

[2] See L.A. Nikolayeva, *Obshchiy nagzor prokuratory v sovetskom gosudarstvennom upravlenii*, M. 1957, p. 12.

of law in all parts of the Soviet Union, powers which were formulated by Lenin in his condemning of "Kazan' " or "Kaluga" legality. [1]

A wide field of activity within the general supervision is the examination of citizens' grievances under which "the prosecutor must not only decide himself on the grievances as to their strict compliance with all requirements of the law, with a great sense of responsibility, but must also "fight bureaucracy and formal treatment of citizen's grievances by any of the state agencies" [2], according to Nikolayeva.

C. PROSECUTOR'S ACTIONS ON LAW VIOLATIONS

a) *Protest*

When the USSR Prosecutor General or a prosecuting subordinate to him discovers in the way of general supervision that laws, orders, instructions, decisions, directions, resolutions and other enactments are violated, he lodges a protest with the organ which issued the legal instrument under protest, or with a higher organ, according to Art. 13 of the Statute of 1955.

The protest paper must contain the text of the protested enactment, the description of the action deemed illegal, and the legal reasons for the protest.

It must be underlined that the prosecuting body is not an administrative agency, and is not included in the Soviet administrative system; just that gives it the possibility to exercise general supervision over agencies, organizations, institutions, officials and private persons in all fields of activity.

This principle has been established by Lenin when he wrote, "It must be remembered that the prosecutor in contradistinction to all other administrative powers, has no administrative power and does not have a deciding voice in any administrative questions". [3] According to Lenin, the prosecuting body has to see to it that no decision of any local power whatsoever should deviate from the law. [4]

---

[1] Lenin, 33, p. 327.

[2] Nikolayeva, *op. cit.*, p. 15.

[3] Lenin, 33, p. 327.

[4] *Ibid.*, p. 328.

The recipient of the prosecutor's protest is not obliged to agree with the protest, but must examine it in due time; then the prosecutor has the possibility to lodge protests with higher instances, including the USSR Council of Ministers and the USSR Supreme Soviet, which would ultimately decide the question.

Although the prosecutor's protest does not automatically inhibit the fulfillment of the decision or order under protest, still state and federal legislation have established dates for the examination of the protest. Thus, the decision of the RSFSR VTsIK and the Council of People's Commissars "On the Suspension of Decisions of the Local Soviets and Executive Committees in Cases of Failure to Examine Protests of the Prosecuting Body Against their Decisions in Due Time" [1] provides that the executive committees and city soviets must examine protests of the prosecuting body—within the shortest time and in any case not later than two weeks after their lodging. Any failure to examine the protest within this term suspends the carrying out of the decision under protest.

A decision of the same bodies of March 30, 1931 established a limit of 15 days for the examination of the protest with the consequence of suspension in the case of non-compliance.

However, individual republics set various terms for the examination of a prosecution body's protest. The Statute on the Prosecutor's Supervision in the USSR of May 24, 1955 [2] established uniformly that "the protest of a prosecutor must be examined not later than within ten days" (Article 13, Par. 2).

Furthermore, if the prosecutor lodges a protest against a decision of a competent administrative organ bringing administrative prosecution against a certain person, the administrative procedure is suspended up to the time when the prosecutor's protest is examined. [3]

The Statute does not repeat the suspension provision of the enactment or action under protest in case of non-observation of the examination term. This is evidently because the suspension is an action of the executive committee and the local provisions of the laws of 1929 and 1931 in this respect have never been repeated. Thus, the

---

[1]   *Sob. uz.*, 1929, Item 686.

[2]   *V.V.S.*, 1955, No. 9.

[3]   *Ibid.*, Article 13, Par. 3.

prosecutor has no power to suspend the decision under protest, but the agency which issued the controversial enactment is bound to do so if the protest is not examined with the period of time presecribed by law.

b) *Representation*

Besides protests, the prosecution body has other means of reaction against the violation of legality. One of them is the representation (*predstavleniye*). [1]

In tsarist Russia representations, as Berezovskaya remarks, "were used to put officially a question before persons having legal power to resolve them, by persons not entitled to do so". [2]

According to Berezovskaya [3], "The demands of the Prosecutors in representations do not differ from demands contained in protests with regard to their legal essence. The essence of these demands is the elimination of any violation of legality committed by this or that administrative organ or officials—these violations may be produced by illegal *action* (author's italics)—or the *failure to act when the law thus requires*" (author's italics).

But being similar in their demands, the protest and the representation differ essentially in respect to their contents and addressees (recipients).

Whereas a protest is lodged against any concrete violation of law established by the prosecuting body, the representation serves to draw the attention of competent agencies to a number of violations of a steady character and to request them to eliminate the reasons and conditions causing or contributing to these violations.

---

[1] In his book on Soviet Administrative Legality (pp. 224 ff.) Glenn G. Morgan uses in English translation the word "proposal" for *predstavleniye*. It seems to me that the word "representation" is more appropriate for *predstavlenye* since, although "predstavleniye" as we shall see later has usually an element of a proposal, still *predstavleniye* is much more than a proposal and cannot be named according to only one of its components. Furthermore, the Russian word does not mean a proposal, whereas the word "representation" may be employed in the sense of a formal protest which *predstavleniye* precisely is.

[2] S. G. Berezovskaya, *Prokurorskiy nadzor, op. cit.*, pp. 81-82. She quotes *Svod zakonov Rossiyskoy Imperii*, Vom. X, Part 2, Articles 106 and 369.

[3] *Ibid.*, p. 87.

The Statute on the Prosecutor's Supervision in the USSR of 1955, in Article 16, provides: "The USSR General Prosecutor and the prosecutors subordinate to him, have the right to make representations to state organs and public institutions about violations of law and the causes contributing to the violation". The recipients of the representation have not more than one month to examine the representation and to take the necessary measures for the elimination of the violations of law and the causes contributing to them.

It may be said that this definition is also valid for the representation of the prosecution body made to an agency in the Soviet Union. The prosecutor is also not entitled to bring remedy to the situation of law violation signalled in his representation as in the case of the protest. He draws only the attention of the agency which has the legal right to eliminate the violation of law. But what distinguishes the representation from the protest are the alleged proposals or recommendations made by the prosecution body in the representation for measures to eliminate the violation.

Are these recommendations an obligatory part of the representation ? Is the representation no representation if the prosecutor does not express his opinion on the measures to be taken for the alleviation of the illegal situation ?

The law and Soviet writers diverge in answering these questions.

As we have seen, the Statute of 1955 provides for a representation on the elimination of the violations of law and the causes contributing to the violation, but does not oblige the prosecutor to make concrete proposals to this effect.

The prosecutor in the exercise of his supervision of legality has only to make his request according to the law to force the liquidation of the illegal situation and causes. Nor were proposals prescribed by legislation preceeding the Statute of 1955. In the Statute on the USSR Prosecution Body of December 17, 1933 [1] the representation was not mentioned at all; but in the Statute on the RSFSR Prosecution Supervision of May 28, 1922 [2] it was said, "that the prosecution has the right" to lodge a representation with the executive committees as to the abrogation or the change of an illegal order and decision published by them and their subordinate organs (Article 11). Then,

---

[1] *Sob. zak., SSSR*, 1934, Item 2.
[2] *Sob. uz., RSFSR*, 1922, Item 424.

again there is no word of a proposal to the offending agency on how to eliminate the violation.

However, Soviet writers are of the opinion that such a proposal is a necessary part of the representation.

Thus Berezovskaya writes : "As prosecutory supervision act, the representation must contain definite proposals directed toward a removal of the discovered violation of law and measures and their prevention. Without proposals there is no representation as an act of prosecutor's supervision". [1]

Thus, Berezovskaya requires of the representation, as its obligatory part, not only proposals for the elimination of the violations but also the suggestion of preventive measures, for which there is no basis whatsoever in the law.

Also P. D. Al'bitsky thinks that the representation must contain "the description of concrete proposals as to measures which, according to (the prosecutor's opinion), must be taken for the removal of violations and their causes...". However, Al'bitsky requires of the prosecutor the inclusion into the representation also of another matter. He does not mention the necessity of preventive measures but asks for a disciplinary punishment of the culprits involved in the violation by the agency or the Party, if criminal proceedings are not started against them. [2] From his viewpoint a representation in which the prosecutor only describes the facts of the law violation, not pointing out the perpetrator and causes of the violations and not advancing concrete proposals directed toward the strengthening of socialist legality, will not have a fortifying effect on legality.

The Legal Dictionary lists among the requirements of a representation "the presentation of a proposal for the taking of concrete measures for the elimination of causes and conditions producing the violation of legality". [3]

V. S. Tadevosyan defines the representation as a report to an agency or organization, usually to a higher directive organ, about the non-compliance or violation of law and the causes contributing to it, also with proposals of measures for the elimination and prevention of such violations in the future. [4]

---

[1] Berezovskaya, *op. cit.*, p. 84.

[2] P.D. Al'bitsky, *Voprosy obshchego nadzora v praktike sovetskoy prokuratury*, M. 1956, p. 100.

[3] *Yuridicheskiy slovar'...*, *op. cit.*, II, 211.

[4] V.S. Tadevosyan, *Prokurorskiy nadzor v SSSR*, *op. cit.*, p. 149.

Nikolayeva is of the opinion that "the basic element of the representation's content is the description of proposals directed toward the liquidation of violations of law, and elimination of causes and conditions contributing to these violations". [1] She also points out the necessity of another element in the representation, asserting that according to the Instruction on the General Supervision, prosecutors are obliged to add to the representation also a draft of decisions to be taken with regard to the violation indicated in the representation by the appropriate agency. [2]

Thus, in his representation the prosecutor should not only suggest the measures to be taken for the elimination of the law violation and the illegal situation but also prepare a draft of the forthcoming decision to this effect.

However, Nikolayeva herself objected to the presentation of drafts. She wrote that "the proposal of such a draft of a decision or resolution of a concrete question pertaining to the operational activity of administrative organs amounts to preparatory work for the completion of legal documents for the leaders of administrative organs" [3], which is not germane to a presentation according to Article 9 of the Statute.

Indeed, let us take an example : The USSR General Prosecutor may present representations to the Presidium of the USSR Supreme Soviet with regard to questions requiring legislative solutions or the interpretation of a law in force, in accordance with point "b", Article 49 of the USSR Constitution. It is difficult to imagine the USSR General Prosecutor presenting proposals, not to mention drafts, for new legislation or the interpretation of an existing law without interfering with the legislative functions of the USSR Supreme Soviet and its Presidium.

It must be agreed with Nikolayeva that the preparation of the drafts of the decision is already the beginning of the action for the removal of the violation and the illegal situation, a function which lies outside the competence of the prosecutor as conceived by Lenin.

It is very questionable as to whether the proposals, presenting drafts of preventive measures and requests for disciplinary prosecution, of which there is no word in the law itself, but are required of the prosecutor as a basic element of the representation according to Soviet

---

[1] Nikolayeva, *op. cit.*, p. 25.

[2] *Ibid.*, p. 28.

[3] *Ibid.*, p. 28.

writers who themselves have differing opinions on the subject, are not an interference with the administrative and legislative competence of state agencies. It is evident that if the proposal were a prerequisite for a representation, the law would not remain silent on this subject. It is self-evident that the representation, as well as the protest, carries, according to its essence, a proposal and a request to eliminate the violations signalled by the representation, but to decide how to do it, by what measures and in what way, is the job of the competent agency.

The duty of the Soviet prosecuting body, as conceived by Lenin, is to assure that legality is not violated by any agency, organization or private person in the Soviet Union. In fulfillment of this general supervision duty the prosecutor has to report the violation to the competent agencies if necessary, but he has no right to stop the violation or put an end to the illegal situation. [1] It seems only reasonable to conclude that the competence of making proposals, to say nothing of the drafting of decisions for the organs invested with the right remedying of any illegality reported by the Prosecutor, is not consonant with his specifically supervisory functions.

D. Suspension of Execution of Sentences, Decisions, Rulings and Resolutions already in Force

Lodging a protest against a sentence, decision or interlocutory order of a court, a prosecutor entitles thereto may suspend the execution of the sentence in force. This right is given to the USSR Prosecutor General with regard to sentences, decisions, interlocutory orders or resolutions and protests of any court in the country until the case is decided in the way of supervision.

The prosecutor of a union republic has the same right with regard to a sentence, decision, interlocutory order or resolution of a court of the union republic and its autonomous republics.

If the USSR Prosecutor General feels a resolution of the Plenum of the USSR Supreme Court does not correspond to law he must lodge a representation with the Presidium of the USSR Supreme Soviet.

---

[1] If the prosecutor judges it necessary to initiate criminal proceedings against an individual violator of legality, he does it not in the way of general supervision but according to provisions of the Code of Criminal Procedure.

He is also entitled to lodge a representation with the Plenum of the USSR Supreme Court asking for guiding instructions to court organs about questions of court practice. [1]

E. Supervision of the Inquest and Preliminary Investigation

The second field of supervisory functions respecting legality assigned to the competence of the prosecuting body is the supervision over the exact fulfillment of the activities of the organs of inquest and preliminary investigation required by law.

To this effect, Article 17 of the Statute of 1955 prescribes that the USSR General Prosecutor and his subordinates must :

1. initiate criminal proceedings against criminals, take measures to the effect that not a single crime should remain undiscovered and not a single criminal avoid responsibility;

2. sharply watch, not a single citizen should be illegally or inadvertantly involved in criminal proceedings or subjected to any other illegal limitation of his rights;

3. watch over the unflinching observance of the rules for investigations set by law, by the organs of inquest and preliminary investigation.

The Statute enjoins the prosecutor to use his supervision right to the effect that nobody should be arrested without a court decision or the sanction of the prosecutor. In deciding on the permission to carry out an arrest, the prosecutor is obliged to thoroughly study the entire material, substantiating the necessity of the arrest and, if needed, to interrogate personnaly the person to be arrested.

The law grants wide powers to the prosecutor in order to enable him to fulfill his duties. He has the right :

1. to give directives to the organs of inquest and preliminary investigation on the investigation of the crime, the choice, change or repeal of measures taken against the suspect, as well as on the search for unknown criminals;

2. to require for checking, from organs on inquest and preliminary investigation, the presentation of files of criminal cases, documents, materials and other information about the committed crimes;

---

[1] For review in the way of supervision of sentences, decisions, rulings and resolutions in force, see Infra pp. 642-650.

3. to participate in the preliminary investigations and inquests in criminal cases and, if necessary, to investigate personally any criminal case.

The prosecutor is empowered to order an additional investigation of a case, to cancel illegal and unfounded decisions of the organs of preliminary investigation and inquest. His rights reach so far as to relieve the investigating magistrate or the person carrying out the inquest of the further work on the case if these persons violated law or the rules of investigation. He may remove a case from organs of inquest and assign it to an investigating magistrate, as well as to transfer cases from one investigating magistrate to another, in order to insure a most complete and impartial investigation. This right includes the assignment of individual investigating actions to inquest organs in cases being investigated by investigating magistrates of the prosecuting body. In particular : to bring about the arrest of the accused, to carry out searches, seizures and the finding of the whereabouts of criminals.

The prosecutor is also empowered to quash criminal cases on the grounds indicated by law.

All the instructions by the prosecutor in connection with criminal cases investigated by them and given in the order as provided by the Codes of Criminal Procedure of union republics, are obligatory for the organs of inquest and preliminary investigation.

Measures were taken for the assuring of legality in the activity of the organs of inquest and preliminary investigation. For instance, according to the Order of the USSR Prosecutor No. 304 of July 31, 1942 "On the Strengthening of the Supervision by the District Prosecutors over the Investigations" the district prosecutors had to get periodically acquainted with cases conducted by investigation magistrates, and give written instruction on them, participate in the most important investigation actions in the most serious and complicated cases, check monthly all cases under investigation still remaining in charge of the investigating magistrate, and to complete notes about all instructions given by the prosecutor in every case.

The territorial and regional prosecutors had to arrange the work of their investigation departments in a way that the guidance of the investigation could be carried out through district prosecutors responsible in the first place for the state of the investigation work in the district. [1]

---

[1] *Rukovodstvo i nadzor za rassledovaniyem*, M. 1947, pp. 253-254; Al'bitsky, *op. cit.*, p. 68.

Thus, the prosecutor has the duties and all necessary rights to control the preliminary investigation and, although the investigating magistrate has a great deal of independence, still he is a subordinate of the prosecutor or, as Tadevosyan puts it, "he is an assistant of the prosecutor" [1], in the carrying out of the preliminary investigation. Ultimate responsibility for the preliminary investigation is with the prosecutor, although the investigating magistrate conducts it and is also responsible for the carrying out of the preliminary investigation.

This responsibility, according to Tadevosyan, causes some prosecutors to avoid the sanctioning of arrests which in turn, produces a milder sentence in some cases, since the court does not supply the punishment of confinement to accused persons who were not put under arrest by the prosecutor before the trial. [2]

With regard to the inquest, the position of the prosecutor is somehow different. Although the prosecutor has the right to request the militia to carry out some acts for the preliminary investigation, as we have seen above, still the militia is not subordinate to the prosecutor as the investigating magistrate is. However, he may remove a case from the inquest and transfer it to the investigating magistrate. The prosecutor retains his rights to watch over every illegal action in general, naturally also with regard to the militia and other organs involved in the inquest.

The position of the prosecutor in respect to the organs of inquest differs from that in his relation to the investigation magistracy because administratively the latter since 1928 has been subordinate to the prosecuting body, whereas the former are not. Nontheless, in matters of investigation, the prosecutor has supervisory and directive powers with regard to the preliminary investigation and the inquest.

Some Soviet writers deny the directive right of the prosecutor in his relation to the inquest, because of lack of administrative subordination of the organs of the inquest to the prosecutor. [3] However, the controversy seems to be made groundless by the provision of Article 19 of the

---

[1] Tadevosyan, *op. cit.*, p. 167.

[2] *Ibid.*

[3] For details, see M. Satvitsky, *Prokurorskiy nadzor za doznaniyem i predvaritel'nym, sledstviyem* M. 1959, pp. 110-117.

Statute of 1955 which reads : "... the prosecutor has the right to give instruction to organs of inquest and preliminary investigation".

One of the duties of the prosecutor is to watch that only legal methods of interrogation of suspects and witnesses are employed by the organs of inquest and preliminary investigation. Coercion of the accused or witness with the purpose of getting from him testimony, or a change in testimony which he is not willing to make, is severely punishable by the old and the new Criminal Codes (Articles 115[2] and 179 respectively).

It is well known that moral and physical coercion of unbelievable cruelty in order to extort confessions and desired testimonies from suspects and witnesses, were systematically used by the investigating organs of the Cheka and similar organizations, especially during the functioning of the "Special Board". There was no sign of any activity of the prosecuting body toward the elimination of the appalling violations of law.

We have seen that in closing the preliminary investigation, the investigating magistrate has to formulate the "accusatory resolution" (obvinitel'noye zaklyucheniye). Article 207 of the new Code of Criminal Procedure provides that "after signing the accusatory decision, the investigating magistrate must, without delay, direct the files to the prosecutor".

The prosecutor is obliged to check all proceedings of the preliminary investigation and the grounds for the accusatory decision.

In particular he has to verify whether : the action charged against the accused took place and represents a crime; circumstances were discovered which could lead to the quashing of the case; the preliminary investigation was carried out thoroughly, completely and objectively; the presented accusation is supported by the evidence produced in the case; the accusation is presented in conformity with criminal actions of the accused established by the preliminary investigation; all those exposed as perpetrators of the crime are made answerable as persons accused; the crime is correctly qualified; the measure of suppression rightly chosen; measures for the insuring of the civil claim and the possible confiscation of property taken; circumstances which contributed to the crime clarified, and measures taken for their elimination; the accusatory decision completed according to the requirements of the Criminal Code; other requirements of the Criminal Code have been observed (Article 213 of the New Criminal Code).

All these circumstances must be checked by the prosecutor also in the case of results presented to him on the basis of an inquest.

The law gives the prosecutor only five days for the study of all these questions and the rendering of a decision. During this short period of time, the prosecutor has to decide :

1. to confirm by a resolution the accusatory resolution of the investigating magistrate and direct the case to the court; or

2. to return the case to the inquest organs or the investigating magistrate with written directions for the carrying out of an additional inquest or preliminary investigation; or

3. to quash the case by a special decision; or

4. in case the accusatory resolution does not conform with requirements of law, to return it to the organs of inquest or the investigating magistrate with a written directive on the rewriting of the accusatory resolution; or

5. to complete a new accusatory resolution and return the old one with an indication of irregularities established by the prosecutor.

The prosecutor also has the right to change the accusatory resolution in individual parts and to qualify the criminal action by a milder provision, or providing a heavier punishment, or, if he considers it necessary to change essentially the accusation with regard to facts, he has to return the accusatory resolution for replacement by another accusatory resolution.

The prosecutor may also change the measure of suppression with regard to the accused, if any measure of suppression was taken before, or order one, and bring changes in the list of persons summoned to the trial session.

The question, as to whether the indictment of the accused is produced by the prosecutor's confirmation of the investigating magistrate's accusatory resolution or by the court, was debated by Soviet writers.

Strogovich is of the opinion that the indictment can be considered as an independent stage of criminal procedure only then, when it is pronounced by the court. He thought that the indictment function of the court is a guarantee for erroneous and unfounded indictments of citizens. [1]

An opposite viewpoint was expressed by Podkovsky, who argued that the indictment belongs to the duties of the prosecution organs and that the transfer of this function to the court would mean an expression

---

[1] M.S. Strogovich, *Ugolovnyy protsess*, M. 1940, p. 210.

of distrust toward the prosecuting body and create another organ supervising the preliminary investigation. [1]

Of the same opinion was Shifman. [2]

It must be said that the old Code of Criminal Procedure did not make of the indictment a separate procedural action.

Indeed, the indictment could be pronounced by four instances : by the people's judge when the case is presented to the court without a forgoing inquest or investigation, by the investigating magistrate, when the case was transferred to him, by the inquest organ, or by the court in an administrative session when the case is submitted to the court by the prosecutor with an accusatory conclusion.

According to Article 234, the cases which immediately reach the court from an investigating magistrate with his "resolution about the indictment" of the accused, are assigned for hearing in the court session without any indictment by the court.

By decision of the VTsIK of October 29, 1929 [3] the pronouncement of the indictment was assigned to the prosecutor, who "confirms the accusatory conclusion by a short resolution on the conclusion which the pronouncing of the indictment of the accused". The indictment by the court in an administrative session, was thus abrogated.

It was, however, reinstated in its indictment functions, by the Plenum of the USSR Supreme Court on June 7, 1934. [4]

The new RSFSR Code of Criminal Procedure is explicit in this subject. The indictment is an individual action of the court provided by Article 221[3] of the Code which reads : "The question of the indictment must be solved by the judge or the court in an administrative session not later than fourteen days from the reception of the case by the court".

If the judge thinks that there is enough ground for the examination of the case in court, without deciding the question of guilt before hand, he takes a decision about the indictment of the accused.

If the judge does not concur with the inference of the accusatory resolution, as well as if it is necessary to change the measure of repres-

---

[1] A. Podkovsky, "An Unnecessary Revival", *Yezhenedel'nik sovetskoy yustitsii*, 1925,

[2] M. Shifman, "The Indictment Almost Became the Function of the Prosecution", *Sots. zak.*, 1946, No. 10, p. 12; see V.P. Rezanov, "The Criminal Procedural Rights", in *40-let sovetskogo prava*, M. 1957, I, pp. 599-610.

[3] *Sob. uz., RSFSR*, 1929, Item 756.

[4] *Sbornik postanovleniy, raz"yasneniy i direktiv Verkhovnogo suda SSSR*, M. 1935, p. 111.

sion, chosen with regard to the accused, the case must be examined in an administrative session of the court.

Grievances about the actions and decisions of a prosecutor are directed to the higher echelon in the hierarchy of prosecutors.

F. Supervision over Court Sentences, Decisions, Rulings and Resolutions [1]

The supervision over all the court acts enumerated in the Subtitle 2 and Article 26 of the Statute of the USSR Prosecuting Body of 1955 is carried out by the prosecutor.

In order to exercise this supervision, the prosecutor participates in the administrative (*rasporyaditel'noye*) sessions of the court [2]; takes part in the examination of criminal cases and civil suits in court sessions and presents conclusions on questions raised during the examination in court; supports the state accusation or drops it in court during the trial; initiates civil actions according to the Code of Civil Procedure on civil actions in criminal cases and supports these actions in court if this is required for the preservation of state or public interests, as well as legitimate interests of citizens; lodges protests as regulated by law, against illegal or non-substantiated sentences, decisions, rulings and resolutions of a court; presents conclusions in criminal and civil cases examined by higher courts on grievances and protests; exercises supervision over the fulfillment of court sentences.

In exercising the rights mentioned above, the prosecutors are entitled within the limits of their individual competence, to require from the courts the handling over of files of criminal or civil cases.

G. Supervision over Places of Detention

The supervision over places of detention is another field of the Prosecuting Body's activity. It entails responsibility for the observance of socialist legality there (Article 32 of the Statute of 1955).

---

[1] If cannot be agreed with the translation into English of the Russian word *postanovleniye* by "decree" used by Glenn G. Morgan in his book *Soviet Administrative Legality*, Stanford, 1962, p. 151 and others. A court does not issue "decrees". The word "decree" means in Russian *dekret*. Decrees are issued only by legislative bodies.

[2] They take place before the trial session for the pronouncing of the indictment and after the sentence for action on some issues raised during the trial.

To this effect, prosecutors are bound to visit places of detention to gain direct knowledge about the activity of the administration of places of detention, to suspend the fulfillment of orders and regulations violating laws on the administration of places of detention, to lodge protests against them and to take measures for the disciplinary or criminal prosecution of persons guilty of violations of legality in those places.

The prosecutor must set at liberty every person illegally arrested or illegally confined to places of detention.

In order to facilitate the carrying out of these duties, the law invests the prosecutor with corresponding rights : he may, at any time, visit the places of detention to check the legality of the order of maintenance of confined persons and has access to all premises of these places; to make himself acquainted with all documents pertaining to the detention of individual persons; to ask for personal explanations from the administrative personnel of the places of detention about violations of legality in maintenance of arrested persons and to free without delay any person who is illegally arrested.

The law permits every arrested person to adress grievances and statements to the prosecutor, and the administration of the place of detention must direct these papers to the prosecutor within 24 hours. The prosecutor on his part is obliged to examine the grievance or the statement within the period of time set by law, to take the necessary measures and inform the agrieved party of his decision.

The prosecutor is also obliged to see that grievances and statements of detained persons should be directed without delay to the organs or the officials to whom they are adressed by the administration of the places of detention.

H. THE PROSECUTOR IN THE TRIAL

Also during the trial the prosecutor exercises supervision over legality and must protest every violation of law which comes to his knowledge.

But, along with the role of a supervisor over legality during the trial, he acts as a party of the trial, namely, he supports the accusation directed by the state against the accused. This accusation is formulated in the accusatory conclusions of the investigating magistrate, approved by the prosecutor, and confirmed by the court in the form of the indictment. Now all the materials collected by the preliminary investigation, and the additionnal evidence, produced in court, is examined and re-examined in the court session. This is the most important examination because no evidence and no circumstance, if not examined in court during the trial, may be used against or for the accused and serve as a basis for the sentence.

The prosecutor takes part in the investigation of evidence, gives his conclusions about legal and other questions raised in court, presents to the court his considerations with regard to the application to the accused of penal law and measures of punishment.

Speaking about the role of the prosecution in the trial, M. S. Strogovich quotes a definition by A. F. Koni, one of the most eminent legal authorities in prerevolutionary Russia, that the prosecutor is a "publicly speaking judge", which means that the prosecutor must be as impartial as a judge.

Strogovich thinks that under conditions of tsarist Russia, Koni must have been sorry to realize that only very seldom he came across prosecutors who corresponded to such a type of prosecutor. But about the Soviet prosecutor, Strogovich writes : "it can be hereby said that he is a publicly speaking judge, since he is an active participant in the administration of Soviet justice in the realization of which he is not less interested than the court". [1]—These words, written in 1948 by one of the most eminent Soviet jurist, also cover evidently all Vyshinsky's accusatory speeches in the famous trials of the thirties, the real character of which were discovered so dramatically by N. S. Khrushchev.

In their book *Chelovek pered sudom*, S. Aver'yanov and A. Zhukov wrote : "Appearing in court as the representative of the Soviet state, the prosecutor fulfills his assignment in the name of the state and in the interest of the state and society. The counsel speaks and acts in the name and in the interest of his client". "The main duty of the state prosecutor, as indicated by law, is the exposure of the criminal".

V. Remnev and O. Temushkin, oppose this definition of the prosecutor's duty.

They argue that according to Aver'yanov's and Zhukov's definition, the interests of the state and society are of importance : "but not the interests of the accused : that may be left to the care of the counsel; in reality no law provides that the main scope of the prosecutor is to expose the accused.

---

[1] M.S. Strogovich, "The Procedural Position and Functions of the Defense", in *Zashchita po ugolovnym delam*, M. 1948, pp. 30-31.

The basic differences between the activity of the counsel and the prosecutor according to these authors, is that the counsel can never shift from the defense to the accusation of his client or plead for a stronger punishment of his client. But for the prosecutor such a shift is completely possible and even obligatory if the results of the preliminary investigation are not confirmed in court. In this case the prosecutor is bound to drop the accusation and seek the acquittal of the accused or the mitigation of the punishment. [1]

But just this obligation makes the activity of the prosecutor more resemblent to that of a judge.

In supporting the accusation the prosecutor must be guided by law and his inner conviction, as based on an evaluation of all circumstances of the case. [2]

In spite of his position as a representative of the accusation, the law requires of the prosecutor impartiality. It requires that, if as a result of the court examination, he comes to the conviction that the results of the court investigation do not confirm the accusation charged to the accused, he is obliged to drop the accusation and explain to the court the reasons for his refusal to accuse (Article 248[3]).

If the preservation of state or public interests requires the initiation of a civil claim, the prosecutor has the right to present such a claim or support the civil claim raised by the victim of the crime.

Gsovski [3] is of the opinion that the soviet prosecutor, because of his supervision activity, developed into a "type of provincial attorney of by-gone days of absolutist Russia, before the Reform of 1864". He thinks the supervision over the observance of law by a centralized bureaucratic machinery is typical for an autocratic regime such as that of the Russian Emperors and of Soviet rulers. Also Harold Berman is of the opinion that "In some respects the Soviet Prosecutor marks a return to the type of prosecutor of the eighteenth century before the 1802 constitutional reform of Alexander I [4], closed the eyes on all the abuses of power during the "cult of personality".

---

[1] V. Remrev and O. Temushkin, "Who is the Prosecutor ?", *Izvestia,* November 23, 1966.

[2] This means "asserts the *Nauchno-prakticheskiy kommentariy*"—that nobody may thrust one's opinion on the prosecutor.—This cannot be done even by the superior prosecutor (*op. cit.,* p. 446).

[3] V.V. Gsovski, *Soviet Civil Law,* Ann Arbor, 1948, I, 851.

[4] *Justice in the USSR, op. cit.,* p. 241.

Also Morgan asserts that "The rulers of Bolshevik Russia found it necessary to return to forms and methods of autocratic Russia". [1]

Certainly, any totalitarian system does not rely on an "independent judiciary, and the combined result of public opinion, free press and free elections", to watch over the observance of legality simply because these features of democracy are non-existent in a totalitarian society. It is true that under the absolutist tsars all the administration, of which the prosecuting body was a part, was highly centralized, as is the Soviet prosecution body now.

But, under the tsars, the prosecuting body was a state agency, whereas the Soviet prosecuting body does not belong to the administrative apparatus.

The comparison is weakened also by the fact that the strong supervisory position created for the prosecuting body by Peter the Great was weakened under his heirs, revived only partially by Katherine II and finally limited under Alexander I.

As we have seen, the USSR prosecuting body occupies a unique position different from that of the tsarist prosecuting body and of all other similar organs in the West.

Finally, the prosecutor's position in court of the time before 1864 greatly differed in comparaison with that of the Soviet prosecutor.

But the most distinctive feature of the Soviet prosecuting body is its independence from state agencies. Theoretically, something as a "fourth power" along the legislative, executive and judicial ones.

I. CONCLUSIONS

It must be agreed with V. S. Tadevosyan when he wrote that : "Nowhere in the whole world is there such a state organ charged with such a wide duty of supervision of law fulfillment, as in the USSR". [2]

Indeed, only in tsarist Russia in the past and in the Soviet Union in the present did and does the prosecuting body exercise such extended supervision duties. In Western Europe the prosecuting body chiefly

---

[1] Glenn G. Morgan, *op. cit.*, p. 43.

[2] V.S. Tadevosyan, "General Supervision of the Prosecuting Body", *S.G.P.*, 1954, No. 4, p. 41.

fulfills the function of state accusation of criminals. And nowhere in the world did the prosecuting body so neglect and violate its supervision duties as in the Soviet Union under the direction of Vyshinsky[1] and also after him.

But while Soviet legal writers puzzled about the question as to whether the activity of the investigating magistrate has an accusatory character or not, an opinion that the accusatory resolution of the investigating magistrate confirmed by the prosecuting body, has a far reaching importance : it establishes, namely, the accused's guilt, was emitted by a prosecutor in the press.

This assertion started a discussion involving Professor Strogovich, G. Filimonov, Assistant Prosecutor of the Chelyabinskiy District, O. Chaykovskaya, a Journalist, A. Gorkin, Chairman of the USSR Supreme Court, an Editorial of *Sotsialisticheskaya zakonnost'*, Professor Perlov and a court action.

The discussion is of great interest because it shows how deeply rooted are notions developed under the cult of personality in the comtemporary opinion of some organs of administration of justice.

The grounds for the argument were provided by Strogovich who interpreted the provision of Article 7 of the Basic Principles of Criminal Procedure of the USSR and the Union Republics of 1958 that "Nobody can be acknowledged guilty of a crime and subjected to a punishment, except by a sentence of a court", in the following words : "Until the court has not spoken, until it has not finally decided upon the case, the person made answerable is not yet considered guilty, is not recognized as a criminal, however serious and convincing the evidence collected against him may be". [2] This provision is, according to Strogovich, an equivalent of the presumption of innocence of the Western Codes.

In a letter to the editor of *Literaturnaya Gazeta* [3] G. Filimonov wrote : "You are mistaken, Comrade Strogovich. You know, if one should admit your interpretation of this law (Article 7 cited above) as correct, the liquidation of the investigating organs and the institution of state accusation in court would be necessary. According to your theory, it results that the prosecutor brings to court an innocent. Can such a thing be admitted ? It would be absurd.

---

[1] Vyshinsky was Deputy Prosecutor of the RSFSR, Prosecutor from 1931-1933 and USSR Prosecutor from 1935 to 1939.

[2] M.S. Strogovich, "A Judicial Mistake", *Literaturnaya gazeta*, May 23, 1964.

[3] August 18, 1964.

No, Comrade Professor, your interpretation will be accepted by nobody and never.

The law gave the right to the investigating organs to present an accusation and interrogate a person as an accused and by this to recognize as a culprit this or that person. And the prosecutor brings to court and accuses in the trial an already culpable person from the viewpoint of the investigating organs, it means from the viewpoint of the state power. And the court only checks in what degree the individual accused by the prosecutor is guilty and as to whether the culprit deserves punishment. That is how this law must be understood, interpreted and applied. The criminal guilt is being proven in the beginning by the investigating organs, and then, the court checks the objectivity of the conclusions made by the investigation organs and takes its decision in the form of a sentence".

In the same issue of the *Literaturnaya gazeta* [1], Strogovich replied to Filimonov emphasizing that Filimonov's viewpoint contradicts the very essence of court and justice. "Just the court has the right and just to the court pertains the duty to solve all the questions in the examined criminal case—the question of the culpability as well as the question of punishment. Just the court has to speak the final and deciding word as to whether a person has committed a crime and deserves punishment."

Strogovich expressed the fear that Filimonov and his colleagues apply their viewpoint also in practice. "The fact is, that Comrade Filimonov is not an exception. He frankly expressed in a somewhat primitive form the views which are still widespread among a number of practical investigating and prosecuting workers", Strogovich wrote.

But an annihilating criticism of his theory Filimonov experienced from the pen of a collaborator of Izvestia—O. Chaykovskaya. [2]

Chaykovskaya begins her article with the question : "What if a surgeon would say that in his profession the main thing is to cut the carotid artery. You would certainly shudder. But a surgeon would not pronounce such words, even under the influence of alcohol. Yet these days, we heard how a jurist said that people could be found guilty without a court...

"It could seem" she continued "... why be terrified. The country is big, there are many people. Among thousands of letters the ignorant

---

[1] *Ibid.*, "Answer to the Prosecutor".

[2] O. Chaykovskaya, "Dangerous Ignorance", *Izvestia*, September 10, 1964.

can be found. However, the case here is much more serious as it could seem on the first sight... When in the years of the cult of personality one was taken away during the night he was named an enemy of the people already on the next morning! I do not suspect Comrade Filimonov of sympathy to the 'cult's' law and order, but still his theory has its source there...

Comrade Filimonov came foreward with his assertion so, as if a defense does not exist in the world, and a court did never return a case for a new investigation or pronounce acquittals. Evidently Comrade Filimonov still seriously thinks the court has no right to acquit if an accusatory resolution exists."

The discrepancy in opinion between Strogovich and Chaykovskaya on one side and Filimonov on the other was deemed of such importance that A. Gorkin, interfered in the dispute taking sides with Strogovich and Chaykovskaya. In his article [1], Gorkin sharply rebuked Filimonov for his assertion that the prosecutor brings to court "an already guilty person" and the court has only to establish the degree of this guilt and set the punishment. He interprets Article 7 of the Basic Principles of Criminal Procedure of the USSR and Union Republics in the same way as Strogovich, declaring the opinion that "a person can be recognized guilty only by a court is correct beyond any doubt".

In this connection Gorkin asserted that the days of the cult of personality are irrevocably passed. "There cannot be a return to such 'order' when for instance, in cases of crimes against the state the question of the guilt of a person was decided in essence by investigating organs", Gorkin wrote. He indicated that a substantial number of sentences are reversed and remanded because judges "blindly, uncritically follow the accusatory resolution putting in essence a rubber stamp on it and passing because of that unsubstantiated court decisions".

An editorial of *Sotsialisticheskaya zakonnost'* [2], periodical of the USSR prosecuting body, was dedicated to the criticism of several writings of O. Chaykovskaya, including the article 'Dangerous Ignorance'.

The Editorial had to acknowledge that Chaykovskaya was right in the main and basic question that the guilt of a person in the com-

---

1 *Izvestia*, December 2, 1964.
2 "Questions of Law and Justice in a Distorted Mirror", *Sotsialisticheskaya zakonnost'*, 1965, No. 1, p. 95-96.

mitting of a crime is finally decided, conforming with the law, by the court. But, says the editorial, "Chaykovskaya has touched upon one of those legal questions which are not simple and easy even for jurists". The question is, namely, about the truth in the preliminary investigation and in court, about "where, on what stages of our united criminal procedure the culpability of the accused is established and the question of his guilt is solved".

It is evident that although the editorial is forced to admit that the guilt of a person is finally established by the court this admission is somehow retracted by the second sentence in which it is declared that even for jurists it is not simple and easy to establish on *which stage* [1] of the criminal procedure the guilt of a person is set.

It seems evident, for everyone that the question is already solved by Strogovich, Chaykovskaya, Gorkin and the acknowledgement of the editorial. The presence of a question with regard to the stage of the procedure can be interpreted only by a concession to Filimonov's opinion. Solution of the question is so complicated, according to the editorial, that it promised to come back to it in a special article, which did not appear, up to the present time.

Chaykovskaya, however, is accused by the editorial of having, without any grounds, extremely belittled the role of the investigation magistrate and the preliminary investigation.

The editorial concluded with the assertion that it does not simply defend the "honor of the uniform", but cannot agree when "our Soviet justice—the most democratic in the world—is presented in a distorted mirror".

The editorial of *Sotsialisticheskaya zakonnost'* prompted Perlov [2] to come forward in defense of Chaykovskaya and with a sharp accusation of the periodical.

Perlov asserts that the Filimonov's position is in crying contradiction to democratic principles of Soviet justice and is able to bring damage to the correct education of staffs of judges, investigating magistrates and prosecutors. "Who else than a legal periodical should look into all that and express a viewpoint scientifically substantiated. The periodical, however, not only does not criticize this position but accuses Chaykovskaya that she, and not Filimonov, presents questions of law and justice in a distorted mirror !", Perlov wrote. He concluded

---

[1]   Italics provided.
[2]   I.D. Perlov, "Why Reproach the Mirrors ?", *Izvestia*, February 14, 1965.

that problems of law and justice have been, indeed, presented in a distorted miror not by the article in *Izvestia* but in the editorial of *Sotsialisticheskaya zakonnost'*.

The argument Strogovich-Filimonov-Chaykovskaya had an aftermath.

Filomonov sued Chaykovskaya in a civil court for defamation and libel, since his personal honor and dignity as a member of the prosecuting body had been defamed by connecting his opinion with the illegal Stalinist methods. He asserted also that Chaykovskaya's article contradicted his opinion of "guilty until proven innocent".

Thus, Filimonov, in spite of all that was writen on the subject, insisted on his viewpoint and brought the whole argument to court. In this way the civil court had to decide as to whether an accused is presumed innocent until proven guilty, or guilty until proven innocent.

The People's Court of the Sverdlov District in Moscow threw out Filimonov's action on December 17, 1964, providing an indirect precedent in favor of the presumption of innocence.

Reporting the suit the correspondent of *Izvzstia* wrote: "It can be agreed with G. A. Filimonov in one thing that he, indeed, needs to rehabilitate his honor and dignity 'as a jurist and prosecuting worker'. But for that, he must follow another path : comprehend his mistake and make conclusions from it without fail for his pratical activity". [1]

The court decision in the case Filimonov vs. Chaykovskaya and the opinion emitted by the Chairman of the USSR Supreme Court sanctioned the application of the principle of presumption of innocence in Soviet administration of justice, although there is not only no such direct provision in Soviet Codes but the inclusion of the provision into the Basic Principles of Court Structure of the USSR and the Union Republics of 1958 was rejected by the Commission of the USSR Supreme Soviet which presented the bill.

The objection against the provision was formulated by the Deputy B. S. Sharkov in the session of the Supreme Soviet of December 26, 1958.

Although the discussion of the "presumption of innocence" is outside of the scope of this book and was touched upon only in connection with interpretation of the activity of the investigating magistry and the prosecuting body, it is not without interest to cite Sharkov's speech

---

[1] *Izvestia*, December 19, 1964.

in order to show that Filimonov's opinion was shared even in the Supreme Soviet.

Sharkov said : "The attempts to introduce into our theory and practice such obsolete dogmas of bourgeois law as the presumption of innocence, deeply contradicts the essence of Soviet socialist law. It was proposed to bring into the Basic Principles—and in the quality of a principle of Soviet criminal procedure too—the presumption of innocence, per example, in such a form : 'The accused is considered innocent, until his guilt is established by a court sentence in force'... ! According to this formula, if it would have been included into the law, the investigating magistrate and the prosecutor are bound to consider a bandit innocent... The absurdity of such a situation is indisputable from the viewpoint of common sense. It cannot be understood only, why this is not clear to the theoreticians, mentioned above ? That is why the Commissions acted quite correctly... in decidingly rejecting such attempts to include into the Basic Principle formal provisions purely declaratory, foreign to Soviet legislation, not reflecting real social relations and only capable of misguiding workers of the investigating magistracy, prosecuting bodies and courts". [1]

----

[1] B.S. Sharkov, "Speech at the Supreme Soviet Session of December 26", *Pravda*, December 27, 1958.

CHAPTER SIXTEEN

THE LEGAL PROFESSION [1]

A. HISTORICAL DEVELOPMENT

a) *Abrogation of the Prerevolutionary Legal Profession*

The Decree No. 1 on Courts of November 21, 1917, abrogated together with all judicial institutions also the Bar and the legal profession. [2] "We have destroyed the bourgeois Bar in Russia and it was right that we destroyed it", Lenin wrote. [3]

On November 26, 1917, the Petrograd Bar decided that the Decree No. 1 on Courts could not be recognized as law, since it was issued by an agency without power to do so. The General Assembly of the

---

[1] The terms "members of the legal profession" and "lawyers" are understood to mean in this book, exclusively attorneys-at-law who have the right to provide legal help to the public, institutions, enterprises, organizations, agencies and kolkhozes. Only they practice law according to this definition. It is admitted that usually in the United States, every one who has a higher legal education is a lawyer, for instance, judges are also lawyers. Barry and Berman, "The Soviet Legal Profession" (*The Harvard Law Review*, 1968, No. 1.), unite under the definition : The Soviet Legal Profession, the Soviet "advocates, advisors to state institutions [jurisconsults] procurators, judges, legal scholars and others". The present writer prefers to name the jurists involved in the administration of justice "Men of Law". The reason for the restricted meaning given in this book to the definition "legal profession" is that the Russian word *advokatura*, as L.M. Friedman and Z.L. Zile, "Soviet Legal Profession : Recent Developments in Law and Practice" (*Wisconsin Law Review*, 1964, No. 1, p. 32) correctly remark, has no precise equivalent in English. The best translation for *advokatura* which means the advocates taken collectively, is, in the opinion of the present writer, "legal profession" used by the present author already in the article "The Legal Profession in Pre- and Post-Revolutionary Russia" (*The American Journal of Comparative Law*, Summer, 1958, No. 3, pp. 443-470). However, Barry and Berman, Friedman and Zile include in the legal profession of the Soviet Union also jurisconsults and the latter authors even the underground law practitioners. It cannot be agreed with these inclusions. The jurisconsults are discussed at the end of this Chapter in order to explain the difference between them and advocates. They are, namely, not members of the legal profession and the underground advocates are the "sharks" of the legal profession, not its members.

[2] On the Legal Profession in Tsarist Russia, see Samuel Kucherov, *Courts, Lawyers and Trials...*, op. cit.

[3] Lenin, 31, p. 95.

Bar directed its members to continue their previous activities in the old law courts. [1]

The decision reads : 1) to recognize that the Decree No. 1 as issued by an organization which is not accepted as an acknowledged power by the country, has no legal force; 2) the members of the Bar must continue their professional activity up to the time when court activities will be stopped by violence.

At the same time a meeting of the judges association took place in the same building of the Petrograd Circuit Court.

This meeting was attended by judges of every rank, from justices of the peace to members of appellate benches.

Also, the judges as we know decided to fulfill the Ukase of the Senate up to the last possibility and not to recognize the Bolshevist power : to adjudicate up to the time when prevented to do so physically by the Bolshevists.

The Judges and advocates merged their meetings later and jointly decided to organize a procession to the Constituent Assembly, on November 28th. [2]

The Moscow Bar reacted to events on December 3, 1917. The General Assembly of the Bar, having discussed the attempts to impede the regular administration of justice and sharing completely the opinion of the Ruling Senate embodied in the resolution of the General Assembly and of the Moscow judicial institutions, decided :

1. to continue the actvity of the sworn advocates on the basis established by the judicial statutes of November 20, 1864 for the sworn advocates and their aids, and by legislation duly published—;

2. to recognize that changes in this organization of courts and the guild of the sworn advocates can be carried out only on the basis which will be established by a freely elected Constituent Assembly—. [3]

The General Assembly of the Moscow Bar concurred with the decision of the Senate [4] and the Petrograd Bar on December 3, 1917. [5]

Similar decisions were taken by the General Assemblies of other Bars. [6]

The quarters of the Council of the Bar in Petrograd were not occupied

---

[1] *Russkiye vedomosti*, November 27, 1917.
[2] *Rech'*, November 29, 1917.
[3] *Russkiye vedomisti*, December 5, 1917.
[4] See above, pp. 25-29.
[5] *Russkiye vedomisti*, December 5, 1917.
[6] See for instance, *Smolensliye Vedomisti*, December 30, 1917.

by the Bolshevists until November 1918. This occasion was used by
the New Government to offer to the former attorneys-at-law a mass
transfer to the new organization of lawyers which was allegedly to
be created in accordance with the old principles of the guild. The
former Council of the Bar received permission to hold a General Assembly of the Bar in order to consider this proposal.

However, already prior to the General Assembly, the Council of
the Bar decided to stop the actvities of the Bar and of all its institutions.

To the General Assembly of the Bar, B.L. Gershun reported the
decision of the Council. He said, "The last hour of the Guild has come:
we cannot commit an act of treason against the principles of the Russian
Guild of lawyers by giving up the most holy tradition of independence
and freedom of the Guild ... it is better to dissolve the Guild : an honest
death is preferable to a disgraceful life". [1] The General Assembly
confirmed the decision of the Council.

b) *Lenin on the Legal Profession*

Although himself a member of the tsarist Bar, Lenin had a poor
opinion of his colleagues. In his letter to "E.J. Stasova and the Comrades in jail" [2] he recommended" to handle the advocates with an
iron rod" and hold them "in a state of siege", since "these intellectual
svoloch' (scum) [3] often mar. They must be told beforehand : if you,
son of a bitch, allow yourself—*political opportunism* to speak
about the *underdevelopment or negation of socialism*—about the
negation of violence by social-democrats (I.L.) about the pacific character
of their doctrine and movement, etc, or something like that, then I,
the accused, shall stop you short, on the spot, publicly call you a
scoundrel and declare that I renounce such a defense ...' "

Thus, Lenin abuses the legal profession not because of its amorality
but because of the liberalism to which the majority in the profession
adhered under the tsars. Defending social-democrats the lawyers
tended to present to the court their political movement in a pacifistic
light which in Lenin's opinion abased this movement. That is why
he recommended to the workers to permit to the counsels, only "to
criticize the witnesses of the accusation" to "catch them" and the

---

[1] B.L. Gershun, "'Russia' in die *Rechtsanwaltschaft*", Leipzig, 1929, pp. 229-230.

[2] Published for the first time in *Proletarskaya revolyutsiya*, 1924, No. 7, Lenin, VII,
pp. 60-61.

[3] A very rude expression in Russian.

prosecutor in matters of facts finding and to discredit the unjust aspects of court activity without touching upon the ideological side of their crime.

But Lenin was not opposed to the legal profession as such. He thought that defense is an indispensable feature of a trial. Stuchka recalled that when the draft of a Code of Criminal Procedure was discussed in 1918, when Steinberg was People's Commissar of Justice, it was Lenin personally who included the provisions on the counsels into the draft. [1]

However, the discarded tsarist Bar had not to be replaced by another institution at once.

c) *Initial Legislation in the Legal Profession*

The Decree No. 1 on Courts simply provided that all citizens of both sexes who enjoyed civil rights may act as counsel for the defense. As a consequence of this freedom for everyone to exercise the age-old profession, some former lawyers, whose organization had been liquidated, continued to act as counsel.

V. Turin relates that, as Soviet rule was strengthened, a steadily increasing number of former members of the bar, joined the new organized Soviet enterprizes and orgnaizations in the quality of jurist-counsults : "It is enough to say that only in the Petrograd Food Administration, ... several tens of former lawyers and their aids worked as legal advisers". [2]

This right of everyone to act as counsel was retained in the draft of the Decree No. 2 on Courts. Article 24 of the draft provided as follows : "Every citizen of either sex in possession of political rights and chosen by the parties involved may particpate in the proceedings in the capacity ... of counsel". However, Lenin changed Article 24 of the draft and formulated it as follows : "Colleges of persons who dedicate themselves to the defense of rights in the capacity of public prosecutors or public defenders are created and attached to Councils of Workers, Soldiers and Peasants Deputies. Only these persons have the right to act in court for remuneration". [3]

---

[1] *Yezhenedel'nik Sovetskoy yustsitsii*, M. 1828, No 4, p. 115.

[2] V. Turin, "From Colleges of Right Defenders to Advocates", *Sov. yust.*, 1957, No. 9, p. 38.

[3] Lenin, XXI, p. 218.

The emphasis here is on "remuneration". Among the persons present at a trial, one person was permitted to speak for the defense and one for the prosecution, besides the remunerated members of the College, provided they were not paid. The retention of this right for any person to assume the defense was termed already by Kursky himself "a remainder of illusion not yet extinct". In his opinion "remuneration" of counsel contains the seed of speculation. Since the members of the old bar were in the great majority against the new regime and did not want to cooperate, the number of persons capable of fulfilling the duties of a "defender of rights" was very limited and the colleges were manned by a not adequate number of members. He writes that these colleges were "a poor copy of the former guild of advocates". [1]

Indeed, the organization created by the Decree No. 2 on Courts did not last. It was considered undesirable to unite the prosecution and defense into one college. The separation first took place in military courts. The decree of May 4, 1918 organized the prosecutors into special colleges attached to military tribunals. In other courts, the prosecution and the defense remained united for a while.

The local Soviets assumed the duty to regulate the activities of the colleges. For instance, the Moscow Soviet issued a regulation on the College of Defenders of Rights, of September 3, 1918, in which it assumed the right to appoint new members of the college and dismiss old ones.

Councils of the colleges were created. Their duty consisted in controlling the activity of the colleges, in the working-out of regulations and instructions concerning the activity of college members, the establishment of a schedule of fees, the assignment of prosecutors and counsel for pleading in court, etc. The remuneration of a counsel who was a member of a college was provided by the client to the counsel himself who has to forward it to the college fund for distribution among all members. [2]

The Statutes on the People's Courts of November 30, 1918 introduced a new form of organization of the legal profession. Colleges of counsel, prosecutors, and representatives of parties in civil proceedings were reorganized and attached to District and Province Executive Committees. Members of such colleges were officials, remunerated by wages corresponding to those of people's judges. They had no right

---

[1] Kursky, *Izbrannyye stat'i...*, *op. cit.*, p. 93.

[2] *Izvestia*, 1918, No. 189.

to accept fees from their clients. The exceptional position of prosecutors in military tribunals, established by the Decree of May 4,1918,
was abrogated and members of colleges became prosecutors and
counsels in military courts as well.

Thus, the tendency to create a monopoly of pleading in court for
the members of colleges, which was constantly developed in further
legislation, is already taking shape in the law of November 30, 1918
and the Instruction mentioned above.

A. Molochkov is of the opinion that the cancellation of the right
of every citizen in possession of civil rights to plead in court without
remuneration was a compensation for the partial elimination of the
monopoly of the old bar with regard to its personal composition.
He argues that "under the cover of a gratuitous activity, the former
lawyers, the well-known inveterate professionals—accustomed to their
complicated way of weaving their 'legal spider's web' would again
appear in court. The court, thinks Molochkov, called upon to direct
itself by its socialits sense of justice would acquire, in theory, not
collaborators, helping to clarify the case in all aspects, but a socially
inimical power, striving by all means to snatch a bit of blessings for
the party represented by them. [1]

Interestingly enough, this opinion, given in the issue of the periodical of November 1, 1918, evidently did not correspond to the views
of the Soviet government on the old bar at that time, to which in
November 1918 it proposed the incorporation en masse of the former
Russioan lawyers into the new organization of the legal profession.

With regard to the salary of the *pravozastupniks*, since they were
not members of a free guild, but state employees, the Second Congress
of Regional and Professional Commissars of Justice of 1918 decided
that their salary should be a fixed monthly remuneration corresponding to that of a judge.

The colleges of *pravozastupniks* were critized on many accounts.
They were mostly accused of having too many prerevolutionary advocates as their members, people opposed to the new regime. As Lenin
puts it : "We have destroyed in Russia the old bar, and acted rightly
in destroying it, but it is reborn ... under the cover of Soviet pravozastupniks". [2]

---

[1] Molochkov, "Advocates-Defenders of Rights and Court Assistants", *Proletarskaya
revolyutsiya i pravo*, November 1918, No. 7, p. 20.

[2] Lenin, 31, p. 95.

Kursky relates that, for instance, in Saratov, an attempt was made to form the College of Defenders of Rights as follows: the local Soviet elected to the College a number of persons, classed them as a Soviet organization, but in other respects left them free to shape their relations with the clients at will, without any reglementation on the part of the authorities.

The "defenders" opened offices, started to receive clients, name sign boards were designed and "the legal profession was reborn in its most undesirable form; mean-spirited people flocked to it, who opened shops and started trafficking in justice", Kursky writes. [1]

According to Kursky the organization of colleges of defenders of rights, was the bearer of germs of its own decomposition: remuneration—in reality speculation—and the evidently small staff of competent defenders, since it was impossible to include into the members of the colleges experienced specialists of the bourgeois legal profession, which stood to a man on the side of the enemies of the working population at that time, reduced the College of *pravozastupniks* to a bad [2] copy of the former guild of the sworn legal profession". [3]

In a letter to the VTsIK's Presidium of August 26, 1920, Kursky suggested that "in view of the evident inadequacy of the college staff, composed almost every-where of cast offs of the old lawyers' bar, and sometimes simply of underground advocates, and since the really capable and competent among the former advocates and jurists in general do not want to saddle themselves with participation in the *pravozastupniks*, which has the tendency to give birth, although in a covered form, to the institution of the bourgeois bar ...".

Kursky sees the way out of this situation in attracting to the legal profession persons capable of carrying out the defense and in the first place, outstanding trial lawyers from the former bar on the basis of a duty to render services. [4]

However, the institution of counsel as special officials was soon considered inefficient. It was therefore liquidated and a new organization created by the Statutes on People's Courts of October 21,

---

[1] D.I. Kursky, *Izbrannyye stat'i i rechi, op. cit.*, p. 57.

[2] A.C. Malone, in his article "The Soviet Bar", *Cornell Law Quarterly*, Winter 1961, No. 2, p. 265, translated the Russian word "skvernaya" (bad) in Kursky's passage quoted above, erroneously with the English word "obscene".

[3] Kursky, *op. cit.*, p. 93.

[4] V. Turin, "From Colleges of Right Defenders to Advocates", *Sov. yust.*, 1957, No. 9, p. 39.

1920. [1] Prosecutors were separated from colleges and attached to the militia.

With regard to counsels, the Decree established provisions unique in the history of the legal profession throughout the world : all persons "capable to act as counsel for the defense" in court were drafted as such and entered in lists prepared by people's judges, councils of people's judges, professional and party organizations, and Departments of justice. [2] District executive committees had to confirm these twice a year on the first of January and of July. The inclusion of a person in the list was tantamount to a draft; such a person was obliged to serve as a counsel whether he wanted to or not. The duty of distributing the draftees among various courts and tribunals was transferred to the departments of justice. Whenever necessary, the courts or tribunals summoned the persons entered on the lists for the performance of duties as counsel. If the number of draftees was insufficient, the court had the right to appoint defense counsels from among consultants to the department of justice.

It is evident that such a system was doomed to failure. The draftees were reluctant to perform duties pressed upon them, and in many instances those who showed up for duty were unable to fulfil it, being unprepared for the legal profession. That is actually why the majority of counsels for the defense were appointed from among consultants to the departments of justice. In this way they remained officials, just as they were between 1918 and 1920.

The system of exercising of the legal profession as a compelling duty to render service lasted until 1922 when it was abolished by the the Statute on the Legal Profession.

d) *The Birth of the Soviet Legal Profession*

The first Statute on the Legal Profession adopted by the VTsIK on May 26, 1922 was promulgated as an amendment to the Statute on the People's Court of 21 October 1920. Articles 43-49 of the latter were replaced by the articles of the Statute on the Legal Profession.

The history of the Soviet legal profession started with this Statute, according to Soviet writers.

---

[1] *Sob. uz.*, 1920, Item 407.

[2] Depts. of justice were created at local Soviets by the Decree of Jan. 30, 1919 and reorganized by Statutes on Local Organs of Justice of Aug. 21, 1920. They were local organs of the People's Commissariat of Justice and at the same time they were subordinate to corresponding Soviets of Workers', Soldiers' and Peasants' Deputies.

The Statute created colleges of defenders in criminal and civil cases attached to provincial departments of justice. The members of the first staff of the colleges had to be confirmed by the presidium of the provincial executive comittees on presentation by the provincial department of justice. In the future the new members of the colleges were to be admitted by corresponding college presidiums. Notice of admission had to be given to the presidium of the provincial executive who had the right of challenge.

Members of the colleges were prohibited to occupy positions on state agencies or enterprizes, with the exception of elected positions and of professors and teachers of law.

The Presidium was elected by the General Assembly of the college, which had the following functions: a) supervision and control of the completion of defenders activites; b) infliction of disciplinary punishments on the college members; appeal of the decision of the presidium was admissible to the provincial executive committee; c) managing of the money paid to the fund of the college; d) appointment of defenders who worked free of charge or were remunerated, according to the tariff; e) organization of consultation offices for legal aid to the population in accordance with instructions of the department of justice.

The remuneration of the college members was carried out according to the following principles: a) persons recognized by the people's court as indigent were freed from any fees for the services of the defenders in criminal and civil cases; b) workers of state and private enterprises and employees of Soviet agencies and enterprises had the right to remunerate defenders according to the tariff established by the People's Commissariat of Justice.

The defenders had to pay to the fund at the college a certain percent from their remuneration set by the People's Commissariat of Justice, for expenses connected with maintenance of the presidium and consultation offices.

Besides the college members, the law admitted as defenders near relatives of the accused or of the victim, accredited representatives of state agencies and enterprises, as well as of the All-Rusisan Central Council of Trade Unions, All-Russian Central Union of Consumers Societies and of other professional and public organizations. Other persons could be admitted as defenders only with the permission of the court, which examined the case.

With the advent of the New Economic Policy (NEP) changes in the administration of justice and, naturally, in the structure of the legal profession, were inevitable.

We have seen that the All-Russian Central Executive Committee adopted the Statutes of the Legal Profession on May 25, 1922, even prior to the Statutes on the Court Structure of November 3, 1922. Certain rights of self-administration were granted to the colleges; their members elected a presidium, which was charged with the control of the activities of the college and of its members. The presidium admitted new members to the college and carried out disciplinary supervision over its members. But provincial, territorial and regional executive committees retained the right to revoke the appointment of anny member of the college. The presidium of these executive committees functioned also as an appelate instance for complaints against decisions of college presidiums in disciplinary proceedings. Thus, the colleges depended upon executive committees, i.e., upon the administration.

Chel'tsov reports that the bourgeois tendencies in the work of the colleges organized in 1922 prompted many workers of the administration of justice to doubt about the possibility for communists to work in these colleges. A special clarification by the Central Committee of the All-Russian Communist Party became necessary.

In the Circular letter of November 2, 1922 No. 97 [1] it was said that the College of Defenders is an institution completely occupied by elements hostile to Soviet power, can represent a threat for the interest of the workers with regard to the solution of every-day property disputes between workers and employers and between state enterprises and private persons.

Agreeing to the participation of communists in the colleges and their presidiums, the Central Committee emphasized that the communist-members of colleges must be defenders of the working population and exercise supervision over anti-Soviet elements; they cannot represent bourgeois elements and defend them in their disputes with workers, state enterprises, institutions, cooperatives, etc.

With regard to criminal cases, the Central Committee stated that "they cannot be guided by the bourgeois principle, that the counsel is not obliged to find out whom he defends ...".

A certain change in the situation was produced two years later, in 1924, when any appeal against the decisions of college presidiums

---

[1] *Yezhenedel'nik sovetskoy yustsii*, 1923, No. 1, p. 24.

was excluded from the jurisdiction of the executive committees and transferred to the competence of provincial, territorial and regional courts. The right to remove members of colleges remained, however, with the executive committees.

During the NEP, or, more exactly, between 1922 and 1930, private law practice was permitted and was the basic activity of the college members. The college presidiums established public legal consultation offices in cities and rural areas. In these offices members of colleges had to render legal assistance to the population free of charge, as a public service, if they were recognized as indigent by a special decision of the court. Workers and employees, as well as peasants and handicraftsmen who did not use paid labor paid the counsel according to a tariff established by the People's Commissar of Justice. Also persons who did not belong to these categories, but had a counsel appointed by the court in cases requirung the participation of counsel, paid the college of defenders in accordance with the tariff. But in all other cases the remuneration of the counsel was set by agreement between him and his client. A part of the remuneration had to be transferred to to the college for expenses.

Every citizen in possession of electoral rights could join the college of defenders provided he had two years of work experience at the organs of justice, in a capacity not lower than that of investigating magistrate or had passed a corresponding examination at a commission attached to the province court. The college presidium handled the admission to the college; however, the presidium of the provincial executive committee had the right to challenge the admitted members of the college within a month after the notification of the admission. The rejection of the admission by the college presidium could be appealed to the province executive committee, the decision of which was final.

Then, in 1929-30, without any special legislation, another major change occured in the structure of the legal profession. After the liquidation of the NEP, a new policy—the drive for collectivization and industrialization—was started.

Not only the peasantry was collectivized, but the legal profession as well. Peasants were forced into collective farms; lawyers were compelled to join collectives of "defenders of rights" (counsels). Individual law practice was forbidden. Legal work was concentrated in collectives, labelled "voluntary" associations of lawyers. Every college had several such collectives.

On paper, collective farms too are "voluntary" cooperatives of peasants. In reality, just as the peasant had to join a collective farm, the lawyer had to become a member of a collective of counsels if he wanted to exercise the legal profession. Karev admits that in many instances "collectivization" was forced upon the lawyers, that the lawyers who did not join the collective were virtually deprived of the possibility to plead in court, that the money of the collectives was often illegally diverted for needs of the organs of prosecution and the courts, etc. [1]

In the Ukraine even remuneration of the counsel according to "work hours" (a parallel to the "workday" in the kolkhoz) was introduced. An item of advice was valued, for instance, at one-half of a work hour, the participation in court session-three work hours, the writing of an appeal for cassation-two hours, and so forth. In this connection the behavior of Ukrainian People's Commissariat of Justice with regard to the legal profession was then criticized by Vyshinsky. He accused the Ukrainian People's Commissariat of Justice of having disposed of the funds for the remuneration of counsels, artificially lowering their income, having organized legal kolkhozes, drafting and directing counsels into villages, dismissing with one stroke of the pen 100 counsels from colleges as not wanted, etc. [2]

A client who needed the services of a counsel signed a contract with the collective, not with the individual counsel who was assigned to help him. Fees were paid to the collective and not to the lawyer. The members of the collective were remunerated according to the quantity and quality of work performed. The schedule of remuneration differed in various collectives.

L. Yurkovsky, a former Soviet advocate, now in the United States, asserts that at a general assembly of the Moscow Provincial College of Defenders in May 1928, Krylenko speaking with foam at the mouth declared that "if the Soviet advocate contradicts the state accusation, he, consequently, opposes the Soviet state and they (the advocate) must be dispersed, and disposed with shooting by a military squad and banishment". [3]

The law of July 20, 1930 created a Department of Legal Defense within the People's Commissariat of Justice. Its duty was to furnish

---

[1] D.S. Karev, *Sudoustroystvo*, M. 1948, p. 290.

[2] A. Ye. Vyshinsky, *Sots. zak.*, 1934, No. 10, p. 31.

[3] L. Yurkovsky, "Slander", *Novoye Russkoye Slovo*, N.Y., September 3, 1964.

general guidance to the lawyers' activities and their organization. Thus, control over the legal profession by the administration was further tightened.

e) *Statute of February 27, 1932*

The Statute on the Colleges of Defenders of February 27, 1932 obliged the colleges to carry out all their work exclusively through the Legal Consultation Offices, to prepare young lawyers through practice for membership in colleges and to propagandize Soviet Law. According to the Statute, clients could choose the counsel to whom they wanted to entrust their case. Although the work of the colleges was directed by their presidiums, the general political guidance and supervision was attributed to the territorial, regional and union courts. For a short time guidance and supervision of the legal profession passed from the hands of the administration to the courts.

Admission was granted out by the collectives themselves under the supervision of college presidiums. The control of the collective belonged to the general assembly of its members and the board. Also a commission was functioning on auditing. The remuneration of the defenders was fixed by a tariff.

The legal profession in general was in such precarious condition that many voices became loud in demanding [1] the abrogation of the profession in general.

Curiously enough, it was A.Ya. Vyshinsky who most effectively defended the legal profession. At the All-Union Conferences of the Leading Workers of the Court and Prosecuting Organs, he declared [2] that those who think that "we can live without the legal profession, that defense is not necessary and even harmful, are mistaken". He described the role of the defense as especially important in court since the working population needs qualified legal help. "The court" said Vyshinsky, "...often cannot concentrate its attention on individual facts and circumstances in a from which is very important for the case and, thus, for the fate of the accused. The role of the counsel, similar to that of the prosecutor, is to draw the attention of the court to such facts and circumstances and to give them an explanation which the court cannot find without their help". [3]

---

[1] Kursky, *op. cit.*, p. 94.
[2] *Sots. zak.*, 1934, No. 5, p. 31.
[3] *Ibid.*

"The situation is so—Vyshinsky declared—that, in the main, the defense is hardly tolerated and, at best, attempts are made to express disregard of the defense, intending to prove by this behavior one's high "revolutionary attitude". [1]

The 1936 Constitution made necessary the reorganization of the administration of justice. Laws on the Court System, of August 16, 1938, and the decision of the USSR government on the Statutes of Advocates, of August 16, 1939, [2] effected this reorganization.

f) *Statutes of August 16, 1939*

The college system was retained. Persons who are not members of colleges may be admitted to exercise the legal profession only by special permission of the People's Commissar (since 1946,Minister) of Justice of the appropriate Federal Republic.

Who had the right to be a member of a college according to the Statute of 1939 ?

1. Persons with higher legal education [3] (attendance at courses for four years). 2) Graduates of law schools (attendance in courses during two years) who have practiced law in the capacity of judges, prosecutors, investigating magistrates, or legal advisors for a probationary period of not less than one year. 3. Persons without legal education but who have worked in the capacity of judges, prosecutors investigating magistrates, or legal advisors for not less than three years.

Persons deprived of electoral rights, or convicted in criminal courts, as well as persons under criminal investigation or indictment are excluded from admission to colleges. These rules have allegedly been amended in that only applicatns for admission who posess a higher legal education are accepted.

Y. Zaitsev, and A. Poltorak, writing in 1959 asserted that 87% of the membership of the Moscow City College consisted of lawyers [4] with higher education. It means that 31% had no higher legal education. The authors who made the assertion about the amendment to the 1939 Statute omitted to indicate whether the exclusive admission to colleges of advocates of persons with higher legal education was practiced by

---

[1] *Ibid.*, p. 30.

[2] *Sob. post., SSSR*, 1939, Item 394.

[3] See the Section, "Legal Education" in this book, pp. 263-312.

[4] Y. Zaitzov and A. Poltorak, *The Soviet Bar*, M. 1959, pp. 52-53.

the Moscow City College only or the admission rules of the law of 1939 were officially amended.

As a matter of fact, L. Lensky, a member of the Moscow College of Advocates, complained that "nobody except a graduate of a medical school may become in 1951 a physician, but an advocate may be a person without a special education. It is time to rule that nobody has the right to join the legal profession without a legal education". [1]

In 1948 D.S. Karev wrote : "The presidiums of the colleges of advocates face the important problem of improving the qualifications of the advocates. [2] Furthermore, in 1959, Karev asserted that during the previous year very much had been said about the inability of the graduates to compose procedural papers and their poor knowledge of criminology, especially in the application of science and technology to crime investigation which was emphasized at the conferences of the RSFSR Ministry of Justice and Prosecuting Agencies. [3]

A college member could be expelled for the following reasons : a crime established by the court, behavior detrimental to the position of a Soviet advocate, and violation of internal order regulations. An appeal against the decision of the college presidium declining admission or ordering exclusion from membership could be made to the People's Commissar of justice of the federal or autonomous republic. The decision of the People's Commissar of Justice of the Federal Republic and the decision of the latter could be appealed to the USSR People's Commissar of Justice, whose decision was final.

According to the law of 1939, the length of the probationary period for persons with legal education but without legal experience had to be established by the USSR People's Commissar of Justice. In Art. 3. of the Istruction No. 47 of the USSR People's Commissariat of Justice of April 23, 1940, the probationary period was fixed at one year. [4]

The same instructions which were dedicated to the problem of "preparation of young lawyers and trainees for independent work" prescribed that the young lawyers should be trained under the direction of experienced advocates who were charged with initiating them into the methods of practical legal work. During the time of probation,

---

1 *Literaturnaya Gazeta*, May 24, 1951.
2 D.S. Karev, *Sudoustroystvo*, M. 1948, footnote 1 on p. 295.
3 D.S. Karev, "Higher Legal Education", *Sots. zak.*, 1959, No. 2, p. 17.
4 *Sovetskaya advokatura*, M. 1942, p. 22.

the trainees were paid wages. If after six months of probation the young lawyer proved unfit for legal work, he was excluded from the college by its presidium. On the other hand, if the results of the year of probation were satisfactory, the trainee became a full-fledged member of the college.

The organs of a college were the general assembly of all the members and the presidium elected by the general assembly. The presidium guided the work of the college, admitted and excluded college members, assigned them to individual consultation units, etc. It exercised disciplinary power over the members, i.e., examined complaints lodged against them and had the right to inflict the following punishments: slight reprimand, rebuke, strong rebuke, suspension from practice for up to six months, and exclusion from college membership. The activity of college members was exercised in legal consultation offices organized by the presidium of the college in district centers and other cities of the republics.

The client who needed legal help turned to the legal consultation office of his city or district. He could not choose the lawyer whom he preferred to entrust with his case but rather, he had to deal with one of the members of the consultation office assigned to him by the chief of the office. The client could, however, express the desire to use the services of a particular lawyer; the final decision remained with the manager of the office.

The fees—at rates established by the USSR People's Commissariat of Justice—were paid to the consultation office. After a deduction of 25-30 percent for expenses (remuneration of the college presidium, salary of the clerical personnel, and the lawyers-in-training, etc.) the money earnings of every member of the legal consultation office were distrubuted to them.

g) *The Number of Advocates*

The number of advocates is uncertain.

Before World War II, there were 127 colleges of advocates, 10,543 advocates and 478 lawyers-in-training, who were distributed among 1,461 legal consultation offices.

As of January 1, 1947, the number of colleges increased to 150, the number of advocates to 13,134, and the number of legal consultation offices to 4,613. Women constituted 30% of the college membership. Among the advocates, only 41.7% had received higher legal education, 20% were graduates of law schools. The remaining 38.3% had no legal education whatsoever.

Writing in 1941 Kruglov [1] reports that 11,000 advocates handled the legal affairs of millions of people. In 1940 they delivered more than 100,000 reports, lectures, and conferences ... In his opinion there were 3,500 advocates in the RSFSR at that time, of whom more than 3,000 had graduated from institutions of higher education.

A. Ya. Sukharev asserts that 7,000 advocates were united in 73 colleges in the RSFSR in 1964, [2] wereas Lapenna estimates their number at 8,000 for the RSFSR and at 18,000 in the Soviet Union in 1963. [3]

Kukarsky calculated the number of advocates in possession of a higher legal education at 80% of the total number in the RSFSR in 1964, whereas the rest had a secondary legal education on studied by correspondence in legal institutes. [4]

However, according to Sukharev, the advocates are unequally distributed in the Republic. Thus, 103 districts in the RSFSR have no advocates at all and their inhabitants are forced to revert to legal consultation offices located tens of kilometers from them. In the Kuybyshev Region, among 152 advocates of the Region, 100 are domiciled in the city of Kuybychev. The Smolensk Region has 34 advocates in 6 cities : but 8 other cities, and 8 rural districts, are served by only 6 advocates. It is peculiar that in a number of former districts centers militia and prosecutors' offices were retained, but legal consultation offices were abolished.

For many years the legal profession was poorly replenished. Sukharev reports that more than one-third of the advocates active in the RSFSR territory, are older than 50 years of age. Advocates under 30 form only 6% of the staff. He calls for the retraining of advocates in special courses and through the exchange of experience between legal consultation offices and colleges and also with the help of teaching by correspondence so that "all the advocates should have higher legal education in the nearest future".

Professor E.L. Johnson of the University of Durham, who visited the Soviet Union in 1954 as a member of a British delegation of

[1] Kruglov, *Sots. zak.*, 1959, No. 2, pp. 17-18.

[2] A. Ya. Sukharev, "Vital Problems of the Soviet Legal Profession", *S.G.P.*, 1964, No. 10, pp. 4 and 12.

[3] Ivo Lapenna, "The Bar in the Soviet Union and Yugoslavia", *International and Comparative Law-Quarterly*, April 1963, p. 646.

[4] I. Kukarsky, "Heighten the Level of the Legal Profession's Activity", *Sov. yust.*, 1964, No. 18, p. 7.

jurists, reports that the Moscow College consists of 1,014 advocates (among them 383 women) and that there are 24 legal consultation offices in Moscow with 30 to 60 advocates attached to each.

According to T. E. Neyshtadt there were 1,125 members in the Moscow City College, including 440 women in 1958. [1] Among this number 481 advocates were members of or candidates for the communist party of the Soviet Union, 145 were reworded by orders of the Soviet Union; 312 participated in World War II and 80 in the Civil War. Among them are members of the Association of Soviet Writers, Composers, Teachers of Higher Institutions of Learning, and 22 have academic degrees and titles.

Twenty-five among the advocates worked in the legal profession since 1922, and some of them were lawyers and assistant lawyers before the revolution. But, according to Sovetskaya Yustitsiya, there were already 1,167 advocates in Moscow from which about 1,000 had a legal education, in 1942. [2]

Neyshtadt gives some other statistical material which may be quoted since such material concerning the legal profession is even more scarce than in other fields.

He relates that in the city of Moscow more than 250,000 persons requested legal aid in consultation offices. In 1957, 132,422 items of advice and information were given on questions of civil, family and labor law, as well as on other legal questions; 41,101 declarations to courts and administrative agencies were made and a great number of civil and criminal cases taken care of.

Let us look into the work of one of the Moscow legal consultation offices in the Krasnopresnenskiy District in 1957: 11,485 persons requested legal aid; 8,874 items of advice were given out and papers written. This amonut was broken down into questions concerning the following topics : dwellings—2234; labor claims—642; pensions—844; family law—1760; civil law—860; criminal law—1630; torts—550 and inheritance law—264. During the same period 2,611 cases, the majority of which were civil, were handled.

Besides legal help to the population, the advocates propagandized Soviet Law by means of reports and conferences at enterprises and institutions. More than 80% of the advocates in Moscow participated in the propaganda work. Advocates—members of the Society for the

---

[1] T.E. Neystadt, *Sovetskiy advokat*, M. 1958, p. 11.
[2] *Sov. yust.*, 1941, No. 6, p. 15.

Dissemination of Political and Scientific Knowledge—delivered 3,060 reports and lectures at important enterprises, agencies and public organizations and agitation points.

The Editorial of Sovetskaya Yustitsiya No. 7, 1957 reports that the lawyers' colleges of the RSFSR had 8,000 advocates, of whom more than one-half were members of the KP and the great majority had legal education. The exact percentage is not indicated.

The advocates delivered 62, lectures and reports in 1956, of which 11,000 went to kolkozniks.

h) *The Basic Principles of Court Structure of 1958 and the Legal Profession*

The Basic Principles of Court Structure of the USSR and Union Republics of 1958 provided that the legal profession will be regulated in the future not by a federal law like the Statute of 1939, but every supreme soviet of the union republics will confirm statutes on the legal profession in accordance with the national characteristics of the republic concerned (Art. 23). Colleges of advocates are defined in the basic principles as voluntary association of persons engaged in the legal profession and functioning according to satutes confirmed by the supreme soviets of the individual Union Republics.

The law of 1958 introduced new principles in the organization of the legal profession. Functioning under the Statute of 1939, it was supervised and directed by the USSR Ministry of Justice through the union republics' ministers of justice until 31 May 1959 when the USSR Ministry of Justice was abolished. After the elimination of the USSR Ministry of Justice the supervision and direction of the legal profession was assigned to the jurisdiction of the individual union republics' ministries of justice. Then the union republics, with the exception of the RSFSR and the USSR, also abolished their ministries of justice. The functions of the ministries of justice with regard to the legal profession were taken over, as a rule, by the councils of ministers of the individual union republics (at the Kazakh SSR these functions are carried out by a special Legal Commission, attached to the Council of Ministers of the Kazakh SSR).

According to law the legal profession is a "voluntary association of persons" under the supervision and direct guidance of the state. Voluntariness as embodied in the principle that nobody may be incorporated into the legal profession without an expression of his or her will to this effect, that everyone meeting the required conditions to exercise the legal profession must be admitted to the college of advocates.

But still, an element of coercion inheres in this principle of voluntariness; namely, the impossibilty of exercising the legal profession without belonging to the college of advocates.

Ye. P. Dubkov thinks that it is doubtful as to whether the prohibition of private practice has even a remote connection with the voluntariness of association, since every association, including those of a voluntariness of association, since every association, including those of a voluntary character, must assume a certain degree of collectivistic activity by its members. On the contrary, the system of associations would be devoid of membership and senseless if private practice would be allowed. [1] The argument, that also in a socialist society there are associations the members of which are occupied with private work, as for instance, the Association of Soviet Writers, Dubkov rejects with the assertion that also the association is working collectively (collective discussion of prepared books, etc.) "Just a greater amount of collectivism is inherent in the lawyer's activity", he writes. For him "The collective form is the highest form of work organization".

According to the Basic Principles of Court Structure of the USSR, the Union and Autonomous Republic of 1958, it is the function of the administration of justice to protect the social and state structure of the country. The socialist system of economy and socialist property established under its Constitution and the Constitutions of the union and autonomous republics must be protected against all encroachments thereon, as well as the political, labor, housing and other personal and property rights and interests of Soviet citizens as guaranteed by the Constitution and the constitutions of the union and autonomous republics ... [2]

The Basic Principles of Criminal Procedure of the USSR and the Union Republics of Dec. 25, 1958 defines the duties of the defense counsels as follows : "The counsel for the defense must use all legal means and ways of defense in order to clarify circumstances vindicating the accused or mitigating his responsibility and extend to the accused the necessary legal help" (Art. 23).

---

[1] Ye. P. Dubkov, "The Democratic Bases of the Organization and Activity of the Soviet Legal Profession", *S.G.P.*, 1962, No. 6, p. 109.

[2] Zeitsev and Poltorak, *op. cit.*, p. 39.

One of the great changes introduced by the law of 1958, was the admission of the advocate to the preliminary investigation in its final stage. [1]

In accordance with these provisions, all union republics enacted statutes for the legal profession between 1960 and 1962. Let us consider the Satute confirmed by the RSFSR Supreme Soviet on July 25, 1962. [2]

i) The RSFSR Statute of July 25, 1962

The definition of the college of advocates is identical with that given in the 1958 Basic Principles : "A voluntary association of persons exercizing the legal profession".

However, the purposes of the colleges are defined more extensively in the RSFSR law of 1962 than in the USSR Statute of 1939. Namely the scope is, according to Art. 1 of the new Statute, "the defense in the preliminary investigations and in court, representation in civil cases in court and in arbitration proceedings, as well as the extending of ohter legal help to citizens, enterprises, agencies, organizations and collective farms in the RSFSR". To this effect republic (in autonomous republics), territorial, regional and city (in Moscow and Leningrad) Colleges of advocates are organized.

The admission of the defense to the preliminary investigation is an innovation produced by the provision of the RSFSR new Code of Criminal Procedure establishing in Art. 201 that after the investigating magistrate has collected the evidence against the accused and formulated the accusation in a special brief, he has to inform the accused that the preliminary investigation is completed and that the accused has the right to make himself acquainted with the material gathered against him or do it "with the help of counsel".

In this connection, the Code provides that the right for counsel to confer with the accused under four eyes, to get acquainted with the material of the investigation and make abstracts from them; to request additional investigative actions, collection of evidence, etc; to challenge the investigating magistrate, the prosecutor, and experts; to lodge complaints against actions of the investigating magistrate which violate or restrict the rights of the counsel or the accused, and to be present, however, only with the permission of the investigating magi-

---

[1]   V.V.S., SSSR, 1959, No. 1.

[2]   V.V.S., RSFSR, 1962, Item 450.

strate, at the performance of investigating actions additionally requested by the accused or by his cousel.

The admission of counsel to the preliminary investigation, although
only at its final stage, is certainly an extension of the rights of the
defense, since Article 13 of the Basic Principles describing the functions
of the advocate in terms of providing defense in court and other legal
help to citizens, enterprises, institutions and organizations does not
mention the preliminary investigation.

Art. 1 of the Statute also underlines the duty of the legal profession
to extend its activity to kolkhozes.

With regard to the legal help to enterpizes and kolkhozes it seems
that the work of the colleges has been extended in this direction greatly
during the last years.

Kukarskiy reports that a substantial part of the advocates' activity
is dedicated to the legal help to enterprizes, institutions, kolkhozes
and sovkhozes. [1] In 1967, legal help by advocates was extended to
7000 enterprizes and institutions, 3000 kolhozes and 1400 sovkhozes,
in the RSFSR. [2]

Furthermore, the Statute adds, to the duty of the legal profession
to protect the rights of the said parties, also the obligation to contribute to the observation and strenthening of socialist legality and administration of justice.

Art. 4 of the Statute states that only members of colleges may exercise the legal profession, as advocates.

The general guidance of and supervision over the colleges is the
function of the RSFSR Ministry of Justice. The organization and guidance of and supervision over the individual colleges is the duty of the
councils of ministres of the autonomous republics, the executive committees of the territorial and regional soviets as well as of the city
soviets, respectively.

The supervision rights of these agencies includes the right of rejecting a newly enrolled member [3] of the college within a month after

---

[1] The legal help provided to enterprizes and institutions by members of colleges
should not be mixed up with the activity of the jurisconsults. (See Infra, pp. 571-572.)

[2] I. Kukarsky, "The Soviet Legal Profession is 45 years old", *Sov. yust.*, 1967,
No. 10, p. 2.

[3] This rejection right is qualified as "*otvod*", challenge, in Soviet legal literature
(cf. K.F. Gutsenko, "On the New Statute on the Legal Profession, Passed by 13 Republics", *S.G.P.*, 1962, No. 3, p. 61) an identical term that is used for the challenge of a
judge or assessor in court. It would be better to say "peremptory challenge" since no

the receipt of the notification of his admission by the presidium of the college.

In contradistinction to the Statute of 1939, the new Law prescribes a higher legal education and two years' experience in legal work as a prerequisite for the admission to the college. If a person who graduated from an institution of higher learning has no experience in legal work or less than two years of experience, the admission to the college takes place after a period of six months of probation. The order of the probation is established by the RSFSR Ministry of Justice.

However, with permission a person lacking a higher legal education, but in possession of five years' experience at legal work, may become a member of the college.

In some of the union republics admission to the college of persons with a secondary legal education and five years of legal experience is exceptionally possible. But in the Lithuanian SSR a person without legal education, but in possession of five years of legal experience, may be admitted to the legal profession without special permission.

The provision permitting exception to one of the basic requirements for the admission to the college—higher legal education—has been criticized by Soviet writers. So Dubkov is of the opinion that "In consideration of the increased requirements posed to the legal profession by the decisions of the XXIInd Congress of the Communist Party of the USSR, it is inexpedient to retain in the new legislation exceptions permitting the admission to the legal profession, of persons without a higher legal education. [1]

Indeed, these exceptions are too numerous. So in 1967, Kukarsky reported that the staff of the RSFSR legal profession has noticibly improved during the last years. "At the present time 80% of the advocates have a higher legal education". [2]

But the same assertion Kukarsky made in 1964. [3] Thus, during

---

substantiation is necessary and the challenge automatically excludes from the college. There is no appeal against the challenge. The right of challenge belongs to the supervising agency also according to some other statutes on the legal profession, such as in Kazakhstan, Uzbekistan and Tadzhikistan. But there the right presupposes the illegality of the admission. The RSFSR Statute does not have such a limitation.

[1] Dubkov, "The Democratic Bases of the Organization and Activity of the Soviet Legal Profession", *S.G.P.*, 1962, No. 6, p. 109.

[2] I. Kukarsky, "The Soviet Legal Profession is 45 years old", *Sov. yust.*, 1967, No. 10, p. 1.

[3] I. Kukarsky, "To Heighten the Level of the Legal Profession's Activity", *Sots. zak.*, 1964, No. 18, p. 7.

the years 1964-1967 the percentage of advocates with a higher legal education has not increased in the RSFSR.

Although admission to the college is granted by the presidium of the college and notice there-of is given to the council of ministers of an autonomous republic or the executive committees of the territorial or regional soviets or of the Soviets in Moscow and Leningrad within seven days of the admission, these agencies, besides the right of peremptory challenge mentioned above, are also entitled, as is the college presidium, to exclude a member of the college in the following cases : a) discovery of unfitness for the fulfillment of the duties of counsel; b) systematic violation of rules of internal order of the college of advocates and the unscrupulous fulfillment of duties; c) the receipt of remuneration apart from that provided by the legal consultation office; d) actions discrediting the name of a Soviet lawyer; e) commission of a crime.

The reasons under a) and c) were not mentioned in the Statute of 1939. The insertion of c) indicates that human nature did not change under Socialism and Krylenko's judgment (see infra p. 502) remained valid.

The decision of the college presidium approving or rejecting the admission to the college may be appealed to the council of ministers of an autonomous republic, to the executive committee of the territorial or regional soviets, or of the City Soviets in Moscow and Leningrad, respectively, which are entitled to reverse the decisions of the college presidium.

Not admitted to the college are persons with criminal records whose moral and business qualities do not correspond to the position of a Soviet lawyer.

The self-governing organs of the legal profession in the RSFSR remained the same as provided by the 1939 statute : the general assembly of college members (called "conference" of the college if it has more than 300 members), the presidium and auditing commission.

1. *Self Government*

The general seembly, or conference, the college's highest organ : 1) elects the presidium and the auditing commission; 2) hears and confirms reports on and takes discussions concerning the work of the college; 3) establishes the number of members of the college, its personnel, the estimate of income and expenses, which are subject to confirmation by the council of ministers of an autonomous republic, or the executive committees of territorial or regional soviets, or of the City Soviets in Moscow or Leningrad, respectively; 4) confirms rules of internal order of the college, in agreement with trade unions; examines other questions related to the work of the college.

The General Assembly or Conference is convoked at least once a year by the Presidium. But also the administrative agencies mentioned above have the right to request the convocation of a general assembly or conference.

The quorum of the general assembly is two-thirds of all attending members of the college whereas a conference is formed by delegates elected by the individual legal consultation offices and is called to order when two-thirds of all delegates are present.

Again the agencies entrusted with the general supervision of the college work are entitled to revoke a decision of the general assembly or conference if it violates the law or the statutes of the legal profession.

The presidium remains the executive organ of the college. Members of the presidium as well as of the auditing commission, are elected by secret ballot. [1] The candidates are elected to membership of the presidium and the auditing commission if they receive a majority of votes cast by college members present at the general assembly or conference. The number of members of the presidium and the auditing commission is established by the general assembly-conference.

The functions of the presidium have been extended in the new statute as compared to those provided by the 1939 statute by some essential provisions. It must now take measures for the increase of the high-minded political level and legal qualifications of college members, to organize the participation of advocates in the propaganda of Soviet legislation, to control the quality of the advocates' work, to generalize the positive experience of the work performed by the legal consultation offices and advocates, to work out and publish methodical text books on the advocates' activities.

The presidium must also study and generalize the material gathered by the college with regard to criminality and other law violations and present appropriate suggestions to state and public organizations.

---

[1] Elections by secret ballot are provided not in all Statutes on the legal profession. For instance, the Presidium and the auditing commission are elected by open voting in the General Assembly in Kazakhstan and Kirgiz Republics and in Azerbaydzhan by the Council of the Legal Profession.

The Presidium elects its Chairman and his Deputies which must be confirmed by the Council of ministers of an autonomous republic or the executive committees of the territorial or regional soviets, or of the City Soviets in Moscow and Leningrad, respectively.

The work of the Presidium is divided between its members. For instance, "In the Presidium of the Moscow Collegium the work is distributed as follows : the President exercises general guidance and has charge of the finances. One of his Deputies attends to admissions to the college, assigns each lawyer to a definite consultation office and prepares the material for the hearing of disciplinary cases. Another Deputy checks on the quality of the professional work and is engaged in generalizing the experience of the most eminent members of the bar. The remaining members of the Presidium take care of the work carried on with young lawyers on probation, look after the social work of bar members, see that the right fees are charged, generalize the work of the meetings in the consultation offices and direct the work of the meetings in the consultation offices and guides the work of the two departments—criminal and civil". [1]

The work of the advocates is, as before, concentrated in the legal consultation offices according to their qualifications and requests of the clients for individual lawyers. The office manager must see to it that some lawyers are not to be overloaded with work when other lawyers have a small amount of work. It is he who sets the amount of remuneration for the work performed by lawyers.

In the following cases no fees are charged : 1) alimony suits; 2) in suits for maiming inflicted during production; 3) writing of requests for pensions and subventions; 4) writing of requests, grievances and other papers on request of soldiers and seamen in the consultation office; 5) for giving oral information and advice.

Besides the enumerated cases, the manager may free the client from fees also in other cases, on the ground of the client's material conditions.

The manager supervises the quality of work and takes measures for its improvement.

He acts on the basis of a delegation of power by the presidium of the college.

New on the 1962 Statute is the enumeration of rights and duties of an advocate. It is brief in detailing the positive rights but expansive

---

[1] Zaitsev and Poltorak, *op. cit.*, p. 72.

in setting restrictions to his rights and the number of his duties. His positive rights are : to elect and be elected to the organs of the college and participate in the discussion of questions connected with the activities of the college. With regard to his participation in the preliminary investigation and sessions of the criminal and civil court he is referred to the Criminal and Civil Codes of the individual republics.

The advocate also has the right to a subsidy in case of a temporary inability to work and to a pension according to general rules.

The advocate is forbidden to take over a case when an official related to him takes part in the preliminary investigation or decision of the case, or if he has rendered legal services to a person before whose interests are opposed to those of the person who asks him to accept the case, or has previously participated in the case, in the quality of a judge, investigating magistrate, prosecutor, public prosecutor, or a charged with the inquest, witness, expert, interpretor or secretary in the court session.

An advocate is prohibited to serve in agencies, organizations or enterprises. Exceptions may be permitted by the presidium with regard to a teaching or scientific activity. [1]

In the field of professional behavior the advocate is not allowed to divulge information given to him by his client in connection with the legal help he has to provide in the case. The Statute also repeats the provision of Article 72 of the 1961 RSFSR Code of Criminal Procedure that the advocate may not be examined as a witness about circumstances known to him in connection with the fulfillment of his duty as counsel on the case, and of Article 51 of the same Code forbidding the counsel to abandon the defense of the accused once it has been accepted.

The duties of an advocate encompass, according to the Statute, the use of all legal means and every manner of defense of the rights and interests of citizens, enterpises, institutions, organizations and kolkhozes which resort to him for legal help.

Article 30 of the Statute describes the moral qualities required of an advocate : he must be an example of the exact and steadfast

---

[1] Some union-republics statutes on the legal profession do not admit the holding of an additional job even in the field of teaching or research. However, the Tadzhik Statute on the legal profession permits plurality of jobs not only in the field of teaching and scientific activity but also in assuming state positions for advocates who work in the remote regions. This holding of two jobs requires the permission of the College Presidium.

compliance with Soviet laws, of moral purity and irreproachable behavior; he must constantly perfect his knowledge, raise the high principled political level of his professional qaulifications and actively participate in the propaganda of Soviet Law.

2. *Probation* [1]

The length of the probation period is two years according to Article 9 of the Statute. The character of probation is established by the RSFSR Ministry of Justice. The presidium conducts the work with the young lawyer during the time of probation. Usually every probationer has a "patron" an experienced lawyer who directs his work. He is made acquainted with the work in special fields of law, criminal, civil, international, etc. The probationers have to prepare briefs in cases handled by the patrons, attend trials in which the patron takes part, assist him during consultations in the office. Gradually the probationer receives cases to work on independently but under the supervision of the patron.

After the probationary period is finished, the presidium accepts him as a full-fledged member of the college, if the results of the probationary work are satisfactory, or refuses admission if the training results are not adequate. The probationary period is then prolonged for a time set by the Presidium.

During the probationary period the probationer is paid fixed wages by the presidium.

With the admission to the college and the assignment to a definite legal consultation office the training of the young lawyer is not completed. In some legal colleges seminars are organized in which very experienced lawyers and university professors train and retrain young and old lawyers in *"les finesses du métier"* and the handling of particularly complicated theoretical questions.

About every month, a conference of the member lawyers is called by the consultation office. It discusses routine problems, but mainly delves deeply into the more intricate problems that arise in current complicated and controversial trials and lawsuits which require competent advice and handling. This is where the expert knowledge of the older members tells.

---

[1] The *stazh.*

Veinberg criticized the poor preparation of the young lawyers for their profession and the lack of efforts to improve their qualfication. "During all these years after the war not a single advocate got a degree of a candidate (corresponding to a Master's Degree), or of a Doctor in Law", writes Veinberg.

He calls for special attention to the training of young advocates and suggests the creation of a position of a "lawyer's assistant".[1] According to him, the young lawyer must work at least one year in this capacity after graduation from a higher institution of learning. During this time of probation the young lawyer should acquire the necessary skill and insight into the work of a lawyer under the direction of a highly qualified lawyer.[2] This work must be supervised by a consultation office manager who, togehter with the instructing lawyer, selects cases for the probationer to be pleaded by him in court. The instructor to whom the young lawyer is attached has to help him in his daily work and is responsible to the college presidium for his training.[3]

It is peculiar that the Statute of 1962 does not definitely regulate the institution of young lawyers (on probation). Neither their position in the college, nor their rights and duties are established.

Sukharev[4] praises the initiative of the Leningrad Regional and City Colleges which organized a Research Institute for Defense in Court. About 70 members teach in the Institute, comprising the most experienced advocates and scholars from the local law schools. The Institute contributed to the solution of many-sided and complicated problems of Soviet legal practice.

The Moscow City College has formed a special commission attached to its Presidium to work with the young lawyers during their probationary time. This commission guides and controls the work of the young advocates in consultation offices and in court, as well as their training in specially arranged courses. Sukharev regrets that not all colleges did organize an adequate training of young advocates and the supervision of their work. Not only do the necessary conditions for

---

[1] Would correspond to the *"pomoshchnik prisyazhnogo poverennogo"* of tsarist times. However, the length of the probationary period in tsarist Russia was 5 years.

[2] The "patron" of the old bar.

[3] E. Veinberg, "Perfection of the Work of the Soviet Legal Prodession", *Sots. zak.*, 1958, No. 10, p. 20.

[4] A. Ya. Sukharev, "Vital Problems of the Soviet Legal Profession", *S.G.P.*, 1964, No. 10, pp. 4, 6, 7.

their training not exist in some colleges, but often attempts are made to get rid of them and all kinds of obstacles are put in the way of their work.

In Sukharev's opinion it is the Legal Commission attached to the RSFSR Council of Ministers, which, having been charged with the supervision over the actvity of the legal profession after the abolition of the RSFSR Ministry of Justice, [1] must seriously occupy itself with the training of the staff of the legal profession; measures for the improvement of the professional, ideological and political preparedness of the staff must be strengthened also materially. Sukharev suggests that a part of the funds of the colleges should be appropriated for the training and retraining of the staffs not only in the regional but also on the republic level, since according to him, "serious improvement is needed not only in the quality of the defense in criminal cases, but also in the representation in civil suits and the legal services rendered to the population.

Sukharev thinks that the quality of the defense as a whole, its professional level, still do not correspond to the requirements. "Individual advocates do not fulfill their obligation skillfully and even apolitically". "In their desire to exculpate the criminals by any means, they resort to inadmissible methods of defense, hinder the establishment of the truth in the case, do not keep the public and state in mind, with many turning the defense of the accused into a defense of the crime".

As mentioned above, Presidiums of the Leningrad City and Regional Colleges have taken steps toward the theoretical and practical training of advocates. They have created a new institution "on public bases", meaning that the work in the institution is honorary, not remunerated. It is the Research Institute on Problems of Court Defense. The Institute has the task to develop forms and methods of defense of lawful rights and interests of citizens, socialist enterprises and organizations. The Institute also intends to study and generalize the experience of the participation of the public in the preservation of legal order and citizens' rights, as well as the prevention of violations of the law. It is meant to contribute to the perfection of the legal profession's activity by putting achievements of Soviet legal science into practice.

---

[1]   V.V.S., RSFSR, 1963, Item 289. The Commission took over all the functions pertaining to the supervision according to the new Statute.

The Institute is divided into four sections : 1) defense in criminal cases; 2) defense in civil, labor law and administrative cases; 3) participation of lawyers in work to prevent violations of the law and propagandize Soviet law; 4) legal services to socialist enterprises and organizations.

The Institute is to pay special attention to the working out of forms and methods for the establishment of reasons of violations of the law and their prevention. The results of the broadening of this approach is to be communicated to corresponding Party, Soviet, economic and prosecuting agencies.

The advocates of the Leningrad City and Regional Consultation Offices will have the opportunity of consulting the Institute and getting its conclusions on the most complicated legal questions in their practice.

Seminars, theoretical conferences, reports and lectures will contribute to the perfection of the professional work of the advocates.

Legal scholars, advocates, members of other legal organs, counsels of enterprises and organizations of Leningrad participate in the work of the Institute in the capacity of scientific workers.

The Learned Council of the Institute, consisting of eminent legal scholars of Leningrad, who are the most experienced and qualified advocates and representatives of the Prosecutor's Offices, take care of the most important questions concerning the Institute's work and plans for its activity.

The Institute is entrusted also with working out and publishing scientific practical and methodical text books written on the basis of the study and broadening of the legal professions's work. An editing and publishing council will publish transactions, scientific works, collections of advocate's court summations and practical textbooks.

The doors of the Institute are open too for legal scientists and advocates of other colleges. It works in close contact with scientific legal institutions and the Legal Commission attached to the RSFSR Council of Ministers.

3. *Disciplinary Responsibility*

Like the 1939 Law, the 1962 Statute prescribes a disciplinary procedure for cases of violations of the internal order, negligent and unscrupulous fulfillment of duties and other actions discrediting the name of an advocate. This provision is under a rule of limitations :

a disciplinary punishment may not be applied if more than one month has passed after the action has become known and more than one year after the action has been committed.

The list of disciplinary punishments is shortened in the new Statute : dropped is the strict reprimand and suspension of activity for not more than six months.

Disciplinary proceedings may be initiated by the presidium of the college but also by the supervising state agencies.

The Presidium sits as disciplinary court. [1] The procedure itself is not described in detail. It is only said that before the session, the presidium has to require a written explanation from the accused advocate, check thoroughly the evidence calling for the initiation of disciplinary proceeding and make him acquainted with the entire material in the case.

There are no other details given on the session of the disciplinary court with the exception of the provision that it must take place in the presence of the accused.

Sukharev thinks that it is now sometimes difficult to recognize the line in the desciplinary practice of the colleges. Cases are not rare when an advocate receives severe punishment for various violations and misdemeanors and then, during the same year, on the occasion of a convention or celebration, he receives a citation or other bonus. Thus, for instance, the Presidium of the Altay College gave awards to almost one-fourth of the advocates for good work on May 1, 1963. But only one month later three among them were punished for poor work and violations of discipline, and the facts that prompted their punishment were already known to the Presidium when it granted the reward. "Certainly", remarks Sukharev, "such practices do not contribute to the educational work". [2]

The decision of the Presidium in disciplinary cases may be appealed to the ministry of justice of an autonomous republic or to the executive committees of territorial or regional Soviets or city Soviets in Moscow and Leningrad, respectively, within two weeks.

By virtue of a special provision of the Statute, if the guilty advocate does not commit a new act subject to disciplinary prosecution within one year, the first conviction is considered not to have taken place.

---

[1] The Latvian Statute of the Legal Profession provides for a special Disciplinary Court.

[2] A. Ya. Sukharev, *op. cit.*, p. 10.

Also, if the advocate shows that he has reformed by conscientious work and irreproachable behavior, the presidium may remit the punishment before he has served it in full. The petition for remission of the punishment can be filled by the manager of the legal consultation office where the advocate works.

It must be emphasized that no disciplinary codes for advocates exist in the Soviet Union. Individual colleges assume different viewpoints on what is a disciplinary violation.

Curiously enough, G. M. Shafir [1] reports that some times it is assumed that if a counsel pleads for acquittal but the court sentences to a punishment, the counsel must be subjected to disciplinary responsibilty, an assertion which certifies to the poor conception of the counsel's work not only by courts and the prosecuting body but by the advocates themselves.

4. *Autonomy*

Although the colleges are a "voluntary" organization according to Soviet definition, they enjoy only a small degree of autonomy. In reality, a tough state supervision is exercised over the legal profession. Indeed, the RSFSR Ministry of Justice is charged wit the general guidance and supervision over the profession. The State Administration, not judicial agencies, are prominantly included in the system of the profession's supervision and administration. It is the RSFSR Ministry of Justice which establishes the order of probation for the young lawyers; the table or remuneration fees for the activity of lawyers are confirmed by the RSFSR Council of Ministers; the council of ministers of an autonomous republic and the executive committees of territorial and regional Soviets, as well as of the City Soviets in Moscow and Leningrad, are appellate instances for decisions of the Presidium excluding lawyers or denying them admission to the college, as well as for decisions of the presidium in disciplinary procedure; these agencies also have the right to make exceptions to the rule requiring higher legal education for the admission to the bar; to call a general assembly (conference) of the college, to reverse a decision of the general assembly and the college and to exclude advocates from the college as result of these proceedings; to confirm elections

---

[1] G.M. Shafir, "Some Suggestions for the Organization of the Soviet Legal Profession", *S.G.P.*, 1965, No. 10, p. 102.

to the presidium, and the right of peremptory challenge of newly admitted members of the college.

All these rights of the government represent not only a supervisory function but active participation in the administration of the legal profession, an authoritative voice in the shaping of its functioning.

However, the RSFSR Statute on the legal profession is not the toughest with regard to the role of the administration in lawyers' affairs. For instance, the new Statute on the legal profession of the Kazakhskaya SSR goes beyond the RSFSR Statute and confers on the Legal Commission, attached to the Kazakh Council of Ministers, even the right to dissolve the presidiums of the colleges if, in its opinion, they do not adequately insure leadership. No Statutes of other union republics contain such a provision. K. F. Gutsenko protests against such a limitation of the democratic bases of the organization and the activity of the legal profession. [1]

When the drafts of the new Statutes of the Legal Profession were submitted to discussion the question was raised as to what agency or institution the guidence and supervision of the legal profession should belong.

In tsarist Russia the individual attorneys-at-law and their councils were attached to the courts of appeal (*sudebnyye palaty*). They remained, so to say, in their own lawyers' family and were tried in disciplinary procedure by their own peers. It is self-understood that lawyers are nearer by their education and activity to judges than to members of administrative agencies and courts are in a better position to guide and supervise them.

However, proposals to entrust this job to the supreme courts of the republics were rejected, and D. Karev finds that just because of this affinity of lawyers' and judges the solution of the question in the way we have seen above is correct.

Karev writes namely that "the supreme court of union republics, especially in republics not having regional administrative division, come in a very near contact in their activity with attorneys-at-law who direct complaint to court colleges and presidiums. It will be difficult to the supreme courts to combine their basic activity with guidance of the colleges of advocates". [2]

---

[1]　Gutsenko, *op. cit.*, p. 61.

[2]　D.S. Karev, "What must be the Statute on the Legal Profession?", *Sots. zak.*, 1960, No. 9, p. 25.

It is peculiar that an advocate in eminent position expressed himself in favor of an adminstrative agency : the Chairman of the Moscow City College of Advocates, V.A. Samsonov, discussed the question of the forms of state guidance of the advocates.

Samsonov opposes the opinion of "some advocates" that the organization of the advocates, as a public and self governing one, like the association of Soviet writers, composers, artists, journalists, etc. [1] does not need state guidance. He argues that although the Soviet advocate organization is, according to its character, a public organization, still to deduce from this fact, that its activity can take place without the control and guidance of the state, means not to understand the peculiarities of the legal profession and of the specific problems faced by it, and, of the same time, not to realize the reasons, why just to the legal profession—one of the responsible links in the adminstration of justice—a public character was attributed in distinction of all other links.

It is evident for Samsonov, that the advocate, a participant in the trial, must be fully independent in the realization of his functions. [2] But at the same time, the state is interested that the advocates fulfill their scope in the best way since their entire activity is indisoluably bound to one of the most complicated and responsible state functions, namely the administration of justice. All that makes a general control and guidance of this activity of the advocates by state organs necessary.

With regard to the question, what organs should realize the control and guidance, Samsonov is of the opinion "that the RSFSR Ministry of Justice which assumed the general direction of colleges' activity in the RSFSR" and which "contributed to their good functioning", should retain it in the future. [3]

It is, of course, pure propaganda when Yudin writes in "The Soviet Union", a Soviet periodical distributed in the United States, that "this independence (of the legal profession) is achieved by the very structure of the college of barristers. Such colleges are self-governing democratic institutions. No one interferes in their everyday activities.

---

[1]   In reality, also these organizations are under the "guidance" of the state when even not officially.

[2]   Samsonov does not state in what extent the advocate must be independent also from his client.

[3]   V.A. Samsonov, "The Soviet Legal Profession and Its Role in the Further Strengthening of Soviet Legality", S.G.P., 1960, No. 11, p. 29.

The Ministry of Justice merely supervises the work of their presidiums". [1]

But Samsonov defends also the system of lawyers' collectivization against criticisms by western writers :

"Bourgeois jurists not seldom assert that the activity of Soviet advocates in the frame of colleges and counsultation offices hinders the correct realization of professional duties of an advocate, depriving the citizens to choose a counsel according to their desire, that the choice of this or that advocate depends not upon the citizen seeking legal help, but from the manager of the consultation office.

The experience of the activity of Soviet advocates discloses the complete failure of such assertions. Furthermore, it eloquently testifies about a number of advantages of the organizational form of advocates activities adopted in the Soviet Union." [2]

But the only argument Samsonov brings forward in support of his assertion is that : "It is well known that in no bourgeois country is legal help so accesible as in the Soviet Union : the Soviet citizens can receive any legal consultation without charge. The principle of advocates work in legal consultation offices itself, creates favorable possibility for good legal service for the population and for the professional growth of the advocate himself, as well." [3]

Legal help without charge is provided also in the Soviet Union not for everyone, but for those who cannot pay only. This last category of citizens get legal help without charge in bourgeois countries also. Unfortunately, Samsonov fails to explain just why collectivization promotes good legal services and professional growth.

G.M. Shafir makes some suggestions for the improvement of the organization of the legal profession in the USSR.

He claims that the counsel's work in court is not sufficiently checked and studied. Not enough attention is paid to the discussion of counsel's summing up and the experience of the best lawyers is not dissiminated among their colleagues. Also the press is paying too little attention to counsels' work.

A main defect in the organization of the legal profession, Shafir sees in the lack of centralized guidance of the profession. Such a Republic, for instance, as the RSFSR, which has 72 regional and city

---

[1] A. Yudin, "Counsel for the Defense", *The Soviet Union*, 1958, No. 100, p. 35.

[2] Samsonov, *op. cit.*, p. 25.

[3] *Ibid.*

colleges of lawyers, or the Ukrainian SSR, have no organizational center uniting the work of the advocates.

"The similarity of problems posed to colleges of advocates, the unity of procedural forms in which the advocates work, the one and the same character and content of their activity requires the union of the colleges at least within a republic". [1]

The author thinks that a unified organizational and methodical guidance of the legal profession could certainly bring the solution of controversial questions in the life of the legal profession; it would produce the necessary unification of court practice of the experience in the serving of state and public enterprises, institutions and organizations, a definite solution of methodical and practical questions of counsel's activity.

However, D. Karev is just of the opposite opinion. He thinks the argument that every regional or territorial college of advocates is left to its own resources, the practice of the lawyers is not generalized and unified methodical guidance is lacking, and there is no one and the same system of remuneration, etc., are not completely founded.

According to him, the advocate can exchange their experience, first of all, on the pages of the legal periodicals, at conferences of legal workers, to which as a rule, representatives of the advocates are invited, by participation in scientific sessions of law institutions of higher learning and legal juridical organizations. [2]

In the line of Shafir's thinking a suggestion was made by Yu. M. Aristakov, M.I. Piskotin, Kh. S. Sulyemanov and L. I. Urakov. [3] They proposed to form an association of all Soviet jurists. The unity of basic problems facing all Soviet jurists, independently where they work, demand regular communication between them, the coordination of their efforts, which is likened to the present time.

The main scope of the association was thought by the author in the unification of Soviet jurists for an active cooperation toward the strengthening of socialist legality, the propagation of Soviet law among the population and the development of friendly relations with jurists of foreign countries.

---

1 G.N. Shafir, "Some Suggestions for the Perfecting of the Soviet Legal Profession Organization", *S.G.P.*, 1965, No. 10, p. 102.

2 D. S. Karev, "What Must be the Statute on the Legal Profession ?", *Sots. zak.*, 1960, No. 9, p. 25.

3 "On the Necessity of the Creation of a Soviet Union Jurists Association", *Sots. zak.*, 1959, No. 10, p. 321.

The association will increase the possibility of more tight contact between the scientific and practical workers and the strenthening of bonds between the legal science and the practice of Socialist construction. [1]

Dubkov is suggesting a more autonomous structure of the legal profession.

According to him the individual territorial, regional and city colleges must be centralized, united in one central college of the republic. The organs of administration must be the congress, presidium and auditing commission.

All the administrative work should be divided between these organs.

Also Dubkov stresses the fact that only 80% of the advocates have a higher legal education. Among the remaining 20% there are persons who have only a general primary or not completed secondary education and some training or legal courses. "As a consequence of the insufficient general and the lack of a special education they cannot fulfill the duties assigned to them. Such persons exist in not every but in many colleges". [2]

However, the realization of Dubkov's and others suggestions would not mean the creation of a national organization of lawyers similar to the American Bar Association. Such centralization would be unacceptable to the Soviet Government.

According to Sukharev, [3] serious defects in the education of the staff, the slackening of the leadership and the control of the activities in some of the colleges made possible such unhealthy phenomena as admission to colleges by favoritism, unscrupulous groveling at elections of functionaries of colleges, misuse of official position, and even such crimes as bribery. Sukharev explains these phenomena in the first place by the lowering of the moral and of the staff of some colleges produced by a defective practice of new members admission. As an example he cites the admission by the Presidium to the Krasnoyarsk College of a certain Valeyev who previously had worked in six colleges from which he was excluded for self-seeking practice and squabbles. In 1961, he was convicted of hooliganism and his behavior was several times discussed in the press.

---

[1] Pp. 32-34, *passim.*

[2] I. Dubkov, "To Perfect the Organization of the Legal Profession's Self Government", *Sov. yust.*, 1965, No. 14, pp. 25-26.

[3] A. Ya. Sukharev, "Vital Problems of the Soviet Legal Profession", *S.G.P.*, 1964, No. 10, p. 10.

Writing in 1967, Kukarsky finds that the Soviet legal profession still suffers from many defects : some members of the colleges fulfill their duties only formally, without the necessary qualfications, are superficially acquainted with their cases, deliver umpersuasive defensive speeches, write illiterate briefs ... In a series of colleges the work of juridical assistance to kolkhozes and sovkhozes is on a low level. [1]

B. COUNSEL'S DUTIES AND RIGHTS IN THE TRIAL

The duties and rights of counsel in the trial are listed in Article 51 of the RSFSR Code of Criminal Procedure.

As we have pointed out above, the duty of counsel is to use all the means and measures of defense indicated by law to clarify the circumstances justifying the accused or mitigating his responsibility and to extend to the accused the necessary legal help.

To this effect, counsel has the right to participate in the case from the moment he is admitted; to confer with the accused; to acquaint himself with all the material of the case, and to prepare abstracts of all necessary information from it; to present evidence; to submit petitions; to participate in court examination; to logde challenges; to make complaints against the actions and decisions of the investigating magistrate, the prosecutor and the court. With permission of the investigating magistrate, defense counsel has the right to be present during the interrogation of the accused and the performance of other investigative actions carried out on petition of the accused or his defense counsel.

Furthermore, when defense counsel is admitted to the participation in the case from the moment of the presentation of the accusation, he is entitled : [2]

1. to attend when the accusation is presented to the accused and he is interrogated; and with the permission of the investigating magistrate to question the accused;

2. to be present when other investigative actions are conducted with

---

[1] I. Kukarsky, "The Soviet Legal Profession is 45 Years Old", *Sov. yust.*, 1967, No. 10, p. 6.

[2] It means only in cases when the accused is a minor, disabled physically or mentally and cannot themselves realize their rights to defense. (Article 47 (2).)

and to put questions to the witnesses, victim or expert, with the permission of the investigating magistrate;

3. to make observations in writing on account of the correctness and completeness of the entries into the minutes of the investigative actions in which he participated.

The investigating magistrate may reject questions of the defense counsel, but is obliged to enter the rejected questions into the minutes.

The participation of defense counsel is mandatory:

1. when a state or public prosecutor participates in the case;

2. when the accused is deaf, dumb, blind or in consequence of his physical or mental defect, cannot realize the defense himself;

3. when the accused is a minor;

4. when he does not understand the language in which the procedure is conducted;

5. when several persons are accused, have contradicting interests and even one of them has a defense counsel;

6. when the accused is brought to court for a crime which is punishable by the death penalty.

If in the cases mentioned above a defense counsel is not hired by the accused himself, his legal representative or by other persons commissioned by the accused, the investigating magistrate or the court are obliged to secure the participation of a defense counsel in these cases.

Counsel is entitled to file an appeal in cassation and to participate in the session of the cassation court when the appeal (or the prosecutor's protest) are examined.

But the right to take part in sessions of the Supreme Courts of the USSR and the Union Republics is conferred on him by law only if he is invited to do so by the court.

The rights and duties of counsel with regard to his client and his position in the procedure are discussed elsewhere in this book.

The provisions mentioned above enumerate the right of counsel, but they do not speak of rights which the counsel has in every Western country and which he is deprived of in the Soviet Union.

Indeed, counsel has no right to collect evidence in favor of his client. He cannot oblige agencies to give information favorable to the accused. Admitted to the trial he has no possibility to study the accusatory material. He cannot summon additional witnesses or experts.

C. Counsel and the Preliminary Investigation

The admission of counsel to the preliminary investigation certainly is a measure of liberalization of the criminal procedure.

Although admitted only to the last phase of the proceedings, the advocate still has the possibility to help his client in this stage of the criminal proceedings.

It must be said, objections against the admission of counsel at an earlier stage were voiced from very authoritative sides. So M. A. Chel'tsov states that "if one considers the real situation, the earlier admission of counsel to the preliminary investigation will hamper the investigating magistrate during the carrying out of the questioning of witnesses, of the accused and confrontation. In the presence of several accused in the case, and, i.e., the admission of several counsels, the normal carrying out of the investigation would be just impossible". [1]

Objections from another viewpoint against the admission of the counsel to the preliminary investigation in general were presented to the Leningrad Executive Committee in 1957 by a group of jurists : they argued that the admission of counsel to the preliminary investigation will mean the expression of distrust toward the prosecuting body and not a guarrantee for the observation of legality.

The admission of counsel from the stage of the presentation of the accusation on will inevitably lead to the disclosure of secrets of the preliminary investigation and will in reality bring to the weekening of the fight against criminality, not mentioning the fact that it will procedure a substantial prolongation of the terms of the investigation. [2]

Objections against the admission of counsel to the preliminary investigation at an earlier stage had an influence on the final content of the law : the first draft of the RSFSR Code of Criminal Procedure submitted to public discussion in 1957 provided namely, the participation of counsel already from the time of the presentation of the accusation, whereas according to Article 201-203 of the RSFSR 1961 Code of Criminal Procedure, counsel begins his functions in the preliminary investigation when the investigating magistrate has collected all the material in the case, virtually completing the investigation, and presents it for acquaintance to the accused and his counsel.

---

[1] M.A. Chel'tsov, *Sovetskiy ugolovnyy protsess* (Textbook), M. 1951, p. 111.

[2] Quoted by A. Rozhansky, "The Participation of the Counsel in the Preliminary Investigation", *Sorok let sovetskoy advokatury*, M. 1962, p. 35.

Although A. G. Peskin comes to the conclusion that practice testifies that the admission of counsels to the preliminary investigation proved its value and that the participation of the counsel has a fruitful influence on the quality of the preliminary investigation, he points out the following defects of the procedure :

1. the investigating magistrate often presents material on the last day of the term assigned by law for the completion of the preliminary investigation so that the counsel has not enough time for a thorough analysis of the material and think out the defense;

2. counsel's demands about additional action in the preliminary investigation are rejected by the investigating magistrate because he has no time to fulfill them;

3. cases occur when individual investigating magistrates take a negative attitude toward the right of the counsel to demand the requalification of the crime and the quashing of the procedure because of lack of evidence. [1]

The negative attitude of some investigating magistrates and prosecutors towards the participation of counsels in the preliminary investigation is psychologically explained by Rozhansky.

He thinks that an investigating magistrate who conscientiously is of the opinion that his work on the case is fully completed and is faced by such requests of the counsel as the collection of additional material, the change of the crime's qualification, i.e., the application of another provision as that he thought appropriate, the exclusion from the accusation of some episodes because of lack of evidence, or even the quashing of the entire procedure, must, in order to comply with such requests, reconsider his own viewpoint.

Such a reconsidering is, psychologically, very complicated.

Also the prosecutor, who supervised all the stages of the preliminary investigation and to whom complaints against the rejections of the counsel's requests are directed, shares the investigating magistrate's opinion.

"That is why", concludes Rozhansky, "such complaints do not bring the desired results in most of the cases, and only the court in a number of trials comply with the counsel's request and pronounce a sentence different to the formulation of the accusatory resolution". [2]

---

[1] A.G. Peskin, "Some Questions of the Practice of the Counsel's Participation in the Preliminary Investigation", in *Razvitiye prav grazhdan SSSR i usloviya ikh okhrany*, Saratov, 1962, pp. 338-339.

[2] Rozhansky, *op. cit.*, p. 36.

But besides psychological grounds, the law itself is imperfect, since it does not set concrete terms for the examination of requests presented by counsels during the preliminary investigation and the lodging of complaints against the decisions posed in the requests.

As a result of these gaps in the legislation, a situation is created, Kalyayev relates, "when at the time the counsel comes in possession of the decision on his request by the investigating magistrate, the case is already under court examination, and a counsel's complaint to the prosecutor becomes objectless". [1]

It is interesting to note that the necessity of the advocate's participation in all stages of the preliminary investigation must be insured to the accused in both procedures, and was stressed by Shafir at the Scientific and Methodical Conference at the USSR Supreme Court in 1966.

In his opinion, the defense must be admitted and at any time during the criminal procedure, including the revision of the case in the way of supervision.

Also Pulatkhod Zhayev, Chairman of the Uzbeck SSR Supreme Court, spoke in favor of the extension of the advocate's participation in criminal procedure. He held it necessary to widen the cases of the obligatory participation of the advocate in the preliminary investigation and in the court of original jurisdiction.

The obligatory participation of the counsel shall be required in cassation procedure at least in cases of minors, persons afflicted with physical or mental defects when the prosecutor lodged a protest against an acquittal or a too lenient sentence. The participation of a qualified defense will help the court of second instance to examine the essence of the case more deeply and objectively, according to Shafir. [2]

Certainly, this liberalization is still not a complete return to the policy of admitting the defense to all stages of the preliminary investigation followed by the first Soviet Decrees on Courts.

However, the demand of extending the admission of the defense to the preliminary investigation is growing among Soviet jurists.

Thus, Shafir [3] raises the question of legislation with regard to counsel's participation in the preliminary investigation and the

---

[1] A. Kalyayev, "From the Experience of the Counsel's Participation in the Preliminary Investigation", *Sov. yust.*, 1964, No. 9, p. 17.

[2] *Ibid.*, pp. 18-19.

[3] G.M. Shafir, "The Right of Defense in Soviet Criminal Procedure and the Possibility of its Enlargement", *S.G.P.*, 1967, No. 2, pp. 47-53.

inquest. Article 120 of the RSFSR Code of Criminal Procedure excludes the defense completely from the inquest, although the same article provides that the inquest in cases not mandatory subjected to a preliminary investigation, have to be guided by "rules established by the Code for the preliminary investigation".

Certainly, he is right when he asserts that there is no difference in principle in the two forms of investigation, and that the exception of Article 120(2) curtailes the rights of the defense of the accused.

Of the same opinion are Strogovich and Grabovenko [1] who wrote that "It is indifferent to the accused what organ will investigate the case of his crime. All the guarantees for the accused must be insured in both procedures, the right of defense must be accessible to all the accused in all cases".

Shafir justly thinks that the right of defense is generated at the time when the accusation is formulated, it means at the beginning of the preliminary investigation and not at its end. Since the right of defense of the accused is realized by his counsel, the latter must be admitted to the preliminary investigation at its beginning rather than at its end. The selection of the time the defense counsel may be admitted to the preliminary investigation made by the Code of Criminal Procedure has no ground what-so-ever, he thinks.

Unjustified, according to him, is also the lack of provision, making the participation of the counsel mandatory in the cassation procedure as it is in some cases during the preliminary investigation and the trial. The extension and the counsel's participation also to this phase of procedure would correspond to the democratic spirit and sense of the Soviet criminal procedure and be an important step in the further democratization of Soviet criminal procedure. [2]

Furthermore, he demands the full admission of counsel to the procedure of re-examination of cases already in force. [3]

A. Piontkovsky is a strong supporter of the increase of counsel's rights in the preliminary investigation.

He asserts that "the time has come, it seems to us, to think over the

---

[1] M.S. Strogovich and Grabovenko, "Guaranties of the Individual's Rights in Criminal Procedure", in *Democraticheskiye osnovy sovetskogo sotsialisticheskogo pravosudiya*, M. 1965, p. 249.

[2] Shafir, *op. cit.*, p. 52.

[3] According to Article 377 of the RSFSR Code of Criminal Procedure, the Court has only the right to summon to its session the convicted or acquitted or their counsels to the session examining a case in the way of judicial supervision.

enlargement of the counsel's rights in the preliminary investigation. We think that the counsel may be admitted from the stage of the presentation of the accusation. This will contribute to the heightening of the preliminary investigation's quality and, thus, to the strenthening of the justice. This would also promote the role and authority of defense in criminal procedure". [1]

Also Kuprishin, is of the opinion that the participation of counsel in the preliminary investigation should be extended. He quotes cases in which the activity of counsel in the beginning of the preliminary investigation would have prevented many errors of the investigating magistrate which according to legislation in force could be corrected only during court procedure in several instances.

Being confined to the demand of additional investigative actions on the part of the investigating magistrate, the accused and counsel have the right of complaint to the prosecuting body if the investigating magistrate declines the demand.

These demands, Kuprishin emphasizes (he is the Chairman of the Kiev Regional College of Advocates) have usually little chance of being satisfied by the investigating magistrate who finished the investigation and came to definite accusatory conclusions. The complaint to the prosecuting body has also no effect usually. The prosecutor often rejects the complaint with the motivation that the files are already transferred to the court. Thus, "the defense rarely complains about the rejection of their demand by the investigating magistrate."

Kuprishin states, that the advocates of the city and region of Kiev complained against 40% of the accusatory resolutions of investigating magistrates in 1963, against 33% in 1964; in 1965 the percentage dropped to 19%, and to 15% in 1966.

Kuprishin asserts that data are already collected permitting one to come to the conclusion about the effectiveness of the participation of counsel in the entire preliminary investigation.

He has in mind the provision of Article 47(2) mentioned above [2] that if the crime is committed by a minor or a person who by reason of his physical or psychic defects cannot realize himself the right to defense, counsel is admitted at the time of the formulation of the accusation, i.e., when the suspect becomes an accused. Thus, the Code of Criminal Procedure already admits counsel to the preliminary investigation in an earlier period, but as an exception. Kuprishin

---

[1] A. Piontkovsky, "Guarantees of Justice", *Izvestia*, August 28, 1965.

[2] P. 486.

claims that the transformation of the exception into a rule would be
of great possitive effect. He refers to comparative statistics which
show that the investigation in the exceptional cases of Article 47(2) is
much more perfect than in general cases and that the referring of
such cases to an additional investigation is extremely rare. He concludes that "the problem of the enlarging of the extention of counsel
participation in the preliminary investigation has overgrown the
limits of the critical arguing a long time ago. Not only jurists have an
interest in its solution. It is a matter of further strenthening of the
guarantees and rights of defense of Soviet citizens and in the end
effect, a measure for the perfecting of the justice apparatus. [1]

D. THE SYSTEM OF REMUNERATION

The system of remuneration of the individual advocates remained
the same as provided by the Statute of 1939. The 1962 Statute dedicates
only 3 lines to the subject, providing that the work of the advocate
is remunerated from the income of the legal consultation office from
fees paid to the office by the clients served. However, the income of
the college is dependent on sums assigned to it by the legal consultation offices. These assignments may exceed not 30% of the office's
income and are established by the general assembly (conferences) of
the college members.

If the fee to be paid by the client did not exceed 500 rubles in criminal cases it is set by the office manager. In complicated cases requiring an unusual amount of legal work the remuneration is set by
the presidium of the college according to the amount of work done.
No limits to such fees are set by law.

In a civil case the fee of the lawyer is calculated in relation to the
sum involved and should not exceed 600 rubles. [2] In civil cases not
involving a definite sum of money, such as divorce, ejection, etc.,
special fees are charged.

In cassation proceedings the lawyer is entitled to 40% of the fee
charged for his work in the first instance; the lawyer handling the

---

[1] V. Kuprishin, "The Advocate and the Preliminary Investigation", *Izvestia*,
September 15, 1967.

[2] Up to 1960, when the "new" ruble was introduced. The figures given in this section
refer to the "old" rubles.

cassation proceedings may charge 80% of the fee established for representation in the court of original jurisdiction.

The remuneration of a lawyer participating in a cassation proceeding in the way of supervision of cases already in force is regulated by special fees.

Let us take an example. The deduction from the fees earned by individual lawyers of the Moscow City College were 25% in 1958. From this 25%, 7% were retained when the advocate took his annual leave, 4% were assigned for social insurance, 1.5% are retained for a fund for the relief of needy advocates, 1% are deducted for the training of young lawyers and their salary (the young lawyer during the probationary period receives a fixed salary of 450 rubles monthly). The rest of the 25% is employed for the maintenance of the presidium staff, the managers of the legal consultation offices, bookkeepers, secretaries, typists and mesengers. [1]

In 1965, the State Committee on Questions of Labor and Wages, attached to the USSR Counsel of Ministers, and the All-Union Council of Trade-Unions, have confirmed a typical statute on the remuneration of advocates, as well as a typical instruction on the charges for assistance extended by advocates to citizens, enterprises, institutions, sovkhozes, kolhozes and other organizations. The individual union republics had to adopt statues and instructions in conformity with the typical statute and instruction. [2]

The system of advocates' remuneration remained the same. However, limits of monthly remuneration of advocates have been established. Up to 160 new rubles in Moscow and Leningrad and their oblasts, not taking into consideration the amount to be transferred to the fund of the college's presidium. In cities of the first category, the level is 150 rubles; in other cities and districts—140 rubles. The exact monthly remuneration is established by the General Assembly of the College according to the financial state of the college. The remuneration of young advocates during their probation (stazh) is 75 rubles monthly.

The earning of the advocate is established as follows:

From the amounts received by the consultation office for the advocates work during the month, 70% is credited to his account, however not more than the remuneration fixed by the statute. At the same time,

---

[1] T.E. Neystadt, *op. cit.*, p. 13.
[2] *Sov. yust.*, 1965, No. 22, pp. 12-15.

a percentage of the earning, as set by the general assembly, is transferred to the college presidiums' fund. From the amount left after the deduction, 50% is additionally credited to the advocate (thosea dvocates who are legal advisors of enterpirses, institutions, sovkhozes, kolkhozes and other organizations receive 70% of the remaining amount). The additional credit cannot exceed one-half of the monthly remuneration set for the advocate.

The chairman of the college presidium cannot earn more than 250 rubles monthly. In Leningrad and Moscow, and the Regions—not more than 300 rubles. The limit of the remuneration of a consultation office manager is 240 rubles monthly.

Also every legal service rendered to the client is strictly regulated : the writing of briefs in simple cases is remunerated by 2 rubles—in complicated questions—by 30. For the writing of a testament the client has to pay 6 rubles. In criminal cases the fee is 15 rubles and the same remuneration is paid in complex civil cases. If the trial lasts not more than 5 days—up to 30 rubles is paid to the advocate; if the duration is 10 days—up to 60 rubles and if more than 10 days—100 rubles. [1]

As all other workers and employees in the Soviet Union, advocates receive a pension at the age of retirement, free medical care and aid in case of temporary or permanent disability.

This system of remuneration of the lawyer has been criticized for a long time. The main defect of the system lies in the principle that only the work of the lawyer for which a fee has been paid by the client and credited to the account of the lawyer is remunerated. However, the work of a lawyer consists not only in pleading in court but also in consultation, advice and also of lectures, reports and conferences on legal subjcets. Although all the lawyers particpate in this work only those are remunerated whose account is credited at the end of the month. It is natural that in consequence of such a system, every lawyer tries to have assigned to him as much of the work as possible which is subject to fees and avoids reports, consultations, writing of complaints, assignment for duty in consultations. The Chairman of a Rostov Regional College of Advocates, N. Abramov, asserts [2] that

---

[1] For details of the advocate's remuneration and the fees paid by the client, see *Sov. yust.*, 1965, No. 20, pp. 12-15.

[2] N. Abramov, "The System of Lawyers Remuneration", *Sots. zak.*, 1957, No. 7, p. 24.

as a result, the income of a lawyer depends not upon the quantity and quality of his work, but upon the number of assignments requiring payment by the client; and "often a highly qualified lawyer, a man of principle, has a much lower income than another, less experienced, but more enterprising lawyer".

The remuneration system creates a serious situation especially for young, unknown lawyers since the paid assignments are, in a high degree, "personal". According to Abramov, the system creates self-seeking among one part of the lawyers and the loss of respect for their work among others.

Faced by growing complaints of their members many regional colleges have undertaken to change the system of remuneration. Abramov reports on the new system introduced in his college and extended to the other colleges of the Rostov Region.

The essence of the new Rostov system is that all the income of the college, after the deduction of 30% for expenses as under the old system, is distributed among *all* members of the college according to the quantity and quality of the work done.

The sytem is applied as follows: From the income produced by the paid legal help during the year 30% is deducted by the college for expenses. The balance is the fund for the remuneration of the members. This fund, divided by 12, is the monthly remuneration of the college members, and the monthly remuneration divided by the number of members is the average montly income of every member for the work he has to accomplish during the month.

In order to figure out the amount of effective work porduced by the individual lawyer, the payments credited to his account for various types of work performed by him are added, and after the deduction of the 30% for expenses, the balance indicates the effective fulfillment of his assignment with regard to the amount of work and the received assignment.

But that is not all. The remuneration is conditioned not only upon the amount of work done, but also upon the qualifications of the individual college member. The qualifications are circumscribed by the education and the number of years served by the lawyer.

According to the amount and complexity of the work, the following bonuses are paid :

a)	If higher education is achieved	10%
b)	If secondary legal education is achieved	5%

c) If the lawyers continuous to work in the same college,

from 3-5 years	3%
from 5-10 years	5%
from 10-15 years	10%
over 15 years	15%

d) If the work is fulfilled

from 100-110%	10%
from 111-120	15%
from 121-130	20%
from 131-150	30%
from 151-200	40%
over 200%	50%

But, if the work assignment is not completed by the individual lawyer, his remuneration is reduced according to the following table :

If fulfilled from 99-90%	reduced by10%
89-75	reduced by 20%
74-50	reduced by 30%
less than 50%	reduced by 40%

If a lawyer's poor work quality is established, the Presidium of the college has the right to deprive him of the qualification increase for a period of up to six months.

This new remuneration system has been introduced at the Rostov Regional College as of May 1, 1957.

The beneficial effect of the new remuneration system was made evident in the first month of its application, according to Abramov. These are the results :

Remunerations of Lawyers according to the old system in April		Remunerations of Lawyers according to the new system in May	
From 300 to 500 rubles	10%	Less than 680 rubles	none
From 500 to 1,000 rubles	23%	From 680 to 1,000 rubles	26.3%
1000 to 1,500 rubles	32%	1,000 to 1,500 rubles	57.8%
1500 to 2,000 rubles	31%	1,500 to 1,700 rubles	15.9%
More than 2,000 rubles	4%		

"The same gratifying results were obtained during the following month of June", writes Abramov.

However, he himself admits that the system needs some corrections. He is not convinced that the educational increases are warranted since "a very small percent of the lawyers lack high education. Questionable are the increases also for the length of service at the college.

On the other hand he thinks that the increased rate for overwork should be revised. [1]

The data quoted by Abramov are really edifying. We see that the category of lawyers earning 300-500 rubles in April disappeared in May and is replaced by a category earning not less than 680 rubles. However, the place of the category remunerated by 1500-2000 rubles monthly, which included 31% of all lawyers in April, is now represented by about only 15.9% of all lawyers earning not more than 1700 rubles monthly, whereas the category earning from 1700-2,000 and more (4% in April) lacks completely.

Thus, although the least qualified earn more, the most qualified earn less than before and certainly feel frustrated, since it is they who accomplish the best work remunerated by clients.

The argument in defense of the new system is that it is based on the same principle of individual earnings of the members of the college, depending on the number of remunerated cases assigned to them. However, in reality, those who are less efficient will earn more, but the best ones, those whose help is personally requested by the client, will earn less. They will form a group dissatisfied with the new system, as another group was alienated by the old one.

The basic defect of the old and new systems of remuneration lies in the collectivization of the work of the legal profession. Workers, engineers, physicians and scientists work individually. Their earnings depend upon their education and capacity. Their advancement in life is usually related to and conditioned by these features. The lawyer is as handicapped in his personal achievement as is the kolkhoznik. Both depend not on their personal achievment only but on the performance of the entire collective to which they belong.

A new remuneration system of lawyers for the entire country will certainly be adopted. But it is difficult to find a system which as applied to collective work, would correspond to legitimate individualistic desires.

The Editorial in No. 7, 1957, of the *Sovetskaya justitsiya* reported that one-half of the colleges shifted to a new system of remuneration for their members.

Unfortunately, the editorial gives no details of this new system. It says only that advantages consist in the guaranty of an average income to the lawyer corresponding to his qualifications and work.

---

[1] Abramov, *op. cit.*, pp. 26-27.

It permits the managers of the legal consultation offices to distribute the work evenly between all advocates. This system is supposed to provide the presidium of the college with the means of reinforcing quality control of the work and organizing the staff of all legal consultation offices.

But this new system has also defects, according to the author of the editorial. He calls for the creation of a perfect, efficient system of remuneration by an effort of all collectives. [1]

In the meantime the old system of remuneration (not changed by the 1962 Statute) is subject to criticism in many ways. For instance, V. Kozlov, Chairman of the Belgorodsky Regional Court, is of the opinion that since the system of remuneration of the advocates seriously weakens the fight for the improvement of lawyer's work quality, the Ministry of Justice should take measures insuring the speedy shift of the advocates' colleges to a new system of remuneration.

Turgalev is of the opinion that the remuneration system generates foreign habits among the advocates of "private-property" frame of mind and opinions, instills a striving for personal enrichment, selfishness, conceit, self-seeking qualities—he thinks that these unhealthy phenomena could be liquidated by the change of the remuneration system. [2]

An article in the *Sovetskaya Yustitsiya* [3] calling "To Eliminate the Defects in the Advocates' Work", reveals a number of abuses and violations of the remuneration order.

Although the remuneration order prescribes the extention of legal help to citizens free of charge in a number of cases and the managers of the consultation offices have the right to free them from paying in all cases in consideration of their material conditions, abnormal conditions have been created in the Moscow City College, under which the help of an advocate to the population is possible only by paying large sums of money. Although in setting the fees, the material conditions of the applicant for legal help must be considered, individual citizens reverting for legal assistance, in particular to insure defense in court, were obliged to sell a part of their property, borrow money from relatives and friends in order to pay the advocate important amounts of money. In confirming substantial fees set by the

---

[1] Editorial, p. 7.
[2] *Sots. zak.*, 1964, No. 11, p. 50.
[3] 1961, No. 5, pp. 4-5.

the manager of the consultation offices, the Presidium of the College did not check the grounds for the setting of high fees. Complaints of citizens about the amount of the remuneration are lodged with the Presidium and were almost always rejected.

There is a group of advocates in the college which is especially often in receipt of high remunerations from the Presidium for participation in cases of important misappropriation, embezzlement, abuses, etc, whereas these advocates were not obliged to take part in the consultation and propaganda work. In the same time, many other advocates had a very low income as a result of irregular distribution of work.

Neither the managers nor the Presidium took measures against advocates who carried out several criminal cases with high remuneration at the same time without indicating the date of the beginning and the end of the case or dividing the amount of earned money in one month between several months.

The article gives the following example in confirmation of its assertions :

The advocate Yefimenko took part in the Nabiyev case in the Moscow City People's Court from February 6 to March 11, 1960 for a remuneration of 2,000 rubles established by the Presidium and, before the case was closed Yefimenko participated in another case at the same time, from Feburary 15 to March 17 receiving a fee of 4,000 rubles. Thus, the advocate Yefimenko was charged with two important cases between February 15 and March 11th simultaneously receiving a groundlessly increased remuneration of 6,000 rubles (in old money).

In order not to reveal such a high earning, Yefimenko did not indicate the beginning and the end of the cases on registration cards, so that he received the amount toghether with his other earnings in the cases during a number of months.

Thus, concludes the article, in results of the deficient practice of the Presidium of the College and individual office managers costs of the legal help to the population were artificially increased, encouraging the self-seeking tendencies of individual advocates.

The advocate Klyuyeva received a honorarium of 42,200 rubles directly from the client, besides her regular fees through the college. She preferred to resign from the College in order to avoid disbarring. [1]

---

[1]   *Ibid.*, p. 6.

A. Ya. Sukharev [1] complained in 1964 that "up to the present time many legal consultation offices lacked the necessary order in settling accounts with clients for the legal help made available to them; uninhibited practices in the assessment of remuneration were tolerated so that cases in which a honorarium was received apart from the office by individual advocates, as well as cases of extortion and other abuses, took place.

Sukharev also protests against the practice of the legal consultation offices of setting maximum fees for all kinds of legal services, without regard to the complexity of the case or amount of work spent. He calls upon the presidiums and the auditing commissions of the college to wage a decisive fight against self-seeking tendencies of some advocates and to insure the necessary control over the financial activity of the legal consultation offices.

He thinks that, in general, legal help in giving advice and negotiating contracts should be extended by the legal profession, especially to the kolkhozes, not only for remuneration, but also, on a public service basis. "It is not normal", he thinks', "when individual advocates attempt to use this great patriotic action of the legal profession for personal, unfounded enrichment". And he gives the following examples: the advocate of the Stavropol' college Dashevsky, privately obtained 560 rubles from the Geological Expedition for the writing of several briefs and complaints. Finkelstein, an advocate in Kuybyshev, besides the fulfillment of assigned work in court, concluded agreements for substantial remuneration with four organizations : a sulphur factory, a sovkhoz, a poultry farm group and a cleaning shop. His colleague of the Tambov College, Trakumovich, received considerable remuneration from a society for the deaf during two years, although there was not a single case during this time which required his help. [2]

---

[1] A. Ya. Sukharev, "Vital Problems of Soviet Legal Profession", *S.G.P.*, 1964, No. 10, p. 12.

[2] *Ibid.*, pp. 9-10.

CHAPTER SEVENTEEN

THE LEGAL PROFESSION

(Continued)

A. LAWYERS' ETHICS

The 1962 Statute resolved two questions belonging to the ethics of the legal profession which were and are extensively debated in the pre-and-post revolutionary legal literature : the questions as to whether counsel has the right to abandon the defense and to divulge circumstances told him by his client. But other aspects of Lawyer's ethics remained unsolved.

The Councils of the pre-revolutionary Russian Bar were very touchy on problems of lawyer's ethics. [1] Ye. V. Vas'kovsky dedicated a monograph to this problem in 1895. He wrote that "The legal profession, more than any other profession, needs an appropriately drafted professional ethics, in other words a system of rules of personal behavior to be followed by lawyers, the violation of which should be subjected to a disciplinary prosecution. Besides common human ethics a special lawyers' ethics must exist". [2]

The existence of a special lawyers' ethics, was denied by Soviet writers in the beginning.

a) The "Mixed" Cases

Unethical behavior of advocates was and is a frequent subject of complaint on the pages of the Soviet press and in Soviet literature.

The most numerous violations of law and discipline are the so-called "mixed" cases. A "mixed" case is a case in which the advocate receives private remuneration from the client in addition to the fixed fee which the latter pays to the legal consultation office.

There have been a few attempts to justify "mixed" cases by explaining the legal essence of the private remuneration as a tip which is

---

[1] See Samuel Kucherov, *Courts, Lawyers and Trials Under the Last Three Tsars*, N.Y., 1953, pp. 161-196.

[2] Ye. V. Vas'kovsky, *Osnovnyye voprosy advokatskoy etiki*, St. Petersburg, 1895, p. 3.

voluntarily given by the client to the advocate in order to stimulate his work. But there is no doubt that the "mixed" cases are a flagrant violation of the law, which prescribes a fixed schedule for advocates' fees. The "mixed" practice was declared illegal by the Moscow People's Court in the Zemtsov and Ordynsky Case. [1] N. V. Krylenko, a famous prosecutor and jurist during the first periods of Soviet rule, said of the "mixed" case : "It cannot be uprooted under our conditions. To achieve this goal, it would be necessary to change human nature itself. Certainly one cannot uproot this kind of thing by any sort of prohibition or written papers". [2]

Krylenko was right. The "mixed" cases exist and will continue to exist, and "money will change hands" [3] illegally, as long as the legal profession remains "collectivized".

"Indeed", Kukarsky wrote in 1964 that "cases of accepting cash amounts from citizens by advocates besides the money paid to the legal consultation office are not yet liquidated".

But acceptance of a private remuneration by the Soviet lawyer was and is a ground for the disciplining of the culprit. Kruglov relates [4] that the Moscow advocate R. received, at home, an additional honorarium from his client V., and this became known to a number of citizens the next day. After the complaint of V. was checked, R. was disbarred.

The same fate was meted out to the lawyer P. who received, in addition to the legal fees, 15 kg of meat from his client. He also was denounced by the client.

Illegal additional remuneration of the advocate may take the form of not only money. Thus the advocate S. had sexual intercourse with his client at the time of the trial and obtained a part of her dwelling space in an apartment. He was evicted from her apartment and excluded from the legal profession. [5]

Kruglov points out another kind of violation of existing rules also by advocates. He tells that the advocate G. in Leningrad ceded the cases assigned to him by the consultation office to other advocates

---

[1] Azimov, *op. cit.*, p. 13.

[2] Quoted by E.S. Rivlin, *Sovetskaya advokatura* (Moskva, 1926), p. 21.

[3] "Nothing prevented persons from making secret agrements with defense attorneys on the panel under which money changed hands." J.N. Hazard, "The Lawyer Under the Soviets", *Wisconsin Law Review* (1946), No. 2, p. 94.

[4] T. Kruglov, "Advocate's Ethics", *Sov. yust.*, 1941, No. 4, p. 10.

[5] Kruglov, *op. cit.*, p. 10.

for a small remuneration. Thus violating the order of the USSR Ministry of Justice, No. 35 of 1938, according to which the manager of the consultation office has to distribute the cases among the lawyers and not the lawyers themselves according to their desire. [1]

It is interesting to note that the USSR Supreme Court decided, in 1938, that the taking of private remuneration is not an offence in the sense of the criminal law. [2] But the Statute on the Legal Profession of 1962 declared such action a ground for disbarring.

b) *Renunciation by Defense*

The question of whether counsel has the right to discontinue the defense during a criminal trial, if he becomes convinced of the culpability of the accused was raised as early as 1925 on the occassion of Counsel L's refusal to continue the defense. [3]

In connection with this case, Yu. Elkin and Vl. Kaufman wrote an article in which they offered the question for public discussion. They argued as follows : Since Article 306 of the old RSFSR Code of Criminal Procedure gives the prosecutor the right "to drop the accusation if he comes to the conclusion that evidence gathered during the trial does not justify the indictment", counsel must have the right to discontinue the defense if he becomes convinced that the trial did not produce any weighty arguments in favor of the defense. The authors' conclusion is based on the interpretation of the position of counsel in the Soviet court. The Soviet counsel, according to them, is an aid to the court who must assist the court in finding the right decision. The Soviet court, they argued, examines the complex intricacy of life from a class viewpoint and combines the law with the class consciousness of judges : the court demands every kind of help from its two aides : the prosecutor and the counsel. In the authors' opinion, the aim of the counsel is not the defense of the interests of the individual considered apart from the class interests of all workers and peasants. They maintained that the defense must be based on the combination of both class and individual interests—which class interests predominating, however; under no circumstances must the counsel search for far-fetched grounds of acquittal; therefore, after Counsel L. came to the conclusion that he had before him a socially

---

1 *Ibid.*, pp. 10-11.
2 See the Decision in another connection, below, p. 535.
3 *Izvestia*, April 4, 1925.

dangerous criminal, he acted lawfully in abandoning the defense instead of trying to find circumstances which could mitigate the defendant's guilt. [1]

This opinion was shared by M. D. Kakitelashvili, who considered that counsel, whether appointed by the court or hired by the accused, has the right to drop the defense if he comes to the conclusion that his client is guilty : in such cases defense counsel challenges himself, like a judge who feels himself unable to fulfill his duty impartially. [2]

M. Stroyev went even further in this respect, asserting that defense counsel has to give a true characterization of the accused and a reliable picture of the crime, even if they are more unfavorable to the accused than those given by the prosecutor. He commends the behavior of a counsel in a trial in which "the prosecutor tried to find extenuating circumstances in favor of the accused, whereas the defense counsel in his summing-up criticized the prosecutor for such groundless attempts and declared that, unfortunately, there are no mitigating circumstances in favor of the accused in this case". [3]

In his book on the criminal court of the RSFSR, D. B. Rubinshtein, after having asserted that the Soviet counsel plays the role of an aid to the court and of a control organ obliged to detect the seak sides of the accusatory argumentation, declared that in cases when the material gathered during the trial is not sufficient to repudiate the assertions of the accusation, the counsel is obliged to declare to the court that he has no remarks or new arguments to add to those presented by the prosecutor. [4]

However, it cannot be asserted that there is unanimity in Soviet legal literature on the question of whether the counsel has the right to drop the defense during the trial. Thus, Al. Levin argued that the Soviet counsel has no right to quit the defense, except in cassation proceedings when there are no sufficient reasons for cassation. He is obliged, according to Levin, to carry out the difficult tasks of collecting all the elements in favor of the accused wherever he can find them

---

[1]   Yu. Elkin and Vl. Kaufman, "May a Counsel Drop the Defense During the Trial ?", *Yezhenedel'nik sovetskoy yustitsii*, 1925, No. 23, pp. 843-845.

[2]   M.D. Kakitelashvili, "Is It Admissible for an Appointed or Selected Counsel to Resign the Defense of the Interests of the Accused During the Trial ?", *Yezhenedel'nik sovetskoy yustitsii*, 1925, No. 29, pp. 992-993.

[3]   M. Stroyev, "The Role of the Defense in a Criminal Trial", *Yezhenedel'nik sovetskoy yustitsii*, 1925, No. 34, p. 1137.

[4]   D.B. Rubinstein, *Ugolovnyy sud RSFSR*, M. 1925, p. 113.

—in the class position of the accused, his personality, ignorance, illiteracy, financial conditions, in the circumstances of the crime, etc. —and must present the collected material to the socialist court. [1] N. N. Polyansky supported Levin's opinion, [2] D. S. Karev also flatly asserted : "The counsel, in contradistinction to the prosecutor who may drop the accusation, has no right to quit the defense". [3]

Also M. Andreyev is of the opinion that defense counsel has no right to lay down the defense during the trial. He distinguishes however, the activity of a lawyer hired by the accused, from that of a counsel appointed by the court. With regard to the first he thinks the question is irrelevant : the hired counsel will defend under any circumstance since he does not want to lose his remuneration. But also the appointed counsel does not need to quit if he comes to the conviction that his client is guilty. If the accused pleads guilty then counsel must find circumstances mitigating his guilt. Such circumstances can be found in every case if examined under this point of view, according to Andreyev's opinion. If the client denies his guilt in spite of the crushing evidence against him, the counsel must tell the court that "If you believe the accused you will acquit him", but, "since I have to admit that you will not believe him, I will bring to your attention circumstances which, in my opinion, can mitigate his guilt. [4]

Strogovich, already in his textbook of Criminal Procedure of 1938, denied the right of counsel to drop the defense.

M. S. Strogovich rejects the analogy between the right of the prosecutor to drop the accusation and of the counsel to discontinue the defense, independently as to whether counsel is of the opinion that the guilt of the accused is proven or not. He values the dropping of the defense as a "desertion to the enemy discrediting the Soviet defense and producing a very negative effect". [5]

Then, in 1948, Strogovich wrote that the time is past when the question of the right of counsel to drop the defense is debatable. Strogovich considered that the reasoning : "If the prosecutor has the right to give up the accusation, the counsel has the right to quit the

1 Al. Levin, "Is the Counsel Allowed to Drop the Defense During the Trial ?", *Yezhenedel'nik sovetskoy yustitsii*, 1925, No. 35, p. 1165.

2 N.N. Polyansky, *Pravda i lozh' v ugolovnoy zashchite*, M. 1927, p. 45.

3 D.S. Karev, *Sudoustroystvo*, M. 1948, p. 292.

4 M. Andreyev, "Does the Defender Have the Right to Drop the Defense ?", *Rabochiy Sud*, 1926, No. 1, p. 3.

5 M.S. Strogovich, *Uchebnik ugolovnogo protsessa*, M. 1938, p. 126.

defense", [1] is a sophism, because the accusation of an innocent person is intolerable and illegal, whereas the defense of every person, even of a guilty one, is admissible and legal, provided the methods of defense are honest.

Contrary to Strogovich's opinion, it must be said that the problem of counsel's right to abandon the defense remained unresolved in the USSR up to the new Statute of 1962. Thus, in a letter to the editor of Literaturnaya Gazeta, the President of the Presidium of the Leningrad Oblast' College, M. Vladimirov, related a case in which counsel during the trial became conscious of the guilt of the accused, although the latter denied it to the end. Abandoning the position taken by the accused, counsel in his summing up did not ask the court for acquittal but for leniency only. The accused charged counsel with treason.

The behavior of counsel was discussed in a session of the College Presidium, and many were of the opinion that counsel was wrong, since it was his duty to present competently the arguments of the accused to the court without giving his own opinion. On the other hand, there were members of the College who approved of his behavior. Was the counsel right or wrong? asks Vladimirov, leaving the question unsolved. [2]

According to the Bulgarian Edict on the Legal Profession of 1958, the lawyer after he has accepted the defense has not the right to withdraw during the trial. [3]

c) Divulging Secrets

The problem as to whether or not counsel should divulge secrets entrusted to him by his client, was also extensively discussed in Soviet legal literature.

T. Kruglov considered that the Soviet counsel has no right to hide from the court what he has learned from his client, since a counsel who would act in this manner would not be an aid to the court; on the contrary, he would deliberately complicate court proceedings and bring confusion into a clear case. Such behavior, according to Kruglov, would be not only improper fulfillment of counsel's duty but a crime

---

[1] M.S. Strogovich, "The Procedural Position and Functions of the Defense", *Zashchita v ugolovnom protsesse*, M. 1948, p. 3.

[2] *Literaturnaya gazeta*, May 24, 1951, p. 2.

[3] See S. Rosoff, *Highlights of Current Legislation*, April 1959, p. 155.

against the state. Exception should be made, Kruglov thinks, only in the case of circumstances of a strictly personal character, without any influence on the outcome of the trial, which counsel is not obliged to disclose to the court.

To the question : "Can the lawyer in fulfilling his professional functions, hide from the court that, which was told him by his client ?" Kruglov answers : "Certainly not".

Kruglov relates that the advocate U. asked him whether he could keep secret in the trial certain facts of which he had just been informed by his client and which should not be made known in the interest of the client. "I recommended to U. that he inform the prosecutor in the trial about these facts before the beginning of the trial, in order that he could receive instructions from the USSR Prosecution Office. In this way", asserts Kruglov, "this case was resolved rightly". [1]

Another opponent of the duty to secrecy of the Soviet counsel was Elkind. He thought that the situation when an advocate should be prevented from denouncing a crime brought to his knowledge is incompatible with the socialist nature of the legal profession. Since defense counsel has to defend only legal interests of his client, the counsel cannot hide, that means silently defend, illegal interests of his client, without coming into conflict with his "socialistic nature".

He refutes also the argument of the necessity to keep, in the interests of the accused, secrets divulged by the accused.

According to Elkind the practice in general does not know such cases where the defense of the legal interests of the accused would require professional secrecy ; the necessity of such a professional secrecy is felt only when the counsel wants to defend some illegal interests of his client.

The necessity of keeping professional secrecy in the public interest is also denied by Elkind, bacause the honorable functions of the legal profession are not based on professional secrecy in the sense that counsel may keep secret from the state crimes devulged to him by the client. In his opinion, the duty of counsel to inform is limited to counter-revolutionary crimes and some crimes against the governmental order and does in no way solve the question from the viewpoint of the lawyer's ethics.

---

[1]   T. Kruglov, "Advocate's Ethics", *Sov. yust.*, 1941, p. 11.

Finally, Elkind asserts that the procedural norms prohibiting the interrogation of defense counsel as a witness (Art. 61 of the old RSFSR Code of Criminal Procedure)" are obsolate and must be changed, in order not to oblige the advocate to hide violations of the law communicated to him by his client". [1]

Elkind holds to his opinion in spite of his own acknowledgement that the principle of professional secrecy of defense counsel, known already to the old Romans, was accepted in theory and practice in all civilized countries in the world. Certainly, Elkind's opinion was expressed at a time when the accused "confessed" to crimes which they had committed and of which they were innocent.

Kruglov's viewpoint became the subject of discussion in an assembly of Moscow lawyers. His thesis that "there is no such thing as an obligation of secrecy for a counsel" was rejected by the majority. It was pointed out that, should counsel be obliged to disclose to the prosecution everything which the accused has confided to him, he would lose all his clients. However, exception was unanimously made for cases of counter-revolutionary crimes, in which it was said that no secrecy could be tolerated. [2]

Strogovich argues that the question of secrecy is a legal problem and not a matter of lawyer's ethics. To confirm his opinion he refers to Art. 61 of the old RSFSR Code of Criminal Procedure, according to which counsel cannot be heard as a witness in a case in which he acted as a defense counsel.

But political cases are an exception also in Strogovich's opinion : if counsel becomes aware of a counter-revolutionary crime, either completed or in preparation, "counsel is obliged, as a Soviet citizen, to transmit the information to the appropriate authorities and resign his activity as a defense counsel in the case". [3]

For N. N. Polyansky "every communication made by the client under four eyes is confidential and that is why it must remain secret" [4]. Like Strogovich, he derives this obligation of defense counsel from Art. 61

---

[1] P.S. Elkind, "Advocate's Ethics", *Sov. yust.*, 1940, No. 4, p. 19.

[2] *Sov. yust.*, 1941, No. 11, p. 17.

[3] Strogovich, "The Procedural Position and Functions...", *op. cit.*, p. 38. Such a provision is contained in the Ukrainian Code of Criminal Procedure (Note to Article 62). Although other Soviet Codes have no similar provisions, Strogovich considers that the matter is self-evident even without specific mention.

[4] N.N. Polyansky, *Pravda i lozh' v ugolovnoy zashchite*, M. 1927, pp. 28-29.

of the old RSFSR Code of Criminal Procedure. But in contradistinction to Strogovich and other authors, mentioned above, he does not make any exception for counter-revolutionary crimes.

Polyansky thinks that the principle of secrecy is also based on its necessity in order to make possible the counsel's task and this has a public value. However, Polyansky admits another exception to the rule of secrecy only when counsel is named a witness in the case of the accused before he receives from the accused the defense commission.

His exception is made for the case when the accused would like to eliminate the lawyer as a witness by naming him his counsel for the trial.

On the other hand, Cheltsov flatly declared that "Professional Secrets as such are not known to the Soviet Criminal Procedure". [1] But, Cheltsov opposes the opinion of some Soviet writers that the provision of Article 61 of the old Code of Criminal Procedure, forbidding the interrogation of a counsel as a witness, is obsolete. The abolition of the provision would undermine the institution of the defense guaranteed by the Constitution, according to him.

S. N. Abramov in his textbook on Soviet civil procedure extended the exception from the secrecy rule to all cases in which failure to denounce is punished by criminal law (Art. 18 of the old RSFSR Criminal Code) "since the protection of the social and political system established in the USSR must prevail over all other interests". [2] In his opinion, the provision established for criminal cases must be applied in civil suits too. [3] In this respect, he disagrees with Chel'tsov, who is against the extension of this provision to civil cases. [4]

With regard to the lawyers obligation of secrecy it is of interest to quote here provisions adopted in some other Communist States.

Before the advent of communism, the organization of the legal profession in Albania was similar to that of West European countries. After the organization of the "People's Republic" in 1946, the Law of Nov. 1946 (No. 354) on the Legal Profession provided that "the lawyer is no longer permitted to keep to himself facts which he has

---

[1] M.A. Chel'tsov, "The Problems of Soviet Defense and the Procedural Position of Counsel", in *Advokat v sovetskom ugolovnom protsesse*, M. 1954, p. 66.

[2] S.N. Abramov and others, *Grazhdanskiy protsess*, M. 1948, p. 213. In the 1952 edition of this textbook, the justification for the extention is omitted (Abramov, *Sovetskii grazhdanskii protsess*, M. 1952, p. 224).

[3] *Ibid.*

[4] M.A. Chel'tsov, *Sovetskii ugolovnyi protsess*, M. 1929, II, p. 133.

learned from the defendent, but is bound to refer them to the investigating authorities". The Law of 1953 (No. 1601) introduced some amendments to this general rule. Article 16 of this Law reads : "Lawyers may keep professional secrets, but they are bound to transmit to the State Security Agency all information learned in connection with their professional activity concerning crimes against the state, as defined in Articles 64 to 75 and Article 83 [1] of the Criminal Code". [2]

Also in Czechoslovakia, where the bar has been similarly sovietized, the keeping of the accused's secrets by the counsel is regulated by law. The Law on the Bar of Dec. 1948 (No. 322) contained the following provision : "A lawyer must divulge a secret confided to him by his client if the Minister of Justice directs him to do so" (Sec. 4) [3] The new Law on the Bar of Dec. 20, 1951, which replaced the Law of 1948, provides that "a lawyer must keep matters confided to him secret unless the party relieves him of this obligation. He is not bound to testify about these matters before a court or an agency of the state unless the Minister of Justice, for an important state reason, relieves him of this obligation. A lawyer may not invoke his obligation to keep a secret if under the provision of the Criminal Code, Sec. 165, Subsection 2, [4] he is bound to inform the authorities of a crime committed ..." [5]

In Yugoslavia, according to the Law on the Bar of Dec. 16, 1946, a lawyer may be ordered to testify about secrets of his client whenever government interests and protection of legality are involved. The Minister of Justice of the individual republics and the Lawyer's Chamber may order the lawyer to testify at their discretion. [6] However, the structure of the Yugoslav bar was different from that of the Soviet Union. Although the law of 1946 was "intended to organize the advocates in Yugoslav, if not wholly, then at least at a great extent,

---

[1] Articles 64-75 and 83 refer to crimes against the Albanian State and economic crimes (including those against the Soviet Union and the People's Democracies), etc.

[2] Kemal Vokopola, "Reorganization of the Bar", *Highlights of Current Legislation and Activities in Mid-Europe*, 1955, No. 7, pp. 169 and 171.

[3] Stefan Kocvara, "The Bar Sovietized", *Highlights of Current Legislation and Activities in Mid-Europe*, 1956, No. 2, p. 36.

[4] Provisions protecting the Republic and its regime.

[5] Kocvara, *op. cit.*, p. 42.

[6] Dr. Franz G. Jupanovich, in *Highlights of Current Legislation and Activities in Mid-Europe*, 1955, No. 5/6, p. 166.

on this Soviet Model", according to Ivo Lapenna, [1] and the legal profession was defined as "a functuon of State Representation", still this profession remained an individual occupation in private advocate's offices. The new Statutes of 1947 did not change this structure.

The comparison of the viewpoints of former Russian and Soviet jurists on the questions whether the counsel has the right to drop the defense during the trial and whether he has the duty to keep the secrets of his client, shows how different is the approach to the problems of lawyers' ethics. A negative answer to the first question and an affirmative answer without any exception to the second one appeared self-evident to pre-Revolutionary Russian lawyers and scholars. These questions, raised on the occasion of two individual cases and definitely solved by Councils of the Bar, the Senate, and the law, did not provoke even a discussion in legal literature. [2]

Quite different was the approach to these questions in the Soviet Union : they gave rise to the expression of divergent opinions by Soviet lawyers and scholars. Unanimity exists only with regard to political cases in which the obligation of secrecy by counsel was excluded.

It is certain that this viewpoint was necessitated by the political situation in the Soviet Union at that time. The 1962 Statute and Art. 72 of the New Code of Criminal Procedure make no exception to the duty of counsel to keep secret the revelations of his client. But even before the publication of the Statute of 1962, after the change of the political climate with Stalin's death, the limitation of the obligation of secrecy of counsel, was dropped. So, for instance, Neystadt, writing in 1958, asserted that the duty of secrecy is imposed upon counsel by law. It has importance in principle since the law guarantees to the accused that he may revert to counsel for help without risking that this help will be used against him. The law, argues Neystadt, insures to the accused the liberty of personal contact with the counsel, allows him to discuss with him defense plans. The basis of such discussion must be the complete trust of the accused in his counsel. [3]

---

[1] Ivo Lapenna, "The Bar in the Soviet Union and Yugoslavia", *International and Comparative Law Quarterly*, April 1963, p. 636.

[2] See Samuel Kucherov, *Courts, Lawyers and Trials...*, *op. cit.*, pp. 181-200.

[3] T.E. Neystadt, *Sovetskiy advokat*, M. 1958, pp. 16-17.

d) *Differing from the Client's Position*

Another question of the lawyer's ethics involving his relations to his client is that whether he may differ from the position taken by his client in the proceeding.

A. Liberman is of the opinion that counsel may not do so. If counsel, after he has studied the case, or during the trial, comes to a conclusion which is opposed or differs from the position of the accused, he must so inform the client, and if the accused does not wish to accept the position taken by counsel, the latter has to drop the defense and the accused may take another lawyer. In no case should counsel, however, do or say anything against the position of the accused. He would join by such an action the prosecution and, in place of one prosecutor, there would be two. [1]

Cheltsov, citing Liberman's opinion, states that "it is doubtful that anyone should adhere to such an openly bourgeois viewpoint now". [2]

He is of the opinion that, the counsel may deny facts asserted by his client, he may agree with the prosecutor that the accusation is proven, although denied by the accused; he may acknowledge that this or that assertion of the accused does not correspond to truth. [3]

Certainly, Strogovich is right when he writes that "it is easy to imagine how the defense will look when these principles are followed; there would be no defense at all, but an accusation conducted by the advocate, even more dangerous for the accused than that of the prosecutor". [4]

In 1960, Cheltsov still maintained his opinion that the counsel can plead for acquittal only if he is convinced that his client is innocent. He extends to the counsel the obligation of "inner conviction" required by Article 17 of the Basic Principles of Criminal Procedure of the USSR and the Union Republics from judges, prosecutors, investigating magistrates, and inquest organs. Cheltsov wrote : "Every suggestion by the counsel must first of all be based on law; secondly, be a conclusion from the evaluation of circumstances of the case, according

---

[1]　A.M. Liberman, "Advocate's Ethics", *Sov. yust.*, 1938, No. 15, p. 14.

[2]　M.A. Cheltsov, "Scopes of Soviet Defense and Procedural Positions of the Advocate", in *Advokat v sovetskom ugolovnom protsesse*, M. 1954, p. 59.

[3]　*Ibid.*, p. 63.

[4]　M.S. Strogovich, *Kurs sovetskogo ugolovnogo protsessa*, M. 1958, p. 439 and footnote 1 on the same page.

to his inner conviction. This criterion, directly indicated in Article 17 for organs of court, prosecution and investigation and underlined in Article 40 with regard to the summing-up of the prosecutor must be extended also to the counsel. We cannot imagine a Soviet counsel-advocate who does not believe himself in the correctness of his conclusion. [1]

Cheltsov is evidently wrong demanding an artificial extention of the "inner conviction" requirement to advocates. The provision of Article 17 is directed to the persons enumerated in it, just because the persons must act objectively, according to their inner convictions. Also the prosecutor in his summing-up must be moved by his inner conviction since the law obliges him to ask for the condemnation or acquittal of the accused according to it. Just because the law does not list the advocate among the persons required to act only under "inner conviction" is a proof that the inner conviction of the advocate has not to play a decisive role in his activity in the trial. Whereas the prosecutor is bound to be two-sided, i.e., objective, the advocate must be one-sided, only to the benefit of his client. The advocate has not to help the court to find the truth as we will see later, but to be of most help to his client to an acquittal or mitigation of the sentence.

"The counsel must diverge from his client in cases when the counsel comes to the conviction that the accused is guilty,—and it is proven, although the client denies it;—the counsel must not deny the guilt before the court,—"he has no right to lie," is asserted by the authors of the New Soviet Criminal Procedural Legislation and the Legal Profession, [2] and they contradict Strogovich's assertion [3] that "the counsel has no right to acknowledge the guilt of the accused if the accused denies it." [4]

Also Elkind criticized Liberman's viewpoint by reproaching his "ignoring of the class nature of the Soviet legal profession as different from the class nature of the bourgeois legal profession." [5]

Elkind asserts that "if having informed the client of the differences in opinion counsel realizes that the accused continues to deny his

---

[1] M.A. Cheltsov, *Foreword to Sudebnyye rechi sovetskikh advokatov*, M. 1960, pp. 18-19.

[2] *Novoye sovetskoye ugolovno-protsesnal'noye zakonodatel'stvo i advokatura*, M. 1960, p. 22.

[3] M. S. Strogovich, *Kurs sovetskogo ugolovnogo protsessa*, M. 1958, pp. 438-439.

[4] Quoted by V. D. Gol'diner, "On Peculiarities in the Methods of Soviet Criminal Defense," *S.G.P.*, 1962, p. 116.

[5] P. S. Elkind, "Advocate's Ethics," *Sov. yust.*, 1940, No. 3, p. 20.

guilt the advocate, an independent party in the trial, must build the defense according to his conscience and understanding".

Elkind comes to the conclusion that "the Soviet advocate is not a servant of his client in a bourgeois selfish sense of the word. Defending only the legitimate rights and interests of citizens, and thus, acting in the interests of the entire society [he] is not bound by the will of his client".

However, Elkind limits the right of defense counsel to take a position independent of the client's in the trial in three ways : he is not permitted to turn directly or indirectly into a prosecutor of the accused; he may not abandon the defense and he is subject to the right of the accused to dismiss his counsel at any time.

Golubovsky does not go as far as Elkind in the acknowledgement of counsel's rights to differ with his client. But, also he comes to the conclusion that "in appropriate cases, with greatest caution in formulation, defense counsel is bound to make the grave decision of diverging from the position of the accused". [1]

The most flagrant case in practice of variance between the position of the accused and his counsel arises when the accused denies his guilt in spite of the clear evidence and the counsel acknowledges the guilt of his client; this happens in the majority of cases allegedly in the interest of the client, in order to plead mitigating circumstances or insanity.

Thus, for instance, in the Arkhangel'skaya case, the eminent Soviet Advocate, N. V. Kommodov, said in his summing-up : "We are fully aware of the great responsibility we assume when, contrary to the accused's assertion, we admit the commission of the crime by her as proved and thereby eliminate the possibility of securing an acquittal on the ground of insufficient evidence. But we face this situation boldly, since according to our lights, our task is not to deny her obvious guilt but to demonstrate her mental deficiency". [2]

Zaitsev and Poltorak comment on Kommodov's speech to the effect that it is "the only correct, honest, and in the long run, effective course to follow" [3]

This passage of Kommodov's summing-up contradicts the opinion

---

[1] D. Golubovsky, "Lawyer's Ethics", *Sov. yust.*, 1939, No. 11, p. 31.

[2] Quoted by Zaitsev and Poltorak, *op. cit.*, p. 136.

[3] *Ibid.*, p. 137.

as to what a defense counsel should do in such a case as maintained by Zaitsev and Poltorak themselves.

Indeed, in discussing the right of counsel to consider the accused guilty in his plea to the court, if the accused categorically denies it, they put the following questions : "Where would it (this right) lead in practice ?" They convincingly argue that if counsel acknowledges the guilt of the accused he must explain his client's motives in denying it. He will then have to analyze the evidence produced for the assertion of his client and criticize it. "This action would be analogous to that of the public prosecutor", the authors conclude.

They must agree that such a solution is against the law.

On the other hand the authors adhere to the opinion that defense counsel is an individual party to the trial he has the right to take an independent stand in the defense of his client. "Then what is to be done ?", they ask, repeating their question.

The authors think a compromise must be found : "The lawyer must set forth his client's point of view accurately and conscientiously giving all the arguments advanced by the client tending to disprove the charge; and it must be made clear to the court, that counsel is not expounding his own position but that of his client. The speech must end in the following alternative proposal; if the court should nonetheless arrive at a verdict of guilty *in camera*, it ought to consider all the attenuating circumstances ..."

Also Perlov recommends the "alternative" when the accused denies his guilt but the counsel finds it impossible, according to all circumstances of the case, to support the assertion of his client. In such cases, —writes Perlov— the counsel can declare to the court that the valuation right of the correctness or incorrectness of the accused's denial of his guilt belongs only to the court, but if the court will on any ground disagree with the accused and admit his guilt in committing the crime, he asks the court to consider the circumstances mitigating the guilt and the responsibilty of the accused". [1]

In the opinion of the present writer, even the "alternative" suggested by Zaitsev and Poltorak and Perlov is damaging to the accused. When counsel in his speech describes the postition of his client and brings forward the arguments of the accused in support of the correctness

---

[1] I.D. Perlov, *Nauchno-praktichiskiy kommentariy k ugolovno-protsessual'nomu kodeksu RSFSR*, M. 1965, p. 355.

of his position, giving, however, to understand to the court by the alternative that he, defense counsel, does not share this position, he delivers a deadly blow to the accused's arguments, since if even the counsel of the accused does not believe in it, how can the court accept it ? In this manner counsel acts against the accused.

It is evident that the "alternative" makes the conclusion of the advocate non-persuasive, weakens his position not only in the trial in the court of first instance, but also before the court of cassation : having not pled for the acquittal of the accused in the first instance, he cannot do it in his appeal for cassation. Zaitsev and Poltorak themselves cite the excellent words of Strogovich that : "Counsel for the defense participates in the trial only to safeguard the interests of the accused, presents only such arguments as benefit the accused, submits only such evidence which conclude".

But Kommodov did not make even a "compromise proposal" to the court. He flatly acknowledged the guilt of the accused.

If the accused stubbornly denies his guilt even against the most obvious evidence, a doubt—may be a shred of a doubt—still can exist in the mind of the judges and it is certainly not up to counsel to destroy this doubt by the acknowledgement of the client's guilt. The law obliges counsel to do everything lawfully admissible for the defense of his client, and nothing to the detriment of the client's position in court. The personal opinion of counsel about the guilt or innocence of the client plays no role in the question. He is not the judge, he needs not decide it. It is evident that Kommodov was not bound to acknowledge the guilt of the accused in spite of her denial, or even offer a compromise, in order to plead mental deficiency. He could have told the court that independently of the fact as to whether or not you accept the evidence produced as proving the guilt of the accused beyond any doubt, you must acquit her because of mental deficiency.

It seems that the "alternative" is definitely eliminated from Soviet practice. According to K. Osipov [1] "It is well known that the alternative defense position in the advocate's summation, is inadmissible, it is justly condemned by advocate's practice. It is known to everyone that the advocate cannot plead with the court : or acquit or mitigate the punishment".

---

[1] *Sov. yust.*, 1967, No. 3, p. 16.

In a recently published monograph on the Soviet advocate, the authors declare "The admission by the advocate of the accused's guilt if the latter denies it, must be considered as a violation of professional duty, a valid form of defense dropping; consequently a rough violation of the defense right" [1] thus, completely confirming the present writer's viewpoint and is a condemnation of Kommodov's plea.

It is interesting to note that the authors, admit only one circumstance, when the counsel can deviate from his client's position; it is when the accused pleads guilty, but the counsel is persuaded by his innocence. [2]

It is peculiar that in speaking of Kommodov's speech in the Arkhangel'skaya case as the only correct, honest and in the long run, effective course to follow, Zaitsev and Poltorak blame Kommodov for having declared in another case that, "I counter the case of the prosecution with an array of facts which raise great doubts ..." They write that Kommodov's declaration "certainly weakened his arguments since it amounts to an admission of the weakness of the lawyer's case and to his lack of confidence in it". [3] Grave doubts in his own argument is still less than the acknowledgement of the accused's guilt.

A case reported by O. Chaykovskaya [4] may be taken as an example of what consequences the acknowledgement of the accused's guilt by counsel may have when his client denies it.

The case of P. accused of misappropriation of gold, was tried in the Magadan Regional Court. Defense Counsel Adriyenko insisted on the guilt of the accused although the latter denied it, and did not appeal in cassation the death sentence pronounced by the court.

On the appeal, of the accused himself, lodged with the assistance of another counsel in Moscow the sentence was reversed.

Another example is the following case : K. and R. were accused of attempting to murder. The prosecutor asserted that R. played the guiding role in the crime and since he had a criminal record of four foregoing crimes, the prosecutor demanded the death penalty for him

---

[1] G.A. Ginzburg, A.G. Polyak and V.A. Samsonov, *Sovetskiy advokat*, M. 1968, p. 8.
[2] *Ibid.*
[3] Zaitsev and Poltorak, *op. cit.*, p. 129.
[4] O. Chaykovskaya, "The Advocates", *Izvestia*, March 2, 1963.

and the highest confining punishment for K. Counsels, although K.
and R. denied their guilt, admitted it in their summings-up, pleading
only that not the death penalty but a confinement should be applied
to R. and a minimum penalty to K.

The Chelyabinsky Regional Court, admitting that R. is a dangerous
recidivist, sentenced him to 15 years in jail and K. was punished with
12 years of confinement.

The sentence was protested with regard to R. by the prosecutor
because of its mildness. Counsels did not lodge appeal in cassation
and R's counsel did not even object against the protest.

Another counsel represented R. in the RSFSR Supreme Court.
The court threw out the sentence, remanded the case for an additional
investigation, the result of which was that the Chelyabinsky Regional
Court again sentenced R. to 12 years of confinement.

On appeal of cassation lodges by the new counsel, the RSFSR
Supreme Court threw out the second sentence and quashed the criminal
procedure because of lack of evidence (K had died in the meantime). [1]

The problem of a particular lawyer's ethics were simply brushed
aside by D. Kudryavstsev, USSR Deputy Minister of Justice, in
1951. In reply to the letters of Lensky and Vladimirov to the editor
of the Literaturnaya gazeta, Kudryavtsev wrote : [2]

"Arguments about the dependence of counsel upon his client, his
duty of secrecy, his right to defend a hopeless and unjust case by all
means ... are intolerable and out of place as far as our Soviet lawyers
are concerned. Under conditions of socialist justice, there is no place
for such problems. The Marxist-Leninist science on state and law and
our communist morality eliminate such questions. ... reasoning about
special moral norms of behavior are characteristic of venal bourgeois
lawyers who are ready to make any deal with their conscience in order
to defend the interests of the money-bag and their own profit". [3]

In 1954, Golyakov still shared the opinion of the Deputy Minister
of Justice. He wrote that "the question of a special lawyer's ethics
has been solved in the Soviet Union a long time ago. There is a single
and one ethics in the Soviet Union. It is the socialist ethics founded

---

[1]   Quoted by I. Sukharev, *Sov. yust.*, 1965, No. 12, p. 16.

[2]   *Literaturnaya gazeta...*, June 7, 1951, p. 2.

[3]   Kudryavtsev made an exception in favor of "those fighting lawyers who accomplish their noble tasks in bourgeois courts of the USA, England or France by defending
participants in the struggle for peace and democracy from persecutions by courts".

on State and the public and state's interests ..." [1] "In his summing up he continued—the counsel may not forget his duty to his fatherland—he must remember that his speech is directed not only to the court but also to Soviet society". Golyakov agreed with Vyshinsky's opinion "that counsel, in his activity just cannot abandon the basis of the interests of socialist construction, the interests of the state". [2]

Also, Zaitsev and Poltorak claim that in the Soviet Union a concept of lawyer's ethics cannot be considered correct as it would imply the existence of special professional norms of ethics as distinct from the ethics and morality of Soviet society as a whole. Socialist ethics are, however, uniform and their norms are binding on all members of society". [3]

Also, T. E. Neyshtadt thinks that, under the conditions of Soviet life, the question of a separate lawyer's ethics must be resolved negatively. "We have only one set of ethics for all Soviet citizens, for all members of public organizations, that means also for Soviet advocates. This ethics is defined by norms of socialist morals. The Soviet advocate must submit completely and without exceptions to those norms of behavior which are obligatory for all citizens of socialist society. Socialist ethics are founded on the interests of the socialist society and state, and the interests of the individual and the public are the one and the same with us. Complete harmony of individual and society —is a problem which has just been solved in our socialist state for the first time in history. That is why by his defending the lawful rights of the accused, the soviet advocate directly and immediately defends the interests of the socialist state". [4]

As a compromise, in 1959 Strogovich asserted that in the first place, the norms of socialist morality, without exceptions, must be extended also to the activity of the soviet advocate. Still, in a conditional sense, a particular advocate's ethics may be recognized as the application of general socialist morality in special sectors of an advocate's activity where ethical problems arise constantly, since the law establishes only the basic principles for an advocate's activity, its fundamental scope and forms. Such problems are the choice of means and methods

---

[1] I.T. Golyakov, Introduction to *Advokat v sovetskom ugolovnom protsesse*, M. 1954, p. 26.

[2] *Ibid.*, p. 28.

[3] Zaitsev and Poltorak, *op. cit.*, p. 118.

[4] T.E. Neyshtadt, *Sovetskiy advokat*, M. 1958, pp. 15-16, passim.

of defense, the establishment of appropriate relations with the court
and his procedural opponent, the prosecutor, and with the client.
The advocate must solve them, according to his understanding and
conscience, in conformity with a correct understanding of the duties
of a soviet lawyer". [1]

Thus, according to the authors cited above, there can be no particular problems of ethics for Soviet lawyers, since their Marxist-Leninist
conscience and morality provides for all norms of behavior. But now
both the abandoning of the defense and the disclosure of secrets,
are unconditionally forbidden in the Statute of 1962, Does it mean
that socialist ethics have changed, or that it was falsely interpreted by
some authors during the "cult of personality" period?

Indeed in 1965, V. D. Gol'diner fully acknowledged the existence
of a counsel's ethics and took position with regard to its problems.
He writes," ... There are some sectors of public activity requiring,
because of their specific features, more detailed elaboration of moral
principles, applied in the given profession. In this sense, often and
rightly, it is spoken about doctor's ethics. In this sense, it is permissible and necessary to speak about the lawyer's ethics, or more exactly,
about the ethics of the Soviet lawyer". [2]

B. Position of Counsel in Criminal Trial

a) *The Advocate—An Assistant to the Court*

The position of the Soviet Lawyer as of an aid of the court has been
asserted by Andreyev in 1926 : he was of the opinion that the prosecutor and counsel are only aids of the court, the first by accusation,
the second in defending the accused. The prosecutor represents the
interests of society and state whereas the counsel—the interests of
the individual in the dock. [3]

With regard to the position and the activity of counsel in the trial,
Vyshinsky considered that counsel has to solve a very difficult problem.

---

[1] M.S. Strogovich, "The Advocate's Procedural Position in the Soviet Criminal
Procedure", *Sots. zak.*, 1959, No. 3, pp. 36-37.

[2] V.D. Gol'diner, "On the Ethics in the Advocate's Activity", *S.G.P.*, 1965, No. 10.
p. 95.

[3] M. Andreyev, "Does the Defender Have the Right to Drop the Defense ?", *Rabochiy
Sud*, 1926, No. 1, p. 34.

"On the one hand, he defends a person who committed a crime against the Soviet state, and on the other, in defending the culprit, he must not lose sight of the interests of the proletarian state". [1]

He admonishes the Soviet lawyer to get rid, in the Soviet court, of the remnants of bourgeois traditions of the legal profession which considered the counsel's work "more from the viewpoint of the interests of his client than of the viewpoint of the interests of the proletarian state as a whole". [2] It is evident to him that State interests must prevail.

Vyshinsky argues that there generally are two methods of defending the accused. According to the first method, the purpose of the counsel only consists in the defense of the accused with all the means available to the defense, without relation to anything else. "I serve the material truth",—thinks the counsel who follows this method.

The second method, cited by Vyshinsky, is the defense which exerts itself "no more than necessary". It means that the defense is only "an outward sign that the counsel conducting such a defense performs it first of all not damaging the interests of the state as represented by the prosecutor. Thus, such a counsel thinks, according to Vyshinsky, "I shall fulfill my public duty if I defend the 'criminal' not very stubbornly and zealously, although I am not convinced that he is guilty".

Vyshinsky rejects both methods. The first method because the "material truth" conscientiously served by the lawyer cannot be detached from all public and political conditions under which the crime was committed and tried. But the main defect of this system is that "limiting his scope exclusively by the interests of his client, as such, without regard to public and state interests, counsel comes to conflict with himself in his capacity as a citizen and, especially, as a Soviet citizen".

The second method is so obviously fallacious that it is not necessary, according to Vyshinsky, to discuss it in detail. It is a completely rotten solution of the problem, harmful and dangerous. "It is a time-serving, bureaucratic, anti-Soviet method", [3] he writes.

Thus, Vyshinsky condemned any counsel who serves the interests of the accused while disregarding public and state interest, but also

[1] A. Ye. Vyshinsky, *Revolutsionnaya zakonnost' i zadachi sovetskoy zashchity*, M. 1934, pp. 29-32, *passim*.

[2] *Ibid.*, p. 32.

[3] *Ibid.*, p. 33.

the lawyer who neglects the interests of his client fearing to act against public and state interests.

Vyshinsky brings forward and supports a third method of defense which is a compromise between the first two. He sees the purpose and the duty of counsel in "helping the court", and consequently, the Soviet State, to find the real essence of the case, the real character of the accused, the real solution of the given case, corresponding to reality and the interests of the proletarian state. To this effect Vyshinsky requests counsel, in defending the accused, to keep in mind that the Soviet state is encircled by enemies, that it is not completely free from many remnants of the capitalist classes who attempt to blow up the state from within, that any important crime has an anti-state character and is an explosive element.

Vyshinsky also advised the Soviet lawyer to keep in mind that "the courthouse is the laboratory where public opinion is formed ; that an unskilled defense may involuntarily become a banner of narrow-minded, petty-bourgeois, counterrevolutionary moods un-friendly to the Soviet country; that, from the professional and political viewpoints, a defense is correct when all the arguments in favor of the accused are presented conscientiously, however, without disregarding ... the basic requirements ... of socialist construction, state interests, and proletarian dictatorship".

The first requirement to be presented to a Soviet lawyer is an intense feeling of political responsibility and a high political qualifi-cation. Vyshinsky thought that in the Soviet Union prosecution and defense do not represent two opposite principles, but only two different viewpoints, based on the same public interest. [1]

In the just-quoted article, Vyshinsky comes again to the defense of the legal profession. He contests the opinion that it is possible to manage without a defense because the court itself can look in to the case and that there is no value in defending a person brought to account, since "if brought to account, the person is guilty".

Vyshinsky opposes the attempt to organize the relation between the defense and the state in such terms, as reflecting the relation between the prosecution and the State. But "he would like defense counsel

---

[1]   A. Vyshinsky, "On New Rails", *Sots. zak.*, 1936, No. 10, p. 10 (a reworked speech delivered at the Conference of the Moscow College of Defenders).

to be a fearless, manful, consistent, and above all, a selfless fighter for Soviet law, for Soviet justice, for Soviet legality". [1]

"We need defenders" exclaimed Vyshinsky, "capable of heroic deeds, because our work is a work which requires heroic efforts at every step and outstanding courage, striking persistence, resolution and political foresight (sic!) And only in possession of these qualities, you and we, the prosecution and the defense, will be good assistants to the courts, not such as those (yesmen) who applaud every move of the prosecutor or every decision of the court, but who can fear-lessly analyze every case and take anyone's position, can with dignity and honor argue it to the end, submitting only to the law and their own conscience and not to any other very harmful and dangerous, so-called local influence". [2]

And this was said and written in 1936, on the eve of the famous political trials carried out by Vyshinsky himself!

Certainly, not one of the Soviet lawyers accomplished the "heroic deeds" required by Vyshinsky in defending the accused in these trials; they had, however, the "political foresight" to abstain from them, in contradistinction to prerevolutionary Russian lawyers. Indeed, prerevolutionary counsels directed to the government such words of censure in political trials which cannot be heard in a Soviet court. [3]

It is also certain that Soviet advocates do not undergo the risk of depicting some gloomy aspects of Soviet life, for instance, the poverty of the peasants so eloquently described by Plevako in the case of the Lyntoricki peasants, or the exploitation of factory workers in the case of the Konshin factory. Some bitter words of criticism of the investigating magistrates, the police and the prosecution would hardly be an appropriate example to follow for the Soviet advocate, "whose conditions of activity are quite different" from those of the tsarist lawyer. [4]

Striking is the complete absence of political trials in the collection of summings-up of tsarist trial lawyers published in the Soviet Union. Five cases defended by Karabchevsky are included in the collection

---

[1] *Ibid.*, p. 11.

[2] *Ibid.*

[3] See, for instance, the summing-up by Karabchevsky in the Sazonov Case or by Maklakov, in the case of the Tolbenkov peasants (Samuel Kucherov, *Courts, Lawyers and Trials...*, op. cit., pp. 227-230 and 235-238 respectively).

[4] See for some political trials of the Tsarist epoch, S. Kucherov, *Courts, Lawyers and Trials...*, op. cit.

but not the Sazonov case. With the exception of the Zasulich case of 1878, in which criticism of the tsarist government was very much milder in comparison with Karabchevsky's speech in the Sozonov case. or V. A. Maklakov's summing-up in the case of the Dolbenkovo peasants, or O. O. Gruzenberg's in the Beilis case. Certainly it is very understandable that such words of criticism of the government as pronounced by Karabchevsky in the summing-up of Sazonov's trial would be a bad example for Soviet advocates from the viewpoint of the publishers of the collection. The mere fact of the possibility of bringing forward such criticism in the capitalist, bourgeois and reactionary Russia, as compared with the complete impossibility of uttering them in a Soviet socialist court would show up the freedom of speech in the tsarist court to the disadvantage of the Sorrehone.

The Soviet lawyer should not be blamed for it : Stalin's regime cannot be compared with that of the tsars, but the extent of Vyshinsky's hypocrisy, also on that subject, is really amazing.

It is also characteristic for Vyshinsky's concept of the position of defense counsel and his work that the interests of the accused are simply not mentioned in his fierce defense of the lawyer. Indeed, defense counsel must "fight for Soviet law, Soviet justice and Soviet legality fearlessly, mindfully and consistently", but should not all these qualities also be applied to the defense of the accused, who, it would seem, must be the main object of his care ? Vyshinsky does not say. Vyshinsky defends the institution of the defense which he thinks necessary, for he presents high requirements for the individual lawyer, the orderly administration of justice, the quality of lawyers and the work performed in the capacity as "court assistants" but he does not define counsel's relation to his client.

In reality, as Kukarsky puts it, Vyshinsky's erroneous assertions on the role of law in the period of socialism's construction as an instrument of repression only, his theory of evidence, according to which the accused's confession was valued as a decisive evidence, had a negative influence on the institution of defense in court.

In many cases the participation of counsels became in essence only formal and helpless. Almost no attention was paid to the strengthening of the legal profession with qualified personnel and the increase of theoretical knowledge and practical experience of its members. [1]

---

[1] I. Kukarsky, "The Soviet Legal Profession is 45 Years Old", *Sov. yust.*, 1967, No. 10, p. 15.

Also Samsonov stresses the fact that in the period of the cult of personality, when legality was crudely violated, it served to demote the counsel to a third rate participant at the trial. He thought that after Lenin's principles of socialist legality triumphed completely,the role of the legal profession had been heightened, its functions widened and greater rights had been given to the counsel in the process of justice administration. [1]

The possibility of "heroic deeds" by counsels required by Vyshinsky, may be better understood in the light of the statement by the Deputy Minister of Justice, N. S. Prusakov, who disclosed that at the time of the cult of personality "defense counsels were not seldom subject to disciplinary prosecution because they defended in principle the rights and lawful interests of citizens". He asserts that, however, an end was put to all of that after the restoration of Leninist norms of Party life. [2]

In Karev's opinion, the position of the Soviet lawyer is a peculiar one, since two elements are involved in his activity : he is a defender of the accused and at the same time a fighter for socialist legality. [3]

I. T. Golyakov believes that the right to defend cannot consist in exculpating the accused in the face of incontestable facts or in minimizing the danger of his crime. Such a defense, he argues, would be directed against the interests of society and the state. [4]

He emphasizes that defense counsel in the Soviet court is not only a representative of the interests of his client, but also an active participant in the trial who cooperates in truth finding, in passing a sentence which conforms to the essence of the case and to the interests of the state, which on the one hand require the strictest punishment of a criminal and on the other, does not tolerate the punishment of an innocent person. "That is why the participation of counsel and his role in the Soviet court extend far beyond the limits of defense in a bourgeois court". [5]

Golyakov asserts that numberless examples of bourgeois justice prove that the role of counsel in court is often reduced to a shameless exculpation of the client in order to avert a more or less heavy punish-

---

1   Samsonov, "Notes on the Legal Profession", *Sots. zak.*, 1964, No. 11, p. 49.

2   *Sovetskaya Rossiya*, August 2, 1964.

3   Karev, *op. cit.*, pp. 291-292.

4   I.T. Golyakov, *Sovetskii sud*, 1947, pp. 62-63.

5   I.T. Golyakov, "On the Importance of Defense in the Soviet Criminal Trial", *Zashchita po ugolovnym delam*, M. 1948, p. 14.

ment for him. To this purpose counsel hides the truth, strives to limit the questioning of persons whose testimony is detrimental to his client, thoroughly challenges jurors who are most competent in the case.

"The complete moral and political unity of Soviet society and the attending democratic bases of Soviet court procedure", continues Golyakov, "eliminate the possibility of such a role of the lawyer in a Soviet court ..." According to him, the work of Soviet lawyers is not reduced to the defense of private interests only : "it rises to a genuine, real service to society and the state and in practical activity becomes one with the activity of the entire Soviet people in the fight for the success and prosperity of the Socialist fatherland ...". It is certainly difficult to see what is immoral in challenging jurors, even competent ones, a practice so widely applied in the United States. For defense counsel to try to limit as much as possible testimonies of witnesses unfavorable to the accused or to discredit them is only natural and belongs to the fulfillment of his defense duties. Is it not a "general, real service rendered to society", as Golyakov puts it, when defense counsel applies all legitimate means to preserve the interests of his client, a member of society, accused perhaps unjustly of having committed a crime?

Now are the bourgeois lawyers so reprehensible when they try to exculpate the client that they cannot serve as examples for Soviet advocates? Why then was a collection of summings-up of some of the foremost pre-revolutionary lawyers published in the Soviet Union in 1956 and why did it have such a success that a second and third edition, four times larger than the first, appeared in 1957 and 1958 respectively? [1] Granted that the art of forensic oratory of the pre-revolutionary lawyers might serve as a model for Soviet advocates, but such oratorical mastery loses its effect because it cannot find imitation in the Soviet court.

To demand the acquittal of an accused who pleaded guilty on grounds not provided by law, is to defend not the "lawful" right of the accused, but the crime itself;" only "lawful' interests of the accused can be defended by his counsel—these statements apply as the leitmotif of Soviet writers dealing with the duties of a Soviet advocate.

This opinion has been expressed also from the tribune of the USSR legislative body. In his report to the Soviet of Nationalities on the

---

[1]   M.M. Vydrya, *Sudebnyye rechi izvestnykh russkikh yuristov*, M. 1956, 1957, 1958.

bills of "The Basic Principles of Legislation on the Court Structure of the USSR, Union and Autonomous Republics, the Statute of Military Tribunals and Soviet Principles of Criminal Procedure of the USSR and Union Republics", the Deputy D. Rasulov, [1] Chairman of the Commission of Legislative Projects of the Soviet of Nationalities, declared that "The Soviet defense counsel must serve the great humanitarian purpose of the defense of the law of the socialist society, of truth and justice. The defense of lawful interests and rights of the accused ... this is the scope of action permitted to counsel, and the defense is not allowed to advance the illegal pretensions of the accused, which inevitably changes the defense of the criminal into the defense of the crime". [2]

It is evident that an accused who pleads guilty, or has been proven the perpetrator of the incriminating action and has no excuse provided by law for his action, has no "lawful" claim to an acquittal, which consequently cannot be supported by his counsel—according to the Soviet conception of a lawyer's duties.

But one of the most eminent Russian jurists, A. F. Koni, of prerevolutionary time, often cited by Soviet writers, wrote : "Almost for everyone the question 'Is he guilty'? is equivalent to the question 'Did he do it'? And when the words 'Not guilty' are addressed to a person who has confessed that he 'did it', clamors arise in society in which the frankness of discontent is equal to the depth of ignorance". [3]

Let us give the following example of the counsel's freedom of speech in prerevolutionary court.

On July 15, 1904, the Minister of the Interior, V. K. Pleve, was assassinated in St. Petersburg. He was killed by a bomb thrown into his carriage by Yegor Sazonov. Characterizing the victim, Karabchevsky said : "All the horror which overtook Russia in the last years was attributed to him. He jailed and banished thousands of innocent people. He flogged and shot peasants and workers. He scoffed at the intelligentsia, he instigated mass massacres of Jews in Kishenev and Gomel', he choked Finland, he oppressed the Poles, he exercised his influence to bring about the war with Japan in which so much blood

[1] D. Rasulov, "The Basic Principles of Legislation on the Court Structure of the USSR, Union and Autonomous Republics, the Statute of Military Tribunals and Soviet Principles of Criminal Procedure of the USSR and Union Republics", *Sots. zak.*, 1959, No. 1, p. 163.

[2] *Ibid.*

[3] A.F. Koni, *Vospominaniya o dele Vera Zasulich*, M. 1933, p. 230.

has already been shed and will continue to be shed in the future...
Sazonov's imagination pictured Pleve as a fatal, sinister, nightmarish
figure, pressing its imperious knee against the chest of the fatherland
and mercilessly choking it. It seemed to Sazonov that this monster
can be annihilated only by another monster—death. And grasping with
trembling hands the bomb which was destined for Pleve, Sazonov
believed, piously believed, that it was filled not so much with dynamite
and fulminate of mercury as with the tears, sorrow and calamity of the
people. And when its splinters burst and scattered in all directions,
it seemed to him that he heard how the chains which bind the Russian
people are jangling and breaking to pieces...

So thought Sazonov... That is why, when he regained consciousness,
he shouted : 'Long live liberty !' " [1]

Indeed, what court in the Soviet Union would bring in an acquittal
in an embezzlement case when the accused pleads guilty ? Summings-
up by tsarist lawyers in trials were designed, in the majority of
cases, to influence the feelings of the jury even when the objective
guilt of the accused was indisputable. The position of the advocate
as defense counsel in a Soviet court makes it reprehensible to plead
for an acquittal in cases when insanity is not invoked. In cases
of admitted or evident guilt of the accused, the limit of the defense
plea in a Soviet court besides mitigation of the punishment, is the
suspension of the sentence or the commitment to the care and supervision of the organization in which the accused worked.

In the method of defense of the priest Kudryavtsev by Plevako,
V. L. Rossel's sees only "the shift of the defense of the criminal to
the defense of the crime itself". [2]

The grounds for such a conclusion are difficult to see. Plevako did
not defend the embezzlement of church money—he asked only for
the pardon of the sinner who during 35 years fulfilled honestly his
duties and once failed to do so. He asked for pardon for a man who
pardoned the jurors' sins which, although not committed in violation
of the provisions of the Criminal Code, violated the precepts of the
religious code, which was no less sacred in the view of many than the
criminal one. The jurors felt themselves not in a position to throw
the first stone at a man who pardoned their own sins.

---

[1] N.P. Karabchevsky, *Delo Sazonova*, St. Petersburg, 1906, p. 25-27.

[2] V.L. Rossel's, "The Problems of a Defense Counsel in the Soviet Court" in *Zashchitnik v sovetskom sude*, M. 1960, p. 11. See above, p. 361.

According to Rossel's, "The old formula of the bourgeois advocate was correct in its time : "All of us are sinners" is exchanged by the thesis of the Soviet advocate which is full of creative hopes : "he [the accused] has sunk deep, but he is a Soviet man, he has the force to rise, society will improve him". [1]

Also, M. A. Chel'tsov-Bebutov and M. D. Shifman adhere to the opinion that counsel, although a party in the trial whose duty it is to establish facts which favor the accused, i.e., prove his innocence or mitigate his guilt, must nevertheless be endowed with the same socialist sense of legality as the prosecution. [2]

In his chapter on the "Problems of Soviet Defense and the Procedural Status of the Advocate", [3] M. A. Chel'tsov asserts that the defense must always be considered as engaged in the performance of a state function by the advocate, independently of whether he is appointed by the court or fulfills his duties at the request of the accused. "Counsel", Chel'tsov wrote, "is an assistant to the court in the establishment of all circumstances of the case necessary for the pronouncement of a lawful and substantiated sentence. His help consists in the defense of the accused, protecting his procedural rights and bringing forward and elucidating to the court, the circumstances which eliminate the responsibility of the accused or mitigate his guilt. [4]

But the second part of Chel'tsov's definition of counsel's position in criminal procedure contradicts the first part, according to which counsel's assistance to the courts extends to the establishment of "all circumstances necessary" for the pronouncement of a lawful sentence substantiated by reasons which literally means that counsel is bound to assist the court also in the establishment of circumstances harmful to the accused. The second part of the definition restricts this help to defensive actions only. [5]

According to him, the prosecution and the defense have a common ground on which to stand : it is socialist legality and Chel'tsov concludes that "evidently he (counsel) may not hinder the court in the

---

[1] Rossel's, *op. cit.*, p. 10.

[2] M.A. Chel'tsov-Bebutov and M.L. Shifman, "Criminal Defenses in the Court Examination", *Zashchita v ugolovnom protsesse*, M. 1948, p. 60.

[3] In *Advokat v sovetskom ugolovnom protsesse*, M. 1954, p. 44.

[4] *Ibid.*, p. 53.

[5] It seems to the present author that the contradiction is produced by an unfortunate wording of the first part of the definition. Chel'tsov did not want to permit to counsel an accusatory activity with regard to his client.

discovery of the truth on which a just and legitimate sentence must be based". But the denial of firmly established facts which the prosecution confirmed by evidence and checked with the participation of counsel, is not much help but just an impediment to the court's activity.

But, times have changed also for Chel'tsov. In 1958, the Basic Principles of Criminal Procedure of the USSR and the Union Republics [1] were promulgated and Article 23 of the Principles defines the lawyer's rights and duties as follows : "Defense counsel is obliged to use all lawful ways and means of defense provided by law in order to clarify circumstances vindicating the accused or mitigating his responsibility and extend to him the necessary legal help".

Consequently, Chel'tsov had to abandon his definition of defense counsel as an assistant to the court and as a state representation in 1960. [2] He had to admit that the activity of the defense lawyer is limited to the clarification of circumstances favorable to the accused and has a one-sided character. Consequently, he must also consider that "the finding and submitting of evidence inculpating the accused or increasing his responsibility do not only not form part of the duties of counsel, but constitute also a violation of his duties". [3]

Chel'tsov clings, however, to the right of counsel to choose his position in the case and in doing so he is not bound by the will of his client. He deducts this right not from the allegedly independent position of counsel as a party to the trial, according to Article 23 of the old Code of Criminal Procedure, but from the "state importance of counsel's function which requires from him complete conscientiousness". [4]

Chel'tsov obviously overlooks that, in assuming a different position in the trial from that of the accused who denies his guilt, counsel, even by suggesting an alternative decision to the court, acts to the detriment of the accused and, acts in violation of his duty as defense counsel.

---

[1] *V.V.S., SSSR*, 1959, No. 1.

[2] M.A. Chel'tsov, "Some Problems of the Defense in the Light of the Basic Principles of Criminal Procedure of the USSR and the Union Republics" in *Sudeyskiye rechi sovetskikh advokatov*, M. 1960, p. 49.

[3] P. 19.

[4] *Ibid.*, p. 23.

The editorial in *Sovetskaya Yustitsiya* No. 7 of 1957 defines the lawyer's position as follows : "The advocate is charged with helping in the establishment of circumstances mitigating the guilt of the accused or diminishing his responsibility, or refuting the accusation. This activity helps the court to look into the accusation from all sides and contributes to the pronouncing of a just verdict. That is why the advocate is rightly called the helper of justice [1] and not of the court.

In 1954, Golyakov stated the opinion that "The legal profession in the USSR is not a private organization, but a public one, fulfilling a function of great state importance. In defending the lawful interests of the accused, the Soviet lawyer helps the court to mete socialist justice". That is why he thinks that [2] "the scope of Soviet counsel must consist in active help to the court in the correct qualification of the crime, in the establishment of truth in the case, in the elucidation of the crime, in clarifying the extent of public danger both of the crime and its perpetrator". [3]

Still, as late as 1954, such antiquated opinions, as the following were voiced in the Soviet Union. Indeed, B. S. Antimonov and S. L. Gerzon, in their book, The Advocate in Soviet Civil Procedure, write :

"The institution of advocates has been created as an aid to the Soviet Court ... The Soviet advocate is a public figure who strengthens socialist legality, aids the Soviet State and Soviet justice and thereby defends the legal interests of citizens and organizations. He, who has forgotten this and who strives to secure, by all means,

---

[1] Editorial, p. 4.

[2] I.I. Golyakov, Introduction to *Advokat v sovetskom ugolovnom protsesse*, M. 1954, p. 17.

[3] *Ibid*. The idea of the "assistance of lawyers to the court" is strongly accented in the Bulgarian Statute on the Legal Profession and Bulgarian legal literature, according to Stephen Risoff, who writes : "The edict of 1952 shows that the lawyer today is mainly to assist, not the client, but the government in strengthening legal order and the socialist legality". He quotes Ivan Boridzhev writing : "... the attorney must bring his defense in the court to the level of the interest of the people's democratic government... The lawyer must not restrict his defense only to the interest of his client or an isolated person, but he must think primarily of the interest of the people and the interests of the government... The attorney is under the obligation not to deviate politically from the interests of the socialist community". (Stephen Risoff, "The Bar", *Highlights of Current Legislation and Activity in Mid-Europe*, Library of Congress Mid-European Law Project, April 1959, pp. 155-156.)

with the help of chicanery, solely the interests of his client, does not
deserve the exalted rank of a Soviet advocate". [1]

We find similar opinions prevailing in another state behind the
Iron Curtain, in Poland. The Polish Bar has been reorganized according
to the Soviet pattern. The Law of June 1950 on the Organization of
the Bar defines in Article 49 the duty of the lawyer as the obligation
"to contribute by all means within his power to protect and consolidate the legal order of the People's State". [2] In the report No. 80
of the Sejm session in which the Law of 1950 was discussed, it is said :
"The practice of the legal profession cannot be based on conflict
between interests of the individual and those of the government, since
in our system there is no such conflict". [3]

A peculiar definition of the position of Soviet advocates has been
given by M. P. Shalamov, who characterizes their organization as a
"subsidiary court agency". [4]

Evidence for the correctness of such a definition from the viewpoint
of a communist government was provided by the speech of the Albanian
Minister of Justice in introducing the bill of the law on the legal profession to the Albanian Parliament :

"The (lawyers) must forget from now on how they attended to
their professional duties in the past ... Lawyers must become accesory
organs of justice. (Courts and lawyers) must work together".

The minister said further that after the reorganization of justice
no opposition between courts and lawyers will exist, since their interests are seen through the prism of the interests of the majority. [5]
The organization of the Albanian legal profession, created by the laws
of 1946, 1950, and 1953, is very similar to that in the Soviet Union. [6]

---

[1]   B.S. Antimonov and S.L. Gerzon, *Advokat v sovetskom grazhdanskom protsesse*,
M. 1954, pp. 3-4.

[2]   S. Rosada, "The Bar", *Highlights of Current Legislation and Activities in Mid-
Europe*, 1955, No. 10, p. 265.

[3]   *Ibid.*

[4]   M.R. Shalamov, *Istoriya sovetskoy advokatury.* Quoted by D.S. Karev, *Organizatsiya
suda i prokuratury*, 1954, footnote 1 on pp. 173-174.

[5]   Vokopola, *op. cit.*, p. 169.

[6]   In Albania, too, the lawyers are "collectivized" and assigned to legal aid offices
the directors of which distribute the cases among lawyers, dispense salaries, etc. (*Ibid.*,
pp. 169-172 *passim.*) Also in Chechoslovakia the Soviet example was followed. The
rapporteur on the Law of December 20, 1951 said : "... as in our whole legal system,
here also (referring to the bill of the new Law on the Bar) the pattern of the Soviet Union
was of great help to us". (Kocvara, *op. cit.*, p. 40.)

O. Chaykovskaya calls attention to the erroneous doctrine that the defense is called upon to assist the court in the clarification of all aspects of the case, regardless of whether they speak in favor or against the accused, which still has adherents, according to the author.

Also, I. Perlov asserts that the opinion, criticized by O. Chaykovskaya, is held by individual judges, prosecutors, investigating magistrates and scholars. "This is a grave mistake", writes Perlov, for "according to the requirements of the Soviet procedural law, defense counsel is bound to expose any circumstances vindicating the accused or mitigating his guilt or responsibility".

With regard to the assertion that defense counsel is an assistant to the court, Strogovich rightly points out that there is no such procedural figure as a "court assistant" and, therefore, it is not correct to define the position of defense counsel in the trial as that of an "assistant to the court". Certainly, in a way counsel helps the court to avoid a judicial mistake to the detriment of the accused but he may not assist in the exposure of the accused. [1]

The qualification of the advocate as an "aid to the court" in the finding of the truth seems to have been abandoned.

Thus, Gol'diner [2] emphasizes that the advocate cannot aid the court to establish all the circumstances necessary for the production of a lawful and motivated sentence", as formulated by Chel'tsov, "since his activity is directed only toward clarification of the circumstances which speak in favor of the accused. The court and defense counsel have separate functions : the court judges, the counsel defends. This makes the counsel an independent figure with regard to the court". He thinks that the thesis, "the defense counsel is an aid to the court", limits and narrows the function of counsel, by "turning him from an independent figure to an assistant". "It is obvious that the time has come to reject decisively this definition". [3] And five years later he asserted that in the light of the Basic Principles, this conception must be definitely moved to the archives. [4]

---

[1] M.S. Strogovich, "The Procedural Position and Functions of the Defense", Counsel in *Zashchita v ugolovnom protsesse, op. cit.*, p. 26.

[2] V.D. Gol'diner, "On the Question of the Procedural Position of the Advocate", *Sov. yust.*, 1957, No. 7, p. 15.

[3] *Ibid.*, p. 16.

[4] V.D. Gol'diner, "On Some Pecularities in the Methods of Soviet Criminal Trial", *S.G P.*, 1962, No. 6, p. 113.

b) *Is The Legal Profession a State or Public Institution?*

It is interesting to note that Chel'tsov elsewhere also brought forward another definition of the function of a Soviet lawyer. He wrote that "the Soviet lawyer performs the function of a state representative of the rights and legal interests of individual citizens acting as persons accused, plaintiffs and defendants in criminal and civil proceedings". [1]

In this definition "state representation" is attributed to the soviet lawyers, a new formula which puts him, indeed, on the same footing with the prosecutor. No distinction is made in this article between a lawyer's representation of his client in civil practice, to which Chel'tsov ascribes great importance.

Chel'tsov, following Vyshinsky, emphasized the public and state character of counsel's activity. According to this opinion, defense counsel, when pleading in court, defends publicly legal interests and is the representative not of a private person, but of the state which entrusts him with the defense of rights and legal interests of a certain accused person, in the same way as it commissions the prosecutor to accuse this person. He defines the juridical character of the legal profession in these words : "The Soviet advocate realizes the function of State representation of the right and legal interests of individual citizens involved in the quality of persons accused, plaintiffs and defendants in criminal and civil proceedings". [2]

Also, N. N. Polyansky puts the question as to whether the Soviet legal profession is a state or public organization. [3] He thinks that, at first glance, there are serious reasons to take the legal profession just for a state organization, since it was created for purposes of importance to the state : to provide legal help for the population; to contribute to the administration of justice and participate in the fulfillment of certain state functions. Also the fact the People's Commissariat of Justice is the second instance in disciplinary case over members of the lawyer's colleges might introduce it into the family of state organs.

However, Polyansky denies the status of a state organ to the legal profession. In his opinion, although under the Soviet regime all the

---

[1] M.A. Chel'tsov, "On the Legal Profession and the Juridical Nature of Soviet Legal Profession", *S.G.P.*, 1940, No. 7, p. 124.

[2] *Ibid.*

[3] N.N. Polyansky, "The Legal Nature of the Soviet Legal Profession", *Sots. zak.*, 1945, No. 3, p. 12.

public organizations participate in the construction of the socialist state and its defense and the purpose they fulfill certainly assume state importance, the fulfillment of state functions, nevertheless, does not make an organization a state organ. Polyansky not only asserts that defense counsel fulfills a function of state importance, but also pertaining in its essentials to the state, and he declares that even in a civil suit the lawyer acts as an organ contributing to the administration of justice. Also in a civil suit "the principle defining his behavior in the court encompasses the subordination of his client's interests to the interests of justice, the supremacy of the public interest over the private one, if they should collide in a concrete case". [1]

In support of his opinion that the legal profession in the Soviet Union is a public organization, Polyansky brings forward the following arguments : 1) according to the 1939 Statute, the legal profession is "a voluntary association of persons involved in a lawyer's activity". "Voluntary" is an attribute of a public and not a state organization. Although Polyansky admits that the concept of "voluntariness" here is a very relative one, since nobody can exercise the legal profession who is not a member of the association, he still thinks that this limited voluntariness, reduced to the right to apply for membership, to resign membership or ask for the transfer from one college to another, is still an attribute of a public and not of a state organization; the members of the colleges are not appointed and not elected, like the state personnel and the deputes of the legislature are; 2) lawyers are not employees and their activity is not the fulfillment of an employee's duties. [2]

He also cites the following decision of the Plenum of the USSR Supreme Court. The member of the College of Defenders, Varshavsky, was held accountable because, besides his activity in the College, he engaged in private practice and was remunerated for it. If the activity of a college member were to be defined as an activity of an official, Varshavsky's action could not have been considered other than an offense committed in office, argues Polyansky.

However, the Supreme Court did not only not consider Varshavsky's action as a delict in office, but did not find any criminal element in the case, finding a disciplinary delinquency only. [3]

---

1 *Ibid.*
2 *Ibid.*, pp. 12-13.
3 *Sobraniye postanovleniy Verkhovnogo suda SSSR*, 1938 and 1939, No. 65.

V. L. Rossel's thinks that, by his legal help to the accused, defense counsel contributes to the administration of justice and the strengthening of socialist legality in the interest of the whole state and the entire people. Considering his activity as a service to the cause of the socialist society, law and justice, defense counsel must raise the defense to the level corresponding to its state importance, not abandoning the ground of principles common to him, to the court and to the prosecutor. This is his opinion of the importance and the immediate scope of the defense counsel in a criminal trial. [1]

According to him, the fight for the accused's rights and for legality is an inalienable feature of the socio-political and moral aspect of the Soviet defense counsel, distinctly derived from the public scope of the Soviet defense. Unflinchingly striving to redress the violated rights of his client, the defense counsel cannot stop before the official position of the person who violated the right or before any other considerations. [2] The question, as to whether the defending activity of the counsel who is bound to discover only the circumstances and bring forward only the arguments capable of rejecting the accusation or mitigating the guilt of the accused, impedes the finding of the truth in the case and the pronouncing of a correct sentence, is answered in the negative by Rossel.

The Soviet doctrine of the court as a political institution of class struggle has been already depicted above. With regard to the Soviet legal profession, Rossel's writes that "in contradistinction to bourgeois lawyers, the Soviet advocates, being a part of the people's intelligentsia, serve the socialist state, guided by the common principles and political scopes. In contradistinction to bourgeois councils of the bar, the Soviet colleges of advocates underline their political essence and, in particular, require from the advocates an active participation in the procedure, the clarification of its political importance and a corresponding ideological preparedness of defense counsel".

Rossel asks of the Soviet defense lawyer to be completely exact in the evaluation of the political importance of the case, "not over ... and not underestimating it and not weakening the effectiveness of the defense at the same time, but departing from principles and the public position common to him and the prosecutor".

---

[1] A.M. Levin, V.A. Ognyev and V.D. Rossel's, *Zashchitnik, v sovetskom protsesse,* M. 1960, p. 17.

[2] *Ibid.,* p. 18.

He underlines also the political importance of the legal profession's activity. He is of the opinion that the bourgeois legal science in Russia did not understand the political value of the court. In support of this opinion he cites the foremost Russian criminalist, of tsarist epoch, Professor Foynitsky, who wrote that the court with jury "is the nearest to the ideal of a court ... because it is remote from the mixing of justice with politics". [1]

Indeed, also another tsarist professor of law who wrote a special work in three volumes on the legal profession, Ye. V.Vas'kovsky, asserted that : "the legal profession is a legal and not a political institution". [2]

Rossel's is right in contrasting the pre-revolutionary Russian court and bar with the Soviet ones with regard to their political character. The prerevolutionary regular courts and the bar in Russia were proud of being apolitical.

One of the main purposes of the great judicial reform of 1864 was to make courts independent of the administration. Certainly this goal was not reached completely. There were instances when, under overwhelming pressure of the government, the courts deviated from their usual apolitical position. This occurred because the Judicial Reform of 1864 based the judicial power on democratic principles whereas the two other powers, the executive and legislative, remained as autocratic as they were before. "Peaceful coexistance" between the three powers proved difficult in the ensuing years of the reactionary governments of Alexander III and Nicholas II.

Also the bar prior to the Revolution had an apolitical character. Independently of their personal political opinions, lawyers defended criminals belonging to parties they opposed outside of the court. Thus, for instance, Karabchevsky, a very moderate liberal, defended Sazonov, the social-revolutionary activist and killer of the Minister of the Interior, Pleve. His summing-up contained accusations of Sazonov's victim and the regime he represented as fiercely as if they had been formulated by Sazonov himself.

And E. O. Gruzenberg, also a moderate liberal, defended Trotsky when he was tried in 1905 as the Chairman of the first Soviet formed in

---

[1] I. Ya. Foynitsky, *Kurs ugolovnogo sudoproizvodstva*, St. Petersburg, 1907, p. 394.
[2] Ye. V. Vas'kovsky, *Organizatisiya advokatury*, St. Petersburg, 1893, I, p. 320.

Russia. Also Gruzenberg's political convictions were as foreign to
Trotsky's as those of Karabchevsky to Sazonov's beliefs. [1]

Accusations of the tsarist government were brought freely by the
defense in political trials. Of course this freedom of speech in court
has a certain political implication since, according to an Ukase of
Alexander II, promulgated on the same day of 20 November, 1864
as the Judicial Reform, the press had the right to reproduce everything
which occurred in the open session of the Court. Therefore also the
summing-up of the defense in full. Thus, these summings-up with
their criticism of the administration penetrated into the remotest
corners of the Empire.

Polyansky amended Chel'tsov's definition of the Soviet advocate's
activity, to wit, that "the Soviet advocate realizes state representation
of rights and legal interests of individual citizens involved in the
capacity of accused, plaintiffs and defendants in criminal and civil
proceedings", in one respect only : he replaces the word "state"
with "publicly-legal". Thus, he underlines the public aspect of the
legal profession's activity.

The position of defense counsel as a representative of the state or
of the public obliges him to defend only the lawful interests of the
accused, which is stressed by Soviet writers.

This opinion was also expressed by the Chairman of the Legislative
Commission of the USSR Soviet of Nationalities, D. Rasulov, in his
report to the Soviet of Nationalities on the drafts of the Basic Principles
of the Court Structure of the USSR, Union and Autonomous Republics, the Statute on Military Tribunals and Basic Principles of
Criminal Procedure of the USSR and Union Republics of 1958,
mentioned above. [2] But the question, what interests of the accused
are "illegal", remains open. Indeed, this is a very debatable question,
subject to arbitrary interpretation. Legitimate is, however, the right of

---

[1] A curious dialogue between Gruzenberg and his former client took place in the
summer of 1917. Gruzenberg was appointed Senator of the Criminal Department of
the Ruling Senate by the Provisional Government. In a political meeting he heard
Trotsky's speech in favor of an immediate peace with Germany. In the intermission,
Trotsky asked Gruzenberg how he liked his speech. The latter answered : "During
your stay abroad... you have not lost your erudition and your brilliant oratorical talent.
But in my capacity of Senator, I have a forced labor sentence ready for you". Trotsky
responded : "You want to correct the mistake you made in having defended me".
(A. Ya. Stolkind, in O.O. Gruzenberg, *Ocherki i rechi*, N.Y., 1944, p. 21.)

[2] See p. 527.

the accused to deny his guilt even when faced by seemingly irrefutable evidence, and this must be taken into consideration by his counsel.

In an editorial of *Sovetskaya yustitsiya* [1], the Soviet advocate is defined as an active public worker whose immediate duty is the service to the cause of social legality, the strengthening and betterment of the administration of justice and showing up its authority, as well as the rendering of legal help to citizens and the defense of their rights and interests.

The author of the editorial does not see a dualism in the advocate's position. On the contrary, he recognizes the internal organic unity of the advocate's functions based on the nature of the socialist structure which, "for the first time solved the most important problem of human history involving the relation of individual and public interests, the conditions of a genuine flourishing and free development of all spiritual and physical capacities of the individual". That is because "only a socialist society most completely satisfies individual interests".

c) *Counsel-Representative of his Client?*

It is Strogovich [2] who brought forward the theory that counsel is a "special kind" of representative of his client.

Let us follow his argumentation. According to him, counsel is a representative of the accused. That means that he pleads in court on behalf of the accused, defends his legal rights, and is active in court as a chosen representative of the accused or, if he is appointed by the court, with the consent of the accused.

Counsel defends the accused in criminal cases, and that is his procedural duty. He takes part in the proceedings only in the interest of the accused and brings forward only those arguments which prove the innocence of the accused, or serve to mitigate the sentence; the accused is bound to counsel by a definite legal relation; the accused has the right to cancel the relation and even to assume his own defense without the help of any counsel in every stage of the proceedings.

However, Strogovich continues, the representation of the accused by counsel in a criminal trial has a function other than the usual representation and, for instance, other than the representation in a civil suit. The position of defense counsel is, in a certain sense, more

---

[1] 1957, No. 7.

[2] M.S. Strogovich, in Foreword to *Zashchititel'nyye rechi Sovetskikh zashchitnikov*, M. 1956, pp. 8-9.

independent than that of any other representative. This follows from
the fact that the function of the defense is a public one, which is of
importance to the state and the counsel is a participant in the administration of socialist justice, that is why he may not employ means
of defense which are illegal, such as lying, cheating, etc, means which
the accused is free to use in his own defense.

But that is not all which makes defense counsel "a special kind"
of representative, according to Strogovich.

In Strogovich's opinion, defense counsel has also rights independent
of his client. For he is himself a party to the proceedings and in this
capacity he represents also "the interests of the defense as a definite
procedural function, as an activity of state importance, carried out
by the organization of the Soviet legal profession : counsel pleads
in court not only as the representative of the accused but also as the
representative of the defense as realized by the Soviet legal profession,
a function which the advocate performs when he pleads in court in
a given case. Because of that defense counsel is not bound completely
by the position of the accused, but defines the line of his behavior,
his procedural position in the case, independently, as an active participant in socialist justice.

When A. Liberman [1], without any reservation, is of the opinion that
defense counsel has no right to deviate from the position of his client
and if he does not agree with this position he must resign the defense,
it is because he is one of the Soviet writers to share the viewpoint
predominant in pre-revolutionary Russia and in the West that defense
counsel is only the representative of the accused and has no other
function than to defend him with all legal means at his disposal.

Also Elkind assumes the viewpoint that defense counsel is the "representative of the individual" in the first place but also of the "institution of the defense" who performs functions of importance to the state
and, thus, may not defend just any interests of the accused but only
the legal ones. Precisely in this Elkind sees "the unification of the individualistic features of counsel's activity with the state and public
ones". [2]

With regard to the position of counsel as a representative of the
entire legal profession as brought forward by Strogovich and Elkind,
Chel'tsov argues that if two or more accused are involved in a trial,
the interests of which collide, their lawyers will make different alle-

---

[1]   See supra, p. 512.
[2]   P.S. Elkind, "Advocate's Ethics", *op. cit.*, p. 19.

gations while representing the same legal profession. But his main reason against such a conception of defense counsel's position in the trial as a representative of a public organization, is, that it is based on the contraposition of public and state interests. But "from the viewpoint of Soviet legal theory the contrasting of state prosecution with public defense is completely inadmissible", writes Chel'tsov.

We have seen that Chel'tsov, writing in 1954, still denied that defense counsel is the representative of the accused. But, whereas in 1940 he made no difference between criminal and civil procedure, in 1954[1] his arguments are based just on the difference between the position of the lawyer in a civil suit and in a criminal trial. In the first he acknowledges that the lawyer is the real representative of his party thus taking his place in the proceedings whereas in a criminal trial this is not the case, according to Chel'tsov, since the substitution of the accused by counsel is not admissible.

But in 1955, M. Ya. Savitsky[2] came out in support of the representation theory. He rejected Chelt'sov's arguments that defense counsel is not the representative of the accused because he does not replace him and cannot assume obligations in his name. Savitsky argues that defense counsel replaces the accused in the court of cassation where the accused is not present. Although the representation is not of the kind practiced in a civil suit, still counsel acts for the accused in the criminal proceeding. He objects to the aplication to criminal proceedings of concepts taken from civil procedure.

According to Savitsky, defense counsel represents the interests of the accused. That is his duty and that is "what the accused expects from him when he enters into relations with his counsel".[3] Thus, he must not drop the defense and he may not transform himself from a defender into an accuser.

Consequently, Savitsky does not admit counsel's right to diverge completely from the opinion of the accused in the evaluation of individual evidentiary facts and circumstances as asserted by Chel'tsov.

Furhtermore he also does not adhere to the theory of the complete independence of defense counsel as an individual party in the trial.

Then, in 1961, also Sinaysky[4] came forward with a flat rejection

---

[1] See supra, p. 529 and footnote 3.

[2] M. Ya. Savitsky, "Problems and Position of Counsel in Soviet Criminal Procedure", *S.G.P.*, 1955, No. 7.

[3] P. 95.

[4] E.D. Sinaysky, "Basic Questions of Defense in Criminal Procedure", *S.G.P.*, 1961, No. 5, p. 71.

of the "assistant" theory and the acknowledgement of representation without its limitation to a character *sui generis*.

With regard to the representation question, Sinaysky thinks that defense counsel is the representative of the accused since he participates in the proceedings only with the consent of the accused and the accused is entitled at any time to renounce the help of the counsel in general [2] or dismiss an individual counsel if he has hired him, or ask the court for other counsel if counsel was appointed by the court.

d) *Is Counsel An Independent Party in the Trial?*

Chel'tsov ascribes great importance to the fact that Article 23 of the old RSFSR Code of Criminal Procedure assigns to defense counsel the position of a party in the trial, making him to a high degree independent of his client.

Analyzing the position of the prosecutor and defense counsel in a trial, Chel'tsov comes to the conclusion that their positions are similar in the following aspects : 1) both are parties to the trial with equal procedural rights; 2) both must be helpers of the court which means their duty to contribute in the search for material truth, the authentic circumstances of the case. Thus, according also to this, Cheltsov's definition, defense counsel must help the court to establish all circumstances of the case, those favorable and unfavorable to the accused. [1]

Nazarov, Chairman of the Moscow Regional College of Advocates and Sokolov, Chairman of Leningrad City College of Advocates, in a joint article, [2] reject both Chel'tsov's theory that the advocate is the assistant of the court and Strogovich's assertion regarding the representation of the accused by the advocate. They do not accept the first theory because the advocate is not bound to aid the court in the finding of the truth since he is limited to the clarification of facts favorable to the defense, and the second because the representatives of the lawful interests of the accused are exhaustively enumerated in Article 23 (7)

---

[1] Chel'tsov, "Some Problems of the Defense...", *op. cit.*, p. 47. The theory of the defense as a public function was created by Vas'kovsky in his work *Organization of the Legal Profession*, St. Petersburg, 1893. For the question of contraposition of State and Public and Vas'kovsky's theory, see Samuel Kucherov, *Courts, Lawyers and Trials...*, *op. cit.*, pp. 197-200.

[2] L. Nazarov and I. Sokolov, "To Heighten the Authority of the Soviet Legal Profession", *Sov. yust.*, 1959, pp. 17-22.

of the (old) RSFSR Code of Criminal Procedure : "the parents, guardians, trustees and representatives of the organizations in the care of which the accused is placed".

Also the authors think that the advocate is an independent party to the trial (Article 23 (6) of the old Code of Criminal Procedure) and the procedural position of the advocate is, thus, an independent one. In consequence, he must pay heed to all remarks, arguments and desires of the accused but, if after a thorough analysis of all circumstances of the case, he comes to the conclusion that the guilt of the accused is proven with undeniable clearness, he must not speak of the innocence of the accused, which the latter maintains, for he may not lie.

"The duty to defend the accused follows for the advocate not from the procedural relation between him (this procedural relation is, according to M. S. Strogovich, the representation) but from the law".

Of the same opinion on the independent position of the advocate in the trial is Ul'yanova. She asserts that the advocate can fulfill his double duty : to defend the rights and the legal integrity of his client on one side and contribute to the observation of socialist legality and the realization of justice on the other, if he is "not bound by the will of the accused and occupies an independent position in the trial". [1]

Admitting the generally accepted principle that the advocate, acting as defense counsel, may not and should not blindly submit to the will of his client and support his unfounded explanations, Strogovich asserts that this principle does not mean at all that defense counsel may leave the accused without defense, worsen his position, contribute to his convictions, etc. "Covered by any seemly plausible pretext such action is unworthy of defense counsel" [2] In general, Strogovich does not hold as "normal the situation when the accused denies his guilt", but counsel admits the accusation and pleads only for mitigation of punishment". "A method of defense which, in reality leaves the accused without defense, cannot be recognized as admissible", he writes. [3]

Asserting that Strogovich gives "in a certain degree" a theoretical

---

[1] L. Ul'yanova, "On the Procedural Position of the Advocate and His Attitude in the Case", *Sots. zak.*, 1966, No. 3, p. 60.

[2] M.S. Strogovich, in foreword to *Zashchititel'nyye rechi sovetskikh zashchitnikov*, M. 1956, pp. 8-9.

[3] *Ibid.*, p. 16.

foundation to "a defense at all costs", S. Natanzon [1] continues the quotation given above with the following sentence : "I could not find in Strogovich's preface to the book *Zashchitilel'nye rechi sovetskikh zashchitnikov, Moscow,* 1956, the words : "All the assertions of some specialists on criminal procedure that defense counsel is not the representative of the accused, but an independent party (to the trial), not bound to the accused by procedural interests, can only belittle the importance conferred on counsel by the legislator".

The reason Natanzon did not find the sentence on Strogovich's preface, is very simple : Natanzon quoted Strogovich not from the original but from a review of the book by R. Rakhunov [2] who correctly gave the quotation ending with the words ... mitigation of punishment". After these words the quotation is closed in the article and the sentence "All the assertions ... etc." belongs not to Strogovich but to Rakhunov. Natanzon evidently did not notice the end of the quotation and ascribed Rakhunov's words to Strogovich.

But Natanzon accuses also the Presidium of the Moscow College of Advocates of adhering to Strogovich's and Rakhunov's opinions about the inadmissibility of variant positions taken by the accused and his counsel, since the Presidium published the book with Strogovich's preface without any reservations. It seems to Natanzon that "the advocates cannot accept to be led by this theoretical position".

As to Natanzon himself, he expounds the theory that counsel may take an independent position in the trial, and if the accused does not agree with him ... the former must relinquish the defense.

Also Sinaysky argues that the advocate helps the court only by defending the accused, and not by establishing the truth. "The widely spread formula the defense counsel is an assistant to the court must be, in our opinion, rejected". [3]

Sinaysky denies the independence of defense counsel and his position as a separate party to the proceedings. The definition of defense counsel as a separate party to the proceedings under Article 23 of the old RSFSR Code of Criminal Procedure, Sinaysky counters with the assertion that the word "parties" (*storony*) is used to define parties having special rights in the criminal proceedings. But the word "par-

---

[1] S. Natanzon, "On the Principles of Soviet Defense in Criminal Cases", *Sots. zak.,* 1958, No. 5, p. 53.

[2] *Sots. zak.,* 1957, No. 3, p. 86.

[3] Sinaysky, *op. cit.,* p. 71.

ties" defines also the two basic groups in the proceedings : the prosecution and the defense. The defense consists of the accused together with his counsels. [1]

Grekov assumes a somehow unclear position on the question of the independence of the advocate in the trial. On one side, he states that the principle of independence dealing with his rights must be extended to all procedural rights of the counsel, without exception whatsoever. If the counsel holds it necessary to make a certain move, he can do it even then when the accused contradicts it. [2] But nevertheless, he declares [3] that all attempts to separate the counsel from the accused to violate the legal bond between those two participants in the trial means an attempt against the same bases of the participation of the advocate in criminal procedure as a form of realization of the accused's right for defense.

Grekov correctly defines the role of the advocate as "the representative of the legal interests of the accused".

But if the advocate is so tightly bound to the accused by the law and represents his interests, how can he move against the desire of his client ?

From the independent position of defense counsel as a party in the trial, Elkind even deducted his right to lodge an appeal in cassation without the consent of the accused and even against his will. In support of his opinion Elkind invokes Article 349 of the Old Code of Criminal Procedure which provided the right of appeal in cassation to every "interested" party to the trial. "The advocate", argues Elkind, "who is deeply convinced of correctness of his viewpoint which he maintained before the court, is interested in acceptance of his viewpoint by the court".

It is obvious that Elkind extends the "independent" rights of defense counsel *ad absurdum*. First of all, if the client is against an appeal in cassation he needs simply dismiss his counsel by which action the counsel's "independent" rights are cancelled according to Elkind himself.

Furthermore, Article 349 of the old Code provided that every party to the trial has the right of appeal in cassation only with regard

---

[1] Sinaysky, *op. cit.*, p. 72.

[2] V. Grekov, "The Advocate's Position in the Trial Must Be Based on Law", *Sots. zak.*, 1965, No. 10, p. 56.

[3] *Ibid.*, p. 55.

[4] *Ibid.*, p. 21.

to formal rights and interests of the complaining party. It is evident that counsel has no interest of his own in the sentence.

The authors who wrote previously to the publication of the new principles of court structure of 1958 and of the Code of Criminal Procedure of 1961, based usually their assertions of the independence of the advocate's position as a party to the trial on the provision of Article 23 (7) of the old Code of Criminal Procedure.

However, the 1961 Code of Criminal Procedure has no provision similar to the interpretations of Article 23 of the old one.

Thus, the adherents to the theory of the advocate's independence try to prove their point by interpretation of the new Code.

For instance, Raginsky, commenting on the provision of Article 51 of the 1961 Code of Criminal Procedure that "counsel is bound to use all the means and methods of defense indicated by law, in order to clarify circumstances disculpating the accused or mitigating his responsibility ...", writes : "pointing to counsel's obligation to use the legal and only the legal means and methods of defense, the law underlines by it his independent position in the trial, independence from the unfounded and illegal request of the accused". [1]

If Raginsky has in mind only the independence of the counsel expressed in the freedom not to support unfounded and illegal requests of his client it is easy to agree with him. But in some lines further, Raginsky speaks of the "procedural independence" of the counsel under which Soviet writers understand the freedom of the counsel to acknowledge the guilt of the accused when he asserts his innocence, to lodge appeals in cassation as against the desire of the accused, etc. Of this kind of procedural freedom there is no sign in the 1961 Code of Criminal Procedure.

But also the reference to Article 23 (7) of the old RSFSR Code of Criminal Procedure by Soviet authors is not convincing.

Article 23 (7) interprets the terms employed in the Code. Under (7) are defined the "legal representatives", such as parents, etc.

Certainly, the advocate is not a "legal" representative of the accused in this sense. But that does not exclude a representation of the accused's interests by counsel. In reality, the participation of the advocate X or Y in the trial is based on a contract between the accused and the legal counsultation office (or an appointment by the court).

---

[1] M. Yu. Raginsky, in *Nauchno-prakticheskiy kommentariy k ugolovno-protsesudl'nomu kodesku RSFSR*, M. 1965, p. 92.

It seems to the present writer erroneous to deduce an independent position of defense counsel from the wording of Article 23 (6) of the old RSFSR Code of Criminal Procedure, as done by Chel'tsov and a score of other Soviet writers.

Indeed, in interpreting the terminology of the Code, Article 23 (6) defines the "party" to the criminal proceedings in court as follows : "the word 'parties' (*storony*) is understood to mean : the prosecutor presenting the accusation in the case, the civil plaintiff and the representatives of his interests, the accused, his legal representatives and counsels, the victim if he has the right to come forward in support of the accusation, and the representative of his interests".

Thus, the provision identifies four possible parties to the trial who form four separate groups : the prosecutor, the civil plaintiff and the representative of his interests, the accused, his legal representatives and counsels, and the victim and his representatives. The wording of this definition does not warrant the assumption that the defense lawyer is an independent party to the proceedings. According to this provision the accused, his legal representatives (for instance, parents when he is a minor *and* (italics provided) defense counsel form one single party. In the foregoing sentence the civil plaintiff and his representatives are defined as one party (according to the knowledge of the present writer, no one asserts that the representatives of the civil complainant in criminal proceedings are an independent party to the prodecure). In the same way, the accused, his legal representatives (if such are admitted in the case) *and* (italics provided) his counsel are one and a single party to the proceedings. The conjunction "and" binds the accused, his legal representatives with the counsels to one party. After the word "counsels" a comma divides the party of the accused from the next party, namely the victim and his representatives, if he is admitted to support the accusation, but the comma between the words "the accused" and "his legal representatives" is put because of the enumeration of three members of the same group : the accused, his legal representative *and* the counsels. The other groups have two or one members, that is why a comma between the first and the second member of the group is replaced by the word "and". It is obvious that if the provision were intended to enumerate the defense lawyers as an independent party, a comma would stand in the place of "and" before the word "counsel". [1]

---

[1] Although, as said before, Strogovich shares the opinion that defense counsel is an independent party to the trial, in his book *Ugolovnoye presledovaniye v sovetskom*

Furthermore, it must be emphasized that Article 34 of the new RSFSR Code of Criminal Procedure, is interpreting its terminology correspondingly to Article of the old Code, does not give a definition of the term "party".

Thus, the alleged legal basis for the assertion of the independent position of the defense counsel as a "party" to the trial, no longer exists.

On the other hand, Article 325 of the new Code of Criminal Procedure which enumerates the parties and persons entitled to an appeal in cassation against the sentence, gives a positive indication of whom the code considers to be a party to the proceedings. Indeed, the provision lists in separate paragraphs of Article 325 of the 1961 Code of Criminal Procedure the groups or parties of the trial who have the right of appeal in cassation. The first paragraph of Article 325 reads : "The accused, his counsel and legal representative, as well as the victim and his representative have the right of appeal in cassation against the court sentence".

It is evident that the first paragraph of Article 325 gives the right to appeal in cassation a court sentence to two persons : the accused represented or not by his counsel or legal representative and the victim represented or not by his "representative" whether appointed or legal.

Thus, with regard to the victim, the provision does not enumerate its representatives, the counsel and the legal representative, and says, "representative". This makes evident that in the first sentences concerning the accused, the counsel and legal representatives are separately mentioned as two kinds of representatives of the accused.

However, a representative only represents the rights of the represented : he has no rights of his own and cannot be an independent party in the proceedings.

In particular, the counsel has no right to appeal in cassation without the consent of the accused, not mentioning against his consent.

Anashkin who wrote the interpretation of Article 325 in the Commentary to the New RSFSR Code of Criminal Procedure is of the opinion that defense counsel does not have the right to lodge a complaint

---

ugolovnom protsesse, M. 1951, p. 144, he asserts that the prosecutor becomes a real party to the trial only in the trial session, "where, in supporting the accusation, he has against him the party of the defense, *which includes both the accused himself and also his counsel*" (italics provided).

in cassation against the will of the accused. [1] This is, of course, a confirmation of the opinion asserted above that defense counsel has no independent position as a party in the criminal proceedings since, on the contrary, he would also have an independent right to appeal the sentence.

All the procedural rights of counsel are derived from those of the accused. There is no procedural right of counsel that the accused would not be entitled to exercise himself if he were to dispense with the services of counsel. Counsel's rights depend completely upon the will of the accused who may dismiss him at any time.

It is the accused who has the right to the defense, according to Article 111 of the Constitution, and he commissions the defense counsel through the Consultation Office to exercise this right to his, the accused's, benefit.

Gol'diner opposing Strogovich's theory of the lawyer as a representative *sui generis* of the accused, bases his arguments on the assertion that any representation, based on civil or public law, "requires the right of the representative to act for the person represented and assume obligations in his name", which counsel does not have. [2]

The entire Gol'diner argumentation is based, however, on the assumption that the advocate is an independent party in criminal proceedings (Article 23(6) of the old RSFSR Code of Criminal Procedure) discussed above. But Gol'diner contradicts himself when he writes: "But being in principle independent in his action, the advocate is most tightly bound to the accused : the accused and his counsel form together *the party* (ital. prov.) [3] of the defense, as opposed to that of the accusation. All attempts to sever this bond, to separate completely the advocate from the accused, is an encroachment upon the very bases, the essence and content of the advocate's activity in the criminal proceeding". [4]

The assertion that the accused and counsel form "together the party of the defense "is correct and obviously contradicts the definition of defense counsel as an independent party in the proceedings.

---

[1] *Nauchno-prakticheskiy kommentariy k ugolovno-protessual'nomu kodesksu RSFSR*, M. 1963, p. 585(3).

[2] Gol'diner, "On the Question of the Procedural Position of Advocates", *Sov. yust.*, 1957, No. 7, p. 17.

[3] This assertion is a confirmation of the present writer's opinion about the interpretation of Article 23 (6) expressed above.

[4] Gol'diner, *op. cit.*, p. 17.

It is precisely this definition which is an attempt to "sever the bond between the counsel and the accused".

Another consequence of the acceptance of the counsel's independent position in the criminal proceedings is the acknowledgement by Gol'diner that when counsel has no logical possibilty to deny the guilt of the accused, although the accused himself does it, the counsel must admit it. Gol'diner acknowledges this duty of the counsel very reluctantly. He understands that the admission of the client's guilt is an action detrimental to the accused if he denies it, independently, from the degree of evidence of his guilt, thus, a violation of the counsel's duty, admitted also by Gol'diner : to defend and never to accuse the client. But Gol'diner is simply forced to this conclusion by his erroneous premise of the counsel's independent position in the trial.

The acceptance of the theory that defense counsel is an independent party to the trial brings Strogovich to acknowledge the possibilty of two complaints in cassation against the judgement of the court of original jurisdiction: one lodged by the accused and the second by defense counsel, "the contents and conclusion of which may not be identical" since "the advocate is not completely bound by the will of his client and the position he occupies is independent and he conducts defense in a way corresponding in his opinion to the purpose of Soviet defense", according to Strogovich. [1] (It seems that in this case the two complaints would have to be based on different considerations, since otherwise there is no reason for two complaints).

In support of this view, Strogovich quotes the decision of the USSR Supreme Court's Criminal Division, of June 21, 1952, in the case of Batenin-Lantsov.

In this case two complaints in cassation against the sentence of the People's Court were filed : by the accused and his lawyer. The Court of Cassation rejected counsel's complaint by an interlocutory order because no power-of-attorney for the lodging of a complaint in cassation was presented by counsel. The Supreme Court reversed the order declaring that "the advocate in defending the interests of the accused is, in accordance with Art. 23 (6) of the RSFSR Code of Criminal Procedure, a party in the case tried by the People's Court and does not need any special power-of-attorney from the accused in order to write and file a complaint in cassation. Since no declaration indicating his

---

[1] M.S. Strogovich, *Proverka zakonnosti i obosnovannosti sudebnykh prigovorov*, M. 1956, pp. 129-130.

withdrawal from the defense was filed in writing, the Circuit Court had no right to ignore the complaint in cassation of the advocate who defended the accused in the court of original jurisdiction". [1]

It seems to the present writer that the question to be examined by the Supreme Court was not as to whether the counsel withdrew from the defense in general, but whether he was dismissed by the accused. The presence of two complaints in cassation is a sign that the accused was not in agreement with his counsel over the complaint in cassation and filed his own complaint, which had to be interpreted as dismissal of counsel. A dismissed counsel, however, has no right to lodge a complaint in cassation. Even the alladged independent position of defense counsel does not reach so far as to permit him to file a complaint in cassation contrary to the will of the accused, also according to Strogovich himself and Anashkin [2]. If the accused has no desire to complain against the sentence counsel loses his "independent right" of cassation because the abstention of the accused from a complaint in cassation is tantamount to the denial to counsel of his further participation in the case.

The abnormal situation which may be created by the wrong interpretation of the term "independence" of defense counsel is well exemplified in *Sovetskaya Justitsiya* [3]

In a case examined by the Moscow City Court, the prosecutor dropped the accusation, but in his summing-up, defense counsel, instead of demanding the acquittal of the accused, pleaded only for the requalification of the criminal action under another provision of the Criminal Code, imposing a lighter punishment, evidently because he was not convinced of the innocence of his client in contradistinction to the prosecutor.

In consequence of this independance the Soviet advocates do not seldom openly disagree with the accused when he denies his guilt in criminal trials which is evident from complaining letters received by the same periodical. In a review of these letters in the periodical mentioned above it is said that in many cases advocates agree with the prosecution without sufficient proof even when the accused does not admit his guilt, because they do not share the viewpoint of their clients, and in this way help the prosecutor and not the accused. The behavior of the counsels is strongly criticized in the letters. [4]

---

[1] *Ibid.*

[2] In contradistinction to Elkind.

[3] *Sov. yust.*, 1941, No. 11, p. 17.

[4] *Sots. zak.*, 1964, No. 11, p. 52.

The Soviet concept of the independent procedural position of defense counsel is completely unknown to Western, including the tsarist, criminal procedures in which counsel acts as a full-fledged representative of the accused, on the basis of a power-of-attorney.

In the new Statutes of the Legal Profession published by all union republics, it is said that the legal profession is bound to contribute by every action : 1) to the defense of rights and legitimate interests of citizens, enterprises, institutions and organizations [1], 2) to the observation of socialist legality; and 3) to the realization of justice.

This definition of the purpose of the legal profession brings K. F. Gutsenko to the conclusion that the place of the legal profession in the system of state and public organizations is established and permits one to define more accurately the position of defense counsel in criminal proceedings. He thinks that this definition puts an end to the controversy as to whether defense counsel is only the representative of the accused or is also bound, in carrying out the defense, to contribute to the work of the court in the correct solution of the case. [2]

According to him, the new law directly establishes that the advocate, in carrying out the defense, is expected to use all means permitted by law in order to clarify the circumstances absolving the accused or mitigating his guilt. Thus contributing to justice.

Gutsenko recommends that all the republics adopt the extension of the functions of the advocates to administrative cases introduced by the Statutes in the Legal Profession in Estonia, Kazakhstan, and Uzbekistan. [3]

He also points out some guarrantees of the interests of the advocate included in the Kazakhstansky and Litovsky Statutes. The Kzakhstanisky Statute provides that if the transfer from one legal consultation office to another is related to the change of domicile, the transfer may take place only with the consent of the advocate.

If an advocate is irregularly separated or excluded from a college he has the right to an indemnity for the time of the forced unemployment, according to the Litovsky Statute. The same statute forbids an advocate to take a case if the advocate of another party of the case, the interests of which are opposed to the interests of the party he has to defend, is related to him.

---

[1] In Article 2 of the RSFSR Statute of 1962, Kolkhozes are added to this enumeration.

[2] K.F. Gutsenko, "On The New Statute of the Legal Profession, Passed by 13 Republics", *S.G.P.*, 1962, No. 3, p. 58.

[3] The RSFSR Statute of 1962 has no such provisions.

C. DEROGATORY OPINIONS ON THE LEGAL PROFESSION

It was already mentioned that Vyshinsky, writing in 1934, first undertook the defense of the "defenders of rights" as the counsels were called at that time.

According to him, some courts cultivate a disdainful view of the legal profession, based on the underestimation of the role of the defense for socialist legality. He argued against the opinion that the defense in the trial is not necessary. He cited a judicial worker who wanted the lawyers to be kicked out "versts" [1] from Moscow. [2]

It was thought then by a number of people, according to Vyshinsky, that the denial of the necessity of the defense in the trial is the most progressive theory of revolutionary criminal procedure. "We must repudiate such opinions", writes Vyshinsky, "we must demand from legal workers, prosecutors and the court, respect and confidence for the legal field".

This was written in 1934. But it seems that the derogatory opinion of the defense and its representatives still persists among judges, prosecutors and other organs of justice.

Twenty-three years after Vyshinsky's article, the Editorial, "The High Political and Public Duty of the Soviet Advocate", in *Sovetskaya yustitsiya* declared that necessary measures must be taken for the uprooting of the slighting attitude toward the lawyers' activity as something impeding the administration of justice. "Facts show", writes the editor, "that some workers of the organs of the administration of justice have not abandoned their views on the lawyers' activity as something foreign and uncharacteristic of our world outlook". In support of this assertion the editorial gives some examples : thus, the Chairman of the Supreme Court of the Dagestan ASSR, Pakalov, forbade judges to greet advocates and set the following rule for the time assigned to the lawyer for his summing-up : five minutes in civil suits and ten minutes in criminal trials, without regard to the complexity of the case. [3]

The derogative viewpoint on the lawyers' activity was condemned from the tribune of the USSR Supreme Soviet by the Representative

---

[1] A *versta* is equal to 3,500 feet.

[2] A. Ye. Vyshinsky, *Revolutyonnaya zakonnost' i zadachi sovetskoy zashchity*, M. 1934, p. 29.

[3] *Sov. yust.*, 1954, No. 7, p. 4a.

I. A. Kairov. He said : "The peculiar attitude toward advocates as to something hindering and not helping justice has not yet been lived down in some places. This attitude toward advocates has nothing to do with the real scope of Soviet justice, but some advocates submit to such an attitude toward them and lose the notion of the importance of their functions ... An end must be put to this situation and the advocates must be seen as real, persistent and bold defenders of truth and justice". [1]

However, A. Gorkin, Chairman of the USSR Supreme Court, writing in 1964 still thought it necessary to remark that a definite underestimation of the role of the Soviet legal profession takes place among individual members of the investigating magistracy and courts. The necessity of correct administration of justice "of the most accurate and all-sided discovery of truth by the court in the case, require both a qualified accusation and an appropriate defense of the accused. Conscienciously fulfilling his duties, indicated by law, the counsel aids the court to come to recognize all the often intricate particulars of the case, and to pronounce a just sentence". [2]

Also Strogovich writes that one encounters "sorry jurists" who think that the defense binds the preliminary investigation and the court, and impedes the exposure of criminals. [3]

Derogatory opinions on the counsels are still expressed by Soviet Judges. So in an article in *Kommunist*, [4] Yury Idashkin reports about a conversation with a friend, an experienced judge and a clever and good jurist, but who "obviously sinned" by a slighting tone with regard to the legal profession in the Soviet Union. The judge confessed to Idashkin that as a young student of law he dreamed of becoming a lawyer and became engrossed with speeches by Urussov, Karabchebsky and Plevako. [5]

But then, during the practice time in court, he came to the conclusion that it is not interesting to be a Soviet lawyer. He gave a very convincing explanation for his idea. "In tsarist Russia",— he said—'almost every speech of an honest counsel converted into an accusation against the existing regime, causing crimes, wa-

---

[1] *Zasedaniya Verkhovnogo Soveta SSSR. Stenograficheskiy otchet*, M. 1957, p. 464.

[2] A.E. Gorkin, *Izvestia*, December 2, 1964.

[3] M.S. Strogovich, "A Judicial Mistake", *Kommunist Literaturnya gazeta*, May 23, 1964.

[4] Yury Idashkin, "Thoughts About the Defense in Court", 1967, No. 5, p. 173 ff.

[5] Famous prerevolutionary trial counsels.

kened public opinion, brought to light the social roots of the crime
—with us there are no social roots of criminality. Every crime is an
individual deviation from the norm. Maybe because of that, the counsel
became shallow, you do not get any help from him, as a rule, you
have a feeling that the advocate is interested only in the material
success of his performance : will his client be acquitted, or not;
will the punishment be mitigated, or not. Indeed, from that depends
his popularity and consequently, his income ...".

Certainly, he acknowledges that there are some good advocates
who are very helpful in the clarification of the case. But, according
to him, this is seldom. That is why, in his capacity of a judge, he strives
to limit the advocate's activity. "Such a Demosthenes gets quite out
of hand-you must stand firm. And all that—only for the public. But
I have four cases scheduled for the day, and have no time to listen
to such exercises in oratory". [1]

Idashkin tries to get an understanding of his friend's viewpoints.
He has to agree that the activity of the prerevolutionary lawyers
had a great social importance, especially in political cases.

He has also to agree that the political sense of the counsel's activity
had basically changed after the October Revolution. That the defense
in cases of class enemies crimes against the Soviet power can search
for mitigating circumstances only in the actions of this or that criminal, or bring to light mistakes of the investigation "since both
parties to the trial agreed about the class character of such crimes",
as he puts it.

With regard to general crimes, although Idashkin admits that as
the consolidation of the socialist society progressed, the social scourges
which inadvertantly produced illegal actions in the past disappeared,
criminality has sharply diminished and the regularity of crime production against which the counsels directed their weapons is replaced
by individual causes. Still he thinks that there are some concrete
circumstances of a social character, caused by the public which under
defnite unfavorably conditions can contribute to this or that illegal
action. To discover these circumstances, to fight them, "to prevent
them,—is the honorable duty, the most important obligation of an
advocate-citizen". [2]

---

[1] *Ibid.*
[2] *Ibid.*, p. 176.

In all these circumstances, the author sees the reasons for the lowering of the authority of the counsel.

A role to this effect could have been played also by the violations of legality which occured in the years when Vyshinsky's "voluntary doctrines" monopolized the entire theoretical thought in jurisprudence and in no way contributed to the authority of the defense in court.

The source of all evil, Idashkin sees, however, in the fact that the extent of the advocate's income depends in essence upon—the personal reputation and popularity of each of them. The more the advocate is known, the shadier his reputation as of a man "able to win cases", the more clients revert for help just to him, and naturally, his income is more. This is the reason for many advocates to achieve purely utilitarian results : to obtain the acquittal of the accused or at least mitigation of his punishment—in result—the lack of a necessary position of principle in the case and the violation of advocate's ethics, and empty speeches.

Here Idashkin indulges into direct propaganda of wage-leveling, of workers and employees—independently of their individual achievements, which Lenin attemtped to introduce during War Communism abandoned by him and disdainfully called "*uravnilovka*" by Stalin.

Under the cover of preventing the advocates of the necessity to "please" the client, and to gain the reputation of a "tough" counsel, able to "win over" from justice a part of the serving time of his client, which brings them to approach the court with clearly nonsensical, and some times obviously illegal demands and to obstruct the cassation instances with unfounded complaints, Idashkin suggests that the legal profession "completing work of state importance", must become a state organization and the lawyers must receive "the usual salary".

Certainly, Idashkin does not deny that the qualification and capacities are different with individual advocates. It would be evidently unjust to equalize their remuneration. And he does not deny the importance of material incentive for the quality and quantity of work, "which is becoming a leading principle in our society".

Still he "ventures to think" that there are kinds of work to which this principle cannot be directly applied. "One cannot pay to a judge for every conviction, to the militiaman and to a controller—for every fined person, because even in the presence of maximal honesty of these categories of workers, the principle itself would be a threat to the lawful right of citizens and even to the authority of the power which these workers represent". [1]

---

[1]   *Ibid.*, pp. 176-177.

The author admits that there will be many difficulties to realize his project, difficulties which always present themselves in remuneration of "so-called workers of free professions". But the Soviet Union has worked out a remuneration system for performers in consideration of the creative character of their work, their qualfications, experience and capacities. The conclusion—why should the sytem not work for advocates ?

Idashkin's suggestion is not new. We know that it was a time when "defenders of rights" were officials and received wages as such.

But the system was abandoned. Although the lawyers were collectivized and lost the right of individual practice, they still retain some features of members of a free profession; to deprive them finally of these features would be not profitable for the work they have to fulfill.

Idashkin himself admits that "the search for every legal possibilty for the mitigation of the fate of the accused—is, certainly, the most important scope of the advocate's participation in the trial". [1] Then, what sense has the leveling of the accusations of "toughness" of "pleasing the client", "to win over from justice", "reduce the time of serving by his client" ?

If this is done by legal means, it is just what is required from the advocate ! Certainly, by doing his job well, the advocate acquires fame, a greater number of clients and a higher income. But do not famous dancers, performers, scientists and writers strive to fame and positions of promise which bring them material rewards ? The system of remuneration does not change anything in essence : the eminent advocate and the famous dancer, performers, scientists and writers also achieve material benefits by their activity in their respective fields.

The source of the descrepancy between the lofty public and state scopes of the legal porfession and the character and organization of its activity, seen by Idashkin, lies in the attribution of the greatest importance to the public and state aspects of the legal profession's activity, in detriment of its real scope—the service of the individual.

"After the XXth Congress the role of the defense improved considerably", the Deputy Minister of Justice Prusakov asserted.

---

[1] *Ibid.*, p. 176.

The declaration seems overly optimistic and for instance, to be inconsistent with the opinions quoted below.

The advocate Malysheva, cited by P. Skomorokhov in his article "Appointed Defense and the Advocate's Duty" [1] remarked : "What is astonishing that the slighting attitude toward advocates is more and more often expressed there where advocates, it seems, should be received with open arms ... [That means in court], for some judges do not value the help of advocates ... The Statute on the Legal Profession is in force, but prejudice against advocates remain the same with some judicial workers".

Skomorokhov himself also underlines the difficulty for the legal profession to clear its way to the stand it has the right to occupy in the administration of justice : "The right to a defense is a constitutional right", writes Skomorokhov, "but up to the present time the question is raised sometimes as to whether the defense is necessary in court".

The American writer, George Pfeifer, who for a short time observed the administration of justice in the Soviet Union, reports in his book *Justice in Moscow*, that lawyers complained to him "that the courts do not listen to their points of law, not even to their closing speeches; that the judge who is usually less literate than they, assumes a disdainful expression when they speak and some even laugh". [2]

Pfeifer asserts that such an attitude is reinforced by the "popular attitude toward the accused and the trial which undermines the lawyer's effectiveness".

Evidently, Pfeifer implies that the people in general do not believe in the possibility of something being changed in the fate of the accused by the lawyer's efforts, since he relates that "even the law students on the floor in any dormitory thought of the trial as something of a formality and consequently of the lawyer's role as superfluous". [3]

Pfeifer used to hear from students that "In case he is really guilty why must the lawyer confuse the jury and waste our time".

It is certain that in political cases, but also in semi-political trials [4] the Soviet lawyer must feel that he is powerless to influence the court decision dictated beforehand by the government or the party.

---

[1] P. Skomorokhov, "Appointed Defense and the Advocate's Duty", *Literaturnaya gazeta*, September 3, 1964.

[2] G. Pfeifer, *Justice in Moscow* N.Y. 1964, p. 255.

[3] *Ibid.*

[4] It means cases where the state or party are interested in bringing forth an accusation, although a direct crime against the state has not been committed, as for instance, in the Brodsky case.

"Most of the lawyers with whom I talked confidentially", continues Pfeifer [1] "murmured that their own influence and the sphere of action is too limited in some intangible way; that, however strenuous their efforts in a given case, the sentence remains pretty much what it would have been without them; that other, bigger forces are at work, so that the decision depends less upon how they are able to work with the facts than upon these bigger political factors".

He concludes that "the idea that guilt is determined only by the court, after all arguments are heard is not firmly embraced". [2]

It could seem that Pfeifer unduly generalizes the situation. Certainly, the attitude toward lawyers described by him or his confidants, exists with some judges, but can be found also elsewhere outside the Soviet Union. Also not the "people" but some people and some students disbelieve the effectiveness of the defense. In reality, they all run to the consultation offices when they are in trouble and to how many do the counsels bring help and comfort in non-political cases?

True it is that the Soviet lawyer has a difficult stand in some cases. In these cases the lawyer certainly plays "second fiddle" as Pfeifer writes. But these cases are exceptions and not the rule. That some judges assume an inadmissible attitude toward the defense is true, but it is also true that this attitude is criticized in the press and is not shared by the courts of higher instances.

Still this negative attitude toward the legal profession must be deeply rooted in the Soviet Judiciary, and officialdom, when such an eminent justice as the Chairman of the Criminal College of the USSR Supreme Court, G. Z. Anashkin, deems it necessary to report in the *Literaturnaya gazetta* [3] that many advocates who plead energetically in favor of their clients are abused for disagreeing with convictions. He writes that it is common for judges to assert that any advocate who dissents from a court sentence is wrong and must be reprimanded. He quotes a recent poll carried out by a Soviet research institution : To the question : "Are defense counsels necessary", 80 of 159 police officers answered negatively. Anashkin asserts that some courts, prosecutors, investigating magistrates and police officers still underestimate the role and importance of defense counsels. But in his

---

1 G. Pfeifer, *op. cit.*, p. 246.
2 *Ibid.*
3 January 7, 1970.

opinion defense is "one of the most important institutions of criminal justice", and "without a defense there cannot be an adequate and impartial justice."

On the other hand, the following example of a defense is in contradiction with the assertion that counsel does not dare to state his opinion when it departs from the imposed line. This is the case of the Drozdov family : M. Drozdov sued his wife, a physician in a Moscow hospital, for a compulsory exchange of apartments, claiming that his wife was fanatically religious, so that life together became unbearable and that the religious frame of mind of the mother began to influence their fourteen year old daughter.

The defendant was represented by the advocate V. Ya. Merkulov who in his summing-up declared : "The religious convictions of my client are of no importance. The religion she adheres to does not harm anyone".

The case is reported by L. Itkin and A. Pereslavtsev. [1] They wrote that the court passed "the only possible decision", ordering the exchange of apartments and giving the custody of the daughter to the father.

But the court also issued a private ruling pointing out the objective harmfulness of the counsel's speech.

A disciplinary proceeding was instigated against Merkulov. But he stubbornly defended his position. In his explanations to the Presidium of the Moscow City College of Advocates, he wrote that he deems it in principle not necessary to come out with anti-religious propaganda in court and asked that the matter be decided without taking into consideration the religious convictions of his client.

The authors of the article condemn Merkulov's position while maintaining that "Merkulov considered his scope only from a narrow professional viewpoint, forgetting that he, as a representative of the Soviet legal profession, was obliged to give a thought to the educational value of his address".

The result of the disciplinary proceeding is not told, but it can be assumed with a high degree of certainty that Merkulov was not acquitted.

It must be said, however, that the mere fact of Merkulov's declaration in court, and his explanations to the Presidium of the College

---

[1] L. Itkin and A. Pereslavtsev, "The Role of the Advocate", *Moskovskaya pravda*, September 20, 1964.

point out some changes which have taken place in the Soviet Union. That people risk disciplinary proceedings in order to express their opinion is certainly a sign for the better.

On the other hand, the private ruling and the disciplinary proceedings against Merkulov prove that there is still no freedom of speech in the court, as nowhere in the Soviet Union. That, "an end of all of that" as the Deputy Minister of Justice Prusakov puts it, has not been reached in the USSR, is evident.

D. ADVOCATES CRITICIZED

Golyakov thinks that in virtue of the counsel's important role in court, it is even more deplorable that some defects still are inherent in the work of the Soviet advocates and brings some examples of their defective actions 1) the advocate defends his client by means of belittling the danger of the crime committed by him. Such methods of defense must be condemned by state and society; 2) some advocates do not lodge appeals in cassation if they are of the opinion that the condemning sentence was just: it happens often that the cassation instance reverses the sentence in virtue of the appeal entered by another advocate. "Assuming the defense", writes Golyakov, "the advocate must carry it out not only in virtue of the received or pro-mised remuneration, but prompted by high-minded reasons, based on the honor of the entire legal profession, which helps the court in meting justice".

In support of the opinion that the counsel is bound to appeal in cassation if the client desires it, Golyakov quotes the decision of the Council of St. Petersburg Bar of 1909 : "The undertaking of the defense in a criminal case creates the assumption of the counsel's obligation also to appeal in cassation, if necessary", but is careful to add that he is doing it "not at all with the scope of a positive evaluation of the role of the Russian legal profession before 1917 since *even* [1] the old leg-al profession saw in the declination to logde an appeal in cassation the violation of the lawyer's ethics". [2] 3) the third criticism, emitted by Golyakov, is the practice of Soviet lawyers to use the supervision

---

[1] Italics provided.

[2] Thus, Golyakov acknowledges the existence of a "lawyer's ethics" in old Russia but denies it for the Soviet Union.

procedure in order to alleviate the fate of the client convicted by a sentence already in force. He asserts that when a criminal is convicted, the appeal in cassation remains fruitless and the sentence remains in force, the same (advocates) still try to help the client by asking all four instances concerned to review the sentence in the way of supervision to apply Articles 51 and 53 of the Criminal Code. [1]

Golyakov argues that the duty of the advocate is to strive for the acquittal of the accused if he thinks that he is not guilty; to obtain mitigation of punishment if legal grounds to this effect exist; and to get mistakes in the qualification of the incriminated action redressed.

But if the sentence is unjust according to the counsel? What if the courts of original jurisdiction and the cassation court both declined to apply Articles 51 and 53 of the Criminal Code, should the advocate try to get the benefit of these provisions for his client in the way of the supervision procedure?

Golyakov gives a negative answer to this question, because the abundance of complaints in supervision procedures undermines the authority of the court sentence, the fight against the most dangerous and most widely spread crimes, prevents the state from fighting effectively for obedience to the law and against the criminal elements.

In his opinion, there is no doubt that society and state are interested that persons who committed crimes should go to jail. And the striving of some advocates to act against public interests is erroneous. [2]

Golyakov is evidently wrong. Although the advocate is not the judge in his client's case, still it is relevant as to whether, in his opinion the sentence is just or not. He fought the sentence in two instances and tried to get Articles 51 and 53 applied in the case and since his duty is to use every legal means to mitigate the fate of his client in the regular procedure, his duty is also to try to do it by the way of the supervision procedure, a means put at his disposal by law, if he thinks that the sentence is unjust. That the abundance of complaints in the way of supervision undermines the authority of court decisions is an argument against the procedure itself and cannot be used in individual cases. Certainly, it is in the interest of state and society to jail sentenced criminals. But the question is for how long and under what conditions.

---

[1] Article 51 of the Criminal Code gives to the court the right in exceptional circumstances to lower the minimal punishment prescribed for the committed crime and Article 53 empowers the court to put the accused on probation.

[2] For Golyakov see his Introduction to *Advocat v sovetskom ugolovnom protsesse, op. cit.*

The advocate does not act against the interests of state and society when he employs lawful means to curtail imprisonment or seeks in any other way to mitigate the fate of his client. This is his sacred duty.

Kozlov, like Golyakov, complained about the misuse of motions for review in the way of supervision. According to him the advocates intend to file such complaints even before the case is decided by the court. [1]

Kozlov is of the opinion that advocates do not attempt to improve their qualifications and legal knowledge, although some of them have a very poor legal education and experience. Flagrant errors are made by advocates in briefs, and cassation complaints. He even asserts that in civil cases some advocates plead in the same case as counsel for the plaintiff and for the defendant. [2]

One of the reasons why the lawyer's activity is not improving is the inadequate control of the activity of the regional colleges of advocates, and their presidiums, which is carried out by the RSFSR Ministry of Justice. Kozlov thinks that an effective control counsel could be conducted from the center; a local state control is necessary which should be entrusted to the executive committees of the regional and territorial soviets. According to Kozlov, a correct organization of the legal profession in the sense of Lenin's teaching was made by the Decree No. 2 on Courts of February 22, 1918, which established the election of defenders of rights by the local soviets.

Complaints against the work of some advocates are also raised by E. Veinberg, Minister of Justice of the Latvian SSR, although the presidum of the college actively fights against violations of lawyer's ethics. The advocate Andreyev was excluded from the college for drunkenness. The same fate was dealt to the advocate Tarvid who illegally raised his remuneration in a civil case; another advocate was disbarred because he influenced witnesses in order to get an acquittal for his client. [3]

A revison of the activity of the Moscow College of Advocates took place in 1960, with the following resuts : It was established that a number of advocates carelessly fulfill their duties and do not extend qualified help to their clients, which can be partly explained by lack

---

[1] For review of sentences already in force see infra, pp. 642-651.

[2] V. Kozlov, "State Control of the Legal Profession's Activity", *Sots. zak.*, 1959, No. 7, pp. 30 ff.

[3] E. Veinberg, "Perfection of the Work of the Soviet Legal Profession", *op. cit.*, p. 20.

of supervision over the quality of their work by office managers.

Individual advocates chose a legally wrong position in the trial in consequence of insufficient preparation for the case and ignorance of its material. They indulge in empty grandiloquence or do not manifest enough principles and do not appeal court sentences although during the trial they plead for an acquittal or the mitigation of the guilt of their client.

Accusation was leveled against individual lawyers by the revision because of their unworthy behavior in court, because they shield, by all means, persons who committed serious crimes.

Unworthy behavior is also shown by advocates offending witnesses, representatives of the prosecution and other participants of the trial in their briefs.

As an example of the inadmissibility of behavior of such advocates, the revision quotes the *Komsomol'skaya Pravda* of August 26, 1960 in which the advocate Itskov, counsel of the accused Berman, accused of speculation with foreign currency "attempted by all means to cheat the court, juggling the facts and making black pass for white". During the trial, Itskov posed provocative questions to witnesses, presented ungrounded challenges to the prosecution and the presiding judge.

Court and prosecution workers repeatedly drew attention to the necessity of taking radical measures with regard to Itskov in order to stop his interfering with the normal court's work by either the Presidium of the Moscow City College or the RSFSR Minister of Justice. [1]

The revision accused the Presidum of the Moscow City College in general of not having paid enough attention to the behavior of the advocates in trials when checking upon their activity; the Presidium did not discuss in its sessions and meetings questions related to advocate's ethics, almost completely neglected the dissemination of experience of the best advocates of the college, rarely generalized the quality of advocate's work in criminal and civil cases, did not use to this effect the large staff of best qualified advocates of the college.

A special reproach was directed to the advocate Kosachevsky who participating in the defense during the preliminary investigations and informed by his client about circumstances connected with criminal actions of other persons also under investigation, but not jailed,

---

[1] *Sov. yust.*, 1961, No. 5, pp. 5-7.

notified them about the deposition of his client and instructed them on how to act in order to avoid responsibility.

The revision expressed regrets that the Moscow City College, which should serve as an example to other colleges in the RSFSR has not yet assumed this role. Disgracing cases of drunkeness, extortion and other amoral actions take place in this college.

According to the results of the revision, the presidium does not fight adequately the advocates who discredit justice by their behavior. It is not occasionally, remarks the revision, that from 34 private rulings about the wrong behavior of advocates which reached the college, only 19 were acknowledged by the presidium and only three advocates were punished. Completely uncondemned remained the advocates who behave tactlessly and rudely at trials.

It is reported in the revision that advocates were arrested by the prosecution body for abuses, bribery and other crimes lately.

Another defect, according to the revision, is the poor work in the propagation of Soviet law and legislation among the population.

The revision expressed regret that, in spite of a great number of qualified jurists, among whom there are thirty candidates of legal sciences and more than four hundred members of the Society for the Dissemination of Political and Scientific Knowledge, mass-work among the population was poorly conducted. Within ten months of 1960, the Moscow advocates delivered only 2088 lectures for the population, whereas the advocates of the Krasnodar College delivered 1809 during only six months of 1960, and the advocates of the Saratov College—1720 lectures.

All the defects mentioned above are attributed by the revision to the poor work of the Presidium of the Moscow City College of Advocates, a wrong reaction to the criticisms of the defects and especially loose connection between the presidium and the staff of the advocates.

Already in 1958, the revision carried out by the RSFSR ministry of Justice established many of the serious defects on the work of the college which are latent in 1960. No adequate measures for the liquidation of these defects were taken by the presidium.

However, it is not only the Moscow City College and its members which were subjected to such sharp criticism by the RSFSR Supreme Court Presidium.

The revision established that the Presidium of the Yaroslav College of Advocates sharply reduced its work. The presidium poorly controlled the activity of its consultation offices, the observation of financial regulations, did not fight the violations of work discipline. Also the defects in the work of advocates of the Yaroslav College, the revision explains by the faulty direction of advocates work by the presidium of the college.

Finally inadequate work was established by the revision in the Regional Chita College of Advocates.

On the other hand, the revision came to the conclusion that "the many thousands of collectives of advocates in the RSFSR had carried out a definitely positive work in 1960 dedicated to the legal help to the population, enterprises, organizations and institutions, and in main to the defense of rights and legitimate interests of Soviet citizens. The advocate actively participated in the propagandizing of Soviet legislation among the population and delivered 75,000 lectures and reports on legal subjects during 1960".

Examples of meritorious work by a number of colleges presidiums are cited by the revision.

The work of the presidiums of colleges and individual advocates is also criticized by some writers.

So A. Blekh gives appalling examples as to how negligently the task of accepting candidates into the colleges of advocates is handled. For instance, a certain Garbuzov was unanimously admitted to the Krasnodar Territory College of advocates simply on recommendation of the chairman of the presidium without any investigation. Less than two years later he had to be disbarred, because it was established that he faked a number of documents, attempted to bribe a judge in a civil suit, etc. The most peculiar feature of his admission to the college was the fact that long articles about Garbuzov's activity were previously published in *Izvestia* and other newspapers and he was recalled as a people's judge before the expiration of his term.

The former member of the prosecution body, S. E. Mal'kovsky, dismissed after serious professional troubles, was admitted to the bar and than excluded for drunkeness and embezzlement.

The former investigating magistrate, G. P. Mikhaylyuk, dishonorably discharged from the prosecuting body became a member of the College of Advocates and was disbarred two years later because of the embezzlement of large amount of money.

"These facts of non-serious attitude toward the selection of staffs of advocates are not casual. They can be explained, in the first place, by wrong, second-rate attitudes toward the legal profession in general and to the role of the advocate in society in particular", Blekh writes. [1]

In Blekh's opinion, the local Soviets under whose control and guidance the colleges of advocates work, must know that advocates according to the essense of their work, must actively help the correct administration of justice and the strengthening of socialist legality. Then, "how is it possible to admit to legal profession", argues Blekh, "vicious persons, who do not inspire absolute confidence?" "The college of advocates", he concludes, "is not a haven for shipwrecked persons. It must be acknowledged that such staff members as Garbuzov and persons similar to him, do not adorn the Soviet legal profession and do not contribute to its authority".

An Editorial of the *Sovetskaya yustitsiya* [2] came forward with various accusations against individual advocates. "The overwhelming majority of Soviet advocates fulfill their professional duties honestly and conscientiously and in an exemplary manner, solve the problems charged to them. ... At the same time, there are not a few advocates who take an unscrupulous attitude toward their professional duties, commit amoral actions and discredit the Soviet legal profession by their behavior".

A number of examples follow : So an advocate appeared at the session of the court intoxicated and the court had to adjourn; another called names to witnesses and other participants in the trial.

"In many cases, advocates in their pursuit of money violated the elementary norms of advocate's ethics, acting sometimes to the detriment of their clients".

As an example of such action, the Editorial cites the case of the advocate Kamensky who defended a client accused of premeditated murder. The advocate pleaded for a mitigated sentence and the court, agreeing with her plea, sentenced the accused only to seven years in prison. But after the trial, the sister of the murdered man, asked Kamensky to appeal the sentence because of the excessive mildness of the punishment. Kamensky agreed and lodge an appeal in cassation to this effect.

The advocate, D'yachenko, represented the plaintiff in a civil suit and then brought an appeal in cassation for the defendant after the judgement was against him.

The Editorial cites facts of irresponsible attitude of some advocates

---

1 A. Blekh, "The Garbuzovs and the Legal Profession", *Sov. yust.*, 1966, No. 17, p. 32.
2 "The Moral Make-up of a Legal Worker", *Sov. yust.*, 1966, No. 16, pp. 2-3.

toward their professional duties, appearing in court unprepared or in possession of a superficial knowledge of the case. The Kaluga Regional Court issued a private ruling against the advocate Bam who appeared in court to defend a criminal ten months before the trial without any knowledge of the case.

Furthermore, the advocates wrote illiterate briefs in many cases and gave legally wrong advice.

It must be noted that the Editorial also ascribes the guilt for these facts to the presidiums of the colleges which do not manifest enough exactness toward individual college members.

In general, the fight against amoral actions and violations of work discipline is conducted very poorly by presidiums of colleges. Often, they avoid troubling advocates not capable of giving qualified legal help to persons reverting to them, according to the Editorial. With regard to advocates mentioned above, only disciplinary measures were taken, even very mild ones, in some cases, whereas some of these advocates deserved much greater punishments, including disbarrment.

Also, Kozlov is of the opinion that the high purpose of the advocate is "The defense of the lawful interests of the accused". But, drawing upon his experience as a chairman of a court of second instance he asserts that individual advocates defend also illegal interests of their clients and in some cases attempt to exculpate the accused by discrediting indisputable evidence and distorting the truth. As an example of such behavior, Kozlov cites defense counsel of a robber gang which committed 37 confessed robberies. As mitigating circumstances the counsel brought forward that the gang operated with "primitive methods of breaking in and transportation", that "they were forced to go to the expeditions on foot and carry the loot on their backs". Certainly, very unusual attenuating circumstances. [1]

E. Summary of the Advocate's Position in Criminal Trials

In defining the position and the function of defense counsel in Soviet criminal procedure, A. Bilinsky writes that "it is not easy to say precisely how far an attorney may go in defending the accused without opening his own political loyalty to question".

Certainly, the risk of a Soviet attorney of endangering himself in

---

[1] V. Kozlov, "State Control of the Legal Profession's Activity", op. cit., p. 32.

defending his client, especially in a political trial and under the Stalin regime, was very substantial. However, the examples cited by Bilinsky seem to me not appropriate to illustrate the real position of things at the present time. A. Bilinsky described the difficult position of the attorney as follows : "If he contests the specifications of the indictment, he puts himself in opposition to the prosecutor, who is both a state official and a party member; if he appeals the conviction of his client, he challenges the correctness of the decision of the court, which is a state agency. These concerns obviously impose restraints upon his freedom of action in conducting the defense of his client". [1]

Now to assert that these concerns are latent as a rule is going too far. Almost in every criminal trial, with the participation of a prosecutor and an attorney for the defense, the latter "contests the specification of the indictment" and contradicts the opinion of the prosecutor. Thousands of appeal in cassation are lodged with the second instance and hundreds reach the Supreme Courts. They all "challenge the correctness of the decision" of the foregoing courts. In the cassation procedure in the way of supervision, it is not unusual that decisions of the highest judicial hierarchy, which have already become final, are challenged again and again. The advocate mentioned infra [2] who eight times challenged a sentence already final was certainly not plagued by the concerns described by Bilinsky.

It cannot be denied, however, that some concerns exist up to the present time, but they must be limited to political cases and questions only. It seems evident that the advocate has more leeway to give his opinions which had to be kept to oneself under Stalin, as we have seen in the Merkulov case.

Analyzing what was said by various Soviet writers about the position of the counsel it must be said that the assertion about his independence from the accused position must be rejected.

However, on this alleged independence is based the assertion that the counsel can deviate from the position of the accused. In absence of an independent position in court vanishes his alleged right to deviate from the position of his client; for the same reason he has no individual right of appeal.

Certainly the counsel has to defend only "legitimate" rights of the accused. This is indisputable. But, what is a "legitimate right of the

---

[1] A Bilinsky, "The Lawyer and Soviet Society", *Problems of Communism*, March-April 1965, p. 69.

[2] Pp. 650-651.

accused"? Does it not include his right to deny his guilt even in presence of a crushing evidence, against him? Obviously, the question is just how far the counsel can follow his client.

It seems to the present writer, that the counsel can go a long way with his client. If, despite the evidence produced in court, his client is innocent his right to deny is legitimate and must be supported by the counsel. But it should never be forgotten that only the court can decide authoritatively if the accused is lying.

The advocate's view about the guilt or innocence of his client is irrelevant. He is not the judge and his job is only to defend his client. The objective truth is not his concern and he is certainly not an aid of the court in the finding of truth. His scope as defined by law is to bring forward everything capable to disculpate his client or mitigate his guilt. Deciding in advance of the court about the guilt of the accused, the counsel assumes functions not assigned to him and violates his sacred duties of defense prescribed by law.

It must be agreed with Gol'diner when he writes : "The extensive interpretation of the notion of 'legitimate interests' by some experts of procedural law ... is objectively directed toward the infringement of the rights and real possibilities of the defense". [1]

The law not only does not assign to the Soviet lawyer an independent position but binds him to the accused forbidding him to lay down the defense of the accused if he has accepted it.

But when is a defense accepted by the trial lawyer?

Soviet writers disagree also on this point. So, for instance, Ul'yanova[2] is of the opinion that a case is accepted when the order of the manager of the consultation office, after he has signed a contract with the accused or his relatives, assigning an individual advocate to the case, is issued.

But Stetsovsky[3] convincingly argues that the defense is accepted by the advocate after he has his first conversation with the accused. During this meeting with the accused, the advocate receives full information on the position the accused wishes to assume in the trial. If this position is not acceptable to the advocate he has the opportunity to reject the assignment.

---

[1] V.D. Gol'diner, "On the Ethics in the Advocate's Activity", *op. cit.*, pp. 96-97.

[2] Ul'yanova, *op. cit.*, p. 61.

[3] Yu. Stetsovsky, "On Procedural Independence of the Advocate-Counsel", *Sov. yust.*, 1966, No. 16, p. 14.

Certainly, the assertion of the accused can be proven untrue during the trial and the client still can deny his guilt. Now, cases when the guilt of the accused is obviously proven, but the accused still sticks to his denial, *without any grounds whatever* (A. I.), are very seldom. In general the accused has some reason to assert his innocence even in the presence of an overbearing evidence against him. Then the advocate must bring forward as convincingly as possible, the version and the arguments of his client and let the court decide.

But not in any event has the counsel the right to acknowledge the guilt of the accused if the latter denies it. That would be a flagrant violation of his defense duty.

The so-called "alternative", is also not admissible. To say to the court that in case you do not believe the denial of his guilt by the accused consider the mitigating circimstances, is to acknowledge that the counsel himself admits this possibility and thus, does not believe the innocence of his client and herewith shatters his position. The indication of mitigating circumstances must be interwoven in the summing-up of the counsel supporting the position of the accused. The court has to consider these circumstances *ex officio.*

The lack of an independent position in the trial evidently deprives also the Soviet counsel of the alleged right to lodge an appeal in cassation without the consent of the accused, not mentioning against his will, but he must lodge an appeal if the accused wishes it. [1]

F. The Position of the Advocate in Civil Suits

No doubt is expressed by the Soviet jurists that the advocate is a full fledged representative of the party who hired him in a civil procedure.

However, also there, he is not only an obedient servant of his client, he has to defend rights of the latter, only when he is convinced of their legality and rightousness. Also the means the advocate applies to this effect must be legal, writes Tobolovskaya. [2]

---

[1] Also Rakhunov writes : "The opinion of the counsel on the essence of the case is not yet the viewpoint of the second instance in the case, and if the accused is not satisfied with the sentence, the counsel is bound to appeal it. R.D. Rakhunov, *Uchastniki ugolov-no- protsessual'noy deyatel'nosti po sovetskomu pravu,* M. 1961, p. 224).

[2] M. Tobolovskaya, "The Defense of Property and Personal Rights of Citizens by the Advocate", *Sov. yust.*, 1965, No. 10, p. 14.

It is evident that the advocate who represents the opposite party is in a civil suit in the same degree persuaded in the rightousness of his client. One of the advocates must be wrong, however, since a civil suit ends usually with the victory of one party and the defeat of the other.

Certainly, a similar situation occurs in every civil suit also in the West.

But there the lawyer is not obliged to be 100% convinced in the rightousness of his client's position.

If the Soviet advocate has not won a positive opinion with regard to his client's claim when he gets acquainted with the case, he must allegedly decline the assignment given to him by the consultation office.

In this case the manager of the office decides as to whether the opinion of the advocate is correct. If the manager does not share this opinion he assigns another advocate to the case.

Thus, the advocate or the manager assumes the function of the judge and decides beforehand on which side are law and right.

It can also happen that the advocate, having accepted the assignment to defend the interests of the client, comes to the conviction during the suit, that he erred, that his client is wrong and the other party right. Then, writes Tobolovskaya, he must resign his activity in the case.

The Soviet advocate has this right in a civil suit in contradistinction to the criminal procedure in which, as we know, the counsel has no right to resign an accepted defense.

Article 401 (2) of the RSFSR Code of Civil Procedure gives the right to the advocate to resign his assignment by a simple notification directed to the court.

G. Juristconsults

Juristconsults are not advocates. They are officials of agencies or employees of organizations, institutions, enterprises or kolkhozes charged with legal affairs.

In this capacity of legal advisers, home counsels, they are consulted in legal matters and represent their employers in regular and arbitrazh litigations in which they are involved. To represent his employer in court or in an arbitrazh suit the juristconsult needs a power-of-attorney.

However the juristconsult is excluded from the participation in criminal cases.

The juristconsult takes part in the conclusion of contracts and agreements, provides information to the employer, and his employees and workers about the current legislation and gives them legal advice.

The juristconsult of a state agency has to watch that his agency or organization functions to the limits of its jurisdiction and in conformity with the legislation in force.

As an employee, the juristconsult is subjected to the provisions of the Labor Code, the collective agreements, his contract and other rules of the inner labor-order of the enterprise, institution, organization or kolkhoz in which he works.

Rights and duties of juristconsults have been regulated by union-republic legislation.

The RSFSR Council of Ministers has confirmed an exemplary statute on the "Legal Department, the Chief (Person) Juristconsult of an Enterprize, Institution and Organization" on March 29, 1963. [1]

Thus, the jurist consult is not an advocate. He also practices law, but as an employee and his client is not the public, but the individual employer.

Not being an advocate, the juristconsult is naturally not subjected to the provisions of the Statute on Advocates, has not the privileges, but also has not the duties of an advocate.

It must be emphasized that a great number of enterprises, organizations, institutions and kolkhozes conclude contracts with legal consultations for a permanent legal help by regular advocates. In virtue of these contracts the consultation office assumes the position of a juristconsult to the contract partner. In these cases, an individual advocate from the consultation office is charged with the legal advise; with the consent of the contract partner, an individual advocate is attached to it. This attachment and steady advising permits the advocate to get nearly acquainted with the activity of the roganization, institution, enterprize or kolkhoz and gives him the opportunity to extend better help to his client.

However, fulfilling the duties of a juristconsult, the advocate attached to an administration, institution, organization, enterprize or kolkhoz, remains a member of the college and the consultation office

---

[1] *Sob. post., RSFSR.*, 1963, Item 44.

which collects fees for his activity and remunerates him. He is an advocate and not an employee.

H. CONCLUSIONS

The Soviet legal profession went through a major evolution during the fifty years of Soviet rule, as did many institutions and administrations in the Soviet areas.

From the freedom for everyone to exercise this profession to the position of an official of the administration of justice, and from there through collectivization to the functions of a "semi-official", obliged to help the court in finding the truth. This duty is reduced according to the great majority of opinions at the present time, to the contribution to the help of truth establishment by presenting to the court everything which can speak for the innocence of the accused or mitigate his guilt. [1]

In matters of counsel's ethics there was also a very significant development.

The right of dropping the defense and revealing client's secrets, asserted in the beginning, was later denied by the legal literature and finally rejected by the 1962 Statute. [2]

Together with the admission of the advocate to the preliminary investigations and some amount of freedom in speech, these provisions of the 1962 Statute marked a distinct change in the defense position.

It must be said that this evolution moved in the direction of liberalization.

Certainly Lipson is right when he stresses that "it was a time when the defense counsel even viewed with the public prosecutor in abusing the defendant especially in political cases". [3]

Certainly, during the cult of personality the defense had to sing in unison with Vyshinsky.

But faced in the beginning of his career with the denying of the

---

[1] Article 2 of the 1962 Statute still enjoins the advocate "to contribute to the strengthening of socialist legality and the realization of justice".

[2] Without excluding secrets pertaining to the safety of the State.

[3] L. Lipson, "The New Face of Socialist Legality", *Problems of Communism*, 1958, August-September, p. 26.

necessity of a defense in court in general, the Soviet advocate is now considered an indispensible link in the administration of justice.

Still he is not a member of a free profession. The Soviet advocate is collectivized into colleges and bound to definite legal counsultation offices. He does not select his clients; it is the manager of the office who assigns cases to him.

His position remains especially ambiguous in political cases. If the advocate wishes to present to the court all the circumstances of the case which can explain the action imputed to his client and mitigate his guilt, he is bound to criticize the regime with its representatives against which the accused has risen. It is obvious that the Soviet lawyer, unlike the Russian lawyer in prerevolutionary court, is in no position yet to do so. Summings-up like the one delivered by Karab-chevsky in the Sazonov case [1] are certainly impossible.

Let us not forget that a situation arose for the Soviet lawyer in political cases when he was forced to acknowledge the guilt of his client even when he knew that he was innocent. Thus, with regard to the famous trials of the thirties, Hazard writes: "Being in a situation where Stalin's own hand had formulated some of the charges and knowing that guilt was dictated by him before the trial began, the defense attorneys limited their defense. They acknowledged that their clients were guilty. They argued only that their clients had not instigated the alleged plot but had been led into it because of their weak wills after years of exemplary living. Clemency was asked and nothing more". [2]

Furthermore, not only was the advocate forced to acknowledge the guilt of his innocent client, but he was also obliged to praise publicly the administration of justice and express feelings toward it which he could not have had at that time.

So his summing-up in the Abramov case, one of the most eminent Soviet trial lawyers, I. D. Braude, said: "In our country where justice stands on such a high level, unknown to the world, all realistic possibilities exist to address oneself for defense to the organs of power, to the defense of Soviet society". [3]

This was said in 1949 when the Special Board of the Ministry of Internal Affairs was in full function, when Vyshinsky's doctrines

---

[1] See Samuel Kucherov, *Courts, Lawyers and Trials Under the Last Three Tsars*, *op. cit.*, pp. 227-230.

[2] John N. Hazard, "The Soviet System of Government", *op. cit.*, pp. 184-185.

[3] *Zashchititel'nyye rechi sovetskikh advokatov*, 1956, p. 25.

were blindly followed by the courts, when MGB exercised unrestricted power over the life and death of Soviet citizens.

Dealing with the Soviet law it must always be kept in mind that the real circumstances in the Soviet Union must be judged not according to the standards on paper existing in this or that aspect of Soviet life, but to the facts of how Soviet laws are applied in reality.

The 1936 Constitution is, for example, a product of democratic legislation. But the real value of provisions in Chapter 10 of the Constitution enumerating the basic rights of the citizens and guaranteeing them the freedom of speech, press, assembly, mass-meetings, street processions and demonstrations is fictitious. What meant the inviolability of the person and his home, the provision that nobody may be placed under arrest except by decision of a court or a warrant of a prosecutor during the functioning of a Special Board is well known.

But if at the present time, the Soviet citizen does not any longer look forward with excitement to a ring of the doorbell at dawn, which means arrest, torture, condemnation and forced labor under appalling conditions without any guilt on his part, still the rights of Chapter 10 remain only on paper in a very great extent.

The organization of Soviet lawyers is not a bar in the western sense of the word and the Soviet advocate is not a "fearless knight" of the individual but an obedient servant of the state ... of the same state against which he has to defend his client.

The present writer concluded his article "The Legal Profession in Pre- and Post Revolutionary Russia" [1] written in 1956, with the quotation from the former RSFSR Deputy Minister of Justice, Kudryavtsev: "The Soviet Lawyers have nothing in common with the bourgeois lawyers; they differ from them fundamentally and in principle". [2]

In 1968, when these lines are written, Kudryavtsev's words seem grossly exaggerated, the Soviet advocates moved "fundamentally and in principle" nearer to the western lawyer. Still, between the Soviet and the western lawyer stand the collectivization, the lack of freedom of speech and the semi-official position of the former.

In 1956, a commission of French jurists visited the USSR at the invitation of the Soviet Government. The French jurists had the

---

[1] S. Kucherov, "The Legal Profession in Pre-and Post-Revolutionary Russia", *The American Journal of Comparative Law*, Summer 1956, No. 3, p. 470.

[2] *Literaturnaya gazeta*, June 7, 1951.

opportunity to become acquainted with different aspects of Soviet administration of justice.

During a joint ssession of the commission with Soviet officials and law professors the question was raised as to what is the position of the counsel in a trial in which the state has an interest. In his answer, Professor Strogovich emphasized that the advocate is also a "social being". [1]

This means in the USSR that the collective has precedence over the individual in criminal as well as in civil cases.

This means that if state interests are involved, the "social being" —advocate—is caught in a dilemma very difficult to solve and, thus, he has to flounder.

That the position of the Soviet advocate in the whirlpool between the Scylla of his duties as a "social being" and the Charybdis of his obligations to his client, in a political trial is still not only difficult but even dangerous has been exemplified by the fate of the advocate Boris A. Zolotukhin, counsel of Alexander Ginsburg, [2] who was excluded from the Communist Party and relieved of his position as Chairman of the legal consultation office in a Moscow Borough as a result of the trial. [3]

---

[1] Pierre Lochak, *Recht und Richter in der Sowjet-union, Bulletin der Internationalen Juristen Kommission*, Den Haag, February 1957, No. 7, p. 52.

[2] See p. 708.

[3] *The New York Times*, April 17, 1968, p. 13.

CHAPTER EIGHTEEN

PUBLIC PROSECUTORS AND PUBLIC COUNSELS

A. HISTORICAL DEVELOPMENT

The way to the activity of prosecutor or counsel was already opened to everyone by the Decree No. 1 on Courts. The reason was the abolition of the former organs of accusation and defense. But a prosecutor and a counsel were still necessary for the conduct of a trial in even distorted conditions of Soviet democracy.

Thus, every unstained citizen had the right to assume accusation or defense of an accused in court. Certainly, they were self-appointed and not elected by any enterprise, institution or organization, but still they can be regarded as the forerunner of the contemporary lay prosecutor and lay counsel.

The succeeding legislation endeavored to give a public character to the activity of these lay prosecutors and counsels.

Article 42 of the Statute on the People's Court of October 21, 1920 conferred the right to Soviet institutions to send their representatives to the trial, with the assignment to function in the capacity of a prose-cutor, and Article 45 permitted the People's Court to admit to the trial as counsels members of organizations to which the accused belonged, assigned to this effect. This right to defend in the trial belonged also to relatives of the accused.

The participation of public prosecutors and public counsels in the criminal procedure was enlarged by the RSFSR Codes of Criminal Procedure of 1922 and 1923, giving the right to a number of organi-zations and institutions to nominate public prosecutors and counsels.

It must be emphasized that according to the old RSFSR Codes there was no difference between the procedural position and rights of the state prosecutor and the public prosecutor, as well as the advocate and the public counsel. [1]

However, tendency to subordinate the public prosecutor to the representative of the state accusation was made distinct by the ad-ministration.

---

[1] See L.I. Urakov, *Obshchestvennoye obvineniye i obschestvennaya zashchita v sovetskom ugolovnom protsesse*, M. 1964, p. 12.

First of all, a second kind of public prosecutor was introduced by the Instruction of the People's Commissariat of Justice No. 1, of January 3, 1923, conferring on province prosecutors the power to attract to the participation in the public accusation, persons not belonging formally to the prosecuting body, selected from among shock workers and members of the VKP (b) and trade unions. These public prosecutors, appointed by the prosecuting body, had to act along side the public prosecutors assigned by organizations or institutions.

The same Instruction established that if a public prosecutor takes part together with the state prosecutor in the examination of a case, the state prosecutor has the duty to guide the accusation during the trial. It is the latter who decides all the controversial questions between him and the public prosecutor, without letting it be known in any way to the public and the court, of these controversies.

Furthermore, the directing letter of the People's Commissariat of Justice of June 14, 1927, established that the public prosecutors shall not be assigned to individual cases, but elected according to the territorial principle for one year and the state prosecutor had to appoint them to the appropriate cases according to his understanding. It was recommended in the letter to let public prosecutors participate in not less than one half of the cases in which a state prosecutor appears himself.

Finally, the Circular Letter of the USSR Prosecuting Body of July 2, 1935 restricted the activity of the public prosecutor to the evaluation of the social and political aspects of the crime, the analysis of the causes and the exposure of the defects in the work of the organization, where the crime was committed. The demand for definite punatative measures belonged exclusively to the competence of the state prosecutor.

"Thus", Urakov writes, "the public prosecutor was definitely transformed into an assistant of the state prosecutor, for the maintenance of the accusation in court under his assignment and control". [1]

With the advent of the late thirties and the growth of the cult of personality, the public participation in the administration of justice experienced a period of stagnation, as we have seen with regard to the comrades' courts.

It is in connection with the participation of public prosecutors

---

[1] *Ibid.*, p. 16.

in the trial that Vyshinsky made his slighting remark about the work of the *obshchestvennost'* in general in 1936, quoted above. [1]

Shifman explained the practical activity elimination of the public prosecutor by the character of the Soviet public-political structure under which base for the activity of a public prosecutor is excluded since an antagonism between the public and the state does not exist, whereas Mokichev sees the reason in the organizational strengthening of the prosecuting body and its replenishing with qualified investigating magistrates and prosecutors making the participation of a public prosecutor in the trial along side the state prosecutor superfluous. [2]

We have already had occasion to discuss the revival of Lenin's doctrine about the participation of wide masses of the population in the administration of the state and, thus, in the administration of justice, advocated by Khrushchev and decided by the XXIst Congress of the Soviet Union Communist Party.

As one of the expressions of this revival prosecutors and public counsels were provided by the Basic Principles of the Court Structure Legislation of the USSR, Union and Autonomous Republics of December 25, 1958 and the Basic Principles of Criminal Procedure of the USSR, the Union and Autonomous Republics of the same date, although "the Soviet public-political structure" remained the same.

On grounds of these principles, the individual union republics adopted codes of criminal procedure between 1959 and 1962 which formulate the rights and regulate the activity of public prosecutors and counsels.

Let us take a look at the corresponding provisions of the RSFSR Code of Criminal Procedure of 1961.

B. The RSFSR Code of Criminal Procedure
on Public Prosecutors and Counsels

a. *Admission to the Trial*

The admission of a public prosecutor or counsel to the trial is related to indictment.

---

[1] See p. 163.

[2] M.L. Shifman, *Prokuror v ugolovnom protsesse*, M. 1948; K. Mokichev, "Against Bourgeois Influence in Criminal Procedure", *Sots. zak.*, 1949, No. 2, p. 7 respectively; Urakov, *op. cit.*, pp. 18-19.

The indictment [1] is namely decided by the judge alone if he thinks that, without preceding upon the guilt or innocence of the accused, there is enough ground for the examination of the case in a trial. But, if he does not agree with the accusatory conclusions of the investigating magistrate or with the measure of suppression taken by the latter, an administrative session of the court with the participation of the judge, the two assessors assigned to the case and the prosecutor, is convoked.

Hence, if the indictment is decided by the judge alone he also has to take all the preparatory decisions. One of them is, according to Article 228 (Par. 2 and 4), the admission of a public prosecutor or counsel. But, if the indictment is resolved in the administrative session of the court—the corresponding resolution is taken by the court.

Thus, Perlov remarks that the court or the judge decide the question of the public prosecutor's or counsel's admission.

However, commenting on Article 250 of the Basic Code of Criminal Procedure, Perlov writes that it "seems" to him, since Article 41 of the Basic Principles of Criminal Procedure establishes that public prosecutors and public counsels are admitted to the trial by resolution of the *court* (italics provided), in cases when they are admitted by a resolution of the judge alone, the court must return to the decision on this question during the trial and take a corresponding resolution. [2]

Thus, in the end effect, it is the court which decides about the admission.

The contradiction in Perlov's statements is caused by the fact that also the judge alone is empowered by law to take the indicting resolution and the preliminary measures to the trial enumerated in Article 228 of the RSFSR Code of Criminal Procedure. [3]

That the legislator wanted the court and not the judge to decide about the admission of the public prosecutor or counsel to the trial follows, in the present writer's opinion, from the wording of the basic article formulating the principles of the admission. Article 250 (1) of the RSFSR Code of Criminal Procedure reads namely : "Representatives of toilers public organizations may be admitted to the

---

[1] *Predaniye sudu.*

[2] I.D. Perlov, in *Nauchno-prakticheskiy kommentariy k ugolovno-protsessual'nomu kodeksu RSFSR, op. cit.*, pp. 408 and 452 respectively.

[3] Urakov (*op. cit.*, pp. 26-27) is of the opinion that only the court has to take a resolution about the admission of a public prosecutor or counsel : in an administrative session of the court or during the trial, if the request for admission is presented before or during the trial, respectively.

participation in court examination of criminal cases in the capacity of public prosecutors or defense counsel by a resolution of the *court* (italics provided)". [1]

b. *Election of the Public Prosecutor or Counsel*

However, in order to be admitted the public participants to the trial must be elected by a public organization to this effect. Usually a collective being informed by the investigating magistrate or the prosecutor about a criminal procedure against one or more of its members convokes an assembly of the collective in which it must be decided as to whether the collective desires to side with the accused reinforcing his defense by a public counsel, or to act against him assigning a public prosecutor to the case.

Unclear also is the question, which organization or public organ is empowered to elect or appoint representatives for the participation in the trial. The RSFSR legislator remained silent on this subject.

It was generally admitted that only the general assembly of the organization has the right to elect these representatives up to a ruling of the Presidium of the USSR Supreme Court Plenum of 1961.

On December 16, 1961, the USSR Plenum of the Supreme Court ruled that a public prosecutor may be assigned for the participation in court examination of a criminal case not only by the general assembly of a public organization, but also in a session of a rightful collegiate organ of the organization if a contrary order is not established by union-republic legislation. [2]

The case which caused the Ruling is the following :

In the Bakker's case, the judicial college of the Kazakh SSR Supreme Court in a private ruling indicated to the chairman of the court of original jurisdiction that the public prosecutor in the trial was assigned illegally to the trial since he was not elected by the general assembly of a public organization or a worker's collective, but by the Worker's Committee of the trade-union organization.

---

[1] The RSFSR Code of Criminal Procedure reproduces literally the provision of Article 41 of the USSR Basic Principles of Criminal Procedure. There is an evident contradiction between the provisions of Articles 288 and 250.

[2] *Bulletin' verkhovnogo suda SSSR*, 1962, No. 5, p. 29. Only three Republics, the Lithuanian, Turkmen and Tadzhik SSR included into their Codes of Criminal Procedure the provision that the court representatives of the public organizations must be elected by the General Assembly of the organizations.

The Prosecutor of the Kazakh Republic lodged a protest against the private ruling with the Plenum of the Kazakh Supreme Court which rejected the protest.

Then, the USSR General Prosecutor protested the rejection to the Plenum of the USSR Supreme Court, which threw out the ruling of the Kazakh Supreme Court and decided as quoted above.

The Ruling of the Plenum of the USSR Supreme Court is based on three grounds :

1) That the Kazakh Code of Criminal Procedure does not provide for a definite order of the election of court representatives of public organizations; 2) That trade-unions are public organizations according to Article 126 of the USSR Constitution; 3) That the Workers' Committee (6 persons) is a collegiate legal organ of the trade-union and since there is no provision that the electing organ must be the general assembly—the election by the Committee was legal.

It remains indisputable that the administrative organs of a public organization have no right to appoint a public prosecutor or counsel.

C. RIGHTS AND POSITION
OF PUBLIC PROSECUTORS AND COUNSELS

Rights of the public prosecutors and counsels are exhaustively enumerated in Article 250 (2) and (3) of the RSFSR Code of Criminal Procedure, respectively :

The public prosecutor has the right to present evidence, to participate in the examination of evidence, to petition and challenge the court, to participate in court pleadings communicating to the court his opinion on the irrefutability of the accusation, the public danger represented in the person of the accused and his actions. The public prosecutor may give his opinion about the application of penal law and the measures of punishment for the accused and with regard to other circumstances of the case. The public prosecutor also may drop the accusation if the result of the court examination gives grounds for such an action.

The public defense counsel has the same rights concerning the presentation of evidence, participation in the examination of evidence, of petition and challenge and pleading as the public prosecutor. Naturally, his pleading has the scope to bring forward all the circumstances which mitigate or exclude the guilt of the accused, or permit a suspended sentence. But his most important right belonging only to him and not to the advocate is the plea for liberation of the accused from punishment, releasing him on bail of the organization in the name of which the public counsel is acting. This move can be made by the public counsel only if the public organization has decided to present the plea to the court.

Article 49 (1) of the RSFSR Code of Criminal Procedures makes the participation of defense counsel obligatory if a state or public prosecutor takes part in the trial, equalizing the state prosecutor with the public prosecutor in the trial. Unfortunately, commenting on Article 49, M. Yu. Raginsky does not give his opinion to the question as to whether also the public counsel is included into the provision of Article 49 (1), i.e., if the participation of a public counsel is sufficient when a state or public prosecutor takes part in the trial.

It seems to the present writer that the provisions of the paragraphs 2, 3, 4, 5, and 6 of Article 49 point out the mandatory participation of defense counsel in the person of an advocate hired or appointed by the court, and not of a public counsel.

Thus, equalizing the positions of the state and public prosecutors, Article 49 makes a difference between the positions of an advocate and public counsel. [1]

The public prosecutor and the public defense counsel have, thus, the same procedural rights in the trial as the state prosecutor and the advocate, respectively.

However, there is no complete identification in their activity.

The state prosecutor must, in the first place, give an analysis of the legal aspects of the case. The public prosecutor may but is not obliged to discuss these aspects. He certainly may confine himself to the public, political and moral sides of the crime and present the opinion of the organization who assigned him to the case on these subjects.

As to whether important discrepancy in opinion on some aspects of the case and questions arising during the trial may occur between the two prosecutors is debatable and there is no unanimity of opinion in the Soviet legal literature on this subject. [2]

But in practice, the public prosecutor will certainly follow the guiding of his legally educated colleague and cases when he would deviate from the line established by the public prosecutor may be very seldom.

---

[1] See Article 49 and Raginsky's commentaries in *nauchno-prakticheskiy kommentoriy...*, *op. cit.*, pp. 122-123.

[2] See Urakov, *op. cit.*, and the authors quoted by him, pp. 59-61.

Although the rights of the public counsel are similar in the trial to those of the advocate with the exception of the plea for bail which is the exclusive right of the public counsel, they differ greatly by their relation to the accused.

We know already that only a small minority of Soviet writers admit that the Soviet advocate is a representative of the accused and the majority even denies a semi-representation of the accused by the counsel, although he is hired or appointed with the consent of the accused and can be dismissed by him at any time.

The present writer has also tried to prove that the advocate is not an independent party to the trial. [1]

However, the unanimous opinion of Soviet authors that the public counsel (as well as the public prosecutor) is an independent party to the trial, although the organization itself, of which he is an undeniable representative is not,—cannot be disputed.

Indeed, the public counsel is not depending upon the accused, and cannot be dismissed by the latter. The accused has to bear his public counsel even if he does not agree with the line of defense of the public counsel and even if the line differs from that of the advocate.

Still, also the public counsel may not transform himself into a prosecutor. His scope remains only the defense of the accused, and in contradistinction to the public prosecutor, who may drop the accusation if during the trial he comes to the conclusion that the accused is innocent, the public counsel cannot renounce the defense similarly to the advocate.

Certainly, Karev is wrong when he asserts that "also the public counsel must speak about the social danger of the commited crime and express the opinion of the collective about the blamableness of the action". [2] He evidently confuses the functions of the public prosecutor and public counsel, and forgets that also the public counsel alike the advocate is bound to bring only that which can contribute to the acquittal of the accused or the mitigation of his guilt.

---

[1] See supra, p. 546 ff.

[2] D.S. Karev, "Public Prosecutors and Public Counsels", in *Sovetskaya obshchestvennost' na strazhe sotsialisticheskoy zakonnosti*, M. 1960, p. 161.

Neither the public prosecutor, nor the public counsel have the right of appeal and participation in the session of the cassation instance. [1]

The participation of a public prosecutor and a public counsel in the same case is possible when they are assigned by two different collectives, for instance, that of the accused sends to the trial a public counsel and of the victim—a public prosecutor.

Also the participation of several public prosecutors and public counsels is possible if several organizations are interested in the case.

It should not be overlooked that the public prosecutor, allegedly representing the public and its opinion, plays herewith a political role in the trial.

That is why Samsonov, the Chairman of the Presidium of the Moscow City College of Advocates, instructed the advocates to observe the greatest tact in presenting their objections against the arguments of the public prosecutors in a trial since he is the bearer of the collective's opinion. "That is why" Samsonov asserted "the criticism of his arguments must be clad in an appropriate form and thought out especially carefully". [2]

On the other hand, the public counsel brings to the defense of the accused the public opinion which contributes to influence the court in his behalf.

D. APPRAISAL

a) *The Assembly's Decision*

The assembly of the public organization which has to decide upon the question of sending its representative to the trial expresses its opinion of the case by sending a public prosecutor or a public counsel to the trial, without having the possibility to examine all circumstances and aspects of the case.

Indeed, the information provided by the investigating magistrate or the prosecutor may be, and often is, one-sided. The culprit himself is already under lock and key in the majority of cases and cannot present his defense to the assembly of the collective.

---

[1] Art. 44 of the Basic Principles of Criminal Procedure.... *Op. cit.*, p. 451, gives the right to appeal the sentence to the state but not to the public prosecutor as to the accused and the advocate but not to the public counsel.

[2] V.A. Samsonov, "Soviet advocates and their Role in the Further Strengthening of Soviet Legality", *S.G.P.*, 1960, No. 11, p. 28.

On the other side, if the intervention is sought by the relatives of the accused the information provided by them to the assembly may be, naturally, also biased and incomplete.

Thus, the decision of the assembly expressing the opinion of the public organization and which is valued as "public opinion" in general by the court, is taken without knowledge of all circumstances of the case and the presented evidence, which can be provided only in a court examination.

This is the weak point in the participation of the public prosecutors and counsels in the trial. For, the case may be frequent when a public prosecutor or counsel becomes aware during the trial that his place is properly speaking on the other side of the barricade and not where he has been put by a too hasty decision of the collective.

In this respect, the position of a public defender is even worse than that of a public prosecutor : the latter may drop the accusation whereas the former cannot quit the defense.

It must be emphasized that a peculiar development in the number of cases with the participation of public prosecution took place after the introduction of the institution into the Code of Criminal Procedure. Indeed, whereas between 1961 and 1965 the number of these cases steadily increased from 7.4% to 15.4%, a regression in the participation of public prosecutors is to be observed : it went steadily down to 10.3% in 1966. A kind of apathy on the part of the public concerning the participation in the trial of criminal cases can be noted. [1]

b) *The Soviet Bail or Probation*

The idea of taking on bail by a public organization, institution, organization, or enterprise was also generated at the XXIst Congress of the Soviet Union Communist Party.

In a speech delivered at the Congress, A. N. Shelepin made the following suggestion : "The question of giving to public organizations, the Komsomal, trade-unions as well as plant, factory and kolkhoz collectives, the right to take on bail, persons who went astray and committed petty offences in order to give them the possibility of rehabilitation within the collective, in place of serving punishment set by the court, should be thought over". [2]

---

[1] See V.I. Baskov, "Public Prosecution and Public Defense", *S.G.P.*, 1968, No. 3, pp. 49, 50.

[2] *Pravda*, February 5, 1959.

Strogovich clarifies that bail is considered not as a change or the measure of suppression but as a particular measure replacing the application of the penal punishment. [1]

The bail suggestion was realized by the provision of Article 52 of the RSFSR Criminal Code and the other Union Republic criminal codes.

The application of the provision of Article 52 by the court produces the inaction of criminal procedure against the accused and his tranfer to the care of the organization which petitioned the action according to Article 9 of the RSFSR Code of Criminal Procedure.

We have seen that Article 51 of the RSFSR Criminal Code empowers the court to transfer, under certain conditions, a case to the comrades' court for examination.

Article 52 of the same Code provides that if according to the circumstances of the case the offense and the offender himself do not represent a great public danger and the action has not caused serious consequences, but the culprit himself did wholeheartedly repent, he can be, on request of a public organization or toilers collective, released from criminal responsibility and punishment and transferred on bail to the public organization or the toilers' collective which presented the request, for re-education and rehabilitation.

The Russian word used by the Soviet legislator is *poruka* usually translated to English by "bail". However, the *poruka* of Article 52 is not a bail in the Western meaning of the word, but is in reality a release on probation, since it is not a change of the measure of suppression (arrest), but the setting of a one year term during which the person on probation must be re-educated and rehabilitated.

Indeed, Par. 4 of Article 52 prescribes that if the person taken on "bail" does not justify the confidence of the collective, violated the promise to prove its rehabilitation by exemplary behavior and honest work, does not submit to norms of socialist life, or left the work collective to escape from public influence, the public organization or the workers' collective which took him on bail, has to take a decision renouncing its guarranty and direct the decision to the prosecutor or the court for the examination of the question of bringing the accused to penal responsibility for the crime in connection with the committing of which he was released on bail.

Soviet writers are concerned with the fact that general assemblies of

---

[1]   M.S. Strogovich, *Osnovnyye voprosy sovetskoy sotsialisticheskoy zakonnosti*, M. 1959, p. 51.

workers and employers not only assign public counsels for the defense of non-workers accused in criminal cases but also request their transfer for reform to the organization or collective, forgetting that such requests are admissible only when the "accused mearly committed an unimportant crime, without bringing great damage to a person or the state". [1] In reality, Prusakov writes, such requests are filed concerning inveterate plunderers of state property" and perpetrators of other crimes against persons and state. Prusakov gives the following example : In Belgorod a group of employees and workers of a plant stole systematically parts of the equipment and sold them with the help of accomplices. After more than one year of such activity, the culprits were arrested and brought before a court. At the general assembly of the City Trade Establishment for the Sale of Manufactured Goods (*Gorpromtorg*), 70 persons were present and they voted unanimously to extend help to the accused and at the general assembly of the Department Store (Univermag), the 62 persons attending the assembly voted for the request to free the accused on bail.

The decision to take the accused on bail is also taken sometimes rashly at the assembly of the collective. The Soviet press publishes many complaints in this respect.

A. Aliverdiyev, Chairman of the Dagestan ASSR Supreme Court, relates the following cases about the rashness of the assembly's decision. [2]

The automobile driver Ashurov was not a bad worker, but had too strongly expressed likeness for alcohol. In a fight he initiated, Ashurov crippled his opponent. He was arrested. An urgently convoked assembly of the collective in which Ashurov worked was convinced by Ashurov's friends to take him on bail.

The tractor driver Semenov, member of a Kolkhoz who was already twice called for responsibility for petty hooliganism, administrated a strong beating to his wife. When neighbors intervened, he attacked them and finally set fire to his house.

Again, intercessors were found. In the Semenov's characteristic, sent to the court by the kolkhoz it was said that he is an outstanding and disciplined man. "It could be thought" writes the author, "that he should not only not be punished but even encouraged".

---

[1] N. Prusakov, "Guarantors", *Izvestia*, August 22, 1966.

[2] A. Aliverdigev, "Taken on Bail", *Pravda*, December 9, 1966.

"Reading such requests", the author continues, "one is marvelled how irresponsible the evaluation of comrades' behavior in some kolkhozes is".

K. P. Gorshenin is of the opinion that the participation of public prosecutors and counsels in court has confirmed the rightness and wisdom of measures directed to produce public influence, increasing many times the educational influence of the court on law violators and playing a tremendous role for the prevention of crimes and the inproving of law consciousness of Soviet citizens.

"The participation in the trial of workers, kolkhozniks, members of the intelligentia in the quality of public prosecutors and counsels, speaking on the crime, expressing the progressive socialist world outlook, the requirement of a society, building communism, have a tremendous social and educational power, the importance of which cannot be underestimated", he writes. [1]

It must be emphasized, however, that a trial is in the first place the examination of an individual criminal action, the decision of the fate of an individual. The accused has the right for an impartial and just sentence. It is only this viewpoint, i.e., as how far the participation of public prosecutor or counsel can contribute to a just sentence, must be considered.

The educational or preventive value of the case is only a consequence of the trial and its salutary influence is in direct proportion to the impartiality and justice of the sentence.

In assigning public prosecutors to political cases, the assemblies of the collectives follow sometimes lines prescribed by the Party and, thus, convict in advance persons over the crime of which they do not have and cannot have sufficient information [2], and allegedly express by it "public opinion".

Nevertheless, with all these restrictions it must be said that the introduction of public counsels, especially when they are justly empowered to plead for a "bail", is a liberalization of the criminal code and the criminal procedure, as it is in the case of the comrades' courts.

---

[1] K.P. Gorshenin, "The Participation of the Public in the Fight Against Law Breaking... is the Further Development of Soviet Democracy", in *Sovetskaya obshchestvennost' na strazhe sotsialisticheskoy zakonnosti, op. cit.*, M. 1960, p. 155.

[2] See, for instance, Brodsky's Case and the trial of Senyavsky, Daniel and other political cases which received great notoriety in 1967-68.

PART THREE

JUSTICE IN OPERATION

CHAPTER NINETEEN

SENTENCE FORMATION

Let us examine the elements which conduct the Soviet court to the formation of the sentence.

A. a) *Revolutionary Law Consciousness*

What is revolutionary law consciousness? According to Stuchka the expression was taken over from bourgeois law where it was coined by Professor Petrazhitsky, the creator of the Intuitive Theory of Law. [1]

Thus, Reisner, a follower of Petrazhitsky, called the revolutionary law consciousness an "intuition".

Also, Hazard is of the opinion that "This revolutionary legal consciousness was nothing other than an intuition which lay at the foundation of Soviet legal "order" [2]

Traynin used the word "instinct" for revolutionary law consciousness. He wrote that in the first years of the proletarian dictatorship, when the old law broke down and the revolution moved gropingly toward the creation of new forms, "the place of law and legality ... was occupied by revolutionary law consciousness. As in previous times, every court decision was based on law, so in the first years of the revolution, the reference to the revolutionary law consciousness was a sufficient ground for any sentence. It was a time of legal improvisation when revolutionary instinct served both as a criterion and a source of judicial truth". [3]

The replacement of law by revolutionary law consciousness was sanctioned by Lenin. In a note to Kursky he declared that "we must apply not the "*corpus juris romanum,* but *revolutionary law consciousness* (I. L.) in our civil relations". [4]

---

[1]   P.I.Stuchka, "Revolutionary Consciousness", *Entsiklopedicheskiy slovar' gosudarstva i prava,* M. 1925-1927, V. III, p. 330.

[2]   John N. Hazard, *The Soviet Legal System,* N.Y. 1962, p. 3.

[3]   A. Traynin, "On Revolutionary Legality", *Pravo i zhizn',* June 1922, No. 1, p. 5.

[4]   Lenin, XXIX, p. 419.

Stuchka is evidently right when he asserted that revolutionary law consciousness did not exist in the beginning of Bolshevist power "either in nature or in human notion". [1]

Indeed, instinct or intuition, law consciousness is an attitude toward law and obviously cannot exist when there is no law system in force. Thus, up to the creation of the law codes, the Soviet judge was directed by his instinct or intuition not toward law but with regard to justice as individually understood by him.

For Vyshinsky the existence of a revolutionary law consciousness even before the publication of the first decrees on courts is made evident enough by Lenin's instruction to apply revolutionary consciousness in the place of law. [2]

It means, thus, if Lenin acknowledges the presence and importance of revolutionary legal consciousness, it suffices, it cannot be denied.

Kursky brings some examples of court decisions taken in the first years of Soviet power, finding them "just in a high degree". [3]

But, Kursky himself had to acknowledge that "these decisions are shot through with the spirit of unhindered imagination. They are as far from the opinion of a legally trained judge as they are from the heartless form of the old written law.

Certainly, "unhindered imagination" based on a fanciful revolutionary law consciousness is a very inappropriate guide on the difficult path of meting justice. They may be sometimes "just" from an individual viewpoint. But law is just there in order to restrain the "unhindered imagination" of a judge. When laws applicable to the case do not exist and the intuition or imagination of the judge has free leave, a situation of lawlessness and willfulness in the work of the court is created.

That administration of justice cannot be based on revolutionary or socialist law consciousness alone was realized very soon and the call for legality, as we will see later, started almost with the beginning of the Soviet state.

However, P. Grishayev [4] sharply criticized Hazard and other

---

[1] Quoted by Vyshinsky in "The Problem of Evidence Valuation in the Soviet Criminal Procedure", *Sots. zak.*, 1936, No. 7, p. 34.

[2] *Ibid.*

[3] D.I. Kursky, "From the Practice of the People's Courts", *Revolutsiya i pravo*, M. No. 1, p. 29; quoted by J. Hazard, *Settling Disputes in Soviet Society*, N.Y., 1960, pp. 68-72.

[4] P. Grishayev, "Against Anti-Communist Slander of Soviet Law", *Sots. zak.*, 1963, No. 6, p. 69.

"bourgeois" authors for the assertion of "lawlessness" in the first period of Soviet power. Qualifying it as "a lie", dissiminated by bourgeois jurists. However, Grishayev can bring in support of his opinion only the assertion that having thoroughly eliminated pre-revolutionary law, the Soviets created new laws at the same time. He has in mind Decrees such as, "On Peace", "On the Land", "On the Abolition of the Death Penalty", "On the order of conformation and Publication of Laws", etc. It is evident that these laws are of a special character and could not replace general law codes.

He also writes that "during 1918-1922 active codification work of Soviet laws was conducted". That is true but this work, with the exception of two codes—Family and Labor Codes—was completed only in 1922-23, as he himself admits.

When the law codes were introduced revolutionary law consciousness could not play the role it played before.

Stuchka wrote, "the revolutionary law consciousness was replaced by revolutionary legality during our retreat, [1] because then, the individual class consciousness was not sufficient anymore. It became necessary to establish its limits, i.e., the maximum and minimum of the retreat in an organized form, in laws and their fulfillment". He added that "law consciousness exist in itself also in the present time, but it does not already coincide with fulfillment of law". [2]

The adjective "revolutionary" was replaced by "socialist", although the Soviet state was not yet a socialist society even according to Soviet writers. [3] But socialist law consciousness had to mean the attitude toward law in an alleged socialist society, as Anashkin puts it.

He defines socialist law consciousness as one of the forms of social consciousness, the totality of views expressing the attitude of the Soviet people toward socialist law—.

The formation of socialist law consciousness is influenced by several elements. According to Anashkin, its basis is formed by the policy of

---

[1] Meant is the retreat to the NEP.

[2] P.I. Stuchka, "Law Consciousness" in *Entsiklopediya gosudarstva i prava*, M. 1925-27, V. III, p. 330.

[3] The present writer is of the opinion that although the completion of socialism is proclaimed in the Soviet Union, socialism, as thought out by Marx and Engels and developed by Lenin, is still not achieved there. (See Samuel Kucherov, "The Soviet Union is Not a Socialist Society" (in defense of V.M Molotov), *Political Science Quarterly*, April 1956.)

the Communist Party, Lenin's teaching on the essence of socialist law, about the unflinching observation and fulfillment of law by all citizens and officials. [1]

Although no more the only basis of the sentence formation socialist law consciousness retains an important place in the procedure and serves as basis for the composition of other elements of sentence finding, such as the evaluation of evidence, the formation of the judge's inner conviction, up to the present time. Thus, Article 23 of the Basic Principles of Criminal Legislation prescribes that the court set the provisions also in conformity with its law consciousness.

Vyshinsky saw in socialist law consciousness "the key to the correct understanding of all the conditions under which the crime was committed, to the sound evaluation of the crime and the right decision, in what degree the crime is really a crime, not only by the outward signs, but to its essense as a socially dangerous phenomenon requiring this or that measure of penal repression or other reaction". [2]

This magic key served Vyshinsky for the opening of many doors leading to the solution of many legal questions.

In his opinion, the socialist consciousness insures to the Soviet judge the possibility of a more flexible, free and wise orientation in the complex circumstances of a civil suit or a crime and in the choice of the necessary decisions in every concrete case, according to the law in force. The conviction of the righteousness of the punishment itself under the factual circumstances of the case, are in direct connection with the judges' law consciousness, with his opinion on the purposes of justice, on the importance of the given crime and the methods to fight criminality.

"In a socialist society," he writes, "the conviction of a judge is fed by the juice of the socialist soil, by principles of the socialist attitude toward society, the surrounding human beings, the duty toward the state. It is determined by the entire world outlook of the mass, by examining occurrences and human actions, and the human beings themselves *from the viewpoint of the interests of the socialist state and socialist construction*, (Italics provided). [3]

---

[1] G.Z. Anashkin, "The Role of Law Consciousness and Public Opinion in Setting Punishment", *S.G.P.*, 1967, No. 1, p. 42.

[2] A. Ye. Vyshinsky, *Revoluytsionnaya zakonnost' na sovremennom etape*, M. 1933, p 74.

[3] *Ibid.*, p. 184.

Thus, in the evaluation of evidence in a trial, Vyshinsky demanded of the judge to be guided by the interests of the socialist state and socialist construction and not by the striving for truth.

But where could the judge acquire this revolutionary or socialist law consciousness during the first period of Soviet power ?

There was no socialist society which could "feed his inner conviction". The overwhelming majority of judges and assessors did not even know what socialism was. The only "law consciousness", if any, they could have was acquired under the old regime. A political revolution is a forcible change from one state power to another ; a social revolution is a violent transition from one economic and social structure to another. But, according to Vyshinsky's definition, the inner conviction or law consciousness of a judge is formed by the society to which he belongs and bourgeois law consciousness is contrasted with socialist law consciousness. The judges and assessors of that time could not have acted under the influence of a socialist law consciousness because there was no socialistic society in the RSFSR. They could, however, still have retained their law consciousness, formed in a capitalistic society, which is true, certainly, for an overwhelming majority of the Russian people.

"Soviet justice", exclaims Vyshinsky, "is socialist justice realized in conformity with principles of Socialism in compliance with socialist law consciousness, and the socialist conviction of judges".

We have seen what role the "revolutionary (socialist)" law consciousness had played in the period preceeding Decree No. 1 and up to publication of the Soviet codes. It simply replaced the law.

But law consciousness retained an important role also after the publication of codes. The steady drive for legality conducted by Soviet leaders and Congresses of the Party described below did not impair its importance. On the contrary, Vyshinsky sees in the socialist law consciousness the only means under some conditions to a correct attitude toward an occurrence and the law, the right cognition how a case should be solved under the given circumstances, according to law and socialist consciousness which must be identical and not oppose each other.

When "demands of life" come, in some cases, in opposition to formal law, then Vyshinsky sees in the law consciousness of the judge the only means to solve or eliminate such contradiction.

The important role ascribed by Vyshinsky to socialist law consciousness and its interpretation permits Vyshinsky, in his capacity as USSR prosecutor, to ask the judges for a sentence based not on truth but on the interests of the socialist state and socialist construction.

The most important role law consciousness of judges played in the formation of sentences is also acknowledged by Anashkin, since law consciousness is in an uninterrupted relation with the inner conviction of the judge having a direct bearing on the evaluation of all factual circumstances of the case and the setting of punishment for the culprit.

But Anashkin does not exaggerate the role of the inner conviction as Vyshinsky does. Anashkin does not give unlimited freedom to the inner conviction. He emphasizes that this inner conviction must be based on the formulation of facts, the proving force of which is beyond doubt, and requirements of legality. [1]

b) *Evaluation of Evidence*

The judicial reform of 1864 in Russia abrogated the doctrine of "formal evidence", based on the inquisitorial principle which set exact rules for the evaluation of the evidence. [2]

The 1864 Code of Criminal Procedure no longer classified the value of evidence in advance and evidence was not divided into admissible and inadmissible as is the case, for instance, in the United States. The bringing forward of any evidence was permitted (including hearsay) and the evaluation corresponded to the inner conviction of the judges.

This principle of free evidence admisssion and evaluation was taken over by Soviet legislation. [3] The court admits and evaluates evidence according to the inner convictions of its members.

The only evidence which is not admitted is the oath. [4]

Article 71 of the new RSFSR Code of Criminal Procedure on the evaluation of evidence reads : "The court, the prosecutor, the investigating magistrate and the person conducting the inquest evaluate evidence according to their inner conviction, based on the all-sided,

---

[1] Anashkin, "The Role of Law Consciousness...", *op. cit.*, p. 43.

[2] For details on the doctrine of formal evidence, see Samuel Kucherov, *Courts Lawyers and Trials Under the Last Three Tsars*, N.Y., 1953, pp. 1-2.

[3] See Article 319 of the Old Code of Criminal Procedure Article 69 of the New Code provide that any factual data may serve as evidence and Article 71 declares that "no evidence has value established in advance". Article 20 of the Basic Principle of Criminal Procedure reads : "The court is not committed by any formal evidence and it depends upon it to admit the evidence according to circumstances of the case".

[4] Article 57 of the old RSFSR Code of Criminal Procedure.

complete and objective examinations of all circumstances of the case in their totality, guided by law and socialist law consciousness.

No evidence has any importance established in advance for the court, the prosecutor, the investigating magistrate or the person conducting the inquest". [1]

The corresponding provision of the old RSFSR Code of Criminal Procedure (Article 319) was much shorter—"the evaluation of the evidence in the case is carried out by the court according to its inner conviction based on the examination of all circumstances of the case in their totality".

Although law consciousness was not mentioned in the provision of the old Code of Criminal Procedure, Soviet writers assert that the judicial inner conviction is in turn based on socialist law consciousness, which as we will see later, is an important source of evaluation of the evidence and formation of the sentence.

c) *The Judge's Inner Conviction*

Thus, the inner conviction of the judge is allegedly based on law consciousness which is, according to Vyshinsky, "the ideology, the system of opinions, world outlook in the field of questions regulated by law, prevailing in a given society, and is one of the most important conditions for the making of the decision, determining the attitude of the judge or the investigating magistrate toward this or that fact". [2]

In Vyshinsky's opinion, the inner conviction of a judge, based on his law consciousness, varies in relation to what society the judge belongs to : in a bourgeois society his law consciousness and consequently his inner conviction differs from that of a judge belonging to a socialist society.

The role attributed to the revolutionary or socialist law consciousness, especially in the first period of Soviet rule, produced a natural reaction in Soviet legal thought, also against the theory of inner conviction based on it.

Thus, N. M. Grodzinsky opposes the use of "inner conviction" by the judge in evaluating evidence and suggests "to eliminate it from the Soviet Code altogether". He thought that the theory of the inner conviction is the sanctification of judicial arbitrariness. [3]

---

[1]   Repudiation of the theory of "formal evidence" of the inquisitorial procedure.

[2]   Vyshinsky, *Revolyutsionnaya zakonnost'*..., *op. cit.*, p. 178.

[3]   Quoted by Vyshinsky in "The Problem of Evidence Valuation in the Soviet Criminal Procedure", *Sots. zak.*, 1936, No. 7, p. 12.

But the elimination of the inner conviction of the judge would exclude the use of the socialist law consciousness which, according to Vyshinsky, is formed by judicial inner conviction. Consequently, Vyshinsky accuses Grodzinsky of an attempt to eliminate, in this covert way, also the socialist law consciousness from the Soviet codes.

"The basic question put by Prof. Grodzinsky", writes, Vyshinsky, "is the following : Is it permissible or not to the judge to have liberty of action in the evaluation of the evidence ? I reply to that : Not only permissible, but necessary, unavoidable. Grodzinsky's response is : Not permissible, impossible, it must be avoided". [1]

Prompted evidently by the same desire to eliminate judicial arbitrariness, M. S. Strogovich called for the "objectivization"of evidence. According to him, facts must decide upon a case and not the inner conviction of the judge.

The call of objectivization by Strogovich is a feature of his theory of "absolute truth" in criminal proceedings, which we will have to deal with later.

d) *Absolute or Relative Truth in Court*

It is evident that the freedom of the judges and assessors to evaluate the presented evidence preconditions their liberty to form the sentence as guided by their inner conviction and inspired by their socialist law consciousness which must correspond to truth and law.

But is absolute truth abtainable in general and can it be established in court ?

1. *Strogovich's Theory*

The finding of absolute-objective-material truth in court decisions and sentences is demanded by Strogovich. He thinks that in Soviet criminal procedure the requirement of truth finding in the investigation of the case is completely immutable and is realized consequently and firmly, without any reservation or limitation. [2]

The material, i.e., objective or absolute truth required by Strogovich is the truth in the full and exact sense of the word : the essentially correct reproduction of all the facts and circumstances of the case

---

[1] Vyshinsky, "The Problem of Evidence Valuation in the Soviet Criminal procedure", in *Problemy ugolovnoy politiki*, 1937, IV, p. 14.

[2] Strogovich, *Material'naya istina i sudebnyye dokazatel'stva*, M. 1955, p. 44.

in the sentence of the court, as they occured in reality. Without reaching this truth, the realization of Soviet Socialist justice is impossible. *"The material truth in criminal procedure is the objective truth, established by the court in the order and by means prescribed by law"*, writes Strogovich (S. I.).

Strogovich starts his argumentation with the criticism of the "agnostic doctrine" which denies the possibility to reach absolute truth also in court procedure and obliges the court to be satisfied with the establishment of a relative truth of high probability by which the judges are persuaded. "This situation", Strogovich argues, "is the acknowledgment of the inevitability and the legality of judicial mistakes—exactly the legality,—since the objective truth is not ascertainable by the court".

The theory of the "legality" of judicial mistakes brings Strogovich to conclusions amazing even for a Soviet professor embroiled in criticism of bourgeois institutions.

"With regard to justice meted in exploiting countries you cannot speak even of judicial mistakes : the sentencing of innocent people—is not a mistake but a regular phenomenon, a constant activity of this justice. If in this or that case it is impossible to arraign the real criminal—it is possbile to satisfy oneself with his 'replacement', i.e., with any appropriate person".

It is true, that these conclusions are formulated not by Strogovich himself, but in a book by Fauconnet—"La *responsabilité*", quoted by Strogovich, but Strogovich adopts them completely providing even the explanation that "clearly, the real perpetrator cannot be replaced by a representative of the predominant class, propertied and privileged: the repression is directed against a toiling dispossessed person or belonging to progressive democratic elements, objectionable to the ruling reactionary circles ... The theory of judicial mistakes undoubtedly serves the practice of bourgeois justice and reflects this practice",[1] Strogovich declares.

The bourgeois justice is accused en masse by Strogovich of wholesale production and even legalization of judicial mistakes arising from the reliance upon relative and not objective truth by the court.

Strogovich asserts that every interpretation of material truth and truthfulness in a subjective sense in criminal procedure, the exchange of material truth for juridical truth, the endowing of the material

---

[1]   *Ibid.*, pp. 30-31.

truth with a conditional sense, the substitution of truth by probability and personal conviction—is nothing else than a bourgeois ideological conception predicated upon the justification of illegal and unjust sentences by class bourgeois justice as a means of the suppression and oppression of the workers' class and the entire toiling population.

Strogovich declares that for the theory and practice of the Soviet criminal procedure such a conception is absolutely inadmissible, arguing that in using the basic principles of Marxist-Leninist theory of gnosiology and the basic purposes of Soviet socialist justice, as a point of departure, Soviet procedural science treats the material truth as the objective truth, as the correspondence between the conclusions of the investigation and the court with the objective reality, and it does not permit its identification or confusion with probability or personal conviction". [1]

Strogovich rejects the inner conviction of judges as a decisive element or as a factor in the formation of the sentence. He thinks that, to rely on the inner conviction of the judge, is to bring arbitrariness in to the meting out of justice.

But how is this material-objective-absolute truth established in Soviet criminal procedrue?

Strogovich gives a plain answer to this question: the objective truth is reached in criminal cases in no way other than by subjective efforts of the judges deciding the case, of the preliminary investigation and of the prosecutor who supervises the investigation.

Thus, all those participating in the investigation and court examination of a case are striving to reach objective truth. And the judges, when they establish material-objective-absolute truth in their sentence, are personally convinced that they have found it. "Objective truth cannot be torn away from the subjective conviction of the judges", Strogovich admits. [2] The judge who searches for truth recognizes it as found only then when he is convinced that it is really the truth. But, as we have seen, only in two lines preceeding this sentence, Strogovich had asserted that the material-absolute-truth cannot be identified with "personal conviction".

Hence, the material truth is in the end effect established according to the subjective conviction of the judge. Consequently, Strogovich

---

[1] *Ibid.*, p. 105.

[2] *Ibid.*, p. 107.

still identifies the material truth with the subjective conviction of the judge—exactly that which he branded "as a bourgeois-idealistic conception".

There cannot be, of course, a guarantee that the truth corresponding to the inner conviction of the Soviet judge, is just the material-objective-absolute one ...

But conscientious bourgeois investigators, prosecutors and judges also are persuaded that their findings are true. This is the conviction of the judge when he pronounces the sentence. Also he strives for truth, the whole truth and notihng but the truth.

Certainly there have been exceptions when biased sentences were passed in the West, but it seems to me that it is not just the Soviet Union which may serve as an appropriate model for material-objective-absolute truth in sentences pronounced there.

That not every sentence is expected to be the absolute truth in a given case is proved by the existence of appeal and cassation in the West and in the USSR, respectively.

This objection against his theory Strogovich meets with the argument that the higher judicial instance which has the right to declare a sentence illegal or unfounded and to rescind it has not the right to indicate to the court of original jurisdiction what sentence it has to pass, what facts to consider true or false. [1]

The argument is not persuasive. Every higher instance which reverses or rescinds the sentence of the lower instance declares by its decision that the sentence does not correspond to the truth.

But the opinion of the second instance may be again reversed by a higher instance, and finally by a special provision of Soviet procedure unknown to the West : a review is provided in the way of supervision of sentences or decisions already final-a decisive proof of complete accordance of the Soviet legislator with Vyshinsky's skepticism in matters of establishment of the absolute truth in a sentence!

Since the absolute truth cannot be "torn away" from the subjective or inner conviction of the judge, let us see how Strogovich explains the formation of this inner conviction.

He thinks that the inner conviction, although individual and subjective in the sense that it is formed and created by individual persons, still cannot be regarded only under its psychological aspect. First of all the conviction of Soviet judges relies upon their socialist

---

[1] *Ibid.*, p. 108.

law consciousness and opinions as Soviet statesmen. But Socialist law consciousness "is the totality of legal opinions, convictions and ideas of the Soviet people", as Strogovich defines it in complete accordance with Vyshinsky. [1]

With regard to the relation between socialist law consciousness and inner conviction Strogovich also refers to Vyshinsky in obvious agreement with the latter.

2. *Vyshinsky's Theory*

Vyshinsky handles this question as follows :

First of all, he rejects the agnostic philosophy prevailing in the West that absolute truth is unknown to men, by quoting Engels'and Lenin's works. Lenin asserted namely, that "from the viewpoint of contemporary materialism, i.e., Marxism, historically conditioned are the *limits* (L.I.) of the approach of our knowledge to the objective and absolute truth, but the existence of this truth is beyond doubt; undoubtedly, we are approaching it. The contours of the picture are historically conditioned, but it is not doubtful that the picture represents an existing model". [2]

Under the influence of the agnostic philosophy, the great majority of legal writers in the West, including tsarist Russia, were of the opinion that the court is not in a position to discover the absolute truth and that evidence in a trial gives the possibility to establish only a degree of probability, but not the certainty of truth.

But, since the foundling fathers of Marxism-Leninism asserted that absolute truth is ascertainable, which was confirmed also by Stalin, saying that "no unknowable things exist in the world, but things not already known, which will be discovered and known by the forces of science and practice", [3] Vyshinsky has to declare that : "a court sentence must be based on trustworthy facts, exactly established, unconditional, not subject to doubt with regard to their veracity. The court cannot base its sentence or decision only on an assumption or probability of these or those actions and occurrences". [4]

From this assertion of the necessity of a sentence or decision based

---

[1]   *Ibid.*, p. 112.

[2]   Lenin, 14, p. 123.

[3]   I.V. Stalin, *Voprosy leninizma*, M. 1952, p. 54.

[4]   Vyshinsky, *Teoriya...*, *op. cit.*, p. 198.

on unconditional and veracious evidence, one could expect Vyshinsky to ask for the establishment of absolute truth in court.

However, the search for absolute truth in court did not suit Vyshinsky's purposes. It would necessarily also diminish the importance of socialist law consciousness of judges and assessors during the process of the formation of their judgments.

Consequently, Vyshinsky argues that the court is not obliged to establish the absolute truth required by philosophy. He cites Lenin's assertion, quoted above, that the limits to the approach to the absolute truth are only historically conditioned and declares that this principal is applicable in any field of knowledge, and, thus, also to judicial activity, taking into consideration the specific conditions under which this activity takes place.

"If Marx admits the conditionality of all our knowledge, and he does so, also the conclusions arrived at by the court in the course of judicial work, have a relative character". [1]

Hence, due respect is paid to Marxism-Leninism and the court is not obliged to search for absolute truth.

Already in 1937, Vyshinsky expressed his opinion by denying the expedience and possibility of demanding of the court the establishment of the absolute truth, because the conditions of judicial activity put the judge into the necessity to evaluate questions not from the viewpoint of absolute truth, but under maximal probability or truthworthiness of these or those factors under judicial evaluation.

He still held to the same opinion in 1950 when he wrote : "It is an obviously impracticable task *to require* (V.I.) from the court decisions embodying *absolute truth* (V.I.) under conditions of judicial activity, also impracticable because the attempt to draw a delimination line between absolute and relative truth is especially difficult and perhaps completely unreal under judicial procedural conditions". [2]

We have seen that Vyshinsky attributed a decisive role to socialist law consciousness in the process of the evaluation of the evidence.

In the matter of formation of the sentence, Vyshinsky confers on socialist law consciousness a greatly exaggerated role, permitting the judge to correct the law in force and to put, under some circumstances, state interests before truth and legality.

---

[1] *Ibid.*, p. 198.

[2] Vyshinsky, *Teoriya sudebnykh dokazatel'stv...*, *op. cit.*, p. 201. An English or American Court requires for a punitative sentence that the accusation should be proved "beyond a reasonable doubt".

Rejecting the "bourgeois" theories of the impossibility to reaching absolute truth in general, Vyshinsky asserts the impossibility to require of the court the establishment of the absolute truth and assigns great importance to the inner conviction of the judge as based on his Socialist law consciousness.

Already in 1936, Vyshinsky reproached Strogovich that his theory of "objectivization of evidence" leads to the elimination of the inner conviction of the judge as a criterion for the evaluation of the evidence and together with it of the socialist law consciousness on which the judicial inner convintion is based.

He rejected also Strogovich's doctrine on the finding of absolute truth by the court.

Vyshinsky argues—and in this case he is right—that the requirement of absolute truth found by the court is wrong because the conditions of a trial put the judge in a situation in which he is obliged to decide the case not from the viewpoint of absolute truthfinding, but from the necessity to establish the maximum probability of these or those facts which are submitted to judicial evaluation. The court is limited in its findings to the evidence presented and by time, since it cannot repeat and repeat its work until it realizes the absolute truth as a scientist can do in his laboratory.

Another of Vyshinsky's arguments, mentioned before, is very convincing : he writes that if every sentence of the Soviet court would establish the absolute truth in the case, the review of the case by a higher instance would be senseless.

He defends the bourgeois theory of the freedom of inner conviction of judges against the accusation by Strogovich that this freedom leads to arbitrariness, but finds that "the bourgeois theory is inconsistent: on the one side it declares the impossibility of absolute truth finding in court and suggests the acceptance of a reliable truth equivalent to the maximum grade of probability, but on the other it declares every sentence truthful, informing that *"res judicata pro veritate habetur"*—a sentence in a case is considered as truth ... That is why ... (the bourgeoisie) does not permit an appeal against the cases examined by a court with a jury". [1]

Unfortunately, the translation of *res judicata* by Vyshinsky is not correct : This expression means "a case definitely decided", [2] so that

---

[1] Vyshinsky, "The Problem...", *op. cit.*, p. 25.

[2] See *Recueil de maximes et citations latines à l'usage du monde judiciaire*, Paris, 1924, p. 374.

not every sentence but only that which is final, is regarded as being "*pro veritate*".

Furthermore, it is only partly true that there was no remedy against sentences of the court with jury in tsarist Russia : only the appeal against a verdict by the jury was excluded. However, an appeal in cassation by both parties was admissible.

Finally Vyshinsky speaks of bourgeois theory in general so that his assertion is completely untrue with regard to the United States where a remedy exists against the decision of a court with a jury in civil and criminal cases.

Thus, Vyshinsky agreed in principle that men can and should reach absolute truth and that relative truth is not truth at all, but emphasized that the court, with regard to the conditions of its work is impeded in striving for absolute truth and must satisfy itself with the finding of the maximal probability established with the help of inner conviction and individual law consciousness.

Also Tadevosyan has criticized Strogovich's theory.

He is of the opinion that it is often impossible to assert with absolute certitude that the sentence or decision completely coincides with factual reality. And this happens not because the judges are agnostics, do not take every measure in order to establish the material truth, do not believe in the possibility of the reaching of absolute truth, but must admit the possibility of errors and delusions. It is the imperfection of human work which impedes the finding of absolute truth according to him. "It is not necessary to be a scientist to understand how far the level of our knowledge is from the shining lights of absolute truth in all fields of science, including jurispurdence. Medicine, chemistry and other branches of science, have not yet reached such heights that the organs of the administration of justice which are using their help could be convinced that also they establish the absolute truth". [1]

Golunsky disagrees with Strogovich's assertion that absolute truth is accessible to the court; he declares it theoretically wrong and dangerous in practice. "It is necessary decidedly to acknowledge", he writes, "that court truth is always a relative truth". But, he demands at the same time, "that we strive toward a condition, that the truthworthiness of the court's conclusions should be *sufficient* (G. I.) to

---

[1] V.S. Tadevosyan, "The Question of Material Truth Establishment", *S.G.P.*, 1948, No. 6, p. 66.

guarantee the rightness of the court's policy and the appropriateness of the penal repression". [1]

We are certainly not concerned here with the philosophical controversy between agnosticism and Marxism-Leninism as to whethera absolute truth can be established in nature or not.

In a court, however, the truth is sometimes established, and sometimes not, and in the latter case in the West, certainly, not because of an alleged bourgeois conspiracy "bent upon the justification of illegal and unjust sentences", but because investigators, prosecutors and judges both in the West and in the Soviet Union are only human beings subject to mistakes.

The sentence is, however, "the truth", according to the inner conviction and understanding of the judge. It may be the "material-objective-absolute truth" required by Strogovich, if the judge has correctly evaluated the presented evidence according to reality. But it may also not be the truth. But in both cases it is the "truth" for the given court instance.

The process of the building of the judge's inner conviction is basically the same in the West and in the USSR : the judge evaluates the evidence submitted by the parties involved and comes to a decision according to his law consciousness which, however, enjoins him, in the Soviet Union, to give preference to State interests in some cases.

To require the court to establish exactly the material-objective-absolute truth is unrealistic, as Vyshinsky puts it, and useless because in the opinion of the judge every sentence pronounced and decision taken by him is the material-objective-absolute truth, and if he errs—it is not his fault if he is honest.

The findings of a Soviet judge are in reality as relative as those of a bourgeois one. Strogovich's diatribe against bourgeois administration of justice is nothing but the obligatory capitalist baiting.

Certainly, Polyansky is right when he remarks that the requirement of exactitude and absolutness in the establishment of the truth by the court must result in the complete negation of truth, the admission that all what the court decided is an error, a lie ... He gives the following example : If it is not exactly established as to whether A committed a theft or a robbery, it means that it is not proven convincingly that he committed either a theft or a robbery. Thus, if

---

[1] S.A. Golunsky, "On Probability and Trustworthiness in Criminal Trial", *Problemy ugolovnoy politiki*, M. 1937, Issue IV, p. 61.

the court has established only that *A* has illegally appropriated a thing belonging to *B*, but it is not exactly proven whether he committed the action secretly [1] or openly, *A* may not be convicted of the action and must be acquitted. "It would contradict the practice and the law", Polyansky concludes. [2]

It seems to the present writer that Grodzinsky's and Strogovich's call for "objectivization" of evidence and material truth in criminal procedure and judicial findings are caused by the desire of the reduction or elimination of the role of socialist law consciousness, as a criteria for judicial decisions and sentences, and was a natural reaction against the arbitrary use of socialist law consciousness as a cover for the great abuses of justice current at that time in the USSR.

There is no point in going further into the details of the controversy here. [3] Let us say only that the restriction of the role of the judges inner conviction as a measure of the value of this or that evidence is strongly opposed by Vyshinsky because that would mean also to diminish the importance of the socialist law consciousness which is the source of the inner conviction. According to Vyshinsky the setting of a punishment, the practical application of analogy, the decision of the necessity to mitigate or increase the punishment—all this is in the field of action of the inner conviction of the judge : "He who does not understand it underestimates the importance of socialist law consciousness ...", [4] he writes.

To advocate the greatest freedom of the judge to evaluate the evidence and consequently to set the sentence according to his inner conviction under guidance by his socialist law consciousness, opens the way to judicial arbitrariness. It means a step back to the unhibited rule of socialist law consciousness and a step forward to the trials of the thirties.

B. OTHER ELEMENTS

a) *Confessions*

A decisive role in the process of sentence formation is played by the confession of the accused.

---

[1] According to tsarist and Soviet criminal law, theft is a "secret" appropriation of a thing belonging to another person.

[2] N.N. Polyansky, *Dokazatel'stva v inostrannom ugolovnom protsesse*, M. 1946, p. 32.

[3] See A. Ye. Vyshinsky, "The Problem of Evidence Valuation, *op. cit.*, p. 21 ff.

[4] *Ibid.*, p. 32.

Soviet law extends to the accused the right to give explanations with regard to the accusation presented to him and other circumstances pertaining to the same case and known to him, as well as about the evidence presented in the case. His testimony is evidence along with that of witnesses and experts. [1]

The word employed by the Code "*pokazaniya*"—testimony—is not quite correct. It is the same used for witnesses, although according to both tsarist and Soviet laws the accused may not "testify" in his own case, may not be put on the stand as it is permitted in England and the United States.

In reality, he has the right to give explanations—obyasneniya—as was provided in the old RSFSR Code of Criminal Procedure (Article 282, Par. II). The accused gives his "testimony" not under oath and not by written pledge and is not obliged to tell the truth : he may or may not do so.

Naturally, his assertion, as of a person standing under no obligation to tell the truth, and most interested in the refutation of the accusation, has diminished weight if he denies his guilt.

But not if he confesses, i.e., if he admits partly or in full, the veracity of the accusation presented against him. Then, generally his assertion becomes most trustworthy, because of the simple consideration that usually no one would accuse oneself if he is innocent. [2]

In the system of formal evidence of the old tsarist law, before 1864, the confession of the accused was considered "the best evidence in the whole world". [3]

The old RSFSR Code of Criminal Procedure also attributed great importance to the confession of the accused. Article 282 reads : "If the accused agrees with the circumstances depicted in the accusatory resolusion, [4] acknowledges the accusation presented to him as correct,

---

[1] See Article 58 of the old and Article 69 of the new RSFSR Codes of Criminal Procedure, respectively.

[2] Of the same opinion is, for instance, M.A. Chel'tsov-Bebutov (*Obvinyayemyy i ego pokazaniya v sovetskom ugolovnom protsesse*, M. 1917, p. 42). Strogovich contradicts this opinion asserting that "If the accused denies guilt, this testimony has no more and no less proving power than the testimony in which he confesses guilt" (M.S. Strogovich, "The Accused's Confession", *Sots. zak.*, 1956, No. 6, p. 16).

[3] *Svod zakonov Rossiyskoy imperii*, ed. 1857, V. XV, Sect. IV, Article 316.

[4] Presented by the investigating magistrate, confirmed by the prosecutor and put forth as basis for the indictment by the court.

and testifies to this effect, the court may not proceed with a further examination and go over to the summation of the parties".

Thus, the court "may", but is not obliged, to drop the examination of the further evidence if the accused confesses to the crime imputed to him.

The provision of Article 282 of the old Code of Criminal Procedure did not create, however, a situation analogous to that when the accused pleads guilty in an English or American court. The Soviet court could only wave the examination of further evidence, and go over to the summation of parties, but not to the passing of a sentence. The parties had to be heard first.

This was confirmed by a ruling of the USSR Suprmee Court which reads : "That the law does not consider the confession of the accused as an indisputable evidence of guilt, is completely clear from the context of Article 282 of the RSFSR Code of Criminal Procedure which indicated that in case of the confirmation by the accused of the circumstances established in the accusatory conclusions, the court may not carry out a further examination and go over to the summation by the parties, but by no means to the pronouncement of a sentence (Ruling of the Plenum of the USSR Supreme Court in the Avachko case, on February 3, 1941). [1]

The new RSFSR Code of Criminal Procedure brings an end to the exaggerated evaluation of the accused's confession. It provides that "the confession of his guilt by the accused may be put on the same footing as the accusation only if it is confirmed by the entire totality of evidence presented in the case" (Article 77, Par. 2).

Thus, the confession of the accused is no more than just another evidence in the case. Obviously the provision is destined to eliminate the abuses with "confessions" of the accused, extensively practiced by investigating organs and courts during the cult of personality period.

It was Vyshinsky who provided the theoretical cover-up for these abuses. He argued as follows : Admitting that the explanations of the accused must, in general, be met with a certain scepticism, keeping in mind his position in the proceedings as the person most interested in the outcome of the trial, still he may not and should not be regarded as not a full-fledged participant of the proceedings, especially as not in possession of full rights of a subject of the proceedings.

---

[1] *Sbornik postanovleniy plenuma verchovnogo suda SSSR, 1944*, M. 1948, pp. 57-58

But Vyshinsky rejects the usual condition for the acceptance of the confession of the accused, that this confession should be corroborated by "other circumstances established" in the case. This principle Vyshinsky held as completely inadmissible for Soviet law court practice.

Indeed, he argued, if other circumstances established in the case *prove* (V.I.) the guilt of the person brought to responsibility, his confession loses the value of another evidence and is in this connection superfluous. Its value may be reduced in this case to the point where it merely furnishes the basis for the evaluation of these or those moral qualities of the accused or the mitigation or aggravation of the punishment to be set by the court.

With amazing hypocracy, Vyshinsky points to Article 136 of the old RSFSR Code of Criminal Procedure forbidding the investigation magistrate to extort from the accused confession by violence, threats and other measures alike. On paper he requires from the investigation organs the exact and checked evaluation of all the evidence presented, including the confession of the accused. [1]

But the most important point of Vyshinsky's argument is the assertion that in cases of conspiracy, of criminal association, of anti-Soviet and counter-revolutionary organizations and groups in particular—"the explanations of the accused in such cases unavoidably acquire the character and importance of basic evidence of a most important, decisive evidence. This is to be explained by the particularity of these circumstances, by the peculiarity of their legal nature". [2] And he adds : "In spite of the caution necessary for the handling of this question it is impossible not to admit the independent importance of such evidence in this kind of cases". [3]

Not only did Vyshinsky give prominent importance to the confession of the accused, but he directed the investigating magistrate to insist on a confession written by the accused and signed by his own hand. Because, Vyshinsky argued, it is much more difficult for an accused to retreat from his confession if it is written by himself, even if he should have signed not only every page of the interrogation record, but even every sentence written not with his hand, but by the inves-

---

[1] A. Ye. Vyshinsky, *Teoriya sudebnykh dokazatel' stv...*, *op. cit.*, pp. 260-263 passim.

[2] *Ibid.*, pp. 263-264.

[3] *Ibid.*, p. 265.

tigating magistrate". [1] "I personally", he declared, "prefer a semi confession put on paper by the accused himself, to a full confession written down by the investigating magistrate".

Certainly, Vyshinsky used his theoretical assertion also in action, in his capacity as the USSR Prosecutor in the famous trials of the thirties.

Thus in the Anti-Soviet Trotskivite Center Case he said : "You cannot require that we approach cases of conspiracy, of state over-throw, presenting you minutes, decisions, membership cards, the numbers of membership cards; you cannot require that conspirators should conspire according to certificates of their criminal activity issued by notaries public. Not a single sober man can put forth such requirements. Yes, we have a score of documents in this connection. But even if we would not have them, we are of the opinion that we have the right to present the accusation on the grounds of the testi-mony and the explanations of the accused ... We have in mind the testimony of the accused who in themselves represent evidence of tremendous importance". [2]

The effect of such assertions is evident since the confessions of the accused were declared, by the leading legal authority and the almighty SSSR Prosecutor, the basic evidence in political cases. The organs of investigation directed all their efforts to produce the necessary confession which served in the majority of cases as the only, but still sufficient, evidence against the accused.

In 1937, Vyshinsky emphasized in an article [3] that one of the pecu-liarities of the bourgeois counter-revolution inside of the USSR is that it is connected by all its threads and by every step of its practical activity with the counter-revolutionary fascist centers abroad, with the headquarters of the foreign intelligences of this or that capitalist state, with the Second Departments of General Staffs quarters of capitalist countries, especially of the fascist ones.

Indeed, the accusation mainly based itself on such confessions in the cases of the United Trotskivite-Zinoviyevite Center, Anti-Soviet

---

[1] A. Ye. Vyshinsky, "On the Scopes of the Investigating Magistrate", Adress at the Third Educational Conference of Investigating Magistrates, on December 11, 1936, *Sots. zak.*, 1937, No. 1, pp. 40-41.

[2] A. Ye. Vyshinsky, *Sudebnyye rechi*, M. 1948, pp. 459-460.

[3] *Sots. zak.*, 1937, No. 11, p. 4.

Trotskivite Center, in the trials of Tukhachevskiy, Jakir, Uberovich and other cases in which Vyshinsky acted as prosecutor.

We know now that all these cases were framed, that no link existed between the accused and the foreign intelligence or military general staffs.

The peculiarity stressed by Vyshinsky was the system on which the framing was carried out : evidence was provided by confessions extorted by torture, and faked documents.

Many Soviet writers adhered to Vyshinsky's interpretation of confessions of the accused in reviewing his book on the theory of evidence in Soviet Law. One of them was Strogovich, the champion of the material-objective-absolute truth in Soviet Courts.

Still in 1955, Strogovich wrote : "A. Y. Vyshinsky justly works also against the underestimation of the accused's testimony which may be of great importance in connection with the concrete circumstances in individual cases, especially in cases of group crimes and criminal associations". [1]

This adherence to Vyshinsky's views on confesssion he had already expressed in 1941. [2]

But when Khrushchev made his sensational divulgation about the legality in Stalins's time under the care of Vyshinsky and the role of "confessions" played in court, Strogovich declared in 1956 that Vyshinsky's assertion about the independent importance of confession as evidence in some cases was wrong :

"There is not and cannot be special rules of evidence for cases of conspiracy or other anti-revolutionary crimes. In these cases, as in any other, the objective material truth must be found with the help of evidence ..." he wrote. [3]

b) *Analogy*

Another element of the formation of the sentence was a peculiar provision of the old RSFSR Criminal Code permitting the use of analogy or the application to an action, not provided for in the Criminal Code of a provision of the Code dealing with an action only analogous to that under examination of the Court.

---

[1] Strogovich, *Material'naya istina...*, *op. cit.*, p. 344.

[2] See *Sots. zak.*, 1941, No. 2, pp. 79-80.

[3] Strogovich, "The Accused's Confession", *Sots. zak.*, 1956, No. 6, p. 17.

Article 16 of the old RSFSR Criminal Code reads : "If a publicly dangerous action is not directly provided for in the present code, the grounds and the limits of responsibility are established therefore according to those articles of the Code which provide for crimes mostsimilarly related to the examined action".

The use of analogy in the Criminal Code was explained by the unavoidable gaps in the penal legislation caused by the raising of new aspects of relations to be regulated by the Criminal Code.

It is evident that the use of analogy gave wide possibilities for judicial arbitrariness and was a flagrant violation of the principle : *"nullum crimen, nulla poena sine lege"*.

That is why analogy was excluded in the Basic Principles of Penal Legislation of 1958 and, thus, did not reappear in the new RSFSR Criminal Code of 1961. [1]

It is only natural that Vyshinsky was for the analogy in the Criminal Code and defended it against criticism.

Thus, in his review of the textbook on "Soviet Criminal Law, General Part ..." M. 1952, he blamed the authors for" not having adequately defended the use of analogy in criminal law, which has, however, great importance". He reproached them for having limited themselves to some approving remarks such as 'the use of analogy has completely vindicated itself in the following years' and that they have not criticized the position of the enemies of analogy, did not defend the necessity of this institution in criminal law. [2]

c) *Onus Probandi*

In the question of the burden of proof Vyshinsky assumes the position (already in the 1946 edition of his book *Teoriya sudebnykh dokazatel'stv v sovetskom prave*) that, although it is the prosecutor who must prove the accusation, since the accused is presumed innocent until the contrary is proved, still situations may be created in the trial when the burden of proof shifts from the prosecutor to the accused. Such shifts may occur several times during the trial.

His formula for the burdon of proof is as follows : a) to prove the circumstances confirming the accusation is the duty of the prosecu-

---

[1] It is peculiar that analogy was retained in the *Basic Principles of Civil law Legislation of 1961* (Article 12).

[2] Vyshinsky : "Some Problems of the Science of Soviet Law", *S.G.P.*, 1953, No. 4, p. 24.

tors; to prove the circumstances repudiating the accusation is included in the duties of the accused : *"actori incumbit probatio"*.

Vyshinsky brings an example in support of his assertion : [1]

A is accused of robbery. The fact of robbery is proved by the prosecutor. But *A* comes with the assertion that the robbery was a joke concocted with the robbed person. At this point, Vyshinsky declares, the *onus probandi* shifts from the prosecutor to the accused. It is he who has to prove the veracity of his assertions. [2]

M. S. Strogovich may be named the promoter of the presumption of innocence of the accused and of the prosecutor's burden of proof in Soviet literature. He asserted both principles as pertaining to Soviet criminal procedure in his work *Ucheniye o material'noy istine v ugolovnom protsesse*. [3]

Strogovich declared that the question of the burden of evidence as formulated by Vyshinsky in his work on evidence, "is maybe the only one on which I am obliged to dissent". [4]

He takes the example brought forward by Vyshinsky and gives the opinion that *A's* declaration has to be examined and checked by the court and may be repudiated if proven by the prosecutor as false, "and not because the accused failed to prove its veracity". [5]

According to him, there is no shift of the burden of proof from the prosecutor to the accused, but the court is simply faced with an assertion of the accused which, as any other statement of the accused must be checked and examined by the prosecutor and the court. "A situation may not be recognized as correct when the accused refers to a fact of importance to the case, but the court asks him to prove it, and repudiates the fact only because the accused could not do so".

Strogovich comes to the conclusion that in Soviet criminal procedure the burden of proof lies always on the prosecutor and is related to the

---

[1] A. Ye. Vyshinsky, *Teoriya sudebnykh...*, *op. cit.*, p. 244.

[2] *Ibid.*, p. 245.

[3] M. 1947. It must be said that in 1934, Strogovich opposed the use of the presumption of innocence in Soviet criminal procedure because "this liberal principle in this abstract form would have undoubtedly a demobilizing, demagnetizing influence in our court and investigating practice, would bring to a weakening of the fight against criminality, from the viewpoint of the scope of our court and investigating organs". (Strogovich, *Obvineniye i obvinyayemyg na predvaritel'nom sledstvii i sude*, M. 1934, p. 30.) He later drastically changed his opinion.

[4] Strogovich, *Ucheniye...*, *op. cit.*, p. 270. It is curious to note the "burden of proof" was the only question on which Strogovich differed with Vyshinsky in 1947.

[5] *Ibid.*, p. 271.

duty of the court to investigate actively all the circumstances of the case and to fill up the gaps in evidence produced by the parties, but never to shift to the accused and his counsel the burden of proof. [1]

But the polemic was continued. In the 1950 edition of his book, Vyshinsky contradicts Strogovich.

He comes back to the example of the case A, "According to my opinion, the accused A must prove that it was a joke, literally *must* (V.I.) if he asserts that it was a joke. Prof. Strogovich says : 'the prosecutor and the court must, are in duty bound, to check this reference of the accused ...' This is not debatable but this does not only exclude *but demands* (V.I.) that facts subject to checking should be provided by the accused. The question consequently is, in the first place, *who* (V.I.) the prosecutor, or the accused is bound to present such facts ?

Vyshinsky thinks that it is the duty of the accused.

Evidently, Strogovich is right. Both parties to the trial, the prosecutor *and* the accused, bring forward evidence for their assertions, but it is still the prosecutor who must prove that the accused is guilty because of the presumption of innocence is in favor of the latter. When the accused presents evidence he does not do so in discharge of his burden of proof, as the prosecutor does, but exercising his right of defense, and it is the prosecutor who has to prove that the evidence brought forward by the accused is not convincing.

In the A case, the accused must present evidence for his assertion in order that this evidence be considered and checked by the court, and if not destroyed by the prosecutor, be used in his favor.

But there is no shift of the burden of proof from the prosecutor to the accused; it always remains with the prosecutor, but the accused exercises his right of defense in presenting the evidence for his assertion.

It is clear that the transfer of the burden of proof from the prosecutor to the accused would be an important worsening of his position in the trial which makes him more accessible to unfounded accusations.

The controversy between Vyshinsky and Strogovich about the *onus probandi* may be explained by the fundamental principle of Soviet administration of justice : the interests of the state take precedence over those of the individual.

In his criticism of Strogovich's book, Tadevosyan pointed out this principle "Defending the interests and rights of the accused", he wrote,

---

[1] *Ibid.*, p. 273.

"the author does it in a one-sided manner and forgets that transferring the burden of proof to the shoulders of the state, the society and the victim of the crime, liberating the accused and not condemning him until the crime is proven as certain as two by two is four, he maybe defends the liberty and inviolability of the individual very attractively and well in an abstract comprehension of this liberty, but he does not put the interests of state and society at the head of his doctrine". [1]

The Basic Principles of the Criminal Procedure of the USSR and the Union Republics of 1958 resolved the question providing that the court, the prosecutor, the investigating magistrate and the person charged with the inquest have no right to shift the burden of proof to the accused. (Article 14).

Still in political cases, when "state interests" prevail it, Tadevosyan's viewpoint is applied and it is the accused who has to prove his innocence.

d) *Complicity*

Vyshinsky's assertions in the field of legal theory, his interpretation of the provisions of the criminal law and procedure which were mandatory during the time of the cult of personality → all tended to enlarge the circle of persons to be made criminally responsible and to widen the law consciousness of the judges to that effect.

One of his interpretations pertained to the doctrine of complicity.

The old Criminal Code did not give a definition of complicity (Article 17). It said only that accomplices of the physical perpetrator of the crime are the instigators and accessories.

In order to be accomplices to a crime the participants must conspire to commit their crime and must have the intent to commit it. [2]

But Vyshinsky denied the necessity of showing the existence of an intent and conspiring for the concerted commitment of a criminal action in order to bring accomplices to responsibility.

He also rejected the requirement of a causal connection in the perpetration of a crime by several persons. He wrote,: "It is not to interpret the conception of complicity as an activity being in casual

---

[1] V.S. Tadevosyan, "The Question of Material Truth Establishment", *S.G.P.*, 1948, No. 6, p. 70.

[2] See *Ugolovnyy kodeks. Nauchno-populyarnyy, prakticheskiy kommentariy*, M. 1927, Article 17 (1).

connection with the criminal result produced by the perpetrator ... Not a casual connection but a relation in general of a given person is necessary for the conception of complicity".

"And the participation in a group committing criminal actions may cause the responsibility of a participant of the group even when he, personally, has no direct connection with these criminal actions and did not express his consent with them". [1]

It is evident that such an interpretation widened extensively the possibility to inculpate persons who have only a very loose connection with the crime.

After Khrushchev's disclosures at the XXth Party congress, Vyshinsky's views came under sharp criticism even of those Soviet writers who shared, or to say better, had to share, his views during the "cult of Vyshinsky's personality".

Officially his viewpoints were repudiated by A. N. Shelepin in his address at the XXIind Congrees of the Party.

Shelepin declared that "the substantial defects in Soviet legal science, its departure from scientific problems, were caused by the cult of Vyshinsky's personality. Vyshinsky's theory on the accused's confession as evidence in cases of crimes against the state justified in essence mass facts of arbitrariness in investigative and court practice which occurred at a certain time". [2]

e) *Public Opinion*

There is another element of influence on the formation of the sentence to which Anashkin correctly attributes great importance: public opinion.

The "public opinion" with regard to a crime or one accused in a trial is often expressed very loudly in the press, meetings, etc., previous to the trial and finally in the court hall during the trial. It is especially loud and even strident with regard to political or semi-political cases and criminals.

The strength of this influence is illustrated by Anashkin in the following example : The Belinogradsky Territorial and the Odessky Regional Courts motivated decisions about the setting of the punish-

---

[1] Quoted in *S.G.P.*, 1962, No. 3, p. 9.

[2] *XXII S'yezd Kommunisticheskoy partii Sovetskogo soyuza. Stenograpicheskiy otchet*, M. 1962, V. II, p. 409.

ments for the accused in criminal cases by the "demand of the public". [1]

Certainly, Anashkin is right when he demands that the question of the guilt or innocence of the accused and the measure of punishment should be exclusively decided by the court only, since if the court should act under the influence of public opinion this "will have a certain effect on the formation of the judges' conviction and will limit their independence". [2]

Unfortunately, Anashkin does not discuss the influence of the Party, Government and Communist ideology on the judge, his decisions and sentences.

But is there a real "public opinion" in the Soviet Union?

It seems to the present writer that a public needs freedom of expression in word and writing, in order to become the real viewpoint of the public or its majority.

Certainly, such a freedom as such does not exist in the Soviet Union.

What is called there "public opinion" is formed under the instigation and the leadership of the Party and then expressed inplant, factory or kolkhoz meeting which number and loudness corresponds to the importance of the case or the question at hand.

But the "people is silent", according to Pushkin's definition, their real opinion is not manifested.

The "public opinion" is in reality only another method for the Party to exercise its influence under the disguise of the manifestation of a "public opinion".

This influence will be discussed later.

---

[1]   Anashkin, "The Role of Law Consciousness...", *op. cit.*, p. 44.
[2]   *Ibid.*, p. 45.

CHAPTER TWENTY

REMEDIES

A. SOVIET APPEAL AND CASSATION

a) *Historical Development*

1. *Legislation 1917-1933*

Remedy to a judgment has a peculiar history in Soviet Administration of justice.

The Decree No. 1 on Courts abrogated appeals of a judgement of the first instance to a court of the second instance (Article 6). Thus, a case could not be reviewed by a higher court on its merits. The examination of any case for a second time, in full, was eliminated from civil and criminal procedure. However, cassation, i.e., an appeal for cassation to a higher court was retained by the Decree.

The abolition of the appeal, and the retaining of cassation was confirmed in the Basic Principles of Criminal Procedure of the USSR and the Union Republics of 1924, where it was said (Article 28): "All cases are examined on their merit only in one instance. Appeals are not admitted". This was a deliberate attempt to exclude the second instance from renewed examination and retrial of a case on its merits.

The appeal in western terminology is the right to petition a higher court of second instance for the re-examination of a decision or sentence of a court of first instance. The higher court re-examines the case not quite *in extenso* on its merits. Witnesses are usually not heard in the appellate procedure and their testimony is only read.

In general, the court of appeal tends to re-examine the case within the frame of the complaint, but its right to hear witnesses and extend the examination beyond the complaint is not excluded.

Cassation, as it is applied in France and functioned in imperial Russia, is the right to ask a higher court of second or third instance to examine the decision or sentence of the preceeding instances with regard to its formal and procedural validity.

On an appeal, the decision or sentence of the court of first instance is reaffirmed, changed or another decision is taken, whereas the court of cassation may only reject the petition for cassation, reaffirming the decision, or sentence of the lower court, or set aside the sentence or decision of the lower court and remand the case to a lower court for a re-examination sentence or retrial.

Since the cassation court does not examine the case on its merit, it may not pass a new decision or pronounce a new sentence or change the decision or the sentence of the lower instance.

Another kind of cassation is represented by the German "Revision". According to the procedure applied by the revision court it may change the decision or sentence submitted to it, if the material collected by the lower court is sufficient for a judgment on the merits of the case. But the revision court does not gather new evidence and does not check the evidence produced in the lower court.

The revision court is of course also entitled to confirm the decision or the sentence and to reverse it, remanding the case for a re-examination or a retrial.

The attempt to completely eliminate a second examination or trial of the case on its merits was successful only for a short time. We will see that in the later development of the Soviet administration of justice, the functions of the cassation court came more and more to resemble those of a court of appeal in the western sense of the word.

Let us examine this development. It seems evident that in establishing the right to petition for a cassation in the Decree No. 1 on Courts, the legislator had in mind the cassation of the old Russian civil and criminal procedures of 1864 since no other definition of the term was given in the Decree. The Decree provided only that the appeal (*apelyatsiya*) is abolished, but cassation (*kassatsiya*) retained.

This opinion is supported by the fact that as we know the Decree No. 2 on Courts permitted the use of the laws of 1864, including the civil and criminal procedure, to the extent that they were not abolished by Decrees of the TsIK or Council of People's Commissars and did not run counter to the legal consciousness of the working classes.

Since the Decree No. 2 on Courts provided only for one court of cassation, namely the Council of Local Judges, and limited the kind of sentences-subject to cassation to those imposing a fine over 100 rubles or arrest over seven days [1] with the provision that the criminal

---

[1] The limitation of the right of cassation was abandoned by the Statute on the People's Court of November 30, 1918 (*Sob. uz.*, *RSFSR*, 1918, Item 889) which simply provided that decisions and sentences may be petitioned for cassation to a higher court.

and civil procedure of 1864 did not run counter to the "legal consciousness of the working classes", the court had laws at its disposal
to handle the cassation as a "pure" cassation.

That it was the intention of the legislator in the first years of the
Soviets rule to exclude the review of a case on its merits completely
from the competence of the cassation court follows also from the
debates of the draft of the RSFSR Code of Civil Procedure in the
VTsIK. The Rapporteur, Brandenburgsky, said in the session of June
30, 1923 : "No appeal (in the Western sense) is admitted in our Republic, that is why there can be only the question in what way a complaint for cassation can be lodged against a decision, i.e., if a law is
violated ... The higher instance (the court of cassation) does not touch
upon the merits of the case. It may only decide as to whether the law
has been violated or not. If it comes to the conclusion that a law is
violated it may reverse the decision". [1]

Such a viewpoint is contested by E. F. Kutsova. She is of the opinion
that cassation as provided by the Decree No. 1 on Courts could not
be similar to the cassation of tsarist law because, also in the Soviet
cassation procedure, the "judges were directed by their revolutionary
legal consciousness". [2] Certainly, the universal principle of judging
according to "revolutionary legal consciousness" could replace the
use of any law, but the legislator's desire made evident in the Decrees
No. 1 and No. 2 was to submit procedure and, hence, cassation to the
regulations of the tsarist codes of procedure.

However, already the Decree No. 2 on Courts, although accepting
the principle of pure cassation, introduced a ground for cassation
obliging the court of cassation to examine the case on its merits although to a limited extent. Indeed, Article 5 of the Decree No. 2 on
Courts provided that, "on cassation complaints, the court has the right
to reverse the sentence not only because of formal violations deemed
substantial, but also if it realizes that the sentence under complaint
is evidently unjust".

Any decision finding an evidently unjustified sentence is a judgment on the merits of the case and certainly does not belong to the

---

The freedom of bringing any decision or sentence before higher courts for cassation
was retained by the subsequent legislation up to the RSFSR Code of Criminal Procedure
of 1923 for a certain kind of crime.

[1] *Sbornik statey i materialov po grazldanskomu protsessu za 1921-1924*, M. 1925, p. 47.

[2] E.F. Kutsova, *Sovetskaya kassatsiya kak garantiya zakonnosti i pravosudiya*, M.
1957, p. 26.

"pure" cassation competence of the French Court de Cassation or the former Russian Ruling Senate.

Still, "evident" injustice is a defect of the decision or sentence when it "springs to the eyes", so to speak, and does not need a thorough examination of the case on its merits by the cassation instance. The case of evident injustice is only an exception to pure cassation. It is significant, however, that already at the time of the Decree No. 2 on Courts, the lack of the re-examination of a case on its merits was felt and an attempt was made to create the possibility of reversal at least because of evident injustice. The ground for cassation of evident injustice re-appears in some further legislation on cassation as we shall see later. [1]

On July 23, 1918, the People's Commissariat of Justice issued an Instruction defining the activity of the cassation court. In Article 54 of the Instruction it was said : "The Council of the Local Judges, as a cassation instance for the Local People's Court, has the right to reverse the decision of the Local People's Court on the grounds of formal violations, recognzied as substantial. It also has the right to reverse sentences and decisions of the Local People's Court if it comes to the conclusion that the sentences and decisions under complaint are evidently unjust. The Council of the Local People's Courts has also the right to mitigate the punishment, and, in exceptional cases, to dispense with punishment completely". [2]

Hence, the instruction retained the cassation grounds of evident injustice but made another step toward the broadening of the competence of the cassation court, permitting the mitigation of the sentence in "exceptional cases", without remanding the case to the court of original jurisidction which is tantamount to the functions of a court of appeal. A definition of "exceptional cases" was not provided.

According to Article 55 of the Instruction, the cassation cases were examined in a session of the Council of People's Judges to which. "the victim, the accused, the parties (of the civil suit) and persons who claimed rights to the items of material evidence", were admitted.

But their absence did not inhibit the examination of the case, if the Council did not deem their presence indispensible. The participation of counsel in the cassation procedure was regulated by the general provisions on counsels of Article 23 of the Instruction.

---

[1] For a list of legislative acts in which evident injustice appears as a ground for the setting aside of sentence, see *Sovetskiy ugolovnyy protsess*, M. 1956, footnote 3 on p. 337.

[2] *Sob. uz., RSFSR*, 1918, Item 597.

It is peculiar that the Soviet legislature, in the same enactment, imits on the one hand the cassation to formal grounds and prohibits the examination of the case on its merits, but on the other, in enumerating the grounds for cassation, lists grounds which lead to the examination of the case on its merits by the cassation court.

The principle of excluding a second instance for the examination of the case on its merits and the right of cassation petition is upheld in the Statutes on the People's Court of November 25, 1918. [1]

The cassation instance—the Council of People's Judges,—had the right to reverse sentences and decisions in cases of essential violations or an incorrect application of decrees, especially of violations of procedural form, but also if the sentences and decisions evidently were unjust or the preliminary investigation incomplete. The cassation right of the court was extended beyond the limits of the complaint and its grounds.

The imperfection of the preliminary investigation appeared in the Statute as a new cassation ground and the cassation court received the freedom to examine any cassation ground, not only those indicated in the cassation complaint. This freedom is of course an obligation: the cassation court had to look into the entire case for cassation grounds, *ex officio*.

The double-tonguing of the law with regard to cassation got its clearest expression in the codification of the twenties, namely in the RSFSR Code of Criminal Procedure of 1922. [2]

Indeed, Article 353 of this Code provides that "Complaints against sentences of the People's Court may be filed by all interested parties exclusively with regard to formal violations of the rights and interests if they occurred in the preliminary procedure or during the examination of the case in court; these complaints are called cassation complaints and cannot touch upon the merit of the sentence".

Evidently, in this article the legislators stand on the ground of the "pure" cassation.

The grounds for cassation are enumerated in Article 354 as follows: 1) Deficiency and error in the preliminary investigation; 2) essential violation of procedural forms; 3) violations or erroneous application of the law; 4) evident injustice of the sentence.

---

[1] *Sob. uz.*, *RSFSR*, 1918, Item 889.
[2] *Ibid.*, 1922, Item 230.

It is equally clear, however, that the grounds under 1 and 4 of Article 354 must lead the cassation court to an examination on the merits of the case.

This is acknowledged by Kutsova who writes with regard to the provision of Article 353 (349) that "Having established a limitation, not inherent to the nature of Soviet cassation, the RSFSR Code of Criminal Procedure of 1922 (as well as that of 1923) could not consequently remain in this position. The right of the higher court to set aside sentences on taking substantiation and evident injustice, confirmed by the same law, assumed the right and duty of the same courts for the checking of the sentences on their merit. Under this condition the limitation of the rights of the parties to complaints and protests against formal violation in sentences lost every sense".[1]

She declares that the limitation provided by Codes of 1922 did not correspond to the scope of Soviet cassation and that also after 1922 the legality of the sentence and its rightlessness were checked on their merits by cassation courts.

The code of 1922 also defined for the first time the meaning of an "evidently unjust sentence", which is held to be present : 1) when no reasons for the sentence can be found in the preliminary investigation and the sentence is, thus, completely unsubstantiated and 2) when the punishment set by the court, although within the limits of the law, with regard to its severity, does not precisely correspond to the criminal action, (Article 363).

The RSFSR Code of Criminal Procedure of 1922 was revised in 1923. [2] The wordings of Article 353 and 354 were retained in Articles 349 and 413 of the revised edition, respectively. But the definition of the evident injustice of Article 363 was shortened by the first paragraph; the second remained in Article 417.

The Basic Principles of Criminal Procedure of the USSR and the Union Republics of 1924 [3] again confirmed the abolition of the appeal, and sanctioned the new revisional character of the soviet cassation procedure, calling it "cassation-revisional" (Article 26). The following grounds for cassation were listed in the basic principles :

---

[1] Kutsova, *op. cit.*, p. 92. The limitation of Article 354 (349) was defended by the argument that "if ...the cassation instance should be bound to check the sentence on its merit every time—the revisional cassation instance would be transformed into an appellate court. (*Vestnik sovetskoy yustitsii*, 1928, No. 24, p. 717.)

[2] *Sob., uz., RSFSR*, 1923, Item 106.

[3] *Sob. zak., SSSR*, 1924, Item 206.

a) violation of procedural forms which hindered the court in examining all the aspects of the case and had or could have an influence on the pronouncing of the right sentence;

b) violation or incorrect application of USSR or union-republic laws, if the error committed by the court caused the use of a different measure of social defense than that which had to be set by the court, if the law had been correctly applied.

The important thing is that the union-republic legislation was left free to establish also other grounds for the reversal of judgments with regard to union-republic judicial institutions, or to exclude cassation in some cases altogether.

The Basic Principles also provided that the cassation court is not bound to the cassation grounds indicated in the complaint. The cassation court, "without checking the factual circumstances established by the court which examined the case on its mertis", was empowered :

a) to reverse the case and remand it to the lower instance for a new trial;

b) to change the sentence, "if this is possible without a review of the evidence" (Article 27).

Thus, the 1923 edition of the Code of Criminal Procedure dropped the "lack of substantiation" of the sentence and the Basic Principles of 1924 eliminated the "evident injustice" as a ground for cassation altogether.

Although, on one hand, this restraining tendency of the legislator could be interpreted as a device to confine cassation to its "pure" form, and such an interpretation can find support in the repeated emphasis of the prohibition to examine the case on its merits or to check the factual findings of the court of original jurisdiction, still, on the other had, some grounds for cassation, as for instance those of paragraphs 1 and 4 of Article 413 of the Code of Criminal Procedure, spoke against such an assumption.

"Actually, however, the cassation courts continued to exercise control not only over the completeness and correction of the investigation of the case, and the equity of the sentence, but also the motivation of the sentence. The substantial percentage of sentences, set aside by the cassation courts on ground of their erroneous motivation confirmed the necessity of such a control", writes N. Ya. Kalashnikova. [1]

---

[1] In *Sovetskiy ugolovnyy protsessu*, edited by D.S. Karev, M. 1956, p. 337.

A legal support for the checking of the motivation of the sentence was given by the Basic Principles of Court Structure of 1938 discussed below.

The new "revisional" character of the Soviet cassation completely confused the question of the exclusion of appeal.

The situation was pointedly characterized by Krylenko quoted here extensively. He wrote :

"This [revisional] principle was taken over into our court system and is in force up to the present time, but from our viewpoint does not represent any gain but brings only confusion. This gain is expressed in our peculiar admission of an appeal under the name of cassation, i.e., in a factual mixture of both principles ... why should an appeal on the merits of the case not be admitted ? Usually two reasons are given. If the appeal of the sentence on its merit should be permitted, procrastination will occur in the case of a complaint against the formal violation of law ... The other argument is that a complaint on the merits is inadmissible because the sentence is pronounced by conscious judges (the former jurors). We have no jurors; our judges decide also according to their consciences. The question of course, is not as to whether judgment is carried out according to the conscience, or not, but is that, should or should not a court as a state organ enjoy a definite grade of confidence in the eyes of the state ? We respond—yes, it must. This resolves the question, and the logical conclusion from all this is *the complete elimination of appeal* (K.I.) But why do we admit the complaint in cassation ? We admit it because we think that every citizen has the right to require that his rightful guarantees should be observed that, judgment should be carried out over him in the form prescribed by law and not in another one ... To re-examine the case on a new merit in the second instance has no sense, for we have no guarantee that the second instance will decide the case better, but the complaint against formal violation of law must take its course, because we do not deny the protection of the rights of the individual as far as these rights are granted to him. But the mistake of the Decree No. 2 on Courts and of the following Decrees consisted in the admission of appeal under the form of cassation, because they admitted as a reason for cassation the passing of an "obviously unjust sentence". [1]

Thus the decisive reason for the exclusion of appeal was, according

---

[1]   N.V. Krylenko, *Sudovstroystvo*, M. 1924, p. 56.

to Krylenko the preservation of state confidence in the decision of its own organ—the court of original jurisdiction. But is not the cassation right also *an expression* of distrust of the court of first instance ? How far is now the Soviet administration of justice from this primary concept when even the review of sentences already in force are permitted ?

2. *Legislation, 1938-1961*

An important change was produced by Article 15 of the Basic Principles of Court Structure of the USSR, and the Union Republics of 1938, [1] providing that the cassation court has to check the "legality and motivation" of the sentence on the grounds of material "filed in the case and presented by the parties".

For M. S. Strogovich this provision definitely settled the character of Soviet cassation. He writes that "the court of cassation has to check all the requirements of law ... as well as review the correctness of the sentence, with regard to the merits of the case". [2] He recognizes that such a review by the court of cassation is a "revision" but the revision is not a form of review different from cassation. "Revisional" is only the form of Soviet cassation. [3] The principal of revision is set out in Article 421 of the RSFSR Code of Criminal Procedure which provides that, independently of the examination of grounds for the cassation of sentences indicated, or the complaints for cassation and protests—the court has to check in every case the entire procedure in the way of revision and, should a violation of the law inviting the reversal of the sentence be established, to reverse it and remand the case for retrial". Quoting Article 421, Strogovich comes to the conclusion that "Such an examination of a case under a complaint for cassation (protest) beyond the limits of the cassation grounds enumerated in the complaint (protest) is called examination of the case *in the way of revision* (S.I.). This revisional order is not a separate order, different from the cassation order, it is a property of the cassation order itself". [4]

This terminology gives rise to a misunderstanding. Indeed, we have seen that the German "Revision" is a form of cassation, distinct from the "pure" cassation of France and tsarist Russia. But the

---

[1] *V.V.S.*, 1938, No. 11.

[2] Strogovich, *Proverka...*, *op. cit.*, p. 53.

[3] *Ibid.*, p. 68.

[4] *Ibid.*

main characteristic of the "revision" that the *Reichsgericht* had the right to undertake in contradistinction to the French Cours de Cassation and the Russian Ruling Senate, lay in the fact that it could change the decision or the sentence or examine the case on its merits without remanding the case to the lower court.

Article 412 of the RSFSR Criminal Procedure of 1923 defines revision as the right of the court of cassation to examine grounds for cassation other than those brought forward in the cassation complaint or in the protest, and then, not to pass a new sentence but to remand the case for retrial. Thus, Article 412 evidently removes the explicit prohibition for the court of cassation to examine the case on its merits as expressed in Article 349 of the Code. The cassation grounds according to this provision found by the court but not listed in the complaint or protest must be of a formal character and not based on the merits of the case. To say, as Strogovich does, that the revisional order is a characteristic of the Soviet cassation in criminal procedure may give the impression that the revisional character of Soviet cassation is merely the right to change the sentence and examine the case on its merits.

The error is abetted, even more by the fact that the Soviet cassation procedure, as developed by decisions of the RSFSR Supreme Court and practice really comes very close to the revision and even to the appeal as understood in the West. The revisional character of Soviet cassation as applied at the present time is based on the right of the cassation court to examine, under this or that legal protest, the case on its merits, and not on the provisions of Article 412, since the going beyond the grounds of the complaint were given to the cassation court by former laws.

But not only has the cassation court the duty to check the entire procedure including the preliminary investigation, thus going beyond the grounds brought forward in the complaint or the protest, but the formulation of a ground for the complaint is in general not necessary, according to Article 412 of the RSFSR Code of Criminal Procedure of 1923. The plaintiff may legitiamtely ask the court of cassation merely to review the case and the court is obliged to review the case and look itself for the presense or absence of grounds for cassation of the sentence. [1]

This is certainly an important peculiarity of Soviet cassation. The liberty to file a complaint for cassation without providing any

---

[1]   See Strogovich, *Proverka...*, *op. cit.*, p. 72.

grounds for the complaint brings the Soviet cassation even closer to the "appeal" in the western sense than to a "revision" in the German sense.

An "appeal" does not need to be provided with grounds in the majority of the western countries. [1] It is simply the expression of the desire for a second examination of the case.

But a cassation, even a revision on the merits is unthinkable in the West without the bringing forward of grounds for the request for a review.

Thus, the Soviet court of cassation is not only not limited to the examination of the grounds for cassation as presented in the complaint for cassation, but it is also not bound to the review of the sentence demanded by the complainer or as protested by the prosecutor. The cassation court checks the entire case in all its aspects, both formal and on the merits. A complaint for cassation or a protest automatically produces the review by the court of cassation acting in the reviewing process *ex officio* also on its own initiative. The review, as Grodzinsky writes, "is all sided, exhaustive, embracing all the contents of the sentence, all the activities of the prosecution, the preliminary investigation and the court in the case". [2]

It is interesting to note that the double-tongued feature of the law forces the Soviet jurists also to reach out to the same method. Thus Strogovich, in his comments to Article 412 of the Code of Criminal Procedure, writes : "The review or cassation is *mainly* (stress provided) a formal procedure and cannot touch upon the merits of the case, and the court of cassation focuses only on formal violations".

Now, Article 413 enumerates the following reasons for cassation : 1) the inexactitude and deficiency of the investigation; 2) substantial violations of procedural forms; 3) violation or mis-application of law; 4) evident injustice of the sentence. The reasons under 2 and 3 are obviously of a formal character.

The reason under 1 makes Strogovich acknowledge that in order to apply this reason for cassation purposes it is "undoubtedly necessary to examine and study all the totality of circumstances of the case, i.e., to examine the case on its merits". [3] Also with regard to the

---

[1] However, according to American law, the Appellant has to prove the violation of law and the damage incurred by the violation.

[2] M. Grodzinsky, *Kassatsionnoye i nadzornoye proizvodstvo v sovetskom ugolovnom protsesse*, M. 1949, p. 17.

[3] *Ibid.*, p. 377.

reason under 4, Strogovich admits that "evident injustice of the sentence is most obviously connected with a number of questions pertaining to the merits of the case". [1]

And Strogovich makes an effort to find a solution to the awkward situation. He wants to find a limit to the reviewing of a case in the cassation instance and writes in italics : "The cassation instance checks as to whether the court of original jurisdiction has done everything in order to find the material truth as to whether the court did it correctly, but as to what exactly it can acknowledge as true, and what is not true—this is the business of the court of original jurisdiction, and the cassation court cannot interfere with the conviction of the court of first instance as to what is true or not true". [2]

This attempt is unsuccessful. It is evident that every examination of a case on its merits results in a judgment by the cassation instance passing upon that which the court of original jurisdiction found as true or untrue. How can, for instance, the findings that a sentence of the court of original jurisdiction is "evidently unjust" be established without such a judgemnt by the court of cassation ? And Strogovich has to admit that "certainly in this case (of evident injustice) the court of cassation partly examines the case on its merits—but in general the merits of a case are not, according to our law, a foreign and restricted field for the court of cassation". [3]

When Article 349 of the Code of Criminal Procedure of 1923 declares that complaints for cassation may be logded only in regard to formal violations of rights and interests of a party and may not touch upon the merits of the case, nothing else is left to Strogovich than to declare that Article 349 "about the impossibility of complaint against the merit of the sentence has a purely declaratory character and is in substantial contradiction with the principles of Soviet cassation, as established in Article 413 of the Code of Criminal Procedure and thus, has no real importance. [4]

Unfortunately Strogovich does not explain why the Soviet legislators deemed it necessary to adopt provisions "of a declaratory character", contradictory to some other provisions of the same Code.

The checking of the "legality and motivation" is another task of the cassation court according to the subsequent Soviet legislation.

---

[1] Ibid.

[2] Ibid., p. 378.

[3] Ibid., p. 391.

[4] Strogovich and Karnitsky, op. cit., p. 337.

It was formulated for the first time in the law on the Court Structure of the USSR, Union and Autonomous Republics of 1938 and retained in the subsequent legislation.

The new RSFSR Code of Criminal Procedure in force as of January 1, 1961, [1] and passed according to the USSR Basic Principles of Criminal procedure of 25 December 1958 [2] also maintains the principle that the court of cassation has to review the "legality and motivation of the sentence" according to the evidence gathered in the court of original jurisdiction [3] and the additionally submitted material presented before and during the session (Article 337). The court of cassation is also not limited to the grounds for cassation as indicated in the complaint for cassation or the protest. The court has to review the case "in its entirety" also with regard to those accused who did not file complaints or whose sentence was not protested (Article 332). [4]

Whereas the check of legality of a sentence is the fundamental task of every court of cassation the check of the motivation of a sentence is the evaluation of the sentence and of the case on its merits : the Soviet court of cassation has to establish whether the conclusions of the court of original jurisdiction correspond to the facts and the evidence established by the court and the preliminary investigation or additionally submitted, and E. F. Kutsova writes : "the results of the evaluation of the evidence by the court of second instance (cassation court) is a judgment of the correctness of the motivation of the court of original jurisdiction, of the reliability of sources of the evidence presented to the court and the value of the facts established according to the evidence". [5] Thus, according to her, the cassation court has to check all the work accomplished by the Preliminary investigation and the court of orignial jurisdiction.

Kutsova makes the correct conclusion that the law charging the cassation court with the checking of legality and motivation of the sentence inevitably obliges this court to examine the sentence on its merit. The checking of the motivation includes not only the valuation

---

[1] *V.V.S.*, *RSFSR*, 1961, No. 31.

[2] *V.V.S.*, *USSR*, 1959, No. 1.

[3] Article 337 speaks precisely of additional material i.e., not known to the preliminary investigation and the court of original jurisdiction.

[4] In contradiction to Article 411 of the RSFSR Code of Criminal Procedure of 1923 which limited the review of the cassation court only to those accused who filed a complaint or whose sentence was protested by the prosecutor.

[5] E.F. Kutsova, *op. cit.*, p. 99.

of the conformity of the court's conclusions with the facts established by the court in the sentence, but also of the entire evidence submitted to the court of original jurisdiction which brought the court to the recognition of the facts serving as basis for the conclusions of the sentence.

Admitting all that, Kutsova still denies that the review of the sentence on its merits has transformed the Soviet cassation court into a court of appeal since the review in the cassation court "is realized with different *scopes*, in other *conditions*, and the possible legal *consequences* of the checking, are different from those in an appeal court." [1]

In its interpretation of Article 339 of the Code of Criminal Procedure of 1961, also G.Z. Anashkin writes that "The cassation court has to check, as to whether the sentence is correct, according to its essense". [2] But to check the essense of a sentence, does it not mean to review it on its merit?

It follows from the practice of the supreme courts that they interpret their duty exactly in this sense. For instance, V. Rostovshchikov and Yu. Feofanov relate that the supreme court of the Kalmyk SSR, reviewing on cassation the sentence of the People's Court in the Sherman case "started everything from the beginning; the witnesses were heard in the Supreme Court a second time", [3] who repudiated their own testimonies given at the preliminary investigation and in the court of original jurisdiction. The accused, sentenced to four years of liberty deprivation by the People's Court, was acquitted by the Supreme Court.

There is no doubt that the Supreme Court, reviewing the hearing of witnesses and other procedural activity of the court of original jurisdiction, examined the case on its merits and acted as a full-fledged court of appeal in the Western sense of the word.

b) *New Evidence*

Article 337 of the new Code of Criminal Procedure confers the right upon persons entitled to file a complaint for cassation or a protest, [4]

---

[1] Kutsova, *op. cit.*, p. 93. (Italics by Kutsova.)

[2] *Nauchno-prakticheskiy kommentariy...*, *op. cit.*, p. 596.

[3] V. Rostovshchikov and Yu. Feofanov, "Law and Law Only", *Izvestia*, August 19, 1964.

[4] Enumerated in Article 325.

to present "additional material" in support or refutation of complaints or protests. [1]

This provision is of great importance for the definition of the character of Soviet cassation. The presenting of new evidence can make necessary the interrogation of new or old witnesses and the examination of evidence unknown to the court of original jurisdiction. This would put the court of cassation in the position of a court of original jurisdiction or a court of appeal.

Although possessing a competence far beyond that of cassation courts in Western Europe, the Soviet cassation court also in the examination of the merits of the case still was confined to the checking of the evidence and material submitted to the court of original jurisdiction. The corresponding Article 410 (note) of the Code of Criminal Procedure of 1923 permitted the presentation of new cassation complaints, i.e., of new grounds for cassation derived from the procedure in the court of original jurisdiction and not mentioned in the original complaint for cassation.

Indeed, Strogovich and Karnitsky write in their interpretation of Article 410 of the Code of Criminal Procedure of 1923 as follows : "It is to assume as undeniably false the bringing forward by the parties of new arguments, new grounds for the complaint against the sentence not mentioned in the basic or additional complaint. The arguments of the parties must be confined to the limits of the complaint i.e., only with regard to the violations indicated in the complaint". [2]

But Article 337 of the new Code of Criminal Procedure provides just beyond that for the bringing forward of new material not known to the court of original jurisdiction.

The wording of Article 337 permitting the presentation of an undefined new material, i.e., also the bringing forward of new grounds for cassation, in general, must lead to the conclusion that the legislator's goal was to enlarge the competence of the court of cassation in checking the "legality" and "motivation" of the sentence by the examination of evidence not checked by the court of original jurisdiction.

In acting so and basing its decision on the new material the cas-

---

[1] The RSFSR Code of Civil Procedure of 1923 provided only the right to bring forward additional complaints and protests and also bring new grounds of cassation.

[2] M. S. Strogovich and D. A. Karnitsky, *Ugolovno-protsesual'nyy kodeks RSFSR*, M. 1928, pp. 372-373.

sation court indirectly assumes the function of a court of original jurisdiction or of an appellate instance in the Western sense.

Since Article 337 does not define what additional "material" may be presented to the court of cassation it must be assumed that any evidence relevant to the case and capable of having influenced the sentence of the court of original jurisdiction, if known to it, is admissible.

In commenting on the new Code of Criminal Procedure, G. Z. Anashkin remarks on this topic : "Written declarations of persons, not interrogated as witnesses in the court of original jurisdiction or the preliminary investigation giving information about circumstances relevant to the case, as well as written declarations or information of experts on the subjects of their examination and other materials, may be presented to the cassation instance". [1]

The question as to whether the court of cassation has the right to interrogate witnesses has been denied by S. N. Abramov in the name of "everyone".

"Everyone agrees, he writes, that the court of cassation cannot hear witnesses and the entire court practice assumes this viewpoint in recent years", [2]

Anyhow before "the recent years" the court practice was not consistent in this question. For instance, the RSFSR Supreme Court, acting as a cassation instance, heard a witness in its session and finding that the witness corroborated the testimony of the accused, reversed the sentence and remanded the case for an additional investigation.

Although the Presidium of the RSFSR Supreme Court set aside the decision of the Cassation Department of the RSFSR Supreme Court in the way of supervision, it acted not because the cassation court interrogated a witness, but on the ground that the Cassation Department reversed the sentence without adequate foundation. [3]

Thus, the RSFSR Supreme Court, in its quality of a cassation instance heard a witness and the Presidium of the same court, in re-examination of the case, did not object to the interrogation of a witness by the cassation court.

---

[1]   *Nauchno-prakticheski kommentariy k UPK RSFSR* M. 1963, p. 601.

[2]   S.N. Abramov, *Proverka obosnovannosti sudebnogo' resheniya sudom po sovetskomu pravu*, M. 1950, p. 63.

[3]   Case No. 22174 of 1933, *Sotz. zak.*, 1936, No. 1, p. 14.

Also N. Kalashnikova asserts that "cases of presentation not only of the most various documents, but also of written testimonies of witnesses and even the summation of witnesses to sessions of cassation courts for an oral interrogation and the carrying out of examinations by experts" is practiced by the cassation courts. [1]

Such cases must have been known to the legislator and it is not to understand why Article 15 of the Basic Principles of Court Structure of the USSR and the Union and Autonomous Republics of 1958 which legalized the presentation of new materials to the cassation court did not exclude the interrogation of witnesses and experts by the cassation courts, and the RSFSR Code of Criminal Procedure of 1961 repeats the same provision in Article 337 without clarification of what kind of evidence is meant under "additional material".

But Abramov also is against the examination by the cassation court of written testimonies about facts relevant for the case, by persons not interrogated in the court of original jurisdiction, in contradistinction to M. A. Chel'tsov, [2] M. S. Strogovich, [3] and M. M. Grodzinsky. [4]

Abramov's objections are based on the argument that written declarations cannot replace oral testimonies. Certainly, they cannot replace oral testimonies received by the court but they might indicate that the preliminary investigation and the court examination during the trial were carried out adequately, and contribute to the decision of the cassation court remanding or quashing the case or changing the sentence.

The change of a sentence according to material unknown to the court of initial jurisdiction would violate the provision of Article 350(2) of the new Code.

Strogovich is of the opinion that the cassation court in general has no right to change a sentence or quash procedure only on the ground of new materials not known to the court of original jurisdiction, because it is not admissible to change the sentence of a court on the basis of material unknown to the court which passed the sentence and because the cassation instance has not the possibility to check

---

[1] N. Kalashnikova, "Presentation of New Material to the Cassation Instance", *Sots. zak.*, 1945, No. 7, p. 13.

[2] M.A. Chel'tsov, *Sovetskiy ugolovnyy protsess*, M. 1951, p. 375.

[3] M.S. Strogovich, *Proverka zakonnosti i obosnovannosti sudebnykh prigovorov, op. cit.*, p. 189.

[4] M.M. Grodzinsky, *Kassatsionnoye i nadzornoye proizvodstvo v sovetskom ugolovnom protsesse*, M. 1949, p. 44 ff. and the quoted court practice.

the new material so, as the court of original jurisdiction can do it during the examination in the trial.

The same reason of the impossibility for the cassation court to adequately check the new material must prevent it from quashing the procedure.

However, he admits exceptions to the rule. He writes that "in cases of complete indisputability and certainty of the facts as established by new materials, corresponding to all the circumstances of the case—it is sometimes possible to mitigate the punishment—or to quash a case, when the groundlessness of the accusation is apparent from the materials of the case is made even more evident by the presentation of an official indisputable document produced by the defense". [1] But, if the court of cassation has no right in general to check the new material presented to it without assuming the function of a court of original jurisdiction, and allegedly may not reverse or quash a sentence or a decision or procedure on the grounds of the new material what is the sense of the provision of Article 337 ?

An answer to this question, it seems to the present writer, can be derived from the foregoing discussion and especially from the provision of Article 339 of the new RSFSR Code of Criminal Procedure, specifying the measures the cassation court has the right to take. As a result of the review the court of cassation is empowered namely : 1) to reject the complaint or the protest and leave the sentence unchanged; 2) to review the sentence and remand the case for a new preliminary investigation or retrial; 3) to reverse the sentence and quash the proceedings; 4) to change the sentence (Article 339). All four decisions inescapably require the examination of the case on its merit.

G. Z. Anashkin gives a list of questions which the cassation court has to solve in the chamber of deliberation :

a) Is the inquest, the preliminary and court investigation carried out completely and thoroughly;

b) Do the court's conclusions described in the sentence correspond to the actual circumstances of the case;

c) Did essential violation of the law of criminal procedure take place;

d) Is the penal law correctly applied;

---

[1]   Strogovich, *Proverka...*, *op. cit.*, p. 190.

e) Does the punishment set by the court correspond to the importance of the crime committed and the person of the convict;

f) Is the kind of colony, in which the convict has to serve his punishment correctly chosen;

g) Are the reasons and conditions which contributed to the comit- of the crime clarified and measures taken for their liquidation? [1]

Indeed, it is difficult to imagine, how the cassation court can take the decisions listed on 339 and anwser the questions enumerated by Anashkin without a thorough examination of the entire case including the preliminary investigation and the new material, on its merit.

Article 337 provides the duty for the cassation court, to go further and, bases its decision not only on the ground of evidence collected by the preliminary investigation and during the trial, but also by new material including testimonies not examined by the court of original jurisdiction and presented to the cassation court.

It cannot be agreed with Anashkin, that the cassation court has to examine only written declarations of new witnesses. How can the cassation court take decisions on grounds of written declaration of witnesses without hearing their testimony in court? Certainly, the cassation court can remand the case to the court of original juris- diction for the interrogation of the new witnesses. But doing so it nonetheless takes a decision of reversing the original sentence on grounds of testimonies not checked by interrogation or confrontation with other witnesses.

Although the instructions of the court of cassation are obligatory for the court of original jurisdiction if a case is remanded for a new investigation or trial, the Code of Criminal Procedure of 1961 (Article 352(1) tries to preserve the liberty of judgment of the trial court. To this effect, Paragraph 2 of Article 352 prohibits the cassation court ...'' from establishing or admitting as proven facts, which were not established or repudiated by the sentence; to decide before- hand the question as to whether the accusation is proved or not; or this or that evidence trustworthy, to give preference to one piece of evidence as compared with another one, as to whether this or that evidence should be applied to this or that criminal law or measure of punishment by the court of first instance''.

The cassation court has only to point out the defects of the reversed sentence without predetermining the guilt or innocence of the accused

---

[1] *Op. cit.*, p. 604.

and the merit of the individual evidence. It is the duty of the court of original jurisdiction to pronounce a new sentence which takes in consideration the indications of the cassation court. But since the cassation court is empowered to quash the procedure or to change the sentence (Article 339) when it comes to the necessary conclusion on grounds of the evidence presented in the first instance or in the cassation procedure, it is obvious that the cassation court remands a case for new retrial only if it cannot come itself to a final decision. The law enumerates the grounds for the remand and the change of the sentence (Article 342).

These grounds are : 1) if the preliminary or court investigation is one-sided or incomplete; 2) if the conclusions laid down in the sentence do not correspond to the factual findings of the case; 3) if the law of criminal procedure is substantially violated; 4) if the criminal law is not correctly applied; 5) if the punishment set by law does not correspond to the importance of the crime and the personality of the convict.

c) *Conclusions*

Started as "pure" cassation, Soviet cassation went through a complicated development.

Having eliminated the appellate instance, a second examination or retrial of a case on its merits, the Soviet legislator soon realized the necessity of giving the opportunity of a redress of the injustice committed in the first instance. This opportunity was given by enlarging the competence of the court of cassation, forcing it to examine the case also on its merits by including in the cassation such reasons which automatically led the court of cassation to enter into the examination also of the merits of the case and to check not only the procedure before the court of original jurisdiction but also the preliminary investigation.

As Strogovich puts it : "... sometimes the cassation instance replaced the courts of original jurisdiction. In such cases the cassation instance was *de facto* converted into a court of appeal". [1]

The Soviet cassation court was charged already from the beginning with the duty to watch over the operation of justice as meted out by the court of original jurisdiction.

---

[1] Strogovich, *Proverka...*, *op. cit.*, p. 51.

Moreover, the application of the revisional principle, which obliged the cassation court to look for cassation grounds not brought forward in the complaint for cassation, provided the necessity to re-examine the entire case with regard to possible violation of law.

Finally, the checking of legality and motivation of the sentence brought the cassation court unescapably to the review of the case on its merits.

Also, in examining additional material, the cassation courts, in reality, fulfill the function of a court of appeal in the Western sense of the word, without repeating the whole procedure carried out by court of original jurisdiction, such as interrogation of witnesses, experts, etc. But sometimes it hears new witnesses and checks new material. Not having theoretically the right to pronounce a "new" sentence or decision it can change the sentence or decision of the court of original jurisdiction, remand or quash the case which is in effect tantamount to a new sentence or decision also on the merit of the case.

It is peculiar that this goal was acheived not by implicit legislation, but indirectly. We have seen that even the old RSFSR Code of Criminal Procedure contained contradictory provisions to the effect that on one side a direct order to the cassation court to confine itself to the checking of formal violations of the law was provided, whereas on the other, grounds for cassation were established which led the cassation court inevitably to the examination of the case on its merits and thus, to the violation of the legislator's prohibition as expressed in the same code.

The end effect was that Soviet cassation developed into a kind of remedy on paper, completely different from an appeal or cassation, and revision as applied in Western Europe. As M. M. Grodzinsky puts it : "the features of Soviet cassation establish it as a completely new means of review of specific sentences and decisions for Soviet criminal procedure differing in principle from review of sentences in bourgeois criminal procedure". [1]

Certainly, it does not repeat the whole procedure carried out by the first instance, and thus, differs substantially from a court of appeal. But on the other hand it pronounces in reality a new sentence when it changes the sentence of the court of original jurisdiction or lowering the punishment (*reformatio in pejus* is forbidden), or even setting

---

[1] M.M. Grodzinsky, *Kassatsionnoye i nadzornoye proizvodstvo v sovetskom ugolovnom protsesse*, M. 1953, p. 17.

aside the sentence and quashing the case on the grounds of an unsubstantiated accusation, which is legally "tantamount to an acquittal
caused by lack of evidence", as M. A. Chel'tsov correctly remarks, [1]
acting not as a cassation court, but as a court of appeal.

In their striving "to tear down the old house in order to build a
new one" in Russia, extended to the administration of justice, the
new regime abolished the appeal, but retained the cassation principle.
When it became evident, however, that the pure cassation was not
a sufficient remedy against unjust sentences it began to widen the
cassation power of the second instance, extending it to the entire
procedure, including the preliminary investigation under the name
of "revision", to the re-examination of the case not only with regard
to formal violation but also on its merit. The final result is a peculiar
institution, not a court of appeal and not a pure cassation court, but
a mixture of both.

Fulfilling the functions of a court of appeal but not having the
purposefulness of repeating the entire procedure of the essential part
of it carried out by the initial court, the Soviet cassation court does
not provide the guarantees for a just sentence inherent in the principle
of appeal in the Western sense.

An additional guarantee, and an efficient one, is, however, provided
by the Soviet legislator, in the possibility of reviewing court sentences,
decisions and resolutions already in force.

B. The Review of Sentences,
Decisions and Rulings Already in Force

a) *Historical Development*

A criminal or civil *res judicata* can be reviewed on protest of an
official empowered to this effect in the way of judicial supervision.

This kind of remedy is a peculiarity of Soviet criminal and civil
procedure deserving a detailed discussion.

Although created for the protection of parties involved in the case,
these parties are not empowered by law to start the review prodecure
in the way of supervision. However, they may petition one of the
officials possessing this right to do so, initiating the procedure *de
facto*. In this way the persons involved in the case have the opportunity

---

[1]   M.A. Chel'tsov, *Sovetskiy ugolovnyy protsess*, M. 1951, p. 376.

to revive a case already finally decided upon. Their action is not the exercise of a remedial right, but only a petition to the official empowered to start the supervision procedure and it is up to him to decide whether he will grant or reject the demand.

It must be noted that the creation of this opportunity was thought as a potential remedy in cases when cassation, the only legal remedy, was excluded. The review in the way of supervision was, namely, introduced into Soviet criminal procedure in the Statute on Revolutionary Tribunals of November 20, 1919. [1]

The next Statute on Revolutionary Tribunals of March 18, 1920 [2] permitted the appeal for cassation of the sentence and retained the review in the way of supervision.

The Statute on People's Courts of October 21, 1920 contained the reveiw in the way of supervision of sentences already in force. [3]

The Law of March 10, 1921 [4] introducing the Statute on the Higher Judicial Control empowered the People's Commissariat of Justice to review sentences and decisions already in force, thus entrusting an administrative agency with the review of court sentences.

This order was not retained in the RSFSR Code of Criminal Procedure of 1923, which returned the review of sentences already in force to judicial institutions and officials of the administration of justice and set the rule that a sentence in force may be reviewed on the same grounds as a sentence under cassation. This provision is applied up to the present time. [5]

The RSFSR Code of Criminal Procedure of 1923 centralized the review of the sentences in force : only the RSFSR Supreme Court was empowered to make such a review. From 1920 to 1938 the list of officials empowered to logde a protest for review in the way of supervision and of judicial institutions entitled for such a review fluctuated greatly.

The Law on Court Structure of the USSR, the Union and Autonomous Republics of August 16, 1938, [6] reduced the number of officials entitled to lodge a protest in criminal and civil cases and centralized the supervision procedure. The right to bring a protest was granted by the Law to the USSR Prosecutor or the Prosecutor of a Union

---

[1] *Sob. uz.*, 1919, Item 40.

[2] *Sob. uz.*, 1920, Item 407.

[3] *Sob. uz.*, 1920, Item 621.

[4] *Sob. uz.*, 1921, Item 97.

[5] Article 379 of the RSFSR Code of Criminal Procedure of 1961.

[6] *V.V.S.*, *SSSR*, 1938, No. 11.

Republic, the Chairman of the USSR Supreme Court, and the Chairman of the Supreme Court of a Union Republic. Correspondingly, only the following judicial institutions could reverse or change a final sentence : The USSR Supreme Court and the Supreme Court of a Union Republic (Article 17).

Again an enlargement of the number of officials and judicial echelons involved in the supervision procedure took place with regard to military tribunals during the war, since sentences of these tribunals could not be appealed for cassation, or protested : protests in the supervision procedure could be lodged also by military prosecutors of fronts and districts and chairmen of front and district military tribunals. The protests were examined by these tribunals.

A further increase in the number of officials and judicial echelons participating in the supervision procedure in the way of decentralization was brought by the Ukase of the Presidium of the USSR Supreme Soviet on "The Formation of Presidiums of the Supreme Courts of the Union and Autonomous Republics of August 14, 1954 : [1] presidiums of the supreme courts of the autonomous republics, the regional and territorial courts and courts of the autonomous regions were empowered to review, in the way of supervision, sentences of people's courts and cassation decisions already in force. The same right was awarded to the military tribunals of fronts and fleets on protests of military prosecutors of fronts and fleets and chairmen of military tribunals of fronts and fleets.

The Statute on Prosecution Supervision in the USSR of May 24, 1955 [2] and the Statutes of the USSR Supreme Court of February 12, 1957 [3] passed on the question as to which officials have the right to lodge protests in the way of supervision as well as the USSR courts entitled to carry out the proceeding.

The latest regulations with regard to the union republics are contained in the codes of criminal and civil procedure of the individual republics.

For instance, Article 371 of the RSFSR Code of Criminal Procedure of 1961 enumerates the officials empowered to lodge protests. These are : 1) the USSR Prosecutor General against sentences and decisions of any RSFSR court; 2) the Chairman of the USSR Supreme Court

---

[1] *V.V.S.*, *SSSR*, 1954, No. ....

[2] *Ibid.*, 1955, No. 9.

[3] *Ibid.*, 1957, No. 4.

against decisions of the Presidium and sentences and resolutions of the Criminal Judicial College of the RSFSR Supreme Court acting as court of original jurisdiction; 3) the Deputies of the USSR Prosecutor General against sentences and decisions of any RSFSR court with the exception of the Presidium of the RSFSR Supreme Court; 4) the Deputies of the Chairmen of the USSR Supreme Court against sentences and resolutions of the Criminal Judicial College of the RSFSR Supreme Court acting as a court of original jurisdiction; 5) the RSFSR Prosecutor, the Chairman of the RSFSR Supreme Court and their Deputies against sentences and resolutions of any RSFSR court with the exception of the Presidium of the RSFSR Supreme Court; 6) the chairman and the prosecutor of an SSR supreme court as well as of territorial, regional, city, autonomous regions and national district courts; the prosecutor of an autonomous republic, territorial, regional and national district—respectively—against sentences and rulings of a district (city) people's court and the ruling of a judicial college of an autonomous supreme court, territorial, regional or city court, courts of an autonomous region and of a national district court which examined the cases in cassation procedure. Protests against sentences of the military tribunals are regulated by Articles 20 and 21 of the Statute on Military Tribunals. [1]

The official who lodged the protest is entitled to recall it. A protest brought by a prosecutor can be recalled by a prosecutor in a higher position. In both cases the recalling can take place not later than before the court session assigned to decide on the protest.

The officials entitled to the protest have, as a rule, also the right to suspend the execution of the protested court action until the decision on the protest is taken by the competent court. However, deputies of the union-republic prosecutors, deputies of chairmen of union-republic supreme courts, of territorial and regional prosecutors and the chairmen of territorial and regional courts, have not this right.

But in civil procedure, all the officials, without exception, any

---

[1] According to these provisions, the USSR General Prosecutor, the Chairman of the USSR Supreme Court and their Deputies, the Chairman of the Military College of the USSR Supreme Court and the Chief Military Prosecutor have the right to protest in the way of judicial supervision, sentences and rulings of any Military Tribunal. Other officials are empowered to protest sentences and rulings of individual military tribunals, according to their competence.

empowered to the protest in the way of judicial supervision, have the right to suspend the execution of the judicial action under protest.

Article 374 of the Code lists the judicial institutions competent for the examination of the protests :

The presidium of the supreme court of an autonomous republic, of territorial, regional, city, autonomous region and national district courts, examines protests against cassation resolutions of these courts and against sentences already in force of district (city) people's courts.

The Criminal Judicial College of the RSFSR Supreme Court examines protests against regulations of the presidiums of autonomous republic supreme courts, territorial, regional, city, autonomous regions and national district courts if they were not reviewed in cassation by the RSFSR Supreme Court.

The Presidium of the RSFSR Supreme Court examines protests against sentences resolutions and decisions of the Criminal Judicial College of the RSFSR Surpeme Court.

With regard to the grounds for review of a sentence or decision already in force, the Code simply refers to Article 342 of the Code which, as we have seen above, enumerates the grounds for cassation. Thus, the grounds for the review of sentences, decisions and rulings not yet in force and already in force are identical.

The Code contains also a provision on rights in the interest of a convicted person. A protest in the way of supervision against too mild a sentence, the quashing of the case or acquittal may be lodged not later than one year after the sentence or the decision went into force (Article 373). There is no provision for other cases : They may be reviewed any time after they gain force on protest in the way of supervision.

The same is true for sentences and resolutions already reviewed in this procedure, by a lower instance against the decision of such a court. A protest may be brought to the attention of a higher court up to the USSR Supreme Court at any time, but the decision of the Presidium of the USSR Supreme Court taken on protest against the decision of the Criminal Judicial College of the USSR Supreme Court may not be further protested.

As a result of its activity the court examining a case referred to it on protest in the way of supervision, may take the following measures : 1) reject the protest; 2) reverse the sentence and abrogate all the resolutions and decisions taken by the court and to quash the case or to refer it to a new investigation or judicial examination; to set aside the resolution of the cassation instance, as well as the subsequent decisions and resolutions, if they were taken and to remand the case for a new examination in the way of cassation; 3) annulate decisions and resolutions passed in the way of judicial supervision and leave without change, or change the sentence and the resolution taken by the cassation instance; 4) introduce changes into the sentence, decision or resolution of the court.

Rules governing the activity of the court of cassation are strictly applied also in the supervision procedure. Thus, when a protest is examined in the supervision procedure, the court is not bound by the grounds brought forward in the protest. The court has to check all the procedure from the beginning to the end also on its merits. If several persons are sentenced and the protest is logded with regard to one or some of the convicted persons, the court is obliged to check the case with respect to other persons convicted.

Also, the rule of *"reformatio in pejus"* is applied in the supervision procedure : the supervision court may mitigate the punishment or apply to the convicted person a punishment for a lesser crime, but has not the right to increase the punishment or make use of a punishment provided for a more serious offense.

If, in the case on hand, several persons have been convicted or acquitted, the supervision court has no right to reverse the sentence or decision in respect to those convicted or acquitted not covered by the protest if the reversal of the sentence or decision would worsen their position.

When the supervision court decides that the acquittal of the accused or the quashing of the case has merit or the punishment set is too lenient with regard to the committed crime, it has the right, under observance of the provisions of Article 373 [1] to reverse the sentence, resolution or decision, and to remand the case for retrial to the court of orignial jurisdiction or the court of cassation respectively. It has also the right to change the sentence with regard to the punatative measure reducing it or applying another provision of the Criminal Code providing a milder punishment. Remanding the case to the court of original jurisdiction, the supervision court has to indicate the stage of procedure from which a re-investigation or re-examination of the case has to be started.

---

[1] One year of prescription in case of acquittal or quashing.

The directives of the supervision court, like those of the cassation court, are binding for any new investigation or re-examination by the court of original jurisdiction.

But, much as in the case of a cassation court, the supervision court in examining a case, has no right to establish or admit as proven, facts which have not been established or rejected in the sentence, as well as to decide beforehand questions about the conclusiveness or failure of the accusation, about the truthfulness or doubt of this or that evidence and about the advantage of one piece of evidence as compared to another.

In the same way, the supervision court, in reviewing a cassation decision, is prohibited from deciding beforehand about the conclusions which may be made by the court of cassation as a result of the re-examination of the case (Article 380).

A new sentence or decision, pronounced after the retrial or re-examination of a case in the way of supervision, is subjected to a new protest in the way of supervison, which may be again carried through all the instances of the supervision prodecure. Theoretically, the third and fourth, and so on, retrial or re-examination may be again protested if officials and grounds can be found for lodging protests.

It must be noted that a repeated protest against a reconfirmed sentence or decision may be filed on grounds independent of those which brought the reversal of the first sentence or decision (Article 383).

According to V. I. Baskov "Practice makes it evident, that the reversion of sentences already in force, the introduction of changes into them, is so widely applied in the practice of court organs, that it became a usual thing...". [1]

He thinks that the exaggerated use of the review in the way of supervision leads to the formation of a kind of "third instance". In his opinion this sort of review can be employed only in exceptional cases and not almost as a rule. He is shocked by the fact that, for instance, in 1964, the Presidium of the USSR Supreme Court quashed, in the way of supervision, the double quantity of cases than was done by cassation courts, and more than one-third of sentences, decisions and resolutions are reversed or changed one year after they were pronounced.

---

[1] V.I. Baskov, "On the Supervision Review Order of Criminal Cases", *S.G.P.*, 1965, No. 10, p. 45.

Baskov sees in the transformation of the special review of sentences already in force into an usual procedure, a great danger because "it undermines the trust in the stability of a sentence".

It is evident that the figures quoted by Baskov speak against his argumentation. The fact that a double number of cases have been quashed by the Presidium of the USSR Supreme Court in the way of supervision as compared with those closed by the cassation instances, can only convincingly show the efficiency of the supervision procedure : the Supreme Court eliminated the double quantity of unjust sentences as compared with the cassation courts. Undermined by the procedure is the stability of unjust sentences which is a blessing and not a danger.

b) *Appraisal*

The review of sentences, resolutions and decisions already in force by way of supervision is a procedure *sui generis*, unknown to Western countries. If the Soviet cassation has some feature which makes it different from the cassation in other countries, the review by way of supervision is a procedure unique in the history of criminal and civil procedures of all times.

Certainly, the revival of a case in which the sentence is already in force, on the grounds of new circumstances remained hidden from courts during the procedure, is knwon to all procedural codes in the world, including the Soviet procedural codes. But this procedure has nothing to do with the review of sentences already in force by way of supervision.

The latter differs greatly also from the cassation. Whereas cassation is a remedy against a sentence not yet in force, open to various persons involved in the case, the review by the way of supervision is a special procedure started and carried out by officials and judicial institutions designed for this purpose by law.

"The essence and the scope of Soviet socialist justice emphatically excludes such a situation, that a court sentence, illegal and incorrect in its essence, should retain its validity only because it is already in force. Certainly, a sentence in force has the power of a law for the individual case. But this power should be attributed only to correct, legal and well-founded sentences. If, however, a mistake occurred when the sentence was pronounced—this mistake must be corrected and a faulty sentence may not remain valid only because the mistake was not corrected at the proper time", writes Strogovich! [1]

It is evident that the review of sentences already in force in the way of supervision is an additional, very efficient guarantee for the quality of a court sentence, decision or ruling in a criminal procedure where a case cannot be reviewed on its merits by a higher court in the way of appeal.

Although it creates a certain instability in the administration of justice since a sentence or decision theoretically never reaches finality if not reviewed by a whole complex of courts and instances, still it must be valued as a positive feature of Soviet administration of justice.

How important the procedure is may be illustrated by the following examples.

The Zhitomir Regional Court sentenced D., Chief Engineer of a mine administration, to eight years in jail for abuses committed in office by a sentence already in force.

However, his counsel, Gorodinsky, was firmly persuaded of his innocence. Counsel had already during the preliminary investigation petitioned, unsuccessfully, the investigating magistrate to quash the procedure.

The cassation court rejected the complaint in cassation as a whole, but acquitted the accused on two counts reducing the punishment to three years of confinement.

All the instances empowered to lodge a protest against the sentence already in force rejected Gorodinsky's demands, with the exception of the USSR Prosecution Body which prescribed to the Prosecutor of the Ukrainian Republic to lodge a protest against the sentence with the Plenum of the Ukrainian Supreme Court which, in its turn, lowered the punishment and released D. from arrest.

However, Gorodinsky striving for a complete acquittal of his client, again petitioned the USSR Prosecution Body to lodge a protest against the decision of the Ukrainian Supreme Court. This time to no avail.

But Counsel continued his efforts. He went to Moscow and persuaded the USSR Supreme Court to request the files of the case.

The Chairman of the USSR Supreme Court lodged a protest with the Plenum of the USSR Supreme Court which threw out the sentence

---

[1] M.S. Strogovich, *Proverka zakonnosti* ..., op. cit., p. 225.

and quashed the criminal procedure against D. rejecting also the civil claim at the same time. [1]

Thus, if not the supervision procedure and the possibility of reviewing sentences already in force, D. would have served an unjust sentence and remained with a soiled reputation and criminal records the rest of his life.

Here is another example :

Nyeladze and Moiseyev were convicted by the People's Court for violating the law of June 4, 1947 "On the Strenthening of the Protection of Citizens' Property". In his motion for cassation, defense counsel demanded the requalification of the crime according to another article of the same law providing a milder punishment. The petition was rejected by the cassation court.

Then, defense counsel lodged complaints in the way of supervision consecutively with the Chairman of the Supreme Court of the Autonomous Republic, with the Chairman of the RSFSR Supreme Court, with the Prosecutor of the autonomous republic, with the Prosecutor of the RSFSR (twice), and with the General Prosecutor of the USSR. The case was taken up four times for review by the competent instances, but the complaint rejected by all. After the second complaint to the procesutor of the USSR, the case was again taken up for review and the General Prosecutor of the USSR lodged a protest with the Presidium of the Supreme Court of the Autonomous Republic which changed the sentence according to the complaint of the defense counsel. [2]

It must be emphasized that the supervision procedure provided a legal ground to the review of a great number of cases after Stalin's death. Camp inmates were rehabilitated and returned to normal life. If for many rehabilitation came only posthumously, the establishment of their innocence had an enormous moral value and at the same time, was a strong condemnation of the administration of justice under Stalin.

---

[1] *Izvestia*, September 15, 1967.

[2] Quoted by A. Levin, V.A. Ognev, V.A. Rossel's, in *Zashchitnik v sovetskom protsesse*, M. 1960, pp. 21-22.

C. THE PRIVATE RULING [1]

a) *History and Scope*

The "private ruling" as described in Article 321 of the new Code of Criminal Procedure, is also a peculiar provision of Soviet legislation with no comparison in the legislation of Western countries.

In the text of the old Code of Criminal Procedure, private rulings were not mentioned literally. But Article 439 provided that the Cassation College "has the right" in passing the cassation resolution to include into it instructions concerning law violations committed by the previous instance. These instructions were mandatory for the given court or tribunal, independently as to whether the sentence under cassation was upheld or not.

This prompted the commentators of the old Code of Criminal Procedure, M. Strogovich and D. Karpinsky, to qualify this right for instructions as "private ruling" of the Cassation College. [2]

The Plenum of the USSR Supreme Court, on its side drew the attention of the courts to the necessity of clarifying the cases and conditions which contributed to the commission of the crime and the raising of questions before the corresponding organizations, and as well as the taking of measures for the elimination of these causes and conditions, by issuing private rulings.

Thus, in the decision of June 7, 1934 "On the Necessity for Strictest Observation of Criminal Procedure Norms by Courts" it was said that "During the examination of every case it is necessary to establish not only the responsibility of these or those persons, but also to expose the economical and organizational defects and shortcomings which created a favorable situation for the commission of the crime. It is necessary to pass particular rulings concerning these defects and

---

[1] Berman and Spindler translate *chastnoye opredeleniye* as "special ruling". It seems to the present author, there is no ground to change the Russian word "private" into special. First of all, because it is against the will of the Soviet legislation who could have chosen the Russian word *spetcial'nyy* or *osobennyy*—if he wanted to qualify the ruling as a special one. Secondly, the wording of paragraphs 3 and 4 of Article 321 which establishes "the right" of the court, not its duty, to issue a private ruling expresses the desire of the legislator to make the issuing of a private ruling conform to the free will of the court, or its "private affair". "Private"—also because this right is separated from the official business of the court in the trial.

[2] See *Ugolovno-protsessual'nyy kodeks RSFSR*, M. 1928, p. 419.

shortcomings and to direct them to corresponding Party and Soviet organs and to check periodically the results of such a signalization". [1]

In another ruling of the Plenum of the USSR Supreme Court of December 19, 1959 "On the Activity of Court Organs in connection with the Heightening of the Role of Social Organizations in the Fighting of Crimes", the Supreme Court recommended to the lower courts to carry out systematically the task of clarification of the causes and conditions contributing to the commission of crimes and to raise the question of the elimination of the exposed defects, on the ground of the available material". [2]

The recommendation of the USSR Supreme Court was used by the Soviet legislator and incorporated into the provisions of Articles 341 and 355 of the new Code of Criminal Procedure.

Indeed, the new Code of Criminal Procedure created a private ruling of the court, *expressis verbis* and provided it with two scopes : a critical and a preventive one.

The private ruling has namely to draw the attention of the leaders of institutions, enterprises and organizations, and other officials to the causes, and conditions which contributed to the preparation of the crime. The court has to denounce the behavior of individual members of public organizations and collectives, the violation of social duties by them. Also officials can be criticized in the private ruling for the violations of law occurring during the preliminary investigation or the trial.

Whereas Article 321 has in view the court of initial jurisdiction, Article 355 confers to the cassation court the right to draw the attention of corresponding officials to the violations of law occurring during the inquest, preliminary investigation or the examination of the case by the court, and also to issue other private rulings, provided by Article 321 of the Code.

The private ruling passed by the cassation court according to Article 439 of the old Code of Criminal Procedure was obligatory only to the court of lower instance.

The private rulings of Article 321 and 355 of the new Code are,

---

[1] *Sbornik deystvuyushchich postonovleniy Plenuma Verkhovnogo Suda, SSSR, 1924-1951*, M. 1952, p. 81.

[2] *Ibid., 1958-1960*, M. 1961, p. 9; *Nauchno-practicheskiy kommentariy k UPK RSFSR*, M. 1963, p. 579.

however, mandatory also to the enterprises, institutions, organizations and officials to whom they are addressed. The addressees have to report to the court within a month about the measures taken to eliminate the defects or violations emphasized in the private ruling. The court is obliged to check the compliance with its private ruling. The private ruling, although not an integral part of the sentence and emitted parallel to the trial and in connection with it, can be appealed in cassation togehter with or separate from the sentence.

Certainly, the clarification of causes and circumstances, which contributed to the commission of the crime, is an integral part of criminal procedure in every country. Hence Article 21 of the new Code of Criminal Procedure provides that during the inquest, preliminary investigation and the trial, of a criminal case, the organs of inquest, the investigating magistrate, the prosecutor and the court have to expose the causes and conditions which contributed to the commission of the crime and take measures for their elimination.

But only Soviet court is charged and empowered by the legislation to react concretely by private rulings not only by the exposure of causes and conditions which generated or contributed to the perpetration of the crime, but also by checking the elimination and redress of these causes and conditions, as well as of every violation of law by all officials involved in the criminal procedure in the case.

The Soviet legislator, provided the court with a powerful preventive weapon against crime. [1]

The court also issues a private ruling when it wants to bring to the attention of institutions, agencies or enterprises deficiencies in their work made evident during the trial. Thus, for instance, in a trial of some employees of the Moscow Specialized Office for Trade in Potatoes, Fruits and Wild Fruits the court issued a private ruling concerning the unsatisfactory storage method of vegetables at the "Mostorg" [2]. This kind of private ruling can play a salutary role attracting the attention of the management at individual enterprises and organizations to defects of their work.

b) *Private Ruling, the Legal Profession and Individual Persons*

Unfortunately, the courts also use the private ruling in order to criticize the professional activity of the counsel during the trial.

---

[1] For examples of this salutary court activity, see V. Kulikov, "The Private Ruling", *Izvestia,* July 16, 1966.

[2] *Moskovskaya pravda,* September 20, 1964, p. 3.

As basis for the private ruling against the advocate, the provision of Article 263 of the new RSFSR Code of Criminal Procedure is applied.

Paragraph 2 of Article 263 reads : "In case the prosecutor or defense counsel do not submit to the order of the presiding judge, the latter issues a warning. If the insubordination with respect to the order of the presiding judge is continued, the examination of the case may be adjourned if it seems impossible to replace the culprit [offending counsel] with another person without detriment to the case. At the same time, the court informs the superior of the prosecutor, the presidium of the college of advocates or the public organization (in the case of a public prosecutor or counsel) respectively of the incident".

Although the provisions deals with disobedience to the orders of the presiding judge, private rulings were and are used by courts in order to express their dissatisfaction with the professional behavior of counsel in the trial.

In such cases the private ruling is directed to the college to which the advocate belongs and the college of advocates has to inform the court of measures taken in consequence of the private ruling.

In the old Code of Criminal Procedure, it was said (Article 260) that the courts notify the presidium of the college of defenders of rights about the behavior of the prosecutor or counsel "for the purpose of the initiation of disciplinary proceedings". However, also Article 260 of the old Code of Criminal Procedure dealt only with the refusal of counsel to submit to the order of the presiding judge.

Private rulings are passed by courts also when the court is of the opinion that the counsel by his motion, violates the Code of Criminal Procedure. So the Supreme Court of the Latvian SSR issued a private ruling on January 24, 1958 bringing to the knowledge of the Presidium of the College of Advocates of the Latvian SSR, that the advocate B. violated Article 108 of the Code of Criminal Procedure in presenting to the court of original jurisdiction 4 photographs of the place of the crime of which his client was accused and asked for the filing of the photographs as exhibits. The court was of the opinion that counsel assumed functions not pertaining to his position but to the competence of the investigating magistrate.

The Presidium of the USSR Supreme Court threw out the private ruling. [1]

The author of a *Sov. yust.* [2] editorial thinks that underestimation

---

[1] *Byulleten' Verkhovnogo Suda SSSR*, 1958, No. 5, p. 34.

[2] *Sov. yust.*, 1957, No. 7, p. 4.

of the advocate's role in the trial, and sometimes fear of criticism by the lawyer of mistakes made by the court or during the preliminary investigation, are the cause for the issuance by courts of unfounded private rulings regarding advocates.

Other examples are brought forward in the editorial. Thus in the People's Court of the Pereyaslav District, Yaroslav Region, the People's Judge, Loginov, issued a private ruling with regard to the advocate of the Moscow City College, X. in which he indicated that in consequence of her not appearing in court the timetable for the hearing of the case was upset. However, it was established that the advocate X. did not get the assignment to handle the case and, thus, was not obliged to appear in court. A completely unfounded private ruling was issued by the court in which the advocate X. was characterized in a completely inadmissible, slighting way.

The advocate S. of the Rostov Colllege, while pleading before the People's Court in the Drozhzhin case, asked for the acquittal of the accused because of the lack of a *corpus delicti*. After the conviction of Drozhzhin, the advocate filed a complaint in cassation, which he supported in the Kamensky Regional Court, asking for the quashing of the case. The court decided accordingly, but instead of pointing out to the People's Court the Prosecutor's violations of the law committed by him, it issued a private ruling with regard to S. who allegedly did not indicate all the mistakes committed by the court of original jurisdiction. [1]

Let us give other examples.

L. and X. were accused of having inflicted serious bodily injuries to the juvenile K. The Counsels, P. and R. denied that the injures inflicted by the accused were serious and pleaded for the qualification of the action according to another Article of the Criminal Code providing a lesser punishment. They argued also that there was no evidence that the accused inflicted the injuries to K.; that K. could have injured himself by falling during his attempts to escape, and asked for an additional examination of K. by an expert.

The People's Court rejected the arguments of the counsels, sentenced the accused according to the provisions for the infliction of serious injuries, and issued at the same time a private ruling informing the Presidium of the Moscow City College of Advocates about the "impermissible" position taken by the two counsels consisting in the

---

[1] *Ibid.*, pp. 6-7.

assertion that the victim could have brought to himself serious injuries by falling during the escape". "This version", wrote the court, "is not only not confirmed by the material of the case but also contradicts the findings of the forensic medical experts".

The Manager of the Legal Consultation Office charged with the investigation of the case by the College Presidium came to the folowing conclusion :

The court, rejecting the viewpoint taken by the counsel cannot give to its disenting opinion the form of a private ruling asking for the punishment of the counsel. According to the investigator, both lawyers not only had the right but also the duty to raise the question of the lack of evidence of the infliction of serious injuries by their clients. The People's Court had no ground for the issuing of a private ruling about the legal position taken by the counsels.

"The right of the defense of free expression of its opinion on the case is doubtless and cannot be violated by the court itself", the investigator concluded.

The Presidium of the College, having checked the material of the investigation, agreed with the investigator and decided : 1) No disciplinary procedure should be conducted against the advocates P. and R. since there is no ground for such a procedure; 2) to ask the Chairman of the Moscow City People's Court to protest against the private ruling of the Proletarian District People's Court being erroneous in principle, and not based on the material of the case.

The private ruling was set aside by the Judicial College on criminal cases of the Moscow City Court in the way of cassation as violating Article 321 of the RSFSR Code of Criminal Procedure. [1]

The case reflects the biased attitude of court toward the defense in some cases, and had also an aftermath. The behavior of the defense in court in the case reported in the private ruling mentioned above was discussed by the Chairman of the Moscow City Court, N. Osetrov, in a newspaper article. [2]

He sharply criticized the defense for having asked for another forensic expert, for the demand to implement the preliminary investigation, the tough examination of witnesses for the accusation, and so on, all actions which are completely legal in a trial. But for Osetrov

---

[1] Cited by V.D. Gol'diner, "On the Ethics in the Advocate's Activity", *op. cit.*, p. 98.

[2] "The Right of Defense", *Moskovskaya Pravda*, May 8, 1964.

the behavior of the defense tended to put the whole case, "upside down", to screen the accused at any costs, to violate the duty of the defense counsel consisting in the help in finding the truth.

The old—as the legal profession itself—accusation of venality was also restored to life by Osetrov, on this occasion.

He thinks the advocate is brought to the necessity of such a behavior by the fact that he is "hired" to defend, that he must justify the expenses of his client.

And it is not in vain, asserted Osetrov, that the proper expression is "to hire" an advocate. "The sense and the ring of this expression, which has its roots in the old bourgeois society, where the labor of a man was hired and paid according to the resources of the employer, ... is renewed and the advocate is still lying in order to get an acquittal ...".

And his conclusion is that it is time to replace the existing system of remuneration of the legal profession by fixed wages.

Osetrov's opinion as of a high judicial official—he is the Chairman of the Moscow City Court,—is characteristic of the wrong and abusive viewpoint on the legal profession discussed above which still has supporters even in high judicial spheres.

It is peculiar, that Gol'diner, in relating the story about the private ruling, does not mention Osetrov's article.

It found, however, a weak echo in an article by Chetunova. [1] But she only very discretely—evidently with regard to Osetrov's high authority—reproaches him for not having substantiated for the readers, in what consisted the arguments of the defense so sharply criticized by Osetrov. But there is no word about the opinion held by him on the legal profession and the scope in general which are, of course, more important than the case itself.

Certainly, with regard to the case, an answer was given to Osetrov by the Criminal College of the Moscow City Court—of which he is the Chairman—by remanding the case for an additional preliminary investigation, what just was demanded by the defense, and so strongly condemned by Osetrov and the private ruling, and the private ruling itself was set aside.

But the legal profession and its scope remained undefended against Osetrov' accusations in the Soviet literature.

---

[1] N. Chetunova, "Slander", *Literaturnaya gazeta*, June 20, 1964.

Also, Shubin, Deputy Chairman of the RSFSR Supreme Court, pointed out the abuse by courts of private rulings, with regard to advocates. He emphasizes that some judges do not understand yet the problems which are assigned by law to the councils. "There are few, but still cases when the court claims that the counsel does not take the right position in the trial, demands the reclassification of criminal action, the lowering of the punitive sentences, or an acquittal". He illustrates this assertion by two examples :

The Novosibirsk Regional Court adopted a private ruling in the case of Klepov and Zhidkov, only because the counsels asked the court to apply Article 43 of the RSFSR Criminal Code. [1] This private ruling was thrown out by the RSFSR Supreme Court.

In another case, the judicial college of the Chita Regional Court passed a private ruling accusing the counsel B. of having inscrupulously studied the case and groundlessly moved for a reclassification of the incriminated action. It was said in the ruling : The court decided "to bring to the attention of the Chita Regional College of Advocates the unscrupulous attitudes of the counsel B. toward the formulation of the cassation complaint and his pleading before the College of Criminal Affairs of the Regional Court, in order that corresponding measures should be taken".

Also this private ruling was dismissed by the RSFSR Court. Shubin found that the counsel B. was right when he wrote in his explanation that the private ruling was the result of the failure of the judges to understand the role of the counsel in the criminal procedure. [2]

This attitude has been repeatedly criticized by the USSR Supreme Court. The Plenum of the USSR Supreme Court, in its decision of March 1967, reminded the courts of the necessity to strictly abide by the norm which guarantees equal rights of the participants of the trial including the prosecutor and the defense counsel.

The Supreme Court emphasized the inadmissibility of a biased action toward them or to the evidence and pleas presented by them.

In its decision of October 14, 1964, "On the Practice of Private Ruling Passing by Court, in Criminal Cases", [3] the Plenum of the

---

[1] Article 43 of the RSFSR Criminal Code empowers the Court to set a punishment milder than the lowest limit prescribed by the Code, taking into consideration the exceptional circumstances of the case and the personality of the accused.

[2] V. Shubin, "To Know and Respect Law", *Sov. yust.*, 1967, No. 7, p. 6.

[3] *Sov. yust.*, 1965, No. 7, p. 8-10 passim.

USSR Supreme Court confirmed the right of the courts of issuing private rulings with the purpose to draw the attention of corresponding officials to law violations, occuring during the inquest or preliminary investigation, basing this right on Article 321 of the RSFSR Code of Criminal Procedure.

The Plenum acknowledged also the right to the cassation court to point to violations of law manifested by the court of original jurisdiction during the trial (Article 355 of the same Code).

It was stressed, however, in the same Decision, that the courts adopt unfounded private rulings in a number of cases concerning the alleged wrong behavior of individual citizens, not taking into consideration the consequences of such private rulings.

For instances, Ch. was convicted of raping E. In a private ruling the court censured the "reprehensible behavior" of E., who passed the night in Ch.'s room. However, as it was proved by evidence, E. could not leave because she was beaten up by Ch. Naturally, E. who is a member of the Komsomal, was damaged in her reputation by the private ruling, which was thrown out in the way of supervision. [1]

Thus, the private ruling is a powerful weapon in the hands of the court. It may have a salutary effect when it is directed to the prevention of offences by drawing the attention of agencies, enterprises, institutions and organizations on the circumstances which caused or facilitated the crime.

But it has a negative characteristic censoring the professional activity of the advocate when no valid proof for such a measure exists. By doing so the court interferes with the activity of the defense in matters beyond its jurisdiction.

---

[1] Article 331[2] of the RSFSR Criminal Procedure excludes a complaint against the ruling in such cases; V. Baskov, *op. cit.*, p. 10.

CHAPTER TWENTY-ONE

REVOLUTIONARY AND SOCIALIST LEGALITY

A. Historical Development

One would assume that legality—zakonnost'—in the proper sense of this word should mean only the strict observance of law. However, the word "*zakonnost*" is used in two senses : 1) as compliance with existing laws, and 2) as the legislation in force in a given epoch.

Furthermore, Traynin was right when he asserted that "*laws* (T.I.) may be liberal and conservative, useful or harmful, but there is no bad or good legality, rightist or leftist, revolutionary or reactionary. Hence, 'revolutionary' legality is juridically unthinkable, as is a 'red capital' economically". [1]

Still, Soviet political leaders and writers distinguish between bourgeois legality and socialist legality, and assert that legality has different aspects in various periods of time. So Vyshinsky thought that "bourgeois legality" is a force which secured the created order after the victory of the bourgeoisie, a force of greatest stagnation and conservation ; whereas revolutionary legality "is a creative force promoting social development, helping toilers in their advance forward—to the construction of a classless socialist society". [2]

For instance, Shlyapochnikov is of the opinion that the content of revolutionary legality changed in connection with conditions and forms of the class struggle at various stages of the proletarian dictatorship". [3]

Stalin differentiated between the legality of the first period of the NEP and the legality of a later period.

In the examples given above, "bourgeois", "revolutionary" and "socialist" legality are understood to comprise the whole complex of laws of a given historical period, and not legality as the compliance with law in force.

---

[1]   A. Traynin, "On Revolutionary Legality", *Pravo i zhizn'*, June 1922, p. 6.

[2]   A. Ye. Vyshinsky, "Revolutionary Legality in the Present Period of Socialist Construction", *Sov. yust.*, 1932, No. 16, p. 4.

[3]   A.S. Shlyapochnikov, "For the Strengthening of Soviet Legality", *Sovetskoye gosudarstvo*, 1934, No. 4, p. 46.

On the other hand, Strogovich gives a definition of socialist legality as strict and unflinching observance and fulfillment of Soviet laws by all organs of the socialist state, public organizations, offices and all citizens, [1] under all regimes and all time. In the same way, as Lenin excluded the existence of a "Kaluga" or—"Ryazan" legality, there cannot be a special revolutionary socialist or capitalist legality.

Rudenko is of the opinion that legality is not identic to law. [2] Certainly, it supposes the existence of laws and is itself based on law. But the notion of legality is wider than that of law. One can have the best laws but if the citizens and the officials do not fulfill them, there will be no legality in the country.

a) *No Legality in the Court Work of the First Period of Soviet Rule*

It is evident that the "revolutionary courts" of the time before the publishing of the Decrees on Courts decided in analogous cases differently, applied various punishments and in general reacted to offenses according to the personal feelings of its members and under the influence of the people in the court hall or at the village assembly.

Their decisions lacked the main feature of a court decision—legality.

These "courts" could and did not observe any law, either tsarist which they did not know, and the use of which was soon prohibited anyhow, or Soviet which did not exist at that time, since the "October Decrees" of the new government had only a general character and did not cover the field of individual cases coming under the judgment of a court.

Consequently, no legality was observed by these courts, which were no courts in the proper sense of the word, and their decisions were self-inspired individual and arbitrary pronunciations, deprived of any legality.

Still, Soviet writers see a constructive value in the activity of the revolutionary "courts".

Thus, T. Mal'kovich even reproaches Soviet legal writers for not paying enough attention to these courts.

Having described the activity of various revolutionary courts

---

[1] M.S. Strogovich, "Socialist Legality", *Entsiklopedishiskiy slovar' pravovykh nauk*, M. 1965, p. 431.

[2] R.A. Rudenko, "On the Problems of the Further Strengthening of Socialist Legality in the Light of the Sessions of the XXIst Congress of the USSR", *Sovetskaya obshchestvennost' na strazhe sotsialisticheskoy zakonnosti*, M. 1960, p. 66.

Mal'kovich comes to the conclusion that, in spite of a great lack of coordination, these courts had, as a whole, all the forms of court and investigation organs and also the functions which were later installed by decrees of the central power. These common features were the election of judges from among the working population; publicity of trials based on democratic principles; furtherance of the accused's right of counsel not only in the trial, but also during the preliminary investigation.

Mal'kovich underlines—evidently as a positive factor—that in the majority of cases, in meting out justice, the courts were not bound by any law. [1]

Also, Ushakov is of the opinion that the organization and activity of the temporary revolutionary courts established on the basis of the "creative initiative" of the revolutionary masses had a positive importance for the further structure of the Soviet court system. "The local courts and revolutionary tribunals provided by the Decree No. 1 on Courts", Ushakov writes" ... were, in the main, constructed on the same principle on which the revolutionary courts were organized on the initiative of the toilers prior to the publication of the Decree No. 1." [2]

Sh. Grinhaus sees in the activity of the courts of the first period, that is to say before the publication of the Decree No. 1 on Courts or the receipt of the Decree at individual localities, a law-making function of the masses on the basis of the general Decrees addressed to the population by the Soviet power. [3]

There is no doubt that the creation of the revolutionary courts and their activity were prompted by Lenin in repeated talks to the masses urging them to take power in their own hands and use it directly.

Indeed, Lenin had said that "we must follow life, we must provide full creative freedom to the masses". [4]

Lenin admonished the masses not to permit the reestablishment of the state power and its administration into the hands of not-elected irremovable officials remunerated according to bourgeois principles:

---

[1] T.K. Mal'kovich, "On the History of the First Decrees on Courts", *S.G.P.*, 1940, No. 8-9, p. 168.

[2] I.A. Ushakov, "The Creation of the First People's Courts in Petrograd", *S.G.P.*, 1957, No. 1, pp. 11-12.

[3] Sh. Grinhaus, "To the Question of Criminal Law and Law Making Work of the Masses in 1917 and 1918", *S.G.P.*, 1940, No. 3, p. 81.

[4] Lenin, XXII, p. 23.

"... Organize yourself, not trusting anyone, relying only on your mind and experience, and then Russia will be able to proceed with steady measured and reliable steps toward the liberation of our country and the entire humanity, as of the terror of the war, so of the yoke of capitalism". [1]

He was of the opinion that only the shift of the entire state power directly into the hands of the majority of the populace could save all the people. [2]

According to him, democracy had to be built at once, from the bottom, on the initiative of the masses themselves, by their real participation in the *entire* (L.I.) state life, without supervision from above, without officials.

"When the people will assume state power, this power will be a dictatorship, i.e., relying not on law, not on the formal will of the majority, but directly, immediately on violence". [3]

On November 5, 1917, in his address to the population, he declared :

"Comrades-Workers ! Remember that you *yourself* (L.I.) are governing the state. Nothing will help you if you do not organize yourselves and take all the affairs of the state into your own hands". [4]

In his article "The Immediate Problems of Soviet Power" he wrote in March-April 1918 : "As the basic problem of the power becomes not the military suppression, but the administration—the typical measure of suppression and caution will be not the shooting on the spot, but the trial. In this connection the revolutionary masses entered the right path after the 25th October 1917 and proved the vitality of the revolution, starting the creation of their own workers-ad-peasants courts, even before the dissolution of the *bourgeois-bureaucratic* (L.I.) judicial apparatus".

He reporached only these courts of being too weak : "there is a feeling" he continued—"that the popular attitude toward the court as of something fiscal-foreign, inherited from the yoke of land-owners and bourgeoisie, is not yet definitely broken. There is not enough feeling that the court is just an organ for the attraction to a man of the poor to the state administration (since the court activity is one of the functions of state administration), that the court is an *organ*

---

[1] Lenin, XX, p. 146.

[2] *Ibid.*, p. 353.

[3] *Ibid.*, p. 248.

[4] *Ibid.*, p. 55.

(L.I.) of power of the proletariate and the poorest peasantry—that the court is an *implement of education to discipline* (L.I.). [1]

In another article, "How to Organize Competition" completed in December 1917 (L.I.) Lenin declared : "The old *incongruous* (L.I.), infamous and loathsome prejudice, as if only the so-called upper classes, only the rich or those who went through the schools of the rich classes can govern the state and deal with the organization and construction of socialist society, must be destroyed by all means". [2]

However, the real value of the "law-making and justice meting work" of the masses may be well illustrated by the example of a decision made by the general assembly of the inhabitants of the village Gremyachy, Voronezh District, acting also as a "court", on March 1, 1918, attended by 1000 persons.

The reason for the assembly were repeated cases of thefts in the village.

The decision reads : "since frequent thefts by our co-villagers occur in our village, we decided unanimously in order to stop losses and thefts of any kind, as soon as a citizen of Gremyachy or a foreigner, will be observed committing a theft, he will be, after investigating, killed—annihilated as unfit for habitation, ... [3] On the basis of this decision several persons were put to death.

Certainly, the death penalty was applied for property crimes in the Law of August 7, 1932 and later in 1962, but to say that this was a reception of the legislation of the "massess" in the first period after the Bolshevist seizure of power and to ascribe to this legislation a law-making character, important for the future Soviet legislation, is devoid of any basis.

The General Assembly of the Gremyachy village acted as legislator and court at the same time by simply taking law into own hands, implementing Lenin's principle of direct administration of justice by the people.

"Indeed, the people, the bulk of the population" wrote Lenin, "gathered in a certain place without any form occasionally directly occupies the stage itself, administers justice, inflicts punishment, applies power and creates new revolutionary law". [4] Already on

---

[1] Lenin, XXII, p. 460.

[2] *Ibid.*, p. 162.

[3] *Materialy narodnoge komissariata yustitsii,* Issue V, 1918, p. 15.

[4] Lenin, IV, p. 119.

November 18(5) 1917 Lenin had exhorted the peasants, in the name of the Counsil of People's Commissars, "to take themselves local power in their own hands". [1]

The result of the "creative activity" of the masses is the creation of such "laws" as the decision of the village assembly mentioned above, which was by far not an isolated fact : executions of criminals on decisions of the village assemblies and lynching on the spot for property crimes became an applied punishment. M. Isayev reports that in the spring of 1918, on decision of the Volost' [2] Committee in Sviyazhesk District, four peasants, among them a woman in the last month of pregnancy, suspected of robbery, were burned alive in a low fire in the presence af almost all inhabitants of the volost' gathered for the spectacle. [3] Isayev gives a whole list of such "judicial and law-making" actions of the masses.

Certainly, Isayev is right when he classified such decisions of the village assemblies in the category of lynch-law and mob-law.

However, Grinhaus does not agree with Isayev. It seems to him that the cruelty of the punishment does not permit by all means to classify [4] the law-making activity of the village assemblies, an organ of justice administration, as lynch law. Village assemblies meting out justice are not an occasional unification of the mob ... but an organized mass guided by organs of local power, he argues.

Of course, in taking the law into their own hands, the peasants followed Lenin's appeal, but Grinhaus forgets that at the time of the decisions of the village assemblies, judicial power was already conferred on the system of new courts by the Decree No. 1 on Courts and hence, the decisions of the village assemblies were not only horrible in essence, but also completely illegal, according to Lenin's legislation itself. They are nothing but pure mob-law. [5]

---

[1] Lenin, XXII, p. 53.

[2] A small rural district.

[3] M. Isayev, *Obshchaya chast' ugolovnogo prava RSFSR*, M. 1925, p. 63.

[4] Grinhaus, *op. cit.*, pp. 89-90.

[5] It is interesting to note that, evidently preference to revolutionary law consciousness before legality is still given by some people in the Soviet Union up to the present time. Thus, the foremost Soviet writer and Nobel Prize Winner, M. Sholokhov, speaking of the Sinyavsky and Daniel trial, at the XXIII Congress of the USSR Communist Party in April 1966, said with regret : "Would these thugs with a black conscience been caught in the memorable twenties when justice was meted not on the grounds of various provisions of the Criminal Code, but according to revolutionary law consciousness, oh, these turncoats would receive quite another measure of punishment", *Novoye Russkoye Slovo*, N.Y., November 22, 1966.

That some features of procedure used by the primary "revolutionary courts" appeared later in the Decrees and Codes, does not prove conclusively a continuity between the revolutionary courts and the subsequent judicial institutions.

Such features of criminal procedure as publicity, electivity of judges, defense counsel etc., arbitrarily applied by revolutionary courts, were known already a long time before the functioning of these courts, and certainly were taken over by Soviet legislation from old Russian or European Codes and not from the shaky, unorganized practice of revolutionary courts.

Furthermore, the first Decrees on Courts re-introduced the observance of legality in the practice of the courts in contradistinction to the activity of the revolutionary courts.

b) *The Drive for Legality in Lenin's Time*

Lenin and other Bolshevist leaders understood that absence of legality is a sure path to chaos, that the abolished court system must be replaced by another one, that the discarded tsarist laws pertaining to the administration of justice must be partially retained in the beginning of soviet rule under certain conditions and later replaced by Soviet legislation.

Thus, in the Decrees No. 1 and 2 on Courts, the use of tsarist laws was partially permitted under certain restrictions.

But beginning with the Decree No. 3 on Courts all reference to tsarist laws was forbidden and the courts had again to rely on their "revolutionary" or "socialist" law consciousness, since up to 1922-23, no Codes (with the exception of the Family Code of 1918 [1] and the Labor Code [2] as well as the first Constitution of 1918 [3]) were published in 1922-23.

Why did the Soviet government wait five years before the adoption and publication of the Codes? Maybe because every law has a double effect; it binds the citizen to the observance of it, but also formally restricts the government in its freedom of action in the field under the law; it is binding upon the citizen and the government as well.

Maybe the Soviet government preferred to pay lip service to legality but not be limited by law in the filed of judicial administration, since

---

[1] *Sob. uz., RSFSR,* 1918, Item 818.

[2] *Ibid.,* Item 905.

[3] *Sob. uz., RSFSR,* 1918.

the dictatorship of the proletariat is based on violence uninhibited by any law, according to Lenin.

Anyhow, the situation in the administration of justice was changed by the Decrees on Courts and the subsequent legislation.

The various Decrees on Courts, and the other legislation pertaining to this field established a definite system of courts and together with judges and other organs of administration of justice legally appointed used a definite procedure in the preliminary investigation and the trial ressembling very much the procedure adopted in other civilized countries.

In Strogovich's opinion, the Bolsheviks acted correctly when they completely abolished the old state with its bourgeois laws.

But it must be stressed that Strogovich seems somehow not at ease with the substitution of law by socialist law consciousness. He says, very cautiously, that "in a very insignificant measure and for a very short time,—a number of old laws could have been kept in force until corresponding new laws were passed, since there were not sufficient new Soviet laws for the regulation of many important social relations". [1]

Certainly, the absence of codes regulating the major branches of human relations and relations between state and individuals to each other were still lacking, but Soviet legislation gradually changed its character with the strengthening of Soviet power from generalities to the regulation of individual aspects of human and state relations. Thus, for instance, Grinhaus counted 40 laws in the field of penal legislation already at the end of July 1918. The number of other laws with penal sanctions was 69 as of the same date. [2] Naturally, the number of laws and regulations grew with time.

Hence, the courts could base their decisions on Soviet legislation and revert to their revolutionary socialist law consciousness only then when there were no laws on which to rely.

In such cases there existed a certain law making activity of the courts, [3] as Kursky said, on the occasion of the publishing of the decree No. 1 on Courts, "a deep revolution took place in the current law

---

[1] M.S. Strogovich, "At the Sources of Soviet Legal Science", *Sots. zak.*, 1957, No. 10, pp. 20-21.

[2] Grinhaus, *op. cit.*, p. 91.

[3] But not as an obligatory precedent; precedent law in general was foreign to tsarist Russia and is to the Soviet Union.

making process itself, since a new creative source was born. Such a source is the people's court, created by the proletarian revolution". [1]

Indeed, the history of Soviet courts begins with the Decree No. 1 on Courts and with the appearance of law codes, "revolutionary conscience" and "revolutionary (socialist) law consciousness" had to co-exist with socialist legality.

But is such co-existence possible ? Vyshinsky asserted that this co-existence is not only possible but necessary.

He is of the opinion that socialist law consciousness cannot be contrasted with legality : "Just the contrary, socialist law consciousness does not only not contradict revolutionary legality, but implements and strengthens it as the legality of the proletarian revolution, foreign and hostile to any formalism".

He also asserted that the contrasting of revolutioanry law consciousness with legality is the usual mistake of bourgeois jurists. [2]

It is striking that parallel to the exaltation of the free creative power of the people, Lenin demanded the observance of strict legality from all instances of the state and party administration. Still, in1922 he bitterly complained that "we live in a sea of illegality". Just in the same year when he wanted revolutionary law consciousness to replace the *corpus juris romanum*.

His urge for legality was so intense that "socialist legality" was identified with his name and called "Lenin's socialist legality". [3]

Already in 1918, on Lenin's initiative, the VIth Extraordinary Congress of Soviets decided "to call upon all citizens of the Republic, all organs and officials of Soviet power for the strictest observation of RSFSR laws published in the district and being published by the Central Power".

Lenin forwarded this decision to all members of the commissariats and their colleges with the following letter : "Enclosing the booklet "Fulfill the Laws of the Soviet Republic". I draw your attention to the *law* (L.I.) printed there and passed by the VIth All-Russian Congress of Soviets. I recall the necessity of strict fulfillment of this law". [4]

---

[1] D.I. Kursky, *Na putyakh razvitiya Sovetskogo prava*, M. 1927, p. 44.

[2] A. Ye. Vyshinsky, *Revolyutsionnaya zakonnost' na sovremennom etape*, M. 1933, p. 74.

[3] By A. Mikoyan at the XXth Congress of the Party (*XX S"ezd kommunisticheskoy partii Sovetskogo soyuza. Stenograficheskiy otchet*), M. 1956, V. I., pp. 326-327.

[4] *Leninskiy sbornik*, VIII, M. 1928, p. 19.

Lenin added to the letter that, "We will punish for the *ignorance* as well as for the *non-application* (L.I.) of this law". [1]

Interesting is the letter he wrote to V.D. Bonch-Bruyevich, Manager of the Council of People's Commissars Affairs, protesting against the illegal setting of his (Lenin's) salary : "Whereas you did not fulfill my urgent demand to indicate the grounds for the raising of my salary from 500 to 800 rubles monthly and whereas the illegality of this raise, undertaken by you arbitrarily in connivence with the Secretary of the Council, Nikolay Petrovich Gorlukov, in direct violation of the Decree of the Council of People's Commissars of November 27, 1917, is obvious, I severely rebuke you. Chairman of the Council of People's Commissars (signed) V. Ul'yanov (Lenin). [2]

Lenin recognized that it would be pure utopianism to admit that after having overthrown capitalism, people we will learn at once to work for society in the absence of any *law norms* (L.I.). [3]

In his "Letter to Workers and Peasants" of August 24, 1919, on the occasion of the victory over Kolchak, Lenin wrote that "it is necessary to keep the strictest revolutionary order". He exacted the strict observance of the decisions and prescriptions of the Soviet power and the watching over the fulfillment of them by all persons ..." Every violation of legality, the slightest breach of Soviet order, produces a gap which shall be used immediately by enemies of the toilers ..." [4]

Furthermore, in his famous letter to Stalin, addressed to the Politbureau, about the "Double Subordination" of May 20, 1922, [5] Lenin declared that "there must be only one and the same legality everywhere in the country, and the basic evil of all our life and of our lack of culture is the connivance with the real-Russian view and the habit of half-savages of those who want to retain Kalugan-legality in contradistinction to legality in Ryazan".

In this way, Lenin insisted not only on legality in general, but on uniform legality for the entire country.

Lenin's call for the observance of legality was especially emphasized when the time came for a retreat from War Communism and the establishment of the New Economic Policy (NEP).

---

1 *Ibid.*, p. 21.
2 Lenin, 35, p. 272.
3 Lenin, 25, p. 439.
4 Lenin, 29, p. 514, and p. 515.
5 *Ibid.*, 33, p. 327.

It is evident that litigations connected with the restoration by the NEP of private and international trade as well as of other features of a semi-capitalistic economy could not depend on "revolutionary consciousness" or "law consciousness". Law codes were indispensible and a feverish production of Codes was started.

In his report to the IXth All-Russian Congress of Soviets on December 23, 1921, Lenin declared : "Before us stands the problem of commodity circulation, development ... this is required by the New Economic Policy ... and this (in its turn) requires ... the necessity to observe a "greater legality" obviously implying the admission that legality was not observed adequately before; and Lenin explains why it could not have been done before. He argues that legality could not have been better observed under conditions of an armed attack when Soviet power "was taken by the throat". "If we would have posed this problem at that time, we would have become pedants, we would have played revolution, but would not have done it. However, the more we enter conditions which are conditions of a strong and firm power, the more the development of commody circulation is going forward, the more it is urgent to advance the firm slogan of the realization of a greater revolutionary legality". [1]

Here Lenin himself confirms that legality had to be enforced and the economy regulated by definite laws with regard to the introduction of the NEP.

However, Krylenko thought that the urge for observance of revolutionary legality and the publication of Codes cannot be connected with the introduction of the NEP only. "Revolutionary legality is certainly an organic part of the NEP, but it is not a specific part pertaining to the period of the NEP only. Revolutionary legality is a method of our socialist construction, inherent in the dictatorship of the proletariate at the epoch of War Communism, the first period of the NEP and the Second Five Year Plan". [2]

Kursky thought that legality was a slogan not predominant among people working with the law who has to apply law directly, but also among wide masses of the worker's and peasants' population. [3]

He warned that "if we will only speak about revolutionary legality

---

[1] Lenin, 33, p. 151.

[2] N.V. Krylenko, "The Draft of a New Criminal Code", *Problemy ugolovnoy politiki*, Issue I, M. 1935, p. 4.

[3] D.I. Kursky, *Izbrannyye stat'i i rechi*, M. 1948, p. 69.

then there will be no laws, it will be a very effective word, but no more. It is necessary to have a regard, in a sufficiently high degree, to a developed system of norms, in order not to speak only about revolutionary legality, but to realize it in life too". [1]

This necessity of stricter observance of legality forced also the reorganization of the OGPU, the transfer of its judicial functions to the courts and the restriction of some of its power, as we have seen.

Hence, the All-Russian Party Conference which had to decide on the introduction of the NEP, emphasized the neccesity to observe principle of revolutionary legality in all fields of activity. All the agencies and governmental institutions and citizens were charged with a strict responsibility for the violation of laws, passed by Soviet authorities. [2]

It must be noted that the necessity of legality was not realized by all men of power among the Bolshevists of that time. Thus, for instance, P. G. Smidovich, Member of the VTsIK's Presidium, declared at the same IXth Congress of the Party that there is no need in general to attribute to law the greatest importance and require the obligatory compliance with it in all cases. [3]

However, Lenin himself made significant efforts toward the observance of legality in individual cases.

Thus, in the case of embezzlement of securities in the State Bank he wrote to G. Yu. Bokio, Member of the VChK Investigation Commission : "You must investigate the case in detail and write me exact data and not generalities". [4]

In the same case, Lenin had previously asked for information about the evidence collected and whether "the evidence is serious". [5]

In another case Lenin inquired as to whether those against whom a correct accusation is not formulated are set free ? Also those who can be released ? Are the expert findings produced by the accusation reliable ? [6]

When Latsis, one of the most blood-thirsty members of the CheKa,

---

[1]   *Ibid.*, M. 1958, p. 111.

[2]   *Kommunisticheskaya partiya sovetskogo soyuza v resheniyakh, rezolyutsiyakh, s"ezdov, konferentsiy i plenumov Ts-K.*, M. 1951, V.I., p. 593.

[3]   Quoted by M.S. Strogovich, *Osnovnyye voprosy sovetskoy sotsialisticheskoy zakonnosti*, M. 1959, p. 37.

[4]   *Leninskiy sbornik*, XXXVI, p. 242.

[5]   *Ibid.*, XXXV, p. 271.

[6]   *Ibid.*, pp. 244-245.

but also "one of the best, well-tried communists" as qualified by Lenin, wrote in his periodical "The Red Terror" (No. 1, p. 2) that "do not look in an accusation case for evidence as to whether he (the accused) did rise against the Soviets by arms or words" Lenin wrote that this was a "nonsense". He explained that Latsis "wanted to say that the red terror is the forcible suppression of exploiters, attempting to reestablish their supremacy, but in the place of that" wrote the sentence quoted above". [1]

Strogovich is of the opinion that Lenin considered criminal even the thought of Soviet law violation on any ground. [2]

Indeed, when somebody proposed to evade a Decree, Lenin wrote on March 4, 1919, "You cannot evade a Decree : for such a proposal alone one is brought to court". [3]

Kocharov [4] relates that even F.E. Dzerzhinsky, the terrible head of the CheKa, greatly contributed to the strengthening of socialist legality, that he consistently required observation of legality, unflinchingly fought arbitrariness and lawlessness and strictly suppressed illegal methods of investigation.

In support of this story, Kocharov relates the following episode :

When at the end of 1919, Dzerzhinsky became aware that one of the members of the VeCheKa permitted himself the rough handling of an arrested man, he personally conducted an investigation of the case and noted on March 11 : "The Commission examined (the case) and decided to reprimand most energetically the culprits and to bring to court in the future every one who permitted himself to touch an arrested person".

Instructions for the agents of the CheKa who carried out searches and a Note concerning the rules of invasion of private apartments and the handling of arrested persons was issued. "They contained these noteworthy words", writes Kocharov: "... let all those who are assigned to conduct a search or deprive persons of liberty and hold them in jail, handle with consideration those people who are arrested and searched; let them (the CheKa members) be much more polite with these people than with a person near to them". [5]

---

[1] Lenin, 28, pp. 365-366.

[2] M.S. Strogovich, *Osnovnyye voprosy sovetskoy sotsialisticheskoy zakonnosti*, M. 1959, p. 22.

[3] *Leninskiy sbornik*, M. 1945, XXXV, p. 60.

[4] G.I. Kocharov, Introduction to *Teoriya dokazatel'stv v sovetskom ugolovnom protsesse*, M. 1966, pp. 6-7.

[5] *Ibid.*

Remarkable words, which remained on paper only. Unfortuantely Lenin's urge for legality did not prevent also him from violating legality when and if appropriate, as we will see later.

The whole story does not correspond to the well-known activity of the CheKa and the personality of its dreaded head.

c) *Further Drive for Legality up to the Cult of Personality*

The XIV Conference of the Russian Communist Party (B) passed a resolution "On Revolutionary Legality" on April 1925. It was said there that "the interests of the consolidation of the proletarian state and the further growth of confidence unto it on the part of wide masses of the peasantry in connection with the policy followed by the Party at the present time, require the maximum of revolutionary legality ... [1]

The ruthless collectivization process [2] brought countless violations of legality protested by the "rightist" opposition and defended by Stalin and Vyshinsky.

Still it was deemed necessary to stress on paper the necessity of legality.

The Decision of TsIK and the Council of People's Commissars of June 25, 1932 served to this effect. [3]

The Decision was taken on the occasion of the tenth jubilee of the creation of the prosecuting body. Thus, it was said in the Decision that "noting" the decade of the prosecuting body organization and the accomplished achievements in the strengthening of revolutionary legality which is one of the most important means to fortify the dictatorship of the proletariat in its class fight against the enemies of the toiling population (kulaks, re-seller-speculators, bourgeois wreckers and their revolutionary political agents), the TsIK and the *Sovnarkom* point to the important number of violations of legality on the part of officials, and distortions in the practice, especially in the villages.

---

[1] *Kommunisticheskaya partiya sovetskogo soyuza v resheniyakh rezolyutsiakh, s"ezdov konferentsiy i plenumov Ts-K.*, Part II, M. 1954, p. 162.

[2] Three million peasants allegedly *Kulaks* perished in the fight against collectivization and three million starved to death during the famine in the Ukraine produced by collectivization.

[3] *Sob. zak., SSSR,* 1932, Item 298.

In order to eliminate the violations of legality, the Decision ordered the proceedings in villages checked by the prosecuting body and required the courts and the prosecution body to impose strict responsibility in all cases of violation of the toilers rights, especially in cases of illegal arrests, searchies, confiscations, withdrawal of property, etc, applying severe punishments of the perpetrators.

This call for legality of the Soviet government generated, naturally, a score of articles, beginning with Vyshinsky [1] and pronouncements by Soviet leaders. Thus, Molotov, per example, spoke on revolutioanry legality at the IIIrd All-Ukrainian Conference of the Communist Party(B) of July 8, 1932. [2] Kaganovich warned against carrying too far administrative measures in villages. [3] Kalinin stated that the prosecution body did little to strengthen revolutionary legality up to the present time and emphasized the importance of just court work. [4]

However, either legislation or authoritative declarations prevented the wave of violation of legality which submerged the Soviet Union under the cult of personality.

d) *Dictatorship of the Proletariat*

The dictatorship of the proletariat is the name given by Marxists to the state and political power in the transition period from capitalism to socialism. In Lenin's opinion, the dictatorship of the proletariat means the following : "only a concrete class, namely the city and, in general, the plant-and-factory-workers, the industrial workers, are in a position to guide the whole mass of the toiling population in the fight for the overthrow of the capitalist yoke, in the process of the overthrow itself and in the struggle for the retention and strengthening of victory, in the task of the creation of a new socialist society, in the entire fight for complete liquidation of classes". [5]

An original interpretation was brought forward by V. Lesnoy.

---

[1] A. Ye. Vyshinsky, "Revolutionary Legality at the Present Stage of Socialist Development", *Sov. yust.*, 1932, No. 19, pp. 2-8; appeared as a monography under the title : *Revolyutsionnaya zakonnost' na sovremennom etape*, M. 1933.

[2] *Sov. yust.*, 1932, No. 20, p. 2.

[3] *Ibid.*, p. 3.

[4] *Ibid.*, p. 1.

[5] Lenin, 29, p. 387.

He asserted, namely, that Lenin in his definition of the dictatorship of the proletariat as a power based exclusively on violence and not on law, has in mind bourgeois law "preserving the supremacy of the capital, defending private property and the exploitation of men by men". [1]

Vyshinsky and Stalin would completely disagree with Lesnoy. For them the dictatorship of the proletariat, as defined by Lenin, was a kind of government, above every law, bourgeois or socialist alike.

Although Lesnoy writes: "Certainly, having brought to life a definite system of laws the state cannot assume a nihilistic attitude toward laws created by itself, it is somehow bound by them until they are abrogated by the state; still during the dictatorship of the proletariat the Soviet state did not consider itself bound by its own laws when any alleged necessity called for the breaking of these laws.

Lenin insisted on the concept that only the proletariat alone exercises the dictatorship. He stated that "the class which took in his hands the basic political supremacy, took it being fully aware that he takes it *alone* (I.L.). This is integrated in the concept of the dictatorship of the proletariat; this concept has only sense when one class knows that it alone takes in its hands the political power and does not deceive itself or others, by talks about all-popular, all-electoral power, sanctified by the entire people". [2]

Thus, in the period between November 1917-the overthrow of the provisional government-and a time not exactly defined by communist leaders and writers when socialism was definitely installed, the type of Soviet government was allegedly a dictatorship of the proletariat.

This dictatorship of the proletariat is a temporary phenomenon, which has to disappear with the installation of socialism when the Soviet State has been transformed from a dictatorship of the proletariat into a socialist state, "expressing the interests and the will of the entire people into an all-people's state", as Kositsyn puts it. [3]

One may conclude from this assertion that the Soviet state, during

---

[1] V. Lesnoy, "The October Revolution and the Formation of Socialist Law", *Sov. yust.*, 1967, No. 4, p. 173.

[2] Lenin, XXVI, p. 286.

[3] A.P. Kositsyn, "Dictatorship of the Proletariate", *Entssiklopedicheskiy slovar' pravovykh znaniy*, M. 1965, p. 107.

the period of the proletariat's dictatorship, did not represent "the interests and the will" of the entire people.

Consequently, it is also said in the new Program of the USSR Communist Party that the dictatorship of the Proletariat has fulfilled its mission in the USSR. It ensured allegedly the full and definite victory of socialism and the shift of the Soviet society to the developed construction of communism.

"This does not mean, however, the weakening of the guiding role of the workers' class in our society. Being the foremost organized power, the USSR workers' class is realizing its guiding role also in the period of developed construction of communism. It will complete its function as the guide of society with the construction of communism when classes will desappear", writes Rad'kov.

"This development extends the guiding influence of the Soviet Communist Party to all aspects of public life even more", Rad'kov adds. [1]

In what consisted the ending of the state of dictatorship of the proletariat and the remaining of the "even extended" guidance of the proletariat by the Communist Party is not clear. The influence it possessed since 1917 cannot and was not enlarged because it was and is omnipresent and omnipotent all the time.

In this definition of the "dictatorship of the proletariat" only the first part, the "dictatorship", came to realization in the Soviet Union, since this dictatorship was carried out not by the proletariat, which as such had no part in the governing of the state, but by the Party. The proletariat had and has no legal means to participate in the government. Even when the proletariat had some privileges in the election to the legislature at the time of the VTsIK, it elected candidates chosen by the Communist Party.

According to the 1936 Constitution : All USSR citizens older than 18 years of age have the same elctoral rights to the legislature and the Society. The legislature itself was never the expression of the will of the people, or of any part of it, but of the Party only.

Indeed, legislation which is initiated by the government under control of the Party is always voted unanimously and during the entire time of the Soviet legislature, never was a single bill rejected, but always passed unanimously.

It is equally obvious that the proletariat never "guided" the other

---

[1] V. Rad'kov, "The Notion and Content of Socialist Legality", *Sots. zak.*, 1961, p. 21.

classes in the development pictured by Lenin. Not the workers, not a single class, and not even the whole people ruled and rules in the Soviet state.

It is obvious that André Gide, the eminent French writer and Nobel Prize winner, is right when he declared after his visit to Moscow : "The dictatorship of the proletariat was promised to us. We are far away from it. Yes, evidently, there is a dictatorship, but of one man"... [1]

Indeed, dictatorship of one man between 1929 and 1953, and of the Communist Party in between from November 1917 up to the present time. [2]

Stalin resorted to the dictatorship of the proletariat for the justification of his strongest coercive measures, especially in the process of collectivization. "A strong and powerful dictatorship of the proletariat—that is what we need now, in order to reduce to dust the last remnants of the dying classes, and to smash their thievish machinations", Stalin declared. [3]

The "extraordinary measures" against the kulaks during collectivization in the Northern Caucasus produced a strong protest by the so-called "rightist deviations" under the leadership of Bukharin and Rykov. Bukharin wrote that these measures violate revolutionary

---

[1] André Gide, *Retour de l'USSR*, Paris, 1936, p. 77.

[2] The question may be raised as to whether a proletariat class exists at all in the Soviet Union. Did not Engels write "The proletariat seizes state power, then transforms the means of production to state property. But in doing this, it puts an end to itself, as the proletariat". (Quoted by Lenin in *State and Revolution, op. cit.*, pp. 15-16.) Engels' idea is quite logical and clear : having in the revolutionary process seized power and the means of production, the proletariat transforms itself, from an exploited into a ruling class. After the October Revolution things happened, however, not as Engels predicted. The means of industrial production were nationalized all right, but power was seized not by the proletariat, but by the Communist Party. In the opinion of the present writer, during the fifty years of communist power the proletariat remained the same *Lumpen Proletariat* which inspired Marx and Engels to their doctrine. It means living on minimum for existence, producing the surplus value as before and exploited by the appropriation of the surplus value by others as allegedly under capitalism. (See Samuel Kucherov, "The Soviet Union is Not a Socialist Society" (in "Defense" of V.M. Molotov), *Political Science Quarterly*, 1956, No. 2, pp. 189-195.) Stalin did not deny the existence of a surplus value in the Soviet economy, but thought that this surplus value is used for things which are as necessary to society and to the worker himself as the labor expended for the satisfaction of his personal needs. (See Stalin, *Ekonomicheskiye problemy sotsialisma v SSSR*, M. 1952, pp. 21-22.)

[3] Stalin, *Voprosy leninizma*, M. 1938, p. 509.

legality, that "revolutionary legality must take the place of all remnants of administrative arbitrariness, even if revolutionary". [1] Bukharin's and Rykov's protests Stalin called "comic howls". [2]

In defending Stalin's extraordinary measures, Vyshinsky did not deny that these measures violate revolutionary legality. "It is completely evident", he wrote, "that extraordinary measures do not fit into the channel of revolutionary legality and are not always and not in all matters consistent with its requirements. Does it follow that these extraordinary measures cannot be applied under specific circumstances"? asks Vyshinsky, and his answer is: "Not at all". [3]

He thought that in the fight against the enemies of Stalin's regime every measure is permitted. Not only the court and juridical sentences, "but also administrative measures of coercion through such organs of the proletarian dictatorship as the Special Board of the People's Commissariat of Internal Affairs which is a mighty weapon in the hands of the Soviet power to fight the enemies". [4]

Thus, the Special Board is also an appropriate instrument of the dictatorship of the proletariat.

In this way, every measure taken in the name of the dictatorship of the proletariat, regardless of whether it corresponds to legality or not, is "legal", according to Vyshinsky.

His conclusion is that *the proletarian dictatorship is the highest law, defining by itself the concrete content of all laws and everyone of them, drawing* (I.V.) its sense and its power from the proletarian revolution". [5]

It must be said that Lenin wanted to give to the dictatorship of the proletariat a content extending beyond the limits of naked violence. "The dictatorship of the proletariat", he wrote ..." is not only violence with regard to exploiters, and even not violence in the main". He saw the essence of the dictatorship of the proletariat and the guarantee of its vitality and success in the representation and

---

[1] Bukharin, *Put' k sotsialismu i raboche-krest'yanskiy soyuz*, M. 1929, p. 79.

[2] Stalin, *Voprosy leninizma*, M. 1938, p. 283.

[3] Vyshinsky, *Rev. zak...*, *op. cit.*, p. 56.

[4] Vyshinsky, *Sudoustroystvo v SSSR*, M. 1940, p. 76.

[5] *Ibid.*

realization of a higher type of public labor organization in comparison with capitalism. [1]

But not being violence itself and "even not violence in the main", the dictatorship of the proletariat still remained a power based on violence and not law, according to Lenin.

Stalin recognized various aspects in the dictatorship of the proletariat, providing in relation to a given period of history.

Thus, during the Civil War the violent aspect of the dictatorship of the proletariat was striking. At times of socialist construction, the peaceful organizational side of the dictatorship, the revolutionary legality prevails most. But in both cases, he emphasized, the "violent side of the dictatorship is present, does not subside". [2]

The violent side of the dictatorship of the proletariat did not subside even during the construction of the socialist society because the class struggle did not only not cease in this period but was even intensified, according to Stalin. "The elimination of classes", he wrote, "is not achieved by the extinction of the class struggle, but by its strengthening". [3]

Echoing his master, Vyshinsky declared : "Stalin always warned and still warns against the lack of understanding and denial of the continuance of the class struggle under triumphant socialist construction—the abolition of class is attained by intensification—not by extinguishing the class struggle. [4]

Thus, the dictatorship of the proletariat as a power based not on law, but direct violence, served for Stalin and Vyshinsky to justify every violation of legality.

B. Discrepancy between Theory and Practice

a) *Caused by and under Lenin*

It is characteristic that preaching legality Lenin did not hesitate to violate it when he thought necessary and to interfere with the process of meting out justice.

---

[1] Lenin, 29, p. 386.

[2] Stalin, *Voprosy leninizma*, M. 1938, p. 113.

[3] *Ibid.*, p. 509.

[4] A. Ye. Vyshinsky, "The Law of the Soviet State", translated by Hugh W. Babb, N.Y., 1948, pp. 39-40.

Thus, in the Spring of 1918, four members of the Investigation Commission in Moscow were sentenced for confessed bribery by the Moscow Revolutionary Tribunal to six months in jail only. Lenin requested the exclusion of the judges from the Party because, "instead of putting bribers before a firing squad, passing of such scoffingly weak and lenient sentences is a disgraceful act for a communist and revolutionary". [1]

His most flagrant and politically important violation of legality, however, was the dispersing of the Constituent Assembly, on January 18, 1918.

Only on November 8, 1917 (after the seizure of power) Lenin had said in his Report on the Land at the IInd All-Russian Congress of Soviets that "the problem of the land may be completely solved only by the All-People's Constituent Assembly ..." "Even if the peasants will further follow the Socialist-Revolutionaries, and even if they will give the majority to this party in the Constituent Assembly, let it be so. Life is the best teacher and it will indicate who is right (the Bolshevists or the Socialist-Revolutionary). Let the peasants from one end and us from the other solve this question." [2]

All the political parties, including the Bolshevists, participated in the electoral campaign and the elections to the Constituent Assembly. In their propaganda speeches before the seizure of power, the Bolshevists accused the Provisional Government of delaying the elections, to the Constituant Assembly, asserting that if they would have been in power these elections would have taken place much earlier.

But two months later, when the Russian people voted an overwhelming majority to Socialist-Revolutionaries in the Constituent Assembly, it was forcibly dissolved by Lenin with the help of bayonets of sailors and Red-Guardists.

The People voted clearly against the Bolshevists. Among the 707 deputies elected to the Constituent Assembly only 175 were communists. The political alignment of the other deputies was : 40 Leftists-Socialist-Revolutionaries who allied themselves with the Bolshevists later; 370 Rightist Socialist Revolutionaries, 86 members belonged to national minorites (all anti-Bolshevists), 16 Mensheviks, 17 Kadets.

---

[1] Lenin, 27, p. 290.
[2] Lenin, XXII, pp. 21 and 23.

To what parties the rest (3 members) belonged, has not been established.

Certainly, every revolutionary act is a violation of the law of the preceding regime. But Lenin and his Party accepted the election of the Constitutional Assembly, took part in its election, submitted, as we have seen, to its decision in advance.

Furthermore, the elections were conducted also under the Bolshevist regime which, thus, acknowledged the legality of the law concerning the election of the Constituent Assembly. The electoral law no longer was only a bourgeois law or the Assembly a capitalist institution, as declared by the Bolshevists when the results of the elections were made known.

Consequently, by forcibly dispersing the Constituent Assembly, Lenin violated a law acknowledged by the Bolshevists and, thus, their own legality.

b) *After Lenin's Death*

After Lenin's death and the liquidation of the NEP, the call for legality did not cease to resound and the discrepancy between declarations and reality became even more flagrant.

On the occasion of the tenth anniversary of the Prosecuting Body, the TsIK and *Sovnarkom* passed a Joint Decision on legality, on June 25, 1932, mentioned above. [1]

It is interesting to note here the care of the decision for the preservation of the fictional rights of citizens.

The Decision namely charged the courts and the prosecution body with the bringing to strict responsibility of all officials in cases of violations of rights of toilers and especially when illegal arrests, searches, confiscations, or deprivation of property, etc., took place, subjecting the culprits to strict punishments.

This was decided when the numberless violations of legality were committed during the forced collectivization process by the administration itself which were protested by the rightist opposition of

---

[1]   Pp. 674-675.

Bukharin-Rykov, and two years before the establishment of the Special Board.

Certainly, the Decision of June 25, 1932 did not stop or prevent any violation of legality. It was simply the next in turn to render lip service to legality.

Indeed, lip service only, because parallel to the exaltation of legality, extraordinary measures were taken against peasants in the process of collectivization by Stalin which were a flagrant violation of legality, as admitted by Vyshinsky himself. Lip service, since, as stated by Stalin at the United Session of the Central Committee and the Central Committee of the All-Russian Communist Party (B), on January 7, 1933, "the basic concern of revolutionary legality, in our time, consists, consequently, in the preservation of public property and not anything else". [1]

This, Stalin's assertion, was duly exemplified by the law of August 7, 1932, On Preservation of State Enterprises, Kolkhozes and Cooperative Property and the Strengthening of Public (Social) Property, [2] which introduced the death penalty for the violation perpetrated against this property. Preservation of public property and not of personal rights was the main purpose of Soviet legislation of that time.

The protection of individual rights was not mentioned as a function of the state also in Stalin's report to the XVIIIth Congress of the Soviet Union Communist Party on March 10, 1939. Then, according to Stalin, the state had to preserve socialist property from thieves and plunderers, to defend the country from attacks of external and internal enemies of the Soviets, to develop the economic and cultural organization of the state. [3]

That Stalin's concept of socialist legality was one-sided, that the protection of citizens' rights and interests, the insurance of a real liberty of the individual, are not a less important state function than the protection of state property was recognized only after Stalin's death. [4]

---

[1]   Stalin, *Voprosy leninizma*, M. 1938, p. 509.

[2]   *Sots. zak.*, 1932, No. 23, p. 1.

[3]   Stalin, *Voprosy leninizma*, M. 1952, p. 646.

[4]   See Editorial "To liquidate the consequences of the Cult of Personality in Jurisprudence", *S.G.P.*, 1962, No. 4, p. 5; M.S. Strogovich, "Some Questions of State and Law", in *Voprosy stroitel'stva kommunizma*, M. 1959, p. 297.

In the meantime the gap between word and deed, theory and practice was widening.

In 1934, which means in the year when the Special Board of the Commissariat of Internal Affairs was established, M. I. Kalinin, Chairman of the TsIK's Presidium, [1] in a speech delivered on the occasion of the 10th anniversary of the USSR Supreme Court, said : "We require—and have the right to do so,—from the prosecutor such kind of work, such organization of the fight for socialist legality, that every citizen worker, every *kolkhoznik*, every Soviet institution, should be insured from bureaucratic perversions, that everyone should be sure that his legal rights and interests are safeguarded ..." [2]

Stalin saw a difference between legality of the first period of the NEP, liquidated by the First Five Year Plan and the post-NEP time. He said in January 1933 that the first was directed against the extremes of communism, against 'illegal' confiscation and extortions. It guaranteed to the private owner, the individual farmer, the capitalist, the safety of their property, under the conditions of strict compliance with Soviet laws.

"The revolutionary legality [3] of our times—Stalin continued—is pointed not against the extremes of War Communism which have not existed for a long time, but against thieves and saboteurs in the public economy, against hooligans and wreckers of public property". Then, he pronounced the sentence quoted above : "The basic care of revolutionary legality of our time consists, consequently, of the preservation of public property and not in anything else".

In 1956, Strogovich found that Stalin's concept of legality of the first period of the NEP was one-sided and incomplete. "First of all', writes Strogovich, "it is not clear as to whether Stalin had in mind just legality in the direct sense of the word or whether he identified by this term simply the legislation in force". [4] Stalin's definition is incomplete, according to Strogovich, because "although legality of this period (first period of the NEP) certainly required the protection of private capitalist rights within limits, as permitted by law for

---

[1]   A position corresponding to the President of the Republic.

[2]   *Sovetskaya prokuratura v vazhneyshikh dokumentakh*, M. 1956, pp. 395 and 396.

[3]   Stalin evidently employs the word "legality" in the sense of "legislation".

[4]   M.S. Strogovich, "Theoretical Questions of Soviet Legality", *S.G.P.*, 1956, No. 4, p. 18 : We have already stated that legality is used in both senses by Soviet leaders and writers. Strogovich himself employes legality in its strict sense and as legislation in general.

private capitalistic relations, but the essence of legality was not at all in that, but in the creation of the necessary conditions for the reconstruction of the national economy and the strengthening of the union between the worker class and the toiling peasantry". [1]

The essence of Soviet legality Strogovich sees in the unflinching abiding by the laws, in the uniformity of their understanding, in their strict observance and exact fulfillment. [2]

On the other hand, legality was necessary in order to carry out the orderly construction of a "socialist" state, and a strict compliance with law was demanded from individual citizens, officials, organizations, institutions and enterprises, with the exception of the Soviet Government and the Communist Party.

Indeed, the law, in reality, never stood above the government and the Party. The Soviet state was never a state under the rule of law. The government and the Party violated legality at any time when they thought it suited their purposes.

The inconsistancy between theory and practice in the question of legality found its most evident expression in the dogmatic assertions of Vyshinsky and his activity as USSR Prosecutor.

C. VYSHINSKY IN THEORY AND PRACTICE

In his address at the IInd Congress on Problems of the Sciences of State and Law, in 1938, Vyshinsky, in criticizing Stuchka for having reduced law to policy, hence, depersonalized law as the totality of statutes ... "suggesting the false idea that the application of the statute is defined in the socialist state by political consideration and not by force and authority of the Soviet statute itself", declared : "Such an idea means bringing Soviet legality and Soviet law into substantial discredit since on this hypothesis, they called upon to develop a 'policy' and not to defend the rights of citizens and they must start from the requirements of policy (and not from the provisions of the statute) in deciding any problems of court practice.

It is evident that Soviet law cannot be reduced simply to policy, the course identified with the effect".

In support of his opinion, Vyshinsky quotes Article 112 of the 1936 Constitution establishing the independence of judges and clearly and

---

[1] *Ibid.* In this sentence "legality" can be understood in both senses.
[2] *Ibid.*, p. 19.

distinctly providing that their court work is subordinate to the statute and to nothing else. [1]

Certainly, Kelsen is right when he states about this assertion of Vyshinsky that "These are statements which might very well be made by a bourgeois legal scientist who describes the law without regarding it as a means in the exercise of political power but in the sole interest of understanding it in its own authority and hence, tries to separate the science of law from politics". [2]

But on the other hand, Vyshinsky expressed views on law and its application intended to cover the atrocities committed during the "cult of personality" with a faked layer of legality.

His task as Stalin's spokesman in the field of law was to create a theoretical basis for the assertions of his boss in the field of law and his desires in matters of the administration of justice.

Indeed, since Stalin asserted that 'legality' is not an empty phrase but does not exclude the use of certain "extraordinary" administrative measures", [3] Vyshinsky declared that in a proletarian state, every measure either "legal" or "extraordinary", has the dictatorship of the proletariat as its source. On the contrary, revolutionary legality would turn into its opposite—into chains on the proletarian revolution". [4]

In this way every measure taken in the name of the dictatorship of the proletariat, irrespective of whether it corresponds to law or not, is legal. If this were not so "revolutionary legality would inescapably put itself in opposition to the dictatorship of the proletariat as a power", and Vyshinsky quotes Lenin's definition of the dictatorship of the proletariat as a power based on violence and not on law, as a deciding argument. [5]

Vyshinsky attributed to Soviet law a degree of "flexibility" and "conditionality" unknown to bourgeois law in democracies, and typical under dictatorships.

---

[1] Quoted and translated in Soviet Legal Philosophy, Cambridge, 1951, p. 329.

[2] Hans Kelsen, *The Communist Theory of Law*, N.Y., 1955, p. 122.

[3] The "extraordinary" measures were directed against kulaks, specifically in the Northern Caucasus, the peasants were deprived of their land, plots, and executed without trial, in the process of collectivization which cost the peasants about 6,000,000 lives and 50% of their livestock.

[4] A. Ye. Vyshinsky, *Revolyutsionnaya zakonnost' na sovremennom etape*, M. 1933, p. 51.

[5] *Ibid.*

Another feature of Soviet law is, according to Vyshinsky, its expediency. But again revolutionary expediency cannot be contrasted with legality. "Such a contrasting is possible only from the viewpoint of bourgeois understanding of legality, excluding the flexibility, the maneuverability, so to speak the *conditionality*, (V.I.) which distinguish the norms of Soviet law ..." [1]

With these special features of Soviet law, Vyshinsky explains the use of analogy in Soviet criminal law which is excluded in bourgeois law. [2]

According to Schlesinger, "From the point of Soviet legality, Vyshinsky's recognition of emergencies, which most states would deal with by emergency measures, is less serious than his tendency to introduce the element of elasticity and revolutionary expediency into the working of law, or at least, of justice itself ... [3]

Certainly, under Vyshinsky's influence, also A. I. Denisov recommends "flexibility" in the interpretation of soviet legal norms. According to him, "flexible tactics must characterize all the activity of the Soviet state as a whole and its institutions, such as courts, executive and administrative organs of state power and the prosecuting body. Soviet law is correct law. Its influence upon the Social development depends upon the persons executing it, upon their flexibility, their ability to interpret law corectly and consider the concrete conditions of its application". [4]

But if the law standing in the way of Vyshinsky's wishes could not be made "flexible" enough, it could be simply ignored, according to him. "If a law lags behind life, it must be changed or, according to Stalin's expression, 'put aside' " [5]

Stalin, however, had in mind laws covering the lease of land and labor hireing rendered obsolete by collectivization and abrogated on February 1, 1930. [6] But "the putting aside of a law in force" was made a dogma by Vyshinsky which he considered a means of overcoming bourgeois and philistine jurisprudence", as Shlyapochnikov puts it. [7]

---

[1] *Ibid.*, p. 62.

[2] See above, p. 615.

[3] Rudolf Schlesinger, *Soviet Legal Theory*, London, 1951, p. 200.

[4] A. Denisov, *Teoriya gosudarstva i prava*, M. 1948, p. 481.

[5] A. Ye. Vyshinsky, *Voprosy teorii gosudarstva i prava*, M. 1950, p. 257.

[6] See Stalin, *Voprosy leninizma*, M. 1952, pp. 329-330.

[7] A.S. Shlyapochnikov, "On Soviet Criminal Law Stabilization", *S.G.P.*, 1957, No. 12, p. 20.

But on the other hand, these features of Soviet law, argued Vyshinsky, make it possible under some conditions not to bring a person
to responsibility in violation of the bourgeois principles of *"nullum
crimen sine lege"*, and *"dura lex sed lex"*, although all signs of a
corpus delicti are present. [1]

Thus, the possibility to indict persons for an action only resembling
an offense described as a serious crime in the Criminal Code is contrasted
by Vyshinsky with the setting free of a culprit accused of an insignificant offense.

The importance of the "flexibility", "conditionality" and "expediency" of Soviet law, as asserted by Vyshinsky, is eivdent. It per
mitted him to interpret provisions of the Code of Criminal Procedure
in a manner suiting his purposes.

It is striking that the 1936 Constitution, Stalin's Constitution, was
published at the threshold of the main actions of the thirties, when
all the individual right including the independence of judges, guaranteed by the Constitution, were systematically violated in a way,
may be unprecedented in history by the creator of this Constitution.
It was, however, deemed necessary to screen these actions by a democratic piece of legislation and it is self-understood that Vyshinsky
undertook the task of its glorification.

> At the third training conference of the Investigating Magistrates, Vyshinsky,
> speaking on the Constitution, declared that "this Constitution secured in the
> legislative way the conquest by the Soviet people of a new Soviet dignity of the
> Soviet people, who are in possession of all rights which are in the far reach of the
> most democratic bourgeois society. This entered the consciousness of our citizens,
> ready to defend these actions with might and main, with their lives—and will
> not permit anyone to scoff at them or to attempt their inviolability—at the immunity
> of the person, inviolability of the home, the privacy of the correspondence, the
> freedom of speach, freedom of the press, freedom of assembly, etc...".
>
> And Vyshinsky added :
>
> "All these are not slogans, but life conquered by the working class and all the
> working population, conquered with their blood." [2]
>
> What a remarkable example of shameless hypocrisy !

---

[1] Vyshinsky refers here to Article 6 of the old Criminal Code providing that an
action is not criminal if, although corresponding to description of a criminal action
in the Special Part of the Code because of an evident insignificance and the lack of evil
consequences is deprived of a publicly dangerous character. It is evident that also
under bourgeois law a culprit under these circumstances would not have been punished
at all or the sentence would be suspended.

[2] Vyshinsky, "On Problems of the Investigating Magistrates", Verbatim Report of
a speech delivered at the 3rd training conference of investigating magistrates on December 11, 1936. *Sots. zak.* 1937, No 1, pp. 12-13.

D. Legality under the "Cult of Personality"

We dwelled at some length on the description of Vyshinsky's views on legal theory and practice because it was he who wielded a dominent influence upon Soviet legal science and administration of justice during the period called the "cult of personality", which lasted from about 1929 to Stalin's death in 1953.

This influence was convincingly characterized by L. Il'yichev who wrote that Stalin himself did not come forward with special works in the field of legal science, leaving the role of theoretical oracle to Vyshinsky who was his mouthpiece, acting for many years as the leading theoretician on questions of law and state. "It is well known to what heights of theoretical violence Vyshinsky reached in the attempts to give legal support to the erroneous and evil theses of Stalin about the intensification of the class struggle during the gradual strengthening of socialist positions in our country, in his striving to adapt legal science to the justification of the violations of socialist legality". [1]

A. N. Shelepin remarked at the XXII Congress of the Party that "even a peculiar cult of Vyshinsky's personality" existed in the legal science for many years". He stated that Vyshinsky's theory on the confession of the accused as decisive evidence in cases of crimes against the state, justified in general, the facts of mass-arbitrariness in court and investigation practices which took place at a certain time. [2]

Thus, a second cult, this time the cult of a "legal" personality!

What really happened with socialist legality under the cover of Vyshinsky's theory was related by N. S. Khrushchev at the XXth Congress of the Soviet Union Communist Party in 1956, three years after Stalin's, and two years after Vyshinsky's death, on November 22, 1954. [3]

Stalin, Khrushchev said, discarded the Leninist method of convincing and educating, he abandoned the method of ideological struggle for that of administrative violence, mass repressions and terror. He acted

---

[1] L. Il'yichev, "The Powerful Factor of Communism Construction", *Kommunist*, 1962, No. 1, p. 24.

[2] *XXII S'yezd kommunisticheskoy partii sovetskogo soyuza, Stenograficheskiy otchet*, M. 1962, Vol. II, p. 409.

[3] Khrushchev's speech of February 25, 1955 was released in English for the press by the State Department on June 4, 1956.

on an increasingly larger scale and more stubbornly through punitive organs, at the same time often violating all existing norms of morality and Soviet laws. Arbitrary behavior by one person encouraged and permitted arbitrariness in others. Mass arrests and deportations of many thousands of people, execution without trial and without normal investigation created conditions of insecurity, fear and even desperation. [1]

Mass repressions and brutal acts involving socialist legality violations were greatly intensified after the murder of S. M. Kirov.

On December 1, 1934, on Stalin's initiative and without the approval of the Politbureau, it was given two days later, the Secretary of the Presidium of the Central Executive Committee, Yenikidze, signed the following directive :

> I. Investigative agencies are directed to speed up the cases of those accused of the preparation of the execution of terroristic acts.
>
> II. Judicial organs are directed not to hold up the execution of death sentences pertaining to crimes of this category in order to weigh the possibility of pardon, because the Presidium of the Central Executive Committee, USSR, does not consider as possible the receiving of petitions of this sort.
>
> III. The organs of the Commissariat of Internal Affairs are directed to execute the death sentences against criminals of the above-mentioned category immediately after the passing of the sentence.

This directive became the basis for mass acts of abuse against socialist legality. In many of the fabricated court cases the accused were charged with the "preparation of terroristic acts "that deprived them of any possibility that their cases might be re-examined, even when they stated before the court that their "confessions" were secured by force, and even when they disproved the accusation against them in a convincing manner. [2]

Still the slaughter-house did not work efficiently enough, according to Stalin's taste, since Khruschev relates that Stalin and Zhdanov cabled from Sochi (a sea-resort) on September 25, 1936, to Kaganovich, Molotov and other members of the Politbureau that Yezhov should replace Yagoda as Commissar of Internal Affairs, since Yagoda "has definitely proved himself to be uncapable of unmasking the Trotskyite-

---

[1] Pp. 8-9. See the account according to her own experience by Eugenia Ginzburg, "Journey into the Whirlwind", translated by Paul Stevenson and Max Hayward, N.Y., 1967.

[2] *Ibid.*, p. 15.

Zinovievite bloc". and that "the OGPU is four years behind in this matter".

Following Stalin's instructions, Yezhov was appointed People's Commissar of Internal Affairs and the February-March 1937 plenary session of the Central Committee of the All-Union Communist Party (B) adopted a resolution stating that "the People's Commissariat of Internal Affairs has fallen behind at least four years in the attempt to unmask these most inexorable enemies of the people (the anti-Soviet Trotskiyite Center and its followers). [1]

The appointment of Yezhov started a period of a tremendous growth of mass repressions in 1936 which were named after its main perpetrator "*Yezhovshchina*", (Yezhov's era).

Convictions were had on the basis of extorted confessions—"decisive" evidence, according to Vyshinsky.

Let us give two examples taken from Khrushchev's speech.

A candidate for the Politbureau, Eikhe, a most eminent worker of the Party and Soviet Government and a Party member since 1905, was arrested on the basis of slanderous materials, without the sanction of the prosecutor, which was received 15 months later.

Eikhe was forced, under torture, to sign a confession of anti-Soviet activity, prepared by the investigating magistrate.

Eikhe sent a letter to Stalin in which he declared : "The confessions which were made part of my file are not only absurd but contain some slander of the Central Committee of the All-Union Communist Party ... Not being able to suffer the tortures which I was submitted to—by Ushakov and Nicolayev—who utilized the knowledge that my broken ribs had not properly mended, and have caused me great pain—I have been forced to confess and accuse myself and others ..."

When brought to court Eikhe stated : "In all the so-called confessions of mine, there is not one letter written by me with the exception of my signature-which was forced from me. I have made my confession under pressure from the investigating magistrate who from the time of my arrest tortured me. After that I began to write all the nonsense—the most important thing for me is to tell the court, the Party and Stalin that I am not guilty. I have never been guilty of any conspiracy. I shall die believing in the truth of Party policy as I have believed in it during my entire life".

---

[1] *Ibid.*, p. 16.

Eikhe was shot and posthumously rehabilitated after Stalin's death when it definitely was established that Eikhe's case was fabricated!

Also Rudzutak, a candidate to the Politbureau and a Party member of 1905, retracted the confession which was forced on him. He asked the Supreme Military Court to inform the Party Central Committee that there is in the NKVD a center which is craftily manufacturing cases, which forces innocent persons to confess; there is no opportunity to prove one's non-particpation in crimes to which confessions of various persons testify. The investigative methods are such that they force people to lie and to slander entirely innocent persons in addition to those who already are accused.

The trial lasted 20 minutes; after the pronouncement of the sentence Rudzutak was shot.

Also he was posthumously rehabilitated in 1955. [1]

"Facts prove, said Khrushchev, that many abuses were perpetrated on Stalin's orders without taking into account any norms of Party and Soviet legality.

Stalin was a very distrustful man, sickly suspicious; we knew this from our work with him, he could look at a man and say : 'why are your eyes so shifty today', or 'why are you turning so much today and avoiding to look me directly in the eyes'.

The sickly suspicion created in him a general distrust even toward eminent Party workers whom he had known for years. Everywhere and in everything he saw 'enemies', 'two-faced persons' and 'spies' ". [2]

Lists of persons whose cases were under the jurisdiction of the Military College and whose sentences were prepared in advance, Yezhov would sent to Stalin personally for his approval of the proposed punishment. In 1937-38 alone, 383 such lists were sent to Stalin, with thousands of names of Party, Soviet, Komsomol, art and economic workers. He approved all these lists. [3]

When Stalin said that one or another should be arrested, it was necessary to accept on faith that he was an "enemy of the people".

Meanwhile, Beria's gang, which ran the organs of state security, outdid itself in proving the guilt of the arrested persons and the truth of the material which it falsified. "And what proofs were offered" ?

---

[1]   *Ibid.*, pp. 21-22.

[2]   *Ibid.*, p. 25.

[3]   *Ibid.*, p. 24.

Khrushchev asked and gave the answer : "the confessions of the arrested, and the investigating magistrates accepted these confesions".

Khrushchev posed another question : "And how is it possible that a person confesses to crimes which he has not committed" ? The answer is : "Only in some way—because of application of physical methods of persecuting him, tortures, bringing him into a state of unconsciousness, deprivation of his judgment, taking-away of his human dignity. In this manner were confessions acquired". [1]

At this point Khrushchev came to the perhaps most monstrous part of his sinister narration.

He told the Congress that when the wave of mass arrests began to recede in 1939, and leaders of territorial Party organizations began to accuse the NKVD workers of using methods of physical pressure on the arrested persons, Stalin dispatched a coded telegram, on January 20, 1939, to the committee secretaries of the republic communist parties, to the People's Commissariat of Internal Affairs and to the heads of NKVD organizations which reads as follows :

"The Central Committee of the All-Union Communist Party explains that the application of methods of physical pressure is permissible, from 1937 on, in accordance with the permission of the Central Committee of the All-Union Communist Party (B) ... The Central Committee of the All-Union Communist Party (B) considers that physical pressure should still be used obligatorily as an exceptional application to known and obstinate enemies of the people, as a method both justifiable and appropriate". [2]

A "justification" of the measure is given in the same telegram. "It is known", Stalin asserted, "that all bourgeois intelligence services use methods of physical influence against the representatives of the socialist proletariat and that they use them in their most scandalous form. The question arises as to why the socialist intelligence service should be more humanitarian in dealing with the mad agents of the bourgeoisie, against the deadly enemies of the working class and of the kolkhoz workers".

Thus, medieval methods of criminal investigation were sanctioned in the name of the highest organ of the Communist Party by a willful despot, by the same Stalin who declared that "socialist legality is not simply words" a couple of years before.

---

[1] *Ibid.*, p. 25.

[2] *Ibid.*, p. 26.

According to Khrushchev, after the war, Stalin became even more capricious, irritable and brutal; in particular his suspicion grew. His persecution mania reached unbelievable dimensions. Everything was decided by him alone, without any consideration for anyone or anything. The extermination of innocent people was continued; Khrushchev disclosed the cases of other eminent communists arrested, accused of crimes they had never committed but confessed, under torture.

Let us cite the last case which did not come to a tragic end, because of Stalins' death.

It is the affair of "Doctor Plotters".

The case was started by a letter to Stalin written by a woman-doctor Timashuk, an unofficial collaborator of the Organs of State Security. She accused a group of doctors of applying supposedly improper methods of medical treatment.

Such a letter was sufficient for Stalin to make an immediate conclusion that there are doctor-plotters in the Soviet Union. He issued orders to arrest a group of eminent Soviet medical specialists, and personally issued advice on the conduct of the investigation and the method of investigation to be applied to the arrested persons. He ordered that the Academician Vinogradov should be put in chains, another doctor be beaten; the Minister of State Security, Ignat'yev, was told by Stalin : "If you do not obtain confessions from the doctors we will shorten you by a head".

Stalin personally called the investigating magistrate, and advised him on the investigative methods to be used; these methods were simple : beat, beat and once again,—beat.

"Shortly after the doctors were arrested—Khrushchev relates—we, members of the Politbureau, received protocols with the doctors' confessions of guilt. After distributing these protocols Stalin told us : 'You are blind like young kittens; what will happen without me ! The country will perish because you do not know how to recognize the enemies' !

The case was so presented that no one could verify the facts on which the investigation was based. There was no possibility of trying to check by contacting those who had made the confessions of guilt.

We felt, however, that the case of the arrested doctors was questionable. We knew some of these people personally because they had treated us. When we examined their 'case' after Stalin's death, we found it fabricated from the beginning to end". [1]

---

[1]   *Ibid.*, pp. 40-41.

Thus, Khrushchev's revelations draw an outrageous picture of the administration of justice in the period of so-called cult of personality under Stalin's dictatorship.

The question of how it was possible that hundreds of well-known communists with a number of members of Lenin's old guard among them, and high among the old Lenin leaders, could confess to be agents of foreign espionage organizations, of conspiracies against communism which they had dedicated their entire lives to promote, how they could confess to crimes obviously incompatible with their psychology and political convictions, has occupied the West for many years, and was answered by Khrushchev : unbearable torture was used as an expedient, medieval method strengthened by contemporary techniques of producing confessions of any crime were employed, however incongruous. But Vyshinsky, as a legal scholar in his works pointed to Article 136 of the old RSFSR Code of Criminal Procedure prohibiting the investigating magistrate "to strive for testimony or a confession of the accused by means of violence, threats or other similar measures". In his capacity of the USSR Prosecutor he used these confessions, extorted by torture, against accused of whom he knew that the cases against them were framed from beginning to end : he asked and obtained the death penalty against people he knew were innocent!

Although Khrushchev disclosed the truth about the investigations and trials before the military tribunal, directed against high members of the Communist Party, its organizations and the government, he did not mention with even a single word, the work of the Special Board of the NKVD from 1934 to 1953 which meted out administrative punishment against thousands of innocent citizens.

In reality, the procedural methods applied by the investigating magistrates of this Board were the same as employed by the investigating magistrates of the Military Tribunal : the producing of a confession extorted by torture.

The administration of justice by the Board was ever more expedient than the Military Tribunal; on the basis of the "confession" the accused, although not executed, was sent to a forced labor camp in the extreme North for 5-15 years of work under most appalling conditions.

To be sure, the Soviet citizen, according to Soviet theory, has no "inalienable" rights acquired from nature by virtue of his birth. Every right of the—individual is only a right granted to him by Soviet law. But fundamental rights of the Soviet citizens were recognized and defined in Chapter X of the 1936 Constitution and still systematically violated during the "cult of personality".

How did these flagrant violations of legality in political cases affect general criminal cases?

It must be assumed that Vyshinsky's interpretation of evidence had a pernicious influence on the work of investigating magistrates, prosecutors and courts. The striving for "confession" by the accused must have become the working method of many investigating magistrates also in general criminal cases. Since the application of methods of physical pressure was officially sanctioned in NKVD practice, why should it not be used against reticent and obstinate accused persons? Physical pressure approved as an investigating method could have been easily used also in non-political cases.

So looked administration of justice during the cult of personality.

This did not prevent, however, M. Kareva to define socialist legality in 1947 in the following words: [1]

"Justice in the USSR—is real justice. Justice in the USSR stands on watch over socialist legality, defending the public and national structure of the state, the socialist legal order, the rule of socialist community and all the numerous rights of the citizens embodied in fundamental laws of the soviet country, from any attempt against them".

E. LEGALITY AFTER STALIN'S DEATH

At the end of his speech at the XXth Congress of the USSR, Khrushchev declared that the evil caused by acts violating revolutionary socialist legality which have accumulated for a long time as a result of the negative influence of the cult of personality has to be made good completely. [2]

He also said that "it is necessary that our Party, State, Military and trade union organizations should stand on guard over Soviet laws and unmask and expose everyone who makes attempts upon the socialist legal order and the rights of Soviet citizens and severely suppress every expression of lawlessness and arbitrariness". [3]

The Special Board was dissolved in September 1953.

Also provisions permitting exceptions from procedural norms regu-

---

[1] M. Kareva, "Socialist Legality", *Bol'shaya Sovetskaya entsiklopediya* (1st Edition), M. 1947, Vol. 52, pp. 217-218.

[2] Department of State, *For the Press, op. cit.*, p. 24.

[3] *XX S'ezd Kommunistiheskoy partii Sovetskogo Soyuza. Stenograficheskiy otchet*, M. 1956, p. 423.

lating the examination by courts of cases involving crimes against the state and establishing special forms of investigation and court examination of sabotage cases, terroristic acts and especially dangerous sabotage (diversiya) were abolished.

In the Resolution of the XXth Congress of the Soviet Union Communist Party (1956) adopted pursuant to the Report of the Central Committee of the Party, it was said : "The Congress completely approves the measures undertaken by the Central Committee of the Party for the strengthening of Soviet legality and the strict observance of citizen's rights as guaranteed by the Soviet Constitution, and charges all the Party and Soviet organs with the watchful guard over legality and the resolute and severest suppression of any expression of illegality, arbitrariness and the violation of socialist order". [1]

The principle of legality has been also stressed in laws published after Stalin's death. Thus, the RSFSR Law on the Basic Principles of Legislation on Court Structure of the USSR, the Union and Autonomous Republics of 1958 provides in Article 20 that justice in the USSR has the scope of insuring the exact and unflinching fulfillment of law by all institutions, organizations, officials and citizens of the USSR.

This provision is repeated in all laws on court structure of the Union and Autonomous Republics (Article 2 of the RSFSR Law of October 27, 1960).

Also the independence of judges and their submission only to law are again asserted in the Statute on Military Tribunals of December 25, 1958 (Article 6) and in the Statute on the USSR Supreme Court of February 11, 1957 (Article 2).

Furthermore, the crimes against the state are no longer examined by Military Tribunals. According to the Statute on Military Tribunals of December 25, 1958, [2] the competence of these tribunals extends to military persons only, with the exception of all cases of espionage which remained under the jurisdiction of the Military Tribunals (Article 9).

The Basic Principles of Criminal Procedure of the USSR and the Union Republic [3] provides (Article 7) that the administration of justice in criminal cases is to be carried out only by courts and that no one

---

[1] *Kommunisticheskaya partiya sovetskogo soyuza v resheniyakh i rezolyutsiyakh, s"ezdov, konferentsiy i plenumov Ts-K.*, Part IV, 1954-1960, M. 1961, p. 138.

[2] *V.V.S., 1959*, Item 14.

[3] *Ibid.*, Item 15.

may be declared guilty of committing a crime and undergo criminal punishment except by virtue of a court sentence.

The inviolability of the person was confirmed by Article 6 of the same Law providing that no one may be arrested except upon a court decision, or with the approval of the prosecutor. The prosecutor is charged with the immediate release of every person illegally deprived of liberty or detained in extension of the term provided by law or a court sentence.

The Basic Principles of Court Structure of the USSR and the Union and Autonomous Republics of December 25, 1958 [1] (Article 6) provides that the administration of justice is realized in the USSR in strict correspondence with the USSR legislation and the legislation of the union and autonomous republics.

The call for legality resounds louder and louder after the liquidation of the cult of personality in legislation and the legal literature. But, in the latter not unanimously.

Thus, Strogovich complains that views are expressed that the task of strengthening legality has only a temporary character, that after the violations of legality disclosed at the XXth Congress have been eliminated, the question of legality has lost its importance. "We are sometimes ironically questioned—Strogovich relates—till when, Comrades, will you cease speaking about the strengthening of legality? How much more time do you need to strengthen this legality? How much longer do you want to occupy yourself with this matter? And we answer : We will speak about the strengthening of legality and strive toward it as long as the Soviet socialist state exists, as long as this state realizes the main role in the construction of communism, as long as Soviet laws are published in which the will of the Soviet people and the policy of the Communist state are expressed, as long as a strong state discipline is necessary. Hence, so long shall we speak about the strengthening of legality and show strengthening by all means". [2]

On June 23 to June 26, 1959, the USSR Academy of Sciences held a session of its Social Science Departments dedicated to questions connected with the transition from socialism to communism.

In his report "On the Role of the Soviet State in Communist Construction", V. V. Nikolayev declared that there is no purpose to be

---

[1] *Ibid.*, Item 12.

[2] M.S. Strogovich, "Some Questions of State and Law", in *Voprosy stroitel'stva kommunisma v SSSR*, M. 1959, p. 300.

served in speaking about the function of the state as consisting in the protection of rights and interests of citizens and socialist legality. Since attempts against these rights and legality were undertaken only by exploiting classes and the international bourgeoisie which strived by united efforts to overthrow the Soviet regime in the first phase of development of the Soviet socialist state, [1] in defending the country and suppressing the resistance of the exploiting classes the Soviet state protected at the same time the Soviet legal order, legality, and the citizens' liberty.

"Who poses the threats to the socialist legal order, citizen s'rights and legality in the second main phase of development of the Soviet Socialist state after the liquidation of exploiting classes, the internal class forces which had the purpose to overthrow the Soviet rule, annihilate the Soviet legal order, the rights and liberty of Soviet citizens" ? asks Nikolayev. His answer to this is that also in the second phase of its development, the Soviet state, in defending the country from the capitalist camp, protects the Soviet legal order, rights and interests of its citizenry from outside attempts against them.

With regard to violations of legality on the part of individual Soviet citizens, they may be taken care of by such organs of the Soviet state as the militia, prosecution body and the courts". [2]

Thus, Nikolayev denies a specific function of the state to protect legality and the citizens' rights and liberty.

Nikolayev's viewpoint was strongly opposed by Strogovich.

The question, from whom legality and citizens' rights should be protected when the exploiting classes have been liquidated, Strogovich answers with the assertion that criminals still exist in the Soviet Union, that antisocial elements make attempts upon interests and rights of Soviet citizens, that there are people who assume a soulless attitude toward the Soviet masses, ignore their interests and their essential needs.

The protection of citizens' rights and legality is, according to Strogovich, not only an essential state function when these rights or legality is violated, but its main duty is the prevention of such violations, the creation of conditions "insuring to the people, the pos-

---

[1] The first phase of development is the transition from capitalism to socialism and the second—from socialism to communism.

[2] V.V. Nikolayev, "On the Role of the Soviet State in the Communist Constitution", in *Voprosy stroitel'stva kommunisma v SSSR*, M. 1959, p. 276.

sibility to live, create, work and participate in public life, to enjoy all the material and spiritual blessings of socialist society, without fear that their rights and legitiamte interests will be violated". [1]

The protection of rights of Soviet Citizens and legality as an important function of the State was emphasized in another report at the same session of the Academy of Sciences.

N. S. Romashkin asserted : "The viewpoint of those who think that the protection of legitimate rights and interests of citizens must be considered as an independent, most important function of the Soviet state is, in our opinion, completely correct". [2]

According to Romashkin, the real democratic character of the Soviet state finds its expression in this protective function, the highest principle of which is the care for the well-being of the Soviet masses, of the physical and spiritual development of the people.

The recognition of the protection of the citizens' rights and legality as major functions of the Soviet state is a new element in Soviet legal thinking. Strogovich wrote (in 1959) that this thought appeared in Soviet literature only recently. [3] He explains the absence of previous recognition of this functions by the cult of personality. [4]

Indeed, we have already underlined that Stalin saw the scope of legality in the protection of socialist property only, and citizens' rights were not even mentioned by him.

It is only natural that in times when the violation of personal rights, liberty and legality occurred "epidemically, sporadically and endemically", no emphasis was put on the preservation of personal rights and liberty, although lip service was paid to legality.

The recognition of the protection of citizens' rights, liberty and legality as a major function of the Soviet State, although only by some scholars, is till a step in the right direction.

Gorkin asserts that, as a consequence of the liquidation of the cult of personality and the adoption of the Basic Principles of 1958, the normal procedure of investigation and examination of criminal cases has been restored. All crimes are examined by court exclusively under

---

[1] M.S. Strogovich, "Some Questions of State and Law", in *Voprosy stroitel'stva kommunisma v SSSR*, M. 1959, p. 295.

[2] N.S. Romashkin, "The Development of Soviet State Functions in the Transition Process to Communism", *ibid.*, p. 114.

[3] The first time in an article "Basic Development Stages and Main Directions of Soviet State Activity", by F.I. Kalinychev, in 1958.

[4] Strogovich, in *Voprosy stroitel'stva...*, *op. cit.*, p. 296.

the observance of all procedural norms, publicly, with the participation of prosecutors and counsel.

Gorkin assures that "now all conditions for a correct administration of justice and the strictest observance of legality by organs of investigation, court, prosecution and militia are created". [1]

"At the present time, no one may be convicted of a crime and undergo punishment except in consequence of a court sentence", confirmed Shelepin, at that time Chairman of the KGB (Committee of State Security), at the XXIInd Congress of the USSR Communist Party in 1961. He added that the KGB has been completely reorganized and that "in our country, the inviolability of the individual is strictly insured not in words but in reality according to our Constitution". [2]

It seems, however, that the first acts of the Party leadership and the Soviet government after Stalin's death, namely the exclusion of Beria from the Party, his trial and execution followed the same line, established by Stalin and vehemently denounced by Khruschhev in 1956.

About the exclusion from the Party we learn from a decision of the Central Committee of the Communist Party of the Soviet Union, disclosed in a speech by Malenkov delivered in July 1953. One of the reasons for the exclusion was "the undermining of the Soviet state to the benefit of the foreign capital". [3]

On December 23, 1953, Beria was tried by the Special Court of the USSR Supreme Court behind closed doors and condemned to death. Since no appeal whatso-ever existed against such sentences, Beria was executed the same day.

In the motivation of the sentence it was said, among other reasons, that the accused : "was guilty of high treason to the benefit of foreign capital ... of secret connections with foreign spy services ... that these connections started already in 1919 ... that during the subsequent years, Beria had continued his connections to foreign spy services and developed ... that Beria had confessed in the preliminary investigation and during the trial that he was guilty of the most serious crimes against the State".

---

[1] A.F. Gorkin, "On the Problems of Soviet Courts in the Period of Intensive Construction of Communism", in *Sovetskaya obshchestvennost' na strazhe sots. zak.*, *op. cit.*, pp. 83-84.

[2] XXII *S"ezd kommunisticheskoy partii Sovetskogo soyuza. Stenograficheskiy otchet*, M. 1962, VII, p. 407.

[3] *Kommunisticheskaya partiya sovetskogo soyuza v resolyutsiyakh i resheniyakh*, M. 1953, V. II, p. 1152.

We found in this sentence all the accusations which played such an important role in the trials of the thirties and subsequently, including the obligatory confession. [1]

Not denying the infamous role of Beria in Soviet life, the conclusion seems near that his alleged relations to foreign spy services is incredible as those of the Soviet leaders of the thirties, and that his confession was obtained by the same means which were applied up to 1953 and so strongly denounced by Khrushchev.

F. CONCLUSIONS

We have seen that no legality was observed by the socialist revolutionary courts in the period between the October Revolution and the publication of the Decree on Courts No. 1 because no laws or only a restricted number of generale laws in force existed and the "courts" had to rely almost completely on the revolutionary law consciousness of judges.

After the publication of the Decree No. 3 on Courts and the prohibition of the use of any tsarist law, the courts had to revert to their revolutionary law consciousness, although a number of Soviet laws were already published but of a general nature and greatly insufficient to cover all aspects of Soviet life.

When the various Codes were introduced in 1922-1923, legality could have been observed, but the activity of the CheKa, GPU and OGPU which was steadily extended beyond the legal limits of the agencies' competence, brought about frequent violations of legality.

During the period of collectivization the law was violated in the process of the forcible liquidation of the kulaks and the collectivization of the peasants.

Then the trials of the thirties and the activity of the Special Board of the NKVD and the steadily increasing cult of personality produced a situation in which legality was constantly violated until Stalin's death.

The post-Stalin era may be characterized as an intensification of the call for legality in legal works and Party pronouncements. The New Criminal Code and the Code of Criminal Procedure were a step

---

[1] "For Lasting Peace, People's Democracy", German Edition, Bukharek, December 23-31, 1958, p. 2; The Documents on the Beria trial cited on preceding page and footnote 1 on this page are quoted in Walter Grottian, *Das Sowjetische Regierungssystem*, Köln and Opladen, 1965, pp. 514 and 515.

toward liberalization of the penal legislation and the strengthening of the rights of the individual in criminal procedure.

But even if flagrant violations of legality "en masse" do occur no longer, nothing is changed in the main feature of Soviet administration of justice : its dependence upon the Party and the administration.

The law never stood above the state under the Soviet regime. The Communist Party and the Soviet government always were free to break the law created by themselves when they deemed it necessary in the interest of the socialist or communist experiment.

All organs of the administration of justice in the Soviet state were and are under the influence of the Party and the government.

It was Marx who worked out the basic principles which had to be applied in the administration of justice and had to replace the "rotten" bourgeois administration :

He prescribed first of all, the election of the justices by the people; secondly, their responsibility to their electors; thirdly, their removability; fourthly, their remuneration on a similar level as the workers.

Another basic principle is that as long as other classes shall exist ... as long as the proletariat is fighting them ... (since with the advent to power by the proletariat its enemies do not disappear at once), it must apply coercion. [1]

But the Soviets cannot pretend that they have realized Marx's principle in the administration of justice. Indeed, what has been carried out from the fundamentals of a socialist administration of justice during the 50 years of Soviet power? Electivity of justices has been postponed 31 years, and when introduced it is still a Soviet brand of election-tantamount to appointment.

The responsibility of judges, i.e., the procedure of their revocation, is not regulated up to the present time.

Revocability of justices as counteropposed to the bourgeois irrevocability makes the Soviet justice even more subject to influence in comparison to their irrevocable predecessors.

Also the remuneration of justices is not put into relation with workers' wages.

Only the principle of coercion has been thoroughly applied and prolonged far beyond the time prescribed by Marx since no classes to be fought by the proletariat exist anymore, and the dictatorship

---

[1] Marx and Engels, *Sochineniya*, M. 1918-1937, XV, 186.

of the proletariat which had to have lost its *raison d'être* with the
disappearance of the enemy classes, was continued up to the present
time.

If Marx called the bourgeois justices indifferently to the political
regime of a capitalist country "inquisitors of legality", "livery valets",
"vile toadies scrawling before state power", "vampires sucking
out the blood of toilers", how is the Soviet judge—a Party's tool
under Party directive pressure—to be called?

Bourgeois philosophers asserted that there are perpetual human
values, unchangeable moral principles, a consciousness above and
beyond class appurtenance, a law above the king and the state equaly
obligatory to the creators and the citizens, whereas Marx asserted
that only class moral, class consciousness and class consciense exist. [1]

Directed by his class moral, inspired by socialist law consciousness,
the Soviet judge must strive to preserve Socialist legality—to this
effect he has, however, to observe the interests of the Party and the
State in the first place of necessity to the detriment of justice.

It is evident that state and party interests are not only involved
in so-called political cases in the Soviet Union, where the state is the
employer, legislator and administrator at the same time.

That the Party line stands over the law has been also stated by
Vyshinsky as far back as 1936. He wrote that in case of colusion
between the formal requirement of law and party policy, law must
be subordinated to Party policy. [2]

Vyshinsky's declaration discloses the particularity of socialist legality as compared to simple legality observed in Western democracies.
There legality means the strict observance of law only. Socialist
legality, however, is the compliance with law only as far as it does
not contradict the Party line in force at the given time. In the latter
case, law cedes its supremacy to Party policy.

Nobody like Vyshinsky has so clearly and definitely formulated the
real essence of socialist legality, and if many of his assertions have
been repudiated after 1956, his definition of socialist legality and
law consciousness and theories on the process of sentence formation
by the judges stand to the present time.

---

[1] L. Mamut and A. Ugryumov, "Karl Marx on Court and Justice", *Sov. yust.*, 1958,
No. 5, p. 8.

[2] See A. Ye. Vyshinsky and V.S. Undrevich, *Kurs ugolovnogo protsesse*, M. 1930,
p. 36.

We must be aware that the call for strengthening of legality, which does not cease in the Soviet Union is an urge for "socialist" legality, exacly as Vyshinsky understood it, since another legality cannot exist in a socialist state under the sovereign rule of the Communist Party.

That is why Vyshinsky required from the judge to watch first of all over the interest of socialist construction in the process of sentence formation. He put the same requirement even to the socialist lawyer. "The counsel"—he wrote—"must present all his arguments in defense of the accused not leaving the soil of principles common to the court, the accusation and the entire country, namely, of the interests of socialist construction, of the interests of the state and the dictatorship of the proletariat",—He asserted that the advocate must be able to defend his viewpoint and to fight fearlessly for that in which he believes proceeding not from the interests of his clients, but from the interests of socialist construction, from interests of the state.

The Polish legal philosopher, Grzegorz Leopold Seidler correctly discerns between legal consciousness and socialist consciousness. Whereas legal consciousness is the knowledge of the law but also positive evaluation of the law expressed by acceptance of all the legal order, as something right and appropriate, socialist consciousness is perhaps tedious to an individual with a definite way of thinking and, consequently, of behaving. His consciousness is the sum of values and attitudes resulting from adoption of Marxist philosophy. This last consciousness is not a fixed and unchangeable quantity that can be reduced to its component parts; it is a dynamic thing always in process of growth, comprized of judgment, inner experience and, hence, outward acts. [1]

Thus, a Soviet judge, who is forming the sentence according to his socialist legal consciousness must be, first of all, a convinced Marxist applying the Soviet law which he knows and accepts as completely right and appropriate. Such a law consciousness overshadowed by its socialist character, is a sure cover for law violations.

We have seen how, "public opinion", shaped by the Party and manifested in the court has influenced the sentence, and thereby did so.

The influence of the "public opinion of the court was denounced by Anashkin". [2]

---

[1] G.L. Seidler, "Marxist Legal Thought in Poland", *The Slavic Review*, 1967, No. 3, pp. 386-387.

[2] G.Z. Anashkin, "The Role of Law Consciousness and Public Opinion in the Setting of Punishment", *S.G.P.*, 1967, No. 1, p. 44.

But speaking of the influence which can be exercised by public opinion, Anashkin states candidly that "public opinion cannot be put in a more privileged position with regard to the court, than the political institutions of the state, the local organs of power, local Party and public organizations, which as it is well known, *cannot* (italics provided) interfere with the solution of criminal and civil cases by the court".

Indeed, they "cannot" but they do.

Feifer reports a conversation he had with a lawyer in Moscow :

"The judges get the word", said his interlocutor.

"From whom? How ?", asked Feifer.

"Don't be so naive : *sverkhu* (from above), from the smell of things, from the way the wind is blowing ... the *rukovodstvo* (leadership or brass) makes known what it wants in a thousand ways and the court makes decisions accordingly ..." [1]

Writing in "General Theory of Soviet Law", Pigolkin bitterly complains against the bourgeois theoreticians and politicians declaring that the Party has completely usurped power, exercises unrestricted dictatorship, controls all aspects of Soviet society, and life requiring blind obedience.

"In legal matters, in particular, many anti-communists", he writes, "attempting to slander the Soviet judicial system by all means, strive to present the situation so as if the Soviet judges, being simple agents of party policy have no authentic independence". [2]

Against the assertions : by Berman that the Soviet legislative body depends completely upon the Party leadership and, thus, cannot be really free; [3] by Ginsburg and Russis that Soviet Law, being a convenient political instrument of the ruling circles in the USSR has lost from the beginning any real independence; [4] by Hazard that "in the routine case involving no politics, the Soviet lawyer seems to feel free to defend his client's interests as he wishes, but in political cases he has to limit his activities to what the Communist

---

[1] George Feifer, *Justice in Moscow, op. cit.*, p. 248.

[2] A.S. Pigolkin, "Basic Features of Contemporary Anti-Communism in the Field of Legal Theory", in *Obshchaya teoriya sovetskogo prava*. Edited by A.N. Bratus' and I.S. Samoshchenko, M. 1966, pp. 454-455.

[3] Harold Berman, "The Comparison of Soviet and American Law", *Indiana Law Journal*, 1959, No. 4, p. 566.

[4] G. Ginsburg and A. Rusis, "Soviet Criminal Law and the Protection of State Secrets", in *Law in Eastern Europe*, Leyden 1963, p. 46.

Party policy-makers feel is permissible defense; and that people's assessors cannot reflect public opinion since the party shares in their selection and they must carry out its decisions and the judges are not free since they have to follow the policy of the Communist Party of the Soviet Union, [1] Pigolkin brings the following argumentation :

Acknowledging the leading role of the Communist Party, he asserts that the Party fulfills the mission of the revolutionary transformation of the society, with honor. Its leading role is to explain by the fact that being the Party of the People themselves, it is armed with the authentic Marxist-Leninist methodology, deeply and correctly realizes the objective regularities of society development, inspires the people and directs their will and energy on the way to the speediest construction of communism ... Furthermore, he asserts that "the leading role of the Party is based on its moral authority and the unlimited confidence of the people".

The Party decisions, "have, namely, an enormous moral authority. [2] *Just in this and only in this* (stress provided) consist the party's power and its capacity to influence the masses and lead them". Candidly, he explains it by the fact that "the Party does not administer, does not publish legally obligatory decisions, Party decisions, being a form of Party leadership, are not sources of law, do not establish legal norms".

Pigolkin comes to the following conclusion : "in the light of that which was said above", Touster's assertion that "Party instructions are highest law in the USSR", [3] is not convincing. [4]

Also Perfil'yev states that "the Party leans upon its moral authority and the acknowledgement of the rightousness of its policy and guidance by the widest liars of the population. [5]

Thus, both authors do not deny the decisive influence of the Party in all aspects of Soviet life, including the administration of justice, declaring, however, that Party influence is based on its moral authority

---

[1] John N. Hazard, The Soviet System of Government", Chicago, 1957, pp. 165, 160, 153, 193. Pigolkin has summarized the viewpoint of the authors under 3, 4, and 5 on the preceding page so that not the original text has been reproduced here but Pigolkin's words retranslated into English.

[2] *Ibid.*, p. 455.

[3] John Touster, *European Political Systems*, N.Y., 1959, p. 604.

[4] Pigolkin, *op. cit.*, p. 455.

[5] M.N. Perfil'yev, *Kritika burzhuaznykh teoriy o sovetskoy politicheskoy sisteme*, M. 1968, p. 138.

only. They evidently forget or have to forget, that this authority is supported also by the entire power of the Soviet State and that Party directions were enforced and implemented by the most subtle and ruthless coercion apparatus invented by mankind.

Khrushchev's revelations at the XXth Congress had a tremendous impact on the Soviet people. Helene Zamoyska relates that Pasternak has said to her : "A world crushed down and a new one will be born". [1]

Certainly, the cult of personality is dead, but not the features which made it possible. The "new world" expected by Pasternak did not bring the loss of the importance of influence of the Communist Party. Declarations about the inviolability of legality are made by Soviet leaders as in the past. Thus, L. I. Brezhnev declared at the XXIIIrd Congress of the Soviet Union Communist Party : "The Party proceeds from the [assumption] that the entire activity of Soviet organs and the wide participation of citizens in the administration of the country's affairs must be based on the strictest observation of socialist legality". [2] Nevertheless, the Party continues to interfere in judicial matters when it deems appropriate, causing flagrant violation of legality.

We have in mind the trials of A. D. Sinyavsky and Daniel in 1966, of V. I. Bukovsky in the fall of 1967 and of Alexandre Ginzburg, Yuriy Galanskov, Aleksey Dobrovol'sky and Vera Lashskova, in January 1968. All these persons have been sentenced to from 1 to 7 years in concentration camps.

Then, the trial of five persons who participated in a protest demonstration against the invasion of Czechoslovakia, on the Red Square in Moscow on August 25, 1968, took place in October 1968.

Accused and convicted were : Pavel Litvinov, who previously protested against the Sinyavsky-Daniel trial and was witness for the defense in the Bukovsky case (banished to a remote region for five years); Larissa Bogoraz-Daniel, wife of the convicted writer, (sent to a prison camp for four years); Konstantin Babitsky, a literary scholar at the Language Institute of the USSR Academy of Sciences, (exiled for three years); Vadim Delone, a poet, already under a one-year suspended sentence in 1967 for protest against the Sinyavsky-Daniel trial (received two and one-half years in jail and must serve

[1] Helene Zamoyska, "Siniavski et sa patrie", Preface to *Sinyavsky i Daniel na skam'ye podsudimykh*, N.Y., 1966, p. 9.

[2] *Materialy XXIII s"ezda KPSS*, M. 1966, p. 77.

four months of the suspended sentence); and Vladimir Dremlyuga, a worker (sentenced to three years in prison).

The accusation was based on the new Article 190³ of the RSFSR Criminal Code providing punishment for "group activity aimed at the undermining of public order".

In contradistinction to the previous trials for literary crimes and protests against them, the demonstration of August 25, 1968, although a peaceful one and completely in the limits permitted by the Constitution, was directed against the foreign policy of the Soviet government and was a manifestation of the striving not only for the freedom of expression, but for liberty in general.

This became evident from the statements of the accused in the trial :

"For the three minutes on Red Square, I felt free, I am glad to take your three years" [demanded by the prosecutor], declared Delone in his final statement.

"Freedom is important for us all. The freer each of us is in a great socialist state, the better it will be for all of us", asserted Litvinov in his statement.

Henry Kamm, the New York Times correspondent in Moscow, wrote that Delone's words represented the sentiments of all five defendents during the three day trial. [1]

A detailed analysis of the accusation and procedure is not necessary to establish flagrant violations of legality before and during the trials. Many well known features of the trials from the "dead world" were repeated in the cases of 1966-1968. It is sufficient to say that Article 70 of the new Criminal Code was applied to the action of accused which does not provide for such actions, thus, in violence of the principle *nullum crimen, nulla poena sine lege*; confessions of an accused, Dobrovol'sky, implying the guilt of co-accused without being supported by other evidence, was used, etc.

Furthermore, in order to punish persons participating in demonstration against the conviction of Daniel and Sinyavsky, Article 190 of the Criminal Code was amended by an Ukase of the Presidium of the USSR Supreme Soviet several months after the trial. Article 190³ forbids the organization of and particpation in group actions

---

[1] *The New York Times*, October 12, 1968, p. 7.

roughly violating public order, or connected with an evident insubordination to legal requests of the authority representing or causing
disruptions by the group of transportation work of state, public
institutions or enterprises. [1]

The provision of Article 190[3], inserted into the section of "Crimes
against the order of Administration" of the Criminal Code, is an evident
violation of Article 125[d] of the Constitution awarding the "freedom
of street procession and demonstrations" to Soviet citizens. Every
street procession and demonstration is a certain disturbance of public
order and Article 190[3] gives the possibility to the administration to
inhibit and punished every undesired street procession and demonstration in violance of Article 125d of the Constitution. [2]

Also the usual "preparation" of the trials took place. The accused
were condemned in advance by an avalanche of propaganda on the
pages of *Izvestia, Literaturnaya gazeta*, etc.

Evidently violated was also the principle of publicity, since only
carefully selected persons were admitted to the trial who established
by their behaviour, uninhibited by the court, the unfriendly atmosphere toward the accused, thought to express the "public opinion"
about their crimes. [3]

As Yakobson and Allen stated : "The procedure of this trial had
all the forms of a Soviet court of law but the essential trait of justice
to the defendants was lacking". [3]

The trial and its conduct were blamed even by some Communist
organs in the West. For instance, the Daily Worker of London wrote :
"The Soviet press attacks on the accused before the trial assumes
their guilt. So did the Tass version of what went on in the court.
Since no full and objective version of the proceedings of the trial
has appeared, outside opinion cannot form a proper judgment on the
proceedings. The court has found the accused guilty but the full
evidence for the prosecution and defense which led the court to the

---

[1]   *V.V.S., RSFSR*, 1966, Item 1038.

[2]   *The New York Times*, July 22, 1968, p. 15. For further details, see also :
Max Hayward (Editor, Translator and Introductory writer), *On Trial*, New York, 1966
and Evanston, 1967 ; Albert Boiter, *The Literary Trial and Soviet Legality*, Radio Liberty
Research (Mimeographed), Munich, February 13, 1968 ; *Survey*, London, 1968, No. 60,
pp. 145 ff.

[3]   Sergius Yakobson and Robert Allen, *Aspects of Intellectual Ferment and Dissent in
the Soviet Union*, Washington, D.C., U.S. Government Printing Office, October 4, 1968,
p. 27.

conclusion has not been made public. Justice should not only be done, but should be seen to be done. Unfortunately this cannot be said in the case of this trial". [1]

Also in the Ukrainian SSR arrest and trials took place caused by protests against violation of civil and cultural liberties. A number of Ukrainian intellectuals, scholars, teachers and writers were prosecuted, convicted and banished to concentration camps.

As in the RSFSR, also in the Ukrainian SSR, citizens protested against the violation of fundamental rights in a score of letters directed to the highest authorities of the Republic and the Prosecuting Body. A very enlightening material is collected in "The Chornovil Papers" published in the United States in 1968. [2]

But the best confirmation of the injustice and legality violations pertaining to these trials, is the tremendous wave of protest against inside and outside the Soviet Union.

Besides mass demonstration, hundreds of Soviet citizens wrote protest letters to the governemnt, the Supreme Soviet, the Central Committee of the Communist Party, and the press giving their full names and addresses. [3]

Let us quote as an example the words of the known Soviet nuclear physicist, Andrey D. Sakharov, Member of the USSR Academy of Sciences, who wrote in his essay "Thoughts on Progress, Peaceful Coexistence and Intellectual Freedom" : [4]

"The Daniel-Sinyavsky trial which has been condemned by the progressive public in the Soviet Union and abroad (from Louis Aragon to Graham Greene) and has compromised the Communist System, has still not been reviewed".

"Was it not disgraceful to allow the arrest, 12-month detention without trial and then the conviction and sentence of five to seven years, to Ginzburg, Galanskov and others for activities that actually amounted to a defense of civil liberties and (partly as an example) of Daniel and Sinyavsky personally".

"Wide indignation has been aroused by the recent decree adopted by the Supreme Soviet of the Russian Republic, amending the Cri-

---

[1] *Daily Worker*, London, February 15, 1966, p. 29. Quoted in *Aspects of Intellectual Ferment...*, *op. cit.*, p. 27.

[2] See *The Chornovil Papers*, Compiled by Viacheslav Chornovil, Foreword by Zbigniew Brzezinski, Introduction by Frederick C. Barghoorn, McGraw-Hill, New York, 1968.

[3] Letters of protest have been published by *Problems of Communism*, June-July, Sept.-Oct. 1968.

[4] *The New York Times*, July 22, 1968, p. 15.

minal Code, in direct confrontation to the civil rights procedures proclaimed by the Constitution".

"The author of these lines", Sakharov continued, "send an appeal to the Party's Central Committee on February 11, 1967, asking that the Ginzburg-Galanskov case be closed. He received no reply and no explanation on the case".

In an appeal to world public opinion, Pavel M. Litvinov and Larissa Daniel denounced the trial of Ginzburg, Galanskov and Lashkova, as a "wild mockery of justice", a "rehearsed spectacle". They wrote that "... the judicial trial has been carried out in violation of the most important principle of Soviet law. The judge and the prosecutor, with the participation of a special kind of audience have turned the trial into a wild mockery ... The defense lawyers are constantly forbidden to ask questions, and witnesses are not being allowed to give evidence that unmasks the Dobrovol'sky's provocation in the case (the man who 'confessed'.)". They concluded their appeal with the following words : "Citizens of our country, this trial is a stain on the honor of our state and on the conscience of every one of us ...

Today it is not only the fate of the accused which is in danger— their trial is no better than the celebrated trials of the nineteen-thirties, which involved us in so much shame and so much blood, that we have not recovered from them". [1]

In spite of the warning by the secutiry police, a protest was sent to the Presidium of the Conference of 66 Communist Parties which took place in Budapest in February 1968.

In thier appeal it was said that "scores of political trials in the recent years have been conducted with gross violence of legality ..." [2]

In the West, the trials have been condemned also by Communists in France and Italy and the United States.

The sentence was strongly protested also by the International Writers Organization of London. [3]

Svetlana Alliluyeva stated about the trials "The Soviet Law has been violated; the basic democratic freedoms of the citizen were ignored and the sentence predetermined by the government and secret police". [4]

---

1 *The New York Times*, January 13, 1968, pp. 1 and 8.
2 *Ibid.*, February 28, 1968.
3 *Ibid.*, January 17, 1968, p. 2.
4 *Ibid.*

Certainly, as remarked above, Traynin was right : there is no such things as "revolutionary", "socialist" or "bourgeois" legality. Legality is the strict observance of law in force in a socialist or capitalist state. However, it can be rigidly observed only in states where law is binding not only on citizens but on the administration as well, where law is above the state, i.e., in states under the rule of law.

The principle of supremacy of law was perfectly expressed in the answer of the miller of Sans-Souci to Friedrich II : "There are judges in Berlin" and by the words of Lord Coke addressed to James I : "The King is under God and law".

The Soviet state is not, and has never been, a state under the rule of law. It is and was always under the rule of individual persons and the Communist Party.

Neither Lenin nor Stalin, nor the Communist Party ever retreated before a law in force, or the absence of a legal norm inhibiting the realization of their desires. In the first case the law was simply broken, and in the second, the Criminal Code retroactively amended in order to *"sauver les apparences"*, and cover arbitrariness with a shine of legality.

A good example for such retroactive action is the law of July 1961 introducing into the RSFSR Criminal Code (Article 88) the death penalty for currency speculation. R. and F. namely, were tried and executed on grounds of this law [1] although their crime was committed before the Ukase of the Supreme Soviet Presidium was issued. Thus, the law of July 1961 was illegally applied to R. and E. retroactively.

In order to "legalize" this evident violation of legality, the Supreme Soviet Presidium issued a special Ukase for this case authorizing the court to apply the law of July 1961 retroactively. This Ukase was never publicized but Harold Berman relates that "a vice president of the USSR Supreme Court showed it to me". [2]

Another example is the amendment of Art. 190 of the Penal Code mentioned above.

In their joint address to "Workers of the Soviet Judicial Organs" on the occasion of the 50th Jubilee of the Soviet court, the USSR Communist Party and the Presidium of the USSR Supreme Soviet declared that "with the victory of the Great Socialist October Revolution, the most democratic and authentically popular court system

---

[1] *Pravda*, July 25, 1961.

[2] Harold J. Berman, "The Role of Soviet Jurists in the Struggle to Prevent a Return to Stalinist Terror", *Harvard Law School Bulletin*, December 1962, No. 3, p. 4.

was created in our country adopted in the first days of Soviet power, the formulation of which was laid out by the Decrees on Courts, on Lenin's initiative". [1]

We have endeavored to describe the development and operation of the Soviet court from its birth to the present time, and cannot adhere to the opinion of the Party and the Presidium of the USSR Supreme Court, quoted above.

The Soviet Court is not "most democratic" because it is subjected to a "most undemocratic" interference of the Party in cases when the Party deems it necessary and its sentences and decisions are influenced by the interests of state prevailing over those of the individual—the accused or plaintiff.

It is also not an authentically popular court since its members are elected, not by the people, but candidates are selected or approved by the Party, one for every position and then elected, which is tantamount to an appointment and not to a popular election.

Although the directional influence of the Party continues unabated up to the present time, still its expressions have lost much of its violence.

The trials of 1966-1968 cannot be compared with those of the thirties, or the activity of the Special Board under the cult of personality, in spite of the presence of some common features.

Of great significance is the reaction of the Soviet people to these trials. During Stalin's life, "the people were silent", according to Pushkin's expression.

But now—they dare to protest in street demonstrations, appeals and letters, signed by hundreds of citizens, giving their full addresses, against trials violating legality,—a phenomenon unknown in the Soviet Union since 1929.

This is an unmistakable sign that the people's aspiration for freedom and justice suppressed during 50 years of communist rule is not dead. Its open expression, although still punishable, testifies to a slackening of means of oppression. Nevertheless, it is to assume that flagrant violation of legality will occur also in the future, but they will not have the magnitude and importance of a recidive of the cult of personality time.

The present writer is deeply convinced that the Soviet Union will not escape the liberalization process already started in some Communist

---

[1] *Izvestia*, December 7, 1967.

countries, under the pressure of the new generation, which firmly desires it and which someday will come to power also in the Soviet Union.

With a real prophetic forsight, Alexander Hertsen wrote in 1860 :

"Maybe a day will come when socialism will prove to be the worst form of tyranny ... then, a new thirst for liberty will awaken in the hearts of the new generation, unknown to us, and it will rise in mutiny against socialism in the name of freedom". [1]

The protests and demonstrations mentioned above is the dawn of the mutiny predicted by Herzen. If not yet against socialism itself, it is directed against its tyranny, in the name of liberty.

As rightly stated by Senator Thomas Dodd : "The Soviet people, despite 50 years of Communist rule, cherishes the same fundamental values as we do. In this lies the best hope for a peaceful evolution of the totalitarian Communist society into a more open society ... The neo-Stalinist tyranny in the Soviet Union may take many victims. Its armed forces may succeed in overrunning defenseless Czechoslavkia. But, ultimately this tyranny is foredoomed to defeat". [2]

This process will bring a relaxation of the grip of the Communist Party over Soviet life, including the administration of justice. How far will this relaxation reach is a matter of guess. Certainly, an effective guarantee against the interference in judicial matters would be a real separation of the judicial power from the other powers including the Communist Party. This, however, would require a fundamental rebuilding of the Soviet state structure, i.e., the downfall of the Communist regime.,,

---

[1] Quoted by S. A. Levitsky, in *Ocherki po istorii russkoy filosofskoy i obshchestvennoy mysli*, *Posev*, Frankfurt-am-Main, 1968, pp. 83-84.

[2] U.S. Senator Thomas Dodd, in "Aspects of Intellectual Fermentation and Dissent", in The Soviet Union, *op. cit.*, Introduction, p. 8.

BIBLIOGRAPHY OF LITERATURE USED

Abramov, S.N., "On Advocates' Wages", *Sov. yust.*, 1957, No. 7.

— —, *Proverka obosnovannosti sudebnogo resheniya sudom po sovetskomu pravu* (The Check of the Validity of a Court Decision by a Higher Court, according to Soviet Law), M. 1950.

"An Advocate has Duties not only Toward the Court But also With Regard to the 'Client'", *Sots. zak.*, 1959, No. 3.

Advokat v Sovetskom ugolovnom protsesse (The Advocate in Soviet Criminal Procedure), M. 1954.

Afonin, A., "People's Assessors Need Text-Books", *Sov. yust.*, 1958, No. 7.

Agapov-Ivanov, A., "The Council of People's Assessors in Action", *Sov. yust.*, 1964, No. 2.

Aleksandrov, G.N., *Pravo i zakonnost' v period razvernutogo stroitel'stva kommunizma* (Law and Legality in the Period of Extensive Communism Construction), M. 1961.

— —, *Za ukrepleniye sotsialisticheskoy zakonnosti* (For the Strengthening of Socialist Legality), M. 1957.

— —. and Anashkin, G.Z., Grun, A. Ya., Michkovsky, G.U., Novikov, S.G., Perlov, I.D., Raginsky, M. Yu., *Nauchno-prakticheskiy kommentariy k ugolovnoprotsesual'-nomu kodeksu RSFSR* (Scientific-Practical Commentary of the RSFSR Code of Criminal Procedure), M. 1963.

Alekseyev, N.S., "Participation of Society in the Preservation of Public Order and the Realization of Justice", in *Voprosy sudoproizvodstva i sudoustroystva v novom zakonodatel'stve S.S.S.R.* (Questions of Court Procedure and Court Structure in the New Legislation of the USSR), M. 1959.

Aliverdiyev, A., "Taking on Bail", *Pravda*, December 9, 1966.

Al'bitskiy, P.D., *Voprosy obshchego nadzora v praktike sovetskoy prokuratury* (Questions of General Supervision in the Practice of Soviet Prosecuting Body), M. 1956.

Alliluyeva, Svetlana, in *The New York Times*, January 17, 1968, p. 2.

— —, *Only One Year*, Translated from the Russian by Paul Chavchavadze, Harper & Row, New York and Evanston, 1969.

Anashkin, G.Z., "Judicial Activity and Objectivity", *Sov. yust.*, 1967, No. 7.

— —, "On Disrespect toward Advocates", *Literaturnaya gazeta*, January 7, 1970.

— —, *Narodnyye zasedateli v sovetskom sude* (People's Assessors in Soviet Court), M. 1960.

— —, "The Role of Law Consciousness and Public Opinion in the Setting of Punishment", *S.G.P.*, 1967, No. 1.

— — and Kalgin, V., "Do Not Weaken the Fight Against Anti-Social Parasitic Elements", *Sots. zak.*, 1963, No. 7.

Andreyev, M., "Does the Defender Have the Right to Drop the Defense ?", *Rabochiy Sud*, 1926, No. 1.

Antimonov, B.S. and Gerzon, S.L., *Advokat v sovetskom grazhdanskom protsesse* (The Advocate in Soviet Civil Procedure), M. 1954.

Arbitrazh v Sovetskom khozyaystve (*Arbitrazh* in the Soviet Economy), M. 1948.

Archer, Peter, *Communism and the Law*, Dufour, Chester Springs, 1963.

Aristakov, Yu. M., Piskotin, M.I., Suleymanov, Kh. S. and Urakov, L.I., "On the Necessity of the Creation of a Soviet Union Jurists Association", *Sots. zak.*, 1959, No. 10.

A.S., "Disbarment", *Sots. zak.*, 1941, No. 15.

Azroll, Jeremy R., "Is Coercion Withering Away ?", *Problems of Communism*, Nov.-Dec. 1962.

Baksheyev, *Narodnyye Zasedateli v sovetskom sude* (People's Assessors in Soviet Court), M. 1951.

Barry, Donald D., and Berman, Harold J., "The Soviet Legal Profession", *Harvard Law Review*, No. 1, November 1968.

Barsukov, M.V., "For the Further Perfection of Militia's Organization and Activity", *S.G.P.*, 1957, No. 2.

"Basic Problems of the Soviet Socialist Legal Science" in *Materialy 1-go S"ezda nauchnykh rabotnikov prava, 10-19 VII, 1938* (Materials of the Congress of Legal Science Workers on July 10-19, 1938), M. 1938.

Baskov, V.I., "On the Supervision Review Order of Criminal Cases", *S.G.P.*, 1965, No. 10.

— —, "Public Prosecution and Public Defense", *S.G.P.*, 1968, No. 3.

— —, *Prokuror osushchestvlyayet nadzor* (The Prosecutor's Realizing of Supervision), M. 1963.

Beerman, R., "Soviet and Russian Anti-Parasite Laws", *Soviet Studies*, 1964, No. 4.

Bedyayev, F. and Kozlov, L., "The Public Prosecutor on the Court Tribune", *Sots. zak.*, 1959, No. 8.

Berezovskaya, S.G., *Prokurorskiy nadzor v sovetskom gosudarstvennom upravlenii* (Prosecution Body's Supervision in Soviet State Administration), M. 1954.

— —, *Prokurorskiy nadzor za zakonnost'yu pravovykh aktov* (Supervision of Legal Actions by the Prosecuting Body), M. 1959.

Berman, Harold J., "Commercial Contracts in Soviet Law", *California Law Review*, 1947.

— —, "The Comparison of Soviet and American Law", *Indiana Law Journal*, Summer 1959, No. 4.

— —, "The Dilemma of Soviet Law Reform", *Harvard Law Review*, 1963, No. 5.

— —, "Justice in Russia", Harvard University Press, Cambridge, 1950.

— —, The Role of Soviet Jurists in the Struggle to Prevent a Return of Stalinist Terror", *Harvard Law School Bulletin*, December 1962, No. 3.

— —, "Soviet Justice or Soviet Tyranny", *Columbia Law Review*, 1955, No. 6.

— —, "Soviet Law Reform-Dateline Moscow", 1957. *Yale Law Journal*, 1957, pp. 191 ff.

— — and Spindler, J.W., "Soviet Comrades' Courts", *Washington Law Review*, 1963.

— —, (Introduction and Analysis); same and Spindler, J.W. (Translators), "Soviet Criminal Law and Procedure", *The RSFSR Codes*, Harvard University Press, Cambridge, Massachusetts, 1966.

Berman, Ya. L., *Ocherki po sudoustroystvu*, with a foreword by N.V. Krylenko (Sketches on Court Structure), M. 1924.

— —, "On the Question of a Criminal Code of a Socialist State", *Proletarskaya revolutsiya i pravo*, February-April 1919, Nos. 2-4.

Berman, Ya. L., and Medvedev, A.S., *Ucheniye o proletarskoy diktature i sovetskoye pravo* (The Doctrine of the Dictatorship of the Proletariat and Soviet Law), M. 1929.

Bilinsky, A., "The Lawyer and Soviet Society", *Problems of Communism*, March-April, 1965.

— —, "The Organization of the Soviet Legal Profession", *Studien des Institutes für Ostrecht*, Vol. 4, München (n.d.).

— —, "Comrades Courts in the Soviet Union", *Osteuropa-Recht*, 1962, No. 4.

— —, "Socialist Legality and the Personality Cult", *Bulletin of the Institute for the Study of the USSR*, 1963, No. 9.

Blekh, A., "The Garbuzovs and the Legal Profession", *Sov. yust.*, 1966, No. 17.

Boiter, Albert, "The Soviet Legal System", *Studies on the Soviet Union*, No. 2, 1967.

— —, The Literary Trial and Soviet Legality, Radio Liberty Research (Mimeographed), Munich, February 13, 1968.

Bol'deskul', K.I., *Organizatsiya i funktsiya sudebnykh uchrezhdeniy* (Organization and Function of Judicial Institutions), Kiev, 1923.

— —, *Organy doznaniya i sledstviya* (Organs of Inquest and Investigation), M. 1923.

Boldyrev, V., "The People's Assessors", *Izvestia*, January 27, 1963.

Borodin, S.V., *Nauchno-prakticheskiy kommentariy k osnovam zakonodstel'stva v SSSR* (Scientific-Practical Commentary on the Basic Principles of Court Structure), M. 1961.

Bovin, A., "On Socialist Legality", *Izvestia*, February 9, 1962.

Bozh'yev, V. and Sukharev, I., "The Advocate as the Representative of the Victim", *Sov. yust.*, 1968, No. 3.

Brandenburgsky, Ya. N., *Yuridicheskaya pomoshch' nasseleniyu* (Legal Help to the Population), M. 1927.

— —, "On the Social Composition of the Soviet Court", *Yezhenedel'nik sovetskoy yustitsii*, 1923, No. 24.

— —, "Court Questions at the 2nd Session of the VTsIK", *Yezhenedel'nik sovetskoy yustitsi*, 1924, No. 39-40.

Braginsky, M., "Execution of Court Decisions", *Yezhenedel'nik sovetskoy yustitsii*, 1922, No. 2.

Bratus', S., "Economy and Law", *Izvestia*, August 27, 1964.

— — and Samoshchenko, I.S. (Editors), *Obshchaya teoriya prava* (General Theory of Law), M. 1966.

Braude, I.V., *V ugolovnom sude* (In the Criminal Court), Khar'kov, 1929.

Brazol, B.L., "Investigating Magistrates" in *Sudebnyye ustavy 20-noyabrya 1864, goda za 50-let* (Fifty years of the Judicial Statutes of November 20, 1864), Vol. 2, Petrograd, 1914.

Brushtein, Yu., *Tovarishcheskiye sudy pri zhilob"yedineniyakh* (Comrades' Courts of Dwelling Associations), M. 1923.

Brezhnev, L.I., Speech at the XXIIIrd Congress of the Soviet Union Communist Party in *Materialy XXIII s"ezda KPSS* (Materials of the XXIIIrd Congress of the Soviet Union Communist Party), M. 1966.

Bryce, James, *Modern Democracies.* 1921, II.

Bukharin, *Put' k sotsializmu i raboche-krest'yanskiy soyuz* (The Way to Socialism and the Union of Workers and Peasants), M. 1929.

Bulleten' MV i SSO (Bulletin of the Ministry of Higher and Secondary Special Education), 1963, No. 4.

Bulleten' Verkhovnogo suda SSSR (Bulletin of the USSR Supreme Court), 1963, No. 3. 1963, No. 3.

Burlatsky, F.M., "Questions of State in the KPSU Program Project", *Kommunist*, 1961, No. 13.

Cardonne, C. de, *L'empereur Alexandre II, Vingt-six ans de règne*, Paris, 1883.

Carson, George B., Electoral Practices in the Soviet Union, N.Y. and London, 1956.

Chak, G.M., "Public and Personal Interests and their Combination Under Socialism", *Voprosy filosofii*, 1955, No. 4.

Chamberlin, William, *Soviet Russia*, Little Brown & Co, London-Boston, 1931.

Chaykovskaya, O., "The Advocates", *Izvestia*, March 21, 1963.

— —, "Dangerous Ignorance", *Izvestia*, September 10, 1964.

— —, "The Foreman", *Izvestia*, November 27, 1963.

— —, "Not in Vain There Are Three of Them", *Izvestia*, May 15, 1963.

— —, "Strict Judges and Silent People's Assessors", *Izvestia*, May 15, 1963.

— —, "This is a Strange Book", *Izvestia*, July 28, 1965.

Chelovek pered sudom (Man Before Court), Symposium, Leningrad, 1965.

Chel'tsov, M.A., "The Development of the Institute of Appeal and Review of Sentences, in the Soviet Criminal Procedure" in *Uchenyye zapiski vsesoyuznogo yuridichskogo zaochnogo instituta* (Scientific Notes of the All-Union Legal Institute Teaching by Correspondence), M. 1948.

— —, "On the Legal Profession and the Juridical Nature of Soviet Legal Profession", *S.G.P.*, 1940, No. 7.

— —, *Obvinyayemyy i ego pokazaniya v sovetskom ugolovnom protsesse* (The Accused and his Testimony in the Soviet Criminal Procedure), M. 1947.

— —, *Polozheniye lichnosti v ugolovnom protsesse* (Position of the Individual in the Criminal Procedure), M. 1948.

— —, "Scope of Soviet Defense and Procedural Position of the Advocate", Forword to *Sudebnyye rechi sovetskikh advokatov* (Court Speeches of Soviet Advocates), M. 1960.

— —, "Some Problems of the Defense in the Light of the Basic Principles of Criminal Procedure of the USSR and the Union Republics" in *Sudebnyye rechi sovetskikh advokatov* (Court Speeches of Soviet Advocates), M. 1960.

— —, *Sotsialisticheskoye pravosoznaniye i ugolovnoye pravo* (Socialist Law Consciousness and Criminal Law), Khar'kov, 1924.

— —, *Ugolovnyy Protsess* (Criminal Procedure), M. 1948 and 1951.

— —, - Bebutov, M.A., "Appeal of the Sentence by the Council", in *Zashchita v ugolovnom protsesse* (Defense in the Criminal Procedure), M. 1948.

— —, - Bebutov, M.A. and Shifman, M.L., "Criminal Defense in the Court Examination" in *Zashchita v ugolovnom protsesse* (Defense in the Criminal Procedure), M. 1948.

— — and Rad'kov, V., "On the Widening of the Legality Guarantee in the Soviet Criminal Procedure", *Sots. zak.*, 1954, No. 9.

The Chornovil Papers, Compiled by Vyacheslav Chornovil, Foreword by Zbigniew Brzezinski, Introduction by Frederick Barghoorn, McGraw-Hill, New York, Toronto, London, Sydney, Johannesburg, Mexico, 1968.

Chetunova, N., "Slander", *Literaturnaya gazeta*, June 16 and 20, 1964.

"Commentary to the New Statute on Comrades' Courts", *Sov. yust.*, 1961, No. 19-24.

Conquest, Robert (Editor), "Legal Systems in the USSR", The Bodley Head, London, Sydney, Toronto, 1968.

Demokraticheskiye osnovy sovetskogo sotsialisticheskogo pravosudiya (Democratic Foundations of Soviet Socialist Justice), M. 1965.

Denisov, A. (Editor), *Istoriya sovetskogo gosudarstva i prava* (History of Soviet State and Law), M. 1949.

— —, "On the Legal Regulation of Social Activity for the Insurance of Legality in the USSR, *Sovetskaya obshchestvennost' na strazhe sotsialisticheskoy zakonnosti*, (Soviet Society on the Watch of Socialist Legality), M. 1960.

DeWitt, *Education and Professional Employment in the USSR*, National Science Foundation, Washington, 1961.

"Disciplinary Procedure for 1926", in *Moskovskaya gubernskaya kollegiya zashchitnikov* (Moscow Province College of Defenders), M. 1927.

Dmitrevskaya, N., "Organizational Questions Must be Reflected in the New Statute on the Legal Profession", *Sots. zak.*, 1957, No. 3.

Dobrovol'skaya, T., "Activity of the Soviet Court in the Period of the Extensive Construction of Communism", *S.G.P.*, 1963, No. 1.

Dodd, Thomas, in Introduction to *Aspects of International Fermentation and Dissent in the Soviet Union*, Washington, 1968.

Dokumenty velikoy oktyabrskoy revolutsii (Documents of the Great October Revolution), M. 1938 and 1942.

Domakhin, L.A. and Stepanov, V.G., *Obshchestvennoye poruchitel'stvo* (Public Guarantee-Bail), M. 1962.

Dubkov, Ye. P., "The Democratic Bases of the Organization and Activity of the Soivet Legal Profession", *S.G.P.*, 1962, No. 6.

— —, "To Perfect the Organization of the Legal Profession", *Sov. Yust.*, 1965, No. 14.

Dyachenko, M.S., "The First Decrees on Courts, Lecture for Students of the All-Union Legal Institute Teaching by Correspondence", *Vsesoyuznyy zaochnyy institut*, M. 1957.

XX-yy S"ezd Kommunisticheskoy Partii Sovetskogo soyuza. Stenograficheskiy otchet (The XXth Congress of the USSR Communist Party. Verbatim Report), M. 1956, V, 5.

XXII-oy s"ezd kommunisticheskoy Partii Sovetskogo Soyuza Stenograficheskiy otchet, (XXII-d Congress of the Soviet Union Communist Party, Verbatim Report), M. 1962.

Dzhanshiyev, *Epokha velikikh reform* (The Epock of Great Reforms), M. 1900.

Elkin, Yu. and Kaufman, V., "May a Counsel Drop the Defense During the Trial ?", *Yezhenedel'nik sovetskoy yustitsii*, 1925, No. 23.

Elkind, P.S., "Advocate's Ethics", *Sov. yust.*, 1940, No. 3 and 4.

— —, "Advocate's Ethics", *Sov. yust.*, 1941, No. 4.

— —, "To Eliminate the Defects in the Work of Advocates", *Sov. yust.*, 1961, No. 5.

Farbstein, A., "*Arbitrazh* and *Arbitrazh* Procedure", *Sov. yust.*, 1957, No. 13.

Feifer, George, *Justice in Moscow*, Simon & Schuster, N.Y. 1964.

Feldbrugge, F.G. and Precarious, M.A., "Legality", *Problems of Communism*, July-Aug. 1964.

Feldmesser, Robert A., "Social Status and Access to Higher Education : A Comparison of the United States and the Soviet Union", *Harvard Educational Review*, 1957, No. 2.

Feofanov, Yu., "Angels, Demons and the Truth", *Izvestia*, January 5, 1966.

— —, "Voice in the Chorus", *Izvestia*, January 18, 1967.

Filimonov, G., "On the Functions of Court and Investigation", *Literaturnaya gazeta*, August 18, 1964.

"For the Further Heightening of Soviet Legal Science" (Editorial), *Sov. yust.*, 1964, No. 18.

"For High Party Spirit in Soviet Legal Science", *S.G.P.*, 1964, No. 1.

Foynitskiy, I. Ya., *Kurs ugolovnogo sudoproizvodstva* (A Course on Criminal Procedure), I and II, St. Petersburg, 1896.

Fratkin, A.V., "All Russian Congress of Soviet Men of Law", *Pravo i Zhizn'*, 1924, No. 3-4.

Freund, Henry, "Soviet Law and Stalinism", *Slavonic and East European Review*, London, 1940, No. 19.

Friedman, Lawrence M. and Zile, Zigurda, L., "Soviet Legal Profession : Recent Developments in Law and Practice", *Wisconsin Law Review*, 1964, No. 1.

"From the Life of the Khar'kov College of Defenders", *Vestnik Sovetskoy yustitsii*, 1923, No. 2.

Galin, L., *Courts and the Penal System in Revolutionary Russia*, Berlin, 1920.

Galkin, I, "Crime Investigation by Groups of Investigating Magistrates", *Sots. zak.*, 1963, No. 4.

Gal'perin, I.M. and Pososhkov, F.A., *Uchastiye obshchestvennosti v sovetskom ugolovnom protsesse* (Participation of the Public in the Soviet Criminal Trial), M. 1961.

Gerchun, Boris, *Russland*, in *Die Rechtsanwaltschaft*, Leipzig, 1929.

Gertsenson, A.A., *Sovetskaya ugolovnaya statistika* (Soviet Criminal Statistics), M. 1957.

Gide, André, *Retour de l'USSR*, Paris, 1936.

Ginsburg, Eugenia, *Journey into the Whirlwind*, translated by Paul Stevenson and Max Hayward, Harcourt Brace and World, Inc., N.Y., 1967.

Ginsburg, G. and Rusis, A., *Soviet Criminal Law and the Protection of State Security*. Articles and Texts, Leyden, 1963.

Ginzburg, G.A., Polyak, A.G. and Samsonov, V.A., *Sovetskiy advokat* (The Soviet Advocate), M. 1968.

Glenny, Michall, "Sinyavsky and Daniel on Trial", *Survey*, London, 1968, No. 66.

Gol'diner, V.D., "The Advocate's Summing up in the Soviet Criminal Trial", *Sots. zak.*, 1957, No. 3.

— —, "On the Ethics in the Advocate's Activity", *S.G.P.*, 1965, No. 10.

— —, "On the Question of the Procedural Position of the Advocate", *Sov. yust.*, 1957, No. 7.

— —, "On Some Peculiarities in the Methods of Soviet Criminal Defense", *S.G.P.*, 1962, No. 6.

Golubovsky, D., "Criminal Questions of Defense", *Sots. zak.*, 1936, No. 6.

— —, *Advokat v sovetskom ugolovnom protsesse* (The Advocate in Soviet Criminal Trial), M. 1954.

— —, and Karev, D.S., *Uchebnik po sudoustroystvu* (Textbook on Court Structure), M. 1939.

Golubovsky, D., "Fundamentals of Soviet Justice", in *Uchenyye zapiski moskovskogo universiteta* (Scientific Notes of the Moscow University, Issue 116. Works of the Legal Faculty, Book No. 2), M. 1946.

Golyakov, I. T., "On the Importance of Defence". Introduction to *Advokat v Sovetskom ugolovnom protsesse* (The Advocate in Criminal Trial), M. 1954.

— — (Editor), *Istoriya zakonodatel'stva SSSR i RSFSR po ugolovnomu protsessu i organizatsii suda i prokuratury* (The History of the USSR and RSFSR Legislations on Criminal Procedure and the Organization of Courts and Prosecuting Body), M. 1955.

— —, "Lawyers' Ethics", *Sov. Yust.*, 1939, No. 11.

— —, "On the 'Inner Conviction' in Soviet Court", *Sots. zak.*, 1936, No. 5.

— —, "On Probability and Trustworthiness in Criminal Trial", in *Problemy ugolovnoy politiki* (Problems of Penal Policy), M. 1937, Issue IV.

— —, "Soviet Justice During 25 Years", in *Uchenyye Zapiski moskovskogo universitet Trudy yuridicheskogo faku'teta vypusk 76* (Scientific notes of the Moscow University, Works of the Legal Faculty, Issue 76), M. 1945.

— —, *Voprosy sudoproizvodstva i sudoustroystva v novom zakonodatel'stve SSSR* (Questions of Court Procedure and Structure in the New Legislation of the USSR), M. 1959.

— — and Golyakov, I.I., "On the Importance of Defense in the Soviet Criminal Trial", in *Zashchita po ugolovnym delam* (The Defense in Criminal Trial), M. 1948.

— —, Karev, D.S., *Sudoustroystvo SSSR* (USSR Court Structure), M. 1946.

Gorbunov, I., "When it is Argued in Detriment of the State", *Sov. yust.*, 1963, No. 2.

Gorkin, A.F., "On the Problems of Soviet Court in the Period of Intensive Construction of Communism", in *Sovetskaya obshchestvennost' na strazhe sotsialisticheskoy zakonnosti* (Soviet Society on the Watch of Socialist Legality), M. 1960.

— —, "On the Cult of Personality", *Pravda*, April 23, 1964.

Gorobenev, V.M., *Uchastiye obshchestvennykh organizatsiy v pravovom regulirovanii* (Participation of the Public in Legal Regulation), M. 1963.

Gorshenin, K.P., "Participation of the Public in the Fight Against Law Breaking is the Further Development of Soviet Democracy", in *Sovetskaya obshchestvennost' na strage sotsialisticheskoy zakonnosti*, M. 1960. *Sovetskiy sud* (The Soviet Court), M. 1957.

Gosudarstvennyy obvinitel' v sovetskom sude (State Prosecutor in Soviet Court), M. 1954.

Goykhbarg, A.G., "Class Politics in Civil Procedure", *Yezhenedel'nik sovetskoy yustitsii*, 1924, No. 12-13.

— —, "Some Remarks on Law", *Sovetskoye pravo*, 1924, No. 1.

Granin, "After the Marriage", *Oktyabr'*, 1959, No. 7.

Gredinger, F. I., "Prosecutor's Supervision During the Fifty Years After Its Reform, According to the Judicial Statutes of Emperor Alexander II", in *Sudebnyye ustavy 20 go. noyabrya, 1864 g. za 50 let.* (Fifty Years of the Judicial Statutes of November 20, 1864), II., Petrograd, 1914.

Grekov, V., "The Advocate's Position in the Trial Must Be Based on Law", *Sots. zak.*, 1965, No. 10.

Gringanz, I.K., "On the Question of Criminal Law and Law Creation in 1917-18", *S.G.P.*, 1940, No. 3.

Grishayev, P., "Against Anti-Communist Slander of Soviet Law", *Sots. zak.*, 1963, No. 6.

Grodzinsky, M.M., *Kassatsionnoye i nadzornoye proizvodstvo v sovetskom ugolovnom protsesse* (Cassation and Supervision Proceedings in Soviet Criminal Procedure), M. 1953.

— —, "Questioning of the Accused in the New Code of Criminal Procedure", *Pravo i zhizn'*, 1922, No. 3.

— —, "Questions of Review in Cassation in Connection With the Project of a USSR Code of Criminal Procedure", *Sots. zak.*, 1954, No. 10.

Gromov, "On the Unsatisfactory Legal Education", *Sots. zak.*, 1957, No. 3.

Grottian, Walter, *Das Sowjetische Regierungsystem* (The Soviet System of Government), Köln and Opladen, 1965.

Grzybowski, K. "*Soviet Legal Institutions*", University of Michigan Press, AnnArbor, 1962.

Gsovski, V.V., *Soviet Civil Law*, Vol. I and II, University of Michigan Law School, Ann Arbor, 1948.

— —, "The Soviet Conception of Law", *Fordham Law Review*, Jan. 1938.

— — and Grzybowski, K. (General Editors), *Government, Law and Courts in the Soviet Union and Eastern Europe*, Vol. I and II, Frederick A. Praeger, N.Y., 1959.

Gureyev, P.P. and Klochkov, V.V., "For the Further Heightening of Soviet Jurisprudence and the Improvement of Legal Education" (Editorial), *S.G.P.*, 1964, No. 8.

Gusev, L.N., "The Procedural Position of the Investigating Magistrate in the Soviet Criminal Procedure", in *Voprosy sudoproizvodstva i sudoustroystva v novom zakonodatel'stve soyuza SSSR* (Questions of Procedure and Court Structure in the New Legislation of the USSR), M. 1959.

Gutsenko, K.F., "Comrades' Court and Some Questions of Their Jurisdiction Enlargement", *Sots. zak.*, 1962, No. 6.

— —, "On the New Statute on the Legal Profession, Passed by 13 Republics", *S.G.P.*, 1962, No. 3.

Hastrich, Alois, "Laity in the Soviet Administration of Justice", *Osteuropa-Recht*, 1965, No. 7/8.

Hayward, Max (Editor, Translator and Introduction's Author), *On Trial; The Soviet State vs. Abram Terz and Nikolai Arzhak*, Harper and Row, New York, 1966.

Hazard, John N., *Communists and Their Laws*, Chicago University Press, Chicago, 1969.

— —, "Draft of New Soviet Code of Law", *Am. Slavic and East European Review*, Feb. 1948, No. 1.

— —, *Introduction to Soviet Legal Philosophy*, Harvard University Press, Cambridge, Mass., 1950.

— —, "The Lawyer Under the Soviets", *Wisconsin Law Review*, Feb. 1946.

— —, "Law and Social Change in the USSR", Stevens, London, 1953.

— —, *Materials on Soviet Law*, N.Y., 1947 (Mimeographed).

— —, *Review of Berman's Justice in the USSR*; Melvin M. Belli's and Danny R. Jone's, *Looks at Life and Law in Russia* and Ivo Lapenna's *State and Law : Soviet and Jugoslav Theory, Slavic Review*, June 1964, No. 2.

— —, *Settling Disputes in Soviet Society, The Formation Years of Legal Institutions*, Columbia University Press, N.Y., 1960.

— —, "Simplicity and Popular Early Dreams", *Problems of Communism*, March-April 1965.

— —, "Soviet Legal Education", *Wisconsin Law Review*, 1938, No. 4.

Hazard, John N., *The Soviet System of Government*, University of Chicago Press, Chicago & London, 4th Edition, 1968.

—— and Stern, W.N., "Bibliography on the Principal Materials on Soviet Law", *American Foreign Law Association Series*, N.Y., 1945.

—— and Shapiro, Isaac, Muggs, Peter B., *"The Soviet Legal System"*. Documentation and Historical Commentary, Oceana Publications Inc., Dobbs Ferry, N.Y., 1969.

Hertsen, A., *Byloye i dumy* (The Past and Thoughts), Leningrad, 1947.

"The High Political and Social Duty of the Soviet Advocate" (Editorial), *Sov. yust.*, 1957, No. 7.

Idashkin, Yu., "Reflections on Court Defense", *Kommunist*, 1967, No. 5.

Il'yichev, L., "The Powerful Factor of Communism Construction", *Kommunist*, 1962, No. 1.

"Improvement of Legal Education" (Editorial), *S.G.P.*, 1956, No. 8.

"In the Kiev College of Defenders : Instruction on Norms of Professional Ethics for College Members", *Vestnik sovetskoy yustitsii*, 1923, No. 5.

Inast'yev, V., "Revolution and Revolutionary Legality", *Izvestia*, May 10, 1922.

Inkeles, Ab., *Public Opinion in Soviet Russia*, Harvard Univ. Press, Cambridge, 1958.

"Innocent Till Proven Guilty, Test Case in Moscow", *New York Herald Tribune*, Dec. 19-20, 1964, p. 5.

Isayev, M., *Obshchaya chast' ugolovnogo prava RSFSR* (The General Part of the RSFSR Criminal Law), M. 1924.

—— and Piontkovsky, *Voprosy ugolovnogo prava, voyenno-ugolovnogo prava i ugolovnogo protsessa v praktike Verkhovnogo suda SSR* (Questions of Criminal Law, Military Criminal Law and Criminal Procedure in the Practice of the USSR Supreme Court), M. 1947.

Istomin, Yu., "The Council of Comrades' Court Chairmen", *Sov. yust.*, 1962, No. 9.

Istoriya zakonodatel'stva SSSR i RSFSR po ugolovnomu protsesu i organizatsii suda i prokuratury 1917-1954. Sbornik dokumentov (History of Legislation of the USSR and RSFSR on Criminal Procedure, Courts and Prosecuting Body Organization, 1917-1954, A Collection of Documents), M. 1955.

Itkin, L. and Pereslavtsev, A., "The Advocate's Role", *Moskovskaya pravda*, Sept. 20, 1964.

Ivanov, V. A., "The Organization of the Courts and the Prosecuting Body", in *40 let sovetskogo suda* (Forty Years of Soviet Courts), V. I and II, M. 1957.

Izvestia TsIK'a i Petrogradskogo Soveta rabochikh i soldatskikh deputatov (News of the Central Executive Committee and the Petrograd Soviet of Worker's and Soldiers' Deputies), Nov. 19, 1917; Dec. 8, 1917.

Kaftanov, S., *Vyssheye obrazovaniye v SSSR* (Higher Education in the USSR), M. 1950.

Kaganovich, L., Speech (excerpt) at the IIId All-Ukrainian Conference of the Ukrainian Communist Party (B) on July 8, 1932, *Sov. yust.*, 1932, No. 20.

Kairov, I.A. (Editor), *Sovetskaya shkola na sovremennom etape* (Soviet School, Comtemporary Stage), M. 1961.

Kakitelashvili, M.D., "Is It Admissible for an Appointed or Selected Counsel to Resign the Interests of the Accused During the Trial ?", *Yezhenedel'nik sovetskoy yustitsii*, 1925, No. 29.

Kalashinikova, N., "Presentation of New Material to the Cassation Instance", *Sots. zak.*, 1945, No. 7.

— —, in *Sovetskiy ugolovnyy protsess* (Soviet Criminal Procedure) edited by D. S. Karev, M. 1956.

— — and Saminski, A.S., "The Problem of Evidence Valuation When Sentences are Reviewed by a Higher Court", *Sots. zak.*, 1950, No. 3.

Kalinychev, F.I. (Editor), *Polozheniye o tovarishcheskikh sudakh* (Statute on Comrades' Courts), M. 1963.

Kalenov, Yu. A. (Editor), *Nauchno-prakticheskiy kommenteriy k zakonu o sudoustroystve RSFSR* (Scientific-Practical Commentary on the RSFSR Court Structure Law), M. 1962.

— — and Perlov, I.D., *Organizatsiya raboty narodnogo suda* (Organization of People's Court Work), M. 1964.

Kalinin, M., "Speech (Excerpts) at the Solemn Session of July 3, 1932 on the Occasion of the 10th Jubilee of the Soviet Prosecution Body", *Sov. yust.*, 1932, No. 20, p. 1.

Kallistratova, R.F., *Razresheniye sporov v gosudarstvennom arbitrazhe* (Settling of Disputes in State *Arbitrazh*), M. 1961.

Kalyayev, A., "From the Experience of Counsel's Participation in the Preliminary Investigation", *Sov. Yust.*, 1964, No. 9.

Kamenka, Eugene, "The Soviet View of Law", *Problems of Communism*, March-April 1965.

— —, "What Must be the Statute on the Legal Profession ?", *Sots. zak.*, 1960, No. 9.

Karabchevsky, N.P. *Delo Sazonova* (The Sazonov Case), St. Petersburg, 1906.

Karev, D.S., *Demokraticheskiye osnovy organizatsii i deyatel'nosti sovetskogo suda* (Democratic Fundamentals of the Soviet Court Organization and Activity), M. 1951 and 1954.

— —, "The Further Perfection of the Soviet Court System", *S.G.P.*, 1959, No. 2.

— —, "Liquidate the Cult of Personality Consequences in the Soviet Legal Science", *Sots. zak.*, 1962, No. 2.

— —, *Organizatsiya suda i prokuratury* (The Organization of Courts and the Prosecuting Body), M. 1954.

— —, "Public Prosecutors and Public Counsels", in *Sovetskaya obshchestvennost' na strazhe sotsialisticheskoy zakonnosti* (The Soviet Public on the Watch of Socialist Legality), M. 1960.

— —, *Sovetskoye sudoustroystvo* (Soviet Court Structure), M. 1951.

— —, *Sovetskaya yustitsiya* (Soviet Justice), M. 1949.

— — (Editor), *Sovetskiy ugolovnyy protsessu* (Soviet Criminal Procedure), M. 1953.

— —, *Sudoustroystvo* (Court Structure), M. 1948.

Kareva, M., "Socialist Legality", *Bol'shaya sovetskaya entsiclopedia* (Great Soviet Encyclopaedia), 1st Ed., V. 52.

Katkov, in *Moskovskiye Vedomosti* (Moscow Gazette), 1885, No. 39.

Kazin, G., "The Court of Comrades", *Pravda*, May 13, 1963.

Kechek'yan, S.F., *Pravootnosheniya v sotsialisticheskom obshchestve* (Legal Relations in a Socialist Society), M. 1958.

Khmel'nitsky, I.A., "The Province Court or the College of Defenders", in *Vestnik sovetskoy justitsii*, 1923, No. 5.

Kholyavchenko, A., "The Fight Against Spongers and Grabbers", *Sots. zak.*, 1963, No. 9.

Khrushchev, N. S., in *XXth S"ezd kommunisticheskoy partii Sovetskogo soyuza. Steno-grafichesiy Otchet* (The XXth Congress of the Communist Party of the Soviet Union. Verbatim Report), M. 1965.

— —, in *Zasedaniya Verkhovnogo Soveta SSSR. Stenograficheskiy Otchet* (Sessions of the USSR Supreme Soviet. Verbatim Report), M. 1957.

— —, "Educate Active and Conscious Constructors of Communist Society", Speech at the XIIth Congress of the Komsomol, on April 18, 1958, *Molodaya gvardiya*, M. 1958.

— —, *O kontrol'nykh tsifrakh razvitiya narodnogo khozyaystva SSSR na 1959-1965 gg.* (On Control Figures of the USSR Economy Development for 1959-1965 years), M. 1959.

— —, *Otchet TsK. KPSS XXI s"ezdu* (Report of the Central Committee of the Soviet Union Communist Party to the XXIst Congress), M. 1961.

— —, *Rech' na sobranii izbirateley Kalininskogo izbiratel'nogo okruga goroda Moskvy 24-go fevralya 1954 g.*, (Speech at the Electoral Meeting of the Kalininskiy Electoral District of the City of Moskow, on February 24, 1959), M. 1959.

— —, Speech at the XXth Congress of the Soviet Union Communist Party, Department of State, for the Press, Washington, D.C., June 4, 1956.

Kiralfy, A.K.R., "The Campaigne for Legality in the USSR", *The International and Comparative Law Quarterly*, October 1957.

Kirichenko, V.F., "Legal Questions of the Fight Against Persons Avoiding Socially Useful Work and Leading an Anti-Social Parasitic Life", *S.G.P.*, 1961, No. 8.

Kirzner, A., "With an Open Visor for the Socialist Legality", *Sots. zak.*, 1935, No. 6.

Kisilev, Ya., "When the Trial is Going On", *Izvestia*, June 14, 1967.

Kleinman, A.F. (Editor), *Arbitrazh v SSSR* (*Arbitrazh* in the USSR), M. 1960.

Koblents, S., "The Advocate Forces an Open Door", *Sots. zak.*, 1962, No. 4.

Kocharov, G.I., Introduction to *Teoriya Dokazatel'stv v sovetskom ugolovnom protsesse* (The Evidence Theory in Soviet Criminal Procedure), M. 1966.

Kocvara, Stefan, "The Bar Sovietized", *Highlights of Current Legislation and Activity in Mid-Europe*, 1956, No. 2.

Kohler, J., *Moderne Rechtsprobleme*, Leipzig, 1913.

Kolmakov, V., "To Know and Fulfill the Law", *Izvestia*, August 2, 1967.

Kommunisticheskaya partiya sovetskogo soyuza v resheniyakh i rezolyutsiyakh s"ezdov, konferentsiy i plenumov Ts-K. (The Communist Party of the Soviet Union in Decisions and Resolutions of Congresses, Conferences and Plenums of the Central Committee), Part II, IV, VII, M. 1954, 1961, 1962, respectively.

Kondrat'yev, V. and Podzorov, A., "Participation of Representatives of the Public in Criminal Cases", *Sots. zak.*, 1964, No. 11.

Koni, A.F., "Court Statutes 1864-1914", *Zhurnal ministerstva justitsii* (Journal of the Ministry of Justice), 1914, No. 9.

— —, "Court With Jury", *Entsiklopedicheskiy slovar' Brokgauza i Efrona*, Vol. 63, St. Petersburg, 1901.

— —, *Vospominaniya o dele Very Zasulich* (Reminiscences of the Vera Zasulich Case), M. 1933.

Kopylovskaya, N.A., Comments to Art. 29 in *Nauchno-prakticheskiy kommentariy k osnovam zakonodatel'stva v sudoustroystve soyuza SSSR., soyuznykh i avtonom-nykh respublik* (Scientific-Practical Comments on Legislation Fundamentals of the Court Structure of the USSR, Union and Autonomous Republics), M. 1961.

Korotkov, V.S., "Education Without Separation from Production", *Entsiklopedicheskiy slovar' pravovykh znaniy* (Dictionary of Legal Knowledge), M. 1965.

— — and Shind, V., *Obshchestvennost' v bor'be s narushitelyami sotsialisticheskoy zakonnosti* (The Public in the Fight Against Violators of Socialist Legality), M. 1962.

Kositsyn, A.P., "Dictatorship of the Proletariate", *Entsiklopedicheskiy slovar' pravovykh znaniy* (Encyclopedic Dictionary of Legal Knowledge), M. 1964.

Korolev, A.I., "Basic Functions of a Socialist State", in *Obshchaya teoriya gosudarstva i prava*, Leningrad, 1968, V.I.

Korovin, S.T., "On Electoral Law", *S.G.P.*, 1954, No. 2.

Kozhevnikov, M.V., *Istoriya sovetskogo suda* (The History of the Soviet Court), M. 1948 and 1957.

— —, "Organs Which Fulfilled the Duties of the Soviet Prosecution Body Before its Establishment", *Uchenyye zapiski Moskovskogo universiteta, Trudy yuridicheskogo fakul'teta* (Scientific Notes of the Moscow University. Works of the Faculty of Law), Issue 144, M. 1949.

Kozlov, V., "State Control of the Legal Profession's Activity", *Sots. zak.*, 1959, No. 7.

— —, "Advocate's Ethics", *Sov. yust.*, 1941, No. 4.

Kruglov, A., "To Heighten the Quality of the Advocates' Work", *Sov. yust.*, 1966, No. 3. "Statistical Data", Sots. Zak. 1959, No. 2.

Krylenko, "The Court Reform", *Sovetskoye pravo*, 1922, No. 3.

— —, "The Court Structure Reform", *Yezhenedel'nik sovetskoy yustitsii*, 1922, No. 37-38.

— —, N.V., "The Draft of a New Criminal Code", *Problemy ugolovnoy politiki*, M. 1935, Issue I.

— —, *Kak ustroyeny i rabotayut sovetskiye sudy* (How the Soviet Courts are Organized and How They Work), M. 1927.

— —, *Lenin i Stalin o revolutsionnoy zakonnosti* (Lenin and Stalin on Revolutionary Legality), M. 1934.

— —, *Lenin o sude i ugolovnoy politike* (Lenin on Courts and Penal Policy), M. 1934, 1935.

— —, *Osnovy sudoustroystva v SSSR i soyuznykh respublikakh* (Fundamentals of Court Structure in the USSR and Union Republics), M. 1927.

— —, Speech at the General Assembly of the College of Advocates, *Sov. yust.*, 1936, No. 27.

— —, *Sudoustroystvo v RSFSR* (Court Structure in the RSFSR), M. 1924.

— —, "To the Situation on the Theoretical Legal Front", *Problemy ugolovnoy politiki*, M. 1937, Vol. IV.

— —, *Za pyat' let 1918-1922* (During Five Years, 1918-1922), M. 1923.

— — and Luzhin, "On the Unification of Courts and Tribunals into one System", Speeches at the IVth Congress of Legal Workers, *Yezhendel'nik sovetskoy yustitsii*, 1922, No. 5.

Kucherov, Samuel, *Courts, Lawyers and Trials Under the Last Three Tsars*, Frederick A. Praeger, N.Y., 1953.

— —, "The Jury of Tsarist Russia and the People's Accessors of the Soviet Union", *Osteuropa-Recht*, 1966, No. 3.

— —, "The Legal Profession in Pre- and Post Revolutionary Russia", *American Journal of Comparative Law*, 1956, No. 3.

Kucherov, Samuel, "Property in the Soviet Union", *American Journal of Comparative Law*, 1962, No. 3.

— —, "The Nature and Status of *Arbitrazh*", *Bulletin of the Institute for the Study of the USSR*, 1966, No. 11.

— —, "The Soviet Union is Not a Socialist Society" (In "Defense" of V.M. Molotov), *Political Science Quarterly*, 1956, No. 2.

— —, "The Vera Zasulich Case", *The Russian Review*, 1951, No. 2.

Kudryavstsev, D., in *Literaturnaya gazeta* (The Literary Gazette), June 7, 1951.

Kukarsky, I., "Heighten the Level of the Legal Profession's Activity", *Sov. yust.*, 1964, No. 18.

— —, "More Attention to the Organizations of the Legal Profession's Work", *Sov. yust.*, 1968.

— —, "The Soviet Legal Profession is 45 years old", *Sov. yust.*, 1967, No. 10.

Kulikov, V., "Guaranty of Legality", *Izvestia*, December 7, 1967.

— —, "Preserving Justice", *Izvestia*, April 23, 1964.

— —, "The Private Ruling", *Izvestia*, July 10, 1966.

Kuprishin, V., "The Advocate and the Preliminary Investigation", *Izvestia*, Sept. 15, 1967.

Kursky, D.I., "From the Practice of the People's Court", *Revolutsiya i pravo*, 1919, No. 1.

— —, "The Fundamentals of a Revolutionary Court", *Materialy Narodnogo komissariyata yustitsii* (Materials of the People's Commissariat of Justice), 1918, No.1.

— —, *Izbrannyye stat'i i rechi* (Selected Articles and Speeches), M. 1958.

— —, "The Nearest Problem of Soviet Law Studies", *Sovetskoye pravo*, 1922, No. 1.

— —, "The New Criminal Law", *Proletarskaya revolutsiya i pravo*, 1919, No. 2-4.

— —, "The Reorganization of Extraordinary Repression Organs and the Scopes of the People's Commissariat of Justice (N.K.Yu.)", *Yezhenedel'nik sovetskoy yustitsii*, 1922, No. 7.

— —, "On the Single and One People's Court", *Proletarskaya revolutsiya i pravo*, 1918, No. 1.

— —, "The Revolution and the Court", *Materialy narodnogo kommissariata yustitsii*, 1918, V. II.

Kutsova, E.F., *Sovetskaya kassatsiya kak garantiya zakonnosti i pravosudiya* (Soviet Cassation as Guaranty of Legality and Justice), M. 1957.

Lapenna, Ivo, "The Bar in the Soviet Union and Yugoslavia", *International and Comparative Law-Quarterly*, April 1963.

— —, *State and Law, Soviet and Yugoslav Theory*, Yale University Press, New Haven, 1964.

Latsis, M. Ya., *Dva goda bor'by na vnutrennem fronte* (Two Years of Fight at the Internal Front), M. 1920.

— —, "Instruction to the Members of the VeCheKa" (All-Russian Extraordinary Commission), *Pravda*, December 25, 1918.

— —, *Chrezvychaynaya kommissiya po bor'be s konterrevolyutsiyey* (Extraordinary Commission for the Fight Against Counterrevolution), M. 1921.

Lavrova, V., Kirsh, G., "Councils of People's Assessors Attitude to the Regional Court", *Sov. yust.*, 1963, No. 10.

Lazarenko, A.N., "Survey of the Basic Features of the Judicial System in Russia and in the Main West European Countries", in *Sudebnyye ustavy 20 noyabrya 1964g.*

za pyat'desyat let (Fifty Years of the Judicial Statutes of November 20, 1864), V. 1 and 2, Petrograd, 1914.

Leludov, B., "For the Effectiveness of the Comrades' Court Work", *Sov. yust.*, 1966, No. 3.

Lenin, V.I., *Sochineniya* (Works) 3d and 4th Editions, Volumes quoted in Roman and Arabic Numerals respectively.

— —, *State and Revolution*, Revised Translation (International Publishers), N.Y., 1935.

— —, *o gosudarstve i prave* (Lenin on State and Law), M. 1958, Vol. I and II.

— —, *o sotsialisticheskoy zakonnosti* (Lenin on Socialist Legality), M. 1958.

Leninskiy sbornik (Collection of Lenin's Writings), Volumes quoted in Roman Numerals.

Lensky, L., "Do We Need the State *Arbitrazh* ?", *Sov. yust.*, 1937, Nos. 10-11.

Levin, A, "Controversial Questions of Advocate's Activity Concerning Complaints in Cassation Procedure", *Sots. zak.*, 1937, No. 2.

— —, "Is the Counsel Allowed to Drop the Defense During the Trial ?", *Yezhenedel'nik sovetskoy yustitsii*, 1925, No. 35.

— —, "Procedural Rights of the Cassation Instance", *S.G.P.*, 1948, No. 8.

— —, Ognev, V.A. and Rossel's, V.A., *Zashchitnik v sovetskom protsesse* (The Counsel in Soviet Trial), M. 1960.

Lepeshkin, A.I., *Kurs sovetskogo gosudarstvennogo prava* (Textbook of Soviet State Law), Vol. I and II, M. 1961.

Lesnoy, V., "The October Revolution and the Formation of Socialist Law", *Sov. yust.*, 1967, No. 4.

Levitsky, S. A., *Ocherki po istorii russkoy filosofii i obshchestvennoy mysli* (Essays on the History of Russian Philosophy and Social Thought), Possev, Frankfurt-am-Main, 1968.

Liberman, A.M., "Advocate's Ethics", *Sov. yust.*, 1938, No. 15.

— —, "Relations Between Judges and Advocates are Improving in Leningrad", *Sov. yust.*, 1940, No. 7.

— —, "There is no Order in the Leningrad College of Defenders", *Sov. yust.*, 1936, No. 1.

Lipson, L., "The Criminal Reconsidered", *Problems of Communism*, July-August, 1961, No. 4.

— —, (Commentary on) *The Future Belongs to the Parasites*, *Problems of Communism*, May-June, 1963.

— —, Hosts and Pests, "The Fight Against Parasites", *Problems of Communism*, March-April, 1965.

— —, "The New Face of Socialist Legality", *Problems of Communism*, July-August, 1958.

"Liquidate to the End the Evil Consequences of the Cult of Personality" (Editorial), *S.G.P.*, 1962, No. 3.

Lisitsyn, A., "To the Abrogation of the CheKa", *Yezhenedel'nik sovetskoy yustitsii*, 1922, No. 7.

Literatura po sovetskomu pravu (Literature on Soviet Law), M. 1960.

Loeber, Dietrich A., "Plan and Contract Performance in the Post-War Practice of the USSR State *Arbitrazh*", in *Law on the Soviet Union*, Urbana (University of Illinois Press), 1965.

Loginov, P.V., *Resheniya gosudarstvennogo Arbitrazha* (Decisions of the State *Arbitrazh*), M. 1964.

Lokhov, N.A., "Some Questions of the Judicial System of the USSR, Union and Autonomous Republics", in *Voprosy sudoproizvodstva i sudoustroystva v novom zakonodatel'stve soyuza SSSR* (Questions of Procedure and Court Structure of the Soviet Union New Legislation), M. 1959.

Loshak, Pierre, "Right and Judge in the Soviet Union", *Bulletin des Internationalen Juristen Kommission* (Bulletin of the International Commission of Jurists), The Hague, 1957, No. 7.

Loshnov, P.V., *Notariat i Arbitrazh v SSSR* (Notaries and *Arbitrazh* in the USSR), M. 1957.

Lucas, Reiner, "Legal Education in the Soviet Union", *Juristenzeitung* (Jurists' Newspaper), 1962, No. 1.

Luk'yanov, A.I. and Lazarev, B.M., *Sovetskoye gosudarstvo i obshchestvennyye organizatsii* (The Soviet State and the Social Organizations), M. 1961.

Lunacharsky, A., "Revolution and Court", *Pravda*, December 6, 1917.

Lunev, A. Ye., Skudenikin, S.S. and Yenipol'skaya, T.F., *Sotsialisticheskaya zakonnost' v sovetskom gosudarstvennom upravlenii* (Socialist Legality in Soviet State Administration), M. 1948.

Lur'ye, S., "Private Arbitration Courts are in Action", *Sov. yust.*, 1961, No. 16.

L'vov, Ye., "On the Soviet Legal Profession", *Sots. zak.*, 1936, No. 12.

Lyublinsky, P.I., "Procedural Questions in the New Law on Court Structure", *Sov. yust.*, 1938, No. 20.

— —, "Public Defense in Criminal Procedure", *Yuridicheskiy vestnik*, 1913, No. 1.

— — and Polyansky, N.N., *Ugolovno-protsessual'nyy kodeks RSFSR* (RSFSR Code of Criminal Procedure) (Commentary), M. 1928.

Magirovsky, D., "Soviet Law and Methods of its Study", *Sovetskoye pravo*, 1922, No. 1.

Malone, Albert C. Jr., "The Soviet Bar", *Cornell Law Quarterly*, Winter 1961, No. 2.

Mal'kovich, T.K., "On the History of the First Decrees on Courts", *S.G.P.*, 1940, Nos. 7 and 8-9.

Malyarov, M.P., *Prokurorskiy nadzor SSSR* (Prosecuting Body's Supervision in the USSR), M. 1966.

Mamut, L. and Ugryumov, A., "Karl Marx on Court and Justice", *Sov. yust.*, 1958, No. 5.

Mandel'shtam, L.A., *Zakonodatel'stvo ob ustroystve SSSR* (Legislation on the Structure of the USSR), M. 1961.

Marx, K. and Engels, F., *Sochineniya* (Works), M. 1928-1939.

Materialy XXIII s"ezda KPSS (Materials of the XXIIId Congress of the Soviet Union Communist Party), M. 1966.

Materialy narodnogo kommissarista yustitsii (Materials of the People's Commissariat of Justice), M. 1918, Issues 1, 2, and 10.

Maurach, Reinhart, *Handbuch der Sowjetverfassung* (Manual of the Soviet Constitution), Isar Publishing House, Munich, 1955.

Mikoyan, A., "Speech at the XXth Congress of the Soviet Union Communist Party", *XX-yy S"ezd kommunisticheskoy partii Sovetskogo Soyuzai*, M. 1956.

Milyukov, P.N., "The University", in *Entsiklopedicheskiy Slovar' Brokgauza i Efrona*, St. Petersburg, 1902, V. 68.

Mironenko, Ya., "Counsel for the Defense", *Bulletin of the Institute for the Study of the USSR*, 1963, No. 9.

Mironenko, Ya., "Counsel for the Prosecution", *Bulletin of the Institute for the Study of the USSR*, 1964, No. 4.

— —, "The People's Courts", *Bulletin of the Institute for the Study of the USSR*, 1959, No. 9.

— —, "The Soviet Legal Profession", *Soobshcheniya instituta po izucheniyu SSSR* (Information of the Institute for the Study of the USSR), 1965, No. 1.

Mironov, N., "The Strengthening of Socialist Legality and Legal Order", *Partiynaya Zhizn'*, 1962, No. 5.

— —, "Vital Questions of the Further Strengthening of Socialist Legality", *Kommunist*, / 1963, / No. / 1.

Mishutin, A.N. and Kalenov, A. Yu., "To Strengthen Socialist Legality by All Means and Improve the Prosecuting Body's Supervision Over the Exact Fulfillment of Law", *S.G.P.*, 1955, No. 3.

Mittermeier, C., *Erfahrungen über die Wirksamkeit der Schwurgerichte in Europa und Amerika, über Ihe Vorzüge, Mängel und Abhilfe*, Erlangen, 1864.

Mokichev, K., "Against Bourgeois Influence in Criminal Trial", *Sots. zak.*, 1949, No. 2.

Molotov, V.M., Speech (excerpt) at the IIId All-Ukrainian Conference of the Ukrainian Communist Party (B), July 8, 1932, *Sov. yust.*, 1932, No. 20

Molochkov, A., "Advocates — Defenders of Rights and Court Assistants", *Proletarskaya revolutsiya i pravo*, November 1918, No. 7.

"The Moral Make-up of a Legal Worker" (Editorial), *Sov. yust.*, 1966, No. 15, p. 11.

Moroshinin, V., "It was an Interesting Rencounter", *Sov. yust.*, 1962, No. 3.

Mozheyko, "On the Legal Nature of Soviet *Arbitrazh*", *S.G.P.*, 1947, No. 6.

— —, V.N. and Shkundin, Z.I., *Arbitrazh* and the Arbitral Examination of Disputes, in *Arbitrazh v sovetskom khozyaystve* (*Arbitrazh* in Soviet Economy), M. 1948.

Nanikishvily, "On the Advocate's Activity", *Sots. zak.*, 1965, No. 6.

Narodnoye Khozyaystvo SSSR v 1964 g.; Same v 1967 g. (National Economy of the USSR in 1964 and 1967), M. 1965 and 1968, respectively.

Narodnoye obrazovaniye v SSSR (National Education in the USSR), M. 1957.

Natanzon, S., "On the Principles of Soviet Defense in Criminal Cases", *Sots. zak.*, 1958, No. 5.

Nauchno-prakticheskiy kommentariy k UPK RSFSR (Scientific-Practical Commentary of the RSFSR Code of Criminal Procedure), M. 1963 and 1965.

Nauchno-prakticheskiy kommentariy ugolovnogo kodeksa RSFSR (Scientific-Practical Commentary of the RSFSR Criminal Code), M. 1964.

Nazarov, L. and Sokolov, I., "To Heighten the Authority of the Soviet Legal Profession", *Sov. yust.*, 1959, No. 7.

Neystadt, T.E., *Sovetskiy advokat* (The Soviet Advocate), M. 1958.

Novoye Sovetskoye ugolovno-protsesual'noye zakonodatel'stvo i advokatura (The New Legislation on Criminal Procedure and the Legal Profession), M. 1960.

Nikitin, K.I., "On the Further Perfectioning of the Investigating Apparatus Activity", *S.G.P.*, 1966, No. 4.

Nikitinskiy, V.I., "Comrades' Courts", *Entsiklopedicheskiy slovar' pravovykh znaniy* (Encyclopaedic Dictionary of Legal Knowledge), M. 1965.

Nikolayev, V.V., "On the Role of the Soviet State in the Communist Construction", in *Voprosy stroitel'stva kommunisma v SSSR* (Questions of Communism Construction in the USSR), M. 1959.

Nikolayev, V.V., "The Overcoming of Wrong Theories in Criminal Law", *Kommunist*, 1956, No. 14.

Nikolayeva, L.A., *Obshchiy nadzor prokuratury v sovetskom gosudarstvennom upravlenii* (The Prosecuting Body's General Supervision in the Soviet State Administration), M. 1957.

Novak-Deker, N.K., "Problems of Soviet Higher Education", Bulletin of the Institute for the Study of the USSR", 1965, No. 3.

Obshchestvennost' v bor'be s pravonarusheniyem (The Public in the Fight Against Law Violation), Irkutsk, 1963.

Odinstov, V., "A Word on the Judicial Qualification of Court Workers", *Yezhenedel'nik sovetskoy yustitsii*, 1922, Nos. 37-38.

Ognyev, P., "Some Questions of the Advocate's Practical Activity", *Sots. zak.*, 1959, No. 6.

"On the Applying of Torture", *Yezhenedel'nik VeCheKa* (Weekly of the All-Russian Extraordinary Commission), October 6, 1918, No. 3.

"On the Improvement of the Legal Profession's Work" (Letters to the Editor), *Sots. zak.*, 1965, No. 5.

"On Measures for the Further Development of the Legal Science and the Improvement of Legal Education", Decision of the Central Committee of the Soviet Union Communist Party, *S.G.P.*, 1964, No. 8.

Osetrov, N., "The Right of Defense", *Moskovskaya Pravda*, May 8, 1964.

Osipov, K., "On the Collections of Advocates' Speeches", *Sov. yust.*, 1967, No. 3.

— —, "Summing-ups of Soviet Advocates", *Sov. yust.*, 1967, No. 3.

Pakalov, A., "How Important is the Knowledge of Law", *Pravda*, August 8, 1967.

Pashkevich, I.F., *Ob"yektivnaya istina v ugolovnom sudoproizvodstve* (Objective Truth in Criminal Procedure), M. 1961.

Pashukanis, E., "The Situation on the Theoretical Legal Front", *Sovetskoye gosudarstvo i revolutsiya prava* (The Soviet State and the Law Revolution), M. 1930, Nos. 11-12.

Pavlov, I.V., "On the Development of Soviet Legal Science During Forty Years", *S.G.P.*, 1957, No. 11.

Perfil'yev, M.N., *Kritika burzhuaznykh teoriy o sovetskoy politicheskoy sisteme* (Criticism by Bourgeois Theory of the Soviet Political System), M. 1968.

Perlov, D., "The Alphabet of Law", *Izvestia*, January 12, 1967.

— —, "In Defense of the Legal Profession", *Izvestia*, August 13, 1959.

— —, "The Independence of Judges", *Entsiklopedicheskiy slovar' pravovykh znaniy*, M. 1965 (Encyclopaedic Dictionary of Legal Knowledge), M. 1965.

— —, *Sudebnyye preniya i posledneye slovo podsudimogo v sovetskom ugolovnom protsesse* (Pleadings in Court and the Accused's Last Word in Soviet Criminal Procedure), M. 1957.

— —, "Why Reproach the Mirror ?", *Izvestia*, February 14, 1965.

— —, *Zakonnost' i pravosudiye* (Legality and Justice), M. 1959.

— — and Raginsky, M. Yu., "Ripe Questions of Inquest and Preliminary Investigations", *S.G.P.*, 1957, No. 4.

Peskin, A.G., "Some Practical Questions of the Advocate's Participation in the Preliminary Investigation", in *Razvitiye prav grazhdan SSSR i usloviya ikh okhrany na sovremennom etape kommunisticheskogo stroitel'stva* (The Development of USSR Citizens' Rights and Their Preservation in the Contemporary Stage of Communist Structure), Saratov, 1962.

Petrov, G.I., *Rol' obshchestvennosti v bor'be s prestupnost'yu* (The Role of the Public in the Fight Against Criminality), Voronezh, 1960.

Petrov, V.S. and Sheydlin, A., "The Marx-Lenin Doctrine of Socialist State and Law", in *40-let sovetskogo prava* (Forty Years of Soviet Law), M. 1957, Vol. I.

Pigolkin, A.S., "Basic Features of Contemporary Anti-Communism in the Field of Legal Theory", in *Obshchaya teoriya sovetskogo prava* (General Theory of Soviet Law), Edited by Bartus', S.N. and Samoshchenko, I.S., M. 1966.

Piontkovsky, A., "Guaranties of Justice", *Izvestia*, August 28, 1965.

— —, "On Some Questions of the Soviet Legal Science", *Izvestia*, April 1, 1957.

— —, "On the Value of Confessions", *Izvestia*, March 1, 1957.

— —, "The Strengthening of the Public's Role in the Fight Against Criminality and Some Questions of Soviet Criminal Law Theory", *S.G.P.*, 1961, No. 4.

— — and Chkhikvadze, J., "Strengthening of Soviet Legality and Some Questions of Soviet Criminal Procedure", *S.G.P.*, 1956, No. 4.

Podkovsky, A., "An Unnecessary Revival", *Yezhenedel'nik sovetskoy yustitsii*, 1925, No. 44-45.

Polnoye Sobraniye Zakonov Rossiyskoy Imperii (Complete Collection of Laws of the Russian Empire), St. Petersburg, 1830, 1866, 1887.

Polozheniye o prokurorskom nadzore v SSSR, (Statute on the Prosecuting Body's Super-vision in the USSR), M. 1957.

Polozheniye o tovarishcheskikh sudakh (Statute on Comrades' Courts), M. 1961 and 1964.

Polozkov, F.A., *Obshchestvennost' v bor'be s narushitelyami sotsialisticheskogo poryadka* (The Public in the Fight Against Violators of Socialist Order), Kyubyshev, 1961.

Polyak, A., "Legal Ignorance", *Izvestia*, July 1, 1965.

Polyansky, N.N., *Dokazatel'stva v inostrannom ugolovnom protsesse* (Evidence in Foreign Criminal Procedure), M. 1946.

— —, "The Legal Nature of Cassation, According to the Code of Criminal Procedure", *Pravo i zhizn'*, 1924, Issue 1.

— —, "The Legal Nature of the Soviet Legal Profession", *Sots. zak.*, 1945, No. 3.

— —, *Ocherk razvitiya sovetskoy nauki ugolovnogo prava* (Essay on the Development of Soviet Penal Science), M. 1960.

— —, *Pravda i lozh' v ugolovnoy zashchite* (Truth and Untruth in Criminal Defense), M. 1927.

— —, "Questions of Criminal Procedure in Connection With the Draft of the USSR Code of Criminal Procedure", *Sots. zak.*, 1954, No. 6.

— —, "Soviet Criminal Court as a Medium of the Party and Soviet Power", *Vestnik moskovskogo universiteta* (Herald of the Moscow University), 1950, No. 11.

— —, "Soviet Legislation on Court Structure in Its Basic Moments", *Pravo i zhizn'*, 1923, No. 2.

— —, "Valuation of Evidence by a Higher Court", *S.G.P.*, 1951, No. 7.

— —, *Voprosy teorii sovetskogo ugolovnogo protsessa* (Questions of Soviet Criminal Procedure Theory), M. 1956.

— — and Perlov, I.D., Independence of Judges, in *Entsiklopedicheskiy Slovar' pravo-vykh znaniy*, M. 1965.

Ponedelkov, M., "To Organize the Work of the Soviet People's Assessors More Widely and Variously", *Sov. yust.*, 1964, No. 7.

Porella, Curt, "The October Overturn and the Youngest Legal Development in Poland", *Osteuropa-Recht*, June 1957.

Posdeef, Eugene, "The Legal Profession in the USSR", *Bulletin of the Institute for the Study of the USSR*, March 1956, No. 3.

Posobiye dlya narodnykh zasedateley (Textbook for People's Assessors), M. 1955.

Pravovyye garantii zakonnosti v SSSR (Legal Guaranties of Legality in the USSR), M. 1962.

Programma i ustav kommunisticheskoy partii Sovetskogo soyuza (Program and By-Laws of the Soviet Union Communist Party), M. 1964.

Prusakov, N., "Guarantors", *Izvestia*, August 22, 1966.

— —, *Narodnyy sud'ya* (The People's Judge), M. 1965.

Pshenichnov, E., "Strengthen the Authority of the Legal Profession", *Sov. yust.*, 1958, No. 6.

"Questions of Law and Justice in a Distorting Mirror" (Editorial), *Sots. zak.*, 1965, No. 1.

Rad'kov, V., "The Notion and Content of Socialist Legality", *Sots. zak.*, 1961, No. 1.

Radzhabov, S. and Panov, G., *Rol' trudyashchikhsya v ukreplenii i okhrane sovetskogo obshchestvennogo poryadka* (The Role of the Working Population in the Strengthening and Preservation of Public Order), M. 1960.

Rakhunov, R.D., "Legality and Justice", *Pravda*, September 22, 1965.

— —, "The Obvious Importance of the Accused's Confession", *S.G.P.*, 1956, No. 8.

— —, *Peresmotr prigovorov, i opredeleniy v prezidiyumakh sudov* (Review of Sentences and Rulings by Court Presidiums), M. 1956.

— —, "To the Question of Controversy in the Stage of Preliminary Investigation", *Sots. zak.*, 1938, No. 3.

— —, Review of the book : *Zashchititel'nyye rechi sovetskikh zashehitnikov* (Defense Speeches of Soviet Counsels), *Sots. zak.*, 1957, No. 3.

— —, "Some Questions of Criminal Procedure", *Izvestia*, March 27, 1957.

— —, "Soviet Justice and its Role in the Strengthening of Legality", *Kommunist*, 1956, No. 7.

— —, *Uchastniki ugolovno-protsessual'noy deyatel'nosti po sovetskomu pravu* (Participants of the Criminal Procedural Activity According to Soviet Law), M. 1961.

— —, *Vozbuzhdeniye ugolovnogo dela v sovetskom ugolovnom protsesse* (Initiation of a Criminal Case in the Soviet Criminal Procedure), M. 1954.

Rasulov, D., "The Basic Principles of Legislation on the Court Structure of the USSR, Union and Autonomous Republics, the Statute of Military Tribunals and Soviet Principles of Criminal Procedure of the U.S.S.R. and the Union Republics", *Sots. zak.*, 1959, No. 1.

"*Recueil de maximes et citations latines à l'usage du monde judiciaire*, Paris, 1924".

"Regulations on the Admission to Institutions of Higher Learning." Order of the USSR Minister of Higher and Secondary Special Education No. 89, of March 7, 1963, *Byuleten' MV and SSO* (Bulletin of the Ministry of Higher and Secondary Special Education), 1963, No. 4.

Reisner, M.A., "Report on the Birth of Power", *Materialy komissariata yustitsii RSFSR* (Materials of the RSFSR People's Commissariat of Justice), 1918, No. 1.

Remnev, V. and Temushkin, O., "Who is the Prosecutor ?", *Izvestia*, November 23, 1956.

"Report of the People's Commissariat of Justice", *Proletarskaya revolutsiya i pravo*, 1918, No. 1.

Rezanov, V.P., "The Law of Criminal Procedure", in *40-let sovetskogo prava* (Forty Years of Soviet Law), M. 1951, V. 1.

Rivkin, M., "On State *Arbitrazh*", *Sov. yust.*, 1937, No. 5.

Rivlin, E.S., *Sovetskaya advokatura* (Soviet Legal Profession), M. 1926.

Robbins, M., "The Soviet Legal System", *American Bar Association Journal*, Nov. 1933.

Rogovin, A., "The Unification of Procedural Norms of Court and *Arbitrazh*", *Sov. yust.*, 1957, No. 17.

"The Role of the Counsel in the Trial is Independent of that of the Accused", *Sov. yust.*, 1959, No. 7.

Romashkin, N.S., "The Development of Soviet State Functions in the Transition Process to Communism", in *Voprosy stroitel'stva kommunizma v SSSR* (Questions of Communism Construction in the USSR), M. 1959.

— —, "Man and Law", *Izvestia*, April 12, 1967.

Rossada, S., "The Bar", *Highlights of Current Legislation and Activity in Mid-Europe*, 1955, No. 10.

Rosoff, S., "The Bar", in *Highlights of Current Legislation and Activities in Mid-Europe*, April 1959.

Rossel's, V.L., "The Problem of a Defense Counsel in the Soviet Court", in *Zashchitnik v sovetskom sude* (Counsel in Soviet Court), M. 1960.

Rostovshchikov, V. and Feofanov, Yu., "Law and only the Law", *Izvestia*, August 19, 1964.

Rozhansky, "The Participation of the Council in the Preliminary Investigation" in *Sorok let sovetskoy advokatury* (Forty Years of the Soviet Legal Profession), M. 1962.

Rubinstein, D. B., *Ugolovnyy sud RSFSR* (The RSFSR Criminal Court), M. 1925.

Rudenko, R.A., "On the Problem of the Further Strengthening of Socialist Legality in the Light of the Sessions of the XXIst Congress of the USSR Communist Party", *Sovetskaya obshchestvennost' na strazhe sotsialisticheskoy zakonnosti*, M. 1960.

Rukovodstvo i nadzor za rassledovaniyem (Guidance and Supervision of the Investigation), M. 1947.

"Rules of Admission to Institutions of Higher Learning", *Bulleten' MV i SSD* (Bulletin of the Ministry of Higher and Second ary Special Education), 1963, No. 10.

Sakharov, A.D. "Thoughts on Progress, Peaceful Coexistence and Intellectual Freedom. (Excerpts), The N.Y. Times, July 22, 1968.

Samsonov, V.A., "The Soviet Advocates and their Role in the Further Strengthening of Soviet Legality", *S.G.P.*, 1960, No. 11; "Notes on the Profession", *Sots. zak.*, 1964, No. 11.

Savitsky, M. Ya., "According to Law, According to Conscience", *Izvestia*, Feb. 12, 1965.

— —, "A New Stage in the Activity of Comrades' Courts", *S.G.P.*, 1959, No. 12.

— —, "The Principle of Liberty of Complaint Against Sentences and Reformation", *Sots. zak.*, 1949, No. 3.

— —, "Problems and Position of Counsel in Soviet Criminal Procedure", *S.G.P.*, 1955, No. 7.

— —, *Prokurorskiy nadzor za doznaniyem i predvaritel'nym sledstviem* (The Prosecutor's Supervision over Inquest and Preliminary Investigation), M. 1959.

— — and Keizerov, N.M., "The Development of Legal Forms of Comrades' Courts Organization and Activity", *S.G.P.*, 1961, No. 4.

Sbornik normativnykh aktov po sovetskomu administrativnomu pravu (Collection of Normative Acts Pertaining to Soviet Administrative Law), M. 1964.

Sbornik postanovleniy plenuma verchovnogo suda SSSR 1924-1951 (Collection of Decisions of the USSR Supreme Court Plenum 1924-1951), M. 1952, 1961, 1962.

Sbornik statey i materialov po grazhdanskomu pravu (Collection of Articles and Materials on Civil Law), M. 1925.

Sbornik statey i materialov po grazhdanskomu protsessu 1921-1924 (Collection of Articles and Materials on Civil Procedure 1921-1924), M. 1925.

Shcheglovitov, I.G., "New Attempts to Change the Court with Jury in Western Europe", in *Sudebnyye ustavy 20-go noyabrya 1864 za 50 let* (Fifty Years of the Judicial Statutes of Nov. 20, 1864), I, II, Petrograd, 1914.

Schapiro, Leonard, "Prospects for the Rule of Law", *Problems of Communism*, March-April 1965.

Schlesinger, Rudolf, *Soviet Legal Theory, Its Social Background and Development*, Routledge & Kegan Paul, Ltd., London, 1951.

— —, "Court Cases as a Source of Information on Soviet Society", *The Slavic and East European Review*, October, 1951.

Schroeder, Friedrich C., "Social Courts and Administrative Justice", *Osteuropa-Recht*, 1962, No. 4.

Seidler, G.L., "Marxist Legal Thought in Poland", *The Slavic Review*, 1967, No. 3.

Semenov, N., *Sovetskiy sud i Karatel'naya sistema* (Soviet Court and the Penal System), Munchen, 1952.

— — and Yakushev, V., "The Public University of Legal Knowledge", *Sov. yust.*, 1960, No. 4.

Serebryakova, V.A., "Discussion of Questions Related to the Application of the RSFSR Supreme Soviet's Ukase of May 4, 1961", *S.G.P.*, 1961, No. 8.

Shafir, G.M., "The Right of Defense in Soviet Criminal Procedure and the Possibility of its Enlargement", *S.G.P.*, 1967, No. 2.

— —, "Some Suggestions for the Perfection of the Soviet Legal Profession Organization", *S.G.P.*, 1965, No. 10.

Shalamov, M.R., "The Question of The Accused's Confession Evaluation", *S.G.P.*, 1956, No. 8.

Sharkov, B.S., "Speech at the Supreme Soviet Session of December 26", 1958, *Pravda*, December 27, 1958.

— —, "The Indictment Almost Became the Function of the Prosecution", *Sots. zak.*, 1946, No. 10.

Shcheylov, V., "On the Connection of Court and *Arbitrazh* Decisions", *Sov. yust.*, 1961, No. 17.

Shebanov, A., "Bring the Training of Jurists Nearer to Practice", *Sov. yust.*, 1957, No. 8.

— —, "To Improve the Preparation of the Legal Staffs", *S.G.P.*, 1955, No. 1.

— —, "Put Soviet Legal Education on a New Stage", *Sov. yust.*, 1959, No. 9.

— —, *Yuridicheskiye vysshiye uchebnyye zavedeniya* (The Legal Institutions of Higher Learning), M. 1963.

Shein, E.A., "The Counsel and the Preliminary Investigation in Soviet Criminal Procedure", *S.G.P.*, 1962, No. 6.

Shelepin, A.N., "Speech at the XXIst Congress of the Soviet Union Communist Party", *Pravda*, February 5, 1959.

— —, Speech at the XXIInd Congress of the Soviet Union Communist Party, in *XXIIoy s"ezd kommunisticheskoy partii Sovetskogo soyuza. Stenograficheskiy otchet* (The

XXIInd Congress of the Soviet Union Communist Party. Verbatim Report), M. 1962, V. II.

Shifman, M.L., "Some Questions Pertaining to the Summing Up", in *Zashchita v ugolovnom protsesse* (Defense in a Criminal Trial), M. 1948.

Shifman, N.A., "A.F. Koni, the Outstanding Jurist and Court Orator", *Sots. zak.*, 1957, No. 9.

Shkundin, Z., "On *Arbitrazh* Procedure", *Sovetskoye gosudarstvo*, 1936, No. 3.

——, "State *Arbitrazh* and Arbitration Procedure", in *Arbitrazh v sovetskom khozyaystve* (*Arbitrazh* in Soviet Economy), M. 1938.

——, "The Unification of Procedural Norms of Court and *Arbitrazh*", *Sov. yust.*, 1937, No. 4.

Shlyapochnikov, A.S., *Bor'ba s tuneyadtsami — vsenarodnoye delo* (The Fight Against Spongers Is An All-People's Affair), M. 1962.

——, "For the Strengthening of Soviet Legality", *Sovetskoye gosudarstvo*, 1934, No. 4.

——, "Legislation and Society in the Fight Against Parasitic Elements", *S.G.P.*, 1961, No. 8.

——, "V.I. Lenin on Problems of Courts and Investigations Organs in the Fight Against Bureaucracy and Procrastination", *Sots. zak.*, 1966, No. 4.

——, "On Soviet Criminal Law Stabilization", *S.G.P.*, 1957, No. 12.

——, "Questions of the Strengthening of the State-Legal and Social Influence in the Fight Against Parasitic Elements", *S.G.P.*, 1963, No. 9.

——, *Tuneyadtsev k otvetu* (Bring Spongers to Responsibility), M. 1964.

Sholokhov, M., "From a Speech at the XXIth Congress of the Soviet Union Communist Party", *Novoye Russkoye Slovo*, N.Y., November 22, 1966.

Shubin, V., "To Know and Respect Law", *Sov. yust.*, 1967, No. 7.

Shubin, V., "In the Name of the Republic", *Izvestia*, December 11, 1965.

Sinaysky, E.D., "Basic Questions of Defense in Criminal Procedure", *S.G.P.*, 1961, No. 5.

Sinyavsky i Daniel na skam'ye podsudimykh (Sinyavsky and Daniel in the Dock), N.Y. 1966.

Sistematicheskiy sbornik uzakoneniy i rasporyazheniy rabochevo i krestyanskogo pravitelstva (Systematic Collection of Legislation and Orders of the Workers' and Peasants Government), M. 1919.

Skomorokhov, P., "Appointed Defence and the Advocate's Duty", *Literaturnaya gazeta*, September 3, 1964.

Slavin, I.K., "The Court and the New Economic Policy", *Yezhenedel'nik sovetskoy yustitsii*, 1922, No. 1.

——, "On The Reform of RSFSR Court Structure", *Yezhenedel'nik sovetskoy yustitsii*, 1922, No. 37-38.

Smelkov, A., "For the Efficiency of the Comrades' Court Work", *Sov. yust.*, 1966, No. 3.

Sobraniye postanovleniy verkhovnogo suda SSSR, 1938-1939 (Collection of Decisions of the USSR Supreme Court 1938-1939), M. 1940.

"Social Courts are the Most Important Form of Fighting the Survivals of the Past" (Editorial), *S.G.P.*, 1959, No. 5.

Sofinov, P.G., *Ocherki istorii Vserossiyskoy chrezvychaynoy komissii (1917-1922)* (Essays on the History of the All-Russian Extraordinary Commission, 1917-1922), M. 1960.

Solopchenko, Vilensky, "For the Heightening of Advocate's Work Quality", *Sots. zak.*, 1957, No. 8.

Sorok let sovetskoy advocatury (Forty Years of Soviet Legal Profession), M. 1962.

Sorok let sovetskoy advokatury (Forty Years of the Soviet Legal Profession), Reports of the Scientific Conference of Leningrad's Advocates, Leningrad, 1962.

Soviet Criminal Law and Procedure, The RSFSR Codes, Introduction and Analysis by Harold J. Berman. Translation by Harold G. Berman and James W. Spindler, Harvard University Press, Cambridge, Mass., 1966.

Soviet Legal Philosophy, with an Introduction by John N. Hazard. Translated by Hugh W. Babb, Harvard University Press, Cambridge, Mass., 1957.

"Soviet Legal Science" (Editorial), *Izvestia*, March 1, 1957.

Sovetskaya advokatura (The Soviet Legal Profession), M. 1939, 1942.

Sovetskaya obshchestvennost' na strazhe sotsialisticheskoy zakonnosti (The Soviet Public on the Watch of Socialist Legality), M. 1960.

Sovetskaya prokuratura v vazhneyshikh dokumentakh (Soviet Prosecution Body in the Most Important Documents), M. 1956.

Sovetskiy ugolovnyy protsess. (Soviet Criminal Procedure), M. 1956.

Sovetskoye ugolovnoye pravo—Chast' obshchaya i osobennaya (Soviet Criminal Law, General and Special Parts), Vol. I and II, M. 1962.

Spektor, E., "The Activity of the Moscow City College of Advocates", *Sov. yust.*, 1940, No. 1.

— —, "Quality of the Legal Profession's Work", *Sov. yust.*, 1940, No. 9.

Spencer, Herbert, *Social Statistics* : or *the Condition Essential to Human Happiness Specified and the First of Them Developed*, N.Y., 1875.

Speransky, A., "The People's Assessors", *Proletarskaya revolyutsiya i pravo*, M., October 1-15, 1918.

Stalin, I.V., *Voprosy leninizma* (Questions of Leninism), M. 1938, 1947, 1952.

— —, *Sochineniya* (Works).

Statute on Post-Graduate Studies at Institutions of Higher Learning, *Byulleten' ministerstva vysshego i srednego spetsial'nogo obrazovanoya SSSR* (Bulletin of the USSR Ministry of Higher and Secondary Special Education), M. 1962, No. 9.

Stavtsev, A.I., "The Problems of the Comrades' Courts Enterprises and Institutions in the Education of Communist Attitude Toward Labor and Rules of Socialist Common Life", *Vsesoyuznyy institut yuridicheskikh nauk, uchenyye zapiski* (All-Union Institute of Legal Sciences. Scientific Notes), 1961, No. 11.

Steinberg, I.N., "Fundamentals of the People's Court", *Znamya truda*, February 23, 1918.

— —, "In the Workshop of the Revolution", N.Y., 1956.

Stetsovsky, Yu., "On Procedural Independence of the Advocate-Counsel", *Sov. yust.*, 1966, No. 16.

Stolkind, A. Ya., "In Memory of O.O. Gruzenberg", in O.O. Gruzenberg, *Ocherki i rechi* (Essayes and Speeches), N.Y., 1944.

Storchenko, A.A., "The Problem of Objective Truth in the Theory of Criminal Procedure", *Voprosy filosofii*, 1956, No. 2.

Stremovsky, V. and Teshinsky, A., "The Positive Results of the Counsel's Participation in the Preliminary Investigation", *Sov. yust.*, 1961, No. 24.

Strogovich, M.S., "The Accused's Confession", *Sots. zak.*, 1965, No. 6.

— —, "The Advocate's Procedural Position in the Soviet Criminal Procedure", *Sots. zak.*, 1959, No. 3.

— —, "An Answer to the Prosecutor", *Literaturnaya gazeta*, August 18, 1964.

Strogovich, M.S., "The Development of Legislation on Court Structure and Procedure",
    Sov. yust., 1961, No. 22.
— —, "A Judicial Mistake", *Literaturnaya gazeta*, May 23, 1964.
— —, *Kurs sovetskogo ugolovnogo protsessa* (A Course of Soviet Criminal Procedure),
    M. 1958.
— —, *Material'naya istina i sudebnyye dokazatel'stva* (The Material Truth and Court
    Evidence), M. 1955.
— —, *Obvineniye i obvinyayemyy na predvaritel'nom sledstvii i sude* (The Accusation
    and the Accused During the Preliminary Investigation and Trial), M. 1934.
— —, *Osnovnyye voprosy sovetskoy sotsialisticheskoy zakonnosti* (Basic Questions of
    Soviet Socialist Legality), M. 1959.
— —, "The Procedural Position and Functions of the Defense", in *Zashchita v ugolovnom
    protsesse* (Defense in Criminal Procedure), M. 1948.
— —, *Proverka zakonnosti i obosnovannosti sudebnykh prigovorov* (The Checking of the
    Legality and Substantiation of Sentences), M. 1956.
— —, "On the Question, How Individual Legal Problems are Presented in the Works
    of P. I. Stuchka, N.V. Krylenko and E.B. Pashukhanis", in *Voprosy obshchey
    teorii sovetskogo prava* (Questions of the General Theory of Soviet Law), M. 1960.
— —, "Socialist Legality", in *Voprosy gosudarstva i prava* (Questions of State and Law),
    M. 1957.
— —, "Some Questions of State and Law", in *Voprosy stroitel'stva kommunizma*
    (Questions of Communism Construction), M. 1959.
— —, "At the Sources of Soviet Legal Science", *Sots. zak.*, 1957, No. 10.
— —, *Sotsialisticheskaya zakonnost'* (Socialïst Legality), in *Entsiklopedicheskiy slovar'
    pravovykh zhaniy* (Encyclopaedic Dictionary of Legal Knowledge), M. 1965.
— —, "Theoretical Questions of Soviet Legality", *S.G.P.*, 1956, No. 4.
— —, *Uchebnik ugolovnogo protsessa* (Text Book of Criminal Procedure), M. 1938, 1958.
— —, *Ucheniye o material'noy istine v ugolovnom protsesse* (The Doctrine of Material
    Truth in Criminal Procedure), M. 1947.
— —, *Ugolovnoye presledovaniye v sovetskom ugolovnom protsesse* (Criminal Prosecution
    in Soviet Penal Procedure), M. 1951.
— —, *Ugolovnyy protsess* (Criminal Procedure), M. 1946.
— — and Grabovenko, Ya. V., "Guaranties of the Individual's Rights in Criminal Pro-
    cedure", in *Demokraticheskiye osnovy sovetskogo sotsialisticheskogo pravosudiya*
    (Democratic Foundations of Soviet Justice), M. 1965.
— — and Karpinsky, D.A., *Ugolovno-protsessual'nyy kodeks RSFSR* (The RSFSR Code
    of Criminal Procedure), M. 1928.
Stroyev, M., "The Role of the Defense in a Criminal Trial", *Yezhenedel'nik sovetskoy
    yustitsii*, 1925, No. 34.
Stuchka, P.I., *Izbrannyye proizvedeniya po marksistsko-leninskoy teorii prava* (Selected
    Works on Marxist-Leninist Theory of Law), Riga, 1964.
— —, Law Consciousness, in *Entsiklopediya gosudarstva i prava* (Encyclopaedia of
    State and Law), M. 1925-1927.
— —, "The Old and the New Court", *Leningradskaya Pravda*, January 3, 4, 5, 1918.
— —, *Revolutsionnaya rol' sovetskogo prava i gosudarstva* (The Revolutionary Role of
    Soviet Law and State), M. 1921, 1923, 1934.
Svod zakonov Rossiyskoy Imperii (Code of Laws of the Russian Empire) 1857, V. 15.

Sudebnyye rechi sovetskikh advokatov (Court Speeches of Soviet Advocates), M. 1962.

Sudebnyye ustavy 20 noyabrya 1864 s izlozeniyem razsuzhdeniy na koikh oni osnovany (Judicial Statutes of Nov. 20, 1864 with the motives on which they are based), Vol. I, II, III, St. Petersburg, 1867.

Survey, London, 1968, No. 60.

Sukharev, A. Ya., "Vital Problems of the Soviet Legal Profession", *S.G.P.*, 1964, No. 10.

— —, "To Improve the Advocates' Work in the Realization of Citizens' Defense During the Preliminary Investigation", *Sov. yust.*, 1962, No. 12.

Tadevosyan, V.S., "General Supervision by the Prosecuting Body", *S.G.P.*, 1951, No. 4.

— —, "The Question of Material Truth Establishment", *S.G.P.*, 1948, No. 6.

— —, *Prokurorskiy nadzor v SSSR* (Prosecutor Body's Supervision in the USSR), M. 1956.

— —, "Soviet Law System", *S.G.P.*, 1956, No. 7.

Tager, L.S., "Notes on the Legal Profession", *Pravo i zhizn'*, 1922, Vol. I.

— —, "On Soviet Legal Profession", *Sots. zak.*, 1936, No. 10.

Tarde, de G., *La philosophie pénale*, Lyon, 1820.

Tarnopol'sky, A.A., *Sistematicheskiy spravochnik dlya narodnykh sudey i sledovateley* (Systematic Reference Book for People's Judges and Investigating Magistrates), M. 1921.

Tarnova, M., "Defense in Soviet Court", *Sov. yust.*, 1936, No. 26.

Tendryakov, V., *Sud* (The Court), M. 1961.

Teoriya dokazatel'stv v sovetskom ugolovnom protsessa, Chast' obshchaya (Evidence Theory in Soviet Criminal Procedure. General Part), M. 1966.

Terebilov, V., "Science and Staff", *Izvestia*, August 20, 1967.

Thorpe, K.M., "Remuneration of the Lawyer in Soviet Russia", *American Bar Association Journal*, 1935.

Timashev, N.S., "Court Structure", in *Sovetskoye pravo*, V. 1-2, Praha, 1925.

— —, "The Impact of the Penal Law of Imperial Russia on Soviet Penal Law", in *Slavic and East European Review*, 1953, No. 4.

Tobolovskaya, M., "The Defense of Property and Personal Rights of Citizens by the Advocate", *Sov. yust.*, 1965, No. 10.

Tonkikh, V.N., *Obshchestvennyy obvinitel' i obshchestvenny zashchitnik* (The Public Prosecutor and the Public Counsel), M. 1961.

Trapeznikov, V., "Disciplinary Responsibility of Defenders", *Ezhenedel'nik sovetskoy yustitsii*, 1923, No. 40.

Traynin, A., "Clarification of the Corpus Delicti. A Question in the Defense Pleadings", in *Zashchita v ugolovnom protsesse*, M. 1948.

— —, "On Revolutionary Legality", *Pravo i zhizn'*, June 1922.

— —, "Socialist Legality and Socialist Law Consciousness", *Sots. zak.*, 1959, No. 7.

Turin, V., "From Colleges of Right Defenders to Advocates", *Sov. yust.*, 1957, No. 9

Tarasov-Rodionov, P.I., *Predvaritel'noye sledstviye* (The Preliminary Investigation), M. 1955.

Ugolovnyy kodeks. Nauchno-populyarnyy prakticheskiy kommentariy (Criminal Code. Scientific Popular Commentary), M. 1927.

Ul'yanova, L., "On the Procedural Position of the Advocate and His Attitude in the Case", *Sots. zak.*, 1966, No. 3.

Umansky, Ya. N., *Sovetskoye gosudarstvennoye pravo* (Soviet State Law), M. 1960.

Urakov, L.H., *Obshchestvennoye obvineniye i obshchestvennaya zashchita v sovetskom ugolovnom protsesse* (Public Accusation and Public Defense in the Soviet Criminal Procedure), M. 1964.

Ushakov, I.A., "Accusation and Defense in Petrograd's Revolutionary Courts", *Sots. zak.*, 1957, No. 6.

—— —, "The Creation of the First People's Court in Petrograd", *S.G.P.*, 1957, No. 1.

V. "At the Meeting of Moscow Advocates", *Sov. yust.*, 1941, No. 6.

Vasil'yev, A.N., "The Inquest in Soviet Procedure", *S.G.P.*, 1959, No. 6.

Vas'kovsk iy, Ye. V., *Organizatsiya advokatury* (Organization of the Legal Profession), St. Petersburg, 1893, 2 Vol.

—— —, *Osnovnyye voprosy advokatskoy etiki* (Basic Questions of Advocate's Ethics), St. Petersburg, 1895.

Veger, V.I., *Distsiplina i etika zashchitnika* (Defender's Discipline and Ethics), M. 1925.

Veinberg, E., "Perfection of the Work of the Soviet Legal Profession", *Sots. zak.*, 1958, No. 10.

Velichkin, K., "Heighten the Level of Comrades' Courts Guidance", *Sov. yust.*, 1963, No. 12.

Vestnik NKVD (Herald of the People'sCommissariat of Internal Affairs), No, 9-IV.

Vestnik TsIK, SNK i STO (Herald of the Central Executive Committee, Council of People's Commissars and Council of Labor and Defense), 1923, No. 8.

Vinberg, A., Kochar ov, G. and Min'kovsky, G., "Actual Questions of Court Evidence Theory in Criminal Procedure", *Sots. zak.*, 1963, No. 3.

—— —, "Against Vyshinsky's Vicious Theories in Soviet Criminal Procedure", *Sots. zak.*, 1962, No. 3.

Vokopola, Kemal, "Reorganization of the Bar", *Highlights of Current Legislation and Activity in Mid-Europe*, 1955, No. 7.

Vol'sky, A., "The Insurance of the Defense Right to the Accused, According to Soviet Law", *Sov. yust.*, 1936, No. 22.

Voprosy sudoproizvodstva i sudoustroystva v novom zakonodatel'stve SSSR (Questions of Procedure and Court Structure in the New Legislation of the USSR), M. 1959.

Voprosy Stroitel'stva kommunizma v SSSR (Questions of Communism Building in the U.S.S.R.), M. 1959.

Voprosy ugolovnogo protsessa v praktike verkhovnogo suda SSSR (Questions of Criminal Procedure in the Practice of the USSR Supreme Court), M. 1955.

Voprosy sovetskogo gosudarstva i prava 1917-1957 (Questions of Soviet State and Law, 1917-1957), M. 1957.

Vroblevsky, A.G., *Postateynyy kommentariy k ugolovno-protsessual'nomu kodeksu RSFSR* (Commentary by Items on the RSFSR Code of Criminal Procedure), M. 1923.

Vydrya, M.M. and Yarzhenets, Z.N., Review of the Book : The Advocate in the Soviet Criminal Procedure, Edited by Golikov, *S.G.P.*, 1955, No. 3.

—— — (Editor), *Sudebnyye rechi izvestnykh russkikh yuristov* (Court Speeches of Well-Known Russian Jurists), M. 1956, 1957, 1958.

—— — (Editor), *Sudebnyye rechi sovetskikh advokatov* (Court Speeches of Soviet Advocates), M. 1960.

Vyshinsky, A. Ye., "For the High Quality of Work", *Sots. zak.*, 1937, No. 2.

—— —, "Higher the Banner of Socialist Legality", *Sots. zak.*, 1936, No. 11.

Vyshinsky, A. Ye., *K polozheniyu na fronte pravovoy teorii* (On the Situation at the Legal Theory Front), M. 1937.

— —, *The Law of the Soviet State*. Translated by H.W. Babb, New York, The Macmillan Company, 1948.

— —, "The Legal Profession", *Entsiklopediya gosudarstva i prava* (Encyclopaedia of State and Law), M. 1933, Vol. 1.

— —, "The Marxist-Leninist Doctrine on Court and the Soviet Court System", in *Ocherki po sudoustroystvu v SSSR* (Essays on Court Structure in the USSR), M. 1934, Vol. 2.

— —, "On New Rails", *Sots. zak.*, 1936, No. 10.

— —, "On Problems of the Investigating Magistrates", *Sots. zak.*, 1957, No. 1.

— —, "The Problem of Evidence Valuation in the Soviet Criminal Procedure", *Sots. zak.*, 1936, No. 7.

— —, "Problems of Socialist Law", *S.G.P.*, 1939, No. 13.

— —, *Revolyutsionnaya zakonnost' i zadachi sovetskoy zashchity* (Revolutionary Legality and Problems of Soviet Defense), M. 1934.

— —, *Revolyutsionnaya zakonnost' na sovremennom etape* (Revolutionary Legality at the Contemporary Stage), M. 1933.

— —, *Sotsialisticheskoye stroitel'stvo, sotsialisticheskaya zakonnost' i zadachi sovetskoy yustitsii* (Socialist Building, Socialist Legality and Problems of Soviet Justice), M. 1935.

— —, *Sovetskaya prokuratura i yeye zadachi* (The Soviet Prosecuting Body and its Problems), M. 1934.

— —, "Speech at the All-Russian Conference of Prosecutors", *Sots. zak.*, 1938, No. 7.

— —, "Stalin's Constitution and the Problems of the Prosecuting Body's Organs", *Sots. zak.*, 1937, No. 1.

— —, *Sudebnyye rechi* (Court Speeches), M. 1948.

— —, *Sud i Procuratura* (Court and the Prosecuting Body), M. 1934.

— —, *Sudoustroystvo v SSSR* (Court Structure in the USSR), M. 1936 and 1940.

— —, *Sudy obshchestvennoy samodeyatel'nosti* (The Social Courts With Independent Activity), M. 1934.

— —, *Teoriya sudebnykh dokozatel'stv v sovetskom protsesse* (The Theory of Court Evidence in the Soviet Procedure), M. 1946 and 1950.

— —, *Voprosy teorii gosudarstva i prava* (Questions of the Theory of State and Law), M. 1950.

Vysshaya shkola (School of Higher Learning), M. 1957.

Wagner, V., "Universities", *Entsiklopedicheskiy slovar' Granata*, M. (n.d.), Vol. 7.

Westen, Klaus, *Die rechtstheoretischen und rechtspolitischen Ansichten Stalins* (Stalin's Theoretical and Political Views on Law), London-Konstanz, 1959.

"Why Are You Sentimentalizing?", *Yezhenedel'nik VeCheKa* (Weekly of the All-Russian Extraordinary Commission for the Fight Against Counterrevolution and Sabotage), October 6, 1918, No. 3.

Wolin, Simon, Slusser, R., *The Soviet Secret Police*, F. Praeger, N.Y., 1957.

Yakimov, P.P., "The Nature and Importance of *Arbitrazh* Organs", in *Uchenyye zapiski sverdlovskogo yuridicheskogo instituta* (Scientific Notes of the Sverdlovsk Law Institute), 1957, V. 5.

Yakobson, Sergius and Allen, Robert V., *Aspects of Intellectual Ferment and Dissent in the Soviet Union*. Prepared at the Request of Senator Thomas J. Dodd, Subcommittee to Investigate the Administration of the Internal Security Act and Other Internal Security Laws, Committee on the Judiciary, United States Senate, U.S. Government Printing Office, Washington, D.C., 1968.

Yakubovich, N.A., *Okonchaniye predvaritel'nogo sledstviya* (The Termination of the Preliminary Investigation), M. 1962.

Yelyutin, V.P., *Higher Education*, Soviet Booklet No. 100, London, 1962.

— —, "The Higher School of Learning Today", *Molodoy kommunist*, 1960, No. 1.

— —, *Vysshaya shkola strany sotsializma* (The Higher School of Learning of the Country of Socialism), M. 1959.

Yesenboyev, M., Klachkov, N., in *Kazakhstanskaya Pravda*, December 7, 1965.

"Yes, The Honor Must be Rehabilitated", *Izvestia*, December 19, 1964.

Yevtikheyev, I.I. and Vlasov V.A., *Administrativnoye pravo* (Administrative Law), M. 1946.

Yezhenedel'nik NKVD (Weekly of the People's Commissariat of Internal Affairs), 1918, V. I.

Yudel'son, K.S., *Polozheniye o tovarishcheskikh sudakh* (Statute on the Comrades' Courts), M. 1962.

— — (Editor), *Prakticheskoye posobiye dlya tovarishcheskikh sudov* (Practical Textbook on Comrades' Courts), M. 1961.

Yudin, A., "Counsel for the Defense," in *The Soviet Union*, M. 1958, No. 100.

Yurburgsky, Yu. V., "New Features of the People's Assessors Organization", *S.G.P.*, 1963, No. 10.

Yuridicheskiy slovar' (Legal Dictionary), M. 1956, Vol. I and II.

Yurkovsky, L., in *Novoye Russkoye Slovo*, *N.Y.*, Sept. 3, 1964.

Zagurskaya, E.I., *Ob uchastii obshchestvennosti v otpravlenii pravosudiya* (On Public Participation in the Administration of Justice), Khar'kov, 1961.

Zaitsov, Y. and Poltorak, A., *The Soviet Bar*, M. 1959.

Zakonadstel'stvo o sudoustroystve soyuza SSR i soyuznykh respublik (Legislation on Court Structure of the Soviet Union and the Union Republics), M. 1961.

Zamoyska, Helene, "*Siniavski et sa patrie*" (Sinyavsky and his Fatherland), in *Sinyavsky i Daniel na skam'ye podsudimykh* (Sinyavsky and Daniel in the Dock), N.Y., 1966.

Zarza, Victor, "On the Brodsky Case", *Manchester Guardian*, May 13, 1964.

Zashchititel'nyye rechi sovetskikh advokatov (Defense Speeches of Soviet Advocates), M. 1956 and 1957.

Zashchita po ugolovnym delam (Defense in Criminal Cases), M. 1948.

Zasedaniya Verkhovnogo Soveta SSSR. Stenografichesiy otchet (Sessions of the Supreme Soviet of the USSR. Verbatim Report), M. 1957.

Zhogin, N., "The Investigating Magistrate and the Preliminary Investigation", *Izvestia*, September 20, 1964.

— —, "The Role of the Investigating Apparatus and Prosecutor's Supervision in Crime Prevention", *S.G.P.*, 1965, No. 10.

— — and Kudryavtsev, V., "Law and Morals in Our Society", *Pravda*, September 21, 1966.

Zhurnal grazhdanskogo i ugolovnogo prava (The Journal of Civil and Criminal Law), 1890, No. 8.

Zhurnal ministerstva yustitsii (The Journal of the Ministry of Justice), 1876, No. 2.

Zhurnal Soyedinennogo departamenta gosudarstvennogo soveta (Journal of the United Department of the State Council), St. Petersburg, 1864.

Zil'berstein, N., "The Prosecuting Body and the Civil Procedure", *Vestnik sovetskoy yustitsii* (Herald of Soviet Justice), M. 1923, No. 7.

Zile, Z.L., "Soviet Legal Profession : Recent Developments in Law and Practice", *Wisconsin Law Review*, 1964, No. 1.

Zinov'yev, B., "Another Time on the New System of Advocate's Work", *Sov. yust.*, 1958, No. 1.

Zivs, S.L., "Against Anti-Communism in Questions of State Theory", *S.G.P.*, 1962, No. 3.

— —, "The Reactionary-Utopian Concept of Socialist and Bourgeois Legal Systems", *S.G.P.*, 1960, No. 6.

Zlobin, I., *Lawyers in the USSR*, M. 1957, No. 9.

Zvantsev, S., *Advokaty* (The Advocates), Rostov-on-Don, 1963.

INDEX

Abramov, S.N., 494-497, 509, 575, 636

Advocates, assistant to the court, 520-533; criticism of, 561-568; position in civil suits, 571-572

Administrative courts, *see* courts administrative

Admoni, 221-222, 228

Adriyenko, 517

Afonin, A., 350

Agapov-Ivanov, A., 351n

Akhmatova, A., 213

Al'bitsky, P.D., 427, 431n

Aleksinsky, 6

Alexander I, 252, 256, 405, 439-440

Alexander II, 254, 263, 314, 336, 405n, 538

Alexander III, 255, 309, 537

Aliverdiyev, A., 589

All-Russian Extraordinary Commission (VeCheKa), 55-77

Allen, Robert, 710

Alliluyeva, Svetlana, 712

Anashkin, G.Z., 348, 350n, 356, 358-359, 548, 551, 559, 595-596, 598, 619-620, 634, 636, 638-639, 705-706

Andreyev, M., 505, 520, 563

Antimonov, B.S., 531-532n

Antonov-Ovseenko, 157

Appeal and cassation, 621-642; historical development, 621-634; legislation, 1917-1933, 621-629; legislation, 1938-1961, 629-634; new evidence, 634-640

Aragon, Louis, 711

Arbitration, 127-153; commissions, 127-128; state, 128-129; reorganization of, decision of 1959, 129-131; new statute of 1960, 131-132; departmental, 133; present structure, 133-134; precontractual disputes, 134-136; arbitral procedure, 136-138; re-examination of decisions, 138-140; maritime commission, 150

Arbitrazh, see arbitration

Aristakov, Yu. M., 483

Arkhangel'skaya case, 514, 517

Arsen'yev, 357

Ashurov, 589

Assessors, 336-372; choice of, 346-350; councils of, 350-353; replace jurors, 343-344; and German Schoeffen, 343-350

Aver'yanov, S., 438

Azimov, 502

Azraell, Yeremy R., 186, 192n

Babb, W., 367

Babitsky, Konstantin, 708

Bail, soviet, 587-590

Bakker case, 582-583

Bam, 568

Barghoorn, Frederick C., 711n

Baria, 102n

Barry, Donald D., 447n

Barsukov, M.V., 383

Baskov, V.I., 587n, 648-649

Batenin-Lantsov, 550

Baxter, Albert, 180n

Beerman, R., 238-239

Beilis, Mendel, 342, 524

Berdyayev, F., 261-262n

Berezovskaya, S.G., 420, 425, 427

Beria, 692, 701-702

Berman, Harold J., 141, 153n, 167, 176n, 180n. 187-188, 191-194, 201, 235-236, 240, 242-243, 247, 404n-405n, 439, 447n, 564, 625n, 706, 713

Berry, Donald D., 235

Bilinsky, Andreas, 176-177n, 194, 568-569n

Binding, 343

Blekh, A., 566-567

Bludov, Count D.N., 336-337

Bogoraz-Daniel, Larissa, 708, 712

Boiter, Albert, 167, 186, 710n

Bokio, G. Yu., 672

Bonch-Bruyevich, V.D., 670

Boridzhev, Ivan, 531n

Braude, I.D., 575

Imprimerie Orientaliste, s.p.r.l., Louvain (Belgique)